LITERACY, TECHNOLOGY, AND SOCIETY

CONFRONTING THE ISSUES

Editors

Gail E. Hawisher
University of Illinois, Urbana-Champaign

Cynthia L. Selfe
Michigan Technological University

PRENTICE HALL, UPPER SADDLE RIVER, NJ 07458

Library of Congress Cataloging-in-Publication Data

Literacy, technology, and society : confronting the issues / editors,
  Gail E. Hawisher, Cynthia L. Selfe.
        p.   cm.
    Includes index.
    ISBN   0-13-227588-0
    1. Technology—Social aspects.   2. Technology and state.
  3. Computer-assisted instruction.   I. Hawisher, Gail E.   II. Selfe,
  Cynthia L. (date).
  T14.5.L58   1997
  303.48'33—dc21   96-39125
                                                              CIP

Editorial Director: Charlyce Jones Owen
Acquisition Editor: Mary Jo Southern
Editorial Assistant: Karen George
Developmental Editor: Kara Hado
Director of Production and Manufacturing: Barbara Kittle
Managing Editors: Bonnie Biller/Mary Rottino
Project Manager: Linda B. Pawelchak
Manufacturing Manager: Nick Sklitsis
Prepress and Manufacturing Buyer: Lynn Pearlman
Creative Design Director: Leslie Osher
Interior and Cover Design: Ximena Piedra Tamrakopoulos
Electronic Art Creation: Asterisk Art
Marketing Manager: Rob Mejia
Proofreader: Nancy Menges
Permission Specialist: Marian Reiner

This book was set in 10/12 Rotis Semi Sans by Carlisle Communications LTD
and was printed and bound by RR Donnelley & Sons Company.
The cover was printed by Phoenix Color Corp.

© 1997 by Prentice-Hall, Inc.
Simon & Schuster/A Viacom Company
Upper Saddle River, New Jersey 07458

Printed in the United States of America
10   9   8   7   6   5   4

ISBN 0-13-227588-0

Prentice-Hall International (UK) Limited, *London*
Prentice-Hall of Australia Pty. Limited, *Sydney*
Prentice-Hall Canada Inc., *Toronto*
Prentice-Hall Hispanoamericana, S.A., *Mexico*
Prentice-Hall of India Private Limited, *New Delhi*
Prentice-Hall of Japan, Inc., *Tokyo*
Simon & Schuster Asia Pte. Ltd., *Singapore*
Editora Prentice-Hall do Brasil, Ltda., *Rio de Janeiro*

CONTENTS

(handwritten: Read over week end p. 399 - List some of the claims you can make/infer from the data)

I. SOCIAL ISSUES AND TECHNOLOGY   1

> Cyberspace, in the sense of being "in the same room" is an experience, not a wiring system. It is about people using the new technology to do what they are genetically programmed to do: communicate with one another. It can be found in electronic mail exchanged by lovers who have never met. It emerges from the endless debates on mailing lists and message boards. It's that bond that knits together regulars in electronic chat rooms and newsgroups. It is, like Plato's plane of ideal forms, a metaphorical space, a virtual reality.
>
> —Philip Elmer-DeWitt, pp. 6–7

II. EDUCATION AND TECHNOLOGY   131

> With the evolution of human society, the communcations medium has changed, and, as a result, the focus of literacy has changed. We must understand that human society is now at the edge of a discontinuity, the end of the Gutenbergian era and the beginning of the "electronic display" era. As we enter this new stage of historical development, we can expect the form and content of our communications to change.
>
> —Paul A. Strassman, p. 135

III. ETHICS, LAW, AND TECHNOLOGY   267

> For everyone from neo-Nazis to anticensorship activists, cyberspace does indeed provide a free
> space. But how free is the speech on the Internet?
>
> —Jon Wiener, p. 272

IV. GENDER AND TECHNOLOGY   345

Women have to be in [the computer world] because decisions about language and culture and access are being made and we should be involved in making them. Women have to be in it because, although nobody really knows what form all this technoloy will take, there shouldn't be any culture we're afraid to climb into.

—Paula Span, p. 417

V. GOVERNMENT AND TECHNOLOGY   471

This is a historic moment in the White House and we look forward to your participation and enthusiasm for this milestone event. We eagerly anticipate the day when electronic mail from the public is an integral and normal part of the White House communications system.

—President Clinton and Vice President Gore, p. 475

PREFACE

The collection of essays, *Literacy, Technology, and Society: Confronting the Issues,* grows out of our perception that computers have touched almost every site in which we live and work in the late twentieth century. Nowhere is this more apparent than on our college campuses where students often meet and study in electronic classrooms for courses ranging from chemistry to sociology to first-year composition. Members of the educational establishment, especially those in departments of English, have looked to these machines not only for help in teaching, but also for help in altering the politics and practices of literacy and composition in classrooms, transforming them into increasingly dynamic intellectual spaces for teachers and students.

However, if computer technology is perceived by many educational reformists as a potential ally, it is also recognized, increasingly, as a hotly contested site of social struggle—a site characterized by a nexus of complex economic, political, and ideological forces. Vying for position within this dynamic landscape are not only English faculty but also school administrators, commercial hardware and software producers, multinational corporations, parents, and federal and state governments. Given the number of occupants within the new electronic landscapes and the range of interests in connection with education and language, English faculty now realize just how dramatically the values of democratic education and literacy will be played out during the next decade—especially within electronic contexts.

For these reasons, the history, the present, and the future of computers are important intellectual spaces for teachers, educators, and students to map. Indeed, the electronic territory comprised by this ideologically laden technology is one of the most important educational landscapes we have available for our profession to explore. Within it, we will face, for the next decade, the challenges associated with global literacy; the problems associated with the nature of education as a complex set of cultural processes and the role of language within such processes; and the historical, unsolved challenges of students marginalized or silenced within our schools due to race, age, ethnicity, sexual orientation, gender, or handicap.

This reader is designed to provide a collection of readings that explore this territory for teachers and students of writing, as well as for graduate students engaged in computers and composition studies. Primarily, we focus our work on published readings—nonfiction articles from around the world appearing in the popular press; journal articles that appear in professional forums; short pieces of fiction that students can compare to the essays; and cartoons and other visual representations that capture the powerful impact that the new technologies are exerting on social change. The readings are intended to provoke responses among students—written and oral conversations—that will take place in traditional face-to-face classroom settings and in electronic classrooms where discussions are continued online, in and out of class, over computer networks. Many of the discussions will also culminate in a variety of student writings. We are thinking here of reflective pieces, thoughtful analyses of issues, argumentative discourse, research proposals, multimedia projects, and other kinds of electronic writing aimed at online discussion groups.

The book, as a whole, is designed to be used primarily in semester-long, first-year writing classes but could easily be adopted for advanced writing classes or for special seminars focusing on technology. Another audience would be those working in computers and composition studies, a growing and increasingly professionalized group of teachers and scholars. There is a sense within this group of a maturing discipline with its own discourse, scholarship, literature, professional forums, and intellectual responsibilities. This text would be a resource for their own scholarship and also for their teaching. We believe the book will also interest graduate students enrolled at institutions that offer advanced degree programs in rhetoric and composition, or technical communication. Many will choose the book as a reference for their own use, as well as for a reader in their classes.

Our primary audience, however, consists of college undergraduates. The essays and accompanying apparatus are intended to immerse students in the kinds of reading, writing, thinking, and activities that foster critical inquiry and response. We know of no group for whom the development of critical perspectives on the uses of computer technology is more important.

The book consists of five sections, each aimed at particular issues surrounding computer technology and each containing readings that could easily be read, discussed, and written about during a one- or two-week period. The selections range in length from one to twenty or so pages, many of them rather short but nevertheless provocative. Each section of the book is preceded by an introduction written by the editors and followed by suggestions for class activities. The class activities are divided into "Thinking and Re-Reading" and "Writing and Learning" segments that we've designed to help students write to actual audiences, oftentimes classmates, fellow students, and members of local committees in their own college communities. Following the assignments for individual readings, we have provided activities aimed at students working in different computer environments. Some of the section overview assignments, for example, are tailored to Stand-Alone Computers (SAC) while others make use of local area networks (LAN) and still others of wide area networks (WAN). By providing different kinds of assignments for various computer contexts, we hope to help students become aware of the many ways in which computers can facilitate research. Each section also contains what we've called "Images of Technology," a selection of photographs and advertisements taken from the popular press that students are asked to read and analyze. A sixth and final section of articles appears on the World Wide Web at Prentice Hall's World Wide Web site. There students will also find additional images for study. Appendices include questions to help students "read" the images, along with a guide to citing electronic sources.

We are grateful to the following reviewers: Eric Crump, University of Missouri; Sarah J. Duerden, Arizona State University; Gary Layne Hatch, Brigham Young University; Will Hochman, University of Southern Colorado; Nancy Kaplan, University of Baltimore; Marcia Peoples Halio, University of Delaware; Evelyn Posey, University of Texas at El Paso; Margaret-Rose Marek, Texas Christian University; and Philip Sipiora, University of South Florida.

Gail E. Hawisher
Cynthia L. Selfe

PART I

SOCIAL ISSUES AND TECHNOLOGY

INTRODUCTION

> *The things we call "technologies" are ways of building order in our world. . . . Consciously or unconsciously, deliberately or inadvertently, societies choose structures for technologies that influence how people are going to work, communicate, travel, consume. . . . According to this view, the adoption of a given technical system unavoidably brings with it conditions for human relationships that have a distinctive political cast—for example, centralized or de-centralized, egalitarian or inegalitarian, repressive or liberating.*
>
> *Langdon Winner, The Whale and the Reactor (28–29)*

TECHNOLOGY is a nexus—a knot—of power in our culture. This is why, when we look closely at computers in America, we can see enacted in various ways the politics of economic status, age, race, sexual orientation, and gender. In our country, for example, computers are used more frequently by males than by females, by whites than by persons of color, by wealthy people rather than poor people, and by younger generations rather than older generations. For those groups of people who have little access to computers, little education in the use of technology, little exposure to advanced computer strategies, little hope of going to schools where sophisticated computer use is taught, the promise of the computer revolution in America has not been borne out. Indeed, for these people, the very promise of computers suggests that those in power will remain powerful and those without power will remain without. The social issues suggested by this belief are disturbing—but understanding these issues can help us understand why people react to technology as they do.

In this section, eleven authors and several artists examine the implications of technology as a social knot. Among them are popular journalists, technology critics, fiction writers, social psychologists, essayists, and graphic/commercial artists and photographers. The contributions in this section can be divided into four major types—although each of these types typically incorporates some elements of the others.

The first kind of article can be described generally as *technology scholarship and criticism*—examples include Kenneth Gergen's "Social Saturation and the Populated Self," Langdon Winner's "Mythinformation," Alvin Weinberg's "Can Technology Replace Social Engineering?," and Lee Sproull and Sara Kiesler's "Computers, Networks and Work." These pieces are aimed at an audience that wants to make a careful, in-depth study of technology issues, going beyond a surface-level treatment to analyze the social implications of technology development and use. These contributions are generally longer than the other pieces we have included; they are typically read by a limited audience; they employ the critical and analytical approaches of scholars; and they focus on complex sets of social issues. They explore such topics as the ways in which technology serves to saturate our lives with images, individuals, and experiences; the implications of describing the recent boom in technology development as a computer "revolution"; the relationship between social problems and technological "solutions"; and the ways in which computer networks alter workplace communications.

The second major type of article in this section can be generally described as *popular journalism about technology*—examples include "Welcome to Cyberspace," by Philip Elmer-DeWitt; "Welcome to Cyberia," by M. Kadi; "We're Teen, We're Queer, and We've Got E-Mail," by Steve Silberman; "Terror On-Line," by Mark Stuart Gill; and "From Captain America to Wolverine," by Mark Oehlert. These pieces are often short, and they share a focus on computer technology as a popularly experienced cultural phenomenon. They typically focus on the lives and interests of a general population not necessarily expert with computers, but interested in them and their use. These contributions, appearing in venues such as *Time, Newsweek, The Weekly World News,* the *Utne Reader, Wired, Vogue, The Washington Post,* and *The New Yorker* are aimed at the general public. These pieces typically focus on human interest stories (e.g., an online community for gay teens, a woman who has been stalked on the Internet) or on technology issues that have been aired via commercial media on a frequent basis (e.g., the cost of hooking up to the Internet, the value of using computers to improve education, and the option of replacing print newspapers with online newspapers).

The third type of article can be described as *technology fiction,* also known as *science fiction.* We have included only one example of technology fiction in this section, "Johnny Mnemonic," by William Gibson. This kind of fiction is typically set in the future, portrays a technologically dependent world, and extrapolates future social phenomena from existing social patterns and events.

The fourth entry we have called *images of technology.* The images we have included generally appear in advertisements published by popular magazines such as *Wired.* These images illustrate in carefully arranged—and sometimes disguised—ways the values and the familiar stories that our culture associates with computers.

A careful reading of all four types of contributions can help readers establish an increasingly robust understanding of computer technology as a social phenomenon and force. One type of article—technology scholarship and criticism—helps to teach you more formal strategies for analysis and critical thinking about the complex social relationships involved in technology issues. The second type of article—popular journalism—provides a living snapshot of computer technology as it is now being experienced in social contexts by a nonspecialist audience. The third type of contribution—technology fiction—provides a rich picture of current cultural concerns about technology, a picture that gains power because it is magnified by the distance of time and highlighted by the absence of familiar contexts. The fourth type—images of technology—reveals the cultural and social values associated with computers in different ways: by focusing on the visual images we connect with technology and its use, by illustrating the social relationships surrounding computer use, and by highlighting the familiar narrative frameworks into which individuals have written technology as a cultural phenomenon.

Welcome to Cyberspace

Philip Elmer-DeWitt

IN 1982, THE COMPUTER WAS FEATURED on the cover of *Time* magazine as the "Man of the Year." That article focused on the early and explosive growth of the microcomputer industry. In 1995, *Time* once again featured computer technology as a cultural phenomenon of interest in our society—this time with the Internet as a focus. The article that follows, because it was published in a popular news magazine aimed at a general and nonspecialist audience, provides a summary gloss of some of the issues connected with the Internet. It does not treat these issues in depth or provide more serious readers enough specific information to explore these issues thoroughly.

This contribution, however, authored by Philip Elmer-DeWitt, does provide a good space to observe how one reporter working for a mainstream news magazine portrayed the Internet in 1995, what knowledge the reporter (and the magazine's editors) assumed average readers had and did not have at that time, what topics were of interest to a general population of readers, and what level of sophistication discussions about the Internet had reached among a larger population. The article, in other words, provides a cultural snapshot of our society and its general understanding of technology—not a complete representation, by any means, but an interesting cultural image of one point in time.

It started, as the big ideas in technology often do, with a science-fiction writer. William Gibson, a young expatriate American living in Canada, was wandering past the video arcades on Vancouver's Granville Street in the early 1980s when something about the way the players were hunched over their glowing screens struck him as odd. "I could see in the physical intensity of their postures how *rapt* the kids were," he says. "It was like a feedback loop, with photons coming off the screens into the kids' eyes, neurons moving through their bodies and electrons moving through the video game. These kids clearly *believed* in the space the games projected."

That image haunted Gibson. He didn't know much about video games or computers—he wrote his breakthrough novel *Neuromancer* (1984) on an ancient manual typewriter—but he knew people who did. And as near as he could tell, everybody who worked much with the machines eventually came to accept, almost as an article of faith, the reality of that imaginary realm. "They develop a belief that there's some kind of *actual space* behind the screen," he says. "Some place that you can't see but you know is there."

Gibson called that place "cyberspace," and used it as the setting for his early novels and short stories. In his fiction, cyberspace is a computer-generated landscape that characters enter by "jacking in"—sometimes by plugging electrodes directly into sockets implanted in the brain. What they see when they get there is a three-dimensional representation of all the information stored in "every computer in the human system"—great warehouses and skyscrapers of data. He describes it in a key passage in *Neuromancer* as a place of "unthinkable complexity," with "lines of light ranged in the nonspace of the mind, clusters and constellations of data. Like city lights, receding . . ."

In the years since, there have been other names given to that shadowy space where our computer data reside: the Net, the Web, the Cloud, the Matrix, the Metaverse, the Datasphere, the Electronic Frontier, the information superhighway. But Gibson's coinage may prove the most enduring. By 1989 it had been borrowed by the online community to describe not some science-fiction fantasy but today's increasingly interconnected computer systems—especially the millions of computers jacked into the Internet.

Now hardly a day goes by without some newspaper article, some political speech, some corporate press release invoking Gibson's imaginary world. Suddenly, it seems, everybody has an E-mail address, from Hollywood moguls to the Holy See. Billy Graham has preached on America Online; Vice President Al Gore has held forth on CompuServe; thousands chose to celebrate New Year's this year with an online get-together called First Night in Cyberspace.

In Washington cyberspace has become a political hot button of some potency, first pressed during the 1992 presidential campaign by Al Gore and Bill Clinton, who rode to the White House in part on the promise that they would build the so-called information superhighway and route it through every voter's district—if not to his home. But the Clinton Administration lost the high ground of cyberspace, having, among other transgressions, come out on the wrong side of the privacy debate when it endorsed the Clipper Chip security device favored by its intelligence services. The Republicans were quick to grab the initiative. No sooner had incoming House Speaker Newt Gingrich taken office than he made his bid, staging a big press conference to unveil a new House computer system. At a Washington confab called "Democracy in Virtual America," attended by his old friends, futurists Alvin and Heidi Toffler, the Speaker talked expansively about wiring the world. "Cyberspace is the land of knowledge," proclaimed an information age Magna Carta issued in his name. "And the exploration of that land can be a civilization's truest, highest calling."

Corporations, smelling a land rush of another sort, are scrambling to stake out their own claims in cyberspace. Every computer company, nearly every publisher, most communications firms, banks, insurance companies and hundreds of mail-order and retail firms are registering their Internet domains and setting up sites on the World Wide Web. They sense that cyberspace will be one of the driving forces—if not the primary one—for economic growth in the 21st century.

All this is being breathlessly reported in the press, which has seized on cyberspace as an all-purpose buzz word that can add sparkle to the most humdrum development or assignment. For working reporters, many of whom have just discovered the pleasures of going online, cyber has become the prefix of the day, and they are spawning neologisms as fast as they can type: cyberphilia, cyberphobia, cyberwonk, cybersex, cyberslut. A Nexis search of newspapers, magazines, and television transcripts turned up 1,205 mentions of cyber in the month of January, up from 464 the previous January and 167 in January 1993.

One result of this drum roll is a growing public appetite for a place most people haven't been to and are often hard-pressed to define. In a *Time*/CNN poll of 800 Americans conducted in January by Yankelovich Partners, 57% didn't know what cyberspace meant, yet 85% were certain that information technology had made their life better. They may not know where it is, but they want desperately to get there. The rush to get online, to avoid being "left behind" in the information revolution, is intense. Those who find fulfillment in cyberspace often have the religious fervor of the recently converted.

These sentiments have been captured brilliantly in an IBM ad on TV showing a phalanx of Czech nuns discussing—of all things—the latest operating system from Microsoft. As they walk briskly through a convent, a young novice mentions IBM's competing system, called Warp. "I just read about it in *Wired*," she gushes. "You get true multitasking . . . easy access to the Internet." An older sister glances up with obvious interest; the camera cuts to the mother superior, who wistfully confesses, "I'm dying to surf the Net." Fade as the pager tucked under her habit starts to beep.

Cybernuns.

What is cyberspace? According to John Perry Barlow, a rock-'n'-roll lyricist turned computer activist, it can be defined most succinctly as "that place you are in when you are talking on the telephone." That's as good a place to start as any. The telephone system, after all, is really a vast, global computer network with a distinctive, audible presence (crackling static against an almost inaudible background hum). By Barlow's definition, just about everybody has already been to cyberspace. It's marked by the feeling that the person you're talking to is "in the same room." Most people take the spatial dimension of a phone conversation for granted—until they get a really bad connection or a glitchy overseas call. Then they start raising their voice, as if by sheer volume they could propel it to the outer reaches of cyberspace.

Cyberspace, of course, is bigger than a telephone call. It encompasses the millions of personal computers connected by modems—via the telephone system—to commercial online services, as well as the millions more with high-speed links to local area networks, office E-mail systems and the Internet. It includes the rapidly expanding wireless services: microwave towers that carry great quantities of cellular phone and data traffic; communications satellites strung like beads in geosynchronous orbit; low-flying satellites that will soon crisscross the globe like angry bees, connecting folks too far-flung or too much on the go to be tethered by wires. Someday even our television sets may be part of cyberspace, transformed into interactive "teleputers" by so-called full-service networks like the ones several cable-TV companies (including Time Warner) are building along the old cable lines, using fiber optics and high-speed switches.

But these wires and cables and microwaves are not really cyberspace. They are the means of conveyance, not the destination: the information superhighway, not the bright city lights at the end of the road. Cyberspace, in the sense of being "in the same room," is an experience, not a wiring system. It is about people using the new technology to do what they are genetically programmed to do: communicate with one another. It can be found in electronic mail exchanged by lovers who have never met. It emerges from the endless debates on mailing lists and message boards. It's that bond that knits together regulars in electronic chat rooms and newsgroups. It is, like Plato's plane of ideal forms, a metaphorical space, a virtual reality.

But it is no less real for being so. We live in the age of information, as Nicholas Negroponte, director of M.I.T.'s Media Lab, is fond of pointing out, in which the fundamental particle is not the atom but the bit—the binary digit, a unit of data usually represented as a 0 or 1. Information may still be delivered in magazines and newspapers (atoms), but the real value is in the contents (bits). We pay for our goods and services with cash (atoms), but the ebb and flow of capital around the world is carried out—to the tune of several trillion dollars a day—in electronic funds transfers (bits).

Bits are different from atoms and obey different laws. They are weightless. They are easily (and flawlessly) reproduced. There is an infinite supply. And they can be shipped at nearly the speed of light. When you are in the business of moving bits around, barriers of time and space disappear. For information providers—publishers, for example—cyberspace offers a medium in which distribution costs shrink to zero. Buyers and sellers can find each other in cyberspace without the benefit (or the expense) of a marketing campaign. No wonder so many businessmen are convinced it will become a powerful engine of economic growth.

At this point, however, cyberspace is less about commerce than about community. The technology has unleashed a great rush of direct, person-to-person communications, organized not in the top-down, one-to-many structure of traditional media but in a many-to-many model that may—just may—be a vehicle for revolutionary change. In a world already too divided against itself—rich against poor, producer against consumer—cyberspace offers the nearest thing to a level playing field.

Take, for example, the Internet. Until something better comes along to replace it, the Internet is cyberspace. It may not reach every computer in the human system, as Gibson imagined, but it comes very close. And as anyone who has spent much time there can attest, it is in many ways even stranger than fiction.

Begun more than 20 years ago as a Defense Department experiment, the Internet escaped from the Pentagon in 1984 and spread like kudzu during the personal-computer boom, nearly doubling every year from the mid-1980s on. Today 30 million to 40 million people in more than 160 countries have at least E-mail access to the Internet; in Japan, New Zealand and parts of Europe the number of Net users has grown more than 1,000% during the past three years.

One factor fueling the Internet's remarkable growth is its resolutely grass-roots structure. Most conventional computer systems are hierarchical and proprietary; they run on copyright software in a pyramid structure that gives dictatorial powers to the system operators who sit on top. The Internet, by contrast, is open (nonproprietary) and rabidly democratic. No one owns it. No single organization controls it. It is run like a commune with 4.8 million fiercely independent members (called hosts). It crosses national boundaries and answers to no sovereign. It is literally lawless.

Although graphics, photos and even videos have started to show up, cyberspace, as it exists on the Internet, is still primarily a text medium. People communicate by and large through words, typed and displayed on a screen. Yet cyberspace assumes an astonishing array of forms, from the utilitarian mailing list (a sort of junk E-mail list to which anyone can contribute) to the rococo MUDS, or Multi-User Dungeons (elaborate fictional gathering places that users create one "room" at a time). All these "spaces" have one thing in common: they are egalitarian to a fault. Anybody can play (provided he or she has the requisite equipment and access), and everybody is afforded the same level of respect (which is to say, little or none). Stripped of the external trappings of wealth, power, beauty and social status, people tend to be judged in the cyberspace of the Internet only by their ideas and their ability to get them across in terse, vigorous prose. On the Internet, as the famous *New Yorker* cartoon put it, nobody knows you're a dog.

Nowhere is this leveling effect more apparent than on Usenet—a giant set of more than 10,000 discussion groups (called newsgroups) distributed in large part over the Internet and devoted to every conceivable subject, from Rush Limbaugh to particle physics to the nocturnal habits of ring-tailed lemurs. The newsgroups develop their own peculiar dynamic as participants lurch from topic to topic—quick to take and give offense, slow to come to any kind of resolution.

But Usenet regulars are fiercely proud of what they have constructed. They view it as a new vehicle for wielding political power (through mass mailings and petitions) and an alternative system for gathering and disseminating raw, uncensored news. If they are sometimes disdainful of bumbling "newbies" who go online without learning the rules of the road, they are unforgiving to those who violate them deliberately. Many are convinced that the unflattering press accounts (those perennial stories about Internet hackers and pedophiles, for example) are part of a conspiracy among the mainstream media to suppress what they perceive as a threat to their hegemony. top of next page

The Usenet newsgroups are, in their way, the perfect antidote to modern mass media. Rather than catering to the lowest common denominator with programming packaged by a few people in New York, Atlanta, and Hollywood and broadcast to the masses in the heartland, the newsgroups allow news, commentary, and humor to bubble up from the grass roots. They represent narrowcasting in the extreme: content created by consumers for consumers. While cable-TV executives still dream of hundreds of channels, Usenet already has thousands. The network is so fragmented, in fact, that some fear it will ultimately serve to further divide a society already splintered by race, politics and sexual prejudice. That would be an ironic fate for a system designed to enhance communications.

The Internet is far from perfect. Largely unedited, its content is often tasteless, foolish, uninteresting or just plain wrong. It can be dangerously habit-forming and, truth be told, an enormous waste of time. Even with the arrival of new point-and-click software such as Netscape and Mosaic, it is still too hard to navigate. And because it requires access to both a computer and a high-speed telecommunications link, it is out of reach for millions of people too poor or too far from a major communications hub to participate.

But it is remarkable nonetheless, especially considering that it began as a cold war postapocalypse military command grid. "When I look at the Internet," says Bruce Sterling, another science-fiction writer and a great champion of cyberspace, "I see something astounding and delightful. It's as if some grim fallout shelter had burst open and a full-scale Mardi Gras parade had come out. I take such enormous pleasure in this that it's hard to remain properly skeptical."

There is no guarantee, however, that cyberspace will always look like this. The Internet is changing rapidly. Lately a lot of the development efforts—and most of the press attention—have shifted from the rough-and-tumble Usenet newsgroups to the more passive and consumer-oriented "home pages" of the World Wide Web—a system of links that simplifies the task of navigating among the myriad offerings on the Internet. The Net, many old-timers complain, is turning into a shopping mall. But unless it proves to be a total bust for business, that trend is likely to continue.

*hegemony = Leadership or dominance
of one State or nation over others*

The more fundamental changes are those taking place underneath our sidewalks and streets, where great wooden wheels of fiber-optic cable are being rolled out one block at a time. Over the next decade, the telecommunications systems of the world will be rebuilt from the ground up as copper wires are ripped up and replaced by hair-thin fiber-optic strands.

The reason, in a word, is bandwidth, the information-carrying capacity of a medium (usually measured in bits per second). In terms of bandwidth, a copper telephone wire is like a thin straw, too narrow to carry the traffic it is being asked to bear. By contrast, fiber-optic strands, although hair-thin, are like great fat pipes, with an intrinsic capacity to carry tens of thousands of times as many bits as copper wire.

It's not just the Internet surfers who are crying for more bandwidth. Hollywood needs it to deliver movies and television shows on demand. Video game makers want it to send kids the latest adventures of Donkey Kong and Sonic the Hedgehog. The phone companies have their eyes on what some believe will be the next must-have appliance: the videophone.

There is a broad consensus in government and industry that the National Information Infrastructure, as the Clinton Administration prefers to call the info highway, will be a broadband, switched network that could, in theory, deliver all these things. But how it will be structured and how it will be deployed are not so clear. For example, if cable-TV and telephone companies are allowed to roll out the new services in only the richest neighborhoods—a practice known as "cream skimming"—that could exacerbate the already growing disparity between those who have access to the latest information and the best intelligence and those who must be content with what they see on TV.

An even trickier question has to do with the so-called upstream capacity of the network. Everybody wants to build a fat pipeline going into the home; that's the conduit by which the new information goods and services will be delivered. But how much bandwidth needs to be set aside for the signal going from the home back into the network? In some designs that upstream pathway is quite narrow—allowing just enough bits to change the channel or order a zirconium ring. Some network activists argue that consumers will someday need as much bandwidth going out of the home as they have coming in. Only then can ordinary people become, if they choose, not just consumers of media but producers as well, free to plug their camcorders into the network and broadcast their creations to the world.

How these design issues are decided in the months ahead could change the shape of cyberspace. Will it be bottom up, like the Internet, or top down, like broadcast television? In the best case, says Mitch Kapor, cofounder (with John Perry Barlow) of the Electronic Frontier Foundation, we could collectively invent a new entertainment medium, one that taps the creative energies of a nation of midnight scribblers and camcorder video artists. "In the worst case," he says, "we could wind up with networks that have the principal effect of fostering addiction to a new generation of electronic narcotics."

*Symbolic distruction of evil / total or near total
destruction*

If Kapor seems to be painting these scenarios in apocalyptic terms, he is not alone. There is something about cyberspace that sets people's imaginations blazing. Much of what has been written about it—in the press and on the networks—tends to swing from one extreme to the other, from hype and romanticism to fear and loathing. It may be that the near-term impact of cyberspace is being oversold. But that does not mean that real change isn't in the works. As a rule of thumb, historians say, the results of technological innovation always take longer to reach fruition than early champions of change predict. But when change finally comes, its effect is likely to be more profound and widespread and unanticipated than anyone imagined—even the guys who write science fiction.

THINKING AND RE-READING

1. In this article, Elmer-DeWitt mentions several indicators of the popular interest in, and knowledge of, the Internet. As you read, think about the indicators that the reporter has selected. Do they accurately reflect the American understanding of the Internet? What messages do these indicators portray to you? What concerns do they raise? Why?

2. As you read, consider who Elmer-DeWitt quotes in this article and why these people have been chosen as spokespersons on this issue. What are their qualifications? Why did Elmer-DeWitt select quotations from these particular people? If you consider this collection of people as a group, what impression does it give you of the Internet?

WRITING AND LEARNING

1. In a two-to-three-page handout written for an informed group of ninth-grade high school students who have read this article, identify a collection of four to five textual images (metaphors, similes, images) that Elmer-DeWitt uses in this article to describe the Internet (e.g., "communication satellites strung like beads in geosynchronous orbit" or ". . . Usenet newsgroups are . . . the perfect antidote to modern mass media."). In your handout—which should be aimed at enriching the ninth graders' understanding of the language used in this piece—discuss the implications of these specific images, the messages (both implicit and explicit) that they convey, and the picture that they construct of the Internet. Taken as a collection, what is the overall picture that these images present? Why did the author select these images and not others? What overarching picture is communicated to readers? What parts of this picture seem most accurate? Least accurate? Explain why.

2. In a written response, choose one claim made within this article with which you disagree. In a letter to the editors of *Time,* explain why you disagree and use examples from your own life or from the lives of individuals you know to support your argument. Explain why this disagreement seems an important one to you, focusing on either the personal or the public implications of the claim, or on both if they are related. Your purpose is to persuade the editors that Elmer-DeWitt's representation of the Internet is faulty, inaccurate, incomplete, or misrepresentative in some way.

3. For your own insight and practice in citing material accurately, divide a piece of paper into three columns, lengthwise, or create a word processing file with three columns running lengthwise on a page. On the right-hand side of the page, summarize the major positive claims about the Internet that Elmer-DeWitt makes in this article. Use quoted material when possible but be sure to cite it correctly. On the left-hand side of the page, list the negative, or problematic, claims about the Internet that this article makes. If a negative claim relates directly to one of the positive claims, put these opposite one another on the page. If not, leave the other side of the page blank opposite the claim. In the middle column, identify stances on technology, drawn from your experience or from other

readings that you have completed, that do not fall into this polarized scheme—stances that are neither negative nor positive, but maybe more complicated. Try to identify stances for this middle column that recognize *both* the positive and negative aspects of technology—all at once—or that identify aspects of technology that are *neither* simply good or bad. Your purpose in this exercise is to examine how the popular media frequently portray issues—as simplistically good or evil—and then to expand and complicate this portrayal to make it more accurate, complete, and fully representative.

Social Saturation
and the Populated Self

Kenneth J. Gergen

KENNETH GERGEN IS THE AUTHOR of *The Saturated Self: Dilemmas of Identity in Contemporary Life,* a book that attempts to understand how we have re-defined ourselves in terms of the multiple images, multiple identities, and multiple technologies that characterize contemporary life and the social condition identified as "postmodern."

For Gergen, the postmodern world has come to look like a real-life version of MTV—a fragmented place saturated with images multiplied and delivered by television, video, computer, and film. As residents of this technological world, we are, Gergen notes, dizzied by the increased speed of global travel and by the exponential growth in the numbers of social relationships that this travel involves us in. At the same time, we are bombarded by information brought to us by increasingly complex telecommunication systems and the pace of our lives is accelerated to an unhealthy speed by the technologies that we have invented to help us cope with social change. As the speed and the complexity of our lives have intensified, so have the numbers of possible trajectories that carry us away from traditional long-term stable relationships. We are exhausted and isolated, distracted and multiplied beyond our capacity to focus.

In this portrait of our times, Gergen provides a vision of the postmodern condition, a social condition that many critics think characteristic of contemporary culture. The postmodernist denies the modernist belief in Self and in Truth. In a postmodern setting, Gergen shows, people do not exist as individual, unified, coherent selves who think, write, or act in a traditionally reasoned way. Rather, people living in a postmodern world exist as saturated collections of multiple, and sometimes contradictory, selves compiled from various social contexts. Nor is there any single identifiable source of Truth in the postmodern world; rather, truths are multiple, contradictory, and entirely dependent on cultural situations and understandings. Although some people believe that the postmodern condition is one of liberation from traditionally established sets of beliefs, others, such as Gergen, believe that such "liberation becomes a swirling vertigo of demands" that confuses, distracts, and misdirects.

As you read this piece of technology criticism aimed at a serious and educated readership, consider the ways in which your life is marked by postmodern influences that deny belief in a single, unified sense of Truth and Self. It will be difficult for you to consider the full import of postmodernism unless you spend some time in class talking about the historical conceptions of unified Truth and Self presented at various times of human history; so do not hesitate to ask your teacher for additional readings or discussions in this area. As you consider these issues in a historical context, also consider the ways in which historical or modern notions of Truth and Self—informed by religion, or family values, or your understanding of science, for example—may still continue to inform your life and system of values. In these ways, the modern and postmodern co-exist, even as they are contradictory.

Living or happening in same period of time

R andom moments from contemporary life: *Comunication by letters*

- You find your mailbox stuffed with correspondence—advertisements for local events, catalogues from mail-order houses, political announcements, offers for special prizes, bills, and, just maybe, a letter.
- You return from a weekend away to find your answering machine overflowing with calls to be returned.
- You try to arrange a meeting with a business colleague in New York. She is attending a meeting in Caracas. When she returns next week you will be in Memphis. When all attempts to arrange a mutually convenient meeting place fail, you settle for a long-distance phone meeting in the evening.
- An old friend calls, passing through on business, and wants to meet for a drink or dinner.
- You think about planning a New Year's Eve party, but most of your good friends are away in Colorado, Mexico, or other vacation spots.
- You are away for the evening, but you program your VCR so that you won't miss a favorite program.
- You are in Montreal for a few days, and are surprised to meet a friend from back home in Atlanta.

Most of these events are commonplace in contemporary life, scarcely worth comment. Yet none of them were commonplace twenty years ago, and several have only entered our lives within the past five years. Such events are manifestations of a profound pattern of social change.

to prove by evidence

plunge into or as into a liquid

The change is essentially one that immerses us ever more deeply in the social world, and exposes us more and more to the opinions, values, and lifestyles of others.

It is my central thesis that this immersion is propelling us toward a new self-consciousness: the postmodern. The emerging commonplaces of communication—such as those just cited—are critical to understanding the passing of both the romantic and modern views of self. What I call the *technologies of social saturation* are central to the contemporary erasure of individual self. This chapter will explore the ways in which social saturation has come to dominate everyday life. However, we shall also see that as we become increasingly conjoined with our social surroundings, we come to reflect those surroundings. There is a *populating of the self*, reflecting the infusion of partial identities through social saturation. And there is the onset of a *multiphrenic* condition, in which one begins to experience the vertigo of unlimited multiplicity. Both the populating of the self and the multiphrenic condition are significant preludes to post-modern consciousness. To appreciate the magnitude of cultural change, and its probable intensification, attention must be directed to the emerging technologies.

dizzyness

THE TECHNOLOGIES OF SOCIAL SATURATION

> Communication . . . defines social reality and thus influences the organization of work,
> . . . the curriculum of the educational system, formal and informal relations, and the use
> of "free time"—actually the basic social arrangements of living.
> —*Herbert I. Schiller*, Communication and Cultural Domination

to multiply rapidly

In the process of social saturation the numbers, varieties, and intensities of relationship increasingly crowd the days. A full appreciation of the magnitude of cultural change, and its probable intensification in future decades, requires that one focus first on the technological context. For in large measure, an array of technological innovations has led to an enormous proliferation of relationships. It is useful to survey two major phases in technological development, specifically what may be roughly called *low-tech* and *high-tech* phases. Preliminary advice to the reader is in order. Read the following section on technological change as rapidly as possible, for an experiential immersion in the enormity of the whole.

Leading up to

Life in Low Tech

Perhaps the most dramatic aspect of the low-tech phase is the simultaneity of its many developments. Here we are speaking of no less than seven sweeping and overlapping developments within the century, each of which casts us further into the social world. Consider their impact on social life:

1. *The railroad* was one of the first significant steps toward social saturation. The first surge in rail travel began in the mid-1800s. In 1869 it became possible for Americans to cross the continent by train.[1] Although rails are less used in the United States than other modes of transportation, most nations continue to improve their systems. Major new track lines are being laid in Russia and China. Fast rail systems have been installed in Japan, France, Italy, and Sweden, and an under-Channel system will soon link London and Paris. The number of rail passengers in Europe reached an all-time high in 1988, almost doubling the volume in 1970.[2] At the same time, urban mass transit—including elevated and underground rail—moves a steadily increasing volume of persons. Underground systems now operate in such diverse cities as Cairo, Prague, Minsk, and Beijing. More than sixty major cities around the world are now expanding their urban rail systems, and twenty-five new systems have opened in the last two years. With the recent development of the "maglev" (or "flying train"), capable of carrying 1,000 passengers at a speed of over 300 mph, rail transportation may be facing a renaissance.

2. Although *public postal services* were available in the eighteenth century, they did not truly begin to flourish until the advent of railroads in the nineteenth century and then airlines in the twentieth. In the early 1800s there were only about two thousand miles of postal routes in the United States[3]; by 1960 the figure had jumped to over two million miles. The volume of mail is also expanding rapidly; Americans receive almost three times more mail now than in 1945. At present the volume of mail is so great that the U.S. Postal Service is considered the largest single business in the world. In the early 1980s it employed over 700,000 workers, and it now moves over eighty billion items a year—nearly four hundred pieces of mail for every citizen of the nation.

3. At the beginning of this century *the automobile* was virtually unknown. Less than 100 cars had ever been produced in the entire world. Production increased only slowly until the assembly line was perfected in the 1920s. By 1930 world production of motor vehicles had reached the four-million mark, with more than three quarters of them produced in the United States. Fifty years later, in 1980, the annual production figure had jumped to almost 40 million—of which approximately a fifth were made in the States.[4] Improvements in roads have also expanded the number of locations within reach. At the turn of the century there were only a hundred miles of hard-surface roads in the United States; by 1970 there were over two million miles of paved roads. Within recent decades the superhighways—more than 44,000 miles of them—have added new dimensions to long-distance travel.[5] Because of the expanding number of cars and people's increased dependency on them, traffic has become a major policy issue. Highway congestion is now so intense that the average speed on the Los Angeles freeways has dropped to 35 mph. In the next twenty years the volume of traffic is expected to rise by another 42 percent.[6]

4. *The telephone* made its entry into daily living at the turn of the century; within five decades there were some 90 million phones in the United States[7]; in the next decade, the number of phones almost doubled. There are now about 600 million telephones in the world (even though two-thirds of the world's population still has no access to telephones). And the miles of telephone wire continue to expand (from 316 million miles of wire in 1960 to 1,290 million miles in 1984). The pattern of telephone relationships is also changing. Most dramatic is the shift in the function of the telephone from a community, to a national, to an international resource. The number of overseas calls from the United States in 1960 was approximately 3 million; by 1984 this figure had multiplied by almost 130 times, to almost 430 million calls.[8] And, within the 1980s, international telephone calls increased sixfold. As we shall see, high tech is in the process of sending this figure upward by untold magnitudes.

5. *Radio broadcasting* began in the United States and Great Britain in 1919. Since that time it has insinuated itself into virtually all aspects of social life. It has altered social patterns in living rooms, dining rooms, bedrooms, automobiles, beaches, workshops, waiting rooms, and city streets. In 1925 there were 600 stations in the world. This figure doubled in the next ten years, and by 1960 there were over 10,000 stations.[9] With miniaturization and mass production radios became increasingly affordable. By the mid-1980s there were some two billion radios in the world. In recent years "personal audio" has also become a major cultural phenomenon. There are now more than 12 million personal stereos moving about the globe, some to the very edges of civilization: An anthropologist visiting hill tribes along the Burmese border recently reported that the tribespeople offer to trade local handicrafts for personal stereos.

6. At the turn of the century *motion pictures* scarcely existed. The first moving pictures were shown in scattered music halls. With improvements in photography, projection, and sound recording, however, motion pictures became increasingly popular. Even during the depression, box-office receipts remained relatively high. By the 1950s the weekly film audience in the United States alone reached 90 million.[10] Although film attendance at theaters has declined substantially as a result of television, both television and videocassettes continue to expose vast numbers of people to commercial films. (Over 60 percent of those American households with television also own a videocassette recorder.) In 1989 more new films were made in the United States than ever before—and even more were produced in India. *to spread widely*

7 *Printed books* have been disseminating ideas, values, and modes of life for over 400 years. By the mid-1700s, for example, England produced some 90 titles a year; a century later, it produced 600.[11] With the development of the rotary printing press and factory production systems, commercial publishing has become a dominant force in the twentieth century. Particularly in the 1950s, with the emergence of paperback books, ownership of books became possible for vast segments of the population: by the 1960s English publishers printed over 20,000 titles a year, and by the 1980s, five nations (Canada, England, West Germany, the United States, and the USSR) were publishing between 50,000 and 80,000 titles a year.[12]

So we find seven technologies of social saturation—rail, post, automobile, telephone, radio, motion pictures, and commercial publishing—all rapidly expanding within the twentieth century. Each brought people into increasingly close proximity, exposed them to an increasing range of others, and fostered a range of relationships that could never have occurred before.

High Life in High Tech   *associated or connected*

The seven low-tech alterations only began the saturation process. The past two decades have added untold potential for relatedness. We must briefly consider, then, the second, or high-tech, phase in the technology of social saturation, specifically developments in air transportation, television, and electronic communication.

Air Headings

> *Airport Gridlock Near, Aviation Experts Warn*
>
> —Headline, New York Times

The stories are told with increasing frequency: An executive flies from Washington, D.C., to Tokyo to represent his firm at a cocktail party; he returns the next day. Frankfurt couples fly to New York for the weekend to watch Boris Becker play in the U.S. Open. A New York executive flies to San Francisco to spend the day in consultation, and returns that night to Scarsdale on "the redeye." University officials wish to meet with candidates for an executive position; all are flown from locations across the continent for a single afternoon of meetings in an airport hotel. For a family reunion, eighteen people fly to St. Louis from five states across the nation.

For steadily increasing numbers air travel is becoming a casual matter. Businesses routinely think in terms of global expansion. Multinational corporations are so powerful that their budgets exceed that of many nations. Large cities are increasingly dependent on revenues from conference centers, international fairs, and tourism. For many academics, global conference-going is now a way of life. The reader of the Sunday *New York Times* in the 1930s would find no travel section. Today the section typically offers low-budget escapes to more than two hundred exotic locations. A high-school class reunion in North Carolina can pull graduates of over thirty years from as far away as Hawaii. Americans of Irish, Italian, German, and Scandinavian descent go to Europe in large numbers to locate relatives they have never met.

Such dramatic changes in social pattern have occurred only within the lifetime of most readers. Passenger travel by air was scarcely available before 1920. By the year 1940, however, there were approximately 3 million passengers in the United States.[13] Within ten years this figure jumped by six times. By 1970 the number of passengers reached almost 160 million. That figure again doubled in the next ten years. Almost eight of ten Americans have now flown. And, even though air traffic approaches gridlock, the FAA estimates 1990's total at 800 million passengers.[14] The number of passengers boarding planes in such cities as Dallas, Denver, Memphis, and Washington is expected to double by the year 2000. The Concorde now reaches speeds of Mach 2, transporting passengers from London to New York in less than four hours; a new generation of SSTs may bring Tokyo as close.[15]

Vistas of Video

passionate

A timid appearing junior college student meets a tall, blond, drug-using house-painter . . . and invites him to dinner. He gets amorous and rapes her in the bedroom of her apartment. She files charges but less than a month later she posts his bail and moves in with him and plans to be Mrs. Rapist. . . . When asked how she could marry [him] after what he did to her, she referred to a soap opera in which one character rapes another and later marries her. "It's like Luke and Laura on 'General Hospital,' " [she] said. . . . In keeping with the . . . TV flavor of the whole affair, [he] asked her to marry him while they were watching the Oprah Winfrey show, and they are considering an invitation to appear on the Phil Donahue show . . .

a decisive turning point

—*Philadelphia Daily News*

The year 1946 is a watershed, the first year of commercial television. In 1949 over a million television sets were sold in the United States. Two years later there were ten million; by 1959, fifty million.[16] By the early 1980s there were some 800 million television sets in use throughout the world. And they are watched. In the United States the average television set brings the outside world into the home for seven hours a day.

All that is well known. But two more subtle issues deserve attention, both significant to the understanding of social saturation.

First, it is important to consider a phenomenon with beginnings in the low-tech period of radio, film, and commercial publishing, but which becomes paramount in the high-tech era of television. This is the phenomenon of self-multiplication, or the capacity to be significantly present in more than one place at a time. In the face-to-face community one's capacities to carry on a relationship or to have social impact were restricted in space and time. Typically one's identity was manifest to those immediately before one's eyes, though books and newspapers made "multiples" of powerful individuals. With the development of radio and film, one's opinions, emotions, facial expressions, mannerisms, styles of relating, and the like were no longer confined to the immediate audience, but were multiplied manifold. Insights murmured into a microphone in Denver's Brown Palace Hotel could be heard by thousands in St. Louis, Minneapolis, and Grand Rapids. Manners of courting, arguing, deceiving, or playing the hero in a Hollywood studio were available for small-town millions across the country.

having many or various forms

Television has generated an exponential increase in self-multiplication. This is true not only in terms of the increased size of television audiences and the number of hours to which they are exposed to social facsimiles, but in the extent to which self-multiplication transcends time—that is, in which one's identity is sustained in the culture's history. Because television channels are plentiful, popular shows are typically rebroadcast in succeeding years. The patient viewer can still resonate with Groucho Marx on *You Bet Your Life* or Jackie Gleason and Audrey Meadows on *The Honeymooners*.

Further, the VCR has made video-rental libraries possible—perhaps 500,000 throughout the country. Now people need not wait for a given film to be screened or televised; it lies waiting close by for the further duplication of its personages. People can choose the actors they wish to identify with or the stories that will bring fantasies to life. Increasingly this also means that in terms of producing a sense of social connection, any given actor may transcend his or her own death; viewers can continue their private relationships with Marilyn Monroe and James Dean long after the physical demise of the performers. With television, a personage may continue a robust life over eternity.

A second issue follows quickly from the first. I am proposing that the media—especially radio, television, and the movies—are vitally expanding the range and variety of relationships available to the population. Yet, the critic may reasonably respond, do such exposures count as *real* or important relationships? After all, there is no give-and-take, no reciprocal interchange. The answer to this challenge depends largely on what one counts as "real or important." Surely face-to-face encounter is not a requirement of what most people would consider "real and important" relationships. Some of the world's most intense affairs of the heart (Héloïse and Abelard, Elizabeth Barrett and Robert Browning) were carried on largely by written word. Nor does reciprocal interchange seem essential for significant bonding; consider people's relationships with religious figures such as Jesus, Buddha, and Mohammed. If palpable presence is not essential to such relationships, then one must be prepared for the possibility that media figures do enter significantly into people's personal lives.

There is good reason to believe so. Social researchers have long been concerned with the impact of televised violence on the attitudes and behavior of the young. Numerous instances of people acting out what they've seen on television have been documented, even when the models engage in theft, torture, and murder.[17] More directly, Richard Schickel's *Intimate Strangers* explores the manner in which the media generate an illusionary sense of intimacy with celebrity figures.[18] Not only are famous people available to us on television, in the movies, in autobiographies, and in celebrity magazines, but often these media furnish intimate details of their personal lives. We may know more about Merv, Oprah, Johnny, and Phil than we do our neighbors. At one point, according to a national survey, newsman Walter Cronkite was the "most trusted man in America." And, because such figures do become so well known, people absorb them into their cast of significant others—loving, sympathizing with, and loathing them. It is thus that David Letterman sought a court injunction against a woman who claimed to be his wife, John Lennon was killed by an unknown fan, President Reagan was shot by John Hinckley, and the television star Rebecca Schaeffer was killed by a fan who had written unanswered letters to her for two years. The columnist Cynthia Heimel argues that because celebrity figures are known by so many people, they serve as forms of social glue, allowing people from different points of society to converse with each other, to share feelings, and essentially to carry on informal relations. "Celebrities," she proposes, "are our common frames of reference, celebrity loathing and revilement crosses all cultural boundaries. Celebrities are not our community elders, they are our community."[19]

Also relevant are the immense amounts of time, money, and personal effort that go into maintaining media relationships. Millions are spent each year on magazines, books, posters, T-shirts, towels, and photographs bearing likenesses of the favored idol. When *Batman* opened, a crowd of 20,000 stood for hours to glimpse celebrities for a few seconds in person. How many of one's neighbors elicit such dedication? It may also be ventured that with the advances in film technology, the movies have become one of the most powerful rhetorical devices in the world. Unlike most of our acquaintances, films can catapult us rapidly and effectively into states of fear, anger, sadness, romance, lust, and aesthetic ecstasy—often within the same two-hour period. It is undoubtedly true that for many people film relationships provide the most emotionally wrenching experiences of the average week. The ultimate question is not whether media relationships approximate the normal in their significance, but whether normal relationships can match the powers of artifice. *a clever scheme*

For many, the powers of artifice may indeed be in the superior position. So powerful are the media in their well-wrought portrayals that their realities become more compelling than those furnished by common experience. The vacation is not *real* until captured on film; marriages become events staged for camera and videotape; sports fans often prefer television because it is more fully lifelike than the eyeball view from the stands. It is to the media, and not to sense perception, that we increasingly turn for definitions of what is the case.

Electronic Innovation and the Proliferation of Relationships

> *Tomorrow's executives will have to feel as "at home" in Sapporo as Strasbourg as San Francisco . . . asserts Lester Thurow, Dean of MIT's Sloan School of Management. . . . "To be trained as an American manager is to be trained for a world that is no longer there."*
> —U.S. News and World Report

Two of the greatest impediments to communicating, and thus relating, over long distances are slowness and expense. In the 1850s it was possible to convey a message across the American continent, but the speed of transmission was approximately ten miles an hour. The Pony Express required nine days to carry mail from Missouri to California, and the cost for half an ounce was $5.[20] The telegraph system later increased the speed of transmission by an enormous magnitude, but it was still expensive. In recent decades, electronic transmission has cut sharply into these two barriers, and current developments stagger the imagination.

In the late 1950s the development of the digital computer brought great advantages: it could store immense amounts of information in a relatively small space, and could process and transmit this information very quickly. The computer has now become a mainstay for most businesses of any magnitude. With the development of the microchip in the late 1970s, the efficiency of information storage, processing, and transmission increased by an additional magnitude. In the space required by a single handwritten letter, the equivalent of 500 books— two good-sized bookcases—can now be stored on a microchip.[21] With the perfection of laser processing, the microchip will be replaced by a process enabling a single disk on a home computer to store the entire works of Shakespeare several times over. In a single suitcase could be deposited the entire contents of the Library of Congress. Where days might be required to transmit the contents of a single book by telegraph or even phone, microprocessing enables such contents to be transmitted within a matter of seconds. Further, the microchip has meant that computers could be cheap enough for home use; the personal computer business is now a major growth industry in many countries. In 1981 there were slightly over 2 million personal computers in America.[22] By 1987 the figure jumped to almost 38 million, some 10 percent of which allows laptop work to continue in trains, planes, and hotel rooms. And sales continue to rise . . .

With low-cost electronic printing equipment (including home printers and copy machines), every computer owner is now a potential book publisher. Through desktop publishing, computer owners become direct agents of their own self-multiplication. Proponents of electronic communication had expected use of paper to dwindle in the 1990s, but largely because of desktop publishing, more paper is now used than ever before. With the development of the modem, any computer could be linked via existing phone cables to any other computer with a modem. This development, in turn, gave birth to electronic mail, computer teleconferences, and on-line databases (or information services).

Electronic mail first served mainly those within one city or organization. Most large cities offer bulletin-board services, which allow individuals to place an announcement of their interests on a file open to all users of the system. In this way computer conversations develop, and fanciful subcultures spring to life, sharing interests—at any time of day or night—in areas ranging from African art to aphrodisiacs, backgammon to banjos, philately to fellatio. There is almost always someone "out there" to talk to. Many local bulletin boards are also connected to national routing services that transmit messages overnight and free of charge from one board to another across the country. Many participants speak of the warm and accepting relations that develop within these contexts—much like a corner bar, where there are always old buddies and new friends. Estimates are that up to a billion messages a year are now being transmitted in the United States by electronic mail.[23]

Teleconference services enable groups of persons from across the country simultaneously to converse with one another. Over a half million Americans also make use of national, on-line information services or videotex—CompuServe, Dow Jones, or the Source—with databases that rapidly inform their users of airline schedules, movie reviews, world weather, the national news, and more. In France there are over 3,000 such home services available, including home banking, shopping, real-estate listings, and magazine contents.

In the 1960s rockets made it possible to place communication satellites into orbits that keep them in a fixed position relative to points on earth. While in orbit, they can bounce continuous electronic transmissions from one point on earth to another over almost one-third of the planet's surface. At present these satellites transmit radio signals, telephone communication, digital data, and the like instantaneously to the far corners of the globe. Governments rely on such services to carry out their foreign policies, multinational corporations to conduct business, and individuals to sustain friendships. In poor rural areas in Mexico, satellite dishes allow Mexican families to receive as many as 130 TV channels from at least seven nations and in five languages. Satellite television reception is only in its infancy. In the mid-1980s it involved 130 satellites; twice as many are anticipated by the early 1990s.[24] To help business and government take advantage of the satellite capabilities, new companies are springing to life. These enterprises, some now boasting over 100,000 employees, install globe-spanning communications networks.

Worldwide electronic linkages, in combination with computer and telephone, have enabled the development of further social linkages via fax machines, which can convey printed matter rapidly and inexpensively throughout the world. A letter written by a political figure in Iran can, within seconds, be received in embassies around the globe. And with the aid of photocopy and mail, the same message can be in the hands of thousands the following day. Fax machines are rapidly gaining the capacity to transmit complex visual materials (such as maps and photographs), and the cost is dropping enough for fax services to be offered in hotels, in airports, and on trains. Low-cost, personal fax facilities are now advertised in flight magazines; the next step is clear.

These developments—computers, electronic mail, satellites, faxes—are only the beginning. Innovations now emerging will further accelerate the growth in social connectedness. At the outset is the digitization of all the major media—phonograph, photography, printing, telephone, radio, television. This means that the information conveyed by each source—pictures, music, voice—is becoming translatable to computer form. As a result, each medium becomes subject to the vast storage and rapid processing and transmission capabilities of the computer.[25] Each becomes subject to home production and worldwide dissemination. We now face an age in which pressing a button will enable us to transmit self-images—in full color and sound—around the globe.

Fiberoptic cables increase the amount of information that can be received a thousandfold. This opens the possibility for a virtual infinity of new television and radio bands. Further, fiberoptic cable will allow the transmission of a television picture of twice the fidelity of what is now available (approximating 35mm motion picture film). Digital phone services can be carried on the cable, not only reproducing the voice with fidelity, but also enabling subscribers to see the other person. So much information can be carried on the cable that all these various services could be taking place while subscribers were simultaneously having their utility meters read and their electronic mail collected. With a home fax receiver, one could also have an instant *Los Angeles Times* or *National Geographic* at one's fingertips.[26] Plans are now under way for people to designate the kinds of news they wish to see, and for computers to scan information services and compose individualized newspapers—to be printed on reusable paper.[27]

Over a hundred nations (including the USSR) are now involved in linking all the world's phone systems. Simultaneously, the development of the cellular phone is mobilizing possibilities for communication. With the development of point-to-point contact around the world, the 12 million cellular phones now in use will represent but a bare beginning. One could be anywhere—from a woodside walk in Maine to a hut in the Malaysian jungle—and speak with a loved one or colleague on the other side of the globe. Plans are now afoot for the world system to carry all electronic signals—including phone, television, recorded music, written text. This would enable a user to plug into the system anywhere from Alabama to Zaire and immediately transmit and receive manuscripts, sound recordings, or videotapes. The process of social saturation is far from complete.

THE PROCESS OF SOCIAL SATURATION

> *Monocultural communication is the simplest, most natural, and—in the contemporary world—most fragile form of communication. At its best, it is a rich, satisfying, and effort-less way of communicating; at its worst, it can be narrow-minded and coercive.*
> —W. Barnett Pearce, Communication and the Human Condition

A century ago, social relationships were largely confined to the distance of an easy walk. Most were conducted in person, within small communities: family, neighbors, townspeople. Yes, the horse and carriage made longer trips possible, but even a trip of thirty miles could take all day. The railroad could speed one away, but cost and availability limited such travel. If one moved from the community, relationships were likely to end. From birth to death one could depend on relatively even-textured social surroundings. Words, faces, gestures, and possibilities were relatively consistent, coherent, and slow to change.

For much of the world's population, especially the industrialized West, the small, face-to-face community is vanishing into the pages of history. We go to country inns for weekend outings, we decorate condominium interiors with clapboards and brass beds, and we dream of old age in a rural cottage. But as a result of the technological developments just described, contemporary life is a swirling sea of social relations. Words thunder in by radio, television, newspaper, mail, telephone, fax, wire service, electronic mail, billboards, Federal Express, and more. Waves of new faces are everywhere—in town for a day, visiting for the weekend, at the Rotary lunch, at the church social—and incessantly and incandescently on television. Long weeks in a single community are unusual; a full day within a single neighborhood is becoming rare. We travel casually across town, into the countryside, to neighboring towns, cities, states; one might go thirty miles for coffee and conversation.

Through the technologies of the century, the number and variety of relationships in which we are engaged, potential frequency of contact, expressed intensity of relationship, and endurance through time all are steadily increasing. As this increase becomes extreme we reach a state of social saturation. Let us consider this state in greater detail.

Multiplying Relationships

In the face-to-face community the cast of others remained relatively stable.[28] There were changes by virtue of births and deaths, but moving from one town—much less state or country—to another was difficult. The number of relationships commonly maintained in today's world stands in stark contrast. Counting one's family, the morning television news, the car radio, colleagues on the train, and the local newspaper, the typical commuter may confront as many different persons (in terms of views or images) in the first two hours of a day as the community-based predecessor did in a month. The morning calls in a business office may connect one to a dozen different locales in a given city, often across the continent, and very possibly across national boundaries. A single hour of prime-time melodrama immerses one in the lives of a score of individuals. In an evening of television, hundreds of engaging faces insinuate themselves into our lives. It is not only the immediate community that occupies our thoughts and feelings, but a constantly changing cast of characters spread across the globe.

Two aspects of this expansion are particularly noteworthy. First there is what may be termed the perseverance of the past. Formerly, increases in time and distance between persons typically meant loss. When someone moved away, the relationship would languish. Long-distance visits were arduous, and the mails slow. Thus, as one grew older, many active participants would fade from one's life. Today, time and distance are no longer such serious threats to a relationship. One may sustain an intimacy over thousands of miles by frequent telephone raptures punctuated by occasional visits. One may similarly retain relationships with high-school chums, college roommates, old military cronies, or friends from a Caribbean vacation five years earlier. Birthday books have become a standard household item; one's memory is inadequate to record the festivities for which one is responsible. In effect, as we move through life, the cast of relevant characters is ever expanding. For some this means an ever-increasing sense of stress: "How can we make friends with them? We don't even have time for the friends we already have!" For others there is a sense of comfort, for the social caravan in which we travel through life remains always full.

Yet at the same time that the past is preserved, continuously poised to insert itself into the present, there is an _acceleration of the future_. The pace of relationships is hurried, and processes of unfolding that once required months or years may be accomplished in days or weeks. A century ago, for example, courtships were often carried out on foot or horseback, or through occasional letters. Hours of interchange might be punctuated by long periods of silence, making the path from acquaintanceship to intimacy lengthy. With today's technologies, however, it is possible for a couple to maintain almost continuous connection. Not only do transportation technologies chip away at the barrier of geographic distance, but through telephone (both stable and cordless), overnight mail, cassette recordings, home videos, photographs, and electronic mail, the other may be "present" at almost any moment. Courtships may thus move from excitement to exhaustion within a short time. The single person may experience not a handful of courtship relationships in a lifetime but dozens. In the same way, the process of friendship is often accelerated. Through the existing technologies, a sense of affinity may blossom into a lively sense of interdependence within a brief space of time. As the future opens, the number of friendships expands as never before.

Bending the Life-Forms

> _Our private sphere has ceased to be the stage where the drama of the subject at odds with his objects . . . is played out; we no longer exist as playwrights or actors, but as terminals of multiple networks._
>
> —Jean Baudrillard, The Ecstasy of Communication

New patterns of relationship also take shape. In the face-to-face community one participated in a limited set of relationships—with family, friends, storekeepers, clerics, and the like. Now the next telephone call can thrust us suddenly into a new relationship—with a Wall Street broker, a charity solicitor, an alumni campaigner from the old school, a childhood friend at a nearby convention, a relative from across the country, a child of a friend, or even a sex pervert. One may live in a suburb with well-clipped neighbors, but commute to a city for frequent confrontation with street people, scam merchants, panhandlers, prostitutes, and threatening bands of juveniles. One may reside in Houston, but establish bonds—through business or leisure travel—with a Norwegian banker, a wine merchant from the Rhine Pfalz, or an architect from Rome.

Of course, it is television that most dramatically increases the variety of relationships in which one participates—even if vicariously. One can identify with heroes from a thousand tales, carry on imaginary conversations with talk-show guests from all walks of life, or empathize with athletes from around the globe. One of the most interesting results of this electronic expansion of relationships occurs in the domain of parent-child relationships. As Joshua Meyrowitz proposes in _No Sense of Place_, children of the preceding century were largely insulated from information about the private lives of adults.[29] Parents, teachers, and police could shield children from their adult proceedings by simply conducting them in private places. Further, books dealing with the misgivings, failings, deceits, and conflicts of the adult world were generally unavailable to children. Children remained children. Television has changed all that. Programming systematically reveals the full panoply of "backstage" trials and tribulations to the child. As a result the child no longer interacts with one-dimensional, idealized adults, but with persons possessing complex private lives, doubt-filled and vulnerable. In turn, parents no longer confront the comfortably naive child of yesteryear, but one whose awe is diminished and whose insights may be acute.

The technology of the age both expands the variety of human relationships and modifies the form of older ones. When relationships move from the face-to-face to the electronic mode, they are often altered. Relationships that were confined to specific situations—to offices, living rooms, bedrooms—become "unglued." They are no longer geographically confined, but can take place anywhere. Unlike face-to-face relationships, electronic relationships also conceal visual information (eye movement, expressive movements of the mouth), so a telephone speaker cannot read the facial cues of the listener for signs of approval or disapproval. As a result, there is a greater tendency to create an imaginary other with whom to relate. One can fantasize that the other is feeling warm and enthusiastic or cold and angry, and act accordingly. An acquaintance told me that he believed his first marriage to be a product of the heavy phoning necessary for a long-distance courtship. By phone she seemed the most desirable woman in the world; it was only months after the wedding that he realized he had married a mirage.

Many organizations are now installing electronic-mail systems, which enable employees to carry out their business with each other by computer terminals rather than by traditional, face-to-face means. Researchers find that employee relations have subtly changed as a result. Status differences begin to crumble as lower-ranking employees feel freer to express their feelings and question their superiors electronically than in person. Harvard Business School's Shoshana Zuboff suggests that the introduction of "smart machines" into businesses is blurring the distinctions between managers and workers. Managers are no longer the "thinkers" while the workers are consigned to the "doing."[30] Rather, out of necessity the workers now become managers of information, and as a result, they considerably augment their power.

Relating in New Keys

Of the new forms of relationship that the saturation process has helped create, two are of special interest. First is the *friendly lover* relationship. For the essential romanticist, the object of love was all-consuming. He or she possessed value of such immense proportion that a lifetime of steadfast commitment could be viewed merely as preparation for an eternity of spiritual communion. The belief in marriage for "true love" is still pervasive, but as the social world is increasingly saturated, such relationships become unrealistic. Rather, men and women (especially professionals) are often in motion—traveling to business meetings, conferences, sales campaigns, consultations, vacations, and so on. Murmurings of "I can't live without you" lose their authenticity when one must add, "except until next Tuesday, and possibly again until the following Wednesday." And because many attractive members of the opposite sex are encountered along the way—providing professional benefits and companionship as well—a multiplicity of low-level, or "friendly," romances is invited. To illustrate, a single professional woman from Maryland disclosed that she was "seeing" a local lawyer (unhappily married) because it was fun and convenient. At the same time, he took a back seat when a favorite "old friend" in her profession came in from Oklahoma. However, especially during the summer, she was keen to spend her weekends with a Boston consultant (relevant to her line of work) whose boat was moored at Martha's Vineyard. Each of these individuals, in turn, had other friendly lovers.

A second interesting pattern, the *microwave relationship*, is found increasingly on the domestic front. The ideal family unit has traditionally included a close, interdependent "nucleus," composed of a father-provider, a caretaking mother, and children whose lives are centered in the home until early adulthood. Social saturation has cut deeply into this traditional view. Husband and wife are now both likely to have work and recreational relations outside the family; day-care and babysitting facilities are increasingly required; children's social activities may be scattered across city and countryside; evening obligations or indulgences are frequent both for parents and for children over the age of six; and family members are typically drawn into outside activities—sports, religious, community, hobbies, visits—on the weekends. Differing television needs often thrust various family members into different trajectories even when they are at home together. In many families the crucial ritual of interdependence—dinner together—has become a special event. (In some households the dining-room table, once a family center, is strewn with books, papers, letters, and other objects dropped there by family members "passing through.") The home is less a nesting place than a pit stop.

At the same time, however, many parents are loath to give up the traditional image of the close-knit family. As a result, a new form of relationship emerges in which family members attempt to compensate for the vast expanses of nonrelatedness with intense expressions of bondedness. As many understand it, quantity is replaced by quality. The microwave oven is more than a technological support for those living a socially saturated life. It is also a good symbol of the newly emerging form of relationship: in both cases the users command intense heat for the immediate provision of nourishment. The adequacy of the result is subject to debate in both cases.

Intensifying Interchange

> Modern society is to be distinguished from older social formations by the fact that it affords more opportunities both for impersonal and for more intensive personal relation-ships.
>
> —*Niklas Luhmann,* Love as Passion

Interestingly, technology also intensifies the emotional level of many relationships. People come to feel more deeply and express themselves more fully in an increasing number of relationships. This proposal may seem suspect. If persons pass through our lives in increasing numbers and speeds, wouldn't the outcome be a sense of superficiality and a disinclination to get involved? The attractive stranger you meet in Seattle is regrettably from Omaha; the fascinating new neighbors are returning in the spring to London; the absorbing seatmate on the plane is flying on to Bombay. What is there to do but keep it light and cool? To be sure, the vast share of the passing parade remains simply that. However, consider two aspects of the traditional, face-to-face community.

First, as relationships continue over a period of years they tend toward normalization. People choose to do things that reliably give them satisfaction. Changes in pattern mean risking these satisfactions. Thus, relationships over time tend toward a leveling of emotional intensity. As many married couples put it, "Exciting romance is replaced by a comfortable depth."

Second, the face-to-face community lends itself to a high degree of informal surveillance. People tend to know what the others are doing most of the time. They see each other across a room, through their windows, passing in the street, and so on. And where the social world remains stable, and new information is scant, the smallest details of one's life become everyone's topics of conversation. Petty gossip and strong community norms walk hand in hand. The intensity generated by the new, the novel, and the deviant is in scarce supply.

In the present context of saturation, neither of these conditions prevails. Because all relationships are constantly being disrupted, it is more difficult for any given relationship to normalize. The evening at home, once quiet, relaxed, and settling, is now—by dint of telephone, automobile, television, and the like—a parade of faces, information, and intrusions. One can scarcely settle into a calming rut, because who one is and the cast of "significant others" are in continuous motion. Further, because relationships range far and wide, largely through various electronic means, they cannot easily be supervised by others who care. One can find the intimacy of "telling all" to a close friend in Chicago, because those who would be horrified in Dallas or Topeka will never know. One can let the internal fires rage in Paris, because the folk in Peoria will never see the glow. One academic colleague spoke of his conversation with a woman while waiting in a check-in line for a return journey to the United States. The plane was to stop over in Iceland, and passengers had the choice of continuing the journey directly or remaining in Iceland and catching the next plane two days later. The professor found himself attracted to the lady and emboldened by the anonymity of the situation. Suddenly he found himself stammering a proposal to the woman to remain with him in Iceland for two days. Her complex smile gave him no answer. They silently approached the baggage carts on which travelers had to place their bags for either the direct flight or the layover. To his speechless amazement, she maneuvered her bag into the latter cart. After two days of bliss they parted company, never to communicate with each other again.

The press toward intensity is not limited to normalization and the breakdown of surveillance. There are also factors of fantasy and fleetingness at play. As the romanticists were well aware, little inspired the pen so much as the absence of the adored one. In the other's absence, one's fantasies were free to roam; one could project onto the favored person all virtues and desires. In this respect, nineteenth-century romanticism can be partially attributed to the combination of a cultural morality that discouraged a free play of relationships and the number of individuals educated in writing. Although standards of morality have liberalized since then, the increased possibility for relationships at a distance has had much the same effect as it did on the romantics. Relations at a distance can thus glow more brightly, and interchanges remain more highly charged.

The occasional meeting is intensified, finally, by its shortness. If it is agreed that the other is a "good friend," "very close," or a "special person," then the short periods of meeting must be similarly expressive. One must somehow demonstrate the significance of one's feelings and the high esteem in which the relationship is held. And, because there is little time, the demonstrations must be loud and clear. The result may be an elegantly prepared dinner, reservations at an unusual restaurant, entertainments or excursions planned, selected guests invited for sharing, and the like. Friends living in a central European city recently complained of what amounted to a delirium and exhaustion. So frequently did visiting friends require a "display of significance" that both spirits and pocketbooks were depleted. Couples in frequently visited cities such as New York and Paris speak of the measures they take to ensure they have no spare bedrooms. With frequent visitors, no time remains for their nurturing capacities; spare rooms risk the evisceration of their private relationship.

POPULATING THE SELF

> The very din of imaginal voices in adulthood—as they sound in thought and memory, in poetry, drama, novels, and movies, in speech, dreams, fantasy, and prayer . . . can be valued not just as subordinate to social reality, but as a reality as intrinsic to human existence as the literally social.
>
> —Mary Watkins, Invisible Guests

Consider the moments:

- Over lunch with friends you discuss Northern Ireland. Although you have never spoken a word on the subject, you find yourself heatedly defending British policies.
- You work as an executive in the investments department of a bank. In the evenings you smoke marijuana and listen to the Grateful Dead.
- You sit in a café and wonder what it would be like to have an intimate relationship with various strangers walking past.
- You are a lawyer in a prestigious midtown firm. On the weekends you work on a novel about romance with a terrorist.
- You go to a Moroccan restaurant and afterward take in the latest show at a country-and-western bar.

In each case individuals harbor a sense of coherent identity or self-sameness, only to find themselves suddenly propelled by alternative impulses. They seem securely to be one sort of person, but yet another comes bursting to the surface—in a suddenly voiced opinion, a fantasy, a turn of interests, or a private activity. Such experiences with variation and self-contradiction may be viewed as preliminary effects of social saturation. They may signal a *populating of the self*, the acquisition of multiple and disparate potentials for being. It is this process of self-population that begins to undermine the traditional commitments to both romanticist and modernist forms of being. It is of pivotal importance in setting the stage for the postmodern turn. Let us explore.

The technologies of social saturation expose us to an enormous range of persons, new forms of relationship, unique circumstances and opportunities, and special intensities of feeling. One can scarcely remain unaffected by such exposure. As child-development specialists now agree, the process of socialization is lifelong. We continue to incorporate information from the environment throughout our lives. When exposed to other persons, we change in two major ways. We increase our capacities for *knowing that* and for *knowing how*. In the first case, through exposure to others we learn myriad details about their words, actions, dress, mannerisms, and so on. We ingest enormous amounts of information about patterns of interchange. Thus, for example, from an hour on a city street, we are informed of the clothing styles of blacks, whites, upper class, lower class, and more. We may learn the ways of Japanese businessmen, bag ladies, Sikhs, Hare Krishnas, or flute players from Chile. We see how relationships are carried out between mothers and daughters, business executives, teenage friends, and construction workers. An hour in a business office may expose us to the political views of a Texas oilman, a Chicago lawyer, and a gay activist from San Francisco. Radio commentators espouse views on boxing, pollution, and child abuse; pop music may advocate machoism, racial bigotry, and suicide. Paperback books cause hearts to race over the unjustly treated, those who strive against impossible odds, those who are brave or brilliant. And this is to say nothing of television input. Via television, myriad figures are allowed into the home who would never otherwise trespass. Millions watch as talk-show guests—murderers, rapists, women prisoners, child abusers, members of the KKK, mental patients, and others often discredited—attempt to make their lives intelligible. There are few six-year-olds who cannot furnish at least a rudimentary account of life in an African village, the concerns of divorcing parents, or drug-pushing in the ghetto. Hourly our storehouse of social knowledge expands in range and sophistication.

This massive increase in knowledge of the social world lays the groundwork for a second kind of learning, a *knowing how*. We learn how to place such knowledge into action, to shape it for social

a first principle
as of subject
to be learn

consumption, to act so that social life can proceed effectively. And the possibilities for placing this supply of information into effective action are constantly expanding. The Japanese businessman glimpsed on the street today, and on the television tomorrow, may well be confronted in one's office the following week. On these occasions the rudiments of appropriate behavior are already in place. If a mate announces that he or she is thinking about divorce, the other's reaction is not likely to be dumb dismay. The drama has so often been played out on television and movie screens that one is already prepared with multiple options. If one wins a wonderful prize, suffers a humiliating loss, faces temptation to cheat, or learns of a sudden death in the family, the reactions are hardly random. One more or less knows how it goes, is more or less ready for action. Having seen it all before, one approaches a state of ennui. — indifference caused by boredom

In an important sense, as social saturation proceeds we become pastiches, imitative assemblages of each other. In memory we carry others' patterns of being with us. If the conditions are favorable, we can place these patterns into action. Each of us becomes the other, a representative, or a replacement. To put it more broadly, as the century has progressed selves have become increasingly populated with the character of others.[31] We are not one, or a few, but like Walt Whitman, we "contain multitudes." We appear to each other as single identities, unified, of whole cloth. However, with social saturation, each of us comes to harbor a vast population of hidden potentials—to be a blues singer, a gypsy, an aristocrat, a criminal. All the selves lie latent, and under the right conditions may spring to life.

The populating of the self not only opens relationships to new ranges of possibility, but one's subjective life also becomes more fully laminated. Each of the selves we acquire from others can contribute to inner dialogues, private discussions we have with ourselves about all manner of persons, events, and issues. These internal voices, these vestiges of relationships both real and imagined, have been given different names: *invisible guests* by Mary Watkins, *social imagery* by Eric Klinger, and *social ghosts* by Mary Gergen, who found in her research that virtually all the young people she sampled could discuss many such experiences with ease.[32] Most of these ghosts were close friends, often from earlier periods of their lives. Family members were also frequent, with the father's voice predominating, but grandparents, uncles, aunts, and other relatives figured prominently. Relevant to the earlier discussion of relations with media figures, almost a quarter of the ghosts mentioned were individuals with whom the young people had never had any direct interchange. Most were entertainers: rock stars, actors and actresses, singers, and the like. Others were religious figures such as Jesus and Mary, fictitious characters such as James Bond and Sherlock Holmes, and celebrities such as Chris Evert, Joe Montana, Barbara Walters, and the president. considered as a positive solution

The respondents also spoke of the many ways the social ghosts functioned in their lives. It was not simply that they were there for conversation or contemplation; they also served as models for action. They set standards for behavior; they were admired and were emulated. As one wrote, "Connie Chung was constantly being used as a role model for me and I found myself responding to a question about what I planned to do after graduation by saying that I wanted to go into journalism just because I had been thinking of her." Or, as another wrote of her grandmother, "She showed me how to be tolerant of all people and to show respect to everyone regardless of their state in life." Ghosts also voiced opinions on various matters. Most frequently they were used to bolster one's beliefs. At times such opinions were extremely important. As one wrote of the memory of an early friend, "She is the last link I have to Christianity at this point in my life when I am trying to determine my religious inclinations." Still other respondents spoke of the way their ghosts supported their self-esteem: "I think my father and I know that he would be proud of what I have accomplished." Many mentioned the sense of emotional support furnished by their ghosts: "My grandmother seems to be watching me and showing that she loves me even if I am not doing so well."

In closely related work, the psychologists Hazel Markus and Paula Nurius speak of *possible selves*, the multiple conceptions people harbor of what they might become, would like to become, or are afraid to become.[33] In each case, these possible selves function as private surrogates for others to whom one has been exposed—either directly or via the media. The family relations specialists Paul Rosenblatt and Sara Wright speak similarly of the *shadow realities* that exist in close relationships.[34] In addition to the reality that a couple shares together, each will harbor alternative interpretations of their lives together—interpretations that might appear unacceptable and threatening if revealed to the partner. These shadow realities are typically generated and supported by persons outside the relationship—possibly members of the extended family, but also figures from the media. Finally, the British psychologist Michael Billig and his colleagues have studied the values, goals, and ideals to which people are committed in their everyday lives.[35] They found the typical condition of the individual to be internal conflict: for each belief there exists a strong countertendency. People feel their prejudices are justified, yet it is wrong to be intolerant; that there should be equality but hierarchies are also good; and that we are all basically the same, but we must hold on to our individuality. For every value, goal, or ideal, one holds to the converse as well. Billig proposes that the capacity for contradiction is essential to the practical demands of life in contemporary society.

a harsh noise

government or religion

This virtual cacophony of potentials is of no small consequence for either romanticist or modernist visions of the self. For as new and disparate voices are added to one's being, committed identity becomes an increasingly arduous achievement. How difficult for the romantic to keep firm grasp on the helm of an idealistic undertaking when a chorus of internal voices sing the praises of realism, skepticism, hedonism, and nihilism. And can the committed realist, who believes in the powers of rationality and observation, remain arrogant in the face of inner urges toward emotional indulgence, moral sentiment, spiritual sensitivity, or aesthetic fulfillment? Thus, as social saturation adds incrementally to the population of self, each impulse toward well-formed identity is cast into increasing doubt; each is found absurd, shallow, limited, or flawed by the onlooking audience of the interior.

page 22

MULTIPHRENIA

> *Modern man is afflicted with a permanent identity crisis, a condition conducive to considerable nervousness.*
>
> —*Peter Berger, Brigitte Berger, and Hansfried Kellner*, The Homeless Mind

It is a sunny Saturday morning and he finishes breakfast in high spirits. It is a rare day in which he is free to do as he pleases. With relish he contemplates his options. The back door needs fixing, which calls for a trip to the hardware store. This would allow a much-needed haircut; and while in town he could get a birthday card for his brother, leave off his shoes for repair, and pick up shirts at the cleaners. But, he ponders, he really should get some exercise; is there time for jogging in the afternoon? That reminds him of a championship game he wanted to see at the same time. To be taken more seriously was his ex-wife's repeated request for a luncheon talk. And shouldn't he also settle his vacation plans before all the best locations are taken? Slowly his optimism gives way to a sense of defeat. The free day has become a chaos of competing opportunities and necessities.

If such a scene is vaguely familiar, it attests only further to the pervasive effects of social saturation and the populating of the self. More important, one detects amid the hurly-burly of contemporary life a new constellation of feelings or sensibilities, a new pattern of self-consciousness. This syndrome may be termed multiphrenia, generally referring to the splitting of the individual into a multiplicity of self-investments. This condition is partly an outcome of self-population, but partly a result of the populated self's efforts to exploit the potentials of the technologies of relationship. In this sense, there is a cyclical spiraling toward a state of multiphrenia. As one's potentials are expanded by the technologies, so one increasingly employs the technologies for self-expression; yet, as the technologies are further utilized, so do they add to the repertoire of potentials. It would be a mistake to view this multiphrenic condition as a form of illness, for it is often suffused with a sense of expansiveness and adventure. Someday there may indeed be nothing to distinguish multiphrenia from simply "normal living."

However, before we pass into this oceanic state, let us pause to consider some prominent features of the condition.[36] Three of these are especially noteworthy.

Vertigo of the Valued

> *Because of the constant change and feeling "off balance," it is essential for men and women to develop . . . coping skills. First, understand that you will never "catch up" and be on top of things and accept this as all right. . . . Put a high priority on spending time relaxing and enjoying life, in spite of all that needs to be done.*
>
> —Bruce A. Baldwin, Stress and Technology

With the technology of social saturation, two of the major factors traditionally impeding relationships—namely time and space—are both removed. The past can be continuously renewed—via voice, video, and visits, for example—and distance poses no substantial barriers to ongoing interchange. Yet this same freedom ironically leads to a form of enslavement. For each person, passion, or potential incorporated into oneself exacts a penalty—a penalty both of *being* and of *being with*. In the former case, as others are incorporated into the self, their tastes, goals, and values also insinuate themselves into one's being. Through continued interchange, one acquires, for example, a yen for Thai cooking, the desire for retirement security, or an investment in wildlife preservation. Through others one comes to value whole-grain breads, novels from Chile, or community politics. Yet as Buddhists have long been aware, to desire is simultaneously to become a slave of the desirable. To "want" reduces one's choice to "want not." Thus, as others are incorporated into the self, and their desires become one's own, there is an expansion of goals—of "musts," wants, and needs. Attention is necessitated, effort is exerted, frustrations are encountered. Each new desire places its demands and reduces one's liberties.

There is also the penalty of being with. As relationships develop, their participants acquire local definitions—friend, lover, teacher, supporter, and so on. To sustain the relationship requires an honoring of the definitions—both of self and other. If two persons become close friends, for example, each acquires certain rights, duties, and privileges. Most relationships of any significance carry with them a range of obligations—for communication, joint activities, preparing for the other's pleasure, rendering appropriate congratulations, and so on. Thus, as relations accumulate and expand over time, there is a steadily increasing range of phone calls to make and answer, greeting cards to address, visits or activities to arrange, meals to prepare, preparations to be made, clothes to buy, makeup to apply . . . And with each new opportunity— for skiing together in the Alps, touring Australia, camping in the Adirondacks, or snorkling in the Bahamas—there are "opportunity costs." One must unearth information, buy equipment, reserve hotels, arrange travel, work long hours to clear one's desk, locate babysitters, dogsitters, homesitters . . . Liberation becomes a swirling vertigo of demands.

In the professional world this expansion of "musts" is strikingly evident. In the university of the 1950s, for example, one's departmental colleagues were often vital to one's work. One could walk but a short distance for advice, information, support, and so on. Departments were often closeknit and highly interdependent; travels to other departments or professional meetings were notable events. Today, however, the energetic academic will be linked by post, long-distance phone, fax, and electronic mail to like-minded scholars around the globe. The number of interactions possible in a day is limited only by the constraints of time. The technologies have also stimulated the development of hundreds of new organizations, international conferences, and professional meetings. A colleague recently informed me that if funds were available he could spend his entire sabbatical traveling from one professional gathering to another. A similar condition pervades the business world. One's scope of business opportunities is no longer so limited by geography; the technologies of the age enable projects to be pursued around the world. (Colgate Tartar Control toothpaste is now sold in over forty countries.) In effect, the potential for new connection and new opportunities is practically unlimited. Daily life has become a sea of drowning demands, and there is no shore in sight.

The Expansion of Inadequacy

> *Now You Can Read the Best Business Books of 1989 in Just 15 Minutes Each!*
> —*Advertisement,* US Air Magazine

> *Information anxiety is produced by the ever-widening gap between what we understand and what we think we should understand.*
> —*Richard Saul Wurman,* Information Anxiety

It is not simply the expansion of self through relationships that hounds one with the continued sense of "ought." There is also the seeping of self-doubt into everyday consciousness, a subtle feeling of inadequacy that smothers one's activities with an uneasy sense of impending emptiness. In important respects this sense of inadequacy is a by-product of the populating of self and the presence of social ghosts. For as we incorporate others into ourselves, so does the range of proprieties expand—that is, the range of what we feel a "good," "proper," or "exemplary" person should be. Many of us carry with us the "ghost of a father," reminding us of the values of honesty and hard work, or a mother challenging us to be nurturing and understanding. We may also absorb from a friend the values of maintaining a healthy body, from a lover the goal of self-sacrifice, from a teacher the ideal of worldly knowledge, and so on. Normal development leaves most people with a rich range of "goals for a good life," and with sufficient resources to achieve a sense of personal well-being by fulfilling these goals.

But now consider the effects of social saturation. The range of one's friends and associates expands exponentially; one's past life continues to be vivid; and the mass media expose one to an enormous array of new criteria for self-evaluation. A friend from California reminds one to relax and enjoy life; in Ohio an associate is getting ahead by working eleven hours a day. A relative from Boston stresses the importance of cultural sophistication, while a Washington colleague belittles one's lack of political savvy. A relative's return from Paris reminds one to pay more attention to personal appearance, while a ruddy companion from Colorado suggests that one grows soft.

Meanwhile newspapers, magazines, and television provide a barrage of new criteria of self-evaluation. Is one sufficiently adventurous, clean, well traveled, well read, low in cholesterol, slim, skilled in cooking, friendly, odor-free, coiffed, frugal, burglarproof, family-oriented? The list is unending. More than once I have heard the lament of a subscriber to the Sunday *New York Times*. Each page of this weighty tome will be read by millions. Thus each page remaining undevoured by day's end will leave one precariously disadvantaged—a potential idiot in a thousand unpredictable circumstances.

Yet the threat of inadequacy is hardly limited to the immediate confrontation with mates and media. Because many of these criteria for self-evaluation are incorporated into the self—existing within the cadre of social ghosts—they are free to speak at any moment. The problem with values is that they are sufficient unto themselves. To value justice, for example, is to say nothing of the value of love; investing in duty will blind one to the value of spontaneity. No one value in itself recognizes the importance of any alternative value. And so it is with the chorus of social ghosts. Each voice of value stands to discredit all that does not meet its standard. All the voices at odds with one's current conduct thus stand as internal critics, scolding, ridiculing, and robbing action of its potential for fulfillment. One settles in front of the television for enjoyment, and the chorus begins: "twelve-year-old," "couch potato," "lazy," "irresponsible" ... One sits down with a good book, and again, "sedentary," "antisocial," "inefficient," "fantasist" ... Join friends for a game of tennis and "skin cancer," "shirker of household duties," "underexercised," "overly competitive" come up. Work late and it is "workaholic," "heart attack–prone," "overly ambitious," "irresponsible family member." Each moment is enveloped in the guilt born of all that was possible but now foreclosed.

Rationality in Recession

> *A group of agents acting rationally in the light of their expectations could arrive at so many outcomes that none has adequate reasons for action.*
> —*Martin Hollis*, The Cunning of Reason

> *Latin Debts: Lack of Consensus*
> *Washington Awash in Arguments,*
> *Dry on Agreements*
>
> —*Headlines*, International Herald Tribune

A third dimension of multiphrenia is closely related to the others. The focus here is on the rationality of everyday decision making—instances in which one tries to be a "reasonable person." Why, one asks, is it important for one's children to attend college? The rational reply is that a college education increases one's job opportunities, earnings, and likely sense of personal fulfillment. Why should I stop smoking? one asks, and the answer is clear that smoking causes cancer, so to smoke is simply to invite a short life. Yet these "obvious" lines of reasoning are obvious only so long as one's identity remains fixed within a particular group.

The rationality of these replies depends altogether on the sharing of opinions—of each incorporating the views of others. To achieve identity in other cultural enclaves turns these "good reasons" into "rationalizations," "false consciousness," or "ignorance." Within some subcultures a college education is a one-way ticket to bourgeois conventionality—a white-collar job, picket fence in the suburbs, and chronic boredom. For many, smoking is an integral part of a risky life-style; it furnishes a sense of intensity, offbeatness, rugged individualism. In the same way, saving money for old age is "sensible" in one family, and "oblivious to the erosions of inflation" in another. For most Westerners, marrying for love is the only reasonable (if not conceivable) thing to do. But many Japanese will point to statistics demonstrating greater longevity and happiness in arranged marriages. Rationality is a vital by-product of social participation.

Yet as the range of our relationships is expanded, the validity of each localized rationality is threatened. What is rational in one relationship is questionable or absurd from the standpoint of another. The "obvious choice" while talking with a colleague lapses into absurdity when speaking with a spouse, and into irrelevance when an old friend calls that evening. Further, because each relationship increases one's capacities for discernment, one carries with oneself a multiplicity of competing expectations, values, and beliefs about "the obvious solution." Thus, if the options are carefully evaluated, every decision becomes a leap into gray vapors. Hamlet's bifurcated decision becomes all too simple, for it is no longer being or nonbeing that is in question, but to which of multifarious beings one can be committed. T. S. Eliot began to sense the problem when Prufrock found "time yet for a hundred indecisions/And for a hundred visions and revisions,/Before taking of a toast and tea."[37]

The otherwise simple task of casting a presidential vote provides a useful illustration. As one relates (either directly or vicariously) to various men and women, in various walks of life, and various sectors of the nation or abroad, one's capacities for discernment are multiplied. Where one might have once employed a handful of rational standards, or seen the issues in only limited ways, one can now employ a variety of criteria and see many sides of many issues. One may thus favor candidate A because he strives for cuts in the defense budget, but also worry about the loss of military capability in an unsteady world climate. Candidate B's plans for stimulating the growth of private enterprise may be rational from one standpoint, but the resulting tax changes seem unduly to penalize the middle-class family. At the same time, there is good reason to believe that A's cuts in defense spending will favor B's aims for a stimulated economy, and that B's shifts in the tax structure will make A's reductions in the military budget unnecessary. To use one criterion, candidate A is desirable because of his seeming intelligence, but from another, his complex ideas seem both cumbersome and remote from reality. Candidate B has a pleasing personality, useful for him to garner popular support for his programs, but in another sense his pleasant ways suggest he cannot take a firm stand. And so on.

Increasing the criteria of rationality does not, then, move one to a clear and univocal judgment of the candidates. Rather, the degree of complexity is increased until a rationally coherent stand is impossible. In effect, as social saturation steadily expands the population of the self, a choice of candidates approaches the arbitrary. A toss of a coin becomes equivalent to the diligently sought solution. We approach a condition in which the very idea of "rational choice" becomes meaningless.

So we find a profound sea change taking place in the character of social life during the twentieth century. Through an array of newly emerging technologies the world of relationships becomes increasingly saturated. We engage in greater numbers of relationships, in a greater variety of forms, and with greater intensities than ever before. With the multiplication of relationships also comes a transformation in the social capacities of the individual—both in knowing how and knowing that. The relatively coherent and unified sense of self inherent in a traditional culture gives way to manifold and competing potentials. A multiphrenic condition emerges in which one swims in ever-shifting, concatenating, and contentious currents of being. One bears the burden of an increasing array of oughts, of self-doubts and irrationalities. The possibility for committed romanticism or strong and single-minded modernism recedes, and the way is opened for the postmodern being.

to link together

NOTES

1. Although rail transportation in the United States accounts for a smaller proportion of public travel, the number of rail passengers continues to mount. The U.S. Department of Transportation's *15th Annual Report, Fiscal Year 1981* (Washington: U.S. Government Printing Office, 1981) reports that from 1972 to 1981, the number of passengers increased from 13.7 million to 20.6 million. See also F. D. Hobbs, "Transportation," in *Encyclopaedia Britannica* (1988).
2. *International Herald Tribune,* 15 May 1990.
3. See Andrew C. Brix, "Postal Systems," in *Encyclopaedia Britannica* (1988). The *Annual Report of the Postmaster General, 1986* (Washington: U.S. Government Printing Office, 1986) says that the annual volume of mail continues to increase at a steady and substantial rate for all classes, including priority, express, second-class, and third-class. The volume within the latter two classes jumped from a total of 45 billion in 1982 to 65 billion by 1986.
4. John B. Rae, *The American Automobile Industry* (Boston: Twayne, 1984).
5. *U.S. News and World Report,* 23 July 1990.
6. Hobbs, "Transportation."
7. Ivan Stoddard Coggeshall et al., "Telecommunications Systems," *Encyclopaedia Britannica* (1988). Calvin Sims, "U.S. Phone Companies Prospering as Costs Fall," *International Herald Tribune,* 23 May 1989, reports that long-distance services are expected to be "the growth industry of the 1990s."
8. *Statistical Abstracts of the United States, 1987* (Washington: U.S. Government Printing Office, 1987).
9. Coggeshall et al., "Telecommunications."
10. For a detailed account, see Tino Balio, ed., *The American Film Industry* (Madison: University of Wisconsin Press, 1985). Also see Elizabeth Weis et al., "Motion Pictures," *Encyclopaedia Britannica* (1988).
11. Philip S. Unwin, George Unwin, and Hans Georg Artur Viktor, "Publishing," *Encyclopaedia Britannica* (1988).
12. *UNESCO Statistical Yearbook,* 1989, and R. R. Bowker Data Services, New York.
13. *Air Transport 1987* (Washington: Air Transport Association of America, 1987). See also F. D. Hobbs, "Transportation."
14. *Statistical Abstracts;* also see Robert Bailey, "Industry Rides Wave of Expansion," *International Herald Tribune,* 11 June 1989.
15. Mark Frankel, "Jets of the Future," *Newsweek,* 3 July 1989, 38–39.
16. Cobbet Steinberg, *TV Facts* (New York: Facts On File, 1985).
17. See, for example, G. Comstock et al., *Television and Human Behavior* (New York: Columbia University Press, 1978) and L. D. Eron, "Prescription for Reduction of Aggression," *American Psychologist* 35 (1980): 244–52.
18. Richard Schickel, *Intimate Strangers: The Culture of Celebrity* (New York: Doubleday, 1985).
19. Cynthia Heimel, *Village Voice,* 2 Jan. 1990.
20. Glenn D. Bradley, *The Story of the Pony Express* (Chicago: McClurg, 1913).
21. Tom Forester, *High-Tech Society* (Cambridge, Mass.: MIT Press, 1987).
22. *USA Today,* 4 May 1989.
23. Stewart Brand, *The Media Lab: Inventing the Future at MIT* (New York: Viking, 1987), p. 24.
24. Ibid., pp. 36–39.
25. The capacity for digitizing information enables TV cameramen to shoot video in Tiananmen Square, for example, and (via live satellite transmission) have it readied for viewing in the U.S. within five minutes.
26. Brand, *The Media Lab.*

27. Joe Bernard, "Tomorrow's Edition," *TWA Ambassador* (July 1990): 38–40.

28. A useful description of communication in the traditional or "monocultural" community is furnished by W. Barnett Pearce in *Communication and the Human Condition* (Carbondale: University of Northern Illinois Press, 1989).

29. Joshua Meyrowitz, *No Sense of Place* (New York: Oxford University Press, 1985). A similar thesis is developed by Neil Postman in *The Disappearance of Childhood* (New York: Delacorte, 1982).

30. Shoshana Zuboff, *In the Age of the Smart Machine* (New York: Basic Books, 1988).

31. Bruce Wilshire describes the process by which humans come to imitate each other as *mimetic engulfment*. See his "Mimetic Engulfment and Self-Deception," in Amelie Rorty, ed., *Self-Deception* (Berkeley: University of California Press, 1988). Many social scientists believe that such tendencies are innate, appearing as early as the first two weeks of life.

32. Mary Watkins, *Invisible Guests: The Development of Imaginal Dialogues* (Hillsdale, N.J.: Analytic Press, 1986); Eric Klinger, "The Central Place of Imagery in Human Functioning," in Eric Klinger, ed., *Imagery, Volume 2: Concepts, Results, and Applications* (New York: Plenum, 1981); Mary Gergen, "Social Ghosts, Our Imaginal Dialogues with Others" (paper presented at American Psychological Association Meetings, New York, August 1987). See also Mark W. Baldwin and John G. Holmes, "Private Audiences and Awareness of the Self," *Journal of Personality and Social Psychology* 52(1987): 1087–1198.

33. Hazel Markus and Paula Nurius, "Possible Selves," *American Psychologist* 41(1986): 954–69. Closely related is Barbara Konig's fascinating novel, *Personen-Person* (Frankfurt: Carl Hanser Verlag, 1981). The narrator realizes that she may be soon meeting an attractive man. The entire volume is then composed of a dialogue among her many inner voices—the residuals of all her past relations.

34. Paul C. Rosenblatt and Sara E. Wright, "Shadow Realities in Close Relationships," *American Journal of Family Therapy* 12 (1984): 45–54.

35. Michael Billig et al., *Ideological Dilemmas* (London: Sage, 1988).

36. See Peter Berger, Brigitte Berger, and Hansfried Kellner, *The Homeless Mind* (New York: Random House, 1973), for a precursor to the present discussion.

37. T. S. Eliot, "The Love Song of J. Alfred Prufrock," in *The Waste Land and Other Poems* (New York: Harvest, 1930).

THINKING AND RE-READING

1. As you re-read this piece, identify the various types of information that Gergen juxtaposes to make his case: bulleted lists of "random moments from contemporary life," quotations from other writers, a historical outline of travel infrastructure in America since the turn of the last century, newspaper headlines and articles, and the text of advertisements. What effect do these sources of information have on you? On your understanding of his argument? What is the relationship between Gergen's main argument and the form in which he has presented this argument?

2. As you re-read this piece, think about the stories that you have been told by family members or others about household life in previous generations. Think back, for instance, to the stories your parents or grandparents have told you about mealtimes in their family settings. Compare these stories with your own experiences during family mealtimes in the household where you grew up or in the households of your friends to Gergen's account of the "microwave relationship." What has remained the same? What has changed? What has been lost? What has been gained?

WRITING AND LEARNING

1. Gergen writes of the "social ghosts" that function in our lives as role models, people (or the memories of people) who set "standards of behavior" and "models for action" by their own action. Write a story that describes one or two of the most important social ghosts in your life—describe where and when you knew, met, or encountered these people and what influences they have had on your life. The story should be one that you could tell a younger sibling, cousin, or relative in your family; its purpose should be instructive in a historical way.

2. Find two or three "texts" (e.g., advertising images, photographs, newspaper articles, headlines) that Gergen could incorporate productively in his essay as examples of our saturated society. Photocopy not only the text/image, but also all the relevant bibliographical information that would allow someone to locate it. Next, write a letter to Gergen and attach these texts/images. Your purpose is to persuade Gergen that he should include them in the next revision of this article or in the next book that he writes about this topic. In the letter, tell him how you think these sample texts/images could contribute to his argument. Also describe how these texts/images relate to your own lived experience with the saturated, postmodern condition that he describes in this essay.

3. Pretend that you have been asked to give a 15- to 20-minute presentation to a group of tenth-grade high school students who have been studying technology in their Social Studies class. The teacher of this class believes that students have focused too narrowly on the technical aspects of technology and have not considered the social issues. She or he also thinks that the students define technology far too narrowly as "computers," and that they do not realize automobiles, televisions, pencils, or telephones are all examples of technologies, as well. She or he has asked you to describe for these students several personal and/or social relationships that you have maintained with the help of technologies—including the telephone, the computer, the fax machine, the pen, the automobile, and the airplane. In the presentation/speech that you write, describe how some of your relationships are helped by these technologies. Or describe how a single relationship that you are able to maintain primarily through face-to-face exchanges differs when you have to maintain it through the mediation of some technology. What changes? What stays the same? What are the effects of technology on the relationship?

Welcome to Cyberia

M. Kadi

THIS CONTRIBUTION ORIGINALLY PUBLISHED by M. Kadi in *h2so4,* a popular 'zine (magazine) that focuses on the world of computer users, has also been excerpted and published in the *Utne Reader.* Both of these publications are aimed at a readership positioned on the political left that is generally informed about technology, but also capable of assuming a critical stance toward it. In this piece, Kadi debunks the myths of openness and diversity in cyberspace. As Kadi points out, only those individuals who can afford the relatively steep entry price for cyberspace involvement (here cited as approximately $120 per month) and have enough free time to spend approximately 30 hours of online time a month are able to participate in online conversations—facts that seriously limit the diversity of the online population.

Worse still, as Kadi notes, constrained by money and time, most individuals limit their online explorations to the topics that they are already interested in or know something about, thereby reproducing their offline preferences and prejudices in cyberspace. As a result, Kadi continues, "Diversity might be out there (and personally I don't think it is), but the simple fact is that the average person will not encounter it because with one brain, one job, one partner, one family, and one life, no one has the time!"

> "Computer networking offers the soundest basis for world peace that has yet been presented. Peace must be created on the bulwark of understanding. International computer networks will knit together the peoples of the world in bonds of mutual respect; its possibilities are vast, indeed."
>
> —Scientific American, June 1994

Computer bulletin board services offer up the glories of e-mail, the thought provocation of newsgroups, the sharing of ideas implicit in public posting, and the interaction of real-time chats. The fabulous, wonderful, limitless world of communication is just waiting for you to log on. Sure. Yeah. Right. What this whole delirious, interconnected, global community of a world needs is a little reality check.

Let's face facts. The U.S. government by and large foots the bill for the Internet, through maintaining the structural (hardware) backbone, including, among other things, funding to major universities. As surely as the Department of Defense started this whole thing, AT&T or Ted Turner is going to end up running it, so I don't think it's too unrealistic to take a look at the Net as it exists in its commercial form in order to expose some of the realities lurking behind the regurgitated media rhetoric and the religious fanaticism of net junkies.

The average person, J. Individual, has an income. How much of J. Individual's income is going to be spent on computer connectivity? Does $120 a month sound reasonable? Well, you may find that a bit too steep for your pocketbook, but the brutal fact is that $120 is a "reasonable" monthly amount. The major on-line services have a monthly service charge of approximately $15. Fifteen dollars to join the global community, communicate with a diverse group of people, and access the world's largest repository of knowledge since the Alexandrian library doesn't seem unreasonable, does it? But don't overlook the average per-hour connection rate of $3 (which can skyrocket upwards of $10, depending on your modem speed and service). You might think that you are a crack whiz with your communications software—that you are rigorous and stringent and never, ever respond to e-mail or a forum while you're on-line—but let me tell you that no one is capable of logging on efficiently every time. Thirty hours per month is a realistic estimate for on-line time spent by a single user engaging in activities beyond primitive e-mail. Now consider that the average, one-step-above-complete-neophyte user has at least two distinct BBS [bulletin board system] accounts, and do the math. Total monthly cost: $120. Most likely, that's already more than the combined cost of your utility bills. How many people are prepared to double their monthly bills for the sole purpose of connectivity?

In case you think 30 hours a month is an outrageous estimate, think of it in terms of television. Thirty hours a month in front of a television is simply the evening news plus a weekly *Seinfeld/Frasier* hour. Thirty hours a month is less time than the average car-phone owner spends on the phone while commuting. Even a conscientious geek, logging on for e-mail and the up-to-the-minute news that only the net services can provide, is probably going to spend 30 hours a month on-line. And, let's be truthful here, 30 hours a month ignores shareware downloads, computer illiteracy, real-time chatting, interactive game playing, and any serious forum following, which by nature entail a significant amount of scrolling and/or downloading time.

If you are really and truly going to use the net services to connect with the global community, the hourly charges are going to add up pretty quickly. Take out a piece of paper, pretend you're writing a check, and print out "One hundred and twenty dollars—" and tell me again, how diverse is the on-line community?

That scenario aside, let's pretend that you have as much time and as much money to spend on-line as you damn well want. What do you actually do on-line?

Well, you download some cool shareware, you post technical questions in the computer user group forums, you check your stocks, you read the news and maybe some reviews—hey, you've already passed that 30-hour limit! But, of course, since computer networks are supposed to make it easy to reach out and touch strangers who share a particular obsession or concern, you are participating in the on-line forums, discussion groups, and conferences.

Let's review the structure of forums. For the purposes of this essay, we will examine the smallest of the major user-friendly commercial services—America Online (AOL). There is no precise statistic available (at least none that the company will reveal—you have to do the research by HAND!!!) on exactly how many subject-specific discussion areas (folders) exist on America Online. Any on-line service is going to have zillions of posts—contributions from users—pertaining to computer usage (the computer games area of America Online, for example, breaks into 500 separate topics with over 100,000 individual posts), so let's look at a less popular area: the "Lifestyles and Interests" department.

For starters, as I write this, there are 57 initial categories within the Lifestyles and Interests area. One of these categories is Ham Radio. Ham Radio? How can there possibly be 5,909 separate, individual posts about Ham Radio? There are 5,865 postings in the Biking (and that's just bicycles, not motorcycles) category. Genealogy—22,525 posts. The Gay and Lesbian category is slightly more substantial—36,333 posts. There are five separate categories for political and issue discussion. The big catchall topic area, the Exchange, has over 100,000 posts. Servicewide (on the smallest service, remember) there are over a million posts.

You may want to join the on-line revolution, but obviously you can't wade through everything that's being discussed—you need to decide which topics interest you, which folders to browse. Within the Exchange alone (one of 57 subdivisions within one of another 50 higher divisions) there are 1,492 separate topic-specific folders—each containing a rough average of 50 posts, but many containing closer to 400. (Note: America Online automatically empties folders when their post totals reach 400, so total post numbers do not reflect the overall historical totals for a given topic. Sometimes the posting is so frequent that the "shelf life" of a given post is no more than four weeks.)

So, there you are. J. Individual, ready to start interacting with folks, sharing stories and communicating. You have narrowed yourself into a single folder, three tiers down in the America Online hierarchy, and now you must choose between nearly 1,500 folders. Of course, once you choose a few of these folders, you will then have to read all the posts in order to catch up, be current, and not merely repeat a previous post.

A polite post is no more than two paragraphs long (a screenful of text, which obviously has a number of intellectually negative implications). Let's say you choose 10 folders (out of 1,500). Each folder contains an average of 50 posts. Five hundred posts, at, say, one paragraph each, and you're now looking at the equivalent of a 200-page book.

Enough with the stats. Let me back up a minute and present you with some very disturbing, but rational, assumptions. J. Individual wants to join the on-line revolution, to connect and communicate. But J. is not going to read all one million posts on AOL. (After all, J. has a second on-line service.) Exercising choice is J. Individual's God-given right as an American, and, by gosh, J. Individual is going to make some decisions. So J. is going to ignore all the support groups—after all, J. is a normal, well-adjusted person, and all of J.'s friends are normal, well-adjusted people; what does J. need to know about alcoholism or incest victims? J. Individual is white. So J. Individual is going to ignore all the multicultural folders. J. couldn't give a hoot about gender issues and does not want to discuss religion or philosophy. Ultimately, J. Individual does not engage in topics that do not interest J. Individual. So who is J. meeting? Why, people who are *just like* J.

J. Individual has now joined the electronic community. Surfed the Net. Found some friends. *Tuned in, turned on, and geeked out.* Traveled the Information Highway and, just a few miles down that great democratic expressway, J. Individual has settled into an electronic suburb.

Are any of us so very different? It's my time and my money and I am not going to waste any of it reading posts by disgruntled Robert-Bly drum-beating men's-movement boys who think that they should have some say over, for instance, whether or not I choose to carry a child to term simply because a condom broke. I know where I stand. I'm an adult. I know what's up and I am not going to waste my money arguing with a bunch of neanderthals.

Oh yeah; I am so connected, so enlightened, so open to the opposing viewpoint. I'm out there, meeting all kinds of people from different economic backgrounds (who have $120 a month to burn), from all religions (yeah, right, like anyone actually discusses religion anymore from a user standpoint), from all kinds of different ethnic backgrounds and with all kinds of sexual orientations (as if any of this ever comes up outside of the appropriate topic folder).

People are drawn to topics and folders that interest them and therefore people will only meet people who are interested in the same topics in the same folders. Rarely does anyone venture into a random folder just to see what others (the Other?) are talking about.

Basically, between the monetary constraints and the sheer number of topics and individual posts, the great Information Highway is not a place where you will enter an "amazing web of new people, places, and ideas." One does not encounter people from "all walks of life" because there are too many people and too many folders. Diversity might be out there (and personally I don't think it is), but the simple fact is that the average person will not encounter it because with one brain, one job, one partner, one family, and one life, no one has the time!

Just in case these arguments based on time and money aren't completely convincing, let me bring up a historical reference. Please take another look at the opening quote of this essay, from *Scientific American*. It was featured in their 50 Years Ago Today column. Where you read "computer networking," the quote originally contained the word *television*. Amusing, isn't it?

THINKING AND RE-READING

1. As you re-read this piece, consider the widely held belief that the Information Super-highway is a prime example of technological "progress," a project that will result in increasingly open and democratic venues for human communication. As you read, consider your own experiences with computer technology. Have these experiences brought you in contact with a wider variety of people? Different ideas? Different systems of values? Has technology changed your life in significant ways? Or has it simply supported more of the same in your life? More connections with people like you? More information about the ideas you already held? More contact with others that hold the same values?

2. Kadi's contention is that money is the primary factor determining who enters and functions in cyberspace. As you read, think of examples from your life that confirm and disconfirm that hypothesis. Make a list of these examples for later use—consider your own experiences, those of friends you know, as well as those of family members. If money is not the primary determining factor, identify others that seem important.

WRITING AND LEARNING

1. Write a letter to M. Kadi about her profile of J. Individual—white, unconcerned about issues of gender or multiculturalism, uninterested in serious exchanges about religion or philosophy, and unwilling to engage in issues that "do not interest J. Individual." In this letter, tell Kadi if this profile matches your own profile as an Internet user or the profiles of those people you know who use the Internet. Given this information, also let Kadi know whether you agree or disagree with the arguments stated in this essay and why.

2. Kadi mentions that a "polite post" is no more than two paragraphs long. Interview several friends who are avid e-mail correspondents or listserv correspondents. Ask about the other characteristics of "polite" exchanges—consider such factors as type of language, tone, content, greeting, salutation, subject line, references to previous conversations, and the use of emoticons (symbols that denote the emotional content of messages). Using the information you glean from these conversations, write a list of rules for e-mail etiquette. Your audience for these rules is the wide range of other users on the Internet, so be as complete, as clear, and as flexible as possible in the rules you present. Remember that people's ideas of acceptable social rules may differ widely depending on age, culture, and social situation. Your goal is to identify a set of rules that is directive enough to prevent major social gaffs and disagreements, but flexible enough to accommodate a wide range of users from different age groups, cultures, and situations.

3. To develop your own sense of historical context and insight, go to the library and find at least three articles written when the technology of television was in its infancy (circa 1945–1955). Find articles that identify promising claims for the new technology of television. In a written response that can be shared with other members of your class, compare the early claims for television with those you have read about computers in various pieces within this collection. Identify the important ways in which the claims are similar and different. In your comparison, be sure to use the correct format for citation, quotations, summary, and paraphrase. Check your handbook for assistance.

Mythinformation

Langdon Winner

LANGDON WINNER IS THE AUTHOR of *The Whale and the Reactor,* a book that looks at the challenges posed by the contemporary age of new technology and tries to identify some social limits that we might productively consider adopting in our headlong rush for "progress." The following contribution by Winner represents one chapter, entitled "Mythinformation," of that book. This chapter, which we can consider as an example of technology criticism, explores the implications of the "computer revolution," calling into question the goals of such a revolution, the participants, their motives, and the resulting social developments.

As you read this chapter—which is written for a serious and educated audience—try to recall all the times when you have heard the term "computer revolution" and considered that movement an inevitable mark of technological progress. When you read Winner's analysis, consider which goals of the computer revolution you would prefer to be associated with, and why.

> Computer power to the people is essential to the realization of a future in which most citizens are informed about, and interested and involved in, the processes of government.
>
> *—J. C. R. Licklider*

In nineteenth-century Europe a recurring ceremonial gesture signaled the progress of popular uprisings. At the point at which it seemed that forces of disruption in the streets were sufficiently powerful to overthrow monarchical authority, a prominent rebel leader would go to the parliament or city hall to "proclaim the republic." This was an indication to friend and foe alike that a revolution was prepared to take its work seriously, to seize power and begin governing in a way that guaranteed political representation to all the people. Subsequent events, of course, did not always match these grand hopes; on occasion the revolutionaries were thwarted in their ambitions and reactionary governments regained control.

Nevertheless, what a glorious moment when the republic was declared! Here, if only briefly, was the promise of a new order—an age of equality, justice, and emancipation of humankind.

A somewhat similar gesture has become a standard feature in contemporary writings on computers and society. In countless books, magazine articles, and media specials some intrepid soul steps forth to proclaim "the revolution." Often it is called simply "the computer revolution"; my brief inspection of a library catalogue revealed three books with exactly that title published since 1962.[1] Other popular variants include the "information revolution," "microelectronics revolution," and "network revolution." But whatever its label, the message is usually the same. The use of computers and advanced communications technologies is producing a sweeping set of transformations in every corner of social life. An informal consensus among computer scientists, social scientists, and journalists affirms the term "revolution" as the concept best suited to describe these events. "We are all very privileged," a noted computer scientist declares, "to be in this great Information Revolution in which the computer is going to affect us very profoundly, probably more so than the Industrial Revolution."[2] A well-known sociologist writes, "This revolution in the organization and processing of information and knowledge, in which the computer plays a central role, has as its context the development of what I have called the post-industrial society."[3] At frequent intervals during the past dozen years, garish cover stories in *Time* and *Newsweek* have repeated this story, climaxed by *Time*'s selection of the computer as its "Man of the Year" for 1982.

Of course, the same society now said to be undergoing a computer revolution has long since gotten used to "revolutions" in laundry detergents, underarm deodorants, floor waxes, and other consumer products. Exhausted in Madison Avenue advertising slogans, the image has lost much of its punch. Those who employ it to talk about computers and society, however, appear to be making much more serious claims. They offer a powerful metaphor, one that invites us to compare the kind of disruptions seen in political revolutions to the changes we see happening around computer information systems. Let us take that invitation seriously and see where it leads.

A METAPHOR EXPLORED

Suppose that we were looking at a revolution in a Third World country, the revolution of the Sandinistas in Nicaragua, for example. We would want to begin by studying the fundamental goals of the revolution. Is this a movement truly committed to social justice? Does it seek to uphold a valid ideal of human freedom? Does it aspire to a system of democratic rule? Answers to those questions would help us decide whether or not this is a revolution worthy of our endorsement. By the same token, we would want to ask about the means the revolutionaries had chosen to pursue their goals. Having succeeded in armed struggle, how will they manage violence and military force once they gain control? A reasonable person would also want to learn something of the structure of institutional authority that the revolution will try to create. Will there be frequent, open elections? What systems of decision making, administration, and law enforcement will be put to work? Coming to terms with its proposed ends and means, a sympathetic observer could then watch the revolution unfold, noticing whether or not it remained true to its professed purposes and how well it succeeded in its reforms.

Most dedicated revolutionaries of the modern age have been willing to supply coherent public answers to questions of this sort. It is not unreasonable to expect, therefore, that something like these issues must have engaged those who so eagerly use the metaphor "revolution" to describe and celebrate the advent of computerization. Unfortunately, this is not the case. Books, articles, and media specials aimed at a popular audience are usually content to depict the dazzling magnitude of technical innovations and social effects. Written as if by some universally accepted format, such accounts describe scores of new computer products and processes, announce the enormous dollar value of the growing computer and communications industry, survey the expanding uses of computers in offices, factories, schools, and homes, and offer good news from research and development laboratories about the great promise of the next generation of computing devices. Along with this one reads of the many "impacts" that computerization is going to have on every sphere of life. Professionals in widely separate fields—doctors, lawyers, corporate managers, and scientists—comment on the changes computers have brought to their work. Home consumers give testimonials explaining how personal computers are helping educate their children, prepare their income tax forms, and file their recipes. On occasion, this generally happy story will include reports on people left unemployed in occupations undermined by automation. Almost always, following this formula, there will be an obligatory sentence or two of criticism of the computer culture solicited from a technically qualified spokesman, an attempt to add balance to an otherwise totally sanguine outlook.

Unfortunately, the prevalence of such superficial, unreflective descriptions and forecasts about computerization cannot be attributed solely to hasty journalism. Some of the most prestigious journals of the scientific community echo the claim that a revolution is in the works.[4] A well-known computer scientist has announced unabashedly that "revolution, transformation and salvation are all to be carried out."[5] It is true that more serious approaches to the study of computers and society can be found in scholarly publications. A number of social scientists, computer scientists, and philosophers have begun to explore important issues about how computerization works and what developments, positive and negative, it is likely to bring to society.[6] But such careful, critical studies are by no means the ones most influential in shaping public attitudes about the world of microelectronics. An editor at a New York publishing house stated the norm, "People want to know what's new with computer technology. They don't want to know what could go wrong."[7]

It seems all but impossible for computer enthusiasts to examine critically the *ends* that might guide the world-shaking developments they anticipate. They employ the metaphor of revolution for one purpose only—to suggest a drastic upheaval, one that people ought to welcome as good news. It never occurs to them to investigate the idea or its meaning any further.

One might suppose, for example, that a revolution of this type would involve a significant shift in the locus of power; after all, that is exactly what one expects in revolutions of a political kind. Is something similar going to happen in this instance?

One might also ask whether or not this revolution will be strongly committed, as revolutions often are, to a particular set of social ideals. If so, what are the ideals that matter? Where can we see them argued?

To mention revolution also brings to mind the relationships of different social classes. Will the computer revolution bring about the victory of one class over another? Will it be the occasion for a realignment of class loyalties?

In the busy world of computer science, computer engineering, and computer marketing such questions seldom come up. Those actively engaged in promoting the transformation—hardware and software engineers, managers of microelectronics firms, computer salesmen, and the like—are busy pursuing their own ends: profits, market share, handsome salaries, the intrinsic joy of invention, the intellectual rewards of programming, and the pleasures of owning and using powerful machines. But the sheer dynamism of technical and economic activity in the computer industry evidently leaves its members little time to ponder the historical significance of their own activity. They must struggle to keep current, to be on the crest of the next wave as it breaks. As one member of Data General's Eagle computer project describes it, the prevailing spirit resembles a game of pinball. "You win one game, you get to play another. You win with this machine, you get to build the next."[8] The process has its own inertia.

Hence, one looks in vain to the movers and shakers in computer fields for the qualities of social and political insight that characterized revolutionaries of the past. Too busy. Cromwell, Jefferson, Robespierre, Lenin, and Mao were able to reflect upon the world historical events in which they played a role. Public pronouncements by the likes of Robert Noyce, Marvin Minsky, Edward Feigenbaum, and Steven Jobs show no similar wisdom about the transformations they so actively help to create. By and large the computer revolution is conspicuously silent about its own ends.

GOOD CONSOLE, GOOD NETWORK, GOOD COMPUTER

My concern for the political meaning of revolution in this setting may seem somewhat misleading, even perverse. A much better point of reference might be the technical "revolutions" and associated social upheavals of the past, the industrial revolution in particular. If the enthusiasts of computerization had readily taken up this comparison, studying earlier historical periods for similarities and differences in patterns of technological innovation, capital formation, employment, social change, and the like, then it would be clear that I had chosen the wrong application of this metaphor. But, in fact, no well-developed comparisons of that kind are to be found in the writings on the computer revolution. A consistently ahistorical viewpoint prevails. What one often finds emphasized, however, is a vision of drastically altered social and political conditions, a future upheld as both desirable and, in all likelihood, inevitable. Politics, in other words, is not a secondary concern for many computer enthusiasts; it is a crucial, albeit thoughtless, part of their message.

We are, according to a fairly standard account, moving into an age characterized by the overwhelming dominance of electronic information systems in all areas of human practice. Industrial society, which depended upon material production for its livelihood, is rapidly being supplanted by a society of information services that will enable people to satisfy their economic and social needs. What water- and steam-powered machines were to the industrial age, the computer will be to the era now dawning. Ever-expanding technical capacities in computation and communications will make possible a universal, instantaneous access to enormous quantities of valuable information. As these technologies become less and less expensive and more and more convenient, all the people of the world, not just the wealthy, will be able to use the wonderful services that information machines make available. Gradually, existing differences between rich and poor, advantaged and disadvantaged, will begin to evaporate. Widespread access to computers will produce a society more democratic, egalitarian, and richly diverse than any previously known. Because "knowledge is power," because electronic information will spread knowledge into every corner of world society, political influence will be much more widely shared. With the personal computer serving as the great equalizer, rule by centralized authority and social class dominance will gradually fade away. The marvelous promise of a "global village" will be fulfilled in a worldwide burst of human creativity.

A sampling from recent writings on the information society illustrates these grand expectations.

> *The world is entering a new period. The wealth of nations, which depended upon land, labor, and capital during its agricultural and industrial phases—depended upon natural resources, the accumulation of money, and even upon weaponry—will come in the future to depend upon information, knowledge and intelligence.*[9]

> *The electronic revolution will not do away with work, but it does hold out some promises: Most boring jobs can be done by machines; lengthy commuting can be avoided; we can have enough leisure to follow interesting pursuits outside our work; environmental destruction can be avoided; the opportunities for personal creativity will be unlimited.*[10]

Long lists of specific services spell out the utopian promise of this new age: interactive television, electronic funds transfer, computer-aided instruction, customized news service, electronic magazines, electronic mail, computer teleconferencing, on-line stock market and weather reports, computerized Yellow Pages, shopping via home computer, and so forth. All of it is supposed to add up to a cultural renaissance.

> *Whatever the limits to growth in other fields, there are no limits near in telecommunications and electronic technology. There are no limits near in the consumption of information, the growth of culture, or the development of the human mind.*[11]

> *Computer-based communications can be used to make human lives richer and freer, by enabling persons to have access to vast stores of information, other "human resources," and opportunities for work and socializing on a more flexible, cheaper and convenient basis than ever before.*[12]

> *When such systems become widespread, potentially intense communications networks among geographically dispersed persons will become actualized. We will become Network Nation, exchanging vast amounts of information and social and emotional communications with colleagues, friends and "strangers" who share similar interests, who are spread all over the nation.*[13]

> *A rich diversity of subcultures will be fostered by computer-based communications systems. Social, political, technical changes will produce conditions likely to lead to the formation of groups with their own distinctive sets of values, activities, language and dress.*[14]

According to this view, the computer revolution will, by its sheer momentum, eliminate many of the ills that have vexed political society since the beginning of time. Inequalities of wealth and privilege will gradually fade away. One writer predicts that computer networks will "offer major opportunities to disadvantaged groups to acquire the skills and social ties they need to become full members of society."[15] Another looks forward to "a revolutionary network where each node is equal in power to all others."[16] Information will become the dominant form of wealth. Because it can flow so quickly, so freely through computer networks, it will not, in this interpretation, cause the kinds of stratification associated with traditional forms of property. Obnoxious forms of social organization will also be replaced. "The computer will smash the pyramid," one best-selling book proclaims. "We created the hierarchical, pyramidal, managerial system because we needed it to keep track of people and things people did; with the computer to keep track, we can restructure our institutions horizontally."[17] Thus, the proliferation of electronic information will generate a leveling effect to surpass the dreams of history's great social reformers.

The same viewpoint holds that the prospects for participatory democracy have never been brighter. According to one group of social scientists, "The form of democracy found in the ancient Greek city-state, the Israeli kibbutz, and the New England town meeting, which gave every citizen the opportunity to directly participate in the political process, has become impractical in America's mass society. But this need not be the case. The technological means exist through which millions of people can enter into dialogue with one another and with their representatives, and can form the authentic consensus essential for democracy."[18]

Computer scientist J. C. R. Licklider of the Massachusetts Institute of Technology is one advocate especially hopeful about a revitalization of the democratic process. He looks forward to "an information environment that would give politics greater depth and dimension than it now has." Home computer consoles and television sets would be linked together in a massive network. "The political process would essentially be a giant teleconference, and a campaign would be a months-long series of communications among candidates, propagandists, commentators, political action groups and voters." An arrangement of this kind would, in his view, encourage a more open, comprehensive examination of both issues and candidates. "The information revolution," he exclaims, "is bringing with it a key that may open the door to a new era of involvement and participation. The key is the self-motivating exhilaration that accompanies truly effective interaction with information through a good console through a good network to a good computer."[19] It is, in short, a democracy of machines.

Taken as a whole, beliefs of this kind constitute what I would call mythinformation: the almost religious conviction that a widespread adoption of computers and communications systems along with easy access to electronic information will automatically produce a better world for human living. It is a peculiar form of enthusiasm that characterizes social fashions of the latter decades of the twentieth century. Many people who have grown cynical or discouraged about other aspects of social life are completely enthralled by the supposed redemptive qualities of computers and telecommunications. Writing of the "fifth generation" supercomputers, Japanese author Yoneji Masuda rhapsodically predicts "freedom for each of us to set individual goals of self-realization and then perhaps a worldwide religious renaissance, characterized not by a belief in a supernatural god, but rather by awe and humility in the presence of the collective human spirit and its wisdom, humanity living in a symbolic tranquility with the planet we have found ourselves upon, regulated by a new set of global ethics."[20]

It is not uncommon for the advent of a new technology to provide an occasion for flights of utopian fancy. During the last two centuries the factory system, railroads, telephone, electricity, automobile, airplane, radio, television, and nuclear power have all figured prominently in the belief that a new and glorious age was about to begin. But even within the great tradition of optimistic technophilia, current dreams of a "computer age" stand out as exaggerated and unrealistic. Because they have such a broad appeal, because they overshadow other ways of looking at the matter, these notions deserve closer inspection.

THE GREAT EQUALIZER

As is generally true of a myth, the story contains elements of truth. What were once industrial societies are being transformed into service economies, a trend that emerges as more material production shifts to developing countries where labor costs are low and business tax breaks lucrative. At the same time that industrialization takes hold in less-developed nations of the world, deindustrialization is gradually altering the economies of North America and Europe. Some of the service industries central to this pattern are ones that depend upon highly sophisticated computer and communications systems. But this does not mean that future employment possibilities will flow largely from the microelectronics industry and information services. A number of studies, including those of the U.S. Bureau of Labor Statistics, suggest that the vast majority of new jobs will come in menial service occupations paying relatively low wages.[21] As robots and computer software absorb an increasing share of factory and office tasks, the "information society" will offer plenty of opportunities for janitors, hospital orderlies, and fast-food waiters.

The computer romantics are also correct in noting that computerization alters relationships of social power and control, although they misrepresent the direction this development is likely to take. Those who stand to benefit most obviously are large transnational business corporations. While their "global reach" does not arise solely from the application of information technologies, such organizations are uniquely situated to exploit the efficiency, productivity, command, and control the new electronics make available. Other notable beneficiaries of the systematic use of vast amounts of digitized information are public bureaucracies, intelligence agencies, and an ever-expanding military, organizations that would operate less effectively at their present scale were it not for the use of computer power. Ordinary people are, of course, strongly affected by the workings of these organizations and by the rapid spread of new electronic systems in banking, insurance, taxation, factory and office work, home entertainment, and the like. They are also counted upon to be eager buyers of hardware, software, and communications services as computer products reach the consumer market.

But where in all of this motion do we see increased democratization? Social equality? The dawn of a cultural renaissance? Current developments in the information age suggest an increase in power by those who already had a great deal of power, an enhanced centralization of control by those already prepared for control, an augmentation of wealth by the already wealthy. Far from demonstrating a revolution in patterns of social and political influence, empirical studies of computers and social change usually show powerful groups adapting computerized methods to retain control.[22] That is not surprising. Those best situated to take advantage of the power of a new technology are often those previously well situated by dint of wealth, social standing, and institutional position. Thus, if there is to be a computer revolution, the best guess is that it will have a distinctly conservative character.

Granted, such prominent trends could be altered. It is possible that a society strongly rooted in computer and telecommunications systems could be one in which participatory democracy, decentralized political control, and social equality are fully realized. Progress of that kind would have to occur as the result of that society's concerted efforts to overcome many difficult obstacles to achieve those ends. Computer enthusiasts, however, seldom propose deliberate action of that kind. Instead, they strongly suggest that the good society will be realized as a side effect, a spin-off from the vast proliferation of computing devices. There is evidently no need to try to shape the institutions of the information age in ways that maximize human freedom while placing limits upon concentrations of power.

For those willing to wait passively while the computer revolution takes its course, technological determinism ceases to be mere theory and becomes an ideal: a desire to embrace conditions brought on by technological change without judging them in advance. There is nothing new in this disposition. Computer romanticism is merely the latest version of the nineteenth- and twentieth-century faith we noted earlier, one that has always expected to generate freedom, democracy, and justice through sheer material abundance. Thus there is no need for serious inquiry into the appropriate design of new institutions or the distribution of rewards and burdens. As long as the economy is growing and the machinery in good working order, the rest will take care of itself. In previous versions of this homespun conviction, the abundant (and therefore democratic) society was manifest by a limitless supply of houses, appliances, and consumer goods.[23] Now "access to information" and "access to computers" have moved to the top of the list.

The political arguments of computer romantics draw upon a number of key assumptions: (1) people are bereft of information; (2) information is knowledge; (3) knowledge is power; and (4) increasing access to information enhances democracy and equalizes social power. Taken as separate assertions and in combination, these beliefs provide a woefully distorted picture of the role of electronic systems in social life.

Is it true that people face serious shortages of information? To read the literature on the computer revolution one would suppose this to be a problem on a par with the energy crisis of the 1970s. The persuasiveness of this notion borrows from our sense that literacy, education, knowledge, well-informed minds, and the widespread availability of tools of inquiry are unquestionable social goods, and that, in contrast, illiteracy, inadequate education, ignorance, and forced restrictions upon knowledge are among history's worst evils. Thus, it appears superficially plausible that a world rewired to connect human beings to vast data banks and communications systems would be a progressive step. Information shortage would be remedied in much the same way that developing a new fuel supply might solve an energy crisis.

Alas, the idea is entirely faulty. It mistakes sheer supply of information with an educated ability to gain knowledge and act effectively based on that knowledge. In many parts of the world that ability is sadly lacking. Even some highly developed societies still contain chronic inequalities in the distribution of good education and basic intellectual skills. The U.S. Army, for instance, must now reject or dismiss a fairly high percentage of the young men and women it recruits because they simply cannot read military manuals. It is no doubt true of these recruits that they have a great deal of information about the world—information from their life experiences, schooling, the mass media, and so forth. What makes them "functionally illiterate" is that they have not learned to translate this information into a mastery of practical skills.

If the solution to problems of illiteracy and poor education were a question of information supply alone, then the best policy might be to increase the number of well-stocked libraries, making sure they were built in places where libraries do not presently exist. Of course, that would do little good in itself unless people are sufficiently well educated to use those libraries to broaden their knowledge and understanding. Computer enthusiasts, however, are not noted for their calls to increase support of public libraries and schools. It is *electronic information* carried by *networks* they uphold as crucial. Here is a case in which an obsession with a particular kind of technology causes one to disregard what are obvious problems and clear remedies. While it is true that systems of computation and communications, intelligently structured and wisely applied, might help a society raise its standards of literacy, education, and general knowledgeability, to look to those instruments first while ignoring how to enlighten and invigorate a human mind is pure foolishness.

"As everybody knows, knowledge is power."[24] This is an attractive idea, but highly misleading. Of course, knowledge employed in particular circumstances can help one act effectively and in that sense enhance one's power. A citrus farmer's knowledge of frost conditions enables him/her to take steps to prevent damage to the crop. A candidate's knowledge of public opinion can be a powerful aid in an election campaign. But surely there is no automatic, positive link between knowledge and power, especially if that means power in a social or political sense. At times knowledge brings merely an enlightened impotence or paralysis. One may know exactly what to do but lack the wherewithal to act. Of the many conditions that affect the phenomenon of power, knowledge is but one and by no means the most important. Thus, in the history of ideas, arguments that expert knowledge ought to play a special role in politics—the philosopher-kings for Plato, the engineers for Veblen—have always been offered as something contrary to prevailing wisdom. To Plato and Veblen it was obvious that knowledge was *not* power, a situation they hoped to remedy.

An equally serious misconception among computer enthusiasts is the belief that democracy is first and foremost a matter of distributing information. As one particularly flamboyant manifesto exclaims: "There is an explosion of information dispersal in the technology and we think this information has to be shared. All great thinkers about democracy said that the key to democracy is access to information. And now we have a chance to get information into people's hands like never before."[25] Once again such assertions play on our belief that a democratic public ought to be open-minded and well informed. One of the great evils of totalitarian societies is that they dictate what people can know and impose secrecy to restrict freedom. But democracy is not founded solely (or even primarily) upon conditions that affect the availability of information. What distinguishes it from other political forms is a recognition that the people as a whole are capable of self-government and that they have a rightful claim to rule. As a consequence, political society ought to build institutions that allow or even encourage a great latitude of democratic participation. How far a society must go in making political authority and public roles available to ordinary people is a matter of dispute among political theorists. But no serious student of the question would give much credence to the idea that creating a universal gridwork to spread electronic information is, by itself, a democratizing step.

What, then, of the idea that "interaction with information through a good console, through a good network to a good computer" will promote a renewed sense of political involvement and participation? Readers who believe that assertion should contact me about some parcels of land my uncle has for sale in Florida. Relatively low levels of citizen participation prevail in some modern democracies, the United States, for example. There are many reasons for this, many ways a society might try to improve things. Perhaps opportunities to serve in public office or influence public policy are too limited; in that case, broaden the opportunities. Or perhaps choices placed before citizens are so pallid that boredom is a valid response; in that instance, improve the quality of those choices. But it is simply not reasonable to assume that enthusiasm for political activity will be stimulated solely by the introduction of sophisticated information machines.

The role that television plays in modern politics should suggest why this is so. Public participation in voting has steadily declined as television replaced the face-to-face politics of precincts and neighborhoods. Passive monitoring of electronic news and information allows citizens to feel involved while dampening the desire to take an active part. If people begin to rely upon computerized data bases and telecommunications as a primary means of exercising power, it is conceivable that genuine political knowledge based in first-hand experience would vanish altogether. The vitality of democratic politics depends upon people's willingness to act together in pursuit of their common ends. It requires that on occasion members of a community appear before each other in person, speak their minds, deliberate on paths of action, and decide what they will do.[26] This is considerably different from the model now upheld as a breakthrough for democracy: logging onto one's computer, receiving the latest information, and sending back an instantaneous digitized response.

A chapter from recent political history illustrates the strength of direct participation in contrast to the politics of electronic information. In 1981 and 1982 two groups of activists set about to do what they could to stop the international nuclear arms race. One of the groups, Ground Zero, chose to rely almost solely upon mass communications to convey its message to the public. Its leaders appeared on morning talk shows and evening news programs on all three major television networks. They followed up with a mass mail solicitation using addresses from a computerized data base. At the same time another group, the Nuclear Weapons Freeze Campaign, began by taking its proposal for a bilateral nuclear freeze to New England town meetings, places where active citizen participation is a long-standing tradition. Winning the endorsement of the idea from a great many town meetings, the Nuclear Freeze group expanded its drive by launching a series of state initiatives. Once again the key was a direct approach to people, this time through thousands of meetings, dinners, and parties held in homes across the country.

The effects of the two movements were strikingly different. After its initial publicity, Ground Zero was largely ignored. It had been an ephemeral exercise in media posturing. The Nuclear Freeze campaign, however, continued to gain influence in the form of increasing public support, successful ballot measures, and an ability to apply pressure upon political officials. Eventually, the latter group did begin to use computerized mailings, television appearances, and the like to advance its cause. But it never forgot the original source of its leverage: people working together for shared ends.

Of all the computer enthusiasts' political ideas, there is none more poignant than the faith that the computer is destined to become a potent equalizer in modern society. Support for this belief is found in the fact that small "personal" computers are becoming more and more powerful, less and less expensive, and ever more simple to use. Obnoxious tendencies associated with the enormous, costly, technically inaccessible computers of the recent past are soon to be overcome. As one writer explains, "The great forces of centralization that characterized mainframe and minicomputer design of that period have now been reversed." This means that "the puny device that sits innocuously on the desktop will, in fact, within a few years, contain enough computing power to become an effective equalizer."[27] Presumably, ordinary citizens equipped with microcomputers will be able to counter the influence of large, computer-based organizations.

Notions of this kind echo beliefs of eighteenth- and nineteenth-century revolutionaries that placing fire arms in the hands of the people was crucial to overthrowing entrenched authority. In the American Revolution, French Revolution, Paris Commune, and Russian Revolution the role of "the people armed" was central to the revolutionary program. As the military defeat of the Paris Commune made clear, however, the fact that the popular forces have guns may not be decisive. In a contest of force against force, the larger, more sophisticated, more ruthless, better equipped competitor often has the upper hand. Hence, the availability of low-cost computing power may move the baseline that defines electronic dimensions of social influence, but it does not necessarily alter the relative balance of power. Using a personal computer makes one no more powerful vis-à-vis, say, the National Security Agency than flying a hang glider establishes a person as a match for the U.S. Air Force.

In sum, the political expectations of computer enthusiasts are seldom more than idle fantasy. Beliefs that widespread use of computers will cause hierarchies to crumble, inequality to tumble, participation to flourish, and centralized power to dissolve simply do not withstand close scrutiny. The formula information = knowledge = power = democracy lacks any real substance. At each point the mistake comes in the conviction that computerization will inevitably move society toward the good life. And no one will have to raise a finger.

INFORMATION AND IDEOLOGY

Despite its shortcomings as political theory, mythinformation is noteworthy as an expressive contemporary ideology. I use the term "ideology" here in a sense common in social science: a set of beliefs that expresses the needs and aspirations of a group, class, culture, or subculture. In this instance the needs and aspirations that matter most are those that stem from operational requirements of highly complex systems in an advanced technological society; the groups most directly involved are those who build, maintain, operate, improve, and market these systems. At a time in which almost all major components of our technological society have come to depend upon the application of large and small computers, it is not surprising that computerization has risen to ideological prominence, an expression of grand hopes and ideals.

What is the "information" so crucial in this odd belief system, the icon now so greatly cherished? We have seen enough to appreciate that the kind of information upheld is not knowledge in the ordinary sense of the term; nor is it understanding, enlightenment, critical thought, timeless wisdom, or the content of a well-educated mind. If one looks carefully at the writings of computer enthusiasts, one finds that information in a particular form and context is offered as a paradigm to inspire emulation. Enormous quantities of data, manipulated within various kinds of electronic media and used to facilitate the transactions of today's large, complex organizations is the model we are urged to embrace. In this context the sheer quantity of information presents a formidable challenge. Modern organizations are continually faced with overload, a flood of data that threatens to become unintelligible to them. Computers provide one way to confront that problem; speed conquers quantity. An equally serious challenge is created by the fact that the varieties of information most crucial to modern organizations are highly time specific. Data on stock market prices, airline traffic, weather conditions, international economic indicators, military intelligence, public opinion poll results, and the like are useful for very short periods of time. Systems that gather, organize, analyze, and utilize electronic data in these areas must be closely tuned to the very latest developments. If one is trading on fast-paced international markets, information about prices an hour old or even a few seconds old may have no value. Information is itself a perishable commodity.

Thus, what looked so puzzling in another context—the urgent "need" for information in a social world filled with many pressing human needs—now becomes transparent. It is, in the first instance, the need of complex human/machine systems threatened with debilitating uncertainties or even breakdown unless continually replenished with up-to-the-minute electronic information about their internal states and operating environments. Rapid information-processing capabilities of modern computers and communications devices are a perfect match for such needs, a marriage made in technological heaven.

But is it sensible to transfer this model, as many evidently wish, to all parts of human life? Must activities, experiences, ideas, and ways of knowing that take a longer time to bear fruit adapt to the speedy processes of digitized information processing? Must education, the arts, politics, sports, home life, and all other forms of social practice be transformed to accommodate it? As one article on the coming of the home computer concludes, "running a household is actually like running a small business. You have to worry about inventory control—of household supplies—and budgeting for school tuition, housekeepers' salaries, and all the rest."[28] The writer argues that these complex, rapidly changing operations require a powerful information-processing capacity to keep them functioning smoothly. One begins to wonder how everyday activities such as running a household were even possible before the advent of microelectronics. This is a case in which the computer is a solution frantically in search of a problem.

In the last analysis, the almost total silence about the ends of the "computer revolution" is filled by a conviction that information processing is something valuable in its own right. Faced with an information explosion that strains the capacities of traditional institutions, society will renovate its structure to accommodate computerized, automated systems in every area of concern. The efficient management of information is revealed as the *telos* of modern society, its greatest mission. It is that fact to which mythinformation adds glory and glitter. People must be convinced that the human burdens of an information age—unemployment, de-skilling, the disruption of many social patterns—are worth bearing. Once again, those who push the plow are told they ride a golden chariot.

EVERYWHERE AND NOWHERE

Having criticized a point of view, it remains for me to suggest what topics a serious study of computers and politics should pursue. The question is, of course, a very large one. If the long-term consequences of computerization are anything like the ones commonly predicted, they will require a rethinking of many fundamental conditions in social and political life. I will mention three areas of concern.

As people handle an increasing range of their daily activities through electronic instruments—mail, banking, shopping, entertainment, travel plans, and so forth—it becomes technically feasible to monitor these activities to a degree heretofore inconceivable. The availability of digitized footprints of social transactions affords opportunities that contain a menacing aspect. While there has been a great deal written about this problem, most of it deals with the "threat to privacy," the possibility that someone might gain access to information that violates the sanctity of one's personal life. As important as that issue certainly is, it by no means exhausts the potential evils created by electronic data banks and computer matching. The danger extends beyond the private sphere to affect the most basic of public freedoms. Unless steps are taken to prevent it, we may develop systems capable of a perpetual, pervasive, apparently benign surveillance. Confronted with omnipresent, all-seeing data banks, the populace may find passivity and compliance the safest route, avoiding activities that once represented political liberty. As a badge of civic pride a citizen may announce, "I'm not involved in anything a computer would find the least bit interesting."

The evolution of this unhappy state of affairs does not necessarily depend upon the "misuse" of computer systems. The prospect we face is really much more insidious. An age rich in electronic information may achieve wonderful social conveniences at a cost of placing freedom, perhaps inadvertently, in a deep chill.

A thoroughly computerized world is also one bound to alter conditions of human sociability. The point of many applications of microelectronics, after all, is to eliminate social layers that were previously needed to get things done. Computerized bank tellers, for example, have largely done away with small, local branch banks, which were not only ways of doing business, but places where people met, talked, and socialized. The so-called electronic cottage industry, similarly, operates very well without the kinds of human interactions that once characterized office work. Despite greater efficiency, productivity, and convenience, innovations of this kind do away with the reasons people formerly had for being together, working together, acting together. Many practical activities once crucial to even a minimal sense of community life are rendered obsolete. One consequence of these developments is to pare away the kinds of face-to-face contact that once provided important buffers between individuals and organized power. To an increasing extent, people will become even more susceptible to the influence of employers, news media, advertisers, and national political leaders. Where will we find new institutions to balance and mediate such power?

Perhaps the most significant challenge posed by the linking of computers and telecommunications is the prospect that the basic structures of political order will be recast. Worldwide computer, satellite, and communication networks fulfill, in large part, the modern dream of conquering space and time. These systems make possible instantaneous action at any point on the globe without limits imposed by the specific location of the initiating actor. Human beings and human societies, however, have traditionally found their identities within spatial and temporal limits. They have lived, acted, and found meaning in a particular place at a particular time. Developments in microelectronics tend to dissolve these limits, thereby threatening the integrity of social and political forms that depend on them. Aristotle's observation that "man is a political animal" meant in its most literal sense that man is a *polis* animal, a creature naturally suited to live in a particular kind of community within a specific geographical setting, the city-state. Historical experience shows that it is possible for human beings to flourish in political units—kingdoms, empires, nation-states—larger than those the Greeks thought natural. But until recently the crucial conditions created by spatial boundaries of political societies were never in question.

That has changed. Methods pioneered by transnational corporations now make it possible for organizations of enormous size to manage their activities effectively across the surface of the planet. Business units that used to depend upon spatial proximity can now be integrated through complex electronic signals. If it seems convenient to shift operations from one area of the world to another far distant, it can be accomplished with a flick of a switch. Close an office in Sunnyvale; open an office in Singapore. In the recent past corporations have had to demonstrate at least some semblance of commitment to geographically based communities; their public relations often stressed the fact that they were "good neighbors." But in an age in which organizations are located everywhere and nowhere, this commitment easily evaporates. A transnational corporation can play fast and loose with everyone, including the country that is ostensibly its "home." Towns, cities, regions, and whole nations are forced to swallow their pride and negotiate for favors. In that process, political authority is gradually redefined.

Computerization resembles other vast, but largely unconscious experiments in modern social and technological history, experiments of the kind noted in earlier chapters. Following a step-by-step process of instrumental improvements, societies create new institutions, new patterns of behavior, new sensibilities, new contexts for the exercise of power. Calling such changes "revolutionary," we tacitly acknowledge that these are matters that require reflection, possibly even strong public action to ensure that the outcomes are desirable. But the occasions for reflection, debate, and public choice are extremely rare indeed. The important decisions are left in private hands inspired by narrowly focused economic motives. While many recognize that these decisions have profound consequences for our common life, few seem prepared to own up to that fact. Some observers forecast that "the computer revolution" will eventually be guided by new wonders in artificial intelligence. Its present course is influenced by something much more familiar: the absent mind.

NOTES

1. See, for example, Edward Berkeley, *The Computer Revolution* (New York: Doubleday, 1962); Edward Tomeski, *The Computer Revolution: The Executive and the New Information Technology* (New York: Macmillan, 1970); and Nigel Hawkes, *The Computer Revolution* (New York: E. P. Dutton, 1972). See also Aaron Sloman, *The Computer Revolution in Philosophy* (Hassocks, England: Harvester Press, 1978); Zenon Pylyshyn, *Perspectives on the Computer Revolution* (Englewood Cliffs, N.J.: Prentice-Hall, 1970); Paul Stoneman, *Technological Diffusion and the Computer Revolution* (Cambridge: Cambridge University Press, 1976); and Ernest Braun and Stuart MacDonald, *Revolution in Miniature: The History and Impact of Semiconductor Electronics* (Cambridge: Cambridge University Press, 1978).
2. Michael L. Dertouzos in an interview on "The Today Show," National Broadcasting Company, August 8, 1983.
3. Daniel Bell, "The Social Framework of the Information Society," in *The Computer Age: A Twenty Year View,* Michael L. Dertouzos and Joel Moses (eds.) (Cambridge: MIT Press, 1980), 163.
4. See, for example, Philip H. Abelson, "The Revolution in Computers and Electronics," *Science* 215:751–753, 1982.
5. Edward A. Feigenbaum and Pamela McCorduck, *The Fifth Generation: Artificial Intelligence and Japan's Computer Challenge to the World* (Reading, Mass.: Addison-Wesley, 1983), 8.
6. Among the important works of this kind are David Burnham, *The Rise of the Computer State* (New York: Random House, 1983); James N. Danziger et al., *Computers and Politics: High Technology in American Local Governments* (New York: Columbia University Press, 1982); Abbe Moshowitz, *The Conquest of Will: Information Processing in Human Affairs* (Reading, Mass.: Addison-Wesley, 1976); James Rule et al., *The Politics of Privacy* (New York: New American Library, 1980); and Joseph Weizenbaum, *Computer Power and Human Reason: From Judgment to Calculation* (San Francisco: W. H. Freeman, 1976).
7. Quoted in Jacques Vallee, *The Network Revolution: Confessions of a Computer Scientist* (Berkeley: And/Or Press, 1982), 10.
8. Tracy Kidder, *Soul of a New Machine* (New York: Avon Books, 1982), 228.
9. *The Fifth Generation,* 14.
10. James Martin, *Telematic Society: A Challenge for Tomorrow* (Englewood Cliffs, N.J.: Prentice-Hall, 1981), 172.
11. Ibid., 4.
12. Starr Roxanne Hiltz and Murray Turoff, *The Network Nation: Human Communication via Computer* (Reading, Mass.: Addison-Wesley, 1978), 489.
13. Ibid., xxix.
14. Ibid., 484.
15. Ibid., xxix.
16. *The Network Revolution,* 198.
17. John Naisbitt, *Megatrends: Ten New Directions Transforming Our Lives* (New York: Warner Books, 1984), 282.
18. Amitai Etzioni, Kenneth Laudon, and Sara Lipson, "Participating Technology: The Minerva Communications Tree," *Journal of Communications,* 25:64, Spring 1975.
19. J. C. R. Licklider, "Computers and Government," in Dertouzos and Moses (eds.), *The Computer Age,* 114, 126.
20. Quoted in *The Fifth Generation,* 240.

21. *Occupational Outlook Handbook, 1982–1983*, U.S. Bureau of Labor Statistics, Bulletin No. 2200, Superintendent of Documents, U.S. Government Printing Office, Washington, D.C. See also Gene I. Maeroff, "The Real Job Boom Is Likely to Be Low-Tech," *New York Times*, September 4, 1983, 16E.
22. See, for example, James Danziger et al., *Computers and Politics*.
23. For a study of the utopia of consumer products in American democracy, see Jeffrey L. Meikle, *Twentieth Century Limited: Industrial Design in America, 1925–1939* (Philadelphia: Temple University Press, 1979). For other utopian dreams see Joseph J. Corn, *The Winged Gospel: America's Romance with Aviation, 1900–1950* (Oxford: Oxford University Press, 1983); Joseph J. Corn and Brian Horrigan, *Yesterday's Tomorrows: Past Visions of America's Future* (New York: Summit Books, 1984); and Erik Barnow, *The Tube of Plenty* (Oxford: Oxford University Press, 1975).
24. *The Fifth Generation,* 8.
25. "The Philosophy of US," from the official program of The US Festival held in San Bernardino, California, September 4–7, 1982. The outdoor rock festival, sponsored by Steven Wozniak, co-inventor of the original Apple Computer, attracted an estimated half million people. Wozniak regaled the crowd with large-screen video presentations of his message, proclaiming a new age of community and democracy generated by the use of personal computers.
26. "*Power* corresponds to the human ability not just to act but to act in concert. Power is never the property of an individual; it belongs to a group and remains in existence only so long as the group keeps together." Hannah Arendt, *On Violence* (New York: Harcourt Brace & World, 1969), 44.
27. John Markoff, "A View of the Future: Micros Won't Matter," *Info-World,* October 31, 1983, 69.
28. Donald H. Dunn, "The Many Uses of the Personal Computer," *Business Week,* June 23, 1980, 125–126.

THINKING AND RE-READING

1. As you re-read this piece, consider Winner's quote from an editor at a New York publishing firm, "People want to know what's new with computer technology. They don't want to know what could go wrong." Think about why such a statement might be true. Why would people avoid an analysis of the problems associated with technology?

2. Furthermore, identify for yourself the specific goals of the computer revolution as it has been manifested in our culture. What is the revolution against? What is it for? Who are the participants? Who are the victims? How do they stand to benefit? To lose?

WRITING AND LEARNING

1. In a letter written to Vice President Albert Gore Jr. or to the current president or vice president of the United States, identify the goals of the computer revolution as you think they have been manifested in our country. You are writing from the point of view of an informed citizen and a taxpayer, so you have both the right and the responsibility to express your opinion on this matter. In your letter, identify which of these specific goals you agree with and think we should be able to attain, which you consider less worthwhile and less attainable, and which you disagree with and believe we will be unable to attain. Explain your opinions about each goal.

2. Winner says that many individuals who believe that technology can benefit our society also believe that computers support the elements of the following formula: information = knowledge = power = democracy. Write a letter to somebody you know—a friend, a younger brother or sister, a family member—who may believe in this simple formula, and in the fact that computers always support this interaction. In your own words, explain why the formula might be false, why it might not yield the expected results, why computers might not support an enhanced democracy. Be sure to use language that your audience would understand and relate to. Your purpose in this letter is to explain to the reader why this seemingly simple formula may not be as accurate, complete, or simple as it initially appears.

3. Winner notes,

> [Computer] systems make possible instantaneous action at any point on the globe without limits imposed by the specific location of the initiating actor. Human beings and human societies, however, have traditionally found their identities within spatial and temporal limits. They have lived, acted, and found meaning in a particular place and time. Developments in microelectronics tend to dissolve these limits, thereby threatening the integrity of social and political forms that depend on them.

In a written response designed to help your classmates understand this complicated idea, explain what you think Winner may mean by these words. Use concrete examples from your own experience or the experiences of individuals you know well to illustrate your explanation.

We're Teen, We're Queer, and We've Got E-Mail

Steve Silberman

THIS ARTICLE DESCRIBES ONLINE COMMUNITIES that have provided gay teens opportunities to exchange views with other gay individuals, explore and create their own identities through discourse, and gather information important to their lives. We have included this article not only because it touches on an issue of cultural importance to a significant proportion of the American population, but also because it richly illustrates the kinds of communities that can be formed online.

The author of this contribution, Steve Silberman, has written *Skeleton Key: A Dictionary for Deadheads.* This piece was originally published in *Wired,* a popular magazine aimed at an informed readership interested in technology.

There's a light on in the Nerd Nook: JohnTeen ∅ is composing e-mail into the night. The Nerd Nook is what John's mother calls her 16-year-old's bedroom—it's more cramped than the bridge of the Enterprise, with a Roland CM-322 that makes "You've got mail" thunder like the voice of God.

John's favorite short story is "The Metamorphosis." Sure, Kafka's fable of waking up to discover you've morphed into something that makes everyone tweak speaks to every teenager. But John especially has had moments of feeling insectoid—like during one school choir trip, when, he says, the teacher booking rooms felt it necessary to inform the other students' parents of John's "orientation." When they balked at their kids sharing a room with him, John was doubled up with another teacher—a fate nearly as alienating as Gregor Samsa's.

The choir trip fiasco was but one chapter in the continuing online journal that has made JohnTeen ∅—or as his parents and classmates know him, John Erwin—one of the most articulate voices in America Online's Gay and Lesbian Community Forum.

> From: JohnTeen ∅
>
> My high school career has been a sudden and drastic
> spell of turbulence and change that has influenced every
> aspect of life. Once I was an automaton, obeying
> external, societal, and parental expectations like a dog,

oblivious of who I was or what I wanted. I was the token child every parent wants—student body president, color guard, recipient of the general excellence award, and outstanding music student of the year. I conformed to society's paradigm, and I was rewarded. Yet I was miserable. Everything I did was a diversion from thinking about myself. Finally, last summer, my subconsciousness felt comfortable enough to be able to connect myself with who I really am, and I began to understand what it is to be gay.

JohnTeen ∅ is a new kind of gay kid, a 16-year-old not only out, but already at home in the online convergence of activists that Tom Reilly, the co-founder of Digital Queers, calls the "Queer Global Village." Just 10 years ago, most queer teens hid behind a self-imposed don't-ask-don't-tell policy until they shipped out to Oberlin or San Francisco, but the Net has given even closeted kids a place to conspire. Though the Erwin's house is in an unincorporated area of Santa Clara County in California, with goats and llamas foraging in the backyard, John's access to AOL's gay and lesbian forum enables him to follow dispatches from queer activists worldwide, hone his writing, flirt, try on disposable identities, and battle bigots—all from his home screen.

John's ambitions to recast national policy before the principal of Menlo School even palms him a diploma (John's mother refers to him as her "little mini-activist") are not unrealistic. Like the ur-narrative of every videogame, the saga of gay teens online is one of metamorphosis, of "little mini" nerds becoming warriors in a hidden Stronghold of Power. For young queers, the Magic Ring is the bond of community.

John's posts have the confidence and urgency of one who speaks for many who must keep silent:

> The struggle for equal rights has always taken place on the frontier of the legal wilderness where liberty meets power. Liberty has claimed much of that wilderness now, but the frontier always lies ahead of us. . . . The frontier of liberty may have expanded far beyond where it began, but for those without rights, it always seems on the horizon, just beyond their reach.

And the messages that stream back into John's box are mostly from kids his own age, many marooned far from urban centers for gay and lesbian youth. Such is Christopher Rempel, a witty, soft-spoken Ace of Base fan from (as he puts it) "redneck farmer hell." Christopher borrowed the principal's modem to jack into a beekeepers BBS and gopher his way to the Queer Resources Directory, a multimeg collection of text files, news items, and services listings.

> My name is Christopher and I am 15 years old. I came to terms that I was gay last summer and, aside from some depression, I'm OK. I am "not" in denial about being gay.

> I would like to write to someone that I can talk to about issues I can't talk about with my friends. I don't play sports very much, but I make it up in my knowledge of computers. I am interested in anybody with an open mind and big aspirations for the future.

A decade ago, the only queer info available to most teens was in a few dour psychology texts under the nose of the school librarian. Now libraries of files await them in the AOL forum and elsewhere—the Queer Resources Directory alone contains hundreds—and teens can join mailing lists like Queercampus and GayNet, or tap resources like the Bridges Project, a referral service that tells teens not only how to get in touch with queer youth groups, but how to jump-start one themselves.

> "If teen organizers succeed," says Tom Reilly, "everyone's gonna hear about it. This is the most powerful tool queer youth have ever had."

Kali is an 18-year-old lesbian at a university in Colorado. Her name means "fierce" in Swahili. Growing up in California, Kali was the leader of a young women's chapter of the Church of Jesus Christ of Latter-day Saints. She was also the "Girl Saved by E-mail," whose story ran last spring on CNN. After mood swings plummeted her into a profound depression, Kali—like too many gay teens—considered suicide. Her access to GayNet at school gave her a place to air those feelings, and a phone call from someone she knew online saved her life.

Kali is now a regular contributor to Sappho, a women's board she most appreciates because there she is accepted as an equal. "They forgive me for being young," Kali laughs, "though women come out later than guys, so there aren't a lot of teen lesbians. But it's a high of connection. We joke that we're posting to 500 of our closest friends."

"The wonderful thing about online services is that they are an intrinsically decentralized resource," says Tom Reilly, who has solicited the hardware and imparted the skills to get dozens of queer organizations jacked in. "Kids can challenge what adults have to say and make the news. One of the best examples of teen organizing in the last year was teens working with the Massachusetts legislature to pass a law requiring gay and lesbian education in the high schools. If teen organizers are successful *somewhere* now, everyone's gonna hear about it. This is the most powerful tool queer youth have ever had."

Another power that teenagers are now wielding online is their anger. "Teens are starting to throw their weight around," says Quirk, the leader of the AOL forum. (Quirk maintains a gender-neutral identity online, to be an equal-opportunity sounding board for young lesbians and gay men.) "They're *complaining*. It used to be, 'Ick—I think I'm gay, I'll sneak around the forum and see what they're doing.' With this second wave of activism, it's like, 'There's gay stuff here, but it's not right for *me*.' These kids are computer literate, and they're using the anger of youth to create a space for themselves."

The powers that be at AOL, however, have not yet seen fit to allow that space to be named by its users—the creation of chat rooms called "gay teen" anything is banned. "AOL has found that the word 'gay' with the word 'youth' or 'teen' in a room name becomes a lightning rod for predators," says Quirk. "I've been in teen conferences where adult cruising so overwhelmed any kind of conversation about being in high school and 'What kind of music do you like?' that I was furious. Until I can figure out a way to provide a safe space for them, I'm not going to put them at risk."

Quirk and AOL are in a tight place. Pedophilia has become the trendy bludgeon with which to trash cyberspace in the dailies, and concerned parents invoke the P-word to justify limiting teens' access to gay forums. At the same time, however, postings in the teens-only folder of

Accessing Queer Teen Cyberspace

> **Accessing Queer Teen Cyberspace**
>
> - The Gay and Lesbian Community Forum, On America Online. Keyword: Gay
> - Queer America. Send e-mail containing your city, state, zip code, area code, and age to *ncglbyorg@aol.com*.
> - Queer Resources Directory. Anonymous ftp or gopher to *vector.casti.com* (look in pub/QRD/youth); On the World Wide Web, go to *http:/vector.casti.com/QRD/.html/QRD-home-page.html*. Or send an inquiry to *qrdstaff@vector.casti.com*.
> - Bridges Project. American Friends Service Committee referral and resource center. E-mail *bridgespro@aol.com*.

the Gay and Lesbian Community Forum flame not only the invasion of teen turf by adults trolling for sex, but also the adults claiming to "protect" them by limiting their access to one another.

One anonymous 17-year-old poster on AOL dissed the notion that queer teens are helpless victims of online "predators":

> There are procedures for dealing with perverts, which most teens (in contrast with most of the adults we've encountered) are familiar with. Flooding e-mail boxes of annoying perverts, 'IGNORE'-ing them in chat rooms, and shutting off our Instant Messages are all very effective methods. We are not defenseless, nor innocent.

The issue is further complicated by the fact that the intermingling of old and young people online is good for teens. The online connection allows them to open dialogs with mentors like Deacon Maccubbin, co-owner of Lambda Rising bookstore in Washington, D.C. As "DeaconMac," Maccubbin has been talking with gay kids on CompuServe and AOL for eight years. One of the young people DeaconMac corresponded with online, years ago, was Tom Reilly. "Deacon was the first openly gay man I'd ever had a conversation with, and he had a very clear idea of what his role was. He was nurturing and mentoring; he sent me articles; and he didn't come on to me," says Reilly. "I'll never forget it as long as I live."

In the past, teens often had to wait until they were old enough to get into a bar to meet other gay people—or hang around outside until someone noticed them. Online interaction gives teens a chance to unmask themselves in a safe place, in a venue where individuals make themselves known by the acuity of their thought and expression, rather than by their physical appearance.

When JohnTeen ∅ logged his first post in the gay AOL forum, he expressed outrage that the concerns of queer teens—who are at a disproportionately high risk for suicide—were being shunted aside by adult organizations. His post was spotted by Sarah Gregory, a 26-year-old anarchist law student who helped get the National Gay and Lesbian Task Force wired up. "I really wanted to hit this kid between the eyes with the fact that a national organization saw what he was saying and cared that gay youth were killing themselves," Gregory recalls. A correspondence and friendship began that would have been unlikely offline—for, as Gregory says, "I don't notice 16-year-old boys in the real world."

Gregory explains: "I remember one particularly graphic letter I sent John in response to his questions. I wrote a *huge* disclaimer before and after it. But then I remembered how desperately I wanted to be talked to as an adult, and a sexual being, when I was 14. Thinking back, that's the point where John stopped sounding so formal, so much like a well-bred teenager talking to an authority figure, and became my friend. It's also the last time he talked about suicide. It scared me how easily his vulnerability could have been exploited, but I'd do it again in a heartbeat."

"I didn't even listen to music," moans John recalling his nerdhood, when the only thing he logged in for was shareware. Now the background thrash for his late-night e-mail sessions is Pansy Division. "To keep myself in the closet, I surrounded myself with people I'd never find attractive. I had two different parts of my life: the normal part, where I worked hard in school and got good grades, and this other part, where I was interested in guys but didn't do anything about it." For many kids, writing to John or to other posters is where a more authentic life begins:

> Dear JohnTeen:
>
> I am so frustrated with life and all of its blind turns. Am I gay? What will happen if I tell friends and my mom? . . . (I still don't 100% know that I am gay only that I am not heterosexual SO WHAT AM I) I really want to fit somewhere and also to love someone (at this point I don't care who). . . . Please EMAIL back and enlighten me. You have been very inspirational to me. I have no idea how you gained the courage to come out. Thanks, James

But John Erwin must guard against JohnTeen ∅ becoming a full-time gig: he not only has the frontiers of liberty to defend and his peers to "enlighten," but like any 16-year-old, he needs space to fuck up, be a normal teenage cockroach, and figure out who he is. And he'd like to find someone to love. Does he have anyone in mind? "Yes!" he grins, pulling out his yearbook and leafing to a photo of a handsome boy who says he's straight.

Is John's dream guy online?

"No, I wish," John says. "If he was online, I could tell him how I *feel.*"

THINKING AND RE-READING

1. As you re-read this piece, consider your own set of beliefs about gay people in our culture. What are your beliefs? Where did they come from? How do they square with your impression of the people that you read about in this particular article? With gay people that you know? How do your beliefs influence the way in which you read and understand this article? The experiences of the people it describes?

WRITING AND LEARNING

1. Contact a member of the gay students' organization on your campus and ask to be put in contact with a gay student who would be willing to participate in an interview with you about this article. Often, gay organizations have an e-mail address on campus, and you can use this address to establish e-mail contact with a spokesperson for the group. After you have identified a person who is willing to have either a face-to-face or an e-mail interview with you, provide him or her a copy of this article in advance. In your interview, ask the person to respond to this article within the context of his or her own experience. Among the questions you might ask are the following: Did this article seem realistic to you? Why? Are the experiences it describes similar to or different from your own? In what ways? Do you participate in similar online exchanges? Do you find those conversations a productive or troubling experience? Why? If you do talk online, how do these online conversations differ from those you can hold in face-to-face situations? How does the electronic setting affect what it is possible for you to express? What does it hinder you from expressing? Summarize both the questions and the responses to this interview for the purpose of reporting them to the other members of your class.

2. To develop your own insight about, and understanding of, electronic conversations, examine the five e-mail excerpts that are included in this article. In a written response, answer the following question: How do these pieces of online conversation differ from pieces of conversation that you might hear in a face-to-face setting? Think not only about the vocabulary and the content of the messages, but also about the tone, frankness, focus, and voice that characterize these excerpts. To answer this question, you may need to determine what characteristics the e-mail messages share and in what ways they differ. What does the electronic setting of these conversations make it possible to express? What does it seem to hinder individuals from expressing?

3. In a letter to a young person whom you know (e.g., a friend, a family member, the child of a friend), write about what life is like for anybody who is different in some important way. In this letter, consider the following questions, among others that you might think of: How does our culture identify *difference?* What cultural values are associated with difference? Why is our culture so concerned with difference? How does difference make individuals feel? What are your own experiences with difference? Your purpose in this letter is to inform the younger reader about what it means to be different in our culture and to inform him or her about how you think he or she should respond to differences.

IMAGES OF SOCIAL ISSUES AND TECHNOLOGY

THINKING AND RE-READING

1. In Appendix A of this reader, you will find a list of questions that will help you read and understand this set of images, and other images that you see, in new ways. Read the questions in this list carefully and use them to "read" the images in this section—carefully and with an increasing sense of thoughtfulness.

WRITING AND LEARNING

1. Choose at least two of the three images to analyze more carefully. For these images, write down your answers to the questions listed in Appendix A.

JUNE 1994 • $5.00

Presentations

TECHNOLOGY AND TECHNIQUES FOR BETTER COMMUNICATIONS

Presentations to Go:

Portable Computers, Peripherals and More

PAGE 21

Multimedia Authoring Software
PAGE 44

Designing Graphics for Video
PAGE 52

Reviews: PowerPoint 4.0, nVIEW Z-Series LCD Panels
PAGE 56

ESCAPE THE OFFICE

WITHOUT LEAVING IT BEHIND.

These days your office can be anywhere you do business. Whether you're downtown or in your dining room, you need to stay in touch. That's why Fujitsu Microelectronics offers a complete family of integrated, world-class PC Cards, to give you immediate access to vital information while in the office or on the road.

Our ultraportable PC Cards offer a wide range of capabilities including multimedia, LAN, and high-speed communications. With Fujitsu, you get instant compatibility with virtually all of today's PCMCIA standard computing platforms in addition to multi-function capability and interoperability. Plus, our intuitive Microsoft® Windows-based installation software automatically

sets up and configures your PC, which means fewer headaches and hassles. With Plug and Play features like hot insertion and removal, there's no need to reboot your system when swapping cards. You even get the ease and comfort of our extensive customer support services that ensure customer satisfaction and help you get the most from your investment.

So, if today's virtual office is leaving you feeling a little detached, call Fujitsu Microelectronics at **1-800-642-7616** and we'll get you connected.

Can Technology Replace Social Engineering?

Alvin M. Weinberg

THIS ESSAY WAS ORIGINALLY PUBLISHED in 1966 in the *University of Chicago Magazine,* a publication read by faculty, students, staff, and alumni of the University of Chicago—an educated and informed readership. As an artifact of that time, this essay reflects an optimism about technological advances characteristic of the 1960s, specifically, and the modern age, generally. In particular, this piece of scholarship makes the claim that humans can employ technology productively to "fix" complex social problems such as overpopulation, drought, and even war.

As you read this article—authored approximately thirty years ago by a physicist who participated in the Manhattan Project (the effort that ultimately resulted in the development of the atomic bomb) during World War II and who served as the director of the Oak Ridge National Laboratory—consider how our cultural understanding of technology's potential has changed over the last thirty years. Also think about how it has remained largely the same.

During World War II, and immediately afterward, our federal government mobilized its scientific and technical resources, such as the Oak Ridge National Laboratory, around great technological problems. Nuclear reactors, nuclear weapons, radar, and space are some of the miraculous new technologies that have been created by this mobilization of federal effort. In the past few years there has been a major change in focus of much of our federal research. Instead of being preoccupied with technology, our government is now mobilizing around problems that are largely social. We are beginning to ask what can we do about world population, about the deterioration of our environment, about our educational system, our decaying cities, race relations, poverty. Recent administrations have dedicated the power of a scientifically oriented federal apparatus to finding solutions for these complex social problems.

Social problems are much more complex than are technological problems. It is much harder to identify a social problem than a technological problem: how do we know when our cities need renewing, or when our population is too big, or when our modes of transportation have broken down? The problems are, in a way, harder to identify just because their solutions are never clear-cut: how do we know when our cities are renewed, or our air clean enough, or our transportation convenient enough? By contrast, the availability of a crisp and beautiful technological *solution* often helps focus on the problem to which the new technology is the solution. I doubt that we would have been nearly as concerned with an eventual shortage of energy as we now are if we had not had a neat solution—nuclear energy—available to eliminate the shortage.

There is a more basic sense in which social problems are much more difficult than are technological problems. A social problem exists because many people behave, individually, in a socially unacceptable way. To solve a social problem one must induce social change—one must persuade many people to behave differently than they have behaved in the past. One must persuade many people to have fewer babies, or to drive more carefully, or to refrain from disliking blacks. By contrast, resolution of a technological problem involves many fewer individual decisions. Once President Roosevelt decided to go after atomic energy, it was by comparison a relatively simple task to mobilize the Manhattan Project.

The resolution of social problems by the traditional methods—by motivating or forcing people to behave more rationally—is a frustrating business. People don't behave rationally; it is a long, hard business to persuade individuals to forgo immediate personal gain or pleasure (as seen by the individual) in favor of longer term social gain. And indeed, the aim of social engineering is to invent the social devices—usually legal, but also moral and educational and organizational—that will change each person's motivation and redirect his activities along ways that are more acceptable to the society.

The technologist is appalled by the difficulties faced by the social engineer; to engineer even a small social change by inducing individuals to behave differently is always hard even when the change is rather neutral or even beneficial. For example, some rice eaters in India are reported to prefer starvation to eating wheat which we send to them. How much harder it is to change motivations where the individual is insecure and feels threatened if he acts differently, as illustrated by the poor white's reluctance to accept the black as an equal. By contrast, technological engineering is simple: the rocket, the reactor, and the desalination plants are devices that are expensive to develop, to be sure, but their feasibility is relatively easy to assess, and their success relatively easy to achieve once one understands the scientific principles that underlie them. It is, therefore, tempting to raise the following question: In view of the simplicity of technological engineering, and the complexity of social engineering, to what extent can social problems be circumvented by reducing them to technological problems? Can we identify Quick Technological Fixes for profound and almost infinitely complicated social problems, "fixes" that are within the grasp of modern technology, and which would either eliminate the original social problem without requiring a change in the individual's social attitudes, or would so alter the problem as to make its resolution more feasible? To paraphrase Ralph Nader, to what extent can technological *remedies* be found for social problems without first having to remove the *causes* of the problem? It is in this sense that I ask, "Can technology replace social engineering?"

THE MAJOR TECHNOLOGICAL FIXES OF THE PAST

To better explain what I have in mind, I shall describe how two of our profoundest social problems—poverty and war—have in some limited degree been solved by the Technological Fix, rather than by the methods of social engineering. Let me begin with poverty.

The traditional Marxian view of poverty regarded our economic ills as being primarily a question of maldistribution of goods. The Marxist recipe for elimination of poverty, therefore, was to eliminate profit, in the erroneous belief that it was the loss of this relatively small increment from the worker's paycheck that kept him poverty-stricken. The Marxist dogma is typical of the approach of the social engineer: one tries to convince or coerce many people to forgo their short-term profits in what is presumed to be the long-term interest of the society as a whole.

The Marxian view seems archaic in this age of mass production and automation not only to us, but apparently to many Eastern bloc economists. For the brilliant advances in the technology of energy, of mass production, and of automation have created the affluent society. Technology has expanded our productive capacity so greatly that even though our distribution is still inefficient, and unfair by Marxian precepts, there is more than enough to go around. Technology has provided a "fix"—greatly expanded production of goods—which enables our capitalistic society to achieve many of the aims of the Marxist social engineer without going through the social revolution Marx viewed as inevitable. Technology has converted the seemingly intractable social problem of *widespread* poverty into a relatively tractable one.

My second example is war. The traditional Christian position views war as primarily a moral issue: if men become good, and model themselves after the Prince of Peace, they will live in peace. This doctrine is so deeply ingrained in the spirit of all civilized men that I suppose it is a blasphemy to point out that it has never worked very well—that men have not been good, and that they are not paragons of virtue or even of reasonableness.

Though I realize it is terribly presumptuous to claim, I believe that Edward Teller may have supplied the nearest thing to a Quick Technological Fix to the problem of war. The hydrogen bomb greatly increases the provocation that would precipitate large-scale war—and not because men's motivations have been changed, not because men have become more tolerant and understanding, but rather because the appeal to the primitive instinct of self-preservation has been intensified far beyond anything we could have imagined before the H-bomb was invented. To point out these things today, with the United States involved in a shooting war, may sound hollow and unconvincing; yet the desperate and partial peace we have now is much better than a full-fledged exchange of thermonuclear weapons. One cannot deny that the Soviet leaders now recognize the force of H-bombs, and that this has surely contributed to the less militant attitude of the USSR. One can only hope that the Chinese leadership, as it acquires familiarity with H-bombs, will also become less militant. If I were to be asked who has given the world a more effective means of achieving peace, our great religious leaders who urge men to love their neighbors and, thus, avoid fights, or our weapons technologists who simply present men with no rational alternative to peace, I would vote for the weapons technologist. That the peace we get is at best terribly fragile, I cannot deny; yet, as I shall explain, I think technology can help stabilize our imperfect and precarious peace.

THE TECHNOLOGICAL FIXES OF THE FUTURE

Are there other Technological Fixes on the horizon, other technologies that can reduce immensely complicated social questions to a matter of "engineering"? Are there new technologies that offer society ways of circumventing social problems and at the same time do *not* require individuals to renounce short-term advantage for long-term gain?

Probably the most important new Technological Fix is the Intra-Uterine Device for birth control. Before the IUD was invented, birth control demanded very strong motivation of countless individuals. Even with the pill, the individual's motivation had to be sustained day in and day out; should it flag even temporarily, the strong motivation of the previous month might go for naught. But the IUD, being a one-shot method, greatly reduces the individual motivation required to induce a social change. To be sure, the mother must be sufficiently motivated to accept the IUD in the first place, but, as experience in India already seems to show, it is much easier to persuade the Indian mother to accept the IUD once, than it is to persuade her to take a pill every day. The IUD does not completely replace social engineering by technology; and indeed, in some Spanish American cultures where the husband's manliness is measured by the number of children he has, the IUD attacks only part of the problem. Yet, in many other situations, as in India, the IUD so reduces the social component of the problem as to make an impossibly difficult social problem much less hopeless.

Let me turn now to problems which from the beginning have had both technical and social components—broadly, those concerned with conservation of our resources: our environment, our water, and our raw materials for production of the means of subsistence. The social issue here arises because many people by their individual acts cause shortages and, thus, create economic, and ultimately social, imbalance. For example, people use water wastefully, or they insist on moving to California because of its climate, and so we have water shortages; or too many people drive cars in Los Angeles with its curious meteorology, and so Los Angeles suffocates from smog.

The water resources problem is a particularly good example of a complicated problem with strong social and technological connotations. Our management of water resources in the past has been based largely on the ancient Roman device, the aqueduct: every water shortage was to be relieved by stealing water from someone else who at the moment didn't need the water or was too poor or too weak to prevent the steal. Southern California would steal from Northern California, New York City from upstate New York, the farmer who could afford a cloud-seeder from the farmer who could not afford a cloud-seeder. The social engineer insists that such shortsighted expedients have got us into serious trouble; we have no water resources policy, we waste water disgracefully, and, perhaps, in denying the ethic of thriftiness in using water, we have generally undermined our moral fiber. The social engineer, therefore, views such technological shenanigans as being shortsighted, if not downright immoral. Instead, he says, we should persuade or force people to use less water, or to stay in the cold Middle West where water is plentiful instead of migrating to California where water is scarce.

The water technologist, on the other hand, views the social engineer's approach as rather impractical. To persuade people to use less water, to get along with expensive water, is difficult, time-consuming, and uncertain in the extreme. Moreover, say the technologists, what right does the water resources expert have to insist that people use water less wastefully? Green lawns and clean cars and swimming pools are part of the good life, American style, . . . and what right do we have to deny this luxury if there is some alternative to cutting down the water we use?

Here we have a sharp confrontation of the two ways of dealing with a complex social issue: the social engineering way which asks people to behave more "reasonably," and the technologists' way which tries to avoid changing people's habits or motivation. Even though I am a technologist, I have sympathy for the social engineer. I think we must use our water as efficiently as possible, that we ought to improve people's attitudes toward the use of water, and that everything that can be done to rationalize our water policy will be welcome. Yet as a technologist, I believe I see ways of providing more water more cheaply than the social engineers may concede is possible.

I refer to the possibility of nuclear desalination. The social engineer dismisses the technologist's simpleminded idea of solving a water shortage by transporting more water primarily because, in so doing, the water user steals water from someone else—possibly foreclosing the possibility of ultimately utilizing land now only sparsely settled. But surely water drawn from the sea deprives no one of his share of water. The whole issue is then a technological one; can fresh water be drawn from the sea cheaply enough to have a major impact on our chronically water-short areas like Southern California, Arizona, and the Eastern seaboard?

I believe the answer is yes, though much hard technical work remains to be done. A large program to develop cheap methods of nuclear desalting has been undertaken by the United States, and I have little doubt that within the next ten to twenty years we shall see huge dual-purpose desalting plants springing up on many parched seacoasts of the world.* At first these plants will produce water at municipal prices. But I believe, on the basis of research now in progress at ORNL and elsewhere, water from the sea at a cost acceptable for agriculture—less than ten cents per 1,000 gallons—is eventually in the cards. In short, for areas close to the seacoasts, technology can provide water without requiring a great and difficult-to-accomplish change in people's attitudes toward the utilization of water.

The Technological Fix for water is based on the availability of extremely cheap energy from very large nuclear reactors. What other social consequences can one foresee flowing from really cheap energy eventually available to every country regardless of its endowment of conventional resources? Though we now see only vaguely the outlines of the possibilities, it does seem likely that from very cheap nuclear energy we shall get hydrogen by electrolysis of water, and, thence, the all important ammonia fertilizer necessary to help feed the hungry of the world; we shall reduce metals without requiring coking coal; we shall even power automobiles with electricity, via fuel cells or storage batteries, thus reducing our world's dependence on crude oil, as well as eliminating our air pollution insofar as it is caused by automobile exhaust or by the burning of fossil fuels. In short, the widespread availability of very cheap energy everywhere in the world ought to lead to an energy autarky in every country of the world; and eventually to an autarky in the many staples of life that should flow from really cheap energy.

WILL TECHNOLOGY REPLACE SOCIAL ENGINEERING?

I hope these examples suggest how social problems can be circumvented or at least reduced to less formidable proportions by the application of the Technological Fix. The examples I have given do not strike me as being fanciful, nor are they at all exhaustive. I have not touched, for example, upon the extent to which really cheap computers and improved technology of communication can help improve elementary teaching without having first to improve our elementary teachers. Nor have I mentioned Ralph Nader's brilliant observation that a safer car, and even its development and adoption by the auto company, is a quicker and probably surer way to reduce traffic deaths than is a campaign to teach people to drive more carefully. Nor have I invoked some really fanciful Technological Fixes: like providing air conditioners and free electricity to operate them for every black family in Watts on the assumption (suggested by Huntington) that race rioting is correlated with hot, humid weather; or the ultimate Technological Fix, Aldous Huxley's soma pills that eliminate human unhappiness without improving human relations in the usual sense.

*Here, as elsewhere, the reader should bear in mind that the essay dates from the mid-1960s.—Ed.

My examples illustrate both the strength and the weakness of the Technological Fix for social problems. The Technological Fix accepts man's intrinsic shortcomings and circumvents them or capitalizes on them for socially useful ends. The Fix is, therefore, eminently practical and, in the short term, relatively effective. One does not wait around trying to change people's minds: if people want more water, one gets them more water rather than requiring them to reduce their use of water; if people insist on driving autos while they are drunk, one provides safer autos that prevent injuries even after a severe accident.

But the technological solutions to social problems tend to be incomplete and metastable, to replace one social problem with another. Perhaps the best example of this instability is the peace imposed upon us by the H-bomb. Evidently the pax hydrogenica is metastable in two senses: in the short term, because the aggressor still enjoys such an advantage; in the long term, because the discrepancy between have and have-not nations must eventually be resolved if we are to have permanent peace. Yet, for these particular shortcomings, technology has something to offer. To the imbalance between offense and defense, technology says let us devise passive defense which redresses the balance. A world with H-bombs and adequate civil defense is less likely to lapse into thermonuclear war than a world with H-bombs alone, at least if one concedes that the danger of the thermonuclear war mainly lies in the acts of irresponsible leaders. Anything that deters the irresponsible leader is a force for peace: a technologically sound civil defense therefore would help stabilize the balance of terror.

[handwritten margin note: If bomb brought Quic peace but now threatens us.]

To the discrepancy between haves and have-nots, technology offers the nuclear energy revolution, with its possibility of autarky for haves and have-nots alike. How this might work to stabilize our metastable thermonuclear peace is suggested by the possible political effect of the recently proposed Israeli desalting plant. The Arab states I should think would be much less set upon destroying the Jordan River Project if the Israelis had a desalination plant in reserve that would nullify the effect of such action. In this connection, I think countries like ours can contribute very much. Our country will soon have to decide whether to continue to spend 5.5×10^9 per year for space exploration after our lunar landing. Is it too outrageous to suggest that some of this money be devoted to building huge nuclear desalting complexes in the arid ocean rims of the troubled world? If the plants are powered with breeder reactors, the out-of-pocket costs, once the plants are built, should be low enough to make large-scale agriculture feasible in these areas. I estimate that for 4×10^9 per year we could build enough desalting capacity to feed more than ten million new mouths per year (provided we use agricultural methods that husband water), and we would, thereby, help stabilize the metastable, bomb-imposed balance of terror.

Yet, I am afraid we technologists shall not satisfy our social engineers, who tell us that our Technological Fixes do not get to the heart of the problem; they are at best temporary expedients; they create new problems as they solve old ones; to put a Technological Fix into effect requires a positive social action. Eventually, social engineering, like the Supreme Court decision on desegregation, must be invoked to solve social problems. And, of course, our social engineers are right. Technology will never *replace* social engineering. But technology has provided and will continue to provide to the social engineer broader options, to make intractable social problems less intractable; perhaps, most of all, technology will buy time—that precious commodity that converts violent social revolution into acceptable social evolution.

Our country now recognizes and is mobilizing around the great social problems that corrupt and disfigure our human existence. It is natural that in this mobilization we should look first to the social engineer. But, unfortunately, the apparatus most readily available to the government, like the great federal laboratories, is technologically oriented, not socially oriented. I believe we have a great opportunity here; for, as I hope I have persuaded you, many of our seemingly social problems do admit of partial technological solutions. Our already deployed technological apparatus can contribute to the resolution of social questions. I plead, therefore, first for our government to deploy its laboratories, its hardware contractors, and its engineering universities around social problems. And I plead, secondly, for understanding and cooperation between technologist and social engineer. Even with all the help he can get from the technologist, the social engineer's problems are never really solved. It is only by cooperation between technologist and social engineer that we can hope to achieve what is the aim of all technologists and social engineers—a better society, and thereby, a better life, for all of us who are part of society.

THINKING AND RE-READING

1. As you re-read this piece, consider your personal response to Weinberg's arguments—understanding that in formulating your own response, you have the benefit of thirty years of historical perspective that he did not have. Do you believe, for example, that the hydrogen bomb provided a "Quick Technological Fix" to the social problem of war? That the IUD provided a technological fix to the problem of overpopulation? Why do you believe as you do? Think about the evidence that supports your answer and how you have come to your conclusions.

2. Weinberg writes that "the availability of a crisp and beautiful technological solution often helps focus on the problem to which the new technology is the solution." Assume, for a minute, that computers may be such a solution. What do you think the problem(s) is (are)?

3. Weinberg talks of two main ways to address complex social problems—that of the social engineer and that of the technologist. These two perspectives are interesting because they assume that complex social problems can be "solved." Are there problems that cannot be solved? That should not be solved? If so, what are they? Why do you believe as you do?

WRITING AND LEARNING

1. Re-read the first selection in this part, "Welcome to Cyberspace," by Elmer-DeWitt. Write down a list of the technological fixes that the author attributes to the Internet. What social problems does he claim the Internet is now addressing? Add to this list other claims that you have heard or read about the social problems that the Internet will solve. In a letter to the editor of your local newspaper or your school newspaper, explain whether or not you think the computer has really addressed two or three of the most important social problems identified on your list. Use your personal experiences

and those experiences of individuals you know to explain, persuasively, why you take each stand that you do.

2. In this article, Weinberg contrasts two ways of dealing with a complex social issue, "the social engineering way asks people to behave more 'reasonably', and the technologists' way tries to avoid changing people's habits or motivations." Write a story of a time when you tried to address an important and complex social problem from one of these two perspectives. Your audience for this story is a class of intelligent tenth-grade high school students who are studying various approaches to problem solving in connection with social problems that they face in their lives—family relationships, social relationships with friends, as well as relationships with adults. Talk about how your approach worked out and whether, given the perspective you have gained from Weinberg's piece and a bit of history, you might now see a different way to approach the problem. You might also consider whether the problem was one that *could* be solved or that *should* be solved. Perhaps, it never needed addressing in the first place; perhaps, it was a problem that one person simply could not address alone. The problem you focus on does not have to be important in the larger sense of the word *social;* it should be a dilemma that was important in your life or the lives of others that you know.

3. Write a letter to the editor of your local paper suggesting a way to address a social problem in your local community. In your suggestion, include some part of the solution that draws on social engineering perspectives and some part of the solution that draws on technological engineering perspectives. If you can think of additional ways to address social problems—strategies beyond the two that Weinberg suggests—you might want to include these as well.

Terror On-Line

Mark Stuart Gill

THIS ARTICLE, ORIGINALLY PRINTED in the January 1995 issue of *Vogue*, describes a form of criminal behavior that is increasingly common on the Internet—stalking. The article is aimed at a general, non-specialist readership comprised primarily of women. Because the topic that this piece focuses on is situated at the intersection of two other important issues in cyberspace—freedom of speech and censorship—it is a complex one. In addition, the issue is connected with sexism, sexual harassment, and the ways in which people in a community govern themselves and others.

As you read this article imagine how you would feel if Laurie Powell were your mother, your sister, or somebody you knew well.

On February 17, 1993, Laurie Powell, a housewife in Greensboro, North Carolina, said good night to her children. She put the house in order. Then she flicked on the computer in her bedroom and, through her phone line, signed on to the on-line service Prodigy, not knowing she was about to open a Pandora's box.

Her family had bought the IBM clone six months earlier, with Prodigy preinstalled on the hard drive. For a monthly fee, Prodigy members can find out the weather, the news, and the latest stock quotations, make plane reservations, or send E-mail to friends and relatives in different states.

But the main draw for 41-year-old Powell, a small attractive woman with brown hair, was the many discussion groups—known as bulletin boards—where people can upload their ideas, experiences, and opinions, and read other people's comments. New users find E-mail powerfully conducive to intimacy. "On-line relationships become intense very quickly," says Powell. "It's about making close connections, finding others that understand you. That's hard to do today."

These days, this is all Laurie Powell is willing to reveal publicly about herself: She was born and went to college in the Midwest. Several members of her family were cops; she once worked as a medical therapist. After 21 years of marriage, she has two teenagers who live at home: a daughter and an adopted son who suffers from fetal alcohol syndrome. Her husband's job in industrial sales is good enough for them to own a three-bedroom home in Greensboro with cathedral ceilings, fireplaces, and a wooded lot. At night, they can sit out on the deck and see rabbits and raccoons. "We're a pretty straight-and-narrow family," she says. "Just dealing with the usual: student drivers, boyfriends, homecoming. We have dinner together almost every night." She loves reading Danielle Steele, hates Stephen King.

Sometimes, when she'd felt the strain of raising a retarded son, she had sought solace on the Home Life and Medical bulletin boards. "A virtual extended family was out there listening to anything you had to say, anytime," she says. But that night, the Home Life Board contained an obscene public message that mentioned Powell by name, signed by someone calling himself "Vito." Powell was shocked: This wasn't what she had signed up for—age-old crimes against women, perpetrated on new technology. What if her kids were to read it? She didn't think to download the message and print it out; it seemed like a random act. Nor could she bring herself to tell her husband about it.

But soon there were more messages, first signed "Vito," then under a variety of names. This one came from a "David Fauhs":

> Laurie Powell AKA snutmuffin. . . . The 'Cracker' who has beer for
> breakfast, lives with a hangover, her underdeveloped AFS child, Mutt's
> claim to fame is screwing 2/3's of the Navy. Seems she is to visit out west
> soon, looking at Monterey. Sadly to report, nearby Fort Ord is an Army
> Base, (and closed) so she will have to keep her pants on.

This message smacked her with the jarring immediacy of a phone call and the stiletto precision of a written letter. She felt sick and confused: Mixed in with the pornographic lies was some vaguely accurate information. In making dozens of faceless electronic friends over a matter of weeks, had she been too forward? Had she mentioned her upcoming vacation or that she had relatives in the navy?

Powell reached out and flipped the computer off. The offending message evaporated, and she instantly felt better. But when she signed on the following day, the message was still there for any of her friends or Prodigy's two million users to read. This time she responded to Vito: "Pls leave me alone."

Later a message came from an "L. Jacques Neaudex," claiming to live in Greensboro, warning: "Laurie, be careful, sometimes even the mailman can be a stalker!" It included her home address. Powell called a Prodigy operator and demanded that the message be deleted, and to know the identity of her harasser. Powell discovered that the sender's ID was fictitious; the message remained on the board for three more hours until Prodigy removed it and kicked the sender off the system.

But the messages continued. What really troubled Powell wasn't the vile personal smears; if all threats and conflicts were confined to cyberspace, the world would probably be a better place. What worried her was that "Vito" seemed to be keeping a personal file on her, culling small bits of information from her on-line conversations and maybe from some unknown sources. How did this person get her home address—and who knows what other personal information? Why was she being singled out? Who was "Vito"?

More than six billion messages flow annually through the global Internet, with few boundaries and no proprietors. Three of the major on-line services, Prodigy, CompuServe, and America Online, reach an audience nearly as large as New York City. And millions more access the Net through independent bulletin boards, corporate hookups, and university links.

The pervasive fear of this electrodemocracy has always been the possibility of terrorists hacking into the U.S. Army's mainframe, or spies datajacking corporate secrets. But instead, the biggest problem has been regular folks arguing, even threatening one another, creating a social meltdown that lawmakers and law-enforcement officials seem incapable of controlling.

Twenty-four hours a day, a large section of the Net is choked with ugly E-mail known as flames. Stumbling across some discussion groups is like seeing the Malibu hillsides after the California firestorms: blackened, apocalyptic, nothing useful left. Maybe it's because the Net has radically thrown together classes of people who've never previously had contact. Or maybe it's the anonymity. The Net is a dizzyingly powerful equalizer: The camouflage of pseudonyms encourages people to say and be what they never could face-to-face or even on the telephone. "E-mail isn't really even writing," says Laurie Powell. "It's written speech. Very intense. Very irrational. You don't think about it, you feel it."

For all Powell knew, Vito could be a woman masquerading as a man. He could be a boyfriend of her daughter's, an office colleague of her husband's, a complete stranger—or even a collection of people. Wanting to learn the truth, Powell helped initiate a manhunt for Vito that has lasted almost two years and foreshadowed the chilling legal showdown concerning how to handle privacy, free speech, and law enforcement in the torrent of words and images gushing through cyberspace. Moreover, her experience highlights the potential for even the most limited E-mail user to be abused by the new technology.

When I first contacted Laurie Powell, she was obsessed with the Vito case. She seemed a bit like one of those Long Island housewives in a Susan Isaacs best-seller—frightened but energized by the prospect of participating in a world more exciting and volatile than her own. At first, Powell had kept the harassment a secret from her family and on-line friends, but she downloaded most of the suspected-Vito notes and pored over them with the precision of a copy editor, hoping to dig up clues about who he was and what motivated him.

There were many intimidating and angry characters on the Internet, but the "Vito" character was the most infamous to ever penetrate the shallow waters of the commercial on-line services. "Vito always used a fake name," says Powell, "but his style and language were unmistakable." The verbal pyrotechnics were sometimes amusing, but also could quickly devolve into gay-bashing and pedophilic references. Prodigy members claiming names like "Rigoberto Gonzaga" targeted Powell's retarded son, Burt, who was small for his age:

> L. Piles is having a 'Come See My 'Soooooo Tiny-Tim-equipped Burt party. Make your reservations now!! Compost Pile will be there with her . . . children. Burt, her 16-year-old son that looks 12 . . . will show off for the girls. . . . Bring your binoculars, you won't want to miss his, well, tiny thing. . . . The little Navy man will demonstrate what lonely sailors do with small, tight, and well-oiled 12-year-olds.

Her teenage daughter was also singled out:

> Amber will be there to show off her latest bra. She will demonstrate how she removes "it" with one hand. Don't miss it!

After receiving several hundred Vito-like messages, Powell could no longer keep the secret from her husband. She also started E-mailing about "Vito" to other Prodigy members whom she had met on a bulletin board for owners of Saturn automobiles. Her friends were starting to get messages, too, including E-mail bombs—on-line junk mail that ties up the machine with garbage data. Since "Vito" seemed to thrive on the attention, why didn't Powell cancel Prodigy and do something else with her $9.95 a month? "A mother's instinct," she says stubbornly. "No one was going to intimidate me and get away with it. No one was going to address my children in sexually graphic terms."

Powell didn't want to admit it, but she also found E-mail fascinating. She had to check her mail and read the boards even when she started to dread what she would find.

And what she found was mind-boggling. Sometimes other members would be impersonated to further confuse matters: the log-on of Powell's cyberfriend Carolyn Fleming, a 37-year-old nurse in El Paso, Texas, was appropriated to lambaste Powell's daughter. And a Vito-like user spooked another acquaintance, Washington housewife Carla Bumpas, by reciting intimate information about her car—mileage, specific dents.

They complained to Prodigy security with little success. "Were any of his ID's canceled?" Powell asks. "They sent us canned E-mail saying 'appropriate action' had been taken. But the messages kept coming."

Powell's Prodigy friends formed an ad hoc anti-Vito group, briefly calling themselves the Coalition for On-line Decency (COLD). They had no more experience with computers than Powell had, but they were infuriated by Prodigy's inadequate response. "We considered ourselves vigilant, but not vigilantes," says one member. They never met one another in person but communicated on-line almost every day.

Comparing their on-line experiences, they theorized that "Vito" had first appeared in early 1993 on Prodigy's Automotive bulletin board, joining a heated debate about the merits of Volkswagens versus Saturns. His interest quickly spread to Prodigy's other boards—Arts, Health, Singles, and Home Life. The average Prodigy user might post a half-dozen E-mail notes a week, but this harassment was relentless, with hundreds of messages generated. Whoever was sending the messages seemed to read and remember everything that appeared on the boards, often lulling people into making themselves vulnerable for attack. After several weeks of correspondence with one of Powell's Jewish friends, one day a "Darbie Lembke" wrote, "It's too bad that Hitler missed one!"

Powell and her friends were determined to persuade Prodigy to prosecute the offender as a criminal. They forwarded the notes to Prodigy security, and even tried to interest the FBI in the case, with little result.

"We thought we were protected by the same laws as other forms of communication," says Powell. That's simply not the case. While most states have computer-crime laws covering misuses like unauthorized access into systems and pirating software, the law is much less definitive when it comes to computer stalking. The nearest Congress has come to a national law directly addressing computer harassment is a still-unpassed bill to update the Communications Act of 1934, which prohibits the use of the telephone to annoy, threaten, or harass people.

The system watchers at Prodigy were aware of the offending messages but took the same hands-off attitude as a telephone company. "We are not responsible for any material a customer submits," points out Prodigy representative Brian Ek. "If someone sends a harassing message, we can help you, but it's not our fault. We can't control it." Besides, "Vito" was a tiny glitch in an on-line ecosystem of 700,000 daily sign-ons that ran nearly trouble-free.

Still, Prodigy's marketing methods did encourage predators indirectly. Free start-up kits—polybagged with newsstand magazines or preinstalled on new computers—were a main strategy in the war with America Online and CompuServe for subscribers. Millions of these kits, consisting of a floppy diskette and a manual, were distributed like trick-or-treat candy. Users generally received ten free hours of on-line time, and weren't billed for 30 days. Prodigy had no restrictions on transferability nor any limits on how many free diskettes a subscriber could use. Initially, Prodigy didn't even request a credit card. Asking for such personal data was a matter of privacy. "It interfered with the rights of the individuals to enjoy this service," according to Ek. The problem was that users could take advantage of this system to create short-term fraudulent accounts. By the time Prodigy realized these accounts had exceeded their limit and were based on false information, the person could easily switch to another start-up kit, another pseudonym.

And the Vito situation was getting out of hand. Dozens of women were both fearful and enraged; one accumulated an entire 80 MB hard drive of Vito-related material. This stalking was the subject of tens of thousands of E-mail messages. But it was still infecting the boards like a sentient virus, feeding off those trying to stop it:

> I will buy ID's. I will trash this board. My friends and cohorts will help
> me as long as it takes. . . I will sue you Greenbaum [Prodigy's director].
> Eric [a Prodigy bulletin board leader] is mine to chop up into little fine
> pieces. I am off right now to buy more ID's. . . I will find your home
> [signed by "S. Fleming"].

Prompted by such taunts and by user complaints, Prodigy's chief of security in White Plains, New York, Alex Bidwell, started an internal investigation in May 1993. According to Prodigy, Bidwell found that the majority of Vito-like messages originated from a local access telephone number for Prodigy in Fresno, California. Someone in Fresno had signed on with free kits again and again, each time typing in a fake ID, fake birth date, fake credit card number, and fake home phone number. In all, as many as 125 start-up kits had been used and discarded, sticking Prodigy with $5,231.34 worth of fraudulent credit card charges.

In July, Bidwell contacted a police detective in Fresno who specializes in computer crime and set up a free on-line account for him. Powell and her friends were not told about this; according to Powell, Bidwell asked them to stay on-line: "Prodigy said they had a way to catch who was doing this," she recalls. "They kept telling us, 'You know how to make him come out. Make him come out.' " (Prodigy denies this.) In November, a "Stephen Lockhart" threatened to toy with Powell's credit rating:

> I love it when people don't know WHO they are REALLY dealing with. (Oh
> if they only knew)<Credit reports are marvelous tools.> HEE HEE!!

A month later, "Lockhart" was even more vengeful:

> This is a loose bunch of feminazi extremists. They represent the worst
> that their gender has to offer mankind. The Paranoid "Coffee Clatch" you
> see in here is an accurate representation of how destructive gossiping
> women can be. In the Middle Ages they used to cut their tongues out.

In January 1994, Powell received a phone call from a pushy man calling himself "Fred" and claiming to be a salesman at a computer company that was distributing low-cost software; he kept demanding her credit card number. Suspicious, Powell told him she'd take down his number and call him back. When she did, there was no Fred at the number.

That night, Powell read a note on a public bulletin board concerning the stalker that said, "I think we should rename it 'Fred.' "

Powell had never in her life encountered such psychological torture: "This was mind rape," she says. Protesting what they considered to be Prodigy's inaction, Powell and her friends went off-line for a week. Messages under various names claimed victory for the stalker, charging that "COLD" had actually been kicked off by Prodigy for harassment.

That wasn't true. In fact, Powell and her cohorts were talking to attorneys about a possible civil lawsuit against "Vito" and Prodigy when, in early February, they received an open letter on-line announcing that an investigation was indeed under way. It was signed Frank Clark, the computer-crimes detective whom Prodigy had contacted.

Clark explained that "real crimes" had been committed, involving electronic harassment, grand theft, and credit card fraud. He signed off ominously: "Everyone using the 'Information Superhighway' should know that they are really in the electronic frontier. They are not talking to their caring next-door neighbor. There are good guys and predators. Very few laws or law enforcement."

At 48, Frank Clark is a serious man, built like Robert Mitchum, with a silver mustache. He started at the Fresno Police Department when Lyndon Johnson was president. In his career, Clark has worked every division, from arson to burglary to SWAT patrol. But he didn't find his real career calling until he became a "cybercop."

Over the past eight years, he's handled hundreds of computer-related cases, from homicides to child pornography, as well as teaching computer investigations to the Secret Service and the IRS. He specializes in covert operations; his biggest computer bust came in 1992, when he posed as a teenager on-line and shut down an operation that solicited sex from minors over a computer bulletin board.

Clark thinks the Internet is "the most significant man-made creation ever." But in the last decade it has undergone a demographic change, with a surge in what he calls "vulnerable people"—women and children. "People like Vito used to be confined to their own neighborhoods," he says.

"I wanted the legal system to start taking computer crime seriously," Clark continues. "When I send a computer case over to the D.A.'s office, they turn pale and green." Prosecutors dread such cases because they're usually black holes: very little established case law, thousands of tedious documents to pore over, not to mention the difficult task of educating a jury on technical issues.

With the stalking on Prodigy, Clark saw the opportunity to set an important precedent. He wanted not only to pursue the credit card fraud but to try to define a standard for stalking-like crimes. Since Clark was eligible for retirement in a few years, spearheading such a case could help if he decided to hire himself out as a private computer-security expert.

By coincidence, Clark says, a month before Prodigy contacted him he had met a local man who had said he was using the name Vito on-line: Mark Johnson, 40, a substitute teacher. Johnson had been helpful in Clark's sex solicitation bust and, Clark says, claimed to have spent time on a Prodigy bulletin board exchanging barbs with Saturn owners and to have been sent thousands of Prodigy start-up kits.

In some ways, Johnson was an unlikely suspect: He had a wealthy, straitlaced Mormon background; he often worked with special-education students; his father is a university professor. On the other hand, Johnson was well versed in computers, having worked at Sperry Univac in the data department and later teaching programming at Volkswagen.

The problem, according to Clark, was pinning all these harassing messages and multiple identities to any one person. Tracing the phone line from Fresno to Prodigy in New York was nearly impossible; it goes through many states and switches. And the nature of bulletin boards is such that an innocent message can be corrupted by a second party, yet to the untrained eye appear to come from the original writer.

Still, based on their previous encounter, Clark felt certain that Johnson was a prime suspect. In late August, Clark contacted Johnson and warned him to stop logging on to Prodigy. Johnson countered that—despite all the start-up kits—he was not using Prodigy anymore, and that he would erase its software from his computer.

Two weeks later, Bidwell called Clark: "Vito" was still at it. On December 6, Clark reviewed nineteen pounds of computer printouts from Prodigy concerning fraudulent accounts. They showed dozens of different user ID's in Fresno, many sent to the same street address and using variations of the same credit card numbers. Was this the source of the messages Powell claimed to have gotten from, variously, a rabbi, a police chief, a blond babe, a French photographer, and others? Clark thought so. He called Johnson again. Johnson claimed *he* was the one being harassed, that people on-line were framing him. But as Clark later explained in an affidavit seeking a search warrant, he then got a call from a woman who he had suspected was a cohort of Johnson's. Clark says she revealed that Johnson—despite his claims of not being on Prodigy—was going on-line using her husband's ID.

Finally, on December 28, 1993, Clark called Johnson and his attorney into his office. Johnson again denied going on Prodigy. He denied using credit cards or sending vulgar messages, and repeated his promise to get rid of all his Prodigy equipment, this time saying his lawyer would witness the act.

Six weeks later, when Frank Clark logged on to read his E-mail, he found two sexually explicit photos of prepubescent boys. But he researched and learned that they hadn't come from Johnson.

On March 7, the Fresno *Bee* ran a story detailing Clark's hunt for Vito, which was picked up by the AP newswire. It ended with quotes from an anonymous caller who "has identified himself as Vito, Oppenheimer, and several other personalities." He admitted only that he "likes to push people's buttons" using on-line services, and that he was victim of a "witch-hunt."

Three days later, Clark received a phone call from a person who had read the article, claimed to know Vito's identity, and wanted to put Clark in touch with a foreign-exchange student who had lived for two months in Johnson's house.

On April 5, Clark interviewed the student, who was a minor. According to Clark's sworn affidavit, the student claimed that Johnson was on the computer virtually all the time when he was home, sometimes as early as 5:00 A.M. He added that Johnson had bragged to him about being Vito, which was also the name of Johnson's cat, and that the license plate of Johnson's decade-old Volkswagen bus was VITOLAW. Also, according to the affidavit, the student told Clark he saw Johnson create user ID's by pulling names out of the Fresno phone book, entering his credit card number, then changing the last four digits until it was accepted; his three favorite passwords were "Diesel," "Molly," and "Mollydog." (Johnson had a car with a diesel engine and a sheepdog named Molly.) The student reported that Johnson had between 500 and 1,000 user ID's in a cardboard box in the trunk of one of his cars. He said that Johnson would often print out messages he had received and store them, and that Johnson would get up early after sending messages to people on Prodigy and say, "Let's see if I pissed enough people off last night," and "All hell broke loose last night because of Vito." The student also made sexual allegations.

Clark checked the student's story by reexamining the names of the fraudulent users and found ten of them in the phone book. He got Bidwell to fax him a list of users whose passwords were Diesel, Molly, or Mollydog. Of the 53 ID's using Diesel, Clark reports, only two listed legitimate credit card numbers—both belonging to Johnson. He ran a Motor Vehicles check on the cars Johnson owned and confirmed the license plate VITOLAW. Frank Clark thought he could now nail his man.

After a year of abuse and fear, Laurie Powell was finally given a name for her suspected stalker. But when she pursued the subject on-line the stalking got more intense. Someone calling himself "Crazy Wright" wrote:

Wrong you fucking bitch, Stalker is still here.

Powell snapped. She entered the flaming fray, writing to others that "Vito" needed a "blow-up doll and a penile implant." "I couldn't help myself," she says today. Others followed suit; this led to a backlash. "Too much virtue is also a vice," one Prodigy member wrote to COLD. "You are as punitive and shrill in pursuing an uncharged man as Vito ever was." In addition, at the request of Mark Johnson, the Fresno Police Department's Internal Affairs Bureau initiated an investigation of Frank Clark for invading Johnson's privacy and releasing confidential information.

Powell was part of one of the ugliest flame wars in cyberspace's young history. Non-Prodigy members began to join in. An entire discussion group on the Internet was devoted to "Johnson as the stalker." Camera crews from CBS's *Eye to Eye* staked out Johnson's house.

Then in April, the sniping seemed to jump the guardrail of the information superhighway. Powell developed an intestinal blockage and had to be rushed to the hospital. "No one but my family knew I was there. I didn't even tell my mother." But within 24 hours a message was posted referring to Powell, including the ward telephone number near her hospital room. The only way she could possibly have been tracked down so fast was by someone getting access to her medical records. If this person could crack into files at a hospital or doctor's office, what damage could be done involving giant, low-security data banks like the Department of Motor Vehicles or her TRW credit rating?

A few days later, Powell's daughter, Amber, got an emergency call at her high school's office: "This is Amber's father, Michael. There's been an emergency. I need to pick up Amber right away." If the person had gotten her father's name right, Amber might have believed it. But no one showed to pick her up. Then over the next several weeks, someone kept removing the screen from Amber's bedroom window.

Laurie Powell blames her on-line experiences for this off-line kidnap threat, although she doesn't believe it was Johnson: "He's not *everywhere*." Still, she called the Greensboro police and asked them to shore up patrols in her area. Other Prodigy members, reading about these events on-line, had had their fill and began poking fun, calling the boards the Stalk Talk Café. Someone was also openly mocking Detective Clark on-line, with messages questioning his intelligence and impugning his character.

Clark felt the situation was out of control. What had started as electronic bickering and name-calling was escalating into a new kind of terrorism.

On April 14, armed with the foreign-exchange student's story and a search warrant, Clark went to Mark Johnson's home in Fresno and CBS cameras were there. He confiscated computers, modems, a fax machine, and dozens of start-up kits, and arrested Johnson for credit card fraud and grand theft.

Powell and her friends believed the reign of terror was over. Some felt they had been a part of history, contributing to a technology that would change the world. One wrote, "Someday our grandchildren can look at us and say grandma/grandpa, thanks for what you did way back then to help bring law and order to the information superhighway."

"I would love to meet 'Vito' in court," Powell said. "Is the word *lawsuit* in his vocabulary? You betcha."

But within a week the case had fallen apart. The Fresno district attorney's office had decided there was insufficient evidence to prosecute. There were many theories as to why the case was dropped. "It's a comedy of errors," says Frank Clark. "When you take a case like that, with thousands of documents, and drop it on the D.A.'s desk and he has 52 cases already that he doesn't have time to read through, which do you think he's going to take on?" By the time *Eye to Eye* aired its segment on May 5, Johnson was back home, not charged. The show provided victims with their first glimpse of their alleged tormentor and seemed to implicate Johnson, but reasserted that it was impossible to prosecute him. (A Federal grand jury is rumored to be reviewing the case.)

"Isn't this the classic nineties mystery?" posited one Prodigy member. "There are no villains. Everyone's a tragically misunderstood victim."

No one can ever be sure of anything in cyberspace. The same technological loopholes that allow stalkers to roam anonymously also allow innocent people to be framed. In a two-hour interview in his lawyer's office in Fresno, Mark Johnson contends that that's exactly what happened to him. Johnson is six feet tall and handsome, with a preppy haircut and boyish blue eyes. He can be gentle, charming, and patient. But as we talked, his charm and patience dissolved. He would launch into ten-minute tirades against his accusers.

"I make no bones about creating or being the personality Vito," he told me. "But I'm not the individual on Prodigy who's harassing these parasites. I think Laurie Powell and her friends are sending the Vito messages to each other. Maybe they'll get on *Oprah*." He blames the whole affair on his accusers' "obscure, bonbon-eating, soap-opera watching, humdrum daily lifestyle. . . . They make me a scapegoat so they can sue Prodigy." He also suggests Vito could be an amalgamation of wanna-bes, like "Elvis lookalikes." Alternately, Johnson theorizes that it could be an ex-tenant of his whom he had evicted, and who knew a lot about computers and Johnson's life. Or perhaps, he says, somebody who had been laid off by Prodigy was creating the situation to make the service vulnerable to lawsuits.

Asked about the similarity between his real credit card numbers and the fraudulent ones Prodigy reported, he said, "[People] knew I lived here. They started posting that on the [bulletin] boards. They found out who owned this place, ran a credit check, and picked a credit card number off the file. What they got was my dad's credit card number. . . . Personally, I don't have any credit card numbers except a gas one." Johnson also claims that his work as a teacher prevented him from sending the sheer volume of messages Vito was responsible for. (But in the past year he has been teaching only a few days a week in the district where he usually works—and some of these schools have access to the Internet.)

Johnson became even more virulent when it came to Detective Clark (who was cleared of any wrongdoing by Fresno Internal Affairs on May 17). "Clark is the real villain in this story," Johnson said, pounding his fist on the table. "He wanted to get his puss on TV. Be the great cybercop no matter who he wounded." Was this the frustrated passion of an innocent man, or the verbal pyrotechnics of the infamous Vito?

With no other suspects and the Internet still ablaze with flame wars, the Vito case has perfectly captured the tyranny and freedom of cyberspace; everyone seems somewhat self-interested and no one knows exactly how to proceed. It's certainly a new kind of investigation, which allows anyone with a computer to contact the principals and join in the discussion. Considering the tsunami of data, evidence, and opinion filling the screen, it's hard to know what to think.

Given the circumstances, Prodigy seems unlikely to recover its money, although it has taken more aggressive steps to prevent fraudulent use of the system. It has updated its validation process to catch bogus credit card use immediately, as well as adding a feature known as a "Bozo filter," which lets members reject messages from specific users. It has software that screens public bulletin boards for obscene language, though the subject of stalking is still quite popular.

Last September, Prodigy felt it no longer needed Frank Clark's services and canceled his free account. Someone began posting bizarre religious parodies on the Internet under the name "Mark Johnson," declaring his innocence and portraying himself as Jesus, the "Cold Gang" as the Twelve Apostles, and Clark as Judas. In real life, Johnson filed a claim for damages against Frank Clark and the City of Fresno for $14.5 million.

The "Vito" mess may be only the tip of the iceberg. This year, market competition will force Prodigy, America Online, and CompuServe to offer not just E-mail but complete Internet access, so tens of millions of newcomers will head past the safety pylons and into informational deep water. That's the largest immigration wave in the history of the world. No one quite knows how to prepare for it or what social problems it will pose.

These days, Laurie Powell is more cautious about her activities both on- and off-line. Although her children are teenagers, she forbids them to play in the yard unless she is home. The harassment "hasn't ruined my life," she says, "but it's changed it. I trust people less." Last November she received a vicious message on the Internet calling her "a cunt" and signed "Mark Johnson," although she says she has no idea who sent it.

Yet Powell still can't seem to resist the pull of E-mail. She continues to go on-line once or twice a week—"just to check my mail," she says. And despite all she's experienced, she's gotten herself involved in another suspected stalker investigation, for which she is cooperating with the FBI.

And where is Vito in all this? Probably still out there in the billion miles of optical microlinks and analogue corridors and packet-switched outdials. Waiting. Lurking.

THINKING AND RE-READING

1. As you re-read this article, think about how you would feel if you were the individual who was the target of such electronic violence. To whom would you turn? How would you cope? With what would you be concerned?

2. Think about the role that law enforcement officials should play in cyberspace. Do you think that cyberspace should be patrolled by such officials? If so, to what extent and why? Do you think that the conversations within cyberspace should be controlled in some way to prevent criminal behavior and/or violence? If so, how and by whom?

WRITING AND LEARNING

1. On a general discussion list on your college's computing system, put out a query asking about online violence or crimes that have been perpetrated against women on your campus. Also, query separately concerning online violence and crimes perpetrated against men. You might want to visit your campus computing office or the archives of your student newspaper to see if you can learn more about the kinds of online crimes or violence that have been experienced by men and women on your campus. After collecting this information, post a summary message online for the information of interested participants; in this message talk about what you have learned. How would you characterize the crimes against women? Against men? How are the crimes against the two different? The same? Why do you think this is so?

2. Re-read this article and conduct a search of articles on electronic stalkings and/or harassments that appeared in your hometown city's newspaper or in a nearby city's newspaper during the last five years. For the latter task, ask for the help of the campus's reference librarian and use an electronic index if possible. Also obtain and read a copy of your campus's computing regulations to see if they contain any relevant guidelines for freedom of speech, harassment, threats of violence, privacy, and so on. In a letter to the editor of your student newspaper, talk about the campus's computing guidelines and whether you believe they are adequate in light of the activities or crimes described in this piece. Provide a clear argument for your stance. If you believe the guidelines need revision, identify the direction these revisions should take.

3. Women and other victims of crime have identified some strategies for fighting back—although such action is often difficult to undertake and sometimes results in additional pain to the victim (as the story about Laurie Powell indicates). Write a letter to high school students who frequently cruise the nets and suggest some strategies for remaining as safe as possible in online conversational contexts and for informing the appropriate people if something happens. This letter should be suitable for publication in the high school newspaper.

Computers, Networks and Work

Lee Sproull and Sara Kiesler

THIS CONTRIBUTION EXPLORES how electronic interactions that take place on a computer network differ significantly from those face-to-face exchanges that occur within work environments. The authors of this article—Dr. Lee Sproull, a social scientist, and Dr. Sara Kiesler, a social psychologist—are communication scholars who focus their research on electronic conversations. As Sproull and Kiesler note, our conceptions of both time and space are altered when electronic conversations become a main means of communication.

This article originally appeared in a special issue of *Scientific American* that focused on "Communications, Computers, and Networks." This special issue, aimed at an informed and educated readership interested in issues broadly associated with science and more specifically acquainted with computers, was published in September 1991, just as electronic global communication systems were beginning a stage of exponential growth and expansion.

Although the world may be evolving into a global village, most people still lead local lives at work. They spend the majority of their time in one physical location and talk predominantly to their immediate co-workers, clients and customers. They participate in only a few workplace groups: their primary work group, perhaps a committee or task force and possibly an informal social group.

Some people, however, already experience a far more cosmopolitan future because they work in organizations that have extensive computer networks. Such individuals can communicate with people around the world as easily as they talk with someone in the next office. They can hold involved group discussions about company policy, new product design, hiring plans or last night's ball game without ever meeting other group members.

The networked organization differs from the conventional workplace with respect to both time and space. Computer-based communication is extremely fast in comparison with telephone or postal services, denigrated as "snail mail" by electronic mail converts. People can send a message to the other side of the globe in minutes; each message can be directed to one

person or to many people. Networks can also essentially make time stand still. Electronic messages can be held indefinitely in computer memory. People can read or reread their messages at any time, copy them, change them or forward them.

Managers are often attracted to networks by the promise of faster communication and greater efficiency. In our view, the real potential of network communication has less to do with such matters than with influencing the overall work environment and the capabilities of employees. Managers can use networks to foster new kinds of task structures and reporting relationships. They can use networks to change the conventional patterns of who talks to whom and who knows what.

The capabilities that accompany networks raise significant questions for managers and for social scientists studying work organizations. Can people really work closely with one another when their only contact is through a computer? If employees interact through telecommuting, teleconferencing and electronic group discussions, what holds the organization together? Networking permits almost unlimited access to data and to other people. Where will management draw the line on freedom of access? What will the organization of the future look like?

We and various colleagues are working to understand how computer networks can affect the nature of work and relationships between managers and employees. What we are learning may help people to exploit better the opportunities that networks offer and to avoid or mitigate the potential pitfalls of networked organizations.

Our research relies on two approaches. Some questions can be studied through laboratory experiments. For instance, how do small groups respond emotionally to different forms of communication? Other questions, particularly those concerning organizational change, require field studies in actual organizations that have been routinely using computer networks. Data describing how hundreds of thousands of people currently use network communications can help predict how other people will work in the future as computer-based communications become more prevalent. Drawing on field studies and experiments, researchers gradually construct a body of evidence on how work and organizations are changing as network technology becomes more widely used. The process may sound straightforward, but in reality it is often full of exciting twists. People use technology in surprising ways, and effects often show up that contradict both theoretical predictions and managerial expectations.

One major surprise emerged as soon as the first large-scale computer network, known as the ARPANET, was begun in the late 1960s. The ARPANET was developed for the Advanced Research Projects Agency (ARPA), a part of the U.S. Department of Defense. ARPANET was intended to link computer scientists at universities and other research institutions to distant computers, thereby permitting efficient access to machines unavailable at the home institutions. A facility called electronic mail, which enabled researchers to communicate with one another, was considered a minor additional feature of the network.

Yet electronic mail rapidly became one of the most popular features of the ARPANET. Computer scientists around the country used ARPANET to exchange ideas spontaneously and casually. Graduate students discussed problems and shared skills with professors and other students without regard to their physical location. Heads of research projects used electronic mail to coordinate activities with project members and to stay in touch with other research teams and funding agencies. A network community quickly formed, filled with friends and collaborators who rarely, if ever, met in person. Although some administrators objected to electronic mail because they did not consider it a legitimate use of computer time, demand grew sharply for more and better network connections.

Since then, many organizations have adopted internal networks that link anywhere from a few to a few thousand employees. Some of these organizational networks have also been connected to the Internet, the successor to ARPANET. Electronic mail has continued to be one of the most popular features of these computer networks.

Anyone who has a computer account on a networked system can use electronic mail software to communicate with other users on the network. Electronic mail transmits messages to a recipient's electronic "mailbox." The sender can send a message simultaneously to several mailboxes by sending the message to a group name or to a distribution list. Electronic bulletin boards and electronic conferences are common variants of group electronic mail; they too have names to identify their topic or audience. Bulletin boards post messages in chronological order as they are received. Computer conferences arrange messages by topic and display grouped messages together.

The computer communications technology in most networked organizations today is fairly similar, but there exist large differences in people's actual communication behavior that stem from policy choices made by management. In some networked organizations, electronic mail access is easy and open. Most employees have networked terminals or computers on their desks, and anyone can send mail to anyone else. Electronic mail costs are considered part of general overhead expenses and are not charged to employees or to their departments. In the open-network organizations we have studied, people typically send and receive between 25 and 100 messages a day and belong to between 10 and 50 electronic groups. These figures hold across job categories, hierarchical position, age and even amount of computer experience.

In other networked organizations, managers have chosen to limit access or charge costs directly to users, leading to much lower usage rates. Paul Schreiber, a *Newsday* columnist, describes how his own organization changed from an open-access network to a limited-access one. Management apparently believed that reporters were spending too much time sending electronic mail; management therefore had the newspaper's electronic mail software modified so that reporters could still receive mail but could no longer send it. Editors, on the other hand, could still send electronic mail to everyone. Clearly, technology by itself does not impel change. Management choices and policies are equally influential.

But even in organizations that have open access, anticipating the effect of networks on communication has proved no easy task. Some of the first researchers to study computer network communications thought the technology would improve group decision making over face-to-face discussion because computer messages were plain text. They reasoned that electronic discussions would be more purely intellectual, and so decision making would be less affected by people's social skills and personal idiosyncracies.

Research has revealed a more complicated picture. In an electronic exchange, the social and contextual cues that usually regulate and influence group dynamics are missing or attenuated. Electronic messages lack information regarding job titles, social importance, hierarchical position, race, age and appearance. The context also is poorly defined because formal and casual exchanges look essentially the same. People may have outside information about senders, receivers and situations, but few cues exist in the computer interaction itself to remind people of that knowledge.

In a series of experiments at Carnegie Mellon University, we compared how small groups make decisions using computer conferences, electronic mail and face-to-face discussion. Using a network induced the participants to talk more frankly and more equally. Instead of one or two people doing most of the talking, as happens in many face-to-face groups, everyone had a more equal say. Furthermore, networked groups generated more proposals for action than did traditional ones.

Open, free-ranging discourse has a dark side. The increased democracy associated with electronic interactions in our experiments interfered with decision making. We observed that three-person groups took approximately four times as long to reach a decision electronically as they did face-to-face. In one case, a group never succeeded in reaching consensus, and we were ultimately forced to terminate the experiment. Making it impossible for people to interrupt one another slowed decision making and increased conflict as a few members tried to dominate control of the network. We also found that people tended to express extreme opinions and vented anger more openly in an electronic face-off than when they sat together and talked. Computer scientists using the ARPANET have called this phenomenon "flaming."

We discovered that electronic communication can influence the effects of people's status. Social or job position normally is a powerful regulator of group interaction. Group members typically defer to those who have higher status and tend to follow their direction. Members' speech and demeanor become more formal in the presence of people who have high status. Higher-status people, in turn, talk more and influence group discussion more than do lower-status people.

Given that electronic conversations attenuate contextual cues, we expected that the effect of status differences within a group should also be reduced. In an experiment conducted with Vitaly Dubrovsky of Clarkson University and Beheruz Sethna of Lamar University, we asked groups containing high- and low-status members to make decisions both by electronic mail and face-to-face. The results confirmed that the proportion of talk and influence of higher-status people decreased when group members communicated by electronic mail.

Is this a good state of affairs? When higher-status members have less expertise, more democracy could improve decision making. If higher-status members truly are better qualified to make decisions, however, the results of consensus decisions may be less good.

Shoshanah Zuboff of Harvard Business School documented reduced effects of status on a computer conference system in one firm. People who regarded themselves as physically unattractive reported feeling more lively and confident when they expressed themselves over the network. Others who had soft voices or small stature reported that they no longer had to struggle to be taken seriously in a meeting.

Researchers have advanced alternative explanations for the openness and democracy of electronic talk. One hypothesis is that people who like to use computers are childish or unruly, but this hypothesis does not explain experimental results showing that the same people talk more openly on a computer than when they are face-to-face. Another hypothesis holds that text messages require strong language to get a point across; this hypothesis explains flaming but not the reduction of social and status differences. The most promising explanation of the behavior of networked individuals is that when cues about social context are absent or weak, people ignore their social situation and cease to worry about how others evaluate them. Hence, they devote less time and effort to posturing and social niceties, and they may be more honest.

Researchers have demonstrated decreased social posturing in studies that ask people to describe their own behavior. In one of our experiments, people were asked to complete a self-evaluation questionnaire either by pencil and paper or via electronic mail. Those randomly assigned to reply electronically reported significantly more undesirable social behaviors, such as illegal drug use or petty crimes. John Greist and his colleagues at the University of Wisconsin found similar decreases in posturing when taking medical histories from clinical patients. People who responded to a computerized patient history interview revealed more socially and physically undesirable behavior than did those who answered the same questions asked by a physician.

These studies show that people are willing to reveal more about undesirable symptoms and behavior to a computer, but are these reports more truthful? An investigation of alcohol consumption conducted by Jennifer J. Waterton and John C. Duffy of the University of Edinburgh suggests an affirmative answer. In traditional surveys, people report drinking only about one half as much alcohol as alcohol sales figures would suggest. Waterton and Duffy compared computer interviews with personal interviews in a survey of alcohol consumption. People who were randomly assigned to answer the computer survey reported higher alcohol consumption than those who talked to the human interviewer. The computer-derived reports of consumption extrapolated more accurately to actual alcohol sales than did the face-to-face reports.

These and other controlled studies of electronic talk suggest that such communication is relatively impersonal, yet paradoxically, it can make people feel more comfortable about talking. People are less shy and more playful in electronic discussions; they also express more opinions and ideas and vent more emotion.

Because of these behavioral effects, organizations are discovering applications for electronic group activities that nobody had anticipated. Computers can be valuable for counseling and conducting surveys about sensitive topics, situations in which many people are anxious and cover their true feelings and opinions. Networks are now being used for applications ranging from electronic Alcoholics Anonymous support groups to electronic quality circles.

Just as the dynamics of electronic communications differ from those conducted orally or by letters, so electronic groups are not just traditional groups whose members use computers. People in a networked organization are likely to belong to a number of electronic groups that span time zones and job categories. Some of these groups serve as extensions of existing work groups, providing a convenient way for members to communicate between face-to-face meetings. Other electronic groups gather together people who do not know one another personally and who may in fact have never had the opportunity to meet in person.

For example, Hewlett-Packard employs human-factors engineers who work in widely scattered locations around the world. These engineers may meet one another in person only once a year. An electronic conference creates ongoing meetings in which they can frequently and routinely discuss professional and company issues.

In some ways, electronic groups resemble nonelectronic social groups. They support sustained interactions, develop their own norms of behavior and generate peer pressure. Electronic groups often have more than 100 members, however, and involve relationships among people who do not know one another personally.

Employees whose organization is connected to the Internet or to a commercial network can belong to electronic groups whose members come from many different organizations. For example, Brian K. Reid of Digital Equipment Corporation reports that some 37,000 organizations are connected to USENET, a loosely organized network that exchanges more than 1,500 electronic discussion groups, called newsgroups. Reid estimates that 1.4 million people worldwide read at least one newsgroup.

Networked communication is only beginning to affect the structure of the workplace. The form of most current organizations has been dictated by the constraints of the nonelectronic world. Interdependent jobs must be situated in physical proximity. Formal command structures specify who reports to whom, who assigns tasks to whom and who has access to what information. These constraints reinforce the centralization of authority and shape the degree of information sharing, the number of organizational levels, the amount of interconnectivity and the structure of social relationships.

Organizations that incorporate computer networks could become more flexible and less hierarchical in structure. A field experiment conducted by Tora K. Bikson of Rand Corporation and John D. Eveland of Claremont Colleges supports the point. They formed two task forces in a large utility firm, each assigned to analyze employee retirement issues. Both groups contained 40 members, half of whom had recently retired from the company and half of whom were still employed but eligible for retirement. The only difference between the two groups was that one worked on networked computer facilities, whereas the other did not.

Both task forces created subcommittees, but the networked group created more of them and assigned people to more than one subcommittee. The networked group also organized its subcommittees in a complex, overlapping matrix structure. It added new subcommittees during the course of its work, and it decided to continue meeting even after its official one-year life span had ended. The networked task force also permitted greater input from the retirees, who were no longer located at the company. Although not every electronic group will be so flexible, eliminating the constraints of face-to-face meetings evidently facilitates trying out different forms of group organization.

Another effect of networking may be changed patterns of information sharing in organizations. Conventional organizations have formal systems of record keeping and of responsibilities for distributing information. Much of the information within an organization consists of personal experience that never appears in the formally authorized distribution system: the war stories told by service representatives (which do not appear in service manuals), the folklore about how the experimental apparatus really works (which does not appear in the journal articles) or the gossip about how workers should behave (which is not described in any personnel policy).

In the past, the spread of such personal information has been strongly determined by physical proximity and social acquaintance. As a result, distant or poorly connected employees have lacked access to local expertise; this untapped knowledge could represent an important informational resource in large organizations. Electronic groups provide a forum for sharing such expertise independent of spatial and social constraints.

One significant kind of information flow begins with the "Does anybody know . . . ?" message that appears frequently on computer networks. A sender might broadcast an electronic request for information to an entire organization, to a particular distribution list or to a bulletin board. Anyone who sees the message can reply. We studied information inquiries on the network at Tandem Computers, Inc., in Cupertino, Calif., a computer company that employs 10,500 workers around the world. In a study we conducted with David Constant, we found an average of about six does-anybody-know messages broadcast every day to one company-wide distribution list.

Information requests typically come from field engineers or sales representatives who are soliciting personal experience or technical knowledge that they cannot find in formal documents or in their own workplace. At Tandem, about eight employees send electronic mail replies to the average question. Fewer than 15 percent of the people who answer a question are personally acquainted with the questioner or are even located in the same city.

Question askers can electronically redistribute the answers they receive by putting them in a public computer file on the network. About half of the Tandem questioners make their reply files publicly available over the company network to other employees. Tandem takes this sharing process one step further by maintaining an electronic archive of question-and-reply files that is also accessible over the company network. The firm has thereby created a repository of information and working expertise that is endlessly accessible through space and time (for example, the expertise remains available when an employee is out of the office or he or she leaves the organization). A study by Thomas Finholt in our research program found that this archive is accessed more than 1,000 times a month by employees, especially those located in field offices away from the geographic center of the company.

The discretionary information sharing we discovered at Tandem and at other networked organizations seems to run contrary to nonelectronic behavior in organizations. The askers openly admit their ignorance to perhaps hundreds or even thousands of people. The repliers respond to requests for help from people they do not know with no expectation of any direct benefit to themselves.

One might wonder why people respond so readily to information requests made by strangers. Part of the explanation is that networks make the cost of responding extremely low in time and effort expended. Also, open-access networks favor the free flow of information. Respondents seem to believe that sharing information enhances the overall electronic community and leads to a richer information environment. The result is a kind of electronic altruism quite different from the fears that networks would weaken the social fabric of organizations.

The changes in communication made possible by networks may substantially alter the relationship between an employee and his or her organization, the structure of organizations and the nature of management. Senior managers and key professionals usually have strong social and informational connections within their organizations and within their broader professional communities. Conversely, employees who reside on the organizational periphery by virtue of geographic location, job requirements or personal attributes have relatively few opportunities to make contact with other employees and colleagues.

Reducing the impediments to communication across both physical and social distance is likely to affect peripheral employees more than central ones. We, along with Charles Huff of St. Olaf College, studied this possibility for city employees in Fort Collins, Colo. Employees who used electronic mail extensively reported more commitment to their jobs and to their co-workers than did those who rarely used the network. This correlation was particularly strong for shift workers, who, because of the nature of their work, had fewer opportunities to see their colleagues than did regular day workers. As one policewoman told us, "Working the night shift, it used to be that I would hear about promotions after they happened, though I had a right to be included in the discussion. Now I have a say in the decision making."

Organizations are traditionally built around two key concepts: hierarchical decomposition of goals and tasks and the stability of employee relationships over time. In the fully networked organization that may become increasingly common in the future, task structures may be much more flexible and dynamic. Hierarchy will not vanish, but it will be augmented by distributed lattices of interconnections.

In today's organizations, executives generally know whom they manage and manage whom they know. In the future, however, managers of some electronic project groups will face the challenge of working with people they have never met. Allocating resources to projects and assigning credit and blame for performance will become more complex. People will often belong to many different groups and will be able to reach out across the network to acquire resources without management intervention or perhaps even without management knowledge.

A recent case in mathematics research hints at the nature of what may lie ahead. Mathematicians at Bell Communications Research (Bellcore) and at Digital Equipment sought to factor a large, theoretically interesting number known as the 9th Fermat number. They broadcast a message on the Internet to recruit researchers from universities, government laboratories and corporations to assist them in their project. The several hundred researchers who volunteered to help received—via electronic mail—software and a piece of the problem to solve; they also returned their solutions through electronic mail.

After results from all the volunteers were combined, the message announcing the final results of the project contained a charming admission:

> We'd like to thank everyone who contributed computing cycles to this project, but I can't: we only have records of the person at each site who installed and managed the code. If you helped us, we'd be delighted to hear from you; please send us your name as you would like it to appear in the final version of the paper. (Broadcast message from Mark S. Manasse, June 15, 1990.)

Networking in most organizations today is limited to data communications, often for economic or financial applications such as electronic data interchange, electronic funds transfer or remote transaction processing. Most organizations have not yet begun to confront the opportunities and challenges afforded by connecting their employees through networks.

Among those that have, managers have responded in a variety of ways to changes that affect their authority and control. Some managers have installed networks for efficiency reasons but ignored their potential for more profound changes. Some have restricted who can send mail or have shut down electronic discussion groups. Others have encouraged using the network for broadening participation and involving more people in the decision-making process. The last actions push responsibility down and through the organization and also produce their own managerial issues.

A democratic organization requires competent, committed, responsible employees. It requires new ways of allocating credit. It increases unpredictability, both for creative ideas and for inappropriate behavior. Managers will have to come up with new kinds of worker incentives and organizational structures to handle these changes.

The technology of networks is changing rapidly. Electronic mail that includes graphics, pictures, sound and video will eventually become widely available. These advances will make it possible to reintroduce some of the social context cues absent in current electronic communications. Even so, electronic interactions will never duplicate those conducted face-to-face.

As more people have ready access to network communications, the number and size of electronic groups will expand dramatically. It is up to management to make and shape connections. The organization of the future will depend significantly not just on how the technology of networking evolves but also on how managers seize the opportunity it presents for transforming the structure of work.

THINKING AND RE-READING

1. As you re-read this piece, focus on some of the questions that Sproull and Kiesler have identified as guiding their research: Can people really work closely and effectively with one another when their only contact is through a computer? If employees interact through telecommuting, teleconferencing, and electronic group discussions, what holds the organization together? Where will management draw the line in freedom of access to electronic mail? What will the organization of the future look like? How do small groups respond emotionally to different forms of communication?

2. Sproull and Kiesler claim that in groups containing both high- and low-status people, the relative influence of high-status people decreased when group members communicated by e-mail. As you read this piece, consider what Sproull and Kiesler mean by high status. How is such a characteristic determined in a group that communicates via face-to-face exchanges? Why? How might status be determined in a group that converses online? Why? How might these different ways of determining status affect Sproull and Kiesler's findings?

WRITING AND LEARNING

1. Conduct your own research project on e-mail communication. First, compose a list of ten or more questions that you'd like answered—some of these questions might be suggested from your reading of the Sproull and Kiesler article. Avoid yes–no questions and questions that yield only single-word answers. Try to focus on questions that get at technology practices as they happen in real social settings and the nature of computer-mediated communication as a form of social exchange. Among them, you might want to ask the following: Do you use e-mail to communicate with others? If so, with whom do you communicate most often via e-mail? Least often? Why? How many e-mail messages do you send a day? How many e-mail messages do you receive? From whom do you receive e-mail on a regular basis? An irregular basis? What features do you like most about e-mail? Least? How do the messages you write on e-mail differ from those you write with a paper and pen/pencil? How do the features of these two sets of technologies (i.e., paper/pen/pencil and computer/e-mail) differ? For what purposes do you think e-mail is best suited? Least well suited? When you have identified a set of at least ten questions that interest you, identify a group of ten people on the same floor of your dorm, or at random in the student union. Ask each of these people to answer the questions you have identified. Either obtain their written permission for you to tape-record their answers, have them write their answers, or take notes of their answers. Finally, in a report written to inform your classmates, summarize your findings about the e-mail practices of these ten people.

2. In a letter to Lee Sproull and/or Sara Kiesler, respond to the following claim: "In an electronic exchange, the social and contextual cues that usually regulate and influence

group dynamics are missing or attenuated. Electronic messages lack information regarding job titles, social importance, hierarchical position, race, age, and appearance." Examine at least ten e-mail messages that you have written or responded to in the last few weeks. Or find a friend who will give you written permission to look at his or her messages and who will answer a few questions about the origins and authors of these messages. In your letter, discuss whether Sproull and Kiesler's claims hold up when you examine these messages and interview the author. Can you see evidence that contradicts their conclusion? If so, explain. If their claims do seem to be true, explain the corroborating evidence that you found. For support, you will want to quote from specific messages; however, make sure you have the written permission of the author before you do so.

3. Sproull and Kiesler note that organizations have both formal systems of record keeping and communication (i.e., communication systems set up by and maintained by the organization for its own official purposes) and informal systems (i.e., systems of communication established primarily by employees for their own purposes). In an observational report written to your teacher, describe one of the more important formal as well as one of the more important informal communication systems within a typical college classroom. Describe the various systems of communication, identify their purposes, and analyze how and why they work as they do. Who generally initiates information within such systems and how? For what purposes? To whom is information communicated? Why? How are responses generated? Why? In what form is the information put? Why? How is information received? What are the social contexts that influence such communications? Why? Your purpose in this report is to provide your teacher with an informative report that includes a student's eye view of classroom communication systems that the teacher might not have noticed or might not have fully analyzed.

From Captain America
to Wolverine

Mark Oehlert

THIS ARTICLE, ORIGINALLY PUBLISHED IN *The Cyborg Handbook* in 1995, targeted an educated readership with a specialist's interest in technology issues—specifically in the cultural icon or symbol of the cyborg, a being that combines the characteristics of both humans and machine technology. Cyborgs are human characters endowed with some technological parts—a computer implant that enhances vision, metal claws, a computer-supported brain, cybernetic links to other artificial and human intelligences, and technologically altered genetic material. Oehlert looks at cyborgs as they are represented, and as they act, in comic books. He speculates on how our culture uses cyborg heroes to reflect on, or to work out, some of the fears associated with living in an increasingly technological age, and some of our concerns about human beings' relationships with technology. Our cultural fascination with cyborgs—in science fiction, in comic books, and in movies—is discussed.

As you read this selection, you might think about the cyborg as a symbol of human beings' uneasy relationship with technology. In the movies you have seen, in the comics you have read, in the fiction you have come in contact with, what themes are typically associated with cyborgs? How are cyborgs represented? What characteristics are associated with them? What do these themes, representations, and characteristics tell us about ourselves? Our experiences with technology? Our concerns about and hopes for technology?

*This paper is dedicated to Jack Kirby. One of the earliest
and greatest comic book artists ever.*

Current comic book cyborgs reveal much about how these characters are perceived. In addition to movies, comic books represent the most prevalent medium in which many children and adults are forming their

impressions of cyborgian culture. One of the more interesting characteristics of this culture is the divisions that comic book cyborgs can be sifted into. These categories are, in order of increasing complexity, simple controller, bio-tech integrator and genetic cyborgs. Comic book cyborgs also expose some of the psychological reactions that these characters evoke in us, ranging from a deep ambivalence towards violence and killing to issues of lost humanity and, finally, to new conceptions of the nature of evil.

GOLDEN AGE TO MARVEL AGE

Comic book cyborgs have a myriad of ancestors. The comic books that we know today can be traced to the 1930's, when Harry Donenfeld, a pulp magazine publisher, bought *New Fun Comics* from its originator, Major Wheeler-Nicholson.[1] Donenfeld's company would eventually become *DC (Detective Comics)* and would go on to publish *Superman* in 1938. To avoid an attempt at a history of the comic book, which would not only shortchange the medium but which is beyond the scope of this essay, it is sufficient to say that *Marvel,* the company that would come to dominate the comic book market, was also born during this time, the "Golden Age" of comics (1939–1950).

This "Golden Age" started at *Detective Comics* with the most well-known hero ever, *Superman.*[2] Interestingly enough, this first hero was not even from Earth but was an alien and an illegal one at that. *Detective Comics (DC)* continued to dominate the early market with their release of *Batman* in 1939.[3] This time *DC* went to the other end of the spectrum from *Superman. Batman* had no super powers and was the son of wealthy parents who were slain in a mugging. The first hero that could be classified as cyborgian[†] appeared two years later.

In 1941, with the world at war, *Marvel* (then called *Timely*) created the super-soldier *Captain America.*[4] *Captain America's* secret identity was Steve Rogers, a 98-pound weakling who was rejected for Army service until he was injected with a "super-soldier serum."[5] This hero's first villain was none other than Adolf Hitler himself. Another anti-Nazi, cyborg-like hero was the *Human Torch.*[6] The original *Torch* was an android that was created in a lab and then rebelled against his creators. The *Torch,* like most of his comic book contemporaries, immediately went to work battling the Nazis.

After World War II ended and the Cold War began, the emphasis of the heroes shifted from Germany and Japan to Russia and China. The very title of *Captain America's* comic book became "*Capt. America . . . Commie Smasher.*"[7] While *Capt. America* was fighting Soviet efforts, *Marvel* created a Chinese communist villain known as the *Yellow Claw* who dabbled in magic and had created a potion to extend his life.[8] A multitude of other heroes and villains were created during this time but these examples illustrate the fairly simplistic origins and conflicts that early characters were involved in. Stories would soon become much more revealing.

Science plays a dominant role in creating both heroes and villains during this time (1961–1970) known as the "Marvel Age."[9] The *Fantastic Four* were a group of heroes who were created by accidental exposure to radiation, a central theme in many of the comics of the time. The *Hulk, Spider-Man* and *DareDevil* were all heroes created by different forms of radiation. This was a definite reflection of the public's fears concerning radiation in the aftermath of World War II. This era also saw the creation of some characters that are discussed below such as the *X-Men, Dr. Doom* and *Iron Man.* The conflicts that these heroes and villains were involved in also took on a cosmic nature. Instead of defending the United States from communism, characters were now trying to save the entire planet.

During the twenty intervening years from 1970 until 1990, comic books were awash with a multitude of super-powered characters. The *Marvel personas* ranged from the *Swamp-Thing* (a swamp creature created by toxic waste), to *Ghost Rider* (half biker/half demon) to the *Punisher* (a Vietnam vet fed up with crime).[10] These individuals not only fought larger external battles but also began to deal with a bagful of personal problems. A shining example of this "realistic" superhero character development came in issue #128 of *Iron Man*, in which a powerful super-hero is forced to come to grips with alcoholism.[11] This maturing of heroes and their problems brings the comic timeline up to the present age, which could almost be known as the "cyborg age," considering their ubiquitous nature.

This section is intended to put to rest any lingering illusions that the comic book industry is still just a kid's game. *Wizard,* a comic industry magazine, reported that U.S. comic book sales for 1993 were over $750,000,000.[12] This same magazine received 285,000 pieces of mail from its readers during the same year.[13] *Wizard* also noted that, as of 1994, in addition to the ongoing animated shows of the *X-Men* and *Exo-Squad,* plans were in the works for a *Youngblood* series as well as a new *Spider-Man* animation.[14] *X-Men* were also the best-sellers in the toy market in 1993.[15] A new journal named *Inks* is being published by the Ohio State University Press, which is devoted to research on cartoons, comic strips, and comic books. *Wizard* lists, from 12/1/93 until 1/15/94, hundreds of shows and conventions in 32 states from Vermont to California, the sheer numbers of which indicate a thriving subculture.[16]

Marvel is the company that has the largest market and dollar share of the comic market and the *Marvel Universe* is a place replete with cyborgs.[17] There will also be several characters examined who are in *Image Comics,* a newer, smaller company but one in which almost every hero or villain is in some way a cyborg. *Detective Comics,* which is the second largest comic company, simply does not seem to have the same variety of cyborgs that are present in the others.

No doubt there are many other comics with cyborgs but the cyborgs that are covered in this paper, by most accounts, are among the most popular comic characters of the mid-1990s and therefore they make ideal subjects for analysis.

CURRENT-DAY CYBORGS

Contemporary cyborg comic characters can be grouped into three broad categories: simple controllers, bio-tech integrators and genetic cyborgs. The rationale for these divisions can be found in the work of Chris Gray, in which the levels of integration are similarly described as:

> *(1) With informational interfaces including computer networks, human-computer com-munications, vaccinations and the technical manipulation of genetic information. (2) With simple mechanical-human relationships as with medical prosthesis, vehicle or weapon man-machine systems, and more general human-tool integration. (3) With direct machine-human connections such as the military's state-of-the-art attempts to hard-wire pilots to computers in DARPA's "pilot's associate" and the Los Alamos Lab's "pitman" exoskeleton. Plans to "download" human consciousness into a computer are part of this nexus as well.[18]*

One thing that makes grouping characters into categories difficult is that many of the heroes and villains fit into multiple divisions, so for the purposes of this analysis the cyborgs are grouped by their primary system.

The first broad category of cyborg is the simple controller group. This label is used to denote cyborgs of two smaller subsets; Implants and Suits. These cyborgs are characterized either by the simplicity of their system or its removability.

Controller

A perfect example of the simple controller/implant cyborg is a *Marvel* character known as *Wolverine*. He is a member of the mutant team, *X-Men*, but his primary cyborg system is surgically attached metal. *Wolverine* was a Canadian mercenary who underwent a series of experimental operations in order for Canada to begin creating its own team of super-heroes. His implants consist of adamantium (the fictional hardest metal in the *Marvel* universe) grafted onto his skeletal structure with some very long, very sharp adamantium claws implanted in his hands.[19] Considering his mutant abilities of super-fast (almost instantaneous) healing and super-sharp senses coupled with a beserker rage, *Wolverine* is a prime example of the newer, darker cyborgs that populate current comics. One of *Wolverine*'s most infamous enemies is also a wonderful illustration of the simple controller/implant type.

Omega Red is a creation of the old Soviet Union and when he was developed he so terrified his creators that they placed him in suspended animation.[20] While *Omega Red* is a powerful villain he is also a cursed one. His cyborg structure is crafted with an artificial metal known as "carbonadium" in order to prevent his "death spore" affliction from killing him.[21] This affliction forces *Omega Red* to drain the life force from others in order to live. While he is not quite remorseful about this, it is a weakness that he would like to correct. While his infection reflects a complicated biological problem, *Omega Red*'s cyborg weapons are still fairly simple. He possesses cables that are similar to *Wolverine*'s claws. These are grafted directly onto and into his nervous system and so are controlled by thoughts, a common cyborgian system. The final character in this category also governs his abilities by thought.

In the *Image* comic, *StormWatch*, the United Nations sends teams of super-powered agents to various trouble spots to act as peacekeepers. The man coordinating these many teams in various global locations is codenamed *Weatherman One*.[22] The *Weatherman* has the ability to "consider huge amounts of data and to make quick, calm decisions" helped along by "cybernetic implants which link his cerebral cortex directly to the SkyWatch computer net."[23] The *Weatherman* is a classic implant/controller who utilizes cyber-technology in concert with the data-processing and decision-making ability of the human brain. The next category are the controller/suit cyborgs, who represent the outermost layer of cyborg culture. These are cyborgs whose abilities are for the most part removable. They may possess some inherent powers but those powers are profoundly augmented by their technological additions.

The first and probably most well-known of this type is *Iron Man* who debuted in 1963 from *Marvel Comics*.[24] In Les Daniels' history of *Marvel*, he mentions that *Iron Man* is not a cyborg simply because of the exo-suit that he wears but he also has additional medical problems.[25] Daniels recounts how *Iron Man*'s armor is not just for battle but was also "created to keep his damaged heart beating" and that a microchip was implanted to correct a later problem insuring that "even without his high-tech costume, Tony Stark is a mixture of man and machine, what science fiction writers call a cyborg."[26] *Iron Man* controls his suit via his thoughts and some form of a cybernetic link. The armor has jets in the feet which allow it to fly, "repulsor beams" that shoot from the palms of the hands and servo-mechanisms which increase the wearer's strength by several orders of magnitude. The present day suit is also modular and can be fitted with several different weapons packages depending on what the immediate mission may be.[27] A testament to *Iron Man*'s continuing popularity is the fact that now there is even a spinoff comic based on a character that had to fill in as *Iron Man* while Tony Stark (the regular *Iron Man*) , entitled "Mythinformation,"was indisposed. This character, aptly named *War Machine,* is a younger more violent model of a controller/suit.[28] One of the most infamous villains in the comic world also belongs to this category, namely *Doctor Doom.*

Victor von Doom is described as "a crazed scientific genius who hid his scarred face behind a mask" and who used his position as the "ruthless ruler of a small country . . . to cloak his plans for world conquest."[29] *Doom* not only exists technologically, within his suit, but he is also a mystic, the ruler of a nation, and a psychotic bent on ruling the world. The final controller/suit in this category is also one of the newest.

Battalion is a super-hero from *Image Comics, StormWatch* series. The suit that he wears is referred to as a "cyber-tran suit" which amplifies his own *psionic* power a "hundred-fold."[30] Additionally the suit is also to be equipped with the "new, experimental tri-kevlar body armour as well as an integrated communication system."[31] This is one of the new directions that suits are taking in comics. Where once the suits of *Iron Man* and *Dr. Doom* simply multiplied their human strength or abilities or allowed them access to a man-machine weapon system, this new suit goes a step beyond. In *Battalion* there is a character whose mental facility is amplified by his suit and his greatest enemy, *Deathtrap,* is a villain whose mental power can focus and improve the performance of machines.[32] These suits then would seem to be the equivalent of mental Waldos.

Other notable controller/suit characters include *Doctor Octopus, Cyber* and *Ahab.* The next category to be discussed is the bio-tech integrator.

Bio-Tech Integrator

Compared to the controller cyborgs mentioned above, the bio-tech integrators are much more complex. Their systems can not be removed and often they are not fully explained either. They are, however, very popular cyborgs. One of the most popular is codenamed *Cable.*[33]

Cable is a character whose very existence is difficult to describe. To make a convoluted story short, *Cable* is the son of two members of the *X-Men.* As a baby, *Cable* is infected with a "techno-organic virus," and is sent into the future in hopes that a cure could be found for his disease.[34] The disease is arrested and *Cable* is left with "techno-organic but not sentient" portions of his molecular structure that can be altered at will.[35] This means that *Cable* can re-configure parts of his body to either a machine or an organic state. As a rule, some visible portion of his body is always portrayed as a machine and when asked about why he would do this, when he could look entirely human, his response is "to get where you want to go . . . it never hurts to remember where you've been."[36] It is obvious that the relationship between *Cable* and his cybernetic system is a more intimate and symbiotic one than exists for the class of controller cyborgs. This is also true for another cyborg member of the bio-tech integrator class named *Weapon X.*

The term *Weapon X* is a confusing element in at least three different comic book series. In its most general term, *Weapon X* is the Canadian government's top secret program for building superheroes; unfortunately for Canada it seems that once imbued with super powers, most of their creations do not feel like working for the government anymore.[37] *Weapon X* was also *Wolverine*'s original designation. The current *Weapon X* is a character named Garrison Kane.[38] The present *Weapon X*'s capabilities include increased strength and the ability to actually shoot parts of his body at opponents as projectile weapons (i.e. a fist or an arm).[39] Again the cybernetic connection is made at a very basic systemic level. A controller such as *Wolverine* cannot alter his cyborg system at will but an integrator like *Weapon X* certainly can.

Genetic Cyborgs

This is the third category of comic book cyborgs and one of the most interesting. Characters in this class may or may not have artificial implants but their primary power rests in a purposeful alteration of their genetic code. The issues of purposefulness and intent are critical and defining ideas for this group. It is intent that distinguishes the genetic cyborg from the comic characters that have been created by accident. These accidental individuals include such notable figures as *Superman*, *Spider-Man*, *Flash* and the *Hulk*.

The first constructed genetic cyborg was one of the comic world's most recognized heroes, *Captain America*. The *Captain* was a product of World War II and his debut, fighting against Hitler, in March of 1941, preceded Pearl Harbor.[40] In the first issue of *Captain America*, the doctor who injected skinny Steve Rogers (*Capt. America's* alter ego) with the "super-soldier serum," declares that the serum "is rapidly building his body and his brain tissues, until his stature and intelligence increase to an amazing degree."[41] During the course of one adventure, *Captain America* was thrown into the icy waters of the North Pole, thanks to the cold and the serum he was preserved until the mid-1960s when he was discovered and revived by the super-hero team, the *Avengers*.[42] Just recently, this original genetic cyborg received the bad news that the serum was beginning to adversely affect his health and that if he continued to perform his super-hero activities, he would eventually become paralyzed.[43] While *Captain America* remains a popular character, his views on violence in comics have become antiquated and mark him as a throw-back to a different era.

Whereas *Captain America* is arguably the first genetic cyborg, the character known as *Supreme* is one of the newest. *Supreme* and *Captain America* are an interesting pair for comparison since these two radically different characters were conceived fifty-three years apart, but in their respective comic universes they were created at essentially the same time. Steve Rogers (a.k.a. *Capt. America*) volunteered for his experiment out of his sense of patriotism but *Supreme* remembers a government that "was playing with civilian lives as usual and I was offered a position with them that I was unable to refuse."[44] During this experiment *Supreme* was given pills and he recalls his handlers "shot me full of experimental drugs, exercised me, exposed me to all sorts of radiation" until they hit upon the right mix which began to increase his strength, mass and weight.[45] When the scientists connected him to computers which "were able to accelerate what had already been started," he became a "genius ten-fold" and eventually realized that he had been "divinely selected for omnipotence . . . to be a supreme being."[46] Not only is *Supreme* portrayed as much more powerful than *Captain America* but his attitude is diametrically opposed to the *Captain's* understated style. *Supreme* has also evidenced the ability to, within a time span of nanoseconds, scan an opponent's weapon and then alter his own biological structure to provide a natural defense against that specific weapon, much like a super-powerful, consciously directed immune system.[47]

Marvel comics has always had a knack for designing characters that were bittersweet and they managed to do it again when they created a mercenary codenamed *Deadpool*. *Deadpool* was facing terminal cancer and had already been "on chemo twice and radiation three times" before he submitted to *Weapon X*' (the government program) "bio-enhancing" experiments.[48] The results included increased strength and an immune system that is constantly healing him while it is, ironically, horribly scarring his body and disfiguring his face.[49] *Deadpool* also fits right in with *Weapon X*'s other projects. As soon as he is cured, he becomes a mercenary and goes freelance.

These three categories represent the most popular and populated classes of cyborgs in comics today. However, they do not encompass all of the characters that could possibly be classified as cyborgian, nor is the listing of heroes and villains in these groups anything more than a representation of entire groups of cyborgs. The current comic book world of *Marvel, Image, DC* and others is literally packed with individuals that could be classed as cyborgs.

A CYBORG'S GREATEST FEARS
OR OUR FEARS OF THEM

Any current hero or villain in comics today faces a multitude of problems that the characters of yesteryear never even dreamed of. Today's super-powered individuals worry about rent, careers, stable relationships, dysfunctional childhoods and even the HIV virus. *Shadowhawk*, a character from *Image* comics, is HIV positive and his creator states that AIDS will cause his death.[50] Among the issues comic book cyborgs confront are violence, consciousness downloading, lost humanity, corporations as evil avatars and the view that obviously robotic creatures are almost entirely evil. Violence is probably the easiest problem to discuss and is certainly the most graphic.

In his classic science fiction novel, *Starship Troopers,* Robert Heinlein's main character declares that the clearly cyborgian "Mobile Infantry" has made future war and violence "as personal as a punch in the nose."[51] Comic book cyborgs are taking that violence and making it as personal as ripping your spine out. In the November 1993 issue of *Bloodstrike,* over a space of six pages, *Supreme* singlehandedly crushes a ribcage, smashes someone's arms off, crushes a hand, gouges eyes out, hits a character in the stomach with such force that his opponent's intestines fly out his back and to finish up breaks a spine.[52] While this is an extreme example of violence, committed by a cyborg against other cyborgs, it is certainly not an isolated instance.

Violence, as a cyborg issue, is a double-edged sword. One edge cuts into society's fears and desires concerning the present level of crime. These cyborg heroes are taking on the drug lords and the terrorists who are keeping us up at night worrying for our safety. Not only are they meeting them head on, but with regenerative tissue and psionically-created weapons, they are violently and graphically destroying these criminals. Instead of waiting or negotiating in a hostage situation, the character *Supreme* simply waded in and chopped them to death with his bare hands.[53] This is cyborg justice. No Miranda rights, no crowded court dockets, no criminals going free on a technicality. If you attract the attention of a cyborg hero, you can probably expect to be killed or maimed.

The opposing edge of the blade lays open our own fears concerning the cyborgs themselves. Are these images of our post-modern Frankenstein monsters? If these cyborgs are so powerful, then how do we, as normal (?) homo sapiens, stand a chance if they ever turn on us? In comic books creatures have been created that are beyond the control of anyone. The fictional *Weapon X* program is a prime example. The very ambiguity with which many of the cyborg heroes and villains are portrayed, good guys become bad guys and vice versa, is indicative of our unease with these creations. The violence depicted on the pages of these comic books may be perceived as warnings as to what might happen if we pursue this line of technology. *Wolverine* once said, "I can't be one hundred percent sure he's lying, but I have to be one hundred percent sure because if I kill him, then he's one hundred percent dead."[54] In the March 1994 issue of *Captain America*, there was a scene involving *Captain America* in civilian clothes intervening in a child's theft of comic books from a local store. *Captain America* looks at the comics and then asks the store owner if he reads them:

> **Store owner:** "Of course I do! I love super-heroes . . . they're at the cutting edge of the counter-culture! I wish I knew some personally! I'd have the Punisher break this punk's hands or I'd have Wolverine carve the word 'thief' on his forehead!"

> **Capt. America:** "Those heroes are your favorites?"

> **Store owner:** "Yep, the more violent they are the better I like them! The better they sell too!"[55]

This is an issue that clearly separates this very cyborgian comic era from previous epochs.

LOST HUMANITY

In his article on cyborg soldiers, Chris Gray notes that while current military thought is "moving towards a more subtle man-machine integration," the vision is still one of "machine-like endurance with a redefined human intellect subordinated to the overall weapons system."[56] While this reflects current military thinking, it is not reflective of the man-machine control issues in comic books.

The hero or villain of today's cyborg comic book is likely to be in control of his weapon system to a greater degree than ever before. A prime example of this would be the character *Supreme*. Here is a genetic cyborg who exercises control over his system at a cellular level.[57] In their article on knowledge-based pilot aids, Cross, Bahnji and Norman approach the issue of control from the aspect of human capabilities. Specifically they state that "Humans have finite capabilities. They are limited by the amount of information they can process and the amount of time required to process that information."[58] Here they seem to be arguing for a preponderance of machine control in a man-machine system because of a lack of human attention span. Cyborgs in comic books seem to be unfettered by this problem and the reason is fairly clear, these characters are participating in Old West shootouts with post-modern weapons. They are not attempting to place a five-hundred-pound bomb on a particular building in a large city while avoiding collateral civilian damage, they are up close and personal.

There also is some disparity between this article and the comic book world in terms of which human capabilities are the lowest limiting factors in a man-machine system. Bahnji, Cross and Norman make it clear that they feel the limit is on "CA . . . cognitive attention." They go on to break down "CA" into "CAs = the cognitive attention required for task accomplishment at the skill-based level, CAr = the cognitive attention required for task accomplishment at the rule-based level and CAk = the cognitive attention required for task accomplishment at the knowledge-based level."[59] Comic book cyborgs are not constrained here because their cyborg system allows them to make a quantum jump forward in skill, their rules are extremely simplified (stop your target before they stop you) and all the knowledge they need is the location of their opponent. As opposed to pilots of fighter aircraft who require a great deal of their attention to be focused on the operation of their system, cyborgs whose systems are managed intuitively require little of their attention to be diverted from the actual combat. The issue of humanity with comic book cyborgs then is not if the machine will take over the human side of the equation but what will the human half choose to do with his new abilities.

The concept of looking and acting like a man and Moravec's more advanced idea of downloading consciousness have both been dealt with in the world of the comic book cyborg. The issue of how much machinery a person must integrate before he becomes a machine, however, has not drawn nearly as much attention as the consciousness issue has. Perhaps the best example of this is a character named the *Vision*.

A *Marvel* comic describes the *Vision* as "a unique form of android known as a synthezoid, who is both composed of mechanical parts and an unknown material that mimics the properties and functions of human tissue and bone but is far stronger and durable."[60] The *Vision* has a long and interesting cybernetic history. He was created by another robot, a villain known as *Ultron*, who originally used him to attack the heroic *Avengers*.[61] The *Vision*'s consciousness was based on "encephalograms from the brain of *Wonder Man* who was then believed to be dead . . . in later years the *Vision* and *Wonder Man* came to regard themselves as 'brothers' of a sort."[62] If all this was not enough, the history of this android becomes even more complicated. Over time the *Vision* managed to develop human emotions and he even married a fellow super-heroine known as the *Scarlet Witch*, which in the comic world "evoked the unreasoning hatred of bigots who would not accept the *Vision*'s claim to be human."[63] Once, due to damage sustained in a battle, he was connected to a giant computer and through this connection came to believe that the way to save humanity was for him "to take absolute control of the planet through linking himself to all the world's computers."[64] Finally, the *Vision* had this connection severed, returned to normal (a hero), was abducted by the government who now feared him, was disassembled, his programming erased (killed?), was rescued by his friends, was reassembled but lost his capacity for emotions, was divorced and is now a reservist for the *Avengers*.[65] From his marriage on there were arguments over whether or not the *Vision* was alive, what relation he had to *Wonder Man* since they shared brain patterns and whether or not he could be trusted. This would be an interesting point to bring up to Moravec. If consciousness could be downloaded and "backup copies" could truly be made, what would happen if a couple of you were in existence at the same time?[66] The question of the *Vision*'s loyalty and the fact that he was created by the evil robot, *Ultron*, brings up the issue of the nature of robots and androids in the comic world.[††]

EVIL, INC.

The great evils in the comic world are the multinational corporations. In their article on the growth of new cyborgian political entities, Gray and Mentor assert that "the age of the hegemony of the nation state is ending."[67] They go on to speak of nation states being "drained of sovereignty by multinational corporations on one side and nongovernmental organizations and international subcultures sustained by world-wide mass telecommunications on the other."[68] This is exactly the situation that has come to pass in comics, especially in the world of *Image* comics. In one particular comic, aptly named *CyberForce*, the great evil is a corporation, again with the appropriate name of *CyberData*. This scenario has *CyberData* implanting its *S.H.O.C.* (Special Hazardous Operations Cyborgs) troops with a micro-circuit implant that forces the recipient's personality into more and more aggressive and lethal pathways.[69] The idea behind the super-hero team is that a doctor, employed by *CyberData*, uncovers its scheme and develops a method for removing the chips. He is promptly killed but by then the team is formed and they still possess the removal method.[70]

Two other teams that were formed by corporate interests were *YoungBlood* and *Heavy Mettle*. These two groups are both genetically engineered humans who are employed by a corporation known as G.A.T.E. International and who are contracted to the government.[71] Gray, in his article on war cyborgs, asserts that "the very possibility of cyborgs is predicated on militarized high technology." While this continues to be true in comic books it is not the government that is in control of this technology.[72] While most of these super-powered teams seem to work for the good of society, there is always the possibility, indeed the implicit danger, that a member or an entire team may go renegade.

The arms race is also clearly present in this new generation of comic books. The twist is that this time the arms are people. In *StormWatch* the race is for "seedlings," children who may have been genetically altered by the close passing of a strange comet.[73] This type of race is in line with the prediction by Gray and Mentor that "the body politic of the future will be those cyborg industries which meld great skill at information processing and personnel management into tremendous profits and powers" as well as their observation that "cyborgs are also the children of war and there is a real chance that the dominant cyborg body politics of the future will be military information societies much like the U.S."[74] It seems that the comic book vision of the future has that dominant body politic resting within the corporate veil.

These issues of violence, downloading, and evil corporations are just a few of the myriad of problems being discussed in cyborg-oriented comics.[†††]

CONCLUDING THOUGHTS

> The poet's eye, in a fine frenzy rolling,
> Doth glance from heaven to earth, from
>   earth to heaven;
> And, as imagination bodies forth
> The forms of things unknown, the poet's
>   pen
> Turns them to shapes, and gives to airy
>   nothing
> A local habitation and a name.[75]

In Shakespeare's time it was the poet who gave wings to visions of the future, later writers such as Verne and Wells took up the burden. More recently, Asimov, Pohl, Clarke and Card have all provided us with their unique interpretations of what the future will look like. Today, science fiction writers still provide a large part of future scenarios but they are also being helped along to a growing extent by comic book artists and writers.

Where those future visions include cyborgs, comic books have seized them tightly. On those multi-colored pages of what were once considered kid's toys are some of the most graphic and vivid images of what cyborgs might look like. Not only are their potential shapes explored but their potential uses as well. The popularity of comic book cyborgs also attests to the growing acceptance and interest in the possibility of such creations. If a search is on for a medium in which cyborgian futures are being explored with great vision and energy, a researcher need look no further than the local comic book store.

NOTES

†For the purpose of this paper a key factor in determining whether or not a hero or villain is a cyborg will be based on design. Changed humans who were created by accident, i.e., *Daredevil*, *Spider-Man*, will not be considered cyborgs, they are more properly mutants.

††If cyborgs in comics seem ambiguous in nature, more overtly robotic creatures do not. A quick look at the most obviously robotic characters such as *Vision, Ultron, Sinsear, Nimrod* and the *Sentinels*, reveals that all at one time were villains and that all but the *Vision* are still considered evil. The question seems to be why do comics regard the creatures that humans should be able to control to the greatest extent, as the creations most likely to run amok? These villains are constantly creating more evil robots and *Ultron*'s plans have grown to include his intention of obliterating not just humanity, but all plants and animals—all organic life on Earth. Since the focus here is on cyborgs, suffice it to say that the robotic position is at least as interesting as that of cyborgs.

†††Some other problems include:

Anti-mutant Hysteria: Glance at any of the pages of comic books involving mutants, particularly in the *Marvel* universe, and examples will be found of sinister-sounding mutant registration programs, and grassroots bigotry against mutants, also known as "homo superior."

Gender/Race/Handicaps: A multitude. The leader of the *Avengers,* one of the oldest super-hero teams, is a woman, the current *Captain Marvel* is a black woman and there are also blind, paraplegic heroes as well as HIV-positive characters and characters fighting cancer.

Comic books also dive into cyberspace, virtual reality addicts, multiple uses of holographic technology and artificial intelligence racing out of control.

1. Les Daniels, *MARVEL* (New York: Harry N. Abrams Inc., 1991) p. 17.
2. Robert M. Overstreet, *The Overstreet Comics and Cards Price Guide* (New York: Avon Books, 1993) p. 48.
3. Ibid., p. 49.
4. Les Daniels, op. cit., p. 39.
5. Ibid., p. 39.
6. Ibid., p. 31.
7. Ibid., p. 71.
8. Ibid., p. 80.
9. Ibid., p. 83.
10. Ibid., p. 163.
11. Robert M. Overstreet, op. cit., p. 206.
12. Jon Warren, "1993: The Year in Review," *Wizard* January 1994: p. 217.
13. Gareb S. Shamus, "Forward Thinking," *Wizard* January 1994: p. 12.
14. Barry Layne, "The Hollywood Beat," *Wizard* January 1994: p. 153.
15. "From the Best of 1993," *Wizard* January 1994: p. 189.
16. "Shows and Conventions," *Wizard* January 1994: p. 291.
17. Jon Warren, op. cit., p. 221.
18. Chris Gray, "Cyborg Citizen: A Genealogy of Cybernetic Organisms in the Americas," Research Proposal for the Caltech Mellon Postdoctoral Fellowship: p. 2.
19. Les Daniels, op. cit., p. 191.
20. Fabian Nicieza, *CABLE,* Vol. 1–No. 9 (March 1994): p. 7.
21. Fabian Nicieza, *CABLE,* Vol. 1–No. 10 (April 1994): p. 1.
22. Jim Lee, *STORMWATCH SOURCEBOOK,* Vol. 1–No. 1 (1994): p. 1.
23. Ibid., p. 1.
24. Les Daniels, op. cit., p. 101.
25. Les Daniels, op. cit., p. 101.
26. Les Daniels, op. cit., p. 101.
27. Ken Kaminski, *IRON MAN,* Vol. 1–No. 300 (January 1994): n. page.
28. Scott Benson, *WAR MACHINE,* Vol. 1–No. 1 (April 1994): p. 1.
29. Les Daniels, op. cit., p. 88.
30. Brandon Choi and Jim Lee, *STORMWATCH,* Vol. 1–No. 0 (August 1993): p. 20.
31. Ibid., p. 20.
32. Jim Lee et al., *STORMWATCH SOURCEBOOK,* Vol. 1–No. 1 (January 1994): p. 27.
33. Matt Ashland, Owner, Matt's Cavalcade of Comics, Cards and Collectibles, Corvallis, OR, personal interview, February 1, 1994.

34. Fabian Nicieza, *CABLE*, Vol. 1–No. 8 (February 1994): p. 15.
35. Fabian Nicieza, *CABLE*, Vol. 1–No. 9 (March 1994): p. 14.
36. Ibid., p. 15.
37. John Byrne, *ALPHA FLIGHT*, Vol. 1–No. 1 (August 1983): n. page.
38. Rob Liefeld, *X-FORCE*, Vol. 1–No. 10 (1992): n. page.
39. Joe Madureira and Fabian Nicieza, *DEADPOOL: THE CIRCLE CHASE*, Vol. 1–No. 4 (December 1993): n. page.
40. Les Daniels, op. cit., p. 37.
41. Les Daniels, op. cit., p. 38.
42. Peter Sanderson, *AVENGERS LOG*, Vol. 1–No. 1 (February 1994): p. 8.
43. Mike Grell, *CAPTAIN AMERICA*, Vol. 1–No. 424 (February 1994): n. page.
44. Rob Liefeld, *SUPREME*, Vol. 1–No. 424 (February 1994) p. 10.
45. Ibid., p. 11.
46. Ibid., p. 13.
47. Rob Liefeld, *SUPREME*, Vol. 1–No. 2 (February 1993): pp. 14–15.
48. Joe Madureira and Fabian Nicieza, *DEADPOOL: THE CIRCLE CHASE*, Vol. 1–No. 3 (November 1993): n. page.
49. Joe Madureira and Fabian Nicieza, *DEADPOOL: THE CIRCLE CHASE,* Vol. 1–No. 4 (December 1993): n. page.
50. Brian Cunningham, "Out of the Shadows," *WIZARD* April 1994: p. 40.
51. Robert A. Heinlein, *STARSHIP TROOPERS* (New York, N.Y.: Ace Books, 1959) p. 80.
52. Keith Giffen, *BLOODSTRIKE*, Vol. 1–No. 5 (November 1993): pp. 16–19.
53. Rob Liefeld, *SUPREME*, Vol. 1–No. 3 (June 1993): p. 17.
54. Peter David, *X-FACTOR*, Vol. 1–No. 85 (1993): n. page.
55. Mike Grell, *CAPTAIN AMERICA*, Vol. 1–No. 425 (March 1994): n. page.
56. Chris Gray, "The Cyborg Soldier: The U.S. Military and the PostModern Warrior," in L. Levidow and K. Robins, eds., *Cyborg Worlds: The Military Information Economy* (London: Free Association Press, 1989) pp. 43–72.
57. Rob Liefeld, *SUPREME*, Vol. 1–No. 4 (July 1993): n. page.
58. Stephen E. Cross, et al., "Knowledge-Based Pilot Aids; A Case Study in Mission Planning" in *Lecture Notes in Control and Information Sciences: Artificial Intelligence and Man-machine Systems* (Berlin: Springer-Verlag, 1986) p. 147.
59. Ibid., p. 148.
60. Peter Sanderson, *AVENGERS LOG*, Vol. 1–No. 1 (February 1994): pp. 24–25.
61. Ibid., p. 44.
62. Ibid., p. 24.
63. Ibid., p. 25.
64. Ibid., p. 25.
65. Ibid., p. 26.
66. Ed Regis, op. cit., p. 167.
67. Chris Gray and Stephen Mentor, "The Cyborg Body Politic Meets the New World Order," in this volume.
68. Ibid., p. 11.
69. Walter Simonson, *CYBERFORCE*, Vol. 1–No. 0 (September 1993): p. 8.
70. Ibid., p. 9.
71. Rob Liefeld, *SUPREME*, Vol. 1–No. 1 (April 1993): n. page.
72. Chris Gray, "The Culture of War Cyborgs: Technoscience, Gender, and PostModern War," in *Research in Philosophy and Technology,* special issue on feminism, ed. by Joan Rothschild, 1993: p. 1.
73. Jim Lee et al., *STORMWATCH SOURCEBOOK*, Vol. 1–No. 1 (January 1994): p. 2.
74. Gray and Mentor, op. cit., pp. 12 and 14.
75. *The Concise Oxford Dictionary of Quotations* (New York: Oxford University Press, 1981) p. 227.

THINKING AND RE-READING

1. As you re-read this piece, think about Shakespeare's poem that Oehlert quotes. Why do you think that cyborgs, and the future, hold such fascination for humans? Why do we portray them so often in literature, comics, and movies? What do our specific portrayals of cyborg characters (e.g., their size, their powers, their appearance, their temperament) reveal about the values/concerns/fears we share as a culture toward technology?

2. As you re-read this piece, consider the fact that most of the cyborgs that Oehlert describes are males. Why do you suppose this is so? Do you know of any female cyborg comic characters? If so, how are they portrayed? Are there major differences between female cyborgs and male cyborgs in their attitudes? The cultural values they portray? In their physical characteristics? In their powers? In their cybernetic parts? Speculate about these differences or the lack of differences.

WRITING AND LEARNING

1. Oehlert identifies three specific cultural and/or social concerns that are revealed in comic-book cyborgs: our concern with the role that technology now plays in supporting crimes and violence; our recognition that machines may control humans as much, or more than, humans control machines within the technologically dependent social systems we have constructed; and our acknowledgment of the role that technology plays in extending the power of multinational corporations/governments/military operations across the globe. Consider some of the cyborg characters that you have seen in a movie or video or television show—Johnny Mnemonic, the Terminator, RoboCop, Edward Scissorhands, and Data. What are the social and/or cultural concerns that they help us play out? Who wins and who loses in these cyborg stories? Who is the enemy? Who is the hero? What similarities do such characters have to the comic book cyborgs that Oehlert describes? What differences? Why? Write a letter to Mark Oehlert describing one of these cyborgs and your observations of their characteristics, relationships with others, and actions. To do a good job in writing this letter, you will have to review the movie or video or television show in which the cyborg character appears and take some careful notes about his or her appearance, actions, and relationships, as well as the story line.

2. Write a letter to one of the major comic book companies describing a new cyborg character that you would like them to initiate for readers ages nine to fourteen. In your letter, describe in detail the cyborg character and his or her attributes. Also indicate in your letter why you think it is important to create this character and how this character would resonate with current cultural concerns that other characters do not address for this particular audience. Consider proposing a female cyborg character.

3. Choose a comic book cyborg that you are familiar with or read at least four issues of a comic book that includes a cyborg character with which you can familiarize yourself. After reading these issues, write a letter to the comic's artist to suggest several future story lines for this cyborg character that you would like to see for readers ages nine to thirteen. Sketch out these story lines as fully as possible and indicate why you think they are important stories to tell the younger generation as they enter the twenty-first century.

Johnny Mnemonic

William Gibson

THIS STORY, ORIGINALLY PUBLISHED by *Omni* magazine in 1981, addresses a popular theme in science fiction—the merger of humans and computers in a single cyborg "body." This theme grows out of our deep-seated cultural concern with the increasingly blurred boundaries between humans and computers—in creating a culture that is so dependent on computer technology, have we also served to link ourselves, our success as a species, and our ability to cope with the world with technology? Can we, even now, afford to separate ourselves from technology—in our work, our play, our communications?

Omni is a popular magazine that offers readers both science fiction and nonfiction essays on related technology issues. In general, the readers of *Omni* are science fiction fans. Many are also informed consumers of technology.

William Gibson, one of the most gifted science fiction writers on the contemporary scene, tackles these questions in "Johnny Mnemonic." After reading this story, you might also want to try some of his novels, among them, *Neuromancer, Count Zero,* and *Mona Lisa Overdrive.*

I put the shotgun in an Adidas bag and padded it out with four pairs of tennis socks, not my style at all, but that was what I was aiming for: If they think you're crude, go technical; if they think you're technical, go crude. I'm a very technical boy. So I decided to get as crude as possible. These days, though, you have to be pretty technical before you can even aspire to crudeness. I'd had to turn both these twelve-gauge shells from brass stock, on a lathe, and then load them myself; I'd had to dig up an old microfiche with instructions for hand-loading cartridges; I'd had to build a lever-action press to seat the primers—all very tricky. But I knew they'd work.

The meet was set for the Drome at 2300, but I rode the tube three stops past the closest platform and walked back. Immaculate procedure.

I checked myself out in the chrome siding of a coffee kiosk, your basic sharp-faced Caucasoid with a ruff of stiff, dark hair. The girls at Under the Knife were big on Sony Mao, and it was getting harder to keep them from adding the chic suggestion of epicanthic folds. It probably wouldn't fool Ralfi Face, but it might get me next to his table.

The Drome is a single narrow space with a bar down one side and tables along the other, thick with pimps and handlers and an arcane array of dealers. The Magnetic Dog Sisters were on the door that night, and I didn't relish trying to get out past them if things didn't work out. They were two meters tall and thin as greyhounds. One was black and the other white, but aside from that they were as nearly identical as cosmetic surgery could make them. They'd been lovers for years and were bad news in a tussle. I was never quite sure which one had originally been male.

Ralfi was sitting at his usual table. Owing me a lot of money. I had hundreds of megabytes stashed in my head on an idiot/savant basis, information I had no conscious access to. Ralfi had left it there. He hadn't, however, come back for it. Only Ralfi could retrieve the data, with a code phrase of his own invention. I'm not cheap to begin with, but my overtime on storage is astronomical. And Ralfi had been very scarce.

Then I'd heard that Ralfi Face wanted to put out a contract on me. So I'd arranged to meet him in the Drome, but I'd arranged it as Edward Bax, clandestine importer, late of Rio and Peking.

The Drome stank of biz, a metallic tang of nervous tension. Muscle-boys scattered through the crowd were flexing stock parts at one another and trying on thin, cold grins, some of them so lost under superstructures of muscle graft that their outlines weren't really human.

Pardon me. Pardon me, friends. Just Eddie Bax here, Fast Eddie the Importer, with his professionally nondescript gym bag, and please ignore this slit, just wide enough to admit his right hand.

Ralfi wasn't alone. Eighty kilos of blond California beef perched alertly in the chair next to his, martial arts written all over him.

Fast Eddie Bax was in the chair opposite them before the beef's hands were off the table. "You black belt?" I asked eagerly. He nodded, blue eyes running an automatic scanning pattern between my eyes and my hands. "Me, too," I said. "Got mine here in the bag." And I shoved my hand through the slit and thumbed the safety off. Click. "Double twelve-gauge with the triggers wired together."

"That's a gun," Ralfi said, putting a plump, restraining hand on his boy's taut blue nylon chest. "Johnny has an antique firearm in his bag." So much for Edward Bax.

I guess he'd always been Ralfi Something or Other, but he owed his acquired surname to a singular vanity. Built something like an overripe pear, he'd worn the once-famous face of Christian White for twenty years—Christian White of the Aryan Reggae Band, Sony Mao to his generation, and final champion of race rock. I'm a whiz at trivia.

Christian White: classic pop face with a singer's high-definition muscles, chiseled cheekbones. Angelic in one light, handsomely depraved in another. But Ralfi's eyes lived behind that face, and they were small and cold and black.

"Please," he said, "let's work this out like businessmen." His voice was marked by a horrible prehensile sincerity, and the corners of his beautiful Christian White mouth were always wet. "Lewis here," nodding in the beefboy's direction, "is a meatball." Lewis took this impassively, looking like something built from a kit. "You aren't a meatball, Johnny."

"Sure I am, Ralfi, a nice meatball chock-full of implants where you can store your dirty laundry while you go off shopping for people to kill me. From my end of this bag, Ralfi, it looks like you've got some explaining to do."

"It's this last batch of product, Johnny." He sighed deeply. "In my role as broker—"

"Fence," I corrected.

"As broker, I'm usually very careful as to sources."

"You buy only from those who steal the best. Got it."

He sighed again. "I try," he said wearily, "not to buy from fools. This time, I'm afraid, I've done that." Third sigh was the cue for Lewis to trigger the neural disruptor they'd taped under my side of the table.

I put everything I had into curling the index finger of my right hand, but I no longer seemed to be connected to it. I could feel the metal of the gun and the foam-pad tape I'd wrapped around the stubby grip, but my hands were cool wax, distant and inert. I was hoping Lewis was a true meatball, thick enough to go for the gym bag and snag my rigid trigger finger, but he wasn't.

"We've been very worried about you, Johnny. Very worried. You see, that's Yakuza property you have there. A fool took it from them, Johnny. A dead fool."

Lewis giggled.

It all made sense then, an ugly kind of sense, like bags of wet sand settling around my head. Killing wasn't Ralfi's style. Lewis wasn't even Ralfi's style. But he'd got himself stuck between the Sons of the Neon Chrysanthemum and something that belonged to them—or, more likely, something of theirs that belonged to someone else. Ralfi, of course, could use the code phrase to throw me into idiot/savant, and I'd spill their hot program without remembering a single quarter tone. For a fence like Ralfi, that would ordinarily have been enough. But not for the Yakuza. The Yakuza would know about Squids, for one thing, and they wouldn't want to worry about one lifting those dim and permanent traces of their program out of my head. I didn't know very much about Squids, but I'd heard stories, and I made it a point never to repeat them to my clients. No, the Yakuza wouldn't like that; it looked too much like evidence. They hadn't got where they were by leaving evidence around. Or alive.

Lewis was grinning. I think he was visualizing a point just behind my forehead and imagining how he could get there the hard way.

"Hey," said a low voice, feminine, from somewhere behind my right shoulder, "you cowboys sure aren't having too lively a time."

"Pack it, bitch," Lewis said, his tanned face very still. Ralfi looked blank.

"Lighten up. You want to buy some good free base?" She pulled up a chair and quickly sat before either of them could stop her. She was barely inside my fixed field of vision, a thin girl with mirrored glasses, her dark hair cut in a rough shag. She wore black leather, open over a T-shirt slashed diagonally with stripes of red and black. "Eight thou a gram weight."

Lewis snorted his exasperation and tried to slap her out of the chair. Somehow he didn't quite connect, and her hand came up and seemed to brush his wrist as it passed. Bright blood sprayed the table. He was clutching his wrist white-knuckle tight, blood trickling from between his fingers.

But hadn't her hand been empty?

He was going to need a tendon stapler. He stood up carefully, without bothering to push his chair back. The chair toppled backward, and he stepped out of my line of sight without a word.

"He better get a medic to look at that," she said. "That's a nasty cut."

"You have no idea," said Ralfi, suddenly sounding very tired, "the depths of shit you have just gotten yourself into."

"No kidding? Mystery. I get real excited by mysteries. Like why your friend here's so quiet. Frozen, like. Or what this thing here is for," and she held up the little control unit that she'd somehow taken from Lewis. Ralfi looked ill.

"You, ah, want maybe a quarter-million to give me that and take a walk?" A fat hand came up to stroke his pale, lean face nervously.

"What I want," she said, snapping her fingers so that the unit spun and glittered, "is work. A job. Your boy hurt his wrist. But a quarter'll do for a retainer."

Ralfi let his breath out explosively and began to laugh, exposing teeth that hadn't been kept up to the Christian White standard. Then she turned the disruptor off.

"Two million," I said.

"My kind of man," she said, and laughed. "What's in the bag?"

"A shotgun."

"Crude." It might have been a compliment.

Ralfi said nothing at all.

"Name's Millions. Molly Millions. You want to get out of here, boss? People are starting to stare." She stood up. She was wearing leather jeans the color of dried blood.

And I saw for the first time that the mirrored lenses were surgical inlays, the silver rising smoothly from her high cheekbones, sealing her eyes in their sockets. I saw my new face twinned there.

"I'm Johnny," I said. "We're taking Mr. Face with us."

He was outside, waiting. Looking like your standard tourist tech, in plastic zoris and a silly Hawaiian shirt printed with blowups of his firm's most popular microprocessor; a mild little guy, the kind most likely to wind up drunk on sake in a bar that puts out miniature rice crackers with seaweed garnish. He looked like the kind who sing the corporate anthem and cry, who shake hands endlessly with the bartender. And the pimps and the dealers would leave him alone, pegging him as innately conservative. Not up for much, and careful with his credit when he was.

The way I figured it later, they must have amputated part of his left thumb, somewhere behind the first joint, replacing it with a prosthetic tip, and cored the stump, fitting it with a spool and socket molded from one of the Ono-Sendai diamond analogs. Then they'd carefully wound the spool with three meters of monomolecular filament.

Molly got into some kind of exchange with the Magnetic Dog Sisters, giving me a chance to usher Ralfi through the door with the gym bag pressed lightly against the base of his spine. She seemed to know them. I heard the black one laugh.

I glanced up, out of some passing reflex, maybe because I've never got used to it, to the soaring arcs of light and the shadows of the geodesics above them. Maybe that saved me.

Ralfi kept walking, but I don't think he was trying to escape. I think he'd already given up. Probably he already had an idea of what we were up against.

I looked back down in time to see him explode.

Playback on full recall shows Ralfi stepping forward as the little tech sidles out of nowhere, smiling. Just a suggestion of a bow, and his left thumb falls off. It's a conjuring trick. The thumb hangs suspended. Mirrors? Wires? And Ralfi stops, his back to us, dark crescents of sweat under the armpits of his pale summer suit. He knows. He must have known. And then the joke-shop thumbtip, heavy as lead, arcs out in a lightning yo-yo trick, and the invisible thread connecting it to the killer's hand passes laterally through Ralfi's skull, just above his eyebrows, whips up, and descends, slicing the pear-shaped torso diagonally from shoulder to rib cage. Cuts so fine that no blood flows until synapses misfire and the first tremors surrender the body to gravity.

Ralfi tumbled apart in a pink cloud of fluids, the three mismatched sections rolling forward onto the tiled pavement. In total silence.

I brought the gym bag up, and my hand convulsed. The recoil nearly broke my wrist.

It must have been raining; ribbons of water cascaded from a ruptured geodesic and spattered on the tile behind us. We crouched in the narrow gap between a surgical boutique and an antique shop. She'd just edged one mirrored eye around the corner to report a single Volks module in front of the Drome, red lights flashing. They were sweeping Ralfi up. Asking questions.

I was covered in scorched white fluff. The tennis socks. The gym bag was a ragged plastic cuff around my wrist. "I don't see how the hell I missed him."

" 'Cause he's fast, so fast." She hugged her knees and rocked back and forth on her bootheels. "His nervous system's jacked up. He's factory custom." She grinned and gave a little squeal of delight. "I'm gonna get that boy. Tonight. He's the best, number one, top dollar, state of the art."

"What you're going to get, for this boy's two million, is my ass out of here. Your boyfriend back there was mostly grown in a vat in Chiba City. He's a Yakuza assassin."

"Chiba. Yeah. See, Molly's been Chiba, too." And she showed me her hands, fingers slightly spread. Her fingers were slender, tapered, very white against the polished burgundy nails. Ten blades snicked straight out from their recesses beneath her nails, each one a narrow, double-edged scalpel in pale blue steel.

I'd never spent much time in Nighttown. Nobody there had anything to pay me to remember, and most of them had a lot they paid regularly to forget. Generations of sharpshooters had chipped away at the neon until the maintenance crews gave up. Even at noon the arcs were soot-black against faintest pearl.

Where do you go when the world's wealthiest criminal order is feeling for you with calm, distant fingers? Where do you hide from the Yakuza, so powerful that it owns comsats and at least three shuttles? The Yakuza is a true multinational, like ITT and Ono-Sendai. Fifty years before I was born the Yakuza had already absorbed the Triads, the Mafia, the Union Corse.

Molly had an answer: you hide in the Pit, in the lowest circle, where any outside influence generates swift, concentric ripples of raw menace. You hide in Nighttown. Better yet, you hide *above* Nighttown, because the Pit's inverted, and the bottom of its bowl touches the sky, the sky that Nighttown never sees, sweating under its own firmament of acrylic resin, up where the Lo Teks crouch in the dark like gargoyles, black-market cigarettes dangling from their lips.

She had another answer, too.

"So you're locked up good and tight, Johnny-san? No way to get that program without the password?" She led me into the shadows that waited beyond the bright tube platform. The concrete walls were overlaid with graffiti, years of them twisting into a single metascrawl of rage and frustration.

"The stored data are fed in through a modified series of microsurgical contraautism prostheses," I reeled off a numb version of my standard sales pitch. "Client's code is stored in a special chip; barring Squids, which we in the trade don't like to talk about, there's no way to recover your phrase. Can't drug it out, cut it out, torture it. I don't *know* it, never did."

"Squids? Crawly things with arms?" We emerged into a deserted street market. Shadowy figures watched us from across a makeshift square littered with fish heads and rotting fruit.

"Superconducting quantum interference detectors. Used them in the war to find submarines, suss out enemy cyber systems."

"Yeah? Navy stuff? From the war? Squid'll read that chip of yours?" She'd stopped walking, and I felt her eyes on me behind those twin mirrors.

"Even the primitive models could measure a magnetic field a billionth the strength of geomagnetic force; it's like pulling a whisper out of a cheering stadium."

"Cops can do that already, with parabolic microphones and lasers."

"But your data's still secure." Pride in profession. "No government'll let their cops have Squids, not even the security heavies. Too much chance of interdepartmental funnies; they're too likely to watergate you."

"Navy stuff," she said, and her grin gleamed in the shadows. "Navy stuff. I got a friend down here who was in the navy, name's Jones. I think you'd better meet him. He's a junkie, though. So we'll have to take him something."

"A junkie?"

"A dolphin."

He was more than a dolphin, but from another dolphin's point of view he might have seemed like something less. I watched him swirling sluggishly in his galvanized tank. Water slopped over the side, wetting my shoes. He was surplus from the last war. A cyborg.

He rose out of the water, showing us the crusted plates along his sides, a kind of visual pun, his grace nearly lost under articulated armor, clumsy and prehistoric. Twin deformities on either side of his skull had been engineered to house sensor units. Silver lesions gleamed on exposed sections of his gray-white hide.

Molly whistled. Jones thrashed his tail, and more water cascaded down the side of the tank.

"What is this place?" I peered at vague shapes in the dark, rusting chain link and things under tarps. Above the tank hung a clumsy wooden framework, crossed and recrossed by rows of dusty Christmas lights.

"Funland. Zoo and carnival rides. 'Talk with the War Whale.' All that. Some whale Jones is. . . ."

Jones reared again and fixed me with a sad and ancient eye.

"How's he talk?" Suddenly I was anxious to go.

"That's the catch. Say 'hi,' Jones."

And all the bulbs lit simultaneously. They were flashing red, white, and blue.

* * *

```
RWBRWBRWB
RWBRWBRWB
RWBRWBRWB
RWBRWBRWB
RWBRWBRWB
```

"Good with symbols, see, but the code's restricted. In the navy they had him wired into an audiovisual display." She drew the narrow package from a jacket pocket. "Pure shit, Jones. Want it?" He froze in the water and started to sink. I felt a strange panic, remembering that he wasn't a fish, that he could drown. "We want the key to Johnny's bank, Jones. We want it fast."

The lights flickered, died.

"Go for it, Jones!"

```
        B
BBBBBBBBB
        B
        B
        B
```

Blue bulbs, cruciform.
Darkness.
"Pure! It's *clean.* Come on, Jones."

```
WWWWWWWWW
WWWWWWWWW
WWWWWWWWW
WWWWWWWWW
WWWWWWWWW
```

White sodium glare washed her features, stark monochrome, shadows cleaving from her cheekbones.

* * *

```
R    RRRRR
R    R
RRRRRRRRR
        R   R
RRRRR   R
```

The arms of the red swastika were twisted in her silver glasses. "Give it to him," I said. "We've got it."

Ralfi Face. No imagination.

Jones heaved half his armored bulk over the edge of his tank, and I thought the metal would give way. Molly stabbed him overhand with the Syrette, driving the needle between two plates. Propellant hissed. Patterns of light exploded, spasming across the frame and then fading to black.

We left him drifting, rolling languorously in the dark water. Maybe he was dreaming of his war in the Pacific, of the cyber mines he'd swept, nosing gently into their circuitry with the Squid he'd used to pick Ralfi's pathetic password from the chip buried in my head.

"I can see them slipping up when he was demobbed, letting him out of the navy with that gear intact, but how does a cybernetic dolphin get wired to smack?"

"The war," she said. "They all were. Navy did it. How else you get 'em working for you?"

"I'm not sure this profiles as good business," the pirate said, angling for better money. "Target specs on a comsat that isn't in the book—"

"Waste my time and you won't profile at all," said Molly, leaning across his scarred plastic desk to prod him with her forefinger.

"So maybe you want to buy your microwaves somewhere else?" He was a tough kid, behind his Mao-job. A Nighttowner by birth, probably.

Her hand blurred down the front of his jacket, completely severing a lapel without even rumpling the fabric.

"So we got a deal or not?"

"Deal," he said, staring at his ruined lapel with what he must have hoped was only polite interest. "Deal."

While I checked the two recorders we'd bought, she extracted the slip of paper I'd given her from the zippered wrist pocket of her jacket. She unfolded it and read silently, moving her lips. She shrugged. "This is it?"

"Shoot," I said, punching the RECORD studs of the two decks simultaneously.

"Christian White," she recited, "and his Aryan Reggae Band."

Faithful Ralfi, a fan to his dying day.

Transition to idiot/savant mode is always less abrupt than I expect it to be. The pirate broadcaster's front was a failing travel agency in a pastel cube that boasted a desk, three chairs, and a faded poster of a Swiss orbital spa. A pair of toy birds with blown-glass bodies and tin legs were sipping monotonously from a Styrofoam cup of water on a ledge beside Molly's shoulder. As I phased into mode, they accelerated gradually until their Day-Glo-feathered crowns became solid arcs of color. The LEDs that told seconds on the plastic wall clock had become meaningless pulsing grids, and Molly and the Mao-faced boy grew hazy, their arms blurring occasionally in insect-quick ghosts of gesture. And then it all faded to cool gray static and an endless tone poem in an artificial language.

I sat and sang dead Ralfi's stolen program for three hours.

The mall runs forty kilometers from end to end, a ragged overlap of Fuller domes roofing what was once a suburban artery. If they turn off the arcs on a clear day, a gray approximation of sunlight filters through layers of acrylic, a view like the prison sketches of Giovanni Piranesi. The three southernmost kilometers roof Nighttown. Nighttown pays no taxes, no utilities. The neon arcs are dead, and the geodesics have been smoked black by decades of cooking fires. In the nearly total darkness of a Nighttown noon, who notices a few dozen mad children lost in the rafters?

We'd been climbing for two hours, up concrete stairs and steel ladders with perforated rungs, past abandoned gantries and dust-covered tools. We'd started in what looked like a disused maintenance yard, stacked with triangular roofing segments. Everything there had been covered with that same uniform layer of spraybomb graffiti: gang names, initials, dates back to the turn of the century. The graffiti followed us up, gradually thinning until a single name was repeated at intervals. LO TEK. In dripping black capitals.

"Who's Lo Tek?"

"Not us, boss." She climbed a shivering aluminum ladder and vanished through a hole in a sheet of corrugated plastic. " 'Low technique, low technology.' " The plastic muffled her voice. I followed her up, nursing my aching wrist. "Lo Teks, they'd think that shotgun trick of yours was effete."

An hour later I dragged myself up through another hole, this one sawed crookedly in a sagging sheet of plywood, and met my first Lo Tek.

" 'S okay," Molly said, her hand brushing my shoulder. "It's just Dog. Hey, Dog."

In the narrow beam of her taped flash, he regarded us with his one eye and slowly extruded a thick length of grayish tongue, licking huge canines. I wondered how they wrote off tooth-bud transplants from Dobermans as low technology. Immunosuppressives don't exactly grow on trees.

"Moll." Dental augmentation impeded his speech. A string of saliva dangled from his twisted lower lip. "Heard ya comin'. Long time." He might have been fifteen, but the fangs and a bright mosaic of scars combined with the gaping socket to present a mask of total bestiality. It had taken time and a certain kind of creativity to assemble that face, and his posture told me he enjoyed living behind it. He wore a pair of decaying jeans, black with grime and shiny along the creases. His chest and feet were bare. He did something with his mouth that approximated a grin. "Bein' followed, you."

Far off, down in Nighttown, a water vendor cried his trade.

"Strings jumping, Dog?" She swung her flash to the side, and I saw thin cords tied to eyebolts, cords that ran to the edge and vanished.

"Kill the fuckin' light!"

She snapped it off.

"How come the one who's followin' you's got no light?"

"Doesn't need it. That one's bad news, Dog. Your sentries give him a tumble, they'll come home in easy-to-carry sections."

"This a *friend* friend, Moll?" He sounded uneasy. I heard his feet shift on the worn plywood.

"No. But he's mine. And this one," slapping my shoulder, "he's a friend. Got that?"

"Sure," he said, without much enthusiasm, padding to the platform's edge, where the eyebolts were. He began to pluck out some kind of message on the taut cords.

Nighttown spread beneath us like a toy village for rats; tiny windows showed candlelight, with only a few harsh, bright squares lit by battery lanterns and carbide lamps. I imagined the old men at their endless games of dominoes, under warm, fat drops of water that fell from wet wash hung out on poles between the plywood shanties. Then I tried to imagine him climbing patiently up through the darkness in his zoris and ugly tourist shirt, bland and unhurried. How was he tracking us?

"Good," said Molly. "He smells us."

"Smoke?" Dog dragged a crumpled pack from his pocket and prized out a flattened cigarette. I squinted at the trademark while he lit it for me with a kitchen match. Yiheyuan filters. Beijing Cigarette Factory. I decided that the Lo Teks were black marketeers. Dog and Molly went back to their argument, which seemed to revolve around Molly's desire to use some particular piece of Lo Tek real estate.

"I've done you a lot of favors, man. I want that floor. And I want the music."

"You're not Lo Tek. . . ."

This must have been going on for the better part of a twisted kilometer, Dog leading us along swaying catwalks and up rope ladders. The Lo Teks leech their webs and huddling places to the city's fabric with thick gobs of epoxy and sleep above the abyss in mesh hammocks. Their country is so attenuated that in places it consists of little more than holds for hands and feet, sawed into geodesic struts.

The Killing Floor, she called it. Scrambling after her, my new Eddie Bax shoes slipping on worn metal and damp plywood, I wondered how it could be any more lethal than the rest of the territory. At the same time I sensed that Dog's protests were ritual and that she already expected to get whatever it was she wanted.

Somewhere beneath us, Jones would be circling his tank, feeling the first twinges of junk sickness. The police would be boring the Drome regulars with questions about Ralfi. What did he do? Who was he with before he stepped outside? And the Yakuza would be settling its ghostly bulk over the city's data banks, probing for faint images of me reflected in numbered accounts, securities transactions, bills for utilities. We're an information economy. They teach you that in school. What they don't tell you is that it's impossible to move, to live, to operate at any level without leaving traces, bits, seemingly meaningless fragments of personal information. Fragments that can be retrieved, amplified . . .

But by now the pirate would have shuttled our message into line for blackbox transmission to the Yakuza comsat. A simple message: Call off the dogs or we wideband your program.

The program. I had no idea what it contained. I still don't. I only sing the song, with zero comprehension. It was probably research data, the Yakuza being given to advanced forms of industrial espionage. A genteel business, stealing from Ono-Sendai as a matter of course and politely holding their data for ransom, threatening to blunt the conglomerate's research edge by making the product public.

But why couldn't any number play? Wouldn't they be happier with something to sell back to Ono-Sendai, happier than they'd be with one dead Johnny from Memory Lane?

Their program was on its way to an address in Sydney, to a place that held letters for clients and didn't ask questions once you'd paid a small retainer. Fourth-class surface mail. I'd erased most of the other copy and recorded our message in the resulting gap, leaving just enough of the program to identify it as the real thing.

My wrist hurt. I wanted to stop, to lie down, to sleep. I knew that I'd lose my grip and fall soon, knew that the sharp black shoes I'd bought for my evening as Eddie Bax would lose their purchase and carry me down to Nighttown. But he rose in my mind like a cheap religious hologram, glowing, the enlarged chip on his Hawaiian shirt looming like a reconnaissance shot of some doomed urban nucleus.

So I followed Dog and Molly through Lo Tek heaven, jury-rigged and jerry-built from scraps that even Nighttown didn't want.

The Killing Floor was eight meters on a side. A giant had threaded steel cable back and forth through a junkyard and drawn it all taut. It creaked when it moved, and it moved constantly, swaying and bucking as the gathering Lo Teks arranged themselves on the shelf of plywood surrounding it. The wood was silver with age, polished with long use and deeply etched with initials, threats, declarations of passion. This was suspended from a separate set of cables, which lost themselves in darkness beyond the raw white glare of the two ancient floods suspended above the Floor.

A girl with teeth like Dog's hit the Floor on all fours. Her breasts were tattooed with indigo spirals. Then she was across the Floor, laughing, grappling with a boy who was drinking dark liquid from a liter flask.

Lo Tek fashion ran to scars and tattoos. And teeth. The electricity they were tapping to light the Killing Floor seemed to be an exception to their overall aesthetic, made in the name of . . . ritual, sport, art? I didn't know, but I could see that the Floor was something special. It had the look of having been assembled over generations.

I held the useless shotgun under my jacket. Its hardness and heft were comforting, even though I had no more shells. And it came to me that I had no idea at all of what was really happening, or of what was supposed to happen. And that was the nature of my game, because I'd spent most of my life as a blind receptacle to be filled with other people's knowledge and then drained, spouting synthetic languages I'd never understand. A very technical boy. Sure.

And then I noticed just how quiet the Lo Teks had become.

He was there, at the edge of the light, taking in the Killing Floor and the gallery of silent Lo Teks with a tourist's calm. And as our eyes met for the first time with mutual recognition, a memory clicked into place for me, of Paris, and the long Mercedes electrics gliding through the rain to Notre Dame; mobile greenhouses, Japanese faces behind the glass, and a hundred Nikons rising in blind phototropism, flowers of steel and crystal. Behind his eyes, as they found me, those same shutters whirring.

I looked for Molly Millions, but she was gone.

The Lo Teks parted to let him step up onto the bench. He bowed, smiling, and stepped smoothly out of his sandals, leaving them side by side, perfectly aligned, and then he stepped down onto the Killing Floor. He came for me, across that shifting trampoline of scrap, as easily as any tourist padding across synthetic pile in any featureless hotel.

Molly hit the Floor, moving.

The Floor screamed.

It was miked and amplified, with pickups riding the four fat coil springs at the corners and contact mikes taped at random to rusting machine fragments. Somewhere the Lo Teks had an amp and a synthesizer, and now I made out the shapes of speakers overhead, above the cruel white floods.

A drumbeat began, electronic, like an amplified heart, steady as a metronome.

She'd removed her leather jacket and boots; her T-shirt was sleeveless, faint telltales of Chiba City circuitry traced along her thin arms. Her leather jeans gleamed under the floods. She began to dance.

She flexed her knees, white feet tensed on a flattened gas tank, and the Killing Floor began to heave in response. The sound it made was like a world ending, like the wires that hold heaven snapping and coiling across the sky.

He rode with it, for a few heartbeats, and then he moved, judging the movement of the Floor perfectly, like a man stepping from one flat stone to another in an ornamental garden.

He pulled the tip from his thumb with the grace of a man at ease with social gesture and flung it at her. Under the floods, the filament was a refracting thread of rainbow. She threw herself flat and rolled, jackknifing up as the molecule whipped past, steel claws snapping into the light in what must have been an automatic rictus of defense.

The drum pulse quickened, and she bounced with it, her dark hair wild around the blank silver lenses, her mouth thin, lips taut with concentration. The Killing Floor boomed and roared, and the Lo Teks were screaming their excitement.

He retracted the filament to a whirling meter-wide circle of ghostly polychrome and spun it in front of him, thumbless hand held level with his sternum. A shield.

And Molly seemed to let something go, something inside, and that was the real start of her mad-dog dance. She jumped, twisting, lunging sideways, landing with both feet on an alloy engine block wired directly to one of the coil springs. I cupped my hands over my ears and knelt in a vertigo of sound, thinking Floor and benches were on their way down, down to Nighttown, and I saw us tearing through the shanties, the wet wash, exploding on the tiles like rotten fruit. But the cables held, and the Killing Floor rose and fell like a crazy metal sea. And Molly danced on it.

And at the end, just before he made his final cast with the filament, I saw something in his face, an expression that didn't seem to belong there. It wasn't fear and it wasn't anger. I think it was disbelief, stunned incomprehension mingled with pure aesthetic revulsion at what he was seeing, hearing—at what was happening to him. He retracted the whirling filament, the ghost disk shrinking to the size of a dinner plate as he whipped his arm above his head and brought it down, the thumbtip curving out for Molly like a live thing.

The Floor carried her down, the molecule passing just above her head; the Floor whiplashed, lifting him into the path of the taut molecule. It should have passed harmlessly over his head and been withdrawn into its diamond-hard socket. It took his hand off just behind the wrist. There was a gap in the Floor in front of him, and he went through it like a diver, with a strange deliberate grace, a defeated kamikaze on his way down to Nighttown. Partly, I think, he took the dive to buy himself a few seconds of the dignity of silence. She'd killed him with culture shock.

The Lo Teks roared, but someone shut the amplifier off, and Molly rode the Killing Floor into silence, hanging on now, her face white and blank, until the pitching slowed and there was only a faint pinging of tortured metal and the grating of rust on rust.

We searched the Floor for the severed hand, but we never found it. All we found was a graceful curve in one piece of rusted steel, where the molecule went through. Its edge was bright as new chrome.

We never learned whether the Yakuza had accepted our terms, or even whether they got our message. As far as I know, their program is still waiting for Eddie Bax on a shelf in the back room of a gift shop on the third level of Sydney Central-5. Probably they sold the original back to Ono-Sendai months ago. But maybe they did get the pirate's broadcast, because nobody's come looking for me yet, and it's been nearly a year. If they do come, they'll have a long climb up through the dark, past Dog's sentries, and I don't look much like Eddie Bax these days. I let Molly take care of that, with a local anesthetic. And my new teeth have almost grown in.

I decided to stay up here. When I looked out across the Killing Floor, before he came, I saw how hollow I was. And I knew I was sick of being a bucket. So now I climb down and visit Jones, almost every night.

We're partners now, Jones and I, and Molly Millions, too. Molly handles our business in the Drome. Jones is still in Funland, but he has a bigger tank, with fresh seawater trucked in once a week. And he has his junk, when he needs it. He still talks to the kids with his frame of lights, but he talks to me on a new display unit in a shed that I rent there, a better unit than the one he used in the navy.

And we're all making good money, better money than I made before, because Jones's Squid can read the traces of anything that anyone ever stored in me, and he gives it to me on the display unit in languages I can understand. So we're learning a lot about all my former clients. And one day I'll have a surgeon dig all the silicon out of my amygdalae, and I'll live with my own memories and nobody else's, the way other people do. But not for a while.

In the meantime it's really okay up here, way up in the dark, smoking a Chinese filtertip and listening to the condensation that drips from the geodesics. Real quiet up here—unless a pair of Lo Teks decide to dance on the Killing Floor.

It's educational, too. With Jones to help me figure things out, I'm getting to be the most technical boy in town.

THINKING AND RE-READING

1. Some people find Gibson's work difficult to read because it makes reference to so many things that exist only in his own imagination—the social contexts, governments, organizations, drugs, and customs of the future. There are elements of his short stories, however, that are fairly traditional and can provide familiar compass points for navigation. As you re-read this piece, identify these familiar components of a short story: Who are the characters? What are their relationships? Their motivations? What is the plot of this story? What kinds of stories is it similar to? What is the setting of this story? What kind of a world does Gibson describe in this setting?

2. As you read this story, consider the kind of future world Gibson describes. What do you find appealing about this world? What do you find distasteful? Think about whether you agree or disagree with Gibson's projection of the future. What makes you think that he is accurate? Inaccurate?

WRITING AND LEARNING

1. Gibson's method of storytelling may be confusing to readers encountering his work for the first time. His style often involves fracturing the traditional plot and timelines that typically characterize stories, including partially explained references to situations, organizations, and social contexts that exist only in the future of his imagination, and using vocabulary that he makes up. In a written response designed to provide a set of crib notes for new readers of this work, write a summary of this story in your own words, in a more traditional form. Share this summary with the members of your writing group and determine where you agree or disagree about the story in terms of your summaries. Where you disagree, go back to the text of the story to see if you can find evidence that resolves the disagreement. Then, revise your own individual summaries to include this information. In considering the format that your response will take, you might want to go to your local commercial bookstore and look for a set of *Cliff Notes* that provides a summary of some other fictional work that you have read. These notes should give you a good idea of the sort of summary that would be useful to a new reader of Gibson's works.

2. Create a glossary of terms that will help other readers interpret this story. To accomplish this, make a list of the important vocabulary words in this story that you didn't understand on your first reading. Include words such as Drome, biz, Squids, and neural disrupter. Next, read the story a second or third time and define as many of these terms as you can, in your own words. Your purpose in this assignment is to provide a reading aid for other students who are approaching this story for the first time.

3. Some people consider Gibson's portrayal of future worlds to be extremely convincing because it is based on a realistic extrapolation of current events. In a written response designed to sharpen your own powers of critical and careful reading, identify those current events and trends that Gibson uses to extrapolate the future in "Johnny Mnemonic." In your response, identify specific links between events and trends happening in our time and events and trends described in Gibson's story. You are writing for your own enlightenment in this assignment.

EXTENDED WRITING ACTIVITIES

BUILDING ON WRITING AND LEARNING

SAC   Writing and learning activities that can be done on a stand-alone computer with access to word processing software.

LAN   Writing and learning activities that can be done on a local area network with access to synchronous or asynchronous conferencing software.

WAN   Writing and learning activities that can be done on a wide-area network, like the Internet, with access to Netscape or Gopher software.

ASSIGNMENT 1: DESIGNING AN INTERFACE

A computer interface is the image/words/environment that you see when you turn on a computer or boot up a piece of software. A primary interface is the first environment that you see when you turn on the computer—often called the operating system—before you start any specific piece of software. Today, two of the most common primary interfaces on personal computers are built around metaphors—*windows* and *desktop*. Both of these environments contain icons (familiar pictures) of file folders, documents, telephones, fax machines, and so on.

One of the interesting features that people have noticed about computer interfaces is that they are *maps* of our cultural values, as well as environments for computing. Like maps, interfaces seem to be particular representations, pictures designed to tell some popular cultural story (or set of stories) about computer technology (generally the most commonly accepted story), but that also necessarily ignore other stories (generally, the less popular ones).

The desktop environment on the Macintosh computer, for example, is a map that tells the social story of computers as machines that were developed and continue to operate primarily within a business or corporate world—all of the images on this desktop are those we associate with business environments. As you know, however, this story is an incomplete one—computers are also used increasingly at home, for leisure, self-instruction, entertainment, and communication among individuals. All primary interfaces in this country also map the story of a culture that speaks English as the "default" language, or the language of choice for individuals. This story is also incomplete because it doesn't represent, for example, the millions of Americans who speak Spanish (approximately 22 million, roughly 10 percent of the population), French (approximately 2 million), German (approximately 1.5 million), or Chinese (approximately 1.3 million) as their first language.

Your assignment is to design two new interfaces that map different cultural stories. For the first new interface that you design, create the map of a space that might be more appropriate to your own life. This space might be based on representations of a kitchen countertop, a mechanic's workbench, a garage, an apartment house, a theater stage, your own room—or any other location that seems comfortable and familiar to you. For the second new interface, map a space that might be more appropriate to someone you know who is under ten years of age. In both interfaces, you are to include icons that are appropriate to the story you are telling with that particular representation or map.

You can design your new interface in any graphic medium—with a drawing program on a computer, with crayons or colored pencils, or with a pen—whatever allows you to create a detailed representation. You can use any language for these interfaces.

In a written response that accompanies each of these new interfaces, explain the cultural story that it represents and try to get at the social implications of this story: How might the story, or the map, change the ways in which you might look at and understand computers? Use computers? Who might this story appeal to? Who might find it useful and familiar? Who might find it strange? Why? **(SAC)**

OPTIONAL ASSIGNMENT

As a class, collect the five or so best interfaces that individuals come up with. Compose a letter to the CEO of IBM or Apple Corporation or to some real third-party software company (such as Microsoft) that explains these efforts and why they are important for major computer hardware/software companies to consider. Try to convince the executive to consider pursuing these alternative interfaces as marketing options. You will need to do a bit of library research to find out the name and the address of the CEOs you want to contact. **(SAC)**

ASSIGNMENT 2: CULTURAL ASSUMPTIONS ABOUT THE INTERNET: A STUDENT'S VIEW

This assignment is designed to help you get at the cultural assumptions that people in your generation have about the Internet, and to think about these assumptions in the context of the social issues we have identified within this section.

First, identify ten individuals, within three years of your own age, who are willing to be interviewed about the Internet or the World Wide Web. These individuals must use the Internet or the World Wide Web on an occasional or frequent basis. Ask these individuals to answer the questions in the following survey. You might want to provide this survey online so that your interviewees can fill it out electronically.

When you have collected all of the completed questionnaires, analyze the answers that you receive to identify interesting patterns and trends that connect with the social issues you have read about in this section. Use whatever methods of analysis are useful to reveal patterns and trends in the data—for example, counting, averaging, summarizing, comparing, figuring percentages.

Your goal is to identify patterns and trends that seem most interesting to you *within the context of the social issues that you have read about in this section* and in this collection as a whole. When you have completed your analysis, write an article suitable for publication in a computer-oriented magazine such as *Wired* that identifies the commonly held assumptions about the Internet or the World Wide Web identified by the students you interviewed. The title of this article should be something like "How the Campus Sees Cyberspace: Students Talk About the Internet as a Social Space." In this article, discuss the relationship between computer experience (in both family and educational background), assumptions about the Internet or the Web, and students' understanding of the social space of the Internet or the Web. You will want to quote from the survey answers you have received, but be sure to use pseudonyms to protect the confidentiality of interviewees and to follow the guidelines for citation contained in your grammar handbook. You will also want to read some of the articles in this collection that were originally published in *Wired* to get a sense of that publication's tone and focus. Among these articles are "We're Teen, We're Queer, and We've Got E-Mail" by Steve Silberman in this section, and "Direct Democracy," by Evan I. Schwartz, in the section focusing on the government and technology.

In the article you write, also make sure to discuss the larger cultural implications of the assumptions that students hold. Among the questions that you may want to ask yourself on this topic are the following: How might the assumptions that students hold change the ways in which they act on the Internet or the Web? Understand what happens on the Internet or the Web? Understand other people's attitudes toward computers and the Internet or the Web? How do they feel about the social issues associated with the Internet or the Web? Think about the official campus policies toward Internet use at your school? React to official government policies enacted to establish the Internet in our country? Spend money on technology in their private lives? Raise their own children to think about technology? **(SAC** or **LAN)**

ALTERNATIVE ASSIGNMENT

Pool the answers to your survey interviews with those of the other members of your writing group. Write a group article as your final product. **(SAC** or **LAN)**

Internet Survey

Name:_____

Age: _____

Background Information   (Circle one choice for each question or fill in the appropriate blank):

I use computers	seldom	occasionally	frequently
I consider myself a	novice user	occasional user	expert user
Members of my family use computers	seldom	occasionally	frequently
Family members are generally	novice users	users with some experience	expert users
My family	does *not* own a computer	owns a computer	owns more than one computer
Members of my family use the Internet or the World Wide Web	seldom	occasionally	frequently

Members of my family use the Internet or the World Wide Web for the following purposes:

_____

_____

At my high school, we used computers   seldom   occasionally   frequently
Students at my high school use the Internet   seldom   occasionally   frequently
At my high school, we used computers regularly in the following kinds of courses:

_____

At my high school, we used computers regularly for the following purposes:

_____

What are the advantages of the Internet or the World Wide Web in our society?
What are the disadvantages of the Internet or the World Wide Web in our society?
What social values characterize the Internet or the World Wide Web?
What kinds of activities or behaviors are generally encouraged on the Internet or the World Wide Web?
What kinds of activities or behaviors are generally discouraged on the Internet or the World Wide Web?
How would you characterize human communication on the Internet or the World Wide Web?
How do you like to use the Internet or the World Wide Web? How do you use it most frequently?
What do you dislike about the Internet or the World Wide Web? What do you avoid in connection with Internet or the World Wide Web use?

I give my permission for _____ to use the information I have provided on this survey for academic purposes only and for this assignment only.

I understand that the investigator is responsible for keeping my name in the strictest possible confidence. I give permission for the investigator to quote from my answers on this survey, but only with the understanding that a pseudonym will be used to protect the absolute confidence and the anonymity of my replies.

Signed: _____

Date: _____

ASSIGNMENT 3: ELECTRONIC TECHNOLOGIES AND THEIR IMPACTS ON HUMAN LIVES

The purpose of this assignment is to encourage you to study the impacts of electronic technologies on your life, and to speculate on how such technologies alter the ways in which you live, interact with others, and experience your environment. It will help you test the "social saturation" theory of Kenneth Gergen, comparing his perceptions to the realities of your own life.

To accomplish this assessment, you will first identify what life is like *without* direct contact with electronic technologies. Thus, for twenty-four hours, live your life as much as possible without contact with—or, at least, direct support from—electronic technologies. (Do not complete this assignment if you are dependent on electronic technologies for health reasons—and do not jeopardize anyone else's health in trying to accomplish it.)

Given that such technologies are now so ubiquitous, this assignment will be difficult; indeed, it will be impossible to avoid all contact with technologies. (After all, toothbrushes are a technology, as are pens, pencils, mirrors, skis, door knobs, and concrete buildings.) However, the more thought you give to planning your day without *electronic* technologies, the more fully you'll be able to appreciate the effects of their absence. For example, you will want to choose a day during which you do not have to go to class or attend any important meetings. You will also want to plan your day so that you stay away from electronic alarm clocks, electronic lighting systems, television sets, air conditioning systems, microwave ovens, computers, calculators, photocopy machines, video games, telephones, concerts with electronically enhanced music, cars with electronic parts—and all other technologies based on components that use electricity as a power source.

During these twenty-four hours, keep a diary of those things you avoided, those familiar activities you missed or changed, and your observations about what life is like without electronic technologies. At the end of this period of time, write a letter to Kenneth Gergen describing the effects that electronic technologies have on your life—drawing on the time you spent away from these devices for examples and support.

In your letter, discuss with Gergen whether his description of the "saturated self"—a self bombarded with millions of electronically generated images, beset by intensified electronic relationships, distracted and driven by the multiplied demands of a technologically enhanced society, marked by the multiple and contradictory identities that grow out of a media-rich environment—seems to hold true in your life.

ASSIGNMENT 4: MAPPING CYBERSPACE

Maps are never absolutely impartial or wholly accurate representations of spaces, landscapes, or places—as Denis Wood points out to us in his 1992 book, *The Power of Maps*. Instead, maps reveal the individual vision of a mapmaker and the values of the culture from which that mapmaker comes. For example, world maps made by mapmakers from the United States often place North and South America at the center of the map, with the continents of Europe and Africa on the right, and those of Asia and Australia on the left. When global maps are made by mapmakers in Asia, however, that continent assumes the central position in the representation of the map. In addition, every mapmaker chooses to show some things and chooses to leave out other things—a topographical map, for example, often leaves out architectural structures and focuses on natural elevations and features of landscape. In fact, maps can be considered a technology themselves—a system or collection of social effects that mediates the world in systematic ways. Examining maps as artifacts of a particular culture can reveal interesting information about social values and about the mapmakers themselves.

This assignment is designed to have you examine the maps of cyberspace provided by either Gopher, Netscape, or Mosaic. Your task is to explore cyberspace using one of these three tools and then to discuss how the particular tool represents the landscape. Among the questions you will want to ask and address are the following:

- How is cyberspace mapped by these tools—what is the systematic view of the landscape that this tool provides? Why has this view been chosen? What does it highlight? What does it ignore?
- What schemes or systems have been borrowed from the "real world" to represent the cyberworld? Why were these particular schemes chosen?
- What kinds of landmarks are represented prominently or centrally within this space? Why? What landmarks are less visible or marginally visible? Why?

- How does this map affect navigation paths in cyberspace? Why? How does it affect the routes that you choose to take? The routes you avoid? Why?
- What action activities does this map make easy? Why? What does it make difficult? Why?
- What social values does this map reveal? What kinds of cultural values does it display? (WAN)

ALTERNATIVE ASSIGNMENT

Examine and analyze the map of your own personal computer's desktop to determine what this artifact says about you as a person, your values, and the culture within which you operate. Among the questions that you might want to address are the following: What are the primary landmarks on your computer's desktop? What are the less important landmarks? How are these landmarks arranged—in what relationship or order? Why? What values does this arrangement, these relationships, imply? What is highlighted by the arrangement, the relationships? What is hidden? Why? (SAC)

PART II

EDUCATION AND TECHNOLOGY

INTRODUCTION

... [T]raditions of pedagogy ... derive from another time, another interpretation of culture, another conception of authority— one that looked at the process of education as a transmission of knowledge and values by those who knew more to those who knew less and knew it less expertly.

Jerome Bruner (122)

ALTHOUGH computers can be found in great numbers at every academic level in American schools, a great deal of controversy continues to accompany their entry into educational settings. On the one hand, they're greeted as revolutionary tools that will cure the ills of American education; and, on the other, they are viewed as expensive instructional delivery systems that have the potential to destroy the human element in education. Clearly both views are extreme.

Our goal for this section is to help you think critically and productively about American schools and the new information technologies. As you read, we hope that you will question, as Bruner does in the epigraph, whether the fit between traditional ways of teaching and computer technology is a good one. As you respond to the selections, we ask that you think carefully about ways in which computer technology can enhance learning and improve the quality of school life. But, at the same time, we ask also that you be wary of the hyperbole that often accompanies the new technologies—that you view computers as cultural artifacts with the potential to support both ineffective and effective ways of teaching and learning. It is your task to develop a critical vision that will enable student-centered rather than teacher-centered curricula and that will encourage the increased participation of all students regardless of color, class, sex, or handicap.

In this section, more than thirteen authors present their views on the relationship between computers and schooling. For our purposes here, "schooling" refers to organized educational activities aimed at fostering intellectual curiosity and critical inquiry. As you read through the selections, you will encounter each author's own perspective on what makes for good schooling. The first three authors, all from the corporate world, discuss the promise of computer technology for educational contexts. Paul Strassmann gives us a historical perspective, whereas both John Sculley and Alan Kay discuss more recent school projects and the types of educational software that they find most promising. None of the three discusses the potential of computers as communication tools, an omission that we think noteworthy. When educators discovered that computers could connect people, rather than only machines, the need for such developments as artificial intelligence and "intelligent computers" became far less pressing. With the advent of computer-mediated communication, students and instructors became able to learn from one another online in ways that were simply not possible before computer technology.

The next two articles in this section are by educators Michael Apple from the University of Wisconsin and David Gelernter from Yale University. Both critique the educational uses of computers, but you will see that their perspectives on schooling and their goals for education are decidedly different.

On the World Wide Web, you will find Douglas Noble's important argument linking the development of educational technology with the military establishment. To let you be the judge as to whether these connections exist and, if they do, to decide what difference they might make to the education of young people, we then present an excerpt from the U.S. Office of Technology Assessment's *Power On!* The excerpt demonstrates the kinds of research various schools and organizations were engaged in before 1988 and lists the funding sources for the research as well.

Rounding out our consideration of some of the controversial issues on the use of computers in schools is Emily Jessup's piece on gender inequities in relation to technology and Barbara Kantrowitz's *Newsweek* essay on the "information gap." Although Jessup's chapter is an academic piece of writing and Kantrowitz's a short essay from the popular press, both make strong cases for the need for equitable distribution of computers. Then, in "A Note from the Future," an anonymous author demonstrates convincingly that all is not equal in this new information age and asks the "Onerabl Acadmy of Computr Sianses" to meet her challenge. These selections should give you a good overview of a few of the many issues that we need to consider if we are to use computers intelligently in educational contexts.

The next four selections are designed to let you explore the potential of different kinds of computer technologies that are becoming increasingly popular on college campuses. David Bennahum provides a vivid picture of his experiences with MOOs, a real-time technology that has been banned at some colleges, whereas John Murphy describes a structured model for teaching with computer networks. (To complement these selections, we've included on the World Wide Web Honan's report of how one university chancellor lost his job over issues related to distance learning and the professoriate.) Following these pieces is Yam's short essay on how "virtual reality," a technology that in the early 1990s was still too costly for schools, can begin to be used in a college physics class.

The last contribution in this section is a fictional account of the place computers might occupy on campuses in the year 2000. We ask you to judge whether the authors of the selection, students themselves, were indeed visionaries when they wrote the piece in 1987 and to decide whether you agree with their vision for computers in education.

Together these pieces are intended to help you develop critical perspectives on technology and education, for without such perspectives it is likely that schools will continue to make costly educational expenditures for new electronic technologies with little assurance that they will abet learning.

Information Systems and Literacy

Paul A. Strassmann

PAUL STRASSMANN'S ESSAY first appeared in a collection titled *Literacy for Life*, which Richard Bailey and Robin Fosheim edited in 1983. In putting together the collection, the editors drew largely from a 1981 conference held in Ann Arbor, Michigan. In the preface, the editors state that "each author was invited to consider the future agenda for literacy with only one constraint: predictions were to be short-term, extending only to the end of the decade" (p. vii). As you read the essay, consider whether Strassmann's predictions have come to pass in our time.

When Strassmann wrote his essay, he was vice president of the Information Products Group at Xerox Corporation and in charge of strategic planning. His position with Xerox over the years had required him to work closely with computer technology while managing data center operations, telecommunications networks, and software development. Because his job was not that of an educator per se, his views are likely to differ from those who have spent their professional lives teaching. Yet Strassmann's professional position required him to think seriously about education and literacy and to look at directions in which the new technologies might lead us as a society. In this article, then, Strassmann places the new information technologies in a historical context and also speculates on the changing requirements of literacy for the upcoming workforce. His views should give you a good summary of how one visionary understood the impact of computers on literacy and education in the United States and the larger global community in the early 1980s.

In this essay, I discuss issues that are related to the interactive-computer medium and suggest how the spreading use of that medium may change some of our traditional concepts of literacy. I deal with four issues:

Progress in Communication

Period	Medium	Economic Organization	Civilization
1 million B.C.–10,000 B.C.	speech	tribal	hunting
10,000 B.C.–A.D. 1500	script	feudal	agriculture
A.D. 1500–A.D. 2000	print	national	industrial
A.D. 2000–	electronic message	universal	information

1. How our ideas concerning the spoken and written language will be influenced as we move from the print medium toward the electronic medium;
2. How the role of the English language may change as the role of electronic communications increases on a global scale;
3. What kind of education we should give our young people now to prepare them for the careers they will follow between 1985 and 2040;
4. What kind of education is needed by educators themselves to help students cope with the electronic culture.

Although literacy has many possible meanings, I prefer a definition that is broad in scope: "the ability of individuals to cope with communications within their civilization." This general definition implies that literacy is a cultural phenomenon dependent on the environment. To illustrate this important point, I will review what literacy has meant at various stages of human development.

With the evolution of human society, the communications medium has changed, and, as a result, the focus of literacy has changed. We must understand that human society is now at the edge of a discontinuity, the end of the Gutenbergian era and the beginning of the "electronic display" era. As we enter this new stage of historical development, we can expect the form and content of our communications to change. Today's ideas are firmly rooted in an industrial civilization defined by national economic interests, and our concepts of literacy are shaped largely by our dependency on printing technology. With the increasing use of new technologies, our concepts of literacy are bound to change.

The likelihood of this impending transition is supported by an examination of trends in the historical patterns of employment. Observing the distribution of the U.S. work force over a period of one hundred years, we see radical changes in the way people earn their livelihood. Since the 1950s our country has become predominantly occupied with the creation, distribution, and administration of information. By 1990, only about fifty percent of the work force will be manufacturing objects and producing food. The rest will occupy most of the time just communicating. From an economic standpoint it is important to be concerned about the effectiveness with which all these people carry out their tasks. Literacy is therefore a special concern since it is one of the underlying capabilities that enable our economy to function effectively.

On a labor-time-weighted basis, we may estimate that in 1980, workplace communications were distributed approximately as follows:

Verbal communications	50% (including telephone)
Written communications	35%
Electronic communications	15% (via computer)

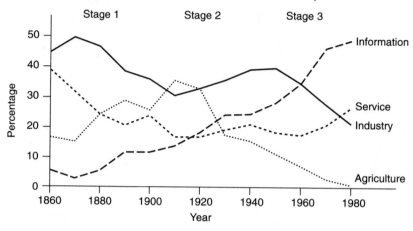

Four-sector aggregation of the U.S. work force by percent

These shares are bound to change. The workplace forecast for 1990 is based on fifty-five million people in "information employment" jobs. The salaries and benefits of these individuals may absorb sixty-five to seventy percent of the total labor value added. Because the labor cost per capita will be so high, there will be a great incentive to increase the output of employees by equipping them with communications-enhancing technology. I believe that about half of the information work force will be equipped with "electronic workstations," an electronic medium through which at least half of their communication will take place. The young people now in schools will have to operate in a work environment dominated by electronics. Will they be adequately equipped to perform well in this environment?

U.S. Office Automation Profile

	1990
Information Employment	55 million
Labor Cost	$2,500 billion
Technology Cost	$480–600 billion
Labor Cost per Capita	$45,500
Technology Cost per Capita	$8,700–10,900
Technology/Labor Ratio	18–22%
Workstations	20–30 million

A few historical examples help to illustrate the problems of literacy at various stages of development.

Literacy in tribal cultures was dominated by the oral medium. Language was poor in form and in content, and communications were limited to tribal concerns. Although script did not exist, there were memory aids to assist in the telling of the tales that represented accumulated human experience, and only a few selected individuals were trusted with handing down oral traditions. This specialization meant that the only information that was retrievable—even to the most literate members of the culture—was that which dealt with the essence of tribal existence: law, tradition, and religion.

If you carefully examine artifacts representing tribal communications—totem poles, notched sticks, Inca quipu, Indian ceremonial robes, and the like—you will be impressed by their graphic richness. By themselves, these graphics are meaningless. They come alive only when supported by a narrator. The feats of memory shown by these narrators were prodigious, and the oral tradition of these storytellers preserved the equivalent of many books for centuries.

The creation of a stable agricultural civilization led to the destruction of tribal forms. Successful agricultural states were based on the oral medium but employed a standardized language aided by syllabic script. The content of messages became increasingly concerned with property and with religion as a means of preserving the stability of society. This change called for standardization of verbal sounds in a geographically bounded feudal domain by means of syllabic notation. Even after the invention of the alphabet, the meaning of written messages remained ambiguous because spelling and vocabulary were not standardized. Each group of scribes created, recorded, and distributed texts in direct support of their limited tasks. The notation and legibility of texts were unimportant since all texts were read aloud and literacy remained the preserve of a few privileged members of society.

The advent of the industrial age coincided with the rise of the nation-state. To communicate in this environment, a much higher level of standardization of language sounds and of written language became necessary. Alphabetic symbols are now restricted in usage even though the phonetic sounds generated from texts still remain imprecise. Schools and information industries continue to concentrate their efforts on standardizing vocabulary, grammar, and syntax, and the role of the commercial printer has been highly significant in establishing and promoting this standardization. Industrial literacy demands universal knowledge of text creation and sophisticated reading skills, while it places decreasing value upon oral skills. Oral language has become too ambiguous to be relied upon for preserving and communicating complex information. As a result, records of legal, legislative, and scientific matters are now stored in writing only.

To illustrate the problems of language representation in the industrial age, let me point to the ambiguity in translating phonetic sounds into a limited set of alphabetic codes. The sound *sh*, for instance, is represented in English by eleven different letters or letter combinations: *sh*oe, *su*gar, *na*ti*on, o*ce*an, ma*chi*ne, mi*ssi*on, fa*ci*al, fa*sci*sm, lu*sci*ous, man*si*on, and luxury. The inability of the written language to represent adequately and unambiguously the spoken language limits its applicability to culturally unified national groups, and, consequently, literacy continues to be defined in a cultural context.

The cultural bias of written languages becomes ever more pronounced when we explore the meaning of words themselves. The ambiguity of words varies in different national languages. For instance, in English a simple sentence like the following can only be understood in a cultural context:

$$\text{Civilized}_{10} \text{ man}_8 \text{ can}_2 \text{ not}_1 \text{ live}_{14} \text{ without}_3 \text{ religion}_9$$

Individual words have a wide range of meaning as indicated by subscripts (e.g., the word "civilized" can be used in ten different meanings). Hence, industrial civilization continually struggles with the problems of meaning, content, ambiguity, and redundant communication. Vast bureaucracies and complex legal and procedural frameworks are constructed to eradicate or compensate for these inadequacies. At the same time, other members of society exploit ambiguity and redundancy in poetry and the arts.

As products of the industrial age enter global markets, there is an increasing need to organize communications on a global scale. Nationally based written languages fail to resolve the problem of ambiguity in meaning and content. Understanding messages without resorting to culture-specific contexts becomes a prerequisite for a global community where international division of labor is accepted. Now that commercial messages flow across national boundaries, we need to be able to understand them without the costly administrative burdens of export bureaucracies, translators, and flocks of lawyers.

The social and economic challenge of literacy in the future is to achieve global understanding and global communications. Therefore, the primary task of the electronic age is to standardize meaning and thus further our ability to deal with complexity in international relationships. The immediate, short-term task of the electronic age is to make possible communication among individuals in a peer group. Such a peer group would be initially defined by interests that include narrow areas of specialization (e.g., molecular biochemists), commercial interests (e.g., all international currency traders), or occupation (e.g., air-traffic controllers). Only after peer-group communications are improved can we hope to improve communication and enhance understanding among interdisciplinary specialists (e.g., product planners, health officers).

The principal means for achieving these objectives are already embedded in the electronic computer technologies that exist today. Voice recognition and speech synthesis permit translation between the digitally encoded medium and verbal expression. Artificial intelligence permits translation between the digitally encoded message and the language-specific context of the recipient.

The vehicle for establishing global literacy will very likely involve group authorship of text. The "group text" will be machine translated into a "carrier" language. The "carrier" language will represent an underlying message that will be machine translated in order to be understood by everyone, regardless of national or cultural context. The "group text" will be written in a language to which each member of the peer group will be able to contribute.

We already have several candidate "carrier" languages that have the attributes of clarity, lack of ambiguity, and simple representation. These languages operate on a scale far exceeding anything previously known and are most widely referred to by the generic name "software." Software, I believe, in its most general definition as an artificial language constructed for communications between human beings and computers, will become the "carrier" language of the future. The language itself—its content, syntax, and grammar—will also become the dominant intellectual asset and property of humankind. Thus, the understanding of software in its total context will be a primary component of literacy in the electronic age.

In what follows, I will explore the literacy requirements that apply to the world of commerce and to the language of the workplace. Private life will continue to use the rich heritage of the past, and the collective use of tribal, feudal, and national forms will continue to be essential. The new literacy should not be a substitute for the old; on the contrary, it should be a new layer on top of a solid understanding of the past.

Education for the electronic age will begin with the tools. Traditional forms of literacy require proficiency with technique—use of reeds for cuneiform script, brush calligraphy for Chinese ideograms, penmanship for script, and typing for printed text. The electronic age requires proficiency in dealing with computer terminals. Information networking is another tool of electronic literacy. In the same way that access to a library and the ability to locate information are essential for contemporary literacy, so familiarity with electronic networking is mandatory for anyone who wishes to participate in exchanging information on a global scale. Computer-aided graphics equipment is another tool of the electronic medium; charts, graphs, diagrams, and logical networks are essential elements in improved communication of messages.

The most important change arising from the electronic medium will be found in the messages it will convey. If we comprehend how the format and language of the older media influenced the vocabulary and the grammar of written messages, it should be easy for us to understand how a totally new medium can influence the language of the future.

The logic on which computer software is constructed can be found in the programming and systems coding that exist today. Almost all the dominant higher-level languages in the world are of English-language origin (e.g., FORTRAN, COBOL, APL). With minor exceptions, data-base definition languages are also of English origin. Most of the documentation in use throughout the world is available only in the original English versions.

Computer-coding languages have the unique attribute that their meaning, definition, and usage are precisely described. The software constructed by means of these codes can be checked for logical consistency and completeness. The procedural and logical message of software is therefore uniquely suited for conveying information that is culturally independent. As a result, computer languages meet the criterion of universality, but their structures are alien and incomprehensible in the traditional sense of literacy.

We need another discipline—presently known in computer science as artificial intelligence—as the intermediary between a culturally comprehending human being and the mathematically logical computer codes. There is now sufficient evidence that artificial intelligence has developed a capability to "understand" ambiguous language and generate intelligible human sentences from logical constructs based on mathematical notation. Great advances also have been made in "problem-definition languages." It is a uniquely human attribute to be able to structure a question and elicit a response. If electronic networks are to serve human needs on a global scale, they must be capable of acting as an intermediary between people who perceive problems in culturally different ways. I see this class of problem-definition languages as a major advance in facilitating computer-aided understanding.

The great power of graphic languages enriches communications. Except for the use of graphics to illustrate a text, existing research almost totally ignores graphics as a way of enhancing understanding of written messages. The new computer medium makes it easy to use graphic means to improve understanding. The electronic medium can also be used as an auxiliary extension of the human mind to scan large volumes of text, data, or pictures. Human beings can now be endowed with vastly enlarged capabilities to deal with massive amounts of data as a way of finding valuable information.

In summary, the future electronic message has completely different attributes from the messages we now routinely send and receive. The ability of our intellectuals to deal with these new experiences will determine whether or not they are literate. Completely new skills are needed to cope with an environment that is rich in electronic messages.

To prepare for the future, our educators must pioneer our understanding of the workplace in which students will operate when they enter careers. Therefore, educating the educators becomes a matter of highest priority. To be effective, educators of electronically literate students need to become proficient in handling text editors, in the use of personal microprocessors, in the ability to search data bases, in skills to address devices and services in complex networks, in the ability to select and connect to the global software marketplace, and in teleconferencing to permit interdisciplinary or international cooperation to create intellectual property on a cooperative basis.

I regard the following as the major challenges to teachers of electronic literacy:

- Recognizing that the electronic medium will be dominant in the workplace after year 2000.
- Equipping our young people to cope with the challenges of the new literacy.
- Teaching electronic medium and electronic message skills in the 1980s so that the class beginning in 1990 will not enter the work force electronically "illiterate."

The literacy of the future involves an augmentation of our past knowledge; it is not a rejection of essential oral, writing, and reading skills. The new electronic medium will most likely cause readjustment in the relative importance and usage of the existing media. What will ultimately matter will be the balanced capability of individuals to cope with the new world of global interdependence.

THINKING AND RE-READING

1. At the outset, Strassmann argues that "literacy is a cultural phenomenon dependent on the environment" and that the requirements for literacy change as societies change. As you re-read, take notes on the various abilities people need in different kinds of societies in order to be considered literate. Make a list of what you consider appropriate roles for teachers in the different societies. And also for students.

2. Strassmann goes on to state that the major "social and economic challenge of literacy" in the future will be to "achieve global understanding and global communications." This can best be done, according to Strassmann, by "standardizing meaning." What does Strassmann mean by this? How does he think such standardization can be achieved? With which claims of Strassmann's prognosis for the future requirements of literacy do you agree? Disagree? In Strassmann's view, what is the purpose of literacy? In other words, why should people become electronically literate?

WRITING AND LEARNING

1. In his essay on the politics of education, literacy scholar C. H. Knoblauch writes, "Literacy never stands alone . . . as a neutral denoting of skills; it is always literacy for something—for professional competence in a technological world, for civic responsibility and the preservation of heritage, for personal growth and self-fulfillment, for social and political change" (p. 76). In a written report prepared for a group of parents visiting your school, discuss how Strassmann's notions of literacy relate to Knoblauch's

statement. Give examples from the article to back up your claims. Be sure to explain to parents some of the differences in the requirements for literacy when they were in school as compared to those for your own generation.

2. Strassmann's article was written at a time when the schools were first adopting computers and when many of us first began using computers as writing tools. In terms of software and hardware development, times have changed radically since Strassmann wrote his essay. E-mail and other forms of computer-mediated communication were not available except to a relatively small group of technology experts who worked with computers on a daily basis. As you consider the changes you see today compared to when Strassmann was writing, make three columns, lengthwise, either on paper or in a word processing file. In the first column, list those observations Strassmann makes that you think are appropriate in today's world; in the second column, list those with which you would disagree. In the third, list changes that have occurred that Strassmann was unable to anticipate. Using your notes, write a response to Strassmann in which you discuss how your revision of his thinking affects our notions of literacy today. What kinds of educational reforms would you recommend based on the unanticipated changes you note?

3. Choose one claim from the article with which you disagree. Explain to the same group of parents why you disagree and use examples from your own life or from the lives of individuals you know to support your contentions. Be sure to write why this disagreement is an important one for you, focusing on either the personal or public implications of the claim, or both if they are related.

Works Cited

Knoblauch, C. H. "Literacy and the Politics of Education." *The Right to Literacy*. Ed. Andrea A. Lunsford, Helene Moglen, and James Slevin. New York: MLA, 1990, 74–80.

The Relationship Between Business and Higher Education: A Perspective on the 21st Century

John Sculley

AS MIGHT BE EXPECTED, John Sculley, the former CEO of Apple Computer, is also interested in the intersection between computers and education, in this case higher education. In his article, first published in 1989 by the Association of Computing Machinery, Sculley argues that as we move toward the twenty-first century three electronic technologies are essential for new learning environments: hypermedia, simulation, and artificial intelligence. In presenting what he calls a "new paradigm for lifelong learning," Sculley outlines educational priorities that many of you will recognize in your own experience with schooling. He also presents an example of a particular kind of software, or courseware, that begins to assimilate the three. He ends his piece with the observation that in the twenty-first century there is the possibility of creating a second Renaissance heralded by the new technologies.

We are privileged to live during an extraordinary time. It is the turning of an era. The world is in passage from the industrial age to the information age. This is a time of profound changes, in which the key economic resources in the world will no longer be capital, labor, and raw materials, but rather knowledge, individual innovators, and information.

Technologies which are emerging today will give us the ability to explore, convey, and create knowledge as never before. This has enormous implications for us as individuals, as well as for our institutions. Our colleges and universities will take on especially heavy responsibilities as we make this transition.

We have an opportunity that is given only to few generations in history. I believe that if we respond with our best creative energies, we can unleash a new Renaissance of discovery and learning.

In our global economy, we are moving from a hierarchical order to one of interdependence. Not long ago the United States stood unchallenged at the top of the world's economic hierarchy. Drawing on the consuming power of an affluent population, this country built a strong industrial base. Our manufacturing companies added value to natural resources through technological know-how. Economies of scale favored the development of large, highly structured institutions.

Today, however, we are not at the top of a pyramid, but rather one node along a network. Our once exclusive know-how is available in many newly industrialized nations, such as Korea, Taiwan, Singapore, Mexico, and Brazil. What is at risk, as the United States loses economic primacy, is not simply our own standard of living, but also the health of the world economy. The global economic system functions like a biological ecosystem. An unbalance in one sector can affect the whole.

A good analogy can be found in the shrinking rain forests of Brazil. Eighty percent of the world's oxygen comes from the Brazilian rain forest. Yet we lose every year, through the cutting of trees and the clearing of land, a land mass the size of the state of Nebraska. If we keep doing that long enough, the decreasing amount of oxygen in the atmosphere will alter the entire ecosystem of the planet.

The United States participates in the world economy not simply as a producer, but also as a marketplace. If our population loses the ability to afford our own products, it also will not afford Japanese automobiles, electronics from the Pacific Rim countries, and so forth. And that would have a tremendous impact on the macroeconomic ecosystem of the world.

Yet it is clear that as a nation, we are living beyond our means. We are no longer creating enough value to sustain our lifestyle, we are falling deeper into debt. There is a compelling need to find new ways to continue to create value in the world.

I believe that in order to do that our businesses and universities must be designed to foster innovation. Yet innovation has never come through bureaucracy and hierarchy. It has always come from individuals.

There is a dangerous timelag built into even the most successful institutions. They are created at one time in response to some particular opportunity in a given historical context. And then as the context shifts, the institution finds itself carrying excess baggage that is no longer useful.

How will the organizations designed to thrive in the 19th and early 20th centuries learn to contribute to the 21st? Only by reinventing themselves through refocusing on *individuals*.

The key strength of 21st-century organizations will be not their size or structure, but their ability to simultaneously unleash and coordinate the creative contributions of many individuals. Unleashing and coordinating may sound like contradictory actions—and in older models they would be—but we must develop new patterns of organization that promote alignment and collaboration while avoiding rigidity and stagnation.

A LIFETIME OF LEARNING

Communication in the new organization will be more fluid, action more spontaneous. Think of the speed and agility of basketball versus the massed force of football. Think of a jazz combo trading solos, versus a marching bank in lock step. The individuals who will succeed as contributors in these new organizations also need to change. In fact, change will be the one constant in their careers.

Over-specialization and a limited perspective can be a dead-end trap. Students today cannot count on finding one smooth career path because jobs that exist today will change radically (by the millions) tomorrow. Individuals will need to have tremendous flexibility to be able to move from one company to another, or from one industry to another. Those who are best prepared to do that will be the most successful.

We used to talk of "taking a position with the firm." Those are revealing words: *position* and *firm* belong to a static model of rigid hierarchy. If you are only going to take one position, you can get by on only one point of view. In the information age, however, a diverse educational experience will be the critical foundation for success. What tomorrow's student will need is not just mastery of subject matter, but mastery of *learning*. Education will be not simply a prelude to a career, but a lifelong endeavor.

Let me list some of the requirements of this new paradigm for lifelong learning:

- It should require rigorous mastery of subject matter under expert guidance.
- It should hone the conceptual skills that wrest meaning from data.
- It should promote a healthy skepticism that tests reality against multiple points of view.
- It should nourish individual creativity and encourage exploration.
- It should support collaboration.
- It should reward clear communication.
- It should provoke a journey of discovery.
- And above all it should be energized by the opportunity to contribute to the total of what we know and what we can do.

Higher education has traditionally defined itself in terms of two missions: instruction and research. In the past, these have been seen as very different activities. Research, which is primarily the domain of faculty and graduate students, is the process whereby we increase the world's store of knowledge. Instruction, which involves all students, is the process whereby we transfer some subset of that knowledge to *individuals.*

But, as we have seen, it is no longer enough simply to transfer knowledge to students. It is not as though we can give young people a ration of knowledge that they can draw on throughout their careers. Instead, we need to give them *access* to the unbounded world of knowledge. That means we must prepare all students, not just professional scholars, to embark on a lifetime of learning and discovery. Which means that our students will not simply be passively absorbing subject matter . . . but be more like researchers actively exploring their environment.

To work in research is to recognize that knowledge does not reside privately in individual minds, or text books, or journals, or libraries, or laboratories, or databases. Knowledge resides in a complex web that encompasses all of these. To work in research is to recognize that knowledge is not static. Everyone in the research community shares the responsibility to test our knowledge and to enlarge it.

The challenge for higher education will be to find ways of bringing to the process of instruction the passion for discovery that drives research. Students today should master the skills and tools of research as part of their basic education. To give our students this mastery, we must create a learning environment in which research and instruction are integrated.

I believe we all can make important contributions to that process. If we succeed we will have found new ways of empowering individuals—not in isolation from each other, but with pathways for rich communication and effective collaboration.

A LESSON IN HISTORY

The transformation I am calling for—shifting focus from the institution to the individual—has a close parallel in history. In medieval Europe people were subservient to the institutions of the church and feudal hierarchies.

Then came the Renaissance, which redefined the individual as the epicenter of intellectual activity. It did more than change people's perspective of the world, it literally invented perspective. The medieval painter depicted great religious events with the most important figures appearing the largest. Composition reflected ideology. Then drawing styles changed. The Renaissance artist drew figures and buildings in perspective, the way they appeared to an individual observer. For the first time, point-of-view came into the world.

The many forces which converged to bring about the Renaissance galvanized around one key technology: printing. The rise of printing led with astonishing speed to an explosion of literacy. The result was a new self-esteem for the individual. A wealth of invention.

An excitement of the power of wonderful ideas. Today, we are in need of a second Renaissance, which like the first can also be galvanized by technology.

We are on the verge of creating new tools which, like the press, will empower individuals, unlock worlds of knowledge, and forge a new community of ideas. These core technologies and the tools they support will help create a new environment of lifetime learning.

We believe the tools that show the most promise for the new learning environment build on three core technologies: hypermedia, simulation, and artificial intelligence. Each of these technologies alone can enrich the educational process. Each gains additional strength when learners can share resources over networks. And when these technologies are fully integrated with each other, they will fuel a 21st-century Renaissance—an outpouring of new learning and achievement.

TECHNOLOGICAL TOOLS

Hypermedia is a new word for many of us. Yet this term and its definition will become increasingly important the more we rely on personal computers to store, manage and retrieve information.

In broad terms, hypermedia is the delivery of information in forms that go beyond traditional list management and database report methods. More specifically, it means that you do not have to follow a predetermined organization for information. Instead you can make instant choices about where to go next. What this means for instruction and research is that content is not bound by particular choices of organization. Instead content and organization become complementary tools that act on each other to deepen our understanding of the world around us.

Hypermedia lets us use a type of cross-reference that can be used to span courses that present related material, like physiology or microbiology. It gives us the capability to explore deeper, linking one idea with another as the student or researcher pursues his own personal learning path.

In a sense, hypermedia is nothing new at all. A researcher using a card catalog and reference materials traditionally had the opportunity to pursue ideas according to insight and interest. Hypermedia does not change that process, it merely *accelerates* it.

It's a natural way of working, but until recently, personal computers were too limited to address it. Today, however, desktop computers can have more information on line than the largest mainframe managed 10 years ago. We are coming to expect high-capacity magnetic hard disks, optical media such as CD-ROM, and high-speed networks as standard in our installations.

Once we have experienced hypermedia, established methods of finding related pieces of information seem cumbersome. Hypermedia can also be seen as a new form of publishing. There are now readily available tools that enable faculty in any discipline to create richly branching presentations. The major obstacles still to be cleared are not technological, but social and economic.

We have not yet devised licensing procedures for the electronic formats of the textbook or journal abstracts.

We must all work together to address such issues as copyright and royalties, and access and security in the information age. Just as hypermedia offers a new paradigm for exploring vast amounts of information, the second core technology, simulation, pushes the boundaries of experimentation. Simulation takes us beyond the "what" to the "how and why." We move from a static picture to dynamic visualization—from limited experience to diverse, multiple experiences.

The excitement in educational simulations today comes from generalized programs which allow professors and students to design their own simulations in particular disciplines, simulations that permit virtually all dynamic phenomena to be modeled and visualized.

Just as the spreadsheet allowed us to ask "what if" questions about financial calculations, this new class of software allows those "what if" questions to act on a dynamic graphic system, whether in physics, chemistry, electronics, or economics.

Another new application of simulation is in the humanities and social sciences, not normally what you would think of as computer-intensive disciplines. At Stanford University, a toolkit built on HyperCard has been designed in deference to a traditionally nonprogramming group: the humanities and social sciences faculty. (See box.)

Using this toolkit, called ALIAS, professors or students in anthropology, history, or sociology can model a culture or period of history by entering their data into the toolkit. ALIAS will in turn create a HyperCard stack that allows students to play the role of an individual of that culture. It is an approach that combines simulation and hypermedia.

In fact, this very simulation has been developed by Stanford Professor Harumi Befu. It's called SHOGAI, which means *life course*. To Professor Befu, SHOGAI means a new territory for his anthropology students; one in which they can explore the richness of Japan's people, its customs, and events, by assuming the roles of characters profiled in the simulation.

Using this simulation, students can make some critical decisions about school, social activities and work that will collectively dictate the character's niche in Japanese society. The point is to understand how and why the choices they make for him will determine the career opportunities he will have and the social status he can achieve. As different choices are made, different results will unfold.

Simulation and hypermedia tools exist today. As they come into more widespread use we will find two things happening. First, authors and publishers will continue to enrich our libraries of linked subject matter. And second, developers will continue to make the underlying tools more powerful. We will have full, three-dimensional motion graphics, and stunning images on CD-ROM. But perhaps the most spectacular advance will not be in the presentation level, but will lie deeper in the programming.

SOONER THAN WE THINK

Just a short way into the future, we will see artificial intelligence (AI) emerge as a core technology. Combined with our core technologies, AI will boost simulations and hypermedia to new levels of realism and usefulness. For example, we will move from building molecules into two- and three-dimensional space, to building the environment in which they combined—where each molecule understands the structure and behavior of the other.

Another important contribution of AI will be intelligent agents that can learn a user's preferences and search strategies. These agents will transform the nature of academic computing. Agents will be sent to prowl among remote databases and bring back the specific information and citations that the user requires.

These future systems are not that far away. Soon, faculty and students will be using systems that enable them to drive through libraries, museums, databases or institutional archives. These tools will not just take you to the doorstep of these great resources, as sophisticated computers do now; they will invite you deep inside its secrets, interpreting and explaining—converting vast quantities of information into personalized and understandable knowledge.

In a (previous) keynote address, Dr. Herb Simon, professor of computer science and psychology at Carnegie Mellon, reminded, "We think of revolutions as being sudden events, producing far reaching changes in a very short period of time. But the revolution launched by the steam engine took, by any reasonable account, 150 years." Changes in computing have been like a whirlwind in the last 40 years. But I think we have only begun to see what innovation and creativity can produce in this industry.

The personal computer could become as galvanizing as the printing press in stimulating change in the world, in creating an environment for innovation and new ideas. Let us remember that the printing press never wrote a single book. Authors write books. So, too, with the new technologies that I have described. This will only be achieved if we work together—universities, corporations and government—and if we recognize the role of the creative individual within these organizations.

We all have a role in making this vision of the future a reality. The technologies I have talked about are only platforms that represent opportunities and possibilities. They are, however, the tallest of platforms, the richest of opportunities, and the broadest of possibilities that I know of.

They will allow us to set loose an avalanche of personal creativity and achievement. Once we have thousands of ideas to harvest, we may have the chance once again to create a second Renaissance, perhaps every bit as important as the first, in the early part of the next century. It would represent a rebirth and revival of learning and culture unleashed by new technologies. It would bridge the gaps between the arts and sciences. And it would signify the emergence of an integrated environment for instruction and research.

It is an exhilarating time to live. I cannot think of any other time in history in which such profound change has gripped each decade. It is destined to be an eventful journey to the 21st century. And there is no place that journey will be more exciting than in higher education.

THINKING AND RE-READING

1. As you re-read, take notes on how Sculley sees education as changing this coming century. What does he see as one of the more important changes that occurred in the historical period commonly referred to as the Renaissance? Why does he think that in the early twenty-first century "we can unleash a new Renaissance of discovery and learning"? Give examples that support his view from the reading and from your experience. What changes in learning does he see as characterizing what he calls the second or twenty-first century Renaissance?

2. The title of Sculley's article talks of "the relationship between business and higher education." List the changes he sees as occurring in business settings. How does his twenty-first-century notion of the "individual" differ from the "individual" he writes of as emerging in the original Renaissance?

3. In what ways do Strassmann and Sculley agree about the future priorities of education? Disagree? What educational activities might be appropriate today that were not possible when Strassmann or Sculley were writing their articles?

WRITING AND THINKING

1. Think back on your educational experiences in high school, and jot down the different ways in which computers were used in a variety of your classes. Imagine now that your high school is considering revamping its curriculum and has asked its alums for help in setting priorities. Choose one area of your high school education and write a letter to the administrators and teachers, suggesting changes to the curriculum based on Sculley's article and your own educational experiences. In your letter, describe one particular use of computers that you find particularly promising for students. What kinds of learning would this activity have that you and your classmates missed out on? Why is such learning important in your opinion? You might begin your letter by first praising or thanking your teachers for the activities and learning experiences they offered that you have come to value.

2. Set up an interview with a college professor or high school teacher whom you regard as being particularly knowledgeable about teaching with the new information technologies. Construct an interview based on Strassmann's, Sculley's, and your own views of the current priorities for education. Share these with another member of your class until both you and your classmate are satisfied with the questions you will ask. If it is acceptable to the person you are interviewing, tape-record the interview, all the while taking notes as well. Write up a report of the interview in which you compare your interviewee's thoughts about technology and education with those you've encountered in the readings, and share it with others in your class.

Computers, Networks and Education

Alan C. Kay

IN SEPTEMBER 1991, *Scientific American* featured several articles in a special issue titled "Communications, Computers and Networks: How to Work, Play and Thrive in CyberSpace." Included among the featured articles were selections devoted to issues surrounding networks and working lives of Americans similar to Sproull and Kiesler's piece in the first section of this volume. But there was also one article by Alan Kay aimed specifically at computers and their potential to bring about changes in schooling. We've selected that article for inclusion here. Four years later, a special issue of the magazine again featured Kay's article as one of "the best computer articles from the pages of *Scientific American* magazine—updated for 1995."

In this selection, "Computers, Networks and Education," Alan Kay turns to the schooling of younger children, because he believes that their thinking can be powerfully shaped in productive ways by the new media if they begin working with the technologies at an early age. In his piece Kay makes several basic criticisms about people's understanding of learning and of the ways in which society uses media. Ultimately, however, he believes that computers, while sharing the same shortcomings of other media, give educators an opportunity to construct richer contexts for learning. He provides several examples of effective and innovative school projects growing out of his and Ann Marion's work with the Open School in Los Angeles.

Alan Kay is certainly one of the century's leaders and visionaries in computing. He was a founder of Xerox Palo Alto Research, a chief scientist at Atari, and at the time he wrote this piece a fellow of Apple Computer, Inc. The article is aimed at educated readers who are interested in a wide range of issues associated with science, education, and the new technologies.

The physicist Murray Gell-Mann has remarked that education in the 20th century is like being taken to the world's greatest restaurant and being fed the menu. He meant that representations of ideas have replaced the ideas themselves; students are taught superficially about great discoveries instead of being helped to learn deeply for themselves.

In the near future, all the representations that human beings have invented will be instantly accessible anywhere in the world on intimate, notebook-size computers. But will we be able to get from the menu to the food? Or will we no longer understand the difference between the two? Worse, will we lose even the ability to read the menu and be satisfied just to recognize that it is one? There has always been confusion between carriers and contents. Pianists know that music is not in the piano. It begins inside human beings as special urges to communicate feelings. But many children are forced to "take piano" before their musical impulses develop; then they turn away from music for life. The piano at its best can only be an amplifier of existing feelings, bringing forth multiple notes in harmony and polyphony that the unaided voice cannot produce.

The computer is the greatest "piano" ever invented, for it is the master carrier of representations of every kind. Now there is a rush to have people, especially schoolchildren, "take computer." Computers can amplify yearnings in ways even more profound than can musical instruments. But if teachers do not nourish the romance of learning and expressing, any external mandate for a new "literacy" becomes as much a crushing burden as being forced to perform Beethoven's sonatas while having no sense of their beauty. Instant access to the world's information will probably have an effect opposite to what is hoped: students will become numb instead of enlightened.

In addition to the notion that the mere presence of computers will improve learning, several other misconceptions about learning often hinder modern education. Stronger ideas need to replace them before any teaching aid, be it a computer or pencil and paper, will be of most service. One misconception might be called the fluidic theory of education: students are empty vessels that must be given knowledge drop by drop from the full teacher-vessel. A related idea is that education is a bitter pill that can be made palatable only by sugarcoating—a view that misses the deep joy brought by learning itself.

Another mistaken view holds that humans, like other animals, have to make do only with nature's mental bricks, or innate ways of thinking, in the construction of our minds. Equally worrisome is the naive idea that reality is solely what the senses reveal. Finally, and perhaps most misguided, is the view that the mind is unitary, that it has a seamless "I"-ness.

Quite the contrary. Minds are far from unitary: they consist of a patchwork of different mentalities. Jerome S. Bruner of New York University has suggested that we have a number of ways to know and think about the world, including doing, seeing and manipulating symbols. What is more, each of us has to construct our own version of reality by main force, literally to make ourselves. And we are quite capable of devising new mental bricks, new ways of thinking, that can enormously expand the understandings we can attain. The bricks we develop become new technologies for thinking.

Many of the most valuable structures devised from our newer bricks may require considerable effort to acquire. Music, mathematics, science and human rights are just a few of the systems of thought that must be built up layer by layer and integrated. Although understanding or creating such constructions is difficult, the need for struggle should not be grounds for avoidance. Difficulty should be sought out, as a spur to delving more deeply into an interesting area. An educational system that tries to make everything easy and pleasurable will prevent much important learning from happening.

a savage state

It is also important to realize that many systems of thought, particularly those in science, are quite at odds with common sense. As the writer Susan Sontag once said, "All understanding begins with our not accepting the world as it appears." Most science, in fact, is quite literally non-sense. This idea became strikingly obvious when such instruments as the telescope and microscope revealed that the universe consists of much that is outside the reach of our naive reality.

Humans are predisposed by biology to live in the barbarism of the deep past. Only by an effort of will and through use of our invented representations can we bring ourselves into the present and peek into the future. Our educational systems must find ways to help children meet that challenge.

In the past few decades the task before children—before all of us—has become harder. Change has accelerated so rapidly that what one generation learns in childhood no longer applies 20 years later in adulthood. In other words, each generation must be able to quickly learn new paradigms, or ways of viewing the world; the old ways do not remain usable for long. Even scientists have problems making such transitions. As Thomas S. Kuhn notes dryly in *The Structure of Scientific Revolutions*, a paradigm shift takes about 25 years to occur—because the original defenders have to die off.

Much of the learning that will go on in the future will necessarily be concerned with complexity. On one hand, humans strive to make the complex more simple; categories in language and universal theories in science have emerged from such efforts. On the other hand, we also need to appreciate that many apparently simple situations are actually complex, and we have to be able to view situations in their larger contexts. For example, burning down parts of a rain forest might be the most obvious way to get arable land, but the environmental effects suggest that burning is not the best solution for humankind. *land being capable of being plowed*

Up to now, the contexts that give meaning and limitation to our various knowledges have been all but invisible. To make contexts visible, make them objects of discourse and make them explicitly reshapable and inventable are strong aspirations very much in harmony with the pressing needs and onrushing changes of our own time. It is therefore the duty of a well-conceived environment for learning to be contentious and even disturbing, seek contrasts rather than absolutes, aim for quality over quantity and acknowledge the need for will and effort. I do not think it goes too far to say that these requirements are at odds with the prevailing values in American life today.

If the music is not in the "piano," to what use should media be put, in the classroom and elsewhere? Part of the answer depends on knowing the pitfalls of existing media.

It is not what is in front of us that counts in our books, televisions and computers but what gets into our heads and why we want to learn it. Yet as Marshall H. McLuhan, the philosopher of communications, has pointed out, the form is much of what does get into our heads; we become what we behold. The form of the carrier of information is not neutral; it both dictates the kind of information conveyed and affects thinking processes. *command w/ and authority*

This property applies to all media, not just the new high-tech ones. Socrates complained about writing. He felt it forced one to follow an argument rather than participate in it, and he disliked both its alienation and its persistence. He was unsettled by the idea that a manuscript traveled without the author, with whom no argument was possible. Worse, the author could die and never be talked away from the position taken in the writing.

Users of media need to be aware, too, that technology often forces us to choose between quality and convenience. Compare the emotions evoked by great paintings and illuminated

implicit = hidden thought

manuscripts with those evoked by excellent photographs of the originals. The feelings are quite different. For the majority of people who cannot make such comparisons directly, there is an understandable tendency to accept the substitution as though nothing were lost. Consequently, little protest has been made over replacing high-resolution photographs of great art (which themselves do not capture the real thing) with lower-resolution videodisc images (which distort both light and space even further). The result is that recognition, not reverie, is the main goal in life and also in school, where recognition is the highest act to which most students are asked to aspire.

When convenience is valued over quality in education, we are led directly to "junk" learning. This is quite analogous to other junk phenomena, pale substitutions masquerading for the real thing. Junk learning leads to junk living. As Neil M. Postman of New York University says, whether a medium carries junk is not important, since all media have junk possibilities. But one needs to be sure that media incapable of carrying important kinds of discourse—for example, television—do not displace those that can.

Media can also lure us into thinking we are creating by design when in fact we are just tinkering. Consider the difficulty of transforming clay—a perfectly malleable and responsive substance—into anything aesthetically satisfying. Perfect "debugability," or malleability, does not make up for lack of an internal image and shaping skills. Unfortunately, computers lend themselves to such "clay pushing"; they tempt users to try to debug constructions into existence by trial and error.

Finally, as McLuhan noted, the instant communication offered by today's media leads to fragmentation. Sequence and exposition are replaced by isolated, context-free factoids, often presented simply because they are recent. Two hundred years ago the Federalist papers—essays by James Madison, Alexander Hamilton and John Jay arguing for ratification of the U.S. Constitution—were published in newspapers in the 13 colonies. Fifty years later the telegraph and its network shifted the goals of news from depth to currency, and the newspapers changed in response. Approximately 100 years after that, television started shifting the emphasis of news from currency to visual immediacy.

Computers have the same drawbacks as other media, and yet they also offer opportunities for counteracting the inherent deficits. Where would the authors of the Constitution publish the Federalist papers today? Not in a book; not enough people read books. Not in newspapers; each essay is too long. Not on the television; it cannot deal with thoughtful content. On computer networks? Well, computer displays, though getting better every year, are not good enough for reading extended prose; the tendency is to show pictures, diagrams and short "bumper sticker" sentences, because that is what displays do well.

But the late 20th century provides an interesting answer to the question: transmitting over computer networks a simulation of the proposed structure and processes of the new Constitution. The receivers not only could run the model but also could change assumptions and even the model itself to test the ideas. The model could be hyperlinked to the sources of the design, such as the constitution of Virginia, so that "readers" might readily compare the new ideas against the old. (Hyperlinking extends any document to include related information from many diverse sources.) Now the receivers would have something stronger than static essays. And feedback about the proposals—again by network—could be timely and relevant.

Five years ago, intent on studying firsthand the strengths and weaknesses of computers as amplifiers for learning, my colleague Ann Marion and I, in collaboration with the Open School: Center for Individualization, in Los Angeles, set up a research project called the Apple Vivarium

Program. We and the principal, Roberta Blatt, were not trying to improve the already excellent school by introducing technology. We were trying to better understand the value computers might have as supporting media.

Children are bused in and, as is the case with other busing schools in Los Angeles, are selected by lot so that the racial balance is roughly in accord with that of the city as a whole. Parents have to be interested enough in their children and the school's teaching approach to put their children on the list for consideration. Parental interest and involvement are key factors that have made the school a success. One could even argue that the educational approach in a classroom is not nearly as important as the set of values about learning found in the home. If those exist, almost any process will work, although some may be more enjoyable and enriching than others.

We particularly wanted to investigate how children can be helped to understand that animals, people and situations are parts of larger systems that influence one another. We therefore focused much of our work on the study of biology and ecology. Studies of the design and functioning of large cities also give children an awareness of such complexity. Doreen Nelson of the California Polytechnic Institute has been teaching city design to children for many years; on the basis of her work, our study group introduced a large-scale city-building project for the third graders. We also helped the school develop a major theater program, so the children might see how art and systems work from the inside.

What does it mean to learn about biology as it relates to us and our world? All creatures consist of and are part of many systems that range from the molecular to the planetary. A weak way to approach this romance—in which we are at once part of the scenery, bit players, star-crossed lovers, heroes and villains—would be a well-meaning attempt to use books, computers or other representational media as "delivery vehicles." There could be videodiscs showing plant and animal growth, and the students could have network access to data about crop yields, taxonomies of animals and plants, and so forth. But why substitute a "music appreciation" approach for the excitement of direct play? Why teach "science and math appreciation," when the children can more happily (and to better effect) actually create whole worlds?

What is great in biology and humankind's other grand investigations cannot be "delivered." But it can be learned—by giving students direct contact with "the great chain of being," so that they can internally generate the structures needed to hold powerful ideas. Media of all kinds can now be used to amplify the learning experience, whereas before they acted as a barrier to the "good stuff."

The Open School is nothing if not straightforward. Because "things that grow" is the essence of what is called the Life Lab program, the children made a garden, tearing up part of their asphalt playground to get good clean dirt. The third graders, while in the midst of their city-building project, spent months modeling and debating designs for the garden. They ultimately arrived at a practical, child-scaled pattern featuring a herringbone-shaped walkway that puts every plot in reach.

Not surprisingly, the children found that the simulation capability of their computers helped them examine the merits of many different walkway designs. Like modern-day architects, they used the computer to help construct models of their ideas. Teachers Dolores Patton and Leslie Barclay facilitated the process, but it was the children who came up with the ideas.

There are many Life Lab schools in California. Because they are engaged in similar pursuits, they have things to say to one another. For them, networks serve as much more than a conduit for retrieving fixed data; they allow students to develop knowledge of their own collaboratively.

For example, it is easy to make one's own weather maps on the basis of simultaneous recordings of temperature and (barometric) pressure and the like and to argue via network about what the maps mean. *indecator of change (usualyin atmospher)*

Computer animation can be used to ponder the patterns more readily. A fairly easy inference is that pressure changes seem to go from west to east. Could this have anything to do with the rotation of the earth? The directions of winds are more complicated, since they are more affected by features of the terrain. Do they match up with pressure changes?

We can go still deeper. Children are capable of much depth and attention to quality when they are thinking about questions that seem important to them. Why do animals do what they do? Why do humans do what we do? These are vital issues. Close observation, theories and role-playing help. Reading books about animal behavior helps. The teacher can even explain some ideas of the Nobel laureate Niko Tinbergen, such as the suggestion that animal behavior is organized into modules of innate patterns. But these are just words. Now the children can make dynamic models of animal behavior patterns to test Tinbergen's concepts themselves. *complacidy of indelegent thought*

Can nine- and 10-year-old children actually capture and understand the (mentality) of a complex organism, such as a fish? Teacher B. J. Allen-Conn spent several summers learning about intricate ecological relations in the oceans. She searched for ways to express how an individual's behavior is altered by interactions with many other animals. At the same time, Michael Travers, a graduate student from the Media Laboratory at the Massachusetts Institute of Technology who was working with us, built several animal simulations, among them fish behaviors described by Tinbergen. Then Scott Wallace and others in our group turned these various ideas into Playground, a simulation construction kit for children. */ Facinated and keeps atention*

Children are particularly (enthralled) by the clown fish, which exhibits all expected fishlike behaviors (such as feeding, mating and fleeing from predators) but also displays a fascinating way of protecting itself. It chooses a single sea anemone and gradually (acclimates) to the *to ajust to something* anemone's poison over a period of several days. When acclimation is complete, the clown fish has a safe haven where it can hide if a predator comes hunting.

It is fairly easy to build a simple behavior in Playground, and so the children produce simulations that reflect how the fish acts when it gets hungry, seeks food, acclimates to an anemone and escapes from predators. Later they can explore what happens when scripts conflict. What happens if the animal is very hungry yet there is a predator near the food? If the animal is hungry enough, will it start eyeing the predator as possible food? Do the fish as a group fare best when each animal is out for itself, or does a touch of (altruism) help the species overall? *unselfish concerned for others*

For an adult, the children's work would be called Artificial Intelligence Programming Using a Rule-Based Expert Systems Language. We researchers and the teachers and children see the (dynamic) *constant activity* simulations as a way of finding out whether theories of animal behavior apply to the real world.

Computers in the Open School are not rescuing the school from a weak curriculum, any more than putting pianos in every classroom would rescue a flawed music program. Wonderful learning can occur without computers or even paper. But once the teachers and children are (enfranchised) *given the right to be* as explorers, computers, like pianos, can serve as powerful amplifiers, extending the reach and depth of the learners.

Many educators have been slow to recognize this concept of knowledge ownership and to realize that children, like adults, have a psychological need for a personal franchise in the culture's knowledge base. Most schools force students to learn somebody else's knowledge. Yet, as

John Holt, the teacher and philosopher of education, once said, mathematics and science would probably be learned better if they were made illegal. Children learn in the same way as adults, in that they learn best when they can ask their own questions, seek answers in many places, consider different perspectives, exchange views with others and add their own findings to existing understandings. *appearing everywhere*

Ten years from now, powerful, intimate computers will become as ubiquitous as television and will be connected to interlinked networks that span the globe more comprehensively than telephones do today. My group's experience with the Open School has given us insight into the potential benefits of this technology for facilitating learning.

The first benefit is great interactivity. Initially the computers will be reactive, like a musical instrument, as they are today. Soon they will take initiatives as well, behaving like a personal assistant. Computers can be fitted to every sense. For instance, there can be displays for vision; pointing devices and keyboards for responding to gesture; speakers, piano-type keyboards and microphones for sound—even television cameras to recognize and respond to the user's facial expressions. Some displays will be worn as magic glasses and force-feedback gloves that together create a virtual reality, putting the user inside the computer to see and touch this new world. The surface of an enzyme can be felt as it catalyzes a reaction between two amino acids; relativistic distortions can be directly experienced by turning the user into an electron traveling at close to the speed of light.

A second value is the ability of the computers to become any and all existing media, including books and musical instruments. This feature means people will be able (and now be required) to choose the kinds of media through which they want to receive and communicate ideas. Constructions such as texts, images, sounds and movies, which have been almost intractable in conventional media, are now manipulatable by word processors, desktop publishing, and illustrative and multimedia systems.

Third, and more important, information can be presented from many different perspectives. Marvin L. Minsky of M.I.T. likes to say that you do not understand anything until you understand it in more than one way. Computers can be programmed so that "facts" retrieved in one window on a screen will automatically cause supporting and opposing arguments to be retrieved in a halo of surrounding windows. An idea can be shown in prose, as an image, viewed from the back and the front, inside or out. Important concepts from many different sources can be collected in one place.

Fourth, the heart of computing is building a dynamic model of an idea through simulation. Computers can go beyond static representations that can at best argue; they can deliver sprightly simulations that portray and test conflicting theories. The ability to "see" with these stronger representations of the world will be as important an advance as was the transition to language, mathematics and science from images and common sense.

A fifth benefit is that computers can be engineered to be reflective. The model-building capabilities of the computer should enable mindlike processes to be built and should allow designers to create flexible "agents." These agents will take on their owner's goals, confer about strategies (asking questions of users as well as answering their queries) and, by reasoning, fabricate goals of their own. *their questions*

Finally, pervasively networked computers will soon become a universal library, the age-old dream of those who love knowledge. Resources now beyond individual means, such as supercomputers for heavy-duty simulation, satellites and huge compilations of data, will be potentially accessible to anyone. *brought together from different places*

to set fuc

8

For children, the (enfranchising) effects of these benefits could be especially exciting. The educator John Dewey noted that urban children in the 20th century can participate only in the form, not the content, of most adult activities; compare the understanding gained by a city girl playing nurse with her doll to that gained by a girl caring for a live calf on a farm. Computers are already helping children to participate in content to some extent. How students from preschool to graduate school use their computers is similar to how computer professionals use theirs. They interact, simulate, contrast and criticize, and they create knowledge to share with others.

concern with, or measured by quality

When massively interconnected, intimate computers become commonplace, the relation of humans to their information carriers will once again change (qualitatively.) As ever more information becomes available, much of it conflicting, the ability to critically assess the value and validity of many different points of view and to recognize the contexts out of which they arise will become increasingly crucial. This facility has been extremely important since books became widely available, but making comparisons has been quite difficult. Now comparing should become easier, if people take advantage of the positive values computers offer.

the appearance of being true or real

Computer designers can help as well. Networked computer media will initially substitute convenience for (verisimilitude) and quantity and speed for exposition and thoughtfulness. Yet well-designed systems can also retain and expand on the profound ideas of the past, making available revolutionary ways to think about the world. As Postman has pointed out, what is required is a kind of guerilla warfare, not to stamp out new media (or old) but to create a parallel consciousness about media—one that gently whispers the debits and credits of any representation and points the way to the "food."

For example, naive acceptance of on-screen information can be combated by designs that automatically gather both the requested information and instances in which a displayed "fact" does not seem to hold.

An on-line library that retrieves only what it is requested produces tunnel vision and misses the point of libraries; by wandering in the stacks, people inevitably find gems they did not know enough to seek. Software could easily provide for browsing and other (serendipitous) ventures.

occurrence of developing events by chance in a beneficial way—"serendipity"

Today facts are often divorced from their original context. This fragmentation can be countered by programs that put separately retrieved ideas into sequences that lead from one thought to the next. And the temptation to "clay push," to create things or collect information by trial and error, can be fought by organizational tools that help people form goals for their searches. If computer users begin with a strong image of what they want to accomplish, they can drive in a fairly straightforward way through their initial construction and rely on subsequent passes to criticize, debug and change.

If the personally owned book was one of the main shapers of the Renaissance notion of the individual, then the pervasively networked computer of the future should shape humans who are healthy skeptics from an early age. Any argument can be tested against the arguments of others and by appeal to simulation. Philip Morrison, a learned physicist, has a fine vision of a skeptical world: ". . . genuine trust implies the *opportunity* of checking wherever it may be wanted. . . . That is why it is the evidence, the experience itself and the argument that gives it order, that we need to share with one another, and not just the unsupported final claim."

spread or be present throughout

I have no doubt that as (pervasively) networked intimate computers become common, many of us will enlarge our points of view. When enough people change, modern culture will once again be transformed, as it was during the Renaissance. But given the current state of educational values, I fear that, just as in the 1500s, great numbers of people will not avail themselves of the opportunity for growth and will be left behind. Can society afford to let that happen again?

FURTHER READING

Understanding Media: The Extensions of Man. Marshall McLuhan. McGraw-Hill, 1965.
Toward a Theory of Instruction. Jerome S. Bruner. Harvard University Press, 1966.
The Structure of Scientific Revolutions. Thomas S. Kuhn. University of Chicago Press, 1970.
Amusing Ourselves to Death: Public Discourse in the Age of Show Business. Neil Postman. Viking Penguin, 1985.
The Ring of Truth: An Inquiry into How We Know What We Know. Philip Morrison and Phylis Morrison. Random House, 1989.

THINKING AND RE-READING

1. As you re-read this piece, make a list of the misconceptions Kay says hinder education today. Also jot down the claims he makes regarding "the pitfalls of existing media." Think about the ways in which he believes the proliferation of "intimate computers" can avoid the pitfalls of other media. Outline the examples he gives of projects that seem particularly promising for education.

2. Kay writes, "Ten years from now, powerful, intimate computers will become as ubiquitous as television and will be connected to interlinked networks that span the globe more comprehensively than televisions do today." What do you think Kay means by "powerful, intimate computers"? Is the language that Kay uses appropriate? What about his prediction? Does it seem accurate? What evidence supports your response?

3. Kay ends his piece by writing,

    When enough people change, modern culture will once again be transformed, as it was during the Renaissance. But given the current state of educational values, I fear that, just as in the 1500s, great numbers of people will not avail themselves of the opportunity for growth and will be left behind. Can society afford to let that happen again?

    According to Kay, who is to blame for "great numbers of people" being left behind? Do you agree or disagree? Why? Think about the steps we as a society can take to avoid the predicament Kay describes. What steps can we take as individuals?

4. As you re-read, make a list of all the people Kay cites and the roles they play in his article. Who are the experts in his essay? Who are the other people in his essay? What do they do? What inferences can you make from his choice of citations?

WRITING AND THINKING

1. Consider the examples Kay provides of productive school experiences in which children can engage, and write an analysis of why you agree (or don't agree) that the projects give students sound educational opportunities. As you write, evaluate at least two of

his examples, illustrating what they have in common. What makes these commonalities promising? Are there some children for whom the projects might have less value? Why? Describe one way in which you think computers should be used to teach children. Your audience for the report should be college professors who help prepare elementary school teachers for using computers in teaching.

2. Talk to one or more elementary school teachers in your community who teach with computers. Note the ways in which the teachers' approaches are similar and dissimilar from the projects Kay describes. Then find out about problems that the teacher(s) may have encountered in trying to use the new technologies for instruction. For example, do the teacher and children have sufficient access to the technologies they need? Does the school administration support the teachers' efforts? What kinds of training are provided for the teacher(s)? Have the teachers been able to give students the kinds of experiences that Kay writes of? Based on your interview(s) and other observations you may have made, write a response to Kay, in care of the editor at *Scientific American*, apprising him of your findings. Let him know how feasible you find his ideas in relation to your own research.

3. Brainstorm for other issues regarding computers and education that Strassmann, Sculley, and Kay neglect in their articles. Choose one, explaining in writing to your classmates and instructor why you think it's an important issue. What problems does it pose? Can they be overcome and, if so, how? Use evidence from your reading, interviews, or your own intellectual life to back up the arguments you present. Your analysis should provide a thoughtful critique for your classmates and teacher to ponder.

4. Although Kay doesn't mention the World Wide Web per se (and, in fact, when he wrote his article in 1991, the browsing software for the Web was rather limited), his description of the electronic publication of the *Federalist* papers seems remarkably suited to the Web. Write a proposal for a project with an educational purpose that you would like to put on the Web. Why is this the best method for showcasing your project? What limitations do print and other media present for your project? What problems might you encounter in constructing your web site? Your proposal should be aimed at faculty members at your college in a particular department or from across departments. It may well be that your project will be cross-disciplinary and able to serve students and faculty working in several different areas at once.

• com. can make dumb learning
  - people learn facts but don't know
  what they mean
• com. can be great tools if people
  only use them to help with research and designe
  not do it for them.

The New Technology: Is It Part of the Solution or Part of the Problem in Education?

Michael Apple

IN THIS ARTICLE, MICHAEL APPLE, a professor of educational studies at the University of Wisconsin, writes about computers in a less favorable light than many of the authors in this section. He worries that schools are incorporating computers into the curriculum without administrators and teachers asking the necessary ethical questions; he fears that the use of computers will widen the rift between the classes in American society, between the poor and the affluent, between women and men, between the "haves" and the "have-nots." Apple's article first appeared in 1991 in an educational journal titled *Computers in the Schools.* The journal is aimed primarily at education professors in colleges, school administrators who seek research to support their thinking, and, in general, those educators who are engaged in educational reform.

For Apple, the connections between corporate and educational settings sometimes appear too close, with the requirements of the workplace driving the curriculum in ways that may not benefit all students. In the name of "progress," such connections tend to push aside ethical and ideological considerations that Apple would have us ponder. He wants to know, for example, why schools are so eager to address the question of "how to" without considering the "why." He wants to know whose interests are best served when computers enter the workplace and become integral to educational contexts. If these questions are not asked, Apple warns that the economic and educational promises made for computers may never be realized. Overall, Apple's article presents a strong argument for examining carefully the consequences of technological innovations and their effects on the infrastructure of society.

THE POLITICS OF TECHNOLOGY

In our society, technology is seen as an autonomous process. It is set apart and viewed as if it had a life of its own, independent of social intentions, power, and privilege. We examine technology as if it was something constantly changing and as something that is constantly changing our lives in schools and elsewhere. This is partly true, of course, and is fine as far as it goes. However, by focusing on what is changing and being changed, we may neglect to ask what relationships are remaining the same. Among the most important of these are the sets of cultural and economic inequalities that dominate even societies like our own.[1]

By thinking of technology in this way, by closely examining whether the changes associated with "technological progress" are really changes in certain relationships after all, we can begin to ask political questions about their causes and especially their multitudinous effects. Whose idea of progress? Progress for what? And fundamentally, who benefits?[2] These questions may seem rather weighty ones to be asking about schools and the curricular and teaching practices that now go on in them or are being proposed. Yet, we are in the midst of one of those many educational bandwagons that governments, industry, and others so like to ride. This wagon is pulled in the direction of a technological workplace, and carries a heavy load of computers as its cargo.

The growth of the new technology in schools is definitely not what one would call a slow movement. In one recent year, there was a 56% reported increase in the use of computers in schools in the United States and even this may be a conservative estimate.[3] This is a trend that shows no sign of abating.[4] Nor is this phenomenon only limited to the United States. France, Canada, England, Australia, and many other countries have "recognized the future." At its center seems to sit a machine with a keyboard and a screen.

I say "at its center," since in both governmental agencies and in schools themselves the computer and the new technology have been seen as something of a savior economically and pedagogically. "High-tech" will save declining economies and will save our students and teachers in schools. In the latter, it is truly remarkable how wide a path the computer is now cutting.

The expansion of its use, the tendency to see all areas of education as a unified terrain for the growth in use of new technologies, can be seen in a two day workshop on integrating the microcomputer into the classroom held at my own university. Among the topics covered were computer applications in writing instruction, in music education, in secondary science and mathematics, in primary language arts, for the handicapped, for teacher record keeping and management, in business education, in health occupation training programs, in art, and in social studies. To this is added a series of sessions on the "electronic office," how technology and automation are helping industry, and how we all can "transcend the terror" of technology.[5]

Two things are evident from this list. First, vast areas of school life are now seen to be within the legitimate purview of technological restructuring. Second, there is a partly hidden but exceptionally close linkage between computers in schools and the needs of management for automated industries, electronic offices, and "skilled" personnel. Thus, recognizing both what is happening inside and outside of schools and the connections between these areas is critical to any understanding of what is likely to happen with the new technologies, especially the computer, in education.

As I have argued elsewhere, all too often educational debates are increasingly limited to technical issues. Questions of "how to" have replaced questions of "why."[6] In this article, I shall want to reverse this tendency. Rather than dealing with what the best way might be to establish closer ties between the technological requirements of the larger society and our formal institutions of education, I want to step back and raise a different set of questions. I want us to consider a number of rather difficult political, economic, and ethical issues about some of the tendencies in schools and the larger society that may make us want to be very cautious about the current technological bandwagon in education. In so doing, a range of areas will need to be examined: Behind the slogans of technological progress and high tech industry, what are some of the real effects of the new technology on the future labor market? What may happen to teaching and curriculum if we do not think carefully about the new technology's place in the classroom? Will the growing focus on technological expertise, particularly computer literacy, equalize or further exacerbate the lack of social opportunities for our most disadvantaged students?

Of course, there are many more issues that need to be raised. Given limited space, however, I shall devote the bulk of my attention to those noted above. I am certain that many of you can and will have many more that you could add to the list.

At root, my claim will be that the debate about the role of the new technology in society and in schools is not and must not be just about the technical correctness of what computers can and cannot do. These may be the least important kinds of questions in fact. At the very core of the debate instead are the ideological and ethical issues concerning what schools should be about and whose interests they should serve.[7] The question of interests is very important currently since, because of the severe problems currently besetting economies like our own, a restructuring of what schools are *for* has reached a rather advanced stage.

Thus, while there has always been a relatively close connection between the two, there is now an even closer relationship between the curriculum in our schools and corporate needs.[8] In a number of countries, educational officials and policy makers, legislators, curriculum workers, and others have been subject to immense pressure to make the "needs" of business and industry the primary goals of the school system. Economic and ideological pressures have become rather intense and often very overt. The language of efficiency, production, standards, cost effectiveness, job skills, work discipline, and so on—all defined by powerful groups and always threatening to become the dominant way we think about schooling[9]—has begun to push aside concerns for a democratic curriculum, teacher autonomy, and class, gender, and race equality. Yet, we cannot fully understand the implications of the new technology in this restructuring unless we gain a more complete idea of what industry is now doing not only in the schools but in the economy as well.

TECHNOLOGICAL MYTHS AND ECONOMIC REALITIES

Let us look at the larger society first. It is claimed that the technological needs of the economy are such that unless we have a technologically literate labor force we will ultimately become outmoded economically. But what will this labor force actually look like?

A helpful way of thinking about this is to use the concepts of increasing proletarianization and deskilling of jobs. These concepts signify a complex historical process in which the control of labor has altered, one in which the skills workers have developed over many years are broken down and reduced to their atomistic units, automated, and redefined by management to enhance profit levels, efficiency and control. In the process, the employee's control of timing, over defining the

162   Part II: Education and Technology

most appropriate way to do a task, and over criteria that establish acceptable performance are slowly taken over as the prerogatives of management personnel who are usually divorced from the place where the actual labor is carried out. Loss of control by the worker is almost always the result. Pay is often lowered. And the job itself becomes routinized, boring, and alienating as conception is separated from execution and more and more aspects of jobs are rationalized to bring them into line with management's need for a tighter economic and ideological ship.[10] Finally, and very importantly, many of these jobs may simply disappear.

There is no doubt that the rapid developments in, say, micro-electronics, genetic engineering and associated "biological technologies," and other high-tech areas are in fact partly transforming work in a large number of sectors in the economy. This may lead to economic prosperity in certain sections of our population, but its other effects may be devastating. Thus, as the authors of a recent study that examined the impact of new technologies on the future labor market demonstrate:

> This transformation . . . may stimulate economic growth and competition in the world marketplace, but it will displace thousands of workers and could sustain high unemployment for many years. It may provide increased job opportunities for engineers, computer operators, and robot technicians, but it also promises to generate an even greater number of low level, service jobs such as those of janitors, cashiers, clericals, and food service workers. And while many more workers will be using computers, automated office equipment, and other sophisticated technical devices in their jobs, the increased use of technology may actually reduce the skills and discretion required to perform many jobs.[11]

Let us examine this scenario in greater detail.

Rumberger and Levin make a distinction that is very useful to this discussion. They differentiate between high-tech industries and high-tech occupations, in essence between what is made and the kinds of jobs these goods require. High-tech industries that manufacture technical devices such as computers, electronic components and the like currently employ less than 15% of the paid work force in the United States and other industrialized nations. Just as importantly, a substantial knowledge of technology is required by *less than one fourth of* all occupations within these industries. On the contrary, the largest share of jobs created by high-tech industries are in areas such as clerical and office work or in production and assembly. These actually pay below average wages.[12] Yet this is not all. High-tech occupations that do require considerable skill—such as computer specialists and engineers—may indeed expand. However, most of these occupations actually "employ relatively few workers compared to many traditional clerical and service fields."[13] Rumberger and Levin summarize a number of these points by stating that "although the percentage growth rate of occupational employment in such high technology fields as engineering and computer programming was higher than the overall growth rate of jobs, far more jobs would be created in low-skilled clerical and service occupations than in high technology ones."[14]

Some of these claims are supported by the following data. It is estimated that even being generous in one's projections, only 17% of new jobs that will be created between now and 1995 will be in high-tech industries. (Less generous and more restrictive projections argue that only 3 to 8% of future jobs will be in such industries.)[15] As I noted though, such jobs will not be all equal. Clerical, secretaries, assemblers, warehouse personnel, etc., these will be the largest occupations within the industry. If we take the electronic components industry as an example here, this is made much clearer. Engineering, science, and computing occupations constituted approximately 15% of

a very typical example

all workers in this industry. The majority of the rest of the workers were engaged in low wage assembly work. Thus, in the late 1970's, nearly two thirds of all workers in the electronic components industry took home hourly wages "that placed them in the bottom third of the national distribution."[16] If we take the archetypical high-tech industry—computer and data processing—and decompose its labor market, we get similar results. In 1980, technologically oriented and skilled jobs accounted for only 26% of the total.[17]

These figures have considerable weight, but they are made even more significant by the fact that many of that 26% may themselves experience a deskilling process in the near future. That is, the reduction of jobs down into simpler and atomistic components, the separation of conception from execution, and so on—processes that have had such a major impact on the labor process of blue, pink, and white collar workers in so many other areas—are now advancing into high technology jobs as well. Computer programming provides an excellent example. New developments in software packages and machine language and design have meant that a considerable portion of the job of programming now requires little more than performing "standard, routine, machine-like tasks that require little in-depth knowledge."[18]

What does this mean for the schooling process and the seemingly widespread belief that the future world of work will require increasing technical competence on the part of all students? Consider the occupations that will contribute the most number of jobs not just in high-tech industries but throughout the society by 1995. Economic forecasts indicate that these will include building custodians, cashiers, secretaries, office clerks, nurses, waiters and waitresses, elementary school teachers, truck drivers, and other health workers such as nurses aides and orderlies.[19] None of these are directly related to high technology. Excluding teachers and nurses, none of them require any post secondary education. (Their earnings will be approximately 30% below the current average earnings of workers, as well.)[20] If we go further than this and examine an even larger segment of expected new jobs by including the forty job categories that will probably account for about one half of all the jobs that will be created, it is estimated that only about 25% will require people with a college degree.[21]

In many ways, this is strongly related to the effects of the new technology on the job market and the labor process in general. Skill levels will be raised in some areas, but will decline in many others, as will jobs themselves decline. For instance, "a recent study of robotics in the United States suggests that robots will have eliminated 100,000 to 200,000 jobs as of 1990, while creating 32,000 to 64,000 jobs."[22] My point about declining skill requirements is made nicely by Rumberger and Levin. As they suggest, while it is usually assumed that workers will need computer programming and other sophisticated skills because of the greater use of technology such as computers in their jobs, the ultimate effect of such technology may be somewhat different. "A variety of evidence suggests just the opposite: as machines become more sophisticated, with expanded memories, more computational ability, and sensory capabilities, the knowledge required to use the devices declines."[23] The effect of these trends on the division of labor will be felt for decades. But it will be in the sexual division of labor where it will be even more extreme. Since historically *women's work* has been subject to these processes in very powerful ways, we shall see increased proletarianization and deskilling of women's labor and, undoubtedly, a further increase in the feminization of poverty.[24]

These points clearly have implications for our educational programs. We need to think much more rigorously about what they mean for our transition from school to work programs, especially since many of the "skills" that schools are currently teaching are transitory because the

short lived

jobs themselves are being transformed (or lost) by new technological developments and new management offensives.

Take office work, for example. In offices, the bulk of the new technology has not been designed to enhance the quality of the job for the largest portion of the employees (usually women clerical workers). Rather it has usually been designed and implemented in such a way that exactly the opposite will result. Instead of accommodating stimulating and satisfying work, the technology is there to make managers' jobs "easier," to eliminate jobs and cut costs, to divide work into routine and atomized tasks, and to make administrative control more easily accomplished.[25] The vision of the future society seen in the microcosm of the office is inherently undemocratic and perhaps increasingly authoritarian. Is this what we wish to prepare our students for? Surely, our task as educators is neither to accept such a future labor market and labor process uncritically nor to have our students accept such practices uncritically as well. To do so is simply to allow the values of a limited but powerful segment of the population to work through us. It may be good business but I have my doubts about whether it is ethically correct educational policy.

In summary, then, what we will witness is the creation of enhanced jobs for a relative few and deskilled and boring work for the majority. Furthermore, even those boring and deskilled jobs will be increasingly hard to find. Take office work, again, an area that is rapidly being transformed by the new technology. It is estimated that between one and five jobs will be lost for every new computer terminal that is introduced.[26] Yet this situation will not be limited to office work. Even those low paying assembly positions noted earlier will not necessarily be found in the industrialized nations with their increasingly service oriented economies. Given the international division of labor, and what is called "capital flight," a large portion of these jobs will be moved to countries such as the Philippines and Indonesia.[27]

This is exacerbated considerably by the fact that many governments now find "acceptable" those levels of unemployment that would have been considered a crisis a decade ago. "Full employment" in the United States is now often seen as between 5–7% *measured* unemployment. (The actual figures are much higher, of course, especially among minority groups and workers who can only get part time jobs.) This is a figure that is *double* that of previous economic periods. Even higher rates are now seen as "normal" in other countries. The trend is clear. The future will see fewer jobs. Most of those that are created will not necessarily be fulfilling, nor will they pay well. Finally, the level of technical skill will continue to be lowered for a large portion of them.[28]

Because of this, we need convincing answers to some very important questions about our future society and the economy before we turn our schools into the "production plants" for creating new workers. *Where* will these new jobs be? *How many* will be created? Will they *equal* the number of positions lost in offices, factories, and service jobs in retailing, banks, telecommunications, and elsewhere? Are the bulk of the jobs that will be created relatively unskilled, less than meaningful, and themselves subject to the inexorable logics of management so that they too will be likely to be automated out of existence?[29]

These are not inconsequential questions. Before we give the schools over to the requirements of the new technology and the corporation, we must be very certain that it will benefit all of us, not mostly those who already possess economic and cultural power. This requires continued democratic discussion, not a quick decision based on the economic and political pressure now being placed on schools.

Much more could be said about the future labor market. I urge the interested reader to pursue it in greater depth since it will have a profound impact on our school policies and programs, especially in vocational areas, in working class schools, and among programs for young women. The difficulties with the high-tech vision that permeates the beliefs of the proponents of a technological solution will not remain outside the school door, however. Similar disproportionate benefits and dangers await us inside our educational institutions as well and it is to this that we shall now turn.

INEQUALITY AND THE TECHNOLOGICAL CLASSROOM

Once we go inside the school, a set of questions concerning "who benefits?" also arises. We shall need to ask about what may be happening to teachers and students given the emphasis now being placed on computers in schools. I shall not talk about the individual teacher or student here. Obviously, some teachers will find their jobs enriched by the new technology and some students will find hidden talents and will excel in a computer oriented classroom. What we need to ask instead (or at least before we deal with the individual) is what may happen to classrooms, teachers, and students differentially. Once again, I shall seek to raise a set of issues that may not be easy to solve, but cannot be ignored if we are to have a truly democratic educational system in more than name only.

While I have dealt with this in greater detail in *Ideology and Curriculum* and *Education and Power*,[30] let me briefly situate the growth of the technologized classroom into what seems to be occurring to teaching and curriculum in general. Currently, considerable pressure is building to have teaching and school curricula be totally prespecified and tightly controlled for the purposes of "efficiency," "cost effectiveness," and "accountability." In many ways, the deskilling that is affecting jobs in general is now having an impact on teachers as more and more decisions are moving out of their hands and as their jobs become even more difficult to do. This is more advanced in some countries than others, but it is clear that the movement to rationalize and control the act of teaching and the content and evaluation of the curriculum is very real.[31] Even in those countries that have made strides away from centralized examination systems, powerful inspectorates and supervisors, and tightly controlled curricula, there is an identifiable tendency to move back toward state control. Many reforms have only a very tenuous hold currently. This is in part due to economic difficulties and partly due as well to the importing of American styles and techniques of educational management, styles and techniques that have their roots in industrial bureaucracies and have almost never had democratic aims.[32] Even though a number of teachers may support computer oriented curricula, an emphasis on the new technology needs to be seen in this context of the rationalization of teaching and curricula in general.

Given these pressures, what will happen to teachers if the new technology is accepted uncritically? One of the major effects of the current (over) emphasis on computers in the classroom may be the deskilling and depowering of a considerable number of teachers. Given the already heavy work load of planning, teaching, meetings, and paperwork for most teachers, and given the expense, it is probably wise to assume that the largest portion of teachers will not be given more than a very small amount of training in computers, their social effects, programming, and so on. This will be especially the case at the primary and elementary school level where most teachers are already teaching a wide array of subject areas. Research indicates in fact that few teachers in any district are actually given substantial information before computer curricula are implemented. Often only one or two teachers are the "resident experts."[33] Because of this, most teachers have to rely on prepackaged sets of material, existing software, and especially purchased material from any of the scores of software manufacturing firms that are springing up in a largely unregulated way.

The impact of this can be striking. What is happening is the exacerbation of trends we have begun to see in a number of nations. Rather than teachers having the time and the skill to do their own curriculum planning and deliberation, they become isolated executors of someone else's plans, procedures, and evaluative mechanisms. In industrial terms, this is very close to what I noted in my previous discussion of the labor process, the separation of conception from execution.[34]

The question of time looms larger here, especially in gender terms. Because of the large amount of time it takes to become a "computer expert" and because of the patriarchal relations that still dominate many families, *men teachers* will often be able to use "computer literacy" to advance their own careers while women teachers will tend to remain the recipients of prepackaged units on computers or "canned" programs over which they have little control.

In her excellent ethnographic study of the effects of the introduction of a district wide computer literacy program on the lives of teachers, Susan Jungck makes exactly this point about what happened in one middle school.

> The condition of time [needs to] be examined in terms of gender differences because it was the women teachers, not the men, in the Math Department who were unprepared to teach about computers and they were the ones most dependent on the availability of the [canned] Unit. Typically, the source of computer literacy for in-service teachers is either college or university courses, school district courses or independent study, all options that take considerable time outside of school. Both [male teachers] had taken a substantial number of university courses on computers in education. Many [of the] women, [because of] child care and household responsibilities . . . , or women who are single parents . . . , have relatively less out of school time to take additional coursework and prepare new curricula. Therefore, when a new curriculum such as computer literacy is required, women teachers may be more dependent on using the ready-made curriculum materials than most men teachers.[35]

The reliance on prepackaged software can have a number of long-term effects. First, it can cause a decided loss of important skills and dispositions on the part of teachers. When the skills of local curriculum planning, individual evaluation, and so on are not used, they atrophy. The tendency to look outside of one's own or one's colleagues' historical experience about curriculum and teaching is lessened as considerably more of the curriculum, and the teaching and evaluative practices that surround it, is viewed as something one purchases. In the process—and this is very important—the school itself is transformed into a lucrative market. The industrialization of the school I talked of previously is complemented, then, by further opening up the classroom to the mass produced commodities of industry. In many ways, it will be a publisher's and saleperson's delight. Whether students' educational experiences will markedly improve is open to question.

The issue of the relationship of purchased software and hardware to the possible deskilling and depowering of teachers does not end here, though. The problem is made even more difficult by the rapidity with which software developers have constructed and marketed their products. There is no guarantee that the mass of such material has any major educational value. Exactly the opposite is often the case. One of the most knowledgeable government officials has put it this way. "High quality educational software is almost non-existent in our elementary and secondary schools."[36] While perhaps overstating his case to emphasize his points, the director of software evaluation for one of the largest school systems in the United States has concluded that of the more than 10,000 programs currently available, approximately 200 are educationally significant.[37]

To their credit, the fact that this is a serious problem is recognized by most computer enthusiasts, and reviews and journals have attempted to deal with it. However, the sheer volume of material, the massive amounts of money spent on advertising software in professional publications, at teachers' and administrators' meetings, and so on, the utter "puffery" of the claims made about much of this material, and the constant pressure by industry, government, parents, some school personnel, and others to institute computer programs in schools *immediately*, all of this makes it nearly impossible to do more than make a small dent in the problem. As one educator put it, "There's a lot of junk out there."[38] The situation is not made any easier by the fact that teachers simply do not now have the time to thoroughly evaluate the educational strengths and weaknesses of a considerable portion of the *existing* curricular material and texts before they are used. Adding one more element, and a sizable one at that, to be evaluated only increases the load. Teachers work is increasingly becoming what students of the labor process call *intensified.* More and more needs to be done; less and less time is available to do it.[39] Thus, one has little choice but to simply buy ready-made material, in this way continuing a trend in which all of the important curricular elements are not locally produced but purchased from commercial sources whose major aim may be profit, not necessarily educational merit.[40]

There is a key concept found in Jungck's argument above that is essential here, that of gender. As I have demonstrated in considerable detail in *Teachers and Texts,*[41] teaching—especially at the elementary school level—has been defined as "women's work." We cannot ignore the fact that 87% of elementary teachers and 67% of teachers over all *are* women. Historically, the introduction of prepackaged or standardized curricula and teaching strategies has often been related to the rationalization and attempt to gain external control of the labor process of women workers. Hence, we cannot completely understand what is happening to teachers—the deskilling, the intensification, the separation of conception from execution, the loss of control, and so on— unless we situate these tendencies into this longer history of what has often happened to occupations that are primarily made up of women.[42] Needless to say, this is a critically important point, for only by raising the question of *who* is most often doing the teaching in many of these schools now introducing prepackaged software can we see the connections between the effects of the curricula and the gendered composition of the teaching force.

A significant consideration here, besides the loss of skill and control, is expense. This is at least a three-pronged issue. First, we must recognize that we may be dealing with something of a "zero-sum game." While dropping, the cost of computers is still comparatively high, though some manufacturers may keep purchase costs relatively low, knowing that a good deal of their profits may come from the purchase of software later on or through a home/school connection, something I shall discuss shortly. This money for the new technology *must come from somewhere.* This is an obvious point but one that is very consequential. In a time of fiscal crisis, where funds are already spread too thinly and necessary programs are being starved in many areas, the addition of computer curricula most often means that money must be drained from one area and given to another. What will be sacrificed? If history is any indication, it may be programs that have benefitted the least advantaged. Little serious attention has been paid to this, but it will become an increasingly serious dilemma.

A second issue of expense concerns staffing patterns, for it is not just the content of teachers' work and the growth of purchased materials that are at stake. Teachers' jobs themselves are on the line here. At a secondary school level in many nations, for example, lay-offs of teachers have not been unusual as funding for education is cut. Declining enrollment in some regions has meant a loss of positions as well. This has caused intense competition over students within the school itself. Social studies, art, music, and other subjects must fight it out with newer, more "glamorous" subject areas. To lose the student numbers game for too long is to lose a job. The effect of the computer in this situation has been to increase competitiveness among staff, often to replace substance with both gloss and attractive packaging of courses, and to threaten many teachers with the loss of their livelihood.[43] Is it really an educationally or socially wise decision to tacitly eliminate a good deal of the choices in these other fields so that we can support the "glamor" of a computer future? These are not only financial decisions, but are ethical decisions about teachers' lives and about what our students are to be educated in. Given the future labor market, do we really want to claim that computers will be more important than further work in humanities and social sciences or, perhaps even more significantly in working class and ethnically diverse areas, in the students' own cultural, historical, and political heritage and struggles? Such decisions must not be made by only looking at the accountant's bottom line. These too need to be arrived at by the lengthy democratic deliberation of all parties, including the teachers who will be most affected.

Third, given the expense of microcomputers and software in schools, the pressure to introduce such technology may increase the already wide social imbalances that now exist. Private schools to which the affluent send their children and publicly funded schools in more affluent areas will have more ready access to the technology itself.[44] Schools in inner city, rural, and poor areas will be largely priced out of the market, even if the cost of "hardware" continues to decline. After all, in these poorer areas and in many public school systems in general in a number of countries it is already difficult to generate enough money to purchase new textbooks and to cover the costs of teachers' salaries. Thus, the computer and literacy over it will "naturally" generate further inequalities. Since, by and large, it will be the top 20% of the population that will have computers in their homes[45] and many of the jobs and institutions of higher education their children will be applying for will either ask for or assume "computer skills" as keys of entry or advancement, the impact can be enormous in the long run.

The role of the relatively affluent parent in this situation does not go unrecognized by computer manufacturers.

> Computer companies . . . gear much of their advertising to the educational possibilities of computers. The drive to link particular computers to schools is a frantic competition. Apple, for example, in a highly touted scheme proposed to "donate" an Apple to every school in America. Issues of philanthropy and intent aside, the clear market strategy is to couple particular computer usages to schools where parents—especially middle class parents with the economic wherewithal and keen motivation [to insure mobility]—purchase machines compatible with those in schools. The potentially most lucrative part of such a scheme, however, is not in the purchase of hardware (although this is also substantial) but in the sale of proprietary software.[46]

This very coupling of school and home markets, then, cannot fail to further disadvantage large groups of students. Those students who already have computer backgrounds—be it because of their schools or their homes or both—will proceed more rapidly. The social stratification of life chances will increase. These students' original advantage—one *not* due to "natural ability," but to *wealth*—will be heightened.[47]

We should not be surprised by this, nor should we think it odd that many parents, especially middle class parents, will pursue a computer future. Computer skills and "literacy" is partly a strategy for the maintenance of middle class mobility patterns.[48] Having such expertise, in a time of fiscal and economic crisis, is like having an insurance policy. It partly guarantees that certain doors remain open in a rapidly changing labor market. In a time of credential inflation, more credentials mean less closed doors.[49]

The credential factor here is of considerable moment. In the past, as gains were made by ethnically different people, working class groups, women, and others in schooling, one of the latent effects was to raise the credentials required by entire sectors of jobs. Thus, class, race, and gender barriers were partly maintained by an ever increasing credential inflation. Though this was more of a structural than a conscious process, the effect over time has often been to again disqualify entire segments of a population from jobs, resources and power. This too may be a latent outcome of the computerization of the school curriculum. Even though, as I have shown, the bulk of new jobs will not require "computer literacy," the establishment of computer requirements and mandated programs in schools will condemn many people to even greater economic disenfranchisement. Since the requirements are in many ways artificial—computer knowledge will not be so very necessary and the number of jobs requiring high levels of expertise will be relatively small—we will simply be affixing one more label to these students. "Functional illiteracy" will simply be broadened to include computers.[50]

Thus, rather than blaming an unequal economy and a situation in which meaningful and fulfilling work is not made available, rather than seeing how the new technology for all its benefits is "creating a growing underclass of displaced and marginal workers," the lack is personalized. It becomes the students' or workers' fault for not being computer literate. One significant social and ideological outcome of computer requirements in schools, then, is that they can serve as a means "to justify those lost lives by a process of mass disqualification, which throws the blame for disenfranchisement in education and employment back on the victims themselves."[51]

Of course, this process may not be visible to many parents of individual children. However, the point does not revolve around the question of individual mobility, but large scale effects. Parents may see such programs as offering important paths to advancement and some will be correct. However, in a time of severe economic problems, parents tend to overestimate what schools can do for their children.[52] As I documented earlier, there simply will not be sufficient jobs and competition will be intense. The uncritical introduction of and investment in hardware and software will by and large hide the reality of the transformation of the labor market and will support those who are already advantaged unless thought is given to these implications now.

Let us suppose, however, that it was important that everyone become computer literate and that these large investments in time, money, and personnel were indeed so necessary for our economic and educational future. Given all this, what is currently happening in schools? Is inequality in access and outcome now being produced? While many educators are continually struggling against these effects, we are already seeing signs of this disadvantagement being created.

There is evidence of class, race, and gender based differences in computer use. In middle class schools, for example, the number of computers is considerably more than in working class or inner city schools populated by children of color. The ratio of computers to children is also much higher. This in itself is an unfortunate finding. However, something else must be added here. These more economically advantaged schools not only have more contact hours and more technical and teacher support, but the very manner in which the computer is used is often different than what would be generally found in schools in less advantaged areas. Programming skills, generalizability, a sense of the multitudinous things one can do with computers both within and across academic areas, these tend to be stressed more[53] (though simply drill and practice uses are still widespread even here).[54] Compare this to the rote, mechanistic, and relatively low level uses that tend to dominate the working class school.[55] These differences are not unimportant, for they signify a ratification of class divisions.

Further evidence to support these claims is now becoming more readily available as researchers dig beneath the glowing claims of a computer future for all children. The differential impact is made clearer in the following figures. In the United States, while over two-thirds of the schools in affluent areas have computers, only approximately 41% of the poorer public schools have them. What one does with the machine is just as important as having one, of course, and here the differences are again very real. One study of poorer elementary schools found that white children were four times more likely than black children to use computers for programming. Another found that the children of professionals employed computers for programming and for other "creative" uses. Non-professional children were more apt to use them for drill and practice in mathematics and reading, and for "vocational" work. In general, in fact, "programming has been seen as the purview of the gifted and talented" and of those students who are more affluent. Less affluent students seem to find that the computer is only a tool for drill and practice sessions.[56]

Gender differences are also very visible. Two out of every three students currently learning about computers are boys. Even here these data are deceptive since girls "tend to be clustered in the general introductory courses," not the more advanced level ones.[57] One current analyst summarizes the situation in a very clear manner.

> While stories abound about students who will do just about anything to increase their access to computers, most youngsters working with school computers are [economically advantaged], white and male. The ever-growing number of private computer camps, after-school and weekend programs serve middle class white boys. Most minority [and poor] parents just can't afford to send their children to participate in these programs.[58]

This class, race, and gendered impact will also occur because of traditional school practices such as tracking or streaming. Thus, vocational and business tracks will learn operating skills for word processing and will be primarily filled with (working class) young women.[59] Academic tracks will stress more general programming abilities and uses and will be disproportionately male.[60] Since computer programs usually have their home bases in mathematics and science in most schools, gender differences can be heightened even more given the often differential treatment of girls in these classes and the ways in which mathematics and science curricula already fulfill "the selective function of the school and contribute to the reproduction of gender differences."[61] While many teachers and curriculum workers have devoted considerable time and effort to equalize both the opportunities and outcomes of female students in mathematics and science (and such efforts are important), the problem still remains a substantive one. It can be worsened by the computerization of these subjects in much the same way as it may have a gendered impact on the teachers themselves.

TOWARDS SOCIAL LITERACY

We have seen some of the possible negative consequences of the new technology in education, including the deskilling and depowering of teachers and the creation of inequalities through expense, credential inflation, and limitations on access. Yet it is important to realize that the issues surrounding the deskilling process are not limited to teachers. They include the very ways students themselves are taught to think about their education, their future roles in society, and the place of technology in that society. Let me explain what I mean by this.

The new technology is not just an assemblage of machines and their accompanying software. It embodies a *form of thinking* that orients a person to approach the world in a particular way. Computers involve ways of thinking that under current educational conditions are primarily *technical*.[62] The more the new technology transforms the classroom into its own image, the more a technical logic will replace critical political and ethical understanding. The discourse of the classroom will center on technique, and less on substance. Once again "how to" will replace "why," but this time at the level of the student. This situation requires what I shall call social, not technical, literacy for all students.

Even if computers make sense technically in all curricular areas and even if all students, not mainly affluent white males, become technically proficient in their use, critical questions of politics and ethics remain to be dealt with in the curriculum. Thus, it is crucial that whenever the new technology is introduced into schools students have a serious understanding of the issues surrounding their larger social effects, many of which I raised earlier.

Unfortunately, this is not often the case. When the social and ethical impacts of computers are dealt with, they are usually addressed in a manner that is less than powerful. One example is provided by a recent proposal for a statewide computer curriculum in one of the larger states in the United States. The objectives that dealt with social questions in the curriculum centered around one particular set of issues. The curriculum states that "the student will be aware of some of the major uses of computers in modern society . . . and the student will be aware of career opportunities related to computers."[63] In most curricula the technical components of the new technology are stressed. Brief glances are given to the history of computers (occasionally mentioning the role of women in their development, which is at least one positive sign). Yet in this history, the close relationship between military use and computer development is largely absent. "Benign" uses are pointed to, coupled with a less than realistic description of the content and possibility of computer careers and what Douglas Noble has called "a gee-whiz glance at the marvels of the future." What is nearly never mentioned is job loss or social disenfranchisement. The very real destruction of the lives of unemployed autoworkers, assemblers or clerical workers is marginalized.[64] The ethical dilemmas involved when we choose between, say, "efficiency" and the quality of the work people experience, between profit and someone's job, these too are made invisible.

How would we counterbalance this? By making it clear from the outset that knowledge about the new technology that is necessary for students to know goes well beyond what we now too easily take for granted. A considerable portion of the curriculum would be organized around questions concerned with social literacy. "Where are computers used? What are they used to do? What do people *actually* need to know in order to use them? Does the computer enhance anyone's life? Whose? Does it hurt anyone's life? Whose? Who decides when and where computers will be used?"[65] Unless these are *fully* integrated in a school program at *all* levels, I would hesitate advocating the use of the new technology in the curriculum. Raising questions of this type is not just important in our elementary and secondary schools. It is even more essential that they be dealt with in a serious way with teachers both in their own undergraduate teacher education programs where courses in educational computing are more and more being mandated and in the many inservice workshops now springing up throughout the country as school districts frantically seek to keep up with the "computer revolution." To do less makes it much more difficult for teachers and students to think critically and independently about the place the new technology does and should have in the lives of the majority of people in our society. Our job as educators involves skilling, not deskilling. Unless teachers and students are able to deal honestly and critically with these complex ethical and social issues, only those now with the power to control technology's uses will have the capacity to act. We cannot afford to let this happen.

CONCLUSION

I realize that a number of my points may prove to be rather contentious in this essay. But stressing the negative side can serve to highlight many of the critical issues that are too easy to put off given the immense amount of work that school personnel are already responsible for. Decisions often get made too quickly, only to be regretted later on when forces are set in motion that could have been avoided if the implications of one's actions had been thought through more fully.
a likely consequence

As I noted at the outset of this discussion, there is now something of a mad scramble to employ the computer in every content area. In fact, it is nearly impossible to find a subject that is not being "computerized." Though mathematics and science (and some parts of vocational education) remain the home base for a large portion of proposed computer curricula, other areas are not far behind. If it can be packaged to fit computerized instruction, it will be, even if it is inappropriate, less effective than the methods that teachers have developed after years of hard practical work, or less than sound educationally or economically. Rather than the machine fitting the educational needs and visions of the teacher, students, and community, all too often these needs and visions are made to fit the technology itself.

Yet, as I have shown, the new technology does not stand alone. It is linked to transformations in real groups of people's lives, jobs, hopes, and dreams. For some of these groups, those lives will be enhanced. For others, the dreams will be shattered. Wise choices about the appropriate place of the new technology in education, then, are not only educational decisions. They are fundamentally choices about the kind of society we shall have, about the social and ethical responsiveness of our institutions to the majority of our future citizens, and to the teachers who now work in our schools.

My discussion here has not been aimed at making us all neo-Luddites, people who go out and smash the machines that threaten our jobs or our children. The new technology is here. It will not go away. Our task as educators is to make sure that when it enters the classroom it is there for politically, economically, and educationally wise reasons, not because powerful groups may be redefining our major educational goals in their own image. We should be very clear about whether or not the future it promises to our teachers and students is real, not fictitious. We need to be certain that it is a future *all* of our students can share in, not just a select few. After all, the new technology is expensive and will take up a good deal of our time and that of our teachers, administrators, and
not real or true, imaginary

students. It is more than a little important that we question whether the wagon we have been asked to ride on is going in the right direction. It's a long walk back.

NOTES

This article is based on a more extensive analysis in Michael W. Apple, *Teachers and Texts: A Political Economy of Class and Gender Relations in Education* (New York: Routledge and Kegan Paul, 1988).

1. David Noble, *Forces of Production: A Social History of Industrial Automation* (New York: Alfred A. Knopf, 1984), pp. xi–xii. For a more general argument about the relationship between technology and human progress, see Nicholas Rescher, *Unpopular Essays on Technological Progress* (Pittsburgh: University of Pittsburgh Press, 1980).
2. Ibid, p. xv.
3. Paul Olson, "Who Computes? The Politics of Literacy," unpublished paper, Ontario Institute for Studies in Education, Toronto, 1985, p. 6.
4. Patricia B. Campbell, "The Computer Revolution: Guess Who's Left Out?" *Interracial Books for Children Bulletin* 15 (no. 3 1984), p. 3.
5. "Instructional Strategies for Integrating the Microcomputer Into the Classroom," The Vocational Studies Center, University of Wisconsin, Madison, 1985.
6. Michael W. Apple, *Ideology and Curriculum,* second edition (New York: Routledge and Kegan Paul, 1990).
7. Olson, "Who Computes?," p. 5.
8. See Michael W. Apple, *Education and Power* (New York: Routledge and Kegan Paul, ARK Edition, 1985).
9. For further discussion of this, see Apple, *Ideology and Curriculum,* Apple, *Education and Power,* and Ira Shor, *Culture Wars* (Boston: Routledge and Kegan Paul, 1986).
10. This is treated in greater detail in Richard Edwards, *Contested Terrain* (New York: Basic Books, 1979). See also the more extensive discussion of the effect these tendencies are having in education in Apple, *Education and Power.*
11. Russell W. Rumberger and Henry M. Levin, "Forecasting the Impact of New Technologies on the Future Job Market," Project Report No. 84-A4, Institute for Research on Educational Finance and Government, School of Education, Stanford University, February, 1984, p. 1.
12. Ibid, p. 2.
13. Ibid, p. 3.
14. Ibid, p. 4.
15. Ibid, p. 18.
16. Ibid.
17. Ibid, p. 19.
18. Ibid, pp. 19–20.
19. Ibid, p. 31.
20. Ibid, p. 21.
21. Ibid.
22. Ibid, p. 25.
23. Ibid.
24. The effects of proletarianization and deskilling on women's labor is analyzed in more detail in Michael W. Apple, *Teachers and Texts* (New York: Routledge, 1988). On the history of women's struggles against proletarianization, see Alice Kessler-Harris, *Out to Work* (New York: Oxford University Press, 1982).
25. Ian Reinecke, *Electronic Illusions* (New York: Penguin Books, 1984), p. 156.
26. See the further discussion of the loss of office jobs and the deskilling of many of those that remain in Ibid, pp. 136–158. The very same process could be a threat to middle and low level management positions as well. After all, if control is further automated, why does one need as many supervisory positions? The implications of this latter point need to be given much more consideration by many middle-class proponents of technology since their jobs may soon be at risk too.
27. Peter Dwyer, Bruce Wilson, and Roger Woock, *Confronting School and Work* (Boston: George Allen and Unwin, 1984), pp. 105–106.

28. The paradigm case is given by the fact that three times as many people now work in low paying positions for McDonald's as for U.S. Steel. See Martin Carnoy, Derek Shearer, and Russell Rumberger, *A New Social Contract* (New York: Harper and Row, 1983), p. 71. As I have argued at greater length elsewhere, however, it may not be important to our economy if all students and workers are made technically knowledgeable by schools. What is just as important is the production of economically useful knowledge (technical/administrative knowledge) that can be used by corporations to enhance profits, control labor, and increase efficiency. See Apple, *Education and Power,* especially Chapter 2.

29. Reinecke, *Electronic Illusions,* p. 234. For further analysis of the economic data and the effects on education, see W. Norton Grubb, "The Bandwagon Once More: Vocational Preparation for High-Tech Occupations," *Harvard Educational Review* 54 (November 1984), 429–451.

30. Apple, *Ideology and Curriculum* and Apple, *Education and Power.* See also Michael W. Apple and Lois Weis, eds., *Ideology and Practice in Schooling* (Philadelphia: Temple University Press, 1983).

31. Ibid. See also Arthur Wise, *Legislated Learning: The Bureaucratization of the American Classroom* (Berkeley: University of California Press, 1979).

32. Apple, *Ideology and Curriculum* and Apple, *Education and Power.* On the general history of the growth of management techniques, see Richard Edwards, *Contested Terrain.*

33. Douglas Noble, "The Underside of Computer Literacy," *Raritan* 3 (Spring 1984), 45. What can actually happen when computers are used in this way is detailed in Michael W. Apple and Susan Jungck, "You Don't Have to Be a Teacher to Teach This Unit," *American Educational Research Journal,* in press.

34. See the discussion of this in Apple, *Education and Power,* especially Chapter 5.

35. Susan Jungck, "Doing Computer Literacy," unpublished Ph.D. dissertation, University of Wisconsin, Madison, 1985, pp. 236–237.

36. Douglas Noble, "Jumping Off the Computer Bandwagon," *Education Week,* October 3, 1984, 24.

37. Ibid.

38. Ibid. See also, Noble, "The Underside of Computer Literacy," 45.

39. For further discussion of the intensification of teachers' work, see Apple, *Teachers and Texts.*

40. Apple, *Education and Power.* For further analysis of the textbook publishing industry, see Michael W. Apple, *Teachers and Texts.*

41. Apple, *Teachers and Texts.*

42. Ibid.

43. I am indebted to Susan Jungck for this point. See Jungck, "Doing Computer Literacy."

44. Reinecke, *Electronic Illusions,* p. 176.

45. Ibid, p. 169.

46. Olson, "Who Computes?," p. 23.

47. Ibid, p. 31. Thus, students' familiarity and comfort with computers becomes a form of what has been called the "cultural capital" of advantaged groups. For further analysis of the dynamics of cultural capital, see Apple, *Education and Power* and Pierre Bourdieu and Jean-Claude Passeron, *Reproduction in Education, Society and Culture* (Beverly Hills: Sage, 1977).

48. Ibid, p. 23. See also the discussion of interclass competition over academic qualifications in Pierre Bourdieu, *Distinction* (Cambridge: Harvard University Press, 1984), pp. 133–168.

49. Once again, I am indebted to Susan Jungck for this argument.

50. Noble, "The Underside of Computer Literacy," p. 54.

51. Douglas Noble, "Computer Literacy and Ideology," *Teachers College Record* 85 (Summer 1984), 611. This process of "blaming the victim" has a long history in education. See Apple, *Ideology and Curriculum,* especially Chapter 7.

52. R. W. Connell, *Teachers' Work* (Boston: George Allen and Unwin, 1985), p. 142.

53. Olson, "Who Computes?," p. 22.

54. For an analysis of the emphasis on and pedagogic problems with such limited uses of computers, see Michael Streibel, "A Critical Analysis of Three Approaches to the Use of Computers in Education," in Landon Beyer and Michael W. Apple, eds., *The Curriculum: Problems, Politics and Possibilities* (Albany: State University of New York Press, 1988), pp. 259–288.

55. Olson, "Who Computes?," p. 22.

56. Campbell, "The Computer Revolution: Guess Who's Left Out?" 3. Many computer experts, however, are highly critical of the fact that students are primarily taught to program in BASIC, a less than appropriate language for later advanced computer work. Michael Streibel, personal communication.

57. Ibid.

58. Ibid.

59. An interesting analysis of what happens to young women in such business programs and how they respond to both the curricula and their later work experiences can be found in Linda Valli, "Becoming Clerical Workers: Business Education and the Culture of Femininity," in Apple and Weis, eds., *Ideology and Practice in Schooling*, pp. 213–234. See also her more extensive treatment in Linda Valli, *Becoming Clerical Workers* (Boston: Routledge and Kegan Paul, 1986).

60. Jane Gaskell in Olson, "Who Computes?," p. 33.

61. Feodora Fomin, "The Best and the Brightest: The Selective Function of Mathematics in the School Curriculum," in Lesley Johnson and Deborah Tyler, eds., *Cultural Politics: Papers in Contemporary Australian Education, Culture and Politics* (Melbourne: University of Melbourne, Sociology Research Group in Cultural and Educational Studies, 1984), p. 220.

62. Michael Streibel's work on the models of thinking usually incorporated within computers in education is helpful in this regard. See Streibel, "A Critical Analysis of Three Approaches to the Use of Computers in Education." The more general issue of the relationship between technology and the control of culture is important here. A useful overview of this can be found in Kathleen Woodward, ed., *The Myths of Information: Technology and Postindustrial Culture* (Madison: Coda Press, 1980).

63. Quoted in Noble, "The Underside of Computer Literacy," p. 56.

64. Ibid, 57. An interesting, but little known fact is that the largest proportion of computer programmers actually work for the military. See Joseph Weizenbaum, "The Computer in Your Future," *The New York Review of Books*, October 27, 1983, pp. 58–62.

65. Noble, "The Underside of Computer Literacy," p. 40. For students in vocational curricula especially, these questions would be given more power if they were developed within a larger program that would seek to provide these young women and men with extensive experience in and understanding of *all* aspects of operating an entire industry, not simply those "skills" that reproduce workplace stratification. See Center for Law and Education, "Key Provisions in New Law Reforms Vocational Education: Focus Is on Broader Knowledge and Experience for Students/Workers," *Center for Law and Education, Inc. D.C. Report*, December 28, 1984, pp. 1–6.

THINKING AND RE-READING

1. As you re-read this piece, list the major claims that Apple makes and consider whether you agree or disagree with him. What experiences have you or those close to you had that confirm his cautionary remarks about the kinds of jobs the new technologies make available? What experiences have you or others had that make you disagree with him?

2. Apple uses the notion of "deskilling" quite frequently. As you re-read his article, copy down the sentences in which the word appears. How would you define the word in the different contexts in which he uses it? Can you think of other examples of deskilling in relationship to work in which you or others have been engaged? Have you had any experiences as a student in which you might apply this word to your teachers' work? Why or why not?

3. One technology that Apple doesn't mention in his article is computer-mediated communication (e-mail, news groups, MOOs, etc.). Do these uses of computers make a difference to Apple's argument that the new technologies will generate further disparities among students in regard to privilege? What difference might they make in regard to his notion of the deskilling of teachers? Why?

WRITING AND LEARNING

1. Apple writes that the new technologies are having an impact on jobs but perhaps not the beneficial impact that we might think. According to Apple, the electronic office doesn't require particularly advanced skills; in fact, the use of technology may be reducing the amount of skill needed to perform various office jobs. To find out more about the contemporary office, your task is to spend some time with local employees and learn more about the qualifications an office worker needs to perform successfully in the office you observe.

   Start off by visiting an office in which the personnel know you and have agreed to let you spend the morning or afternoon. Take notes about what you see going on in the office: Who works there? What tasks do they seem to be engaged in? What abilities or skills do these tasks require? Then interview one or two who have worked in the office for some time. (The office manager might also be appropriate.) Find out how the jobs have changed over the past ten or fifteen years. Also ask the employees how well their schooling prepared them for their work. Then write an account of today's electronic office in which you describe the kinds of technologies that characterize it, the day-to-day routine of those who inhabit it, and the reactions of the employees to their work. Target the report for your teacher and classmates, but also ask the office manager and employees whether they would be interested in reading your report. If they are, revise the report you've written for your class so that it is suitable for the office personnel. Jot down the kinds of changes you needed to make for the new audience, and share your revision decisions with your teacher and classmates.

2. Apple writes that "[t]he language of efficiency, production, standards, cost-effectiveness, job skills, work discipline, and so on—all defined by powerful groups and always threatening to become the dominant way we think about schooling—has begun to push aside concerns for a democratic curriculum, teacher autonomy, and class, gender, and race equality." Find two or three articles on the new technologies in one of the weekly newsmagazines or your local newspaper. Do you see evidence to support Apple's contentions? Is there evidence to refute them? Using these articles and your own school experiences if appropriate, write a response to Apple's claim that notions of efficiency and progress may be taking precedence over concerns for a democratic curriculum. Direct your response to Apple or to a "letters to the editor" section of the journal in which the article appeared. Let readers know where you agree with him, where you disagree, and be sure to include the necessary evidence to back up your claims.

3. Apple believes that teaching students "how" to use computers is only one enterprise in which schools should be involved, and it may not be the important one insofar as the new technologies are concerned. For Apple, the more critical task is for students to explore how social relationships may or may not be changing as a result of the wide-scale use of computers. His argument is that although the new technologies affect the social structures of society, they may not lead to improved conditions for its people. For Apple, there are several critical questions that must be asked, among them:

Where are computers used? What are they used to do? What do people actually need to know in order to use them? Does the computer enhance anyone's life? Whose? Does it hurt anyone's life? Whose? Who decides when and where computers will be used?

4. Construct a short e-mail survey in which you ask classmates and friends about their use of computers on campus. How are computers used in their different courses? Are they making a positive difference in their lives? Are there some students who benefit more than others from their use? Use Apple's questions as a guide. Then write a response in which you assess the impact of computers on the educational climate of your school. After you've revised your report, ask your instructor and classmates whether it would be appropriate to send your report to the school newspaper or to a committee on campus concerned with issues surrounding computer access. Make the necessary revisions and either send your piece off to the school newspaper or set up a time when you and your classmates can give an oral report to one of the computer committees at your school.

Unplugged

David Gelernter

DAVID GELERNTER'S ARTICLE FIRST APPEARED in 1994 in *The New Republic,* a magazine aimed at an educated readership. A professor of computer science at Yale University, Gelernter is also author of *Mirror Worlds,* a book that shows us how computers can provide representations of reality on screen and how they can allow us to visit and interact with others in places where we have never been. Yet despite Gelernter's farsighted views on computers, when it comes to education he is very conservative, and in "Unplugged," he argues strongly against particular uses of computers in the schools. *Perceptible by touch*

O ver the last decade an estimated $2 billion has been spent on more than 2 million computers for America's classrooms. That's not surprising. We constantly hear from Washington that the schools are in trouble and that computers are a godsend. Within the education establishment, in poor as *Delving in religion* well as rich schools, the machines are awaited with nearly religious awe. An inner-city principal bragged to a teacher friend of mine recently that his school "has a computer in every classroom . . . despite being in a bad neighborhood!"

Computers should be in the schools. They have the potential to accomplish great things. With the right software, they could help make science tangible or teach neglected topics like art and music. They could help students form a concrete idea of society by displaying on-screen a version of the city in which they live—a picture that tracks real life moment by moment.

In practice, however, computers make our worst educational nightmares come true. While we bemoan the decline of literacy, computers discount words in favor of pictures and pictures in favor of video. While we fret about the decreasing cogency of public debate, computers dismiss linear argument and promote fast, shallow romps across the information landscape. While we worry about basic skills, we allow into the classroom software that will do a student's arithmetic or correct his spelling.

Take multimedia. The idea of multimedia is to combine text, sound and pictures in a single package that you browse on screen. You don't just *read* Shakespeare; you watch actors performing, listen to songs, view Elizabethan buildings. What's wrong with that? By offering children candy-coated books,

multimedia is guaranteed to sour them on unsweetened reading. It makes the printed page look even more boring than it used to look. Sure, books will be available in the classroom, too—but they'll have all the appeal of a dusty piano to a teen who has a Walkman handy.

So what if the little nippers don't read? If they're watching Olivier instead, what do they lose? The text, the written word along with all of its attendant pleasures. Besides, a book is more portable than a computer, has a higher-resolution display, can be written on and dog-eared and is comparatively dirt cheap.

Hypermedia, multimedia's comrade in the struggle for a brave new classroom, is just as troubling. It's a way of presenting documents on screen without imposing a linear start-to-finish order. Disembodied paragraphs are linked by theme; after reading one about the First World War, for example, you might be able to choose another about the technology of battleships, or the life of Woodrow Wilson, or hemlines in the '20s. This is another cute idea that is good in minor ways and terrible in major ones. Teaching children to understand the orderly unfolding of a plot or a logical argument is a crucial part of education. Authors don't merely agglomerate paragraphs; they work hard to make the narrative read a certain way, prove a particular point. To turn a book or a document into hypertext is to invite readers to ignore exactly what counts—the story.

The real problem, again, is the accentuation of already bad habits. Dynamiting documents into disjointed paragraphs is one more expression of the sorry fact that sustained argument is not our style. If you're a newspaper or magazine editor and your readership is dwindling, what's the solution? Shorter pieces. If you're a politician and you want to get elected, what do you need? Tasty sound bites. Logical presentation be damned.

Another software species, "allow me" programs, is not much better. These programs correct spelling and, by applying canned grammatical and stylistic rules, fix prose. In terms of promoting basic skills, though, they have all the virtues of a pocket calculator.

In Kentucky, as *The Wall Street Journal* recently reported, students in grades K-3 are mixed together regardless of age in a relaxed environment. It works great, the *Journal* says. Yes, scores on computation tests have dropped 10 percent at one school, but not to worry: "Drilling addition and subtraction in an age of calculators is a waste of time," the principal reassures us. Meanwhile, a Japanese educator informs University of Wisconsin mathematician Richard Akey that in his country, "calculators are not used in elementary or junior high school because the primary emphasis is on helping students develop their mental abilities." No wonder Japanese kids blow the pants off American kids in math. Do we really think "drilling addition and subtraction in an age of calculators is a waste of time"? If we do, then "drilling reading in an age of multimedia is a waste of time" can't be far behind.

Prose-correcting programs are also a little ghoulish, like asking a computer for tips on improving your personality. On the other hand, I ran this article through a spell-checker, so how can I ban the use of such programs in schools? Because to misspell is human; to have no idea of correct spelling is to be semiliterate.

There's no denying that computers have the potential to perform inspiring feats in the classroom. If we are ever to see that potential realized, however, we ought to agree on three conditions. First, there should be a completely new crop of children's software. Most of today's offerings show no imagination. There are hundreds of similar reading and geography and arithmetic programs, but almost nothing on electricity or physics or architecture. Also, they abuse the technical capacities of new media to glitz up old forms instead of creating new ones. Why not build a time-travel program that gives kids a feel for how history is structured by zooming you backward? A spectrum program that lets users twirl a frequency knob to see what happens?

Second, computers should be used only during recess or relaxation periods. Treat them as fillips, not as surrogate teachers. When I was in school in the '60s, we all loved educational films. When we saw a movie in class, everybody won: teachers didn't have to teach, and pupils didn't have to learn. I suspect that classroom computers are popular today for the same reasons.

Most important, educators should learn what parents and most teachers already know: you cannot teach a child anything unless you look him in the face. We should not forget what computers are. Like books—better in some ways, worse in others—they are devices that help children mobilize their own resources and learn for themselves. The computer's potential to do good is modestly greater than a book's in some areas. Its potential to do harm is vastly greater, across the board.

THINKING AND RE-READING

1. Gelernter, like Michael Apple, is critical of the uses of computers in schools, but his reasons are very different from Apple's. As you re-read his piece, make a list of his claims. Do you agree with them? Why or why not?

2. Jot down the examples Gelernter uses to support his claims. List others you can come up with that either support or refute his basic argument. Write down the overall gist of his argument in one sentence.

3. Gelernter writes, "Most important, educators should learn what parents and most teachers already know: you cannot teach a child anything unless you look him in the face." Do you agree? Does anything trouble you about Gelernter's own use of language in this particular sentence and in other sentences in the article? Explain.

WRITING AND LEARNING

1. Using your notes, write a response in which you compare Apple's and Gelernter's attitudes toward the use of computers in schools. How can Apple's objections be met? Gelernter's? Which arguments do you agree with? Why? What support can you provide for your conclusions? Help your teacher and classmates organize a debate in which one side argues for Gelernter's views and the other for Apple's. Summarize the debate in a notebook you keep for the class. What other views can you adopt that support neither Gelernter nor Apple?

Power On! New Tools for Teaching and Learning

Congress of the United States, Office of Technology Assessment

POWER ON! IS A 1988 PUBLICATION that the U.S. Congress commissioned from its Office of Technology Assessment. It presents a good overview of the field of instructional technology in the 1980s. Here is how the almost 250-page book is introduced in the foreword:

> *It has been less than a decade since the first personal computers appeared on the education scene. Schools have acquired computers rapidly since then, but most elements of the instructional process remain the same. This contrasts with other sectors of society, where technology has changed the way business is transacted, medical problems are analyzed, and products are produced. During this same decade calls for improving the quality of education for all children have increased. To better understand the potential of new interactive technologies for improving learning, the House Committee on Education and Labor, and its Subcommittee on Select Education, asked the Office of Technology Assessment to do this study.*
>
> *Teachers, administrators, parents, software publishers, hardware manufacturers, researchers, policymakers at all levels of government, and students all play a role in turning on the power of new tools for teaching and learning. This report examines developments in the use of computer-based technologies, analyzes key trends in hardware and software development, evaluates the capability of technology to improve learning in many areas, and explores ways to substantially increase student access to technology. The role of the teacher, teachers' needs for training, and the impact of Federal support for educational technology research and development are reviewed as well. (iii)*

There are eight chapters in the book with titles such as "Interactive Technology in Today's Classrooms," "Cost Effectiveness: Dollars and Sense," "The Teacher's Role," and "Research and Development: Past Support, Promising Directions." We have chosen here to include a section from the research and development chapter to give you an idea of the kinds of studies funded at the time and of the ways in which the authors of the report understand the relationship between research and classroom applications.

A new technology competition under the Programs of National Significance in the Title II Program for Mathematics, Science, Computer Education, and Critical Foreign Languages will have a funding level of $1 million. There is also a new competition for an Educational Technology Center. However, the RFP calls for less support ($5 million over 5 years, versus $7.7 million from 1983 to 1988 under the current contract) with a much broader research agenda. The new center will be responsible for all curriculum areas, not just mathematics and science, and its mandate will cover not only technology, but also teaching, learning, assessment, and school leadership. Despite the limited budget, interest in the center competition has been very strong. Indeed, the new technology center is perceived as "the only game in town" by the educational technology research community.

No new educational television initiatives are planned, and although the new congressionally mandated Star Schools Program for distance learning projects is authorized at a level of $19.1 million for 1988, no funds are requested in the Department's 1989 budget.

OTA concludes that these efforts fall short of focused, long-term commitments called for by the National Governors' Association, the National Task Force on Educational Technology, and the National School Boards Association.[43]

PROMISING DIRECTIONS FOR RESEARCH[44]

OTA finds that both recent research results and current demands for change in schools make increased research on technology and education especially promising at this time.[45] Three major factors make this so:

1. *The technology makes possible the testing and trying of new ideas.* Some of the best and the brightest scientists and researchers today see education as an important frontier for

[43]See National Governors' Association, Center for Policy Research and Analysis, *Time for Results: The Governors' 1991 Report on Education* (Washington, DC: 1986); National Task Force on Educational Technology, op. cit., footnote 35; and National School Boards Association, *A National Imperative: Educating for the 21st Century* (Alexandria, VA: 1988).

[44]Much of this discussion comes from Roy D. Pea and Elliot Soloway, "Mechanisms for Facilitating a Vital and Dynamic Education System: Fundamental Roles for Education Science and Technology," OTA contractor report, December 1987.

[45]See Dean Brown et al., "Influences on Development and Innovation in Educational Technology," OTA contractor report, October 1987. Both this report and Pea and Soloway, ibid., draw heavily on research documents, and personal and written interviews with preeminent researchers in the field. For a complete bibliography, see the contractor reports.

research because of the potential offered by interactive technologies.[46] Work in psychology, computer science, and artificial intelligence is contributing to understanding coherent theories of how people think and learn. These theories can now be tested on powerful computers.[47]

2. *Experimentation at all levels is leading to new uses of technology and demands for increased capabilities.* As the installed base of technology in the schools grows and becomes more powerful, new applications will become possible. Administrators want the technology to be used, and publishers want to exploit markets. As teachers become more sophisticated users of technology, they will demand better products.

3. *Critical educational needs are not being met.* The American public is painfully aware that too many students are dropping out of school, test scores are declining in relation to those of students in other industrial nations, industry is demanding a more skilled and technologically competent work force, and the number of difficult to teach students (special education students, non-English speaking students, and those from homes where educational support is lacking) is increasing. These problems, coupled with a shortage of teachers in some locations and subject areas, and growing concern over whether we can produce and keep the most talented teachers, all create a demand for change and for a more productive system for schooling.

Research in the cognitive, social, instructional, and computational sciences is changing the understanding of learning and teaching. This different focus is important—education viewed from the learner's perspective, not from the traditional curriculum/subject matter perspective (see box 7–D).

Some of the areas where current research shows promise for educational applications include the development of intelligent tutoring systems, tools which act as intelligence extenders, microworlds for learning, multimedia learning systems, new measures of testing learning, and research on how technology affects teaching and the social structure of schools (see table 7–5).

Intelligent Tutoring Systems

Much of the research on human learning and effective teaching has been channeled into developing artificial intelligence technologies that could simulate human tutoring. There is no question that human tutoring produces the most effective learning. For example, one researcher found that only 11 hours of individual tutoring produced the same level of mastery of the LISP programming language as 43 hours of traditional classroom instruction with supplementary student homework. What is also obvious is the prohibitive expense of one-on-one tutoring. The technological opportunity lies in the potential applications of artificial intelligence in simulating human tutoring.[48]

[46]Alan Collins, Bolt, Beranek and Newman, Inc., personal communication, December 1987. For example, Xerox has sponsored, with $5 million in startup funds, an Institute for Research on Learning. One of the goals of the Institute is "... to forge a synthesis of technology and learning theory so that the instructional capacity of new tools can be exploited." From Institute for Research on Learning, op. cit., footnote 24.

[47]"The ability of today's scientists to model the mind on computers was made possible by generations of psychologists who watched and recorded people at work on mental tasks of all sorts, and by the accumulated efforts of artificial intelligence researchers who have been trying to understand the nature of intelligence for over 30 years. Researchers, finding thousands of regularities in the mind's handling mental tasks, are now using the computer to try to assemble those regularities into a larger picture of how the mind performs." David L. Wheeler, "From Years of Work in Psychology and Computer Science, Scientists Build Theories of Thinking and Learning," *The Chronicle of Higher Education*, Mar. 9, 1988, p. A4.

[48]Susan F. Chipman et al., "Personnel and Training Research Program: Cognitive Science at ONR," *Naval Research Reviews*, vol. 38, 1986, p. 14.

BOX 7–D

Guided Discovery: Teaching From a Learner's Level of Understanding

The learner-centered approach looks at the learner's prior level of understanding, how preconceptions or misconceptions from earlier formal or informal experience may affect understanding, and where conceptual stumbling blocks exist. Recent research has focused on diagnosing the understanding, preconceptions, and interests a learner brings to formal instruction, so that additional instruction can build upon this base and deal with specific areas of difficulty.

Studies of how students learn science illustrate this approach. Students' preconceptions about concepts such as light, gravity, motion, heat and temperature, weight and density, and other physical phenomena are being examined. The Educational Technology Center at Harvard has identified "targets of difficulty," curricular topics both critical to students' further progress in science and widely recognized as difficult to teach and learn. For example, in the Weight/Density Project, the research group began by analyzing students' beginning conceptions. Although most middle school students do not know what density means, they do have related ideas about "heaviness for size" and what makes some objects sink or float. Most youngsters have one undifferentiated concept for thinking about weight v. density where physicists require two. The distinction physicists make is hard to teach because an object's density, unlike its weight, is not directly observable. The researchers are therefore exploring the use of interactive computer models to help students observe density in a simulated environment they can manipulate and explore. These activities are combined with hands-on activities with objects of different weights, sizes, and densities, along with problems posed by teachers to guide the students as they consider the connections between their experiences with real materials and the computer representations.[1]

[1]Educational Technology Center, Harvard Graduate School of Education, "Making Sense of the Future," a position paper on the role of technology in science, mathematics, and computing education, January 1988, pp. 7–8.

Cognitive science research is focusing on those aspects of human learning that could be used to develop intelligent tutoring systems. Work supported by the Personnel and Training Research Program at ONR indicates these include:[49]

- understanding how novices and experts solve problems in order to create an "ideal student" model;
- understanding where misconceptions occur when a real student does not perform as the "ideal student" would;
- defining the strategies of effective human tutors (knowing how to present information, what problems to present next, when to interrupt, when to explain);
- developing representations of real systems which learners can manipulate and explore, to try out hypotheses and "what if?" kinds of thinking. (What if I change this variable? What if it breaks down? What if I want to make another like it?)

[49]Ibid., pp. 15–16.

TABLE 7–5

**Promising Directions for Research: Selected Examples
of Intelligent Tutoring Systems, Intelligence Extenders,
Complex Microworlds, and Multimedia Learning Environments
in K–12 Education**

Project[a]	Topic	Grade level	Institution	Funding source
Algebra Workbench	Early algebra instruction using LOGO.	Sixth grade	Lesley College Bolt, Berenak & Newman (BBN)	NSF
Boxer	Programming environments for educators, students, and others	Middle school to adult	University of California, Berkeley (earlier MIT)	NSF
Chips	Tool kit to create graphics intensive programs.	Designers of instructional software	Learning, Research and Development Center (LRDC)	DoD
CMU Tutor	Authoring language to create instructional programs that help diagnose student responses.	Educators and in-structional designers	Carnegie-Mellon University (CMU)	NSF
Debuggy	Uses artificial intelligence and cognitive theory to diagnose subtraction errors.	Elementary school	Xerox PARC (earlier BBN)	DoD
Earth Lab	Collaborative learning and experiments in earth science using LANs.	Sixth grade	Bank Street College	NSF
Geometric Supposer	Hypothesis exploration in plane geometry.	Middle school	Harvard University Educational Technology Center	ED
Geometry Tutor	Uses cognitive theory to diagnose student errors in creating geometry proofs.	Tenth grade	CMU	NSF DoD Carnegie Foundation
Green Globs	Uses games and multiple representations to foster understanding of relationship between algebraic functions and graphs.	Middle school	University of Illinois	ED NSF
Heat and Temperatures	Helps students understand heat and temperature through microcomputer lab activities with dynamic visual representations.	Ninth grade	Harvard University, Educational Technology Center	ED
IDEA	Helps students learn to use systematic decision methods to solve problems.	Middle school to adult	New York University	Spencer Foundation

Project[a]	Topic	Grade level	Institution	Funding source
Inquire	Tool programs for active investigation of scientific phenomena.	Middle school	Bank Street College	NSF
INTERMEDIA	Hypermedia environment to create programs linking images, text, and other representations.	Undergraduate	Brown University	Annenberg Apple
Kids Network	Collaborative science experiments using telecommunications networks.	Fourth–sixth grade	Technical Education Resource Centers (TERC) National Geographic Society (NGS)	NSF NGS
LegoLOGO	Children control Lego machines using the LOGO programming language.	Elementary school and up	MIT BBN	DoD NSF
LISP Tutor	Intelligent tutoring system that provides instruction on introductory LISP programming.	High school and up	CMU	DoD
LOGO	Introductory programming language.	Elementary school and up	MIT BBN	DoD NSF
Macro-contexts	Uses interactive video technologies to provide functional contexts for science learning.	Middle school	Vanderbilt University	IBM DoD
Micro-computer-based laboratory	Inquiry-oriented science tools that connect data collection hardware to graphing software.	Elementary school and up	TERC	NSF ED
Modeling	Computer-based tools that let students build models of systems to learn calculus.	Tenth grade	TERC Lesley College	NSF
PALENQUE	Prototype using digital-video interactive technology that lets user "explore" a Mayan archeological site.	Elementary school	Bank Street College	GE/RCA
Proust	Diagnoses bugs in students' Pascal programs.	Middle school and up	Yale University	DoD
QUEST	A simulation environment for teaching basic electrical theory.	High school	BBN	DoD
Quill	A set of computer-based writing activities that use real documents to teach writing skills.	Elementary school	BBN	ED
Rat	Microworlds that allow children to interact with representations of everyday objects to learn basic arithmetic concepts.	Elementary school	LRDC	NSF

(Continued on next page)

187

TABLE 7-5 *(continued)*

Project[a]	Topic	Grade level	Institution	Funding source
Reasoning under uncertainty	Introductory statistical reasoning.	High school	BBN	NSF
Sketch	Tutor to help teach graphing of simple algebraic expressions.	Middle school and up	Carnegie-Mellon University	NSF
Smithtown	Discovery world using simulations to teach micro-economics.	High school and up	LRDC	DoD
SOPHIE	Electronic troubleshooting skills.	High school and up	Xerox PARC (earlier BBN)	DoD
STEAMER	Uses simulation to teach about operation of a steam propulsion power plant.	Vocational training	BBN	DoD
Tinker Tools	Uses game format to help learn basic concepts in Newtonian mechanics (mass, energy, and velocity).	Sixth grade	BBN	NSF
Vivarium	Computer-based models for ecology.	Elementary	MIT Los Angeles elementary school	Apple
Voyage of the Mimi	Uses multimedia materials for informal and class-room-based learning of mathematics and science.	Fourth grade and up	Bank Street College	ED NSF CBS Sony
West	Employs the coaching paradigm and a computer game format to teach basic arithmetic skills.	Elementary	BBN	DoD
Word Learning	System that helps children learn the meaning of words by providing different characterizations of the meaning of words in a passage.	Elementary school and up	Princeton University	DoD Spencer Foundation
Word Problems	Prototype using multiple representations to help students learn about reasoning with intensive quantities.	Elementary	Harvard University Educational Technology Center	ED

Abbreviations: NSF = National Science Foundation, DoD = U.S. Department of Defense, ED = U.S. Department of Education, GE = General Electric, MIT = Massachusetts Institute of Technology, LANs = local area networks

[a]Projects listed represent the broad range of innovative applications of technology to problems central to cognitive, social, and instructional sciences of education, particularly in the area of K–12 education. This is by no means an exhaustive list.

SOURCE: Office of Technology Assessment, 1988.

- trying out various student-tutor interfaces to determine how easily the student can get at the knowledge contained in the tutor's ideal student model;[50]
- showing various graphic means which can illustrate ways of solving problems; and
- studying how instruction can be adapted to limitations in the student's attention span or ability to absorb information.

An example of an intelligent tutoring system which incorporates at least limited capabilities in all these areas is the Geometry Tutor developed at Carnegie-Mellon University. ONR funding for early research, later supplemented by NSF support for development and the Carnegie Foundation support for testing in the schools, brought this concept from basic research to classroom trials in the Pittsburgh public schools. Other intelligent tutors are being supported by NSF for Pascal programming and an intelligent tutor for high school algebra.

Intelligence Extenders

There is a major class of tools for learning and problem solving, variously described as "cognitive technologies," "intelligence extenders," "cognitive workbenches" or "mental prostheses." These software tools enhance the utility of computers by their capacity to quickly and accurately manipulate symbols, including pictures, text, diagrams, numbers, and sound. They can be used in various combinations as needed.

For example, text editors and graphics tools in word processors enable the writer to manipulate language with new ease and grace. Using these tools, writers find that revisions come more easily, thoughts can be reformatted, rearranged, and given new expressive shapes previously not possible in the world of erasures and cut-and-paste editing. These adjustments and revisions in writing are techniques that are associated with expert performance among writers, yet even the most inexperienced of students can benefit from the assistance these intelligence extenders provide to help them write more fluently.

As these tools now approach second-generation or integrated tool levels, they can be customized by teachers and publishers for different curricular areas and topics. Like *dBase III*, a powerful general tool for various database applications, or *Lotus 1-2-3*, which offers multiple spreadsheets and modeling applications for business, comparably powerful "engines" for education could spawn customized development and applications by the teacher for classroom use. *HyperCard*, the latest associative tool, allows the user to create and link together "cards" of intermixed text, graphics, videodisc images, and sound. This software tool also includes a powerful, but simple, programming language. *HyperCard*'s lineage can be traced back to Memex,[51] the forerunner of today's "hypertext," "idea processing," and outline processing systems. Much of the work creating tool "engines" has been taking place at the university level over the past 5 years, as in Project Andrew at Carnegie-Mellon University, Project Athena at the Massachusetts Institute of Technology, and Brown University's IRIS Project.

Among the most promising uses of technology tools are those for exceptional students. Innovative projects include braille word processors for the blind, specially designed materials for

---

[50]"The interface between the user and the computer may be the last frontier in computer design." James D. Foley, "Interfaces for Advanced Computing," *Scientific American,* October 1987. Examples of interfaces are touch-sensitive, plasma-panel screens, the "mouse" pointing device, the chorded key set, and on-screen windows; icons, menus, browsers, overlapping windows, and the bitmapped display; eyetracking; and the Dataglove. (See Brown et al., op. cit., footnote 45, app. III.)

[51]See Vannevar Bush, "As We May Think," *Atlantic Monthly,* July 1945.

teaching English syntactic structure to improve the reading and writing skills of the deaf, and synthesized speech generated by touching graphics tablets, enabling students with little or no capacity for oral language to communicate.

Increasingly Complex Microworlds

In increasingly complex microworlds a computer representation of a situation or environment enables the student to learn about the content area by exploring the representation, and to practice a skill in progressively more complex computer-generated simulated environments.

Microworlds are valuable learning tools because students can learn by doing, by acting on the microworld rather than merely observing phenomena. They can be very powerful stimuli for understanding how things work. Some microworld systems let students build or program their own worlds, allowing them to explore the properties of the system and their relationships by examining the consequences of changes to these properties.

For example, in the LegoLOGO project, students write LOGO programs to control Lego machines, connecting programming and real-world objects such as gears, levers, and sensors, to introduce key concepts in physics, engineering, and robotics through an experimental approach. In microcomputer-based laboratories students learn science by doing it. Alternatively, imaginary microworlds can also be constructed (e.g., non-Newtonian universes) which offer new opportunities to bring to life things that students could never see or imagine without the technologies. The microworld can offer novel opportunities going beyond the limits of the real world, allowing the learner to delve into created worlds of fantasy and exploration. Examples of microworld R&D include systems for early physics learning (Dynaturtle; Thinker Tools); systems for exploring electrical circuit behavior (SOPHIE; QUEST); economic systems (Smithtown); physical systems (STEAMER); and ecosystems (The Vivarium Project).

Multimedia Learning Environments

Print remains the medium of instruction in schools today, just as it was a century ago. Video, audio, graphics and other representation of information are used far less, despite the fact that they are highly motivating and effective for learning, and most often the sources of the learning that takes place outside the schoolroom.

Researchers are studying ways learners process information presented in nontext media, and how various symbols (pictures, diagrams, graphs, flowcharts, etc.) affect understanding.[52] As discussed in chapter 8, new developments make it possible to combine video, audio, and graphics to provide information in varying formats that the teacher can control and access quickly. Object-oriented graphics editors, digital scanners for photos and video frames, and animation tools are available for computers at reasonably low cost, and are being used in learning technology development work in the research laboratory.

A future scenario illustrates how these multimedia tools could be used in the classroom. Picture the elementary school teacher discussing earth science and plate tectonics with the class. Using the computer as a multimedia control device, the teacher pulls up for computer projection dramatic online video clips of volcanoes. Students use an interactive microworld to examine how continental drift operates, and slides of fossil remains from different continents show how now-dispersed land masses were once connected. One student has the idea of photographing local geological strata, another

---

[52]See Mary Alice White, *What Curriculum for the Information Age* (Hillsdale, NJ: Lawrence Erlbaum Associates, 1987).

brings in a home video of television footage on volcanoes he thinks might be relevant, another tapes the sound of storms to produce an audio soundtrack. When they return the next day these auditory and visual images are scanned into the classroom archives for other students to use. Electronic messages flow between students and from teachers to students when difficulties arise or to share new ways of thinking about what is being learned. Students work at multimedia composition work stations, revealing what they have learned by constructing and revising their own reports about plate tectonics from these and other materials they have found and pulled together.

New Measures of Assessing Learning

Tests play a role in the learning process by telling students what in the curriculum is important. If, for example, testing is confined to memorizable end results, teachers will teach facts and students will memorize them to score well on tests, ignoring the more sophisticated levels of understanding and reasoning which education aims to foster. At present, very little school testing is directed toward measuring students' conceptual understanding. Researchers suggest the need to devise new assessment strategies that analyze the attainment of nontrivial skills, with particular attention to "complex thinking skills" such as the ability to generalize appropriately, to invent analogies and use them critically, to take problems apart into interacting parts, to effectively manage and deal with complexity, to lay out a procedure as a sequence of approximations which converge to a solution, and to analyze a situation from a viewpoint other than one's own.

Another important feature of testing should be the ability to diagnose the student's present level of conceptual understanding, taking into account the preconceptions or misconceptions he or she brings to the learning situation. These prior beliefs may frustrate traditional instruction and need to be identified so that the teacher can address them appropriately. Research is needed to develop instruments for measuring deep conceptual understanding and diagnosing prior understandings.

An additional approach to assessment calls upon learners to evaluate themselves as they are learning (e.g., testing comprehension in reading) and to work strategically to overcome difficulties as they are experienced. Here, too, today's tests are inadequate for self-assessment of understanding or skills.

Research on How Technology Affects Teaching and the Social Structure of Schooling

A last but important area of educational research focuses on the social context in which learning takes place. For example, teachers can make a difference by creating and maintaining an open environment in which making mistakes is an accepted part of the learning process, and in which different approaches to problems are welcomed as opportunities for group learning. Such an environment appears to influence whether a student treats work on a problem as an opportunity for learning or as an occasion for failure and low self-image. And a teacher's negative expectations for a student's performance often become self-fulfilling. The computer, with its immediate and private response to the student's input, can be one antidote.

Social relations with peers in the classroom can also be harnessed to contribute to cognitive growth. Numerous studies indicate that group discussions of strategies for solving a problem can be important vehicles for learning, by making explicit to each member the merits of different approaches and viewpoints.

All the ways technology can enhance what students learn, how learning is measured and how the curriculum can be reconfigured will have major implications for the teacher's role (see chapter 5).

Without new training efforts to teach with, not about, technology, the innovations discussed above will make little impact on education. As one researcher said:

> The problem with education now is not what students are capable of, but what teachers are capable of, given their previous education. The main problem of educational research and development is to educate teachers to teach to students' conceptual understanding, and to teach them to diagnose students' alternative frameworks for thinking about what is being taught.[53]

Few experts see the technology replacing the teacher. Some believe that this is what intelligent tutors are being designed to do, but most think only a small part of formal education can be mechanized in that fashion. Instead, most experts see ways in which the computer can be used to revitalize the teaching profession. For example, the computer could provide better ways for teachers to see incremental changes in students' understanding of concepts to diagnose areas of special difficulty. This will improve teachers' abilities to teach based on an understanding of the student's particular stumbling blocks.

Computers could also help make the teacher's role more one of "coach" than delivery agent of learning. Such tools as microworlds, word processors, and database programs enable students to work individually or in small groups focusing on problem solving activities. In this mode, peer learning is facilitated, while the teacher guides the students in a process of discovery learning. (See box 7–D.) Some see this as an even more intellectually challenging role for teachers than that required in the lecturer/test-deliverer teaching model common today. Computers could also promote more effective learning for the teachers themselves as they use technology in preservice, inservice, and networking activities.

Technologies may have a special role to play in research on the "microsystems" of schooling, which deal with the social organization of instruction and curriculum content. For example, networking technologies could fundamentally change the communication systems of classrooms, connecting teachers and students to a nearly limitless number of learning and teaching resources, including information databases and teachers, specialists, and other students, as close as the next seat and as far as across the ocean.

BARRIERS TO IMPLEMENTATION

A number of barriers stand in the way of moving from research to application in the classroom. Many educators fear that without major restructuring of schools, such as allowing teachers much more flexibility in controlling the curriculum, opening up the time-in-grade system to that of student movement based on individual progress in meeting instructional goals, and other improvements to the educational system, no significant changes will or can be made, with or without technology R&D.[54]

---

[53]Susan Carey, "Cognitive Science and Science Education," *American Psychologist,* vol. 41, 1986, pp. 1123–1130.

[54]"Technology can never replace teachers. But the lack of new technologies in our schools—or the use of technology as if it were no more than a modern blackboard or drill sheet—is certainly squelching real teaching and learning. We've always talked about getting out of the rut of teaching as information dispensing and overcoming a 'one best system' of student learning that denies individual differences and needs, despite all our rhetoric to the contrary. Well, in technology we have the opportunity. The question is, will we take it and what will we do with it?" Al Shanker, president, American Federation of Teachers, personal communication, Mar. 22, 1988.

Problems of funding, leadership, and strategic planning have been highlighted in previous sections of this chapter, while others are discussed in detail in other sections of this report (see chapter 5 on the teacher's role and chapter 6 on software). There are additional barriers:

- The lack of consistent stable funding means that ideas rarely can be sustained through experimental and applied development with appropriate classroom testing and evaluation. Prototype development is not enough to bring the results of basic research into classrooms.

- The hardware necessary to conduct sophisticated artificial intelligence research is extremely expensive. Small grants or contracts to researchers will not suffice.

- The installed base of technologies in the schools today is not powerful enough to run some of the more sophisticated software applications produced by advanced research. In order to experiment with advanced applications, research projects need to be allied with schools and make the necessary advanced hardware systems available to them.[55]

- There is need for long-term comprehensive evaluations of different approaches, including those utilizing technology. Schools are justifiably cautious about using real students as "guinea pigs" for radical approaches without some track record of success.

- There is a shortage of research scientists to do this kind of interdisciplinary research. Currently we have not infused ". . . enough sense of national emergency into the work to attract them away from other attractive projects."[56]

- Differing design features in the technology bedevil the education R&D community and practitioners. Many argue for standards in interface design so research can translate across machines, to ensure compatibility, to reduce learning time for users, and to make finding and storing data easy for even the youngest students.

THINKING AND RE-READING

1. As you re-read the excerpt, note the problems that the authors think the use of computers might solve. Do the claims seem reasonable to you? Why or why not?

2. Write down five sentences in which the word "computer" appears. One that we noted, for example, appears in Chester Finn's quotation when he states, "The computer will deepen its presence in schools and classrooms." What is the effect of using the word "computer" in this manner? How is it used in the other sentences you've listed? What consequences are there in talking and writing about computers like this?

[55]For example, in order to test the *Geometry Tutor* in schools, the researchers at Carnegie-Mellon University had to loan computers to the test sites in the Pittsburgh schools. The Geometry Tutor's high-level software required more powerful machines than the schools had. Although the final version has been adapted to run on a Macintosh, even these are rare in high schools at this time.

[56]George Miller, Princeton University, personal communication, December 1987.

WRITING AND THINKING

1. The authors write of several educational applications of computers that they think seem especially promising: intelligent tutoring systems, intelligence extenders, microworlds for learning, multimedia learning systems, and new measures for testing learning. Make up a short list of questions and arrange to meet with three high school or college instructors teaching in different disciplines. (An alternative would be to ask them if you can query them through e-mail.) Find out if any of these instructional applications are being used in their fields. Are the instructors themselves using these applications for teaching? If so, ask that they describe how they use them with students. What changes do they see in their teaching and in the schools' social structures that they attribute, at least in part, to the use of the new technologies? Prepare an oral report of your findings to share with the rest of your class.

2. In his article on computers and the schools earlier in this section, Michael Apple writes, "In our society, technology is seen as an autonomous process. It is set apart and viewed as if it had a life of its own, independent of social intentions, power, and privilege." Consider this statement in relation to the excerpt from *Power On!* Find examples that support Apple's claim. Are there other examples that contradict his claim? Write an extended e-mail message to another person in your class in which you discuss the possible consequences of viewing technology from this perspective.

3. In his article on "Mental Material," which you can access at the Prentice Hall web site, David Noble writes that his arguments about the close connections between the military establishment and educational research might seem somewhat extreme. Look over the table of funded research projects included in this excerpt from *Power On!* Is there evidence to support Noble's arguments? Choose two of the claims he makes and argue for their validity based on evidence you find in the whole of the excerpt included here. Your audience is your instructor, a critical but fair-minded reader.

IMAGES OF EDUCATION AND TECHNOLOGY

THINKING AND RE-READING

1. In Appendix A of this reader, you will find a list of questions that will help you read and understand this set of images, and other images that you see, in new ways. Read the questions in this list carefully and use them to "read" the images in this section—carefully and with an increasing sense of thoughtfulness.

WRITING AND LEARNING

1. Choose at least two of the three images to analyze more carefully. For these images, write down your answers to the questions listed in Appendix A.

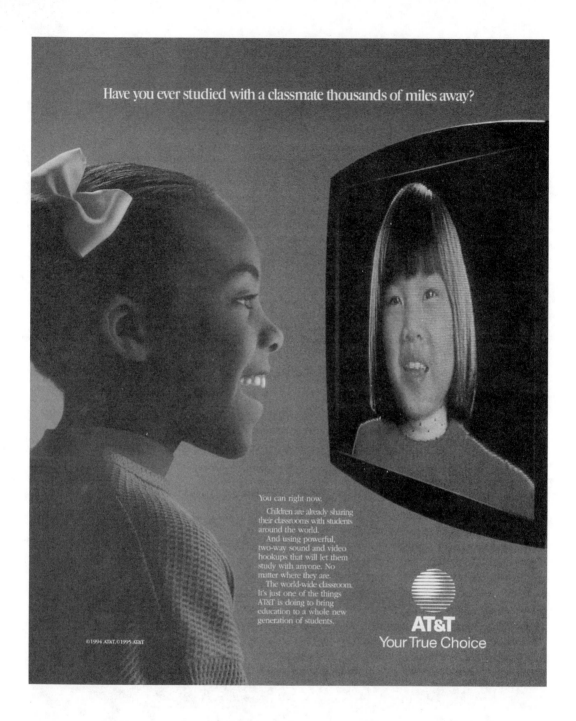

Have you ever studied with a classmate thousands of miles away?

You can right now.

Children are already sharing their classrooms with students around the world.

And using powerful, two-way sound and video hookups that will let them study with anyone. No matter where they are.

The world-wide classroom. It's just one of the things AT&T is doing to bring education to a whole new generation of students.

©1994 AT&T. ©1995 AT&T

AT&T
Your True Choice

198

Feminism and Computers in Composition Instruction

Emily Jessup

IN HER ARTICLE ON THE "GENDER GAP" and computers in education, Emily Jessup describes a number of inequities existing between the sexes regarding the new technologies. She tells us that not only are women underrepresented at all levels of learning about computers, but that the disparities become greater as a girl or woman advances through school. She also argues that a feminist research methodology, that is, a methodology that pays close attention to its own biases and attempts to give those who are "researched" a say in the research, would be more amenable to addressing research questions on computers. Because Jessup's article was written a number of years ago, it provides us with a good opportunity to re-examine the issues she raises and to document any progress that schools have made in regard to the "gender gap."

> *A gender gap in computer use appears as early as elementary school, and persists in some form into our college writing classes. What impact has the computer gender gap had on the use of computers in composition? How has the computer gender gap affected teachers of writing? What are the consequences of this gap for our students? What can we do in our classrooms to try to minimize its effect? What can we do to try to close the computer gender gap?*

The land of computing is a frontier country, and, as in the development of most frontier territories, there are many more men than women. Indeed, it appears that at all levels of learning about computers—in school, in higher education, in further education, in training, in adult education classes, and in independent learning—women tend to be strikingly underrepresented. The extent of their underrepresentation varies from sector to sector and to some extent from country to country, but the fact of it is so ubiquitous that the evidence tends to become monotonous (Gerver, 1989, p. 483).

In 1980, Cindy Selfe and Billie Wahlstrom visited a computer store in Houghton, Michigan. Five years later, they described their experience of trying to join the "computer revolution." Selfe and Wahlstrom (1985) discovered that

> We couldn't even read the enlistment material. . . . [T]he variety of English spoken by the computers, the people who talked to them, and those who ministered to their needs were as foreign to us as the untranslated Aeneid is to most first-year college students. Indeed, these people had taken the same language we used every day in our scholarly pursuit of the humanities and transformed it into a language of mechanistic violence. (p. 64)

Selfe and Wahlstrom appear to attribute their lack of comfort in this technological world to their training as humanists. They contrast their experience using computers with that of "a skinny lad . . . [who] tippity-taps his way through a paper for first-year English; the machine seems friendly enough to him" (p. 67). In this article, Selfe and Walhstrom do not discuss gender explicitly; however, they do identify the computer-using student as a skinny *lad*, not a *lass*, while describing themselves as (female) outsiders. Ten years after Selfe and Wahlstrom's foray, many more women are participating in the "computer revolution." Unfortunately, most of the people in the vanguard of this revolution appear to be men. For example, according to *Women Computing* (1988, p. 2), women constitute a relatively small percentage of the readers of popular computing magazines:

Magazine	% of women readers
Lotus	19.6%
Personal Computing	19%
PC Resource	15%
InfoWorld	10%

The "gender gap" in computer use is visible as early as elementary school. For instance, a participant in EDU:WIT, a computer conference focusing on women in technology that grew out of the 1989 EDUCOM conference, reported in November 1989 that her daughter was encouraged to play with computers but was discouraged from programming them in her elementary classroom. The child's teacher explained that because girls are not as good in math as are boys, it made more sense to let the boys try their hands at programming. Reviewing the results of several different research projects, Hawkins (1985) claims that "sex was the most obvious factor affecting differential use of the machines at all grade levels across sites" (p. 171). Gerver (1989) describes a pattern in which the age of females in both the United Kingdom and the United States is inversely proportional to their computer use. At the elementary level, the percentage of girls and boys using computers is approximately equal. By high school, girls make up only one-third of computer users. In higher education, far more men than women pursue degrees in computer science; the more specialized the degree, the lower the percentage of women (p. 484).

The gender gap in computer use in school is not simply a quantitative one. For instance, use of word-processing software does not appear to be linked to sex (Hawkins, 1985; Becker, 1987). Girls in elementary school are as likely as boys are to play computer games, although this changes in middle and high school (Becker, p. 152). The difference in computer use appears to be greatest in after-school and self-sponsored use. More boys than girls use computers before and after school; more boys than girls use computers at home; more boys than girls attend computer camps (Peer Computer Equity Report, 1984; Hawkins, 1985; Elmer-DeWitt, 1986; Sanders, 1986; Becker, 1987;

Gerver, 1989). Girls also have less confidence in their abilities to use computers than boys do (Peer Computer Equity Report, 1984; Gerver, 1989). Hawkins argues that to understand sex differences in computer use, investigators need to look deeper, to "examine functional uses of the material in particular situations" (p. 178). Stephen Marcus (1987) argues that the sociocultural context of computers leads to the dominance of white middle-class males as computer users:

> Gender, race, and socioeconomic status profoundly influence the experience students have with computers before they reach college classrooms, and these experiences establish the foundation of what students (and faculty) think computers are for. What our students think about computers (their prethinking and their patterns of thinking) and how they think with computers are conditioned by their early experiences with computers. (p. 134)

Some researchers believe that this situation is changing. Strickland, Feely and Wepner (1987) believe that the gender biases surrounding computers are a function of this particular time:

> Our experience suggests that the sexual stereotypes surrounding the use of computers are gradually eroding. In schools where computers are used extensively for word processing as well as other types of activities, students readily see the usefulness of the computer in their lives. . . . We agree that as the computer is given wider and more personal use in the curriculum it is less likely that these sexual distinctions will persist. (pp. 179–80)

Others disagree, claiming that expanding the uses of the computer in the classroom does not do enough to challenge traditional images of sex-appropriate behavior and sex-linked abilities (Sanders, 1986; Stanworth, 1983; Gerver, 1989).

Concerted efforts to make computers more appealing to girls and women have been successful. Some schools, looking for ways to upset the social stereotype of the computer as a "boy's toy," have tried to encourage girls to use computers by initiating clubs and summer sessions for girls, by hiring female computer teachers, and by screening software for gender bias (Elmer-DeWitt, 1986; Sanders, 1986). Other good examples of this effort are Deborah L. Brecher's (1985) book, *The Women's Computer Literacy Handbook* and the computer literacy project for women from which it grew. After working in the computer industry as an "insider," Brecher founded the National Women's Mailing List using a PC and a commercial software package. As she traveled across the country meeting with representatives of women's groups, she found that women who were outside the computing world were having trouble finding a way in. Brecher (1985) states, "There was nothing available that made it easy for women to gain these skills without being patronized, put down, or paralyzed by unnecessary fears" (p. 2). Brecher opened a computer school in San Francisco and began The Women's Computer Literacy Project. The premise of the project is that the language of the computer industry is deliberately exclusive; the goal of the project is to make this language accessible. Before using a technical term, Brecher defines the term, often by making an analogy to something—like cooking—with which women are likely to be more familiar. The Women's Computer Literacy Project's goal is to help women break into the world of computers.

Despite efforts like these, a gender gap in attitudes toward computers and in computer use persists. Without careful scrutiny of gender issues in the area of computers, we in composition risk replicating this gender gap. Unfortunately, composition teachers appear to be doing just that. Seventeen panels at the 1989 annual convention of the Conference on College Composition and Communication focused on computers and composition. Approximately three-fifths of those presenting papers in that area were men, and two-fifths were women (i.e., 30 men, 21 women). On ten of the panels, men and women presented papers together; on seven panels, the speakers were the same sex. Five of the seven same-sex panels were comprised of men; only two same-sex panels were comprised of women. The numbers are significant in themselves, for they reinforce a wider cultural stereotype that links computers with the realm of science and math—a traditionally masculine area. The topics of these same-sex panels are also telling: men spoke about computers and composition with an emphasis on the technology—two panels discussed hypertext, one panel discussed computers and text analysis, one panel discussed the technology of networked computers, and one panel discussed the national project on computers and writing. Women spoke about teaching with computers, emphasizing the social implications of using computers in composition classes—one panel discussed computers and basic writers, and one panel discussed the "social rhetoric of empowerment in computer-supported writing communities."

Clearly, when gender differences are so acute among the most computer-literate members of our field, we need to ask ourselves about the ways in which the fact of gender has been and is influencing composition instructors' use of computers in classrooms. We also need to ask ourselves about the implications of this gender gap for our students. How and when do writing faculty and students begin using computers for writing? What kinds of formal support do male and female composition students and teachers receive for using computers? What kind of informal networks facilitate or hinder teachers' and students' work with computers? What kinds of mentoring go on for men and women, students and teachers, as they use computers for writing? We need to ask questions about the access male and female students and teachers have to computers, at school and at home. We need to learn more about the ways academic and nonacademic computer experts interact with novice male and female students and faculty as they attempt to learn more about using computers in composition classes. We need to ask questions about the attitudes teachers and students have toward the use of computers for writing, as well as ask questions about the origins of those attitudes.

AN EPISTEMOLOGICAL APPROACH
TO FEMINISM AND COMPUTERS

Feminist research in other disciplines suggests that because we live in a patriarchal society, men and women tend to develop different epistemological frameworks that shape the way they think about the world as well as the way they learn. These frameworks will inevitably influence the way men and women conceptualize computers. In *Women's Ways of Knowing: The Development of Self, Voice, and Mind,* Belenky, Clinchy, Goldberger, and Tarule (1986) argue against claims for universal stages in intellectual development. Based on their interviews with 135 women, Belenky et al. take issue with William Perry's scheme for intellectual development:

> In Perry's (1970) account of intellectual development, the student discovers critical reasoning as "how They (the upper case "T" symbolizing authority—here, the professors) want us to think," how students must think in order to win the academic game. The student uses this new mode of thinking to construct arguments powerful enough to meet the standards of an impersonal authority. (p. 101)

Belenky et al. characterize this way of knowing as "separate knowing" (p. 98), and contrast it with the "connected knowing" (p. 100) described by women:

The focus is not on how They want you to think, as in Perry's account, but on how they (the lower case "t" symbolizing more equal status) think; and the purpose is not justification but connection. (p. 101)

In *Learning Styles: Implications for Improving Educational Practices,* Claxton and Murrell (1987) suggest that the distinction between separate and connected knowing resonates with distinctions other researchers have made: separate knowers, like the "splitters, field independents, serialists, and abstract, analytical learners are more in the objectivist mode of knowing" while connected knowers, like "lumpers, field sensitives, holists, and concrete learners are more in the relational mode" (p. 75). Claxton and Murrell claim that to improve current educational practice,

teaching practices are needed that honor both analytic and relational knowing. . . . By honoring both analytical and relational ways of knowing, we may make our greatest contribution—not only to effective learning but also to building a greater sense of community as well. (p. 76)

Sherry Turkle's (1984) research suggests that the computer can play a special role in legitimizing this relational way of knowing when students are allowed to develop their own approaches to computers. In a study of children, Turkle observed differences in programming styles which she characterized as "hard" and "soft." Hard mastery "is the imposition of will over the machine through the implementation of a plan" (p. 104); soft mastery envisions the computer's formal system "not as a set of unforgiving 'rules,' but as a language for communicating with, negotiating with, a behaving, psychological entity" (pp. 108–109). Soft mastery exemplifies an alternative approach, Turkle observes, providing "a model of how women, when given a chance, can find another way to think and talk about the mastery not simply of machines but of formal systems" (p. 118). To what extent are we encouraging students to find their own ways of using computers in our classrooms? Are we doing enough to ensure that computers act as catalysts for a range of learning styles and writing processes, or are we unwittingly using computer applications to reinforce a single way of approaching tasks?

The research on learning styles and on epistemology is also important for composition teachers and students because the kinds of thinking we value get translated into specific kinds of writing. To date, at least one strand of composition studies has resisted the dominant objectivist epistemology that emphasizes a clear separation between subject and object, through its emphasis on the importance of personal writing. As Elizabeth Flynn (1988) writes,

James Britton . . . reverses traditional hierarchies by privileging private expression over public transaction, process over product. In arguing that writing for the self is the matrix out of which all forms of writing develop, he valorizes an activity and a mode of expression that have previously been undervalued or invisible. (p. 424)

The emphasis on the self as the matrix, on subjectivity, creates tension, for even though composition teachers and researchers recognize the need to reverse the traditional hierarchies, as a field they also wrestle with trying to legitimize their work in the eyes of the rest of the academic community, and composition teachers are terribly conscious that their students need to "master" objectivist prose. Importing the computer from its traditional home in analytic culture may tip the balance. The computer can easily become merely a tool to help teachers help students become assimilated into the dominant academic culture if, for example, composition teachers relinquish journal writing to spend more time writing essays with the computer; if the layout of computer labs makes it easier for teachers to focus on the production of texts rather than on the creation of community; and if teachers are not comfortable using available technology to create electronic settings for genuine collaboration. Composition teachers need to ask about the kinds of thinking computers are used to support. For instance, when teachers or researchers develop tutorials, do they focus on academic arguments that assume the stance of a separate knower? Do they develop programs that build on relational knowing, that encourage students to make connections between themselves and their material, between themselves and their audience? Do they work as hard to develop programs that facilitate collaborative writing as they do to develop (more marketable) programs that guide individuals through a process of writing with a special emphasis on editing?

Computers can help make connections between students and between teachers and students through collaborative writing and computer conferencing. Gerrard (1988) argues that

> For women, computers in the writing course may be particularly congenial: research has shown that while many female students dislike the isolation typical of programming, they enjoy collaborative uses of computers. (p. 8)

Computers can have this effect when they are used for collaboration, but composition teachers need to ask questions about how computers are used. Some writing instructors are finding that classes meeting in computer labs without local area networks may do more individual work and less collaborative work than classes in traditional classrooms. Are teachers and researchers developing software and designing computer labs that facilitate interaction among students? Are teachers training male and female writing instructors to use the technology to promote collaboration? Are teachers making certain that both male and female students are confident about using the technology?

RESEARCH ON FEMINISM AND COMPUTERS IN COMPOSITION INSTRUCTION

Very little research on feminism and computers in composition has been done, but at least one study supports the general observations made by Marcus and Gerver. Selfe, Ruehr, and Johnson (1988) report that their modified case study of twenty-three computer lab users at Michigan Technological University confirmed both of their initial hypotheses:

> Age and gender determine the amount of computer-related experience individuals bring to the task of learning a word-processing package and, thus, the attitude with which they approach this task and the instructional methods they prefer to use in learning the package. . . .
>
> Age and gender influence the instructional methods individuals prefer to use when they learn a word-processing package. (p. 75)

According to this study, younger subjects had more experience with computers than did older ones and male subjects had a more positive attitude and less apprehension about using computers than did females. Men also found on-line instruction more effective and enjoyable than did women. Selfe, Ruehr, and Johnson conclude that "teachers cannot expect learners of different ages and genders to approach word processing with the same experience, attitudes, or skills" (p. 82).

Other studies (Selfe, 1990; Cooper & Selfe, 1990) that directly address feminist issues in computers and composition focus on the potential of computers to subvert traditional classroom hierarchies. Selfe (1990) argues that the "value of computers in our classrooms is due as much to their power as tools for social and political reform of literacy education as it is to their power as tools of communication" (p. 121). Her emphasis is on the power of computer networks to facilitate interactions among people when standard markers—sex, age, race—are invisible, and when conventional patterns of turn-taking no longer exist. As Selfe states,

> In this vision, computer networks become human networks, electronic circles that support alternative, non-traditional dialogue and dialect, communities that value re-vision and reinterpretation of traditional educational structures. (p. 123)

The potential of computers to reform education is limited, however, as long as the visions of those who have power to make decisions remain limited. Selfe goes on to say,

> School boards and administrators, privileging individual achievement over group communication, will pay for computers but not the essential software and cables needed to link them together. (pp. 131–132)

The research on feminism and computers in composition instruction completed to date has focused on two central areas: the potential of computers to subvert traditional hierarchies and to enfranchise diverse populations of learners, and on different attitudes among actual computer users. As we enter the 1990s, more research needs to be done that self-consciously asks questions about the impact of gender on computer development and use, and on the sociocultural context surrounding computers. As we consider the place of computers in our society, researchers or teachers of composition might ask what impact computers are having on women, and what the implications of this are for education. What roles are women in the computer industry playing? What are the implications of this for us and for our students? As we think about computers within our own institutions, we might ask how decisions about computers get made, and who makes them. What influences those decisions? As we think about computers within the context of our writing programs, we need to ask whether female teachers and students are as confident in their abilities to use technology as male teachers and students are. Is this true across applications (i.e., word processing, computer conferencing, data retrieval, CAI)?

THE RESEARCH AGENDA FOR THE 1990S

Among the necessary questions we need to ask in the 1990s are a set of questions that focus on the institutional contexts of computers in composition. Researchers or teachers of composition need to ask questions about institutional hierarchies and decision-making processes. Andrea W. Herrmann (1989) argues that because most school systems are paternalistic in the full sense of the word—the administrators still predominantly male, the teachers female—women are being excluded from making decisions about incorporating technology into the curriculum (p. 113). Within the realm of academia, conversations about computers—about the development of new products, about adopting already-developed state-of-the-art products, about applications of new products, and about access to new developments—quickly establish an elite group of insiders and a much larger group of outsiders. Men are more likely to have the background needed to participate in these conversations, and men without a formal background in technology may find it easier to bluff their way into this realm of techno-talk than women will. (See Herrmann in this collection.) Specific questions we need to ask include the following:

- We need to explore the decision-making processes of institutions with respect to technology: Who makes decisions about technology? How are decisions made? Whose values do those decisions represent? To what extent are women excluded from making institutional decisions about the kinds of technology that will be available for writing instruction, and the uses to which the technology may be put?
- What steps can we take to ensure that women will be involved in these institutional decisions in increasing numbers?
- What can we do to ensure that women gain both the technical background and the self-confidence it takes to have access to decision-making circles?

We need to look more carefully at teachers as users of technology, and we need to ask ourselves what the repercussions are for not using (or for using) computers. As status begins to accrue to instructors using technology, those most likely to be penalized are those with the most limited background in technology (older women) and those with the fewest opportunities for using computers outside the writing classroom itself (teachers with family responsibilities—likely to be women; underpaid writing instructors—also likely to be women). Herrmann (1989) suggests that "until they feel confident using [word-processing] technology for themselves, teachers are unlikely to teach others to use it" (p. 115). Selfe, Ruehr, and Johnson (1988) report that women, especially older women, are less likely to feel comfortable with a range of instructional modes in learning to use technology. Questions we need to ask about teachers as users of technology include:

- Within our writing programs, are we inadvertently creating a caste system of elite technology users and lower-status computer avoiders?
- How can we develop teacher-training programs that enable women and men of different ages with different experiences to become comfortable using technology in a variety of ways?
- How can we change the statistics in our Conference on College Composition and Communication program, so that women are as likely to be presenting papers on the programs they are developing, the networks they are building, the conferences they are running, as men are to be presenting papers on the social dynamics in the computer classroom, or the rhetoric of empowerment?

We need to think more about the impact of the computer gender gap on the students in our classes. Margaret Benston (1988) claims that

> Men and women have different access to training, knowledge and confidence about technology. One result of this difference is that men have access to much more of the technological realm than women have and their potential for action is correspondingly much larger. (p. 19)

We are likely to teach students the rudiments of the computer applications we use in our classrooms, but in many cases what we teach students to do represents only a fraction of available computing resources. Therefore, we must ask the following:

- What "potential for action" do our male and female students have? Students who explore the technology on their own are likely to benefit from it—who are the explorers?

- What can teachers do to ensure that female students are as likely to investigate computer resources as male students are?
- What kinds of role modeling go on in computer classrooms? What kinds of attitudes toward computers and themselves as users of technology do female and male teachers intentionally or unintentionally portray?

Communication about technology is also likely to be influenced by gender. As Benston says, "The information flow is almost entirely one-sided: men may explain a technological matter to women but they do not discuss it with them; that they do with other men" (p. 26).

- What happens in classrooms as teachers talk about technology? Do teachers talk with male and female students about technology in similar or different ways? Do teachers discuss with males, explain to females? Do teachers make more eye contact with males when they talk about technology?
- How do students talk with each other about technology in classrooms?
- Are the people to whom students turn with technical questions explaining or discussing ideas with them? Does this vary? According to what variables?

Further questions arise as teachers consider the kinds of software and hardware we are using or developing for use in writing classes:

- Are teachers affirming the epistemological frameworks students bring into the classroom, or are they using computers in ways that reinforce an "objectivist" epistemology?
- Are teachers privileging one way of knowing over another, or are they finding ways to use computers to help students (women and men alike) develop their abilities to think in different ways?

Teachers tend to assume that teaching in computer labs can help them change the social dynamics of their classes in constructive ways, by increasing the emphasis on collaborative learning.

- Are teachers using computers in ways that disrupt the conventional academic emphasis on the individual? That disrupt traditional patterns of teacher-student and student-student interaction? Does the use of the computer make class participation more equitable across sexes, or is it privileging those who feel more confident about using the technology?
- As teachers relinquish authority in the classroom, who assumes power?
- Are female students as likely as male students to assert their authority in the classroom? For instance, as students use, or teachers assign, computer conferences, are women as active as men? Are women assuming a wide spectrum of roles in their responses on computer conferences (i.e. initiating topics as well as supporting other students' contributions)?
- As teachers consider student participation, they need to consider students' access to technology. For example, the need to travel across campus at night to get to a computer may seriously limit women's willingness to use technology. Teachers need to consider other physical aspects of computer use as well; a pregnant woman trying to avoid sitting in front of a video display terminal for long stretches of time will not participate in a computer-intensive course to the extent that her male peer will.

As teachers learn more about addressing the gender gap within their own classrooms, they need to ask questions about the kinds of experiences with computers students have had before coming to college. Teachers also need to learn more about efforts being made to narrow the gender gap among computer users outside institutions of higher education:

- What kinds of programs are being established in K–12 classrooms to achieve computer equity? What can teachers learn about teaching from those efforts? For instance, what can teachers learn from publications like *The Neuter Computer: Computers for Girls and Boys* (Sanders & Stone, 1986)? What have teachers learned from their experiences that might support those efforts? What mechanisms need to be developed to ensure that conversations about computer equity in schools cross age and institutional boundaries?

- What kinds of efforts are going on outside schools to achieve computer equity? What can writing teachers learn from programs like the Women's Computer Literacy Project in San Francisco, and publications like *Women Computing?* What can teachers learn from the women who formed a special-interest group at the 1989 EDUCOM to meet and discuss "strategies to deal with issues facing women in higher education and information technology" (p. 12) at a time when all nine speakers at general sessions were men, and men outnumbered women as speakers in other sessions by a ratio of nearly 2.5 to 1? What kinds of links can teachers forge with groups like these, combining efforts to make the gender gap smaller?

FEMINIST METHODOLOGY

The set of questions writing teachers decide to explore in the 1990s is important; of equal importance, however, are the ways they go about exploring them. Teachers cannot use traditional research methodologies without examining the origins of these methodologies and their underlying assumptions, if they hope to uncover insights into the field of computers and composition. One of the most important tasks facing such researchers in the 1990s will be to develop feminist research methodologies. Although no one research methodology is inherently "more feminist" than any other, all feminist research is likely to share certain characteristics. The first feature will be a shared concern with effecting genuine social change. Feminism began as a social movement, not an academic vantage point. Feminist work begins with the premise that we live in a patriarchal society that privileges some groups (most frequently white, wealthy men) at the expense of others. The intent of feminist work is to change this inequality. Feminist perspectives on computers in composition instruction will be informed by issues of power and shaped by the desire to disrupt conventional social hierarchies. The questions researchers ask will necessarily include considerations of how to use knowledge to make changes—to open up the world of computers and the power it holds to more people, particularly women, and to make use of computers to explore previously discounted ways of thinking and learning. Sandra Harding (1987) argues that

> The class, race, culture, and gender assumptions, beliefs, and behaviors of the researcher her/himself must be placed within the frame of the picture she/he attempts to paint . . . [because] the beliefs and behaviors of the researcher are part of the empirical evidence for (or against) the claims advanced in the results of the research. (p. 9)

The beliefs and behaviors of the researcher shape the questions they ask, the evidence they consider, and the relationships they establish with the group they are studying. This fact is particularly important for people working in computers and composition because of the striking differences in teaching situations in terms of instructors' access to and comfort with technology. Some teachers will be running writing centers equipped with only a few computers, while others will be working with advanced workstations; some teachers will be learning about computers from their students, while others will be collaborating with computer scientists and computer engineers. What teachers learn about computers and composition will invariably be deeply tied to specific contexts because these contexts determine the kinds of questions they can ask. Teachers need to understand these contexts, and work to appreciate the differences that context—including differences between teachers, students, hardware, software, access, even writing programs—makes.

A third characteristic of feminist research in the 1990s will be an interactive and honest relationship between the researcher and the "researched." By refusing to accept an androcentric perspective that posits white middle-class male experience as the norm, teachers can create situations in which both the researcher and the researched can formulate and reformulate their stories. In computers and composition, this reformulation is particularly important. Computers make people vulnerable because while they are associated with power and status in our culture not everyone has equal access to them. It may be "too costly" for a teacher or a student to speak frankly about being fearful of computers. Conversely, the student who loves computers because of the fonts and the laser printer might fear sounding "not serious" if he or she were to report this. Consequently, as Klein (1983) notes, feminist researchers need to develop methodologies that

> open ourselves up to using such resources as intuition, emotions and feelings both in ourselves and in those we want to investigate. In combination with our intellectual capacities for analyzing and interpreting our observations, this open admission of the interaction of facts and feelings might produce a kind of scholarship that encompasses the complexity of reality better than the usual fragmented approach to knowledge. (p. 95)

Cooper and Selfe (1990) claim that computer technology may provide a liberating set of tools:

> We can draw on the revolutionary potential of computer technology to create nontraditional forums that allow students the opportunity to re-examine the authoritarian values of the classroom, to resist their socialization into narrowly conceived forms of academic discourse, to learn from the clash of discourses, to learn through engaging in discourses. (p. 867)

Teachers can draw on that revolutionary potential, but they won't be able to unless they look carefully at the whole configuration before them—at the technology itself, at the users of the technology, and at the ways teachers of writing go about trying to understand both.

REFERENCES

Becker, H. J. (1987, February). Using computers for instruction. *Byte*, pp. 149–162.

Belenky, M. F., Clinchy, B. M., Goldberger, N. R., & Tarule, J. R. (1986). *Women's ways of knowing: The development of self, voice, and mind*. New York: Basic Books.

Benston, M. L. (1988). Women's voices/men's voices: Technology as language. In C. Kramarae (Ed.), *Technology and women's voices: Keeping in touch* (pp. 15–28). New York: Routledge & Kegan Paul.

Brecher, D. (1985). *The Women's Computer Literacy Handbook*. New York: New American Library.

Claxton, C. S., & Murrell, P. (1987). *Learning styles: Implications for improving educational practices*. College Station, TX: Association for the Study of Higher Education.

Cooper, M., & Selfe, C. L. (1990). Computer conferences and learning: Authority, resistance, and internally persuasive discourse. *College English*, 52, 847–869.

EDUCOM '89 (program book). (1989). Ann Arbor, MI: The University of Michigan.

Elmer-Dewitt, P. (1986, November 3). From programs to pajama parties. *Time*, p. 88.

Flynn, E. A. (1988). Composing as a woman. *College Composition and Communication, 39*, 423–435.

Gerrard, L. (1988). *The politics of computer literacy.* Paper presented at the 39th annual convention of the Conference on College Composition and Communication, St. Louis, MO.

Gerver, E. (1989). Computers and gender. In T. Forester (Ed.), *Computers in the human context: Information technology, productivity, and people* (pp. 481–501). Cambridge: The Massachusetts Institute of Technology Press.

Harding, S. (1987). Introduction: Is there a feminist method? In S. Harding (Ed.), *Feminism and methodology* (pp. 1–14). Bloomington, IN: Indiana University.

Hawkins, J. (1985). Computers and girls: Rethinking the issues. *Sex Roles 13,* 165–180.

Herrmann, A. W. (1989). Computers in public schools: Are we being realistic? In G. E. Hawisher & C. Selfe (Eds.), *Critical perspectives on computers and composition instruction* (pp. 109–121). New York: Teachers College Press.

Klein, R. D. (1983). How to do what we want to do: Thoughts about feminist methodology. In G. Bowles & R. D. Klein (Eds.), *Theories of women's studies* (pp. 88–104). London: Routledge & Kegan Paul.

Marcus, S. (1987). Computers in thinking, writing, and literature. In L. Gerrard (Ed.), *Writing at century's end* (pp. 121–138). New York: Random House.

Peer Computer Equity Report. (1984). *Sex bias at the computer terminal–How schools program girls.* Washington, DC: National Organization for Women Legal Defense and Education Fund.

Sanders, J. (1986, January/February). The computer gender gap: Close it while there's time. *The Monitor,* pp. 18–20.

Sanders, J., & Stone, A. (1986). *The neuter computer: Computers for boys and girls.* New York: Neal–Schuman.

Selfe, C. L. (1990). Technology in the English classroom: Computers through the lens of feminist theory. In C. Handa (Ed.), *Computers and community: Teaching composition in the twenty-first century* (pp. 118–139). Portsmouth, NH: Boynton/Cook-Heinemann.

Selfe, C. L., Ruehr, R. R., & Johnson, K. E. (1988). Teaching word processing in composition courses: Age, gender, computer experience, and instructional method. *The Computer-Assisted Composition Journal* 2(2), 75–88.

Selfe, C. L., & Wahlstrom, B. J. (1985). Fighting in the computer revolution: A field report from the walking wounded. *Computers and Composition* 2(4), 63–68.

Stanworth, M. (1983). *Gender and schooling: A study of sexual divisions in the classroom.* London: Hutchinson Education.

Strickland, D. B., Feely, J. T., & Wepner, S. B. (1987). *Using computers in the teaching of reading.* New York: Teachers College Press.

Turkle, S. (1984). *The second self: Computers and the human spirit.* New York: Simon and Schuster.

Women Computing. (1988). San Diego, CA: Women Computing.

THINKING AND RE-READING

1. As you re-read this selection, think about what Jessup means by the "gender gap." List five examples of this phenomenon that she gives in the course of her article.

2. Jessup tells us that there are good reasons as to why girls and women are less involved with computers than boys and men. What reasons does she give? Can you think of others? List them.

3. Jessup suggests that girls and women use different frameworks for thinking than their male counterparts. What evidence does she use to support her argument? Do you agree? Why or why not?

4. What does Jessup mean by a feminist research methodology? How does it differ from current approaches to research? Why does she say that methods of research need to change?

WRITING AND THINKING

1. Jessup gives a number of statistics regarding the percentages of men and women who subscribe to computing magazines, reports on the different uses of computers among girls and boys across grade levels, and details the number and kinds of presentations given at the 1989 *Conference on College Composition and Communication* by the different sexes. Using your library or other resources on the World Wide Web, find more up-to-date studies on computer usage and gender. Does there seem to be a closing of the gender gap or do the statistics paint a similar picture to Jessup's? What steps can be taken to improve the picture the current statistics present? Prepare a short report in which you present your findings to the class. Then post your findings to an electronic discussion group (a listserv) where the other participants will be interested in your results.

2. Think of your experiences with computers in high school. Describe a time when you thought you might have been discriminated against in some way because of your sex. How might the incident have been avoided by the teacher or school? If you believe that you weren't discriminated against because of your gender, describe the procedures that were taken to ensure equity for all students as far as computers were concerned. If there weren't any explicit procedures, explain why they were unnecessary. Discuss your piece of writing in small groups with other students in your class.

3. Go to a computer lab on your campus, preferably one that serves students in the humanities and social sciences. Count the number of men and women in the lab and briefly ask the lab users what projects they are working on. Then do an informal survey of your friends and find out what computer sites they use for their work. Why do they use these sites? Also ask them about the most frequent uses that they make of their computers.

4. Use your findings as a basis for a class discussion on the "gender gap" and computers at your college. Now write a letter to the college newspaper in which you detail your findings and suggest recommendations to remedy the inequitable use of computers on your campus or, if your findings so indicate, write a letter in which you commend your school for providing a safe and welcoming computer environment for both genders.

The Information Gap

Barbara Kantrowitz

UNFORTUNATELY, IF THERE IS A GENDER GAP in the use of computers, there is also what Barbara Kantrowitz calls an "information gap": children of privilege often have more knowledge of and experience with computers than children not so privileged. Schools in poor inner city neighborhoods and rural areas frequently have outdated technologies, whereas their richer suburban counterparts exhibit the most up-to-date equipment and networking. And even within individual schools, the use of technology is often parceled out inequitably. Through the rigors of a tracking system, many high school students are placed in "basic" classes where drill and practice programs are the standard computer fare. Those students deemed the "brightest," on the other hand, often work with the newest multimedia programs and construct sites on the World Wide Web. These are the kinds of inequities that Kantrowitz chronicles in her article, which first appeared in *Newsweek* in 1994.

Jonathan Hee, 15, and Michael Tran, 16, attend the same suburban high school, Montgomery Blair in Silver Spring, Md., outside Washington. Both hope to use computers at work someday. Tran would like to be a programmer or an engineer; Hee wants to be an engineer. But the similarity ends there. Hee is in Montgomery Blair's 400-student magnet science program, which boasts two state-of-the-art computer labs, Internet access and teachers who have been trained in the latest technology. Tran goes to the nonmagnet section of the school, which has 2,000 students, a few dozen obsolete computers and teachers who are struggling with too few resources for too many students. Jonathan has studied binary code and logic; he has his own computer at home. Michael took his first computer class this year; he has no machine of his own to hone his skills.

Students like Hee and Tran represent what many educators fear is becoming an all-too-pervasive trend in American public schools, the creation of two separate and very unequal classes of computer haves and have-nots. "The folks who are getting left out," says Margaret Honey, associate director of the Center for Children and Technology/Education Development Center, "are going to be poor urban districts or rural districts with limited resources or blue-collar districts with very tight budgets." At Montgomery Blair, most of the magnet students are upper-middle class and white; most of the students in the regular school are minorities or immigrants. The school set up the magnet to lure white students into a largely minority school (although the suburban district itself is mostly white). The school now has many more white students, but there's little contact between the two groups. The consequences of such inequity could be grave. Last month Laura D'Andrea Tyson, chairman of the Council of Economic Advisers, released a study showing that in all job categories, from clerks to professionals, people who know how to work with computers earn more than those who don't. In fact, the difference between the two groups accounts for half the increasing wage gap between high-school and college graduates.

The information gap is a problem not only for educators, but for industries and even nations locked out of the technological revolution. But it's especially acute in financially strapped public schools. In a 1992 report, Macworld magazine, a respected trade publication, visited schools around the country and concluded that "computers ... perpetuate a two-tier system of education for rich and poor." Sally Bowman Alden, executive director of the Computer Learning Foundation in Palo Alto, Calif., says that the national ratio of students to computers is 16 to 1. "On the surface that doesn't sound as bad as it really is," she concedes. "But if you think of what would happen in a business where 16 people were sharing one computer, it's the equivalent of having a pencil for every 16 children."

Even when schools manage to get their hands on computers, the machines often gather dust in a locked room because teachers don't know how to use them. "School districts spend 90 percent of funds on new equipment, 10 percent on teacher training," says Charles Piller, the Macworld editor who conducted his magazine's study.

Savvy teachers: Their students miss out on new and innovative learning techniques. A few years ago machines were just for routine drills, and students frequently found them boring. Now savvy teachers focus more on giving kids access to the Information Highway. Bonnie Bracey, a fourth- and fifth-grade teacher at Ashlawn Elementary School in Arlington, Va., is a technophile. With the help of several grants, Bracey and her students use the five computers in her classroom to hook up to the Internet where they study such subjects as the ecology and geography of the rain forest and Mayan civilization. They communicate with students in other countries and tap into sophisticated data banks. The computers inspire her students to transfer what they learn in other subjects. "We have eaten our way through tropical fruits, costed out the price of spices and researched coral bleaching," Bracey says.

To less fortunate students, the Information Highway is about as real as the yellow brick road to Oz. Mischa Porter, a 17-year-old junior in the regular program at Montgomery Blair, talks wistfully about the magnet program. "They're the smart people," he says. Lyn Shiery, a computer teacher in the regular school, points to a service room behind his classroom. It's filled with the carcasses of donated computers that no longer work because he can't get the funds for spare parts. On a bulletin board in his classroom, Shiery has posted a story about Apple IIe computers, declared officially obsolete last year. Shiery's hope is that his students won't share that same fate.

THINKING AND RE-READING

1. As you re-read Kantrowitz's article, identify the major claims she makes about the use of computers in the schools. Have you had any experience with "magnet" programs or "magnet" schools? Why have communities created magnet schools? In your experience, do they achieve the community's intended goals?

2. How does Kantrowitz say that computer usage in schools has changed over the years? Do her observations correspond with your experiences?

WRITING AND LEARNING

1. Go to the library and find a recent magazine that's aimed at computer educators. We're thinking here of *The Computing Teacher, Technological Horizons in Education (THE)*, or another education magazine of your choice. Collect two or three advertising images or photographs from the magazine that reflect others' ideas as to how computers can be used in schools. Look over the images carefully to determine what messages they send to readers. For example, what signs and symbols are present in the image? What role do the various signs play? If there are human figures in the image, what are they like? What conclusions can you draw from the arrangement of all the components in the image? (See additional questions in Appendix A, "How to Look at an Image.") Using both the images and Kantrowitz's piece as sources, write an article for the readers of the magazine from which you culled the pictures, or a piece for your own school newspaper, that compares the different views of the ways in which computers are currently used in the schools. You may want to incorporate into your article other pertinent research you've done in this section on education and technology.

A Note from the Future

Passed on to *Wired* by Cathy Camper

In January of 1995 *Wired* published this letter in its *idées fortes* section. There was no introduction to it and no commentary following it. We could also find no letters from readers written to the magazine in response to it. As you read the letter, think of reasons *Wired* may have featured "A Note from the Future" in quite this way.

To the Onerabl Acadmy of Computr SIANSES:

BAK theN, sum histery boks, long ago tim bak, think **NOW** be IN the futur. SAyIN futur babys har is all in mohaks. Or som picters showd rockits and weal on the mon. Big soots on an wakking jus lik sno. Or tak plastik. Sad axvaly we yoos it to wear clos,

HA HA Wish they cold truly see how futvr isrelly. Al rich foks plug in to a vertul reelity masheen, wich is lik wakin into a bilbord whats cleen with a fatry goin on an peepl not sik but hapy in there Nis cartuon.

Now, spoz to rit a ~~say easy~~ thim SAy why yo let me in scool for this contes yo hav. Why ho cum this scool be somethin I ned. Lik you cant not see it in the way I rite, Like I wood got an equal chans with computer joks, who can typ an go to scool longer than I new how to writ, sur Im svr, we get the same dog cor chans wen it cor cums to a job. Ha evan a dog no, shet on that.

How do yo think, see a sistim an lis job an I don evaN no envf mumers to pvnch in AN git insid the dor? What kin of felings about microwaf clos drirs, on tv, or drivin rok'it soler car or envf mony to pay my clen air bils, So Tri Stats Air compnis don cvttin me of evry month crs I don hef a job.

Yes, trv naf the worl be waKK in on air, be zoming on a compouter scren, buzz an evry dog cor thin jes lik olen tim books did say. But the other haf, they me, livin in the reel wirl, wich you lef a mes. Yes, we werin plastik clos. Bvt they slimmy 1970 poly eser from the yvsd clos stor. Yeh we vizoolizin reelity. Bvt it a dvm karaty gam for 25 sent. An they shet rong abot 1 thing, We not werin any mohaks, in this futvr now, WE so crisdog col, we grow har lon jes kep us warm.

Probly I AM what you cal colerd, aa liK wity wAs the blank pags of a colering bok, An al the waksy flashy brite scribly outta lin stuf, that wAs us. Probly I AM femal, probly I got No job And lotsA kids. Probly. But how yo gonna now? Im Not pluged iN. I AM still A Bod E. Some bodee stuk in AxtuAl reelity.

So I Ask yo plez, to red this wel AN I hop I can be iN yur skool. I do not ask to be a computr jok or a sistim anilis, but jes can I beter myself, AN mAbe sAy enuf my husbAnd An me by A kid. Be sum kin of tru blu family be jus lik the boks, only I ned axses to a computr soon, or to bad, I be loss an it will be to lat.

THINKING AND RE-READING

1. As you re-read the letter, think about the other articles you've read in this section. Think about the images you've collected or seen in magazines and other places. What picture of "axtual reelity" is portrayed in the letter? The writer of the letter conveys a certain wistfulness when she writes that she wants to "besum kin of tru blu family be jus lik the boks, only I ned axses to a computr soon, or to bad, I be loss an it will be to lat." How should the "Onerabl Acadmy of Computr Sianses" respond to her?

WRITING AND THINKING

1. Although the letter presented here might be considered as written by an "illiterate," it is nonetheless a poignant piece of writing. To hone your own skills of critical reading, paraphrase the letter in its entirety. What reactions do you have to the original letter and your own paraphrasing of it? Does re-writing the prose in conventional English improve it? Write an e-mail response to the writer of the letter and send it to one of your classmates. Ask your classmate whether your intended response letter is appropriate. What problems are there in responding to the letter? As a collaborative project with your classmate, devise a plan of action that would address some of the concerns expressed in the letter.

Fly Me to the MOO:
Adventures in Textual Reality

David Bennahum

MOOS ARE VIRTUAL TEXTUAL SPACES that are technically
called Object Oriented MUDs (Multi-User Dungeons). The term "object oriented" characterizes a computer architecture that allows users to program
while in the virtual environment. MOO participants can invent their own
personas with short programming scripts that tell others what they look
like and what other objects they've created to outfit their online world. Like
e-mail, MOOs are conducted through phone lines connected to the
Internet, but, unlike e-mail, participants create virtual rooms, cafes, hotels,
or other e-spaces in which they interact with one another. Participants
commonly take pseudonyms, select a gender (female, male, neuter, sometimes more), and enter into the spirit of the particular MOO. According to
David Bennahum, MOOs are increasingly being used as electronic educational spaces. In "Fly Me to the Moo," the first extended article to appear
about MOOs in the popular press—in *Lingua Franca* in 1994—Bennahum
gives us a feel for what it's like to write and communicate with other participants in a MOO space.

I've been invited to join a freshman composition class at Mott Community
College in Flint, Michigan. I live in New York; we're going to be meeting
halfway, in Mushville. I was told to take the Internet and get off at
palmer.sacc.colostate.edu 6250. My beat-up Mac gets me there in a couple of
seconds. This is what I see:

> A large cornfield ringed by trees, somewhat misty
> around the edges. You notice that there is a cheery
> bonfire in the middle, surrounded by large logs perfect
> for sitting on and roasting marshmallows . . .

I walk into town; there's no one around. I'm a few minutes early. The town
runs along a north-south street. I read signs pointing to the park, the library,

a theater, and something called Writer's Block Café. I wait for velo to appear. Velo is a sentient bicycle—red, with shiny fenders. It is also the Mushville persona of Steve Robinson, the teacher running the class (which should be here any minute now). He warned me that he might be late—he still has to help some of the students log on.

I am waiting for velo and his class of thirty students in a MUSH called WriteMUSH. A MUSH is like a MOO, which is like a MUD. A MUD is a multi-user dungeon—a computer game. MUSHes (Multi-User Shared Hallucinations) and MOOs (MUD Object Oriented) are more fluid than games—they are virtual towns, or clubs, or cafés, or frontier lands, whose rules and personalities evolve over time. What makes this possible is the Internet.

MOOs, like e-mail, work through computers linked by phone lines, but unlike e-mail they allow users to have real-time, multiparty conversations rather than just leave messages for each other. Logging on to a MOO is like walking into a virtual room in which you find a number of objects (a description of the space is written into the program) and other people, sometimes hundreds of them, who are sitting at their terminals, logged on to that MOO, at that moment.

The first MUDs were built around 1978. At the time there was a popular text-based adventure game called, appropriately, Adventure, which ran on a university computer. At first, players played alone, against the machine, going from room to room collecting treasure, killing monsters, until they eventually won the game. After a while it got boring. Computers are predictable. So a few programmers decided to network several games and let people play together, simultaneously. Then, something unexpected happened. People no longer played to win the game; they played to be with other people. A virtual community began to form.

There are now more than 400 of these MUDs and their descendants running on the Internet. MOOs are significant because their creation allowed users to build their own rooms and write their own programs within the virtual world. MUDs were fixed places, most definitely games; MOOs took control from the head programmer and distributed it to every user. The point was not to play a game but to build a social space in a permanent state of evolution.

I get fidgety waiting for velo and his class and decide to explore Mushville. I head north, up the street. I pass by a church, a pizza parlor, a school. Up ahead is a lighthouse and the beach. The beach is the end of this part of Mushville. It doesn't have to be—Mushville could go on forever—but over the years, virtual architects have learned to use boundaries. People like them. It keeps the space intimate, real.

Trying to go farther north than the beach dumps you in the ocean:

> You find yourself swimming in the restless ocean, the waves moving you effortlessly, the sun warm overhead. The ocean moves in a long, soft wave of sound, a great rushing, like wind through a thousand trees in a long, calming rush.

Going any farther is impossible. I swim back to shore and stare out to sea.

> You find yourself captivated by the view and feel as though you were able to join the seagulls in flight. You are reminded of your earthly ties by the lapping of the waves and the fishing boats bobbing upon the ocean waves.

As I look out at the fishing boats bobbing on the waves, Teldorn pages: Hi there. I go back to the town square, hoping Teldorn (one of velo's students) will be there—I want to know where the class is. Teldorn must have checked to see who was logged on and found me. Teldorn and I bump into each other in the town square. He offers to take me to class, telling me that the students are at last arriving. As he speaks, a steady stream of characters hurry past us: Bruno, niki, Smurf, kurt, Ronda. It is a virtual stampede. They are headed to school. The school is a block north, sharing an intersection with the church and the pizza parlor.

> You go up the stairs and into the school.
> Schoolhouse Hallway
> A short hallway, leading to rooms where you can almost smell the
> learning taking place. The floors are parquetry, the varying shades of
> wood making a starburst design. A small crystal chandelier hangs
> overhead, and on the wall ahead of you is a portrait of some man who
> obviously gave a lot of money to the school. Probably donated this
> house, too.

I type, go class

> You open the doors and head into class.
> WriteMUSH Classroom
> A roomy classroom, with a large whiteboard in the front, soft red carpet
> on the floor, and lots of sturdy wooden tables and extremely comfortable
> chairs.
> Contents:
> Teldorn
> kurt
> niki
> Bruno
> kid
> Smurf
> lectern

I find myself surrounded by students busy transforming themselves from character to character, poking at each other, and asking me what I am doing here. I tell them I was invited by velo to sit in. By the time velo arrives, I have gathered that he wants them to write an argumentative essay. He divides us into small groups and sends us off into different rooms to discuss it.

I find myself with Jasmine, crista, and tanis the elf. Jasmine is studying business administration, crista is preparing to be a paralegal, and I can't figure out what tanis wants to do. He may be a netsurfer who has come to crash the party. I type, look at Jasmine, and I read this description:

> Jasmine is looking very smart today. She is wearing a white silk blouse
> and button fly Guess jeans. Her hair is pulled back, showing off her
> emerald earrings. She returns your look with a friendly smile.

I check crista's prose:

> red hair, light tan, wearing blue jeans, western boots, and a western shirt.

Telegraphic; reminds me of the personals. I wonder if these are cross-dressers. I ignore the elf. I ask them what their essays are on. Jasmine is very talkative. Her title is "Not All Pit Bulls Are Vicious Animals." I agree. Crista won't answer the question, so I ask her again. Finally she says,

> I really can't think of what I could write about. I'm not one to put up an argument on anything.

I try a different approach: Crista, can you think of anything you disagree with? For the next few minutes she is very quiet. Jasmine and I discuss why she likes using MOOs as part of her education. Then crista drops a whopper in my lap:

> crista says "I really don't like mixed marriages, but that would offend my sister. I'm not against blacks, I have made lots of friends that are black, and I like them."

I wonder why crista told me this. It's not the kind of comment one makes in casual conversation with strangers. I ask what it is about MOOspace that leads people to be so direct.

> Jasmine says "well it is a time to be alone and yet be with others you can let down your guard and share things, or act in ways you wouldn't normally do."
> Tanis the elf smiles.
> The elf metamorphs into a Dragon.
> Jasmine says "Another thing i think it helps with self esteem. Sometimes I have a hard time opening up to people or trusting others, and this lets me learn to communicate in a way that wont offend me if someone laughs, I can always leave them behind and talk to someone else. The social pressure is not here as much as in real life."
> crista says "It is easier to be honest about what you think or how you feel. I would never say I don't like mixed marriages to someone in person."
> The dragon says "You see people are more self-assertive here."
> Jasmine says "Who will judge you here? Nobody."

When I started researching this article I had no experience with MOOs or MUDs or M-anythings, but I understood what it was like to be totally absorbed in a text-based reality. As a kid in the early 1980s I used to play a variation of Adventure called Zork on my Atari computer. This led to Zork II and III and a steady stream of convoluted fantasy games with names like Deadline and Planetfall. I became obsessed with them, spending months at a time solving puzzles, trying to get to the end. I'd pick up another game and keep going. I'd swap tips with friends. It was a way of life for a while, a sort of living science-fiction fantasy. I abandoned it when puberty diverted my interests elsewhere, and not until last December did I come back to that world: That's when I opened an Internet account from my home in Manhattan ($20 a month) and canceled cable television to pay for it. Ignoring all other Internet distractions, like newsgroups and e-mail, I headed for the closest MUD, a place called Thunderdome. This is a classic hack-and-slash game, except unlike in Zork, Planetfall, and all the rest, *there were other people all around me.*

It was a strange sensation. I felt very happy. I canceled my appointments. I had people to meet, places to go. But a day later I experienced something unexpected, the last thing I ever thought I would feel in something as cool as a MUD: boredom. I kept accosting players named Ranger, Black_Knight, and Black_Magik, asking them where they were from. Answers like "the castle" and "Lórien" (a forest in the Tolkien books) just wouldn't do. I kept prodding, accusing them of taking this all too seriously. After all, isn't this a *game?* I didn't want to talk about slaying trolls. I got yelled at (as much as one can yell with text). I was shunned. I ruined the party. I was back-stabbed by a thief. My character, named Bored, was assassinated.

Then a few days later I telephoned Jennifer Grace, a cultural-anthropology graduate student at Duke University who studies virtual communities. Jennifer does not spend much time on MUDs—she does all her research on MOOs. She warned me that this kind of research quickly bleeds into your real life, taking it over. Everything in a MOO begs to be catalogued by an anthropologist, because people in MOOs come there to be with other people. They do not decapitate elves—they socialize. They lie. They become painfully earnest. Since I'm a former practitioner of anarchic improv comedy, for me the lies became theater. In a MOO, the lying is role-playing, turning MOOs into wild metaphorical playpens where subtext becomes preposterously magnified and released. They are a strange surrealist hybrid of the sweetness of self-help and the raging braggadocio of hacker subculture.

When I spoke with Jennifer the first time, our conversation was very serious—no jokes allowed. Jennifer didn't seem like the kind of person you'd want to get drunk with in a bar. That is, until I did, at least virtually speaking, when she invited me to join her at Club Dred on LambdaMOO. Lambda was the first MOO. Lambda is the biggest MOO. LambdaMOO is a wonderful dance to witness.

To enter Lambda is to visit the hive of the reigning MOO Queen. Like some giant, overstuffed termite mom, Lambda is fed and fattened by a small horde of slave workers. In return, Lambda's parent, Xerox, gives anyone who wants it free access to the MOO software—a policy that has bred the MOO infestation that now riddles the Internet. Xerox is studying the future of networked virtual realities, a technology that didn't exist four years ago, by giving the software away and letting overeducated hackers improve on it. The slave workers are computer types of various kinds—students, postdocs, Xerox PARC employees—who voluntarily manage the 8,000 or so permanent characters on Lambda and vainly try to track new additions to the 5,000-plus "rooms" that make up the hive. The slaves are called wizards—a term left over from hack-and-slash days.

These wizard/slaves wield a magic wand: the programmer's bit. Ownership of a programmer's bit allows a wizard (or even a puny Lambda-mite, if she is given one) to program new kinds of objects into LambdaMOO. People with bits are cool. People who give out bits are even cooler. To add to the insanity of the mix, the father of the Queen, Pavel Curtis (a.k.a. Lambda and Haakon), Xerox employee extraordinaire and creator of the MOO software, permitted Lambda to become a democracy. Now even newcomers like me can vote on various propositions, like *Ballot:mpg (#75104): 'Minimal Population Growth' (I voted no on that one—I want the population to explode). The irony of this is ignored. This is not a democracy. LambdaMOO sits on a hard drive in the belly of the Xerox Corporation. A little tug and the plug comes out.

To log on to Lambda, I type, telnet lambda.parc.xerox.com 8888 into my Internet account. All that means "Get me over to Lambda, now."

> PLEASE NOTE:
> LambdaMOO is a new kind of society, where thousands of people voluntarily come together from all over the world. What these people say or do may not always be to your liking; as when visiting any international city, it is wise to be careful who you associate with and what you say. The operators of LambdaMOO have provided the materials for the buildings of this community, but are not responsible for what is said or done in them. In particular, you must assume responsibility if you permit minors or others to access LambdaMOO through your facilities. The statements and viewpoints expressed here are not necessarily those of the wizards, Pavel Curtis, or the Xerox Corporation and those parties disclaim any responsibility for them.

I type, connect solomon joviso, and I get this annoying message:

> *** The MOO is too busy! The current lag is 14; there are 182 connected.
> WAIT AT LEAST 5 MINUTES BEFORE TRYING TO CONNECT AGAIN! ***

Five minutes. Forget it. I speed-dial, immediately cycling through ten attempts. Finally the lag dips below five—the magic pressure level—and I'm in. The connect solomon joviso tells the Lambda computer to let me in as Solomon (my Lambda character); "joviso" is my password (not anymore, for you hackers out there). That little word "lag" is the bane of the virtual universe. It is an omnipresent subject of conversation. As the termites multiply, the hive they crawl in—disk space and processing time—gets crowded. The Xerox computer tries to serve everyone, stacking us into a huge queue; the time between an entry request and the computer's completing it is the lag. Sometimes it goes up to 40 seconds. That's when it's time to go to one of the other 400 M-whatevers out there.

I tumble into Lambda and straight into a coat closet.

> The lag is approximately 3 seconds; there are 178 connected.
> ***Connected ***
> The Coat Closet
> The closet is a dark, cramped space. It appears to be very crowded in here; you keep bumping into what feels like coats, boots, and other people (apparently sleeping). One useful thing that you've discovered in your bumbling about is a metal doorknob set at waist level into what might be a door.

It's a good thing the closet is dark. Those other people (apparently sleeping) are the 7,922 souls not currently logged on. The closet is where Lambda stores virtual corpses. With the lights on, you'd have to sit through a long list of sleeping names scrolling down your screen.

That would really make the lag bad. Some cool MOOers build their own, personalized rooms, and when they log on to Lambda they appear in them. It's eerie to walk into someone's room and find him there sleeping. Unfortunately, LambdaMOO prevents you from wreaking any mayhem on the sleeper, but you can build objects and leave them behind, like love notes and flowers.

First-time users connect as guests by typing connect guest guest, where "guest" serves as both name and password. Since the name "guest" is usually already taken, you wind up with some modification of it, such as Blue_Guest. Making your own character is easy. I type, @request Solomon for davidsol@panix.com. A few hours later LambdaMOO e-mails me confirmation that no one else has the name Solomon, and gives me a password. Now I'm Solomon. The @ sign means that what follows is a computer command. I am essentially programming. To be a name without a description is unacceptable. When people type look at Solomon they want to see what I look like. Associating a description with my name is equally simple: I just type, @describe me as . . . and then whatever I want my description to be. If you were to look at me, you would see:

> Solomon is a little stressed out from being indoors too much, but happy to be here. Wearing a jacket, shirt, and jeans with heavy brown shoes. Tall with disheveled black hair. He is awake and looks alert.

The final product requires gender—male, female, or neuter (I met a giant carrot the other day; it was neuter). To give myself my gender I type, @gender male. That's it. That made me Solomon. More advanced players create a set of names and descriptions, each very different. Cycling through them is called morphing. Now, after a few weeks on the MOO scene I am not only Solomon—I am Pepe, chia_pet, and my_little_pony. But Solomon is my parent character, my first MOO self. The other characters come in handy, depending on the situation. Pepe is a six-foot-tall, oversexed French skunk, chia_pet is a quiet 400-pound plant, and my_little_pony is a very sweet, sincere, two-inch-high pink plastic toy.

Typing open door will get you out of the closet and into the living room. The people in the living room will see on their screens the words Solomon comes out of the closet (sort of). The living room is the heart of Lambda. The original space was designed to look like a California house, the kind a successful Palo Alto Xerox employee might have. It has a pool, a hot tub, a kitchen, a dining room, and lots of bedrooms. Things have changed since then. Under the pool there is now a warren of caves filled with a couple of headless elves and hack-and-slash knights, but don't tell the neighbors. Stare too closely at the postcard of Paris on the fridge and you'll find yourself tumbling into it . . . and out onto the Boulevard St. Germain. Outside, past the garden by the pool, is a path leading into deep South American jungle. Flights to Brazil leave from there. As long as there is disk space, there can be rooms. Build a room, convince a wizard it's good, and he (rarely she) will link it up to the rest of the MOO for you. There are a lot of half-finished rooms sitting in limbo in Lambda's memory, waiting to be connected—only they never will be. They are abandoned.

As a character you can do three basic things. First, you can speak, by typing "Hello. The computer takes the double quote mark as an instruction to print what follows it as speech, so that other people in the MOO room see Solomon says "Hello." Second, you can emote. Emoting allows you to take on a narrative voice and show emotions, actions, thoughts. If I type, emote yawns loudly, what you are saying is tedious, the computer prints out, Solomon yawns loudly, he thinks what you are saying is tedious. Third, you can build—anything from rooms to virtual accessories.

Building rooms is easy. It's the same as making a character, except here the name is associated with a "space" (on the Internet, space is a rather abstract concept). Once the space has a name, associate a description with it and you have a room. You can then create objects to place inside the room, like newspapers, cookies, chairs—anything you can think of. You can also program a set of verbs to go with each object. I was in the kitchen speaking with Freya and du_Nord when Grump, a person in another room, commanded the housekeeper to deliver a plate of cookies:

> At Grump's request, the housekeeper sneaks in, deposits plate of cookies, and leaves.

I type, eat cookies

> You eat one of the cookies on the plate.
> The taste of choc-chip cookie fills your mouth.

The verb "eat" was associated with the object "cookie." Typing eat cookies (I wanted all of them) prompted the computer to describe me eating one. I could also have typed take cookies and then give cookie to du_Nord. In each case the computer would have understood what I wanted to do, because the creator of the room programmed it to respond to the verbs "eat," "take," and "give," among others. The housekeeper in this case was not a real character but a robot programmed by the room's creator to perform certain actions. Between the rooms, the robots, the objects, and the characters, you have a complete text-based virtual reality that evolves over time, creating history and a virtual community.

MOOspace exists only as text flowing down your computer screen. Sometimes I spend eight hours at a time staring at the moving words, typing back at the people typing at me. My mind has accepted that this is real. As Jennifer warned, the "research" took over my life—for a few weeks I logged on every day. It also brought me closer to Jennifer. The nerd on the phone became an alluring woman named amazin (as in amazin Grace) in Lambda. Ours became my first MOO friendship. Now I spend several nights a week with her. She has become a confidante. That's the strange thing about MOOs—they pop up like trapdoors in your life and connect you to people you would otherwise have nothing to do with. All the context that separates two people like Jennifer and me disappears, leaving an illusion of intimacy: an intimacy devoid of life's accessories, the baggage that we carry around with us. Some MOO friends try to take a relationship out of virtual space, but veteran MOOers are wary—they've been burned too often by net friendships that collapsed once the stuff of real life came in.

I was sitting in the Lambda living room when I received a page from amazin. Paging is a way of speaking to people not in the same room with you; it's also a way to keep messages private. I found her in Club Dred.

> amazin pages, "type @join amazin"

I type, page amazin with "okay"
amazin hears you and smiles sublimely.

I type, @join amazin
You visit amazin.
A bouncer comes up to you and says, "Hey! Think you can crash the Club without paying, eh? Don't think so! Try using the door."

This is the corner of Main Street and Queens Boulevard. . . To the northwest you can see a large castlelike building with a large neon sign reading: "Club Dred." A long line of people wait to get in.
(from Club Dred) amazin hugs you

This nightclub appears to be the new in-spot. Like all nightclubs, it is dimly lit, and very loud. Music and noise from all the conversation around is frankly deafening. But one might manage to find a more quiet corner to gather and talk, if one can find a way through the crowd! You see Gothic Dave, sign, and Abigail here.
amazin and Dred are here.
Dred says, "amazin!"
Princess_Buttercup pays the cover and enters the club.
The DJ makes a smooth transition from AC/DC into a song by The Lemonheads.
amazin hugs Dred warmly.
amazin [to Dred]: hiya, cutie.
Princess_Buttercup says, "The Lymone heads!!"
Some guy jumps up on a table and drops his pants, mooning the entire club. But he jumps down and disappears before the bouncers can find him.
amazin hugs you.
Princess_Buttercup says, "I mean Lemonheads."

This is the kind of detail that keeps people coming back. That and the robots—like the bouncer and Abigail, the waitress—that seem human. Typing order milk from Abigail will get you just that, a glass of milk. And that glass can be passed around, chugged, sipped, thrown.

In this world, writing defines your position in the social hierarchy. Good writers, intelligent writers, get lots of attention. Your sex appeal depends on your prose. I look at amazin.

amazin is a 5'4" buxom blonde with grey-blue eyes and a soft pageboy haircut. Silver earrings drop delicately from her earlobes and tinkle when she walks, and the faint scent of orchid perfume trails behind her. Don't be fooled by her appearance though. She can be alternately overbearingly esoteric or downright bawdy, depending on her mood. She carries Michel Foucault's "History of Sexuality, Part 1" tucked under her arm and she takes to reading it when she is bored. amazin is wearing a mood ring with a lovely umber-colored stone (signifying you have grown tiresome).
She is wearing an elegant red dress which barely hides the black orchid tattoo on her left shoulder blade. Sheer black stockings cover her shapely legs, and she is wearing elegant low-heeled black pumps on her petite feet.

Jennifer has told me she is short and heavy IRL (in real life). That phrase, "IRL," comes up a lot, to separate what happens in MOOspace from out there. I don't believe there is actually a difference between real life and MOOspace—especially when you spend most of your waking hours in a MOO. Then again, I am a novice. I haven't been burned yet.

Some people cling to this IRL distinction not because they've been burned but because they prefer not to acknowledge the humanity of the person behind a character. That way the whole experience remains separate, compartmentalized, dehumanized. MOOers like that can be abusive—groping you, hitting you, making fun of you. For some reason MOOs bring out that kind of behavior in many people. Because of that, many MOO users cloak their gender and race. I've noticed that a lot of guests are women—they come on as guests to be left alone, keeping their gender hidden. Others cross-dress, claiming they are male when they are female IRL. But more often than not it is the IRL males that come on as females. I still don't understand what it is that excites men about coming on as absurdly oversexed Jessica Rabbit female clichés. One MOO pastime is "outing" cross-dressers. Their prose often gives them away, as in the case of the "homosexual woman" I met in a hot tub at LambdaMOO. Everyone in the tub with us picked up on her description, screaming, "A lesbian would not call herself a homosexual woman." She turned out to be a teenage boy.

Social MOOs like Lambda outnumber all other kinds. Their growth has been so rapid that some colleges (Amherst, for one) have outlawed MOOing from their computers. At one point Australia banned MOOing altogether—the MOO load on its few long-distance trunk lines was so heavy that "legitimate" activities, such as currency trading, had slowed to a crawl. The range of social MOOs is endless; some are completely unrelated to anything in real life. The FurryMuck is a MOO where half-human, half-animal creatures come together and have netsex—usually a process of rapid one-handed typing. BayMOO is a squeaky-clean Bay Area MOO where emote lights a cigarette and takes a long drag gets you in big trouble. Dhalgren MOO is postapocalypse New York City, where dogs run wild and street hustlers try to make you part with whatever virtual currency you may be carrying. And then there are the professional MOOs, the ones intended for teaching and research. These are struggling to become more than curiosities; they want to be useful.

MediaMOO and BioMOO, for instance, are serious MOOs used mainly by researchers to share information, network, and exchange job tips. Job listings cover their virtual bulletin boards, electronic greeting cards are swapped, research ideas shared. Unlike with e-mail, there is an element of serendipity to MOOs—maybe you'll run into someone unexpected, with useful information. MediaMOO was created by Amy Bruckman, a graduate student in the Epistemology and Learning Group of the Media Lab at MIT, in the fall of 1992. Bruckman held an inaugural ball for the MOO on January 20, 1993, that competed with that other inaugural ball in Washington, D.C.; some 400 celebrants attended the virtual dance. Now, more than 1,000 people—mostly professors and students of communications and researchers in corporate labs—have permanent characters there. To have a permanent character on MediaMOO, you must submit an application that is reviewed by a committee of seven MediaMOO users; if two vote no, you are denied a permanent character. Like many other MOOs, MediaMOO is in the process of becoming a democracy. Bruckman no longer makes all the decisions; running MediaMOO is now up to elected officials, chosen by members in a secret ballot.

MediaMOO's most popular event is the Tuesday Café, which thirty or more people log on to every Tuesday night for a discussion.

Tuesday Cafe
A cheerful but quiet and peaceful cafe overlooking the lobby of the Nhetoric Headquarters. Sunlight pours through the skylights, and out the windows you see a well-kept English garden. The smells of fresh coffee and tea drift toward you as you join your colleagues for some shoptalk. Lots of comfortable chairs and tables are scattered about, and when more of your colleagues arrive, you simply push more tables together. Each Tuesday at 8:00 p.m. Eastern, the computers and writing crowd gather here to discuss—what else?—issues related to the use of computers in the teaching of writing.

BioMOO is based in Rehovot, Israel, at the Weizmann Institute of Science. It contains a laboratory filled with virtual machines that can manipulate virtual atoms, combine virtual enzymes, code virtual proteins into RNA, and display periodic tables. Anyone can log on to BioMOO and use it as a gateway to supercomputers around the world. I was given a tour by Gustavo Glusman, a graduate student in biology at the Weizmann Institute and BioMOO's founder, whom I found in the woods outside the biology building. Glusman explained that while BioMOO was a professional space for biologists, anyone could have a character here. Everyone with a character enters a description of his or her research interests. I started checking through lists and found descriptions like this:

Isolation and characterization of the DNA encoding the 5' end of the human/gabaa benzodiazepine alpha-1 subunit gene. Characterization of the promoter and control of gene transcription.

Later I found the scientist whose description this was; his BioMOO name is Martin. IRL Martin is Martin David Leach, a graduate student at the Boston University School of Medicine, where he is working on his Ph.D. in molecular pharmacology.

Martin's bifunctional office (MBO)
This room appears to be a lavatory but is in fact Martin's office. Feel free to relieve yourself. Although i don't recommend sitting on the seat as it appears someone forgot to lift it. Say no more! You can enter the double helix by going east.

You see a toilet, Martin's Protein and DNA database, a Notice from martin, a chalkboard, a programming shortcut, a Tue Mar 15 20:21:51 1994 IST, and a sequence editor here.

Scientists have a rough life. I type a few toilet jokes and we move on.
Martin asks me if I want to see the machine he built in the lab, which analyzes genetic sequences. I say yes. This database is a search facility for scientists who want to compare a protein or DNA sequence they isolated in a lab with known sequences stored in large databases around the world. The idea is that a scientist who discovers a genetic sequence can find out whether someone else has already catalogued it. Martin gives me a sequence to type

in: agatcagcgactgactgactatcatcagagacac. I send my sequence off to the European Molecular Biology Laboratory (EMBL), a computer in Heidelberg, Germany, for analysis. EMBL is supposed to e-mail me the results in a couple of hours or days.

In addition to research and informal-networking MOOs there are many virtual classrooms in academic MOOspace. Some, like those in MUSHville, are components of small-time, relatively simple MOOs. Others borrow space in a large, complex MOO called Diversity University. This MOO is a virtual campus: DU's founder, Jeanne McWhorter (who is getting her master's degree in social work from the University of Houston), built the streets and buildings, and offices and classrooms spring up as users require them. This is what the campus looks like:

```
_____1_____2_____3_____
|  _____    ___JASON_ROAD____   _____(Jason's Ct.->)
| |  .------------------. |  |  Football field |  |                           |  |
6| |    |Cllge of Agrcultr| |  |_____| |   (Gym)                   |  |6
| |    |_____-----' |  ____BOB_STREET____                            |  |
| |              Villa   | |   Northern        |  |                           |  |
5| |(grad dorm)  Villekulla | |   Quadrangle | |   (Pool)                     |  |5
| |_____| |                | |  |_____|  |  |
|   _____   ____7th_STREET_____   _____         |
| |     |Cfetria|  _____  |  |.----+-.f.------.|   |   .-.__.-.   .----'|W|
4|M|     `----:   Dorm |Hlth |  | Student|s| Admin|  |(         |  |        ||E|4
|O| Hotel Schl I 2   |Ctr. | |  | Union  |a|   | |  |[ Library |  |Educatn||S|
|G|_____|----|_____  | |_____/  `------'|  |[_____|  |       ||T|
|U|    _____   ____LSU_STREET___   |.---.           `----'|H|
|E|.---------..---------.  | |                | |   |  Engl.|.---.::::::::|E|
3|'|| Business || Communcatn\ |H|              |S|      ||     |.---.|I|3
|S||_____||____ ____| |0|              |A|_____||Cltrl||      ||M|
| |.------. .-------''-----.|U| Southern Quad   |N|.---.|Studs||    Law ||E|
|R||Engin-| | Tech Complex ||S|              |D|Hist.||    ||_____||R|
|U||eering| |  _____/  |T|              |0|_____||_____.|--.| |
2|N||_____|  `--'.---------.|H|              |Z|.--. .-.    |Poli ||S|2
| |.----------.  | Medical | |N|              | |        |_|Soc | |Sci ||T|
| ||Archtcture|  | Complex | | |              |S||Psych_  Work| |_____/|R|
| |`----------'   _____| |S|   .'N`.       |T|  _-----'_`--'_____||I|
| |(Construction .---------. ||T|   W-+-E       | |_____JEANNE'S_LANE____ P|
| |.-. trailer) | Science|||  `.S.'            | |.-----.              |  |
1| ||__|<-'     | Bldg. |  | |              | || M&DA   | Ampithtr | |1
| |_____`-------' | |              | |`-----'_____| |
|_____6th_STREET_____|
                    1                         2                          3
```

Without this kind of structure, MOOs quickly sprawl outward, following the contours of communal fantasy. Many find this element of MOOs exciting. So what if you pass from a closet to a cloud to a bar? This is a virtual world. In MOOs like DU, though, created for professional purposes, structures are useful.

Anyone can log on to DU, including students not registered in any classes. For now, use of DU is also free. To prevent uninvited guests from crashing, teachers can "lock" rooms to users who haven't asked their permission to enter. DU students are mostly American, but there are some Canadians as well. As the number of Internet nodes expands internationally, DU plans to create virtual events linking students around the world. At the moment there are no students attending DU or any other virtual university exclusively. That may change soon with the creation of GNA, the Global Network Academy.

GNA is vying to become the world's first accredited virtual university. Incorporated in the state of Texas in November 1993, GNA hopes to graduate its first degree-holding class by 2005. This April, GNA will begin teaching its first extension courses. Classes take place in a virtual campus, which is really a link between four different MOOs: Diversity University, MediaMOO, BioMOO, and the GNA lab. GNA contains a virtual library, which is a keyword-searchable index of information on the

Internet, and which will make texts in the public domain available for course work. At the moment GNA offers only two courses—Introduction to the Internet and Introduction to Object-Oriented Programming Using C++—but in the future it will offer Renaissance Culture, Introduction to C Programming, and creative writing. Until copyright laws clearly define how electronic media should be billed for and distributed, virtual classes are limited to subjects whose texts tend to be in the public domain—subjects like math, writing, and "the classics."

Cynthia Wambeam, an instructor at the University of Wyoming, is one of the fifteen teachers who is borrowing classroom space at DU at the moment, and she has designed the courses she teaches there to double as investigations into the effect of virtual communication on writing. Wambeam teaches two freshman composition classes of twenty-three students. One uses the MOO; the other—the control group—does not. Both sets of students are required to keep journals. The control students write their entries in notebooks; the MOO students post theirs on an electronic bulletin board.

Wambeam devised this experiment with Leslie Harris, an assistant professor at Susquehanna University in Pennsylvania. What Wambeam and Harris want to know is: At the end of the class, which group will be better writers? At the end of the semester, all forty-six students will write an essay, and several outside evaluators, who do not know which students were in which group, will pore over the essays and try to discern differences in the students' prose. (Their results will be presented at the Computers and Writing conference in Missouri in May.)

Harris has found, in his own MOO classes, that computer mediation changes the nature of classroom dialogue: The role of the teacher shifts from conversation controller to facilitator, and the students have to take charge of the discussion. Harris is asking his sophomore-level Western-literature students to re-create Dante's five levels of hell in MOO-space. The class is divided into five groups, each of which is programming a different level of hell, complete with scenery, characters, and dialogue, and will then perform the piece for the other groups. Students will view the performance from computers scattered around the campus, following the story as it appears on the screen—a textual theater. All this is supposed to give them an intimate experience of *The Inferno* through reenactment.

At Brown, Robert Coover teaches hypertext fiction in a MOO called the Hypertext Hotel. Students create virtual rooms in the hotel, each of which is a story, which can be added to by other students posting new text there. Since the hotel is on the Internet, they can also be added to by the MOO public. Usually "hypertext" describes writing where there is a dynamic link between two or more texts: Clicking on a word in one text transports you immediately to another text, from which you can click on another word and arrive at yet a third text. The Hypertext Hotel is more static than that—it is really just a conventional MOO, where each room contains a story instead of a description. Coover says the hotel is meant to be "playful, not a great literary document," and in fact the "stories" posted there are less experimental fiction than a kind of cyber-toilet-stall graffiti. Room names read like subheadings in a De Sade crib—titillation, abstinence, prostitution, quietude, servitude, necessity, electrocution, gesticulation, malnutrition, flotation, perambulation, and so forth.

I type, follow titillation

You enter titillation
titillation
dripping iron clits

```
lipping dry tits
tripping
slits.

follow abstinence

abstinence
hardcore ram function
extreme unction.
```

A few users of the hotel, led by hypertext-fiction author Carolyn Guyer, are trying to reclaim some literary integrity for it. Guyer has created "Hi-Pitched Voices," a wing of the hotel that has somehow remained free of graffiti. I wandered around there, through rooms with names like "want," "inspiration," and "mouth."

```
follow mouth
mouth
        This is the mouth
            of a cave
                of a river
                    of a sea
                of a child
            of a gutter
                at a restaurant
                    in breath
                        in life
                            in sleep.
```

The text scrolls down my screen, waving from side to side as it appears. The movement is a surprise—it is even a little eerie—but otherwise the poem is obviously pretty bad. Coover agrees that much of the stuff in the hotel is bad. The lack of editorial control, he has realized, leads to a reading experience that is "very diffuse, and seems totally undirected, and is finally kind of a bore to move around in." As is the case with other MOOs, the very things that make the medium interesting—easy access and unrestricted participation—have also made it boring. Coover hopes that the hypertext created in the hotel will at least hold some sort of historical interest for future literary theorists. "Maybe thirty years from now, it will be like the Mickey Mouse watch," he suggests. "Maybe it will retain a kind of aura of its time that people will find compelling."

John Unsworth, director of the Institute for Advanced Technology in the Humanities at the University of Virginia (an organization started with a large grant from IBM intended to foster and develop computer-mediated research in the humanities), first used MOOs to teach composition classes at North Carolina State University at Raleigh. He has since become famous in certain circles as the creator of the Post Modern Culture MOO, or PMC. As far as Unsworth knows, PMC is the only MOO affiliated with a peer-reviewed electronic journal in the humanities, the journal being *Postmodern Culture*, whose editorial board includes such luminaries as Kathy Acker, Henry Louis Gates Jr., bell hooks, Avital Ronell, and Andrew Ross.

PMC is meant to be a serious MOO, a social space for intellectual discussion. It contains a library from which you can get articles from the Internet, a coffeehouse for casual conversation, individual rooms built by members, and a central lobby where everyone arrives. Discussion covers issues like "embodiments" and "cyber-subjectivity." PMC-MOO is frequented by pomo types of all ages—highschool students, graduate students, professors—and on any given night forty or so can be found there. I logged on as a guest, hoping to find out what Post Modern Culture means.

> PMC-MOO is a virtual space designed to promote the exploration of post-modern theory and practice, a place for intellectual meandering. Here, we mix the unstable "real world" of postmodernity with the solid virtuality of MOOspace.
>
> *** Connected ***
> The Welcome Mat
> This is the welcome mat, outside the lobby of PMC-MOO. Above the northern door, a beady electric eye watches to see who will pass the sliding glass door. To the SOUTH, the wind whistles across the abandoned meadow, whipping little sales receipts across the weeds and waste. Stick-a-fork-in-me-baby (asleep), netsurfer (asleep), Roger_Wilco (asleep), and Tree (asleep) are here.

Although twenty-one people were logged in with me, none of them could be found in the area described by the main PMC map; they had retreated to their respective private rooms. The only way to get to these rooms is by "teleporting" in, which requires a command like @join Shrimp-Fried.Ninja. Hoping to find out more about the postmodern condition, I joined the crustacean as a guest. There I discovered pomo culture is better experienced than described.

> I type, @join Shrimp-Fried.Ninja
> The Wanderer's Home
> Home is where the heart is. In this case, you stand at the top of a tall, lonely hill. To the NORTH is the merriment of the Loche, and to the SOUTH is a gloomy cave, but here is only peace and serenity. Kick back and stay a while.
> You see a Small Flightless Rodent here.
> Taran, Larktongue, ANHOLLEMAN@vassar.edu, Slash, and Shrimp-Fried.Ninja are here.
> Taran waves to Guest.
> Shrimp-Fried.Ninja bows to Guest.
>
> I type, emote wave back.
> Shrimp-Fried.Ninja throws a Small Flightless Rodent into the air, for anyone to catch.
>
> I type,
> "Hello Post Modern travelers ANHOLLEMAN@vassar.edu catches the Small Flightless Rodent!
> ANHOLLEMAN@vassar.edu throws a Small Flightless Rodent toward Guest. Catch it!
> Shrimp-Fried.Ninja smiles.
> Shrimp-Fried.Ninja says, " 'lo guest. Catch it!"
> ANHOLLEMAN@vassar.edu [to Guest]:
> PoMo sucks (sorry)

Larktongue waves.
Shrimp-Fried.Ninja says, "catch it!"
INTERCEPTION! Taran jumps out in front of you and catches the Small
Flightless Rodent!
Shrimp-Fried.Ninja jumps up and down, cheering in admiration for
Taran!

I type, "What's the point of this moo? Taran throws a Small Flightless
Rodent toward Shrimp-Fried.Ninja. Catch it!
Shrimp-Fried.Ninja catches the Small Flightless Rodent.
Taran [guest]: Point to life is to have fun.

I type, emote wonders what makes PMC-MOO special, if anything. Shrimp-
Fried. Ninja says, "The people! we make it special"
Shrimp-Fried.Ninja throws a Small Flightless Rodent towards Guest.
Catch it!

I type, eat the rodent. Yum. ANHOLLEMAN@vassar.edu [to Guest]: We are
more creative here, and there is more contiguity . . .
Taran is rolling on the floor laughing!
You fail to catch the Small Flightless Rodent, and it falls to the ground.
Shrimp-Fried.Ninja says, "you have to catch it guest, otherwise it falls on
the ground."
Shrimp-Fried.Ninja says, "duh."
Shrimp-Fried.Ninja throws a Small Flightless Rodent toward Taran.

I type, "I thought I ate the damn thing.
Taran makes a leaping catch of the Small Flightless Rodent!
Taran claps in admiration for Taran.
Taran throws a Small Flightless Rodent toward Slash.
INTERCEPTION! Shrimp-Fried.Ninja jumps out in front of Slash and
catches the Small Flightless Rodent! Shrimp-Fried.Ninja throws a Small
Flightless Rodent into the air, for anyone to catch.
ANHOLLEMAN@vassar.edu catches the Small Flightless Rodent!
ANHOLLEMAN@vassar.edu [to Guest]: just type 'catch rodent'

I type, "AHH ANHOLLEMAN@vassar.edu throws a Small Flightless Rodent
toward Guest. Catch it!
It's too high in the air for you to catch right now!

I type, catch rodent
You jump up into the air and catch the Small Flightless Rodent!
Taran claps in admiration for Guest.

PMC-MOO is also home to postmodern "events." One such event was hosted by a player called
Ogre.

Tarquin says, "ok everyone"
Tarquin says, "I am going to turn the floor over to Ogre in a second"
lazarus sips quad mocha.
Tarquin says, "According to _The Autonomedia Calendar of Jubilee

Saints_, April Fools' Day originated with the calendar change of 1752.
They call it 'A day of pranks and fool's errands.' "
Tarquin says, "I hope we are in for a treat tonite"
Tarquin says, "Ogre the show is all yours"
Ogre hugs smack and flipper briefly . . .
Ogre climbs up onto the stage and turns and faces the crowd.
Tarquin jumps down from the stage into the crowd.
Tarquin walks back into the dim lite corner and takes a seat at a table.
Ogre drops a petition (#715) to the stage floor.
Ogre drops a can of gasoline.
Ogre seriously considers a suicide of protest . . .
Ogre sits cross-legged on the ground . . .
Ogre unscrews the cap on the can of gasoline . . .
Ogre douses himself with the gasoline . . .
Ogre strikes a match and is immediately engulfed in flames!
Smack gets up from the back row.
Smack looks at Ogre
#2938 does not exist.
Sheila climbs up onto the stage and turns and faces the crowd.
Tarquin wonders if he should call the fire department
Skeeter's_Best_Morph climbs up onto the stage and turns and faces the crowd.

<Clap Clap>

Flipper claps
Flipper claps
Flipper claps
    <Clap Clap>
Flipper claps
Flipper claps
  ps

                                          <Clap Clap>
    <Clap Clap>
Hawke claps, and stands.

                       <Clap>

                                                <Clap Clap>
                                             <Clap Clap >

  aps

                                                <Clap Clap>

Flipper claps

                                              <Clap Clap >

Ogre's "suicide" was the culmination of a nasty PMC-MOO fight involving a group of MOO terrorists who fled PMC after their experiments with virtual society began to seriously annoy John Unsworth and the PMC wizards. The terrorists claim these experiments were meant to probe the nature of existence in a virtual community.

The trouble began when Ogre and a few other players created what they called a terrorist class. The purpose of the terrorist class, according to Ogre, was to "experiment with factioning the community, developing semi-tangible classes which mimicked history or real life." People wishing to become terrorists read the following manifesto:

%% TERRORIST CLASS PLAYER INSTRUCTIONS %%
Welcome to the Terrorist Player Class. Wear it proudly. You are part of an elite cadre now, with special powers and a duty to squash the bourgeois Programmer Class once and for all! We must keep them off balance by striking often. We must disseminate fear and confusion.

Terrorists acquired a whole set of nasty verbs, including "steal" (for robbing other players of their virtual objects), "ditch" (for planting stolen goods on an innocent player), "slogan" (for spewing a set of predetermined neo-Mao terrorist slogans), "kill <player>," and "bomb <player>." The bombs at first killed only wizards; then they were upgraded to kill anyone in the room, including well-meaning guests. Dropping a bomb set off a spewing of several lines of text—

```
!!
!! You hear the screeching of tires, a black sedan roars by filled !! with
ski-masked terrorists! A Molotov cocktail is launched into !! your midst!!
!! YOU'RE BEING HIT BY THE PMC-MOO TERRORISTS !!
!! before you can think —
BOOOOOOOOOOOM!!!!
!!
```

—after which hapless players were transferred against their will to room #310 as "eMOOgency services" carted them off to the hospital to recover.

The terrorists wanted to confront the older, more staid PMC users. "They complained that new users were more interested in playing around and making things than talking about Post Modern Culture," says Ogre now. "I thought this was a shallow take on the situation, because we were living pomo, and more often than not it was a chance to explore it more deeply than by exchanging notes with other people verbally. I've always objected to the paper trail of academe. Experience fortifies theory." Ultimately, the wizards removed the terrorist class, and that's when things got nasty. A battle ensued between the few truly angry players and the wizards. A character named Smack created an object called the DarkWhole that, when activated, would sense who was in the room with it and produce disturbing messages. Here is a sample of what happened when a guest was "fed" into the DarkWhole:

```
Feed DarkWhole with Guest

You choose the simulacrum of Guest and drop it on the floor.
A large black rat runs out of a pile of burned debris, grabs the tiny Guest,
and leaps down one of the DarkWhole of holes.
Smack says, "This is Live."
The DarkWhole emits <Guest pulls you close inserting his hot hard
        rod in your tight wet crack
The DarkWhole emits <Violet_Guest kisses lightly at the sides of
        your abs. . obliques. .
and farther up to your
        chest her hot tongue
plays with your nipples
The DarkWhole emits <Guest pulls you to the ground, there's no
        going slow this time he
```

wants you so bad he
        begins to thrust his
hips against yours faster
        and faster
The DarkWhole emits <Violet_Guest feels the pain and wants it
        more . . . more, more

This is the kind of programming that gets you in trouble. The solution adopted at first was punishment without due process. Offenders could be kicked off the system by being @toaded ("@toad" tells the computer to destroy someone's character. Only wizards have access to that command). One player, Sedate, created devices similar to the DarkWhole, except his were invisible; if a hapless player triggered one of them, the player would then be "locked" in place, unable to exit a loop of violently offensive text. Seeming to come from nowhere, the assault would go on for a half hour or more, spewing hundreds or thousands of lines of text, leaving the victim immobile, mute, and terminally frustrated. In the end these stunts proved too unpleasant, and Sedate was @toaded without warning. This angered a lot of other PMC members, and a number of them went into voluntary exile. So, like so many other MOOs dealing with these kinds of problems, PMC instituted a democratic method of dealing with offenders. Now, if a player is offensive, the victim can type @banish. A character with a certain number of @banishes associated with its name could get @toaded. Things seem to have settled down now over at PMC-MOO.

Meanwhile, some of the former PMC terrorists have set up camp at Point MOOt, Texas—a MOO created by Allan Alford, an undergraduate English major at the University of Texas at Austin. Point MOOt provides settlement space for long-term MOO users. Situated at a Texas crossroads, Point MOOt is open to homesteading—with a catch: There is a price for everything. First-time users are granted a small amount of credit to build objects, which corresponds to disk space and processing time. If an object is used by a lot of people, its creator is rewarded with more credits.

Point MOOt opened in February and already has more than 250 players, who have built some 4,000 objects using their credits. These include a university, a radio station, a TV station (MTV, MOO Television, which has put together a history of the town), several strip malls, an electronics outlet store, and a finance magazine called *FOOrbes* (which maintains a list of Point MOOt's ten wealthiest citizens). Alford is "contracting" to have utilities, roads, and other public services built. Since time is the only real commodity in cyberspace, the time that players invest in creating their objects is the real currency of Point MOOt's economy. The price of time is reflected in the prices people (or groups of people) charge for their objects.

Players are divided into three classes. Players who build nothing are considered to be on welfare. Their homes are in public housing ("drab," Alford admits), and they get one building credit per week from the computer. Most players belong to the working class. They go down to the city "job bank," examine the list of objects that need to be built, and contract to take on the public work; in return the city pays them and gives them credit to build. (Objects built by the city are communal and free for everyone to use.) The last class is the capitalist class. These players build objects and "sell" them to other players. Useful objects get sold often.

One player, named Warhol, has taken this one step further: Players "invest" in Warhol by giving him credits. He then builds very useful objects and sells them, using his profits to repay his investors. It is a sort of virtual stock offering. Even the wizard class is for sale—really successful players can "buy" the position. Alford predicts that as more players join Point MOOt, the community will evolve in unexpected ways. He thinks issues of governance will arise soon (at the moment, Point MOOt is still controlled by wizards), as more players invest time in the system.

Point MOOt is monitored more or less constantly by social scientists interested in virtual communities—a group likely to grow rapidly as MOOs become a more important part of everyday life. Jennifer Grace, for one, believes that MOOs are part of a general transition to a postindustrial world where information is the primary commodity, and that today's primordial virtual worlds provide a preview of what we may expect, IRL, in the future.

Every day the number of people using networked virtual spaces in education increases. The Internet as a whole now has 20 million users. At current rates (doubling every two years), the total could reach 160 million by the year 2000. These users will be not only Americans—they will be spread over the globe. In the course of writing this article, word got around, and I soon found myself receiving half a dozen e-mails daily from teachers telling me about another class, another project, another MOO.

Educators of all stripes are beginning to explore what it means to teach in a virtual environment, and preliminary results from these early experiments are trickling in. They will be delivered at a variety of conferences—the MLA and the Computers and Writing Conference among them. Teachers using MOOs report that almost all students enjoy using virtual space. For many of them, creating MOO prose is the first time writing is not a chore. They need to write to communicate with one another. They describe themselves and name themselves. Some build rooms of their own. What excites them is what excites so many of us: They have an audience. People read what they write. They have to in a MOO.

MOOs have their limitations. They discriminate against people who can't touch-type. They also require students to "multitask." As John Unsworth explains, "The people who grew up listening to music on the headphones with the television going while doing their homework have a decided advantage here. They are able to handle three or four conversations at once, following the threads, while other people who are used to doing one thing at a time find it very stressful." Teaching students in a MOO can be difficult; fortunately there are several mechanisms for controlling MOO conversations. One, called "stage talk," allows people to speak to one specific person rather than the whole room; saying hello to David in stage talk appears as "Scott [to David]: Hello." Another, "the yell," or "microphone," gags an entire class and allows only the teacher to speak. Perhaps most importantly, in MOOspace, faculty often lag behind students and allow unchecked information to be disseminated as fact. In virtual environments, metaphor easily becomes truth, and the truth is rarely screened.

Unlike other information-dispensing innovations such as the photocopier and the videocassette, networked virtual spaces are likely to fundamentally change academia, since as a mode of information distribution, MOOs may well prove as revolutionary as the movable-type press. Already, you can "publish" information without a publisher, certain that thousands may read your posting. How many people read you depends not on the decision of an editor but on how "useful" your information is, and how accessible you make it. Electronic information is uncontrolled—it resembles a virus, passing from one medium to the next, using computers as hosts and telephone lines as the means of infection. It grows, it is built upon layer by layer, and no one person owns it—it is too ethereal, too mercurial, to possess. It belongs to everyone.

There is no way to shut off this process. Soon, text-based networks will be complemented by image-based networks and hybrids of both. More and more information will be created and disseminated in cyberspace, and academic institutions will develop new tools to channel it. When history revisits this era, Pavel Curtis and his MOO may well deserve more than a footnote. He may find himself alongside Gutenberg.

THINKING AND RE-READING

1. As you re-read this piece, note the different ways in which Bennahum depicts his participation on a MOO (e.g., "I tumble into Lambda."). What effect does this sort of language create for the reader? Does Bennahum's article make you want to participate in a MOO? Why or why not?

2. Some of the other authors in this section have written about the promise of computer simulations for creating effective learning environments. How do MOOs differ from these other microworlds?

3. Make a list of the different kinds of MOOs Bennahum describes. Some educators have argued that MOOs create egalitarian spaces where all participants can interact equally without being discriminated against because of their race, sex, age, or any of the many other differences that distinguish us from one another. What evidence can you find in the article that supports this contention? What evidence can you find to refute it? Write a short paragraph for your own use, summarizing your findings.

WRITING AND LEARNING

1. To develop your own strategies for thinking and writing critically, jot down the kinds of abilities you think one might need to participate effectively in a MOO. Do you agree that "in this world writing defines your position in the social hierarchy. Good writers, intelligent writers, get lots of attention. Your sex appeal depends on your prose"? How does the rest of Bennahum's article argue for or against this perspective on MOOs? Write a paragraph for your own use in which you encapsulate the support you find in the article for your thinking. Use material from the text to back up your conclusions, making sure that you use the correct citation form for your quotations and paraphrases.

2. Bennahum writes:

> MOOs have their limitations. They discriminate against people who can't touch-type. They also require students to "multitask." As John Unsworth explains, "The people who grew up listening to music on the headphones with the television going while doing their homework have a decided advantage here. They are able to handle three or four conversations at once, following the threads, while other people who are used to doing one thing at a time find it very stressful."

Do you agree? What other more serious limitations can you locate in the article? Based on your experiences MOOing and/or from your reading of Bennahum's article, write a letter to your mother and father or older sibling, explaining what they should expect from a MOO. Also give them advice as to how they should conduct themselves as MOO participants.

3. Write a response in which you discuss some of the advantages and disadvantages of using MOOs in a college curriculum. What subjects might be best suited for MOOs? Which students, in your opinion, will function most successfully in a MOO environment? Whenever possible use your own experiences with MOOs along with your reading to provide evidence for your claims. Your response should be directed to your instructor.

Virtual Time Computer-Mediated Distance Learning Versus the Carnegie Model

John D. Murphy

IN HIS ARTICLE ON "VIRTUAL TIME" computer-mediated distance learning, John Murphy, senior vice president for the Apollo Group, describes a different model for using electronic networks in educational settings. He suggests that asynchronous, or virtual-time, electronic learning environments hold more promise for students than real-time electronic settings. He goes on to describe *Apollo CyberEd Systems (ACEDS)*, a multimedia delivery system that he sees as a structured approach to teaching. In comparing it to the traditional Carnegie Unit instructional model, he underscores some of the shortcomings with current college teaching models. Murphy's article was first published in the summer of 1995 in the *Adult Assessment Forum: A Journal of Quality Management in Adult-Centered Education.*

Higher education professionals are both attracted to and repelled by the thought of utilizing technology to provide education. The attraction is the value of being able to communicate and discuss great ideas to a virtually unlimited number of people without geographical and time barriers. The repellant is that technology will prove the undoing of the academic republic through the liberation of the control of information from the professorate. The reality is much less volatile.

Since 1989 the University of Phoenix has provided the opportunity for qualified working adult students to earn their undergraduate and graduate degrees solely through their personal computer. *UOP Online* currently enrolls over 1100 degree-seeking students and, unlike many other computer-mediated educational programs, has a 65 percent graduation rate. One of the primary reasons for this success is that the programs are delivered via virtual, rather than real, time electronic learning environment.

Building on the success of *UOP Online*, Apollo Group, Inc., has developed a multimedia educational delivery system called *Apollo CyberEd Systems (ACEDS)*,

which will be made available to organizations, corporations and institutions to enable them to provide educational and training products and services electronically.

The following ten characteristics demonstrate the distinct advantages of the ACEDS model over the traditional Carnegie Unit instructional model. I recognize that each of these distinctions does not apply to all instances of instruction based on the Carnegie Unit or the ACEDS model. The predication for this discussion is that these attributes are *common* to each approach.

Evidence of Student Participation/Learning Engagement. In the Carnegie Unit model (CU), which is the nationally recognized measure of instruction in the United States, the student must occupy a seat in classroom with an instructor for a minimum of 15 hours for each credit earned. For a typical three credit course, a student is expected to spend 45 hours physically occupying a seat in a classroom with an instructor. Attendance policies vary by institution and instructor, but simply by physical presence, a student is usually accorded status as a participant, and is judged, de facto, to be actively engaged in the learning process.

In ACEDS, students must evidence their participation and engagement in the learning process through text-based communication. For students utilizing ACEDS, whether studying or documenting knowledge through text, their learning engagement is virtually constant. Students receive no credit or acknowledgment for the time they spend at a computer screen, but rather for what they have electronically archived through their text-based communication. No text? No participation, learning, grade or credit.

Primary Instructional Method. CU-based courses and programs use the lecture as the primary mode of instruction. Generally, students are passive participants in this model because their participation and learning engagement is primarily manifested by sitting and listening to, not interacting with, the instructor. Verbal interactions between and among the instructor and students are limited both in number and duration. Interactions for which the students are held accountable are restricted to the instrumentalities of papers and tests at isolated points in time. No record of verbal interactions is kept by either the student or the instructor.

The ACEDS curricular and teaching/learning interface specifies both learning outcomes and activities, and requires the instructor to organize the course material into very specific and manageable components. The instructor focuses the students on discrete elements of the curriculum which each student is required to address in a text-based response. Following the directions provided in the instructor's text-based lecture, students read and reflect upon the related material; engage in text-based discussions with the instructors, members of the class and members of their 2–3 person study group; and demonstrate their knowledge of the subject matter through text-based responses in virtual, rather than real, time.

Class Location and Time. CU courses are, by definition, restricted to a specific time and place. If a student is available at the time and place at which the course or program is offered, then he or she can take advantage of the learning opportunity. If the student is not available, he or she usually can't take advantage of it.

Most educational institutions utilizing the CU model provide the bulk of their educational offerings between September and December and February and May, primarily during the day at a central location. This schedule of learning opportunities suits full-time students and the employees of the educational institution, but anyone who lives at a distance from the site where the education is being offered, or who has specific learning needs and requirements related to their personal circumstances and/or professional responsibilities, will often have to make extraordinary compromises to take advantage of the education, or will have to forgo it entirely.

With ACEDS, courses and programs can be made available 24 hours a day, every day of the year through a PC. Because ACEDS communications are text-based, students may communicate through their PC whenever they have time available. This allows persons living in widely dispersed geographical locations and time zones to interact electronically whether at their homes or offices, or on the road.

Although students and instructors communicate in virtual time, courses and programs offered through ACEDS are highly structured, and both students and instructors are generally required to evidence electronically archived communication several times weekly.

The elimination of the time- and place-dependent learning through the utilization of ACEDS provides almost universal educational access to persons of all ages who have access to and the use of the requisite hardware and conferencing software configuration, curriculum and teaching/learning interface.

Communications Timeframe.   The CU model of instruction is predicated on the oral communication from the instructor and the student between two narrowly prescribed points in time. This lecture is primarily a monologue by the instructor from which the student is expected to derive the body of their understanding of the subject matter.

The interaction between the lecturer and the student is "real time," since the student must be present if he or she ever wishes to ask a question or engage in dialogue with the instructor. Since no record of spontaneous verbal interaction is maintained, any benefit that might be derived from such interactions is not available to the student who misses a class.

Students in ACEDS are able to achieve the learning outcomes because they must regularly evidence constructive engagement in the learning process. The virtual time educational dynamic provides a sustained level of critical interaction since all students are required to evidence their knowledge of the course material through text-based communication within a prescribed timeframe. Mandated interaction is only possible in a virtual time learning environment, since in a real time classroom—depending on the personality of the student and the instructor—only a limited number of students can interact meaningfully.

With ACEDS, all communications are archived, enabling both the student and the instructor to review previous discussions to help maintain continuity in an interactive learning process that occurs at different places in time over an extended period.

Communications Methodology.   In the CU teaching/learning model, the instructor generally serves as the sole source of knowledge. Students participate passively for the bulk of the time spent in the classroom and demonstrate their knowledge through written tests or papers at isolated points in time.

With ACEDS, students and the instructor communicate in virtual time. This requires and allows students to read and reflect upon the instructor's discussion of specific elements of the curriculum; place that discussion in context through the reading of related course material and text-based interactions with other students, and commit their understanding of the material to text. Unlike real time interaction, once students have committed their understanding to text, they are able to review and modify it before sending it off electronically.

Communications in ACEDS are electronically archived so that both the student and the faculty member can build upon previous understandings of the subject matter. Each time a student commits his or her thoughts to text and uploads it electronically, he or she has effectively published his or her understanding of the subject matter. If a student hasn't read the material, completed the exercises, or reflected critically, it will be plainly evident to the instructor and other students. Each student utilizing ACEDS must take responsibility for his or her own learning or he or she will be considered neither a participant nor engaged in the learning process. No student is anonymous in a course taken through ACEDS.

Learning Environment. In a lecture-based course, students have limited interactions with the instructor and among themselves. Because cooperative learning is minimal, students effectively compete against each other. In many courses, instructors grade students on the curve, thus perpetuating the competitive nature of the learning process. Students uncomfortable with expressing themselves verbally in a large class, who do not wish to call any attention to themselves, or who engage in what they perceive as verbal competition with other students may choose not to interact with only marginal, if any, consequences. As the result, both their interactions and learning are often narrowly confined to written papers and tests. Students who desire to actively engage in an in-depth discussion of the course material are usually denied the opportunity because such discussions would interfere with the delivery of the lecture material, or dominate, and thus skew, the discussion because of minimal participation by the other students in the class.

> Gender, appearance, mannerism, and personality play a circumscribed role, since it is the quality of the knowledge and understanding reflected in the text-based communication upon which both participation and performance are both perceived and evaluated.

With ACEDS, each student is both required and guaranteed the opportunity to present his or her opinion and understanding without undue influence or duress from others who might happen to disagree, or verbally dominate the discussion. Because communication is text-based, everyone's ideas, understandings, and opinions are perceived as having equal merit. The only discriminating factor is the clarity of the written text and evidence of the mastery of the subject matter.

The virtual time communications structure of ACEDS guarantees each student the opportunity to participate equitably and democratically in the learning process. Gender, appearance, mannerism, and personality play a circumscribed role, since it is the quality of the knowledge and understanding reflected in the text-based communication upon which both participation and performance are both perceived and evaluated.

Student Participation. In courses and programs structured on the CU equation, particularly with large enrollments, the interaction between and among the instructor and the students is highly circumscribed, and probably voluntary. Most students only evidence their engagement in the learning process when required to submit a paper or take a test.

With ACEDS, students evidence their engagement in the learning process through regular text-based communications. The requirement of affirmative engagement places the responsibility for learning on the student. Unlike a traditional classroom where the student must only demonstrate learning at isolated points, with ACEDS, all students are required to demonstrate their knowledge and understanding on an actively ongoing basis to both the instructor and the other students. This socialization of the learning process helps ensure a high level of student participation and accountability.

Student–Instructor Interaction. The interaction between the instructor and the student in the CU classroom is unstructured, with student-faculty interaction usually being spontaneous. Despite being primarily passive recipients of the knowledge provided by the instructor, students are perceived and judged to be actively engaged in the learning process if they are physically present. As a result, the instructor gains limited knowledge of, or personal interest in, the individual strengths and weaknesses of each student, which limits his or her role in helping improve individual academic performance.

> If a student hasn't read the material, completed the exercises, or reflected critically, it will be plainly evident to the instructor and other students.

Students utilizing ACEDS are required to interact with the instructor and other students for a minimum number of times during any given course. Because this interaction is text-based, both student and instructor develop well-informed understandings of each other. By nature, virtual time communication is intense because of the requirement that communications be clear and concise.

The ACEDS instructor is required to respond to all communications from the students, and must critically respond within a prescribed timeframe in a very detailed manner. Because of this requirement, over the duration of a course, an instructor is able to assist students in improving their performance in very specific ways. The result is heightened performance both on the part of the instructor and the student. This communications dynamic also ensures that participants remain highly focused and involved in the learning process.

Student–Student Interaction. In the conventional classroom, student participation is unstructured rather than structured. While students are not precluded from responding directly to the lecture subject matter, the one-way communications bias of the lecture format dampens the interaction dynamic. If interaction does occur, it is almost exclusively between an individual student and the instructor. Rarely, unless organized as one of the major components of a particular course, is student-to-student interaction required.

All students utilizing ACEDS are required to interact with other students in direct relationship to the issues identified by the instructor in the context of the course requirements. This interaction is cooperative, and provides an opportunity for students to share ideas and the responsibility for researching and providing information about specific areas of the subject matter of the course. Student-to-student interaction is mandated for both the learning group, i.e., all students enrolled in the course, as well as for each student's respective study group. As with the interactions with the instructor, all communications are text-based. This helps ensure that students maintain a high level of interest and engagement.

Educational Access. Almost without exception, all courses and programs conformed to the CU equation are restricted in both time and place. If an individual wishes to enroll in a particular course, he or she must attend that course at the time and place specified by the institution or entity offering it.

Courses and programs provided through ACEDS are available without restriction as to time and place, thus allowing most individuals to take advantage of the educational opportunity in the context of their personal and professional lives. The elimination of these restrictions provides extraordinary educational access that cannot possibly be duplicated in the traditional CU course structure.

REFLECTION

With the ACEDS computer-mediated model, students are required to take responsibility for their own learning and may not remain an anonymous member of the class often mistakenly thought to be engaged in learning simply by physical presence. ACEDS and other forms of electronically delivered education programs offer great promise in helping restore much of what has been lost in the practice of education.

It should be clear from the above discussion that I believe the Carnegie Unit is no longer an appropriate model for structuring the classrooms of higher education, virtual or physical. Advancements not only in technology, but in the sciences of instruction and curriculum development as well as the sciences of assessment have made instruction based on demonstrated learning the desirable and efficient alternative.

There is certainly much more to be said on all sides of this issue. I invite other views from all who have a stake in the future of higher education in our technologically permeated knowledge society.

THINKING AND RE-READING

1. As you re-read Murphy's article, make a list of the advantages Murphy sees in his "virtual time" model of learning. Go back through the article and begin to make a list of possible disadvantages based on your own experiences in electronic settings. What shortcomings does Murphy include regarding the Carnegie Unit model? Can you add to this list? Why is Murphy such a strong supporter of *ACEDS?* How does his approach to setting up electronic learning environments compare to Bennahum's description of educational MOOs?

WRITING AND LEARNING

1. Think about a class that you are interested in and would like to see improved. Make a list of basic resources you find lacking in the class that electronic networks might begin to provide. Find examples in Bennahum's and/or Murphy's pieces that could enhance the class. How would you apply them to the class you have in mind? Would the class be effective if it were entirely online? Why or why not? Write a description of your ideal class based on your experiences and reading. Be sure to include any electronic activities you think appropriate. Aim your report at a student and faculty committee on campus that is interested in curriculum reform (oftentimes such a committee is called the "General Education Board").

Surreal Science

Philip Yam

IN THE ANONYMOUS LETTER you read earlier in this section, the writer implicitly contrasts her notions of "axtual reelity" with what has become known as "virtual reality." In the short piece included here, Philip Yam informs readers of the potential that such virtual realities have for the teaching of physics. The article first appeared in a 1995 special issue of *Scientific American,* a magazine that appeals to a broad range of educated readers.

High school physics might have been more fun—and more instructive—if the ability to bounce balls on Jupiter were a laboratory option. Well, now it is, at least in principle. Using his experience in developing virtual-reality environments to train National Aeronautics and Space Administration astronauts, R. Bowen Loftin, a physicist at the University of Houston-Downtown, has developed a virtual-physics laboratory in which this and other improbable exercises are as easy as making a slam-dunk shot on a wastepaper basket.

Students enter virtual reality by donning headgear and a control glove hooked up to a computer. A panoramic view of the virtual laboratory is projected through small screens inside the headset. There is a table, a pendulum, some balls as well as a few odd devices that govern the actions in the laboratory. Users see a computer-generated image of their hand, which duplicates the motion of the real thing. Certain gestures of the control glove are reserved for special actions. Pointing the index finger, for example, will send the virtual physicist flying across the room.

In this artificial environment, students can conduct simple experiments in mechanics that are impossible to perform in a real world. Parameters such as friction and drag can be controlled; gravity can even be turned into a negative force. Computer-generated trajectory lines and freeze-time capability enable users to measure the effects of the changes in the variables on swinging pendulums and bouncing balls. Balls, for example, can bounce so that they increase in energy with every skip.

Amusement, however, is not Loftin's primary goal. He and other developers of educational technology are trying to create an interactive environment that challenges students' often mistaken ideas about the physical world. "Kids build misconceptions about the world that are difficult to dislodge," points out Christopher Dede, who directs the center for interactive educational technology at George Mason University.

Loftin notes that many people think constant motion always requires force. This perception—a violation of Newton's first law—comes about because friction almost always plays a role in the motion of objects. "Newtonian mechanics is not easily detected in the world around you," he says.

The immersive quality of virtual reality, Dede says, makes it ideal for such subjects as physics. "We can get a direct intuitive qualitative sense of physical laws. Such simulations are not possible with a mouse running around on a flat screen." Furthermore, the virtual-physics laboratory is not so dangerous as some real physics experiments, as anyone who has gotten a shock from a spark generator or has been bopped by a pendulum knows.

Although most virtual-reality systems retain a certain level of unbelievability, they have proved to be especially useful in situations that would otherwise be difficult to simulate. The near weightlessness of space is one such obvious example. The more conventional techniques all have shortcomings.

In underwater tanks, the viscosity of water affects the training. Freely falling aircraft such as the KC-135 can produce true weightlessness for only about 20 or 30 seconds. Air-bearing floors that levitate astronauts on a cushion of air do not provide the full three-dimensional motion of floating in zero gravity. Virtual reality, on the other hand, can accurately simulate all the conditions of space, so NASA is now using that technology for such tasks as training astronauts to grapple wayward satellites and use robotic arms.

It may take a few years before such computer simulations become commonplace in the classroom. The virtual-physics laboratory is still rather rudimentary. Even by the standards of video games and television cartoons, the images have a stilted quality. Also, the computational speed limits the system's repertoire to a few simple mechanics experiments. But Loftin has been developing a version that will enable users to explore such concepts as angular momentum and energy conservation.

The future could bring virtual laboratories for other domains of science, such as chemistry, biology and medicine. Indeed, Loftin says that medical schools have shown interest in virtual reality for anatomy courses. "It could be like *Fantastic Voyage*," Loftin observes, referring to the movie based on Isaac Asimov's story of scientists shrunk and injected into a human body.

Prices, too, will have to come down before virtual laboratories become widespread. Loftin's headgear and control glove cost several hundred thousand dollars. Researchers are confident, however, that within 10 years, virtual-reality circuit boards should become available for desktop computers. Then, coupled to modest peripheral devices, the fidelity would be sufficient to do some really surreal science.

THINKING AND RE-READING

1. Think about how the virtual reality laboratory that Yam describes compares with the other learning environments we've read about in this section. Reflect on your own experiences in labs in physics and in other science classes. How do they compare with Yam's description? What have been your experiences with virtual reality? What kinds of support are needed for the professors and students in order for these new approaches to be effective? How do your college's resources measure up?

WRITING AND LEARNING

1. Make a list of all the online instructional software systems you've encountered so far in the first twelve selections in this section. Identify two that you find ineffective and explain why. Then choose two that you would like to see incorporated into your own college classes. Why would these applications be effective? How are these instructional uses of computers alike and different? Using your comparison of effective and ineffective computer environments, design with a classmate a system that would enhance the course for which you're using this reader. Share your written recommendations with the rest of your class.

Academic Computing in the Year 2000

Luke Young, Kurt Thearling, Steven Skieno, Arch Robison, Stephen Omohundro, Bartlett Mel, and Stephen Wolfram

THIS SELECTION IS WRITTEN by a group of college students who entered Apple Corporation's "Project 2000" competition held in 1987–1988. According to John Sculley, Apple's chairman and chief executive officer at the time, "Project 2000 extended a challenge for students to visualize how computer technology will be used in the year 2000. At the same time we wanted to engage them in an enriching educational experience that would lead them to explore the possible social, economic, and technological climate of the world at the turn of the century" (9). Students at the University of Illinois, Urbana-Champaign, submitted *Tablet*, the entry we've included here, and were judged the winners. Judges included futurist Alvin Toffler, science fiction writer Ray Bradbury, educator Diane Ravitch, and computer pioneers Steve Wozniak and Alan Kay. The article was originally published in 1988 in *Academic Computing*, a magazine that was aimed at college teachers but is no longer in circulation. This piece should provide you with a good opportunity to look at how a group of students of the 1980s envisioned computers as populating the collegiate landscape in the year 2000.

INTRODUCTION

Computers today represent a powerful tool for education. The computer of the year 2000 will be an even more powerful tool. But it is not the tool that gets the job done, the person using it does. This essay discusses the task of education from the vantage point of Tablet, our vision of computing in the year 2000. While we are very optimistic about the potential of Tablet, it is not by itself a solution to the problems of education. No tool can be unless applied by proper craftsmen.

Any reasonable vision of the future must be bound by two distinct constraints. The first constraint is technological—what will we know, and what will we be able to build at that particular moment? For computers, how powerful will they be, and how much will they cost? Will they be bigger than a bread box? Can they be made portable? How can such a machine communicate with its world—both with its immediate environment as well as the global community? It is this aspect of our design which won us the Apple competition.

The second and more fundamental constraint is how this technology can be used meaningfully by people. A person's density does not double each year, the way VLSI circuitry does. There are only twelve years remaining before the year 2000, and for massive changes to happen in education in this time more people must get involved in an exciting way with the creation of this technology. We mean the educators, scholars, and administrators—the people who are running the classrooms of today. Without significant and enlightened participation from this community, the computer of the year 2000 will be doing the same thing in the classroom that the computer of 1988 is doing: sitting there, running a few games, tabulating grades, and filling out reports inspiring only to a stray hacker wandering into the vicinity.

> **However, there is reason to hope that technical progress by the year 2000 will animate the human side of education.**

However, there is reason to hope that technical progress by the year 2000 will animate the human side of education. As computers become more powerful, it becomes reasonable to mold them in the image of people. The computer as a tool will fit naturally into the lives of the masses instead of being shoehorned in under the oxymoron of "computer literacy." Only when educators need not strain to realize the potential of their classroom machines will computers revolutionize the way things are done. This will happen by the year 2000. Hypertext systems are already beginning to allow the structuring of knowledge with a flexibility that makes it accessible to both student and teacher.

In this essay, we give our vision of Tablet, a machine unquestionably feasible for twelve years from now. We present a brief look at how Tablet will change the life of both the professor and the student. Finally, we elaborate on the challenges education will have to meet for our vision to become reality.

TABLET: THE PERSONAL COMPUTER OF THE YEAR 2000

Tablet will have the same dimensions as a standard notebook. This rectangular slab will look like an 8" × 11" monolith from the movie *2001* and weigh but a few pounds. Having neither buttons nor knobs, the front surface will be a touch-sensitive display screen. One side will have a credit card sized slit, while the other three sides support ruby-colored ridges. Here, we describe our vision in terms of its components, leaving the rest of the essay to prove that the sum is greater than its parts.

The I/O Surface   The most important part of any computer is its user interface. The front surface of Tablet is a high-resolution touchscreen, which yields slightly to pressure. With this single input device, we get the tremendous flexibility of a soft interface: from the low-resolution but traditional means of pointing with your finger to the higher-resolution available using a stylus. The touchscreen can emulate a mouse, or a soft keyboard—customized to the user's finger size and taste.

But if we are holding a stylus, why bother with the keyboard? We can write and draw directly on the surface of the screen, integrating text and graphics. And, if we wish, handwriting recognition software will convert our scrawl to typed text. Finally, this color display is more than just an imitation notebook page, it will be fast enough to support video communications.

Without question this is technologically achievable. Liquid crystal displays are inherently pressure sensitive, and the density is increasing fast enough that by 2000 they will be of laser printer quality and in color. The touchscreen resolution will mimic the finest ball point. Cursive character recognition systems with training and spelling correction techniques can achieve nearly 100% accuracy. Of course, no human or silicon system will recognize all handwriting, particularly from the medical community, but what isn't recognized will be highlighted in a different color and reentered by the user.

It might seem surprising that voice is not a major interface. Science fiction seems to specialize in talking to computers and listening to what they have to say. However, in many of the contexts where Tablet will be used, such as the classroom, the airplane, or a shared office, talking out loud will not be appropriate. This is not to say that speech is not a viable form of input for our design. A microphone and speech recognition processor will allow a user to communicate via speech if he or she chooses. Although dictating letters and memoranda is a skill which takes time to master, a system allowing the user to alternate between a speech-to-text mode and a text editor could spare the user a great deal of time in preparing reports—especially when the words that are spoken match words already appearing somewhere on the screen. In addition, there are circumstances where speech may be the only way a physically handicapped user could communicate with our computer. Our design has the flexibility of allowing the user to communicate in whatever way is desired.

The LaserCard Mass Storage Unit   To replace classical rotating-disk/movable head media, we propose LaserCard. These credit card sized optical RAMs will be a convenient, inexpensive, and physically robust data storage medium. Through data compression techniques, a single one gigabyte card will hold four hours of video or two thousand books from a personal library. People will carry them in their shirt pockets and trade them like baseball cards. The only moving part in the whole machine will be the lid which keeps the optics dry if we use it in the rain.

One gigabyte is a healthy chunk of memory. However, it is only twice the capacity of a compact disk. We will use LaserCard for convenience, but it is clear that the real databases of the world will have to be elsewhere but still easily accessible.

The DataLink   To get this easy access, we need communication capabilities. Thus, Tablet integrates a cellular telephone link. This will not only support voice but data communications as well. The ISDN standard combined with compression techniques is sufficient to transmit video at conference quality rates today.

To use this link for voice communications, we will need a microphone and speaker built into the unit. These are inexpensive and justified by other applications. However for privacy, in most applications we will use a headset attachment clipped onto the infrared bar.

The Infrared Interface   Along three sides of Tablet will be an infrared bar interface through which Tablet will talk to its local environment: printers and projectors, stereo headsets and video cameras, toasters and roasters, other Tablets and just about anything else. Every smart device in the world will have its own unique 256 bit key so a simple protocol will enable devices to talk intelligently to each other. There are nowhere near 2^{256} atoms in the universe, so we need not worry about running out of keys. With infrared light, low bandwidth devices need not be physically connected while indoors. The infrared interface may be extended by repeaters stationed in large offices and clip-on optical cables to boost bandwidth to gigabaud rates.

What types of peripherals will people need? One of the most widely owned peripherals will be a tactile keyboard. The handwriting interface and simulated keyboard will suffice for portable applications, but for rapid text entry, nothing beats a good solid keyboard. Another extremely popular peripheral will be a lapel sized video camera. Charge-coupled devices (CCDs) make inexpensive and rugged solid-state cameras. The cameras will record meetings, electronic mail videos for instruction and personal communication, and digitize those printed documents which remain in the year 2000. The notion of digitizing documents is important, because a substantial number of printed documents will remain, such as old books and new contracts. After digitization, an image can be processed to cleanup and recognize the text to allow searching by keyword and context.

Tablet will have a GPS (Global Positioning System) receiver as a built-in component. GPS is an existing satellite-based system which enables objects to locate themselves in the world to within a few meters. By plugging in the *Rand McNally Road Atlas* LaserCard before a drive, it can provide us with the ideal route and parking place for that new French restaurant in the city. Its usefulness extends well beyond driving, however.

Theft is a significant problem in an academic environment; anything valuable that isn't nailed down vanishes. And Tablet is valuable. However, with the Global Positioning System (GPS), the machine will know where it is and with the cellular phone DataLink, it will be able to communicate this information to the proper authorities. Try and fence merchandise this hot!

The Traditional Computer   That aspect of our vision which deals with what we today call the computer, i.e. the processor and its memory, is rather mundane. It is clear that there will be mega-MIPs and giga-bits available to work with, but whatever processor we have under the hood is irrelevant to the rest of the design. Thus we avoid the temptation to guess the exact number of MIPs, the memory size, or the degree of parallelism of our machine.

We expect microprocessors to converge on generic designs, coming in fast, extra fast, and economy sizes as do memory chips today. There will also be standardization among user interfaces, to the extent that all will be constructed in layers, where all but the highest layer will be a universal standard. Running on these generic processors might be a standard version of UNIX coming out of its shell into a PostScript interface.

All circuitry will sit on the same six-inch wafer of silicon. Though silicon may sound old fashioned, more exotic technologies such as optical computers, molecular or chemical computers, or superconductors will not mature by 2000. Improvements in semiconductor processing and design technology of our wafer will make room for large graphics processors, analog and digital hardware for image processing, and much more.

> **Sexy technology is nice, but how will Tablet fit into the lives of the academic community?**

Perhaps the most interesting special purpose processor will be a data compressor sitting between the memory and the main processors. This will permit video to be stored on LaserCards and transmitted over cellular phone links, because image expansion will occur at video rates. It is ironic that compression becomes even more important as memory capacity increases, because there is so much more to transmit and access.

Rechargeable lithium batteries will deliver all the power we will be able to use without running into heat dissipation problems.

A DAY IN THE LIFE

Sexy technology is nice, but how will Tablet fit into the lives of the academic community? Here, we take a brief look into the future for the student and professor of the year 2000.

A Day in the Life of a Student   The date is October 5, 2000. Alexis Quezada is a freshman at a prestigious institution of higher learning. Her classes are typical for a freshman of the year 2000: Algorithmic Mathematics, Physical Science, Art History, English Composition, and Conversational Japanese. On her first day of classes she was given her own Tablet, the personal computer used at the university.

Today Alexis has three classes: Physical Science, Japanese, and Algorithmic Mathematics. It is a nice day, so Alexis rides her bike over to the park before the lecture starts. At 10:00 A.M. sharp Tablet informs her that the Physical Science lecture is about to start. She directs her attention toward the screen as the lecture begins. When the lecture is over, she begins the laboratory experiment. It involves determining the equilibrium for a chemical reaction. She sets up the simulated experiment apparatus and starts it going. But it isn't working. She instructs Tablet to search today's lecture for "the stuff about setting up today's experiment." Within seconds the requested portion of the lecture is displayed on the screen.

Because of the problem with setting up the experiment, Alexis missed the beginning of her Japanese lecture. Instead of jumping into a lecture that has already started, Alexis's computer contacts the university's lecture database again and instructs the database to display the current lecture from the beginning. Time-shifting the start of the lecture by fifteen minutes has allowed her to see the lecture from the beginning, at the cost of not being able to ask the professor a question if she doesn't understand. Fortunately, the lecture is still in progress and should last another forty minutes, so Alexis invokes the "catch-up" facility. Over the next fifteen minutes,

Alexis watches thirty minutes of lecture as Tablet squeezes out the times of slow movement and silence. Through signal processing, the lecture looks and sounds fast-paced but is otherwise normal. Now up to speed, she watches the rest of the lecture and participates in asking questions, performing an occasional "instant replay/catch-up" sequence on material that she found confusing.

Once Japanese is over, Alexis heads back to the dormitory for lunch. Some things never change, and dorm food is one of them. Fortunately, the social aspects of lunch will still be important even in a world where one can communicate with friends by video email. Afterwards Alexis returns to her room to start reading her LaserCard edition of G. B. Trudeau's *Republic*, complete with art, text, and extensive commentary. She scrawls notes directly on the simulated page which she can search or hide at will.

In English Comp class at 2:00 P.M., the professor indicates that she has finished grading the previous assignment and returns them. Instantly, the corner of the display contains a copy of Alexis's graded paper—B+, not too bad. Alexis pages through the paper by touching the screen. She touches the video-mail icon for comments about a particular page. Segments of her text become highlighted in color as they are discussed. Unfortunately, her teacher is pretty boring, and so she turns on her soap opera instead.

That evening, Alexis starts her math homework due the next day. She makes her computer plot a portion of the Riemann Zeta function to show that most of the zeros lie on a line and completes her assignment by including the counter example discovered in 1993. After finishing her math, she decides to have a look at the *Newsweek* LaserCard she got today. She reviews the headlines: "Last U.S. Nuclear Power Station Closes," "NeXT Buys Apple Computer," "Air America Announces New Boeing Spaceplane Service Between Chicago and Shanghai"—nothing exciting, so she checks the Sports. A fan of Debbie Gibson oldies, Alexis is pleased to learn that Ms. Gibson will be leading the opening ceremonies at the Third Annual Frisbee Olympics.

Now it's time to work on her art history term paper comparing Salvador Dali's surrealist images in his paintings and the images he developed for the movies *Un Chien Andalou* and *Spellbound*. Alexis tells Tablet to find the films in available film databases. It seems that there are three films with the title *Spellbound*. Alexis says to find "the one by Hitchcock." The scenes she is interested in analyzing are being copied directly into her paper—a hypertext document. Alexis expounds on the meaning of the images in the films and their importance with respect to Dali's symbolism until it's time to call it a night.

A Day in the Life of a Professor We now concentrate our attention on Xiao-Lin Zhang, a professor of Complex Systems Science at the same university as Alexis. He starts the day at home by checking his electronic mail. There are a number of questions from his students and a request from a colleague to give a speech at an upcoming conference. He responds to the students' questions and checks his electronic calendar to see if he can attend the conference. It appears that there are no conflicts so he accepts the invitation. He then instructs the computer to make the travel arrangements. After a few seconds, Tablet responds that the airline and hotel reservations have been made and that he is registered for the conference. His calendar is automatically updated.

He heads to his office and prepares his Theoretical Economics lecture. He could work at home but he feels more comfortable working in his office. Tablet retrieves his version of the textbook. Apart from the handwritten marginal notes and solution sets, his copy is identical to the student's copy. These notes will be used with his lecture. An old fogy, he prefers lecturing from the classroom. Upon entering the classroom, the "electronic blackboard" recognizes his Tablet as an authorized host and links in. About a third of the students are physically present, but his Tablet shows that the rest are tuning in. A student calls in with a question about the rent control case study included in the textbook. Xiao-Lin illustrates the effect of rent control on the Campbell curve by plugging values for rent into the graph. As the value for rent is changed, the curve on the graph changes appropriately. The reasoning behind these changes is sufficient to clear up the misunderstanding.

With lecture over, it's time for some high-powered research. He needs to find some data about the effect of political turmoil on debt in fourth-world nations. A database search through Tablet comes up with three sources, one of which is useful but six years old. He needs data that is more up-to-date and contacts the author to see if anything is available. Tablet finds that Professor Moore is no longer at Oxford and has moved to Buckingham. After a few seconds, Professor Moore's face appears on the screen. Xiao-Lin introduces himself and learns his work is at a dead end—an internal Buckingham technical report produced last year solved his very problem. Thank God, he hadn't invested more time in this project.

It is now time to attend the Complex Systems Science department staff meeting. Tablet contacts the other members of the department and the meeting begins. The new budget is the current order of business. On the screen of every department member's computer appears the tentative budget. After a number of arguments and changes to the budget, it appears that a consensus has been reached. Each professor has his or her computer apply a digital signature to the budget acknowledging final approval. There is no other business to cover, so the meeting ends and Xiao-Lin can eat a late lunch.

After lunch it is time to head home and work on his car. Xiao-Lin prides himself on being able to handle himself under the hood and is confident that he will be able to fix whatever is wrong. Once he gets home, he has his computer run diagnostic tests on the engine. The computer responds that there are two possibilities and diagrams of the engine appear on the screen with the possible faulty parts highlighted. Xiao-Lin checks the two parts and determines that both are broken. He then has the computer contact the parts stores in the area to see if they have any replacement parts in stock. There are five local stores with both parts in stock, and the store with the lowest prices is just a couple blocks away. He heads over to the store and picks up the parts.

Tablet in the Classroom   We have presented a vision of radical change in the structure of the classroom. Why have a physical classroom where you must go to learn when, with Tablet, you can take it with you? Tablet makes this vision possible, but what is not clear is to what extent this future is desirable. Do all the changes improve the quality of education, or do they simply change the set of problems?

The essence of education is interaction, and this does not mean canned programs and canned classes. This interaction will not come between a person and their computer because it will take far more than ten years progress in artificial intelligence to create programs which will communicate with people in a meaningful way. This interaction will have to come from people. We hope that Tablet will remove enough of the drudgery associated with education to enable people to interact in a more powerful way.

Disclaimers aside, there is great merit in the idea of the Tele-University. Lectures need no longer be situated in auditoriums with an army of students facing a lone professor. Using the cellular DataLink and image processing capability of their Tablet, students will be able to take part in lectures from any point in the academic world. The class notes produced by the professor will automatically be transferred from their "electronic blackboard" to a window on the student's screen. These notes need not be limited to text. Why not multimedia class notes incorporating video, text, and audio? It is vital that these be two-way lectures—any student must be able to interrupt the professor with a question by simply raising the hand icon on the screen. If you happen to be in the hospital with a broken leg, there is no need to miss an important lecture. To go over a topic covered in lecture at a later date, simply access the file for that lecture in the university database and play back that portion at your own pace.

These days, if you want to be a major player in a particular research area, you have to go where the action (or advisor) is. The Tele-University will enable the best teachers to lecture to thousands of students at dozens of universities simultaneously. However, the real advantage is that eminent researchers will be able to teach extremely specialized courses to small groups scattered around the globe. Perhaps there may not be enough people at Illinois to appreciate a Herbert Edelsbrunner course on "Combinatorial Geometry in E^3" to justify offering it. But by including stray graduate students from NYU and McGill, as well as a few others from here and there, a quorum can be made and maintained. This has exciting possibilities for breaking down the barriers between institutions—geographically and politically. Perhaps different branches of a state university will indeed start acting as members of a system—with faculty and students moving easily between them.

At the university level, most learning happens in front of an open textbook at home, instead of an open notebook at lecture. Because of the availability of Tablet, textbooks in the year 2000 will only partially resemble those used in universities today. Most courses will have online multimedia textbooks available. For example, a "book" on Orson Welles could contain video excerpts from the movie *Citizen Kane* as well as audio from his "War of the Worlds" radio broadcast. A math textbook will include living formulae for the student to manipulate. For example, a student encountering Taylor series can specify his or her favorite function to be expanded, along with evaluating the first several terms to get a feel for the rate of convergence. A chemistry textbook discussion of the Belousov-Zhabotinskii reaction could include a simulation of the reaction with chemical parameters input by the student. The textbook would also include video of the actual reaction as viewed in a laboratory.

In addition to textbooks, other sources of information such as scholarly journals will be stored online. A current and inevitable trend in publishing is to submit articles via electronic means. Once display formats become standardized, it will also be possible for journals to be electronically published. This means more than just desktop publishing—it means the student from a university with a crippled library will be able to get the material they need online. The technology will not only speed the publication process, it will dramatically reduce the cost of publishing a journal. Reducing the cost threshold for starting a journal means more specialized journals will spring up like weeds—again, enhancing our ability to communicate. Doctoral theses and technical reports normally published by universities will also be available online. If a particular piece of information is in a language which you do not understand, your computer will make a rough translation with which you can work.

The organization of such vast amounts of information will dictate the extent to which it will be usable. Imagine a tremendous hypertext encyclopedia where every expert in every field maintains his or her knowledge online. Such a document can only keep growing and assimilating more and more information, pushing older and less popular information to lower levels while maintaining a hierarchical structure. A student can plunge deeply into superstring theory or skim the surface of modern physics by following different paths of links in the document. New links will be formed by remembering the path of previous searches. Thus every student becomes an explorer blazing another trail for all to follow.

To efficiently search the available databases, automatic indexing programs will be used. These programs might map all English words and proper names into, say, 2^{16} different classes. A bit vector of this size can be prepended to each document, where a bit is set if a member of the corresponding word class appears in that document. Thus, we can quickly identify the set of documents relevant to our query by comparing the document vector against a vector of all possible aspects, spellings, and synonyms for our search. Such a system can "infer" by analyzing the similarities between the vectors of related documents. Similar indexing techniques can be used for music and video, so we can search for songs similar to our favorite Beatles tune.

In addition to the ease of access for specific volumes of information, the computer will allow quick and simple searches for a particular item. You can search an art textbook for a painting by drawing a sketch of the painting on your screen. The computer would then try to match your sketch with one of the paintings in the book.

Of course, there will exist problems for which the processing power available in a Tablet will not be great enough to solve a particular problem. In these situations, it will be necessary to tap into "computing power stations." By pulling the plug on the six billion dollar supercollider, we could build a thousand-processor Cray or a billion-processor Connection Machine. Students will be able to use a few processors whenever they need, and the entire machine can be set aside for one hour a week to do the national weather forecast.

The way programming is done must change dramatically for educators to cash in on the computer revolution. Programs in low-level languages like C will die out like dinosaurs. Filling their ecological niche will be scripts for high-level interpretive systems. These programs will not be created by entering a sequence of lines of code, but rather by linking together operations using a graphical representation of the program's function. At the simplest level, a program will be just "replaying" a sequence of commands to a high level system. Thus, a classical literature major should have no more trouble programming the computer than an electrical engineering major.

THE EFFECT ON CURRICULUM AND COURSEWORK

When calculators entered the classroom in the 1970s, they resulted in a dramatic rethinking of the philosophy of education. Is it worthwhile for students to spend time learning long division when a calculator from a box of breakfast cereal will do the job better? Access to a tool like Tablet will have to cause an even greater revolution in what is considered worth knowing.

By the year 2000, computers will have forever become an integral part of doing science. Just as all arithmetic is done on portable calculators today, algebra, calculus, and all aspects of mathematical calculation will be relegated to computers. Yesterday's science followed one of two paths: hands-on physical experimentation or pure theory. Computers make possible a third path: computer experimentation, which will become the dominant method for investigating many kinds of systems. Such experimentation is the method by which one uses an algorithm to simulate a physical system and then finds out what happens by watching the program run. For many systems, this approach is not only fast and convenient, but fundamentally necessary. There will be very few scientists in 2000 who do not spend the majority of their time in front of their computer.

Knowing that each student has available the computational power of Tablet changes the ground rules for homework assignments and exams. The brute force attack applied to traditional math and physics problems will become obsolete. In its place, an algorithmic paradigm, stressing how a problem is to be solved rather than the mechanics of getting to the actual solution, will be adopted by many disciplines. Homework problems will become increasingly open-ended. When students can explore a wide variety of different assumptions through simulation or online retrieval, the enlightened teacher will encourage them to make reasonable choices themselves.

Word processors have revolutionized the way papers are written at the college level. This will inevitably filter down to the lower grades. We laughed at Mr. Dobko in eighth grade for telling us how important rough drafts were—but now that the technology makes iterative writing possible without excessive drudgery, these styles must be emphasized from the beginning of school. It is not clear to what extent spelling and grammar will be taught in the primary grades—when Tablet can check them better than Mr. Dobko, what is the point?

Despite the interactive nature of current word processing programs, almost all writers print out a draft and scratch corrections upon it before pronouncing it ready. In the year 2000, editing papers will be a snap. With stylus in hand and a page of text on the display screen, corrections will be made the old-fashioned way, only faster. By drawing revision symbols directly over that offending participle or comma splice, editing will occur naturally and automatically. Graphs, images, tables, and mathematical formulae will likewise be integrated into such editors.

Through online databases, each student will have easy access to most of the world's words. Since it will be easy to obtain obscure references, the opportunities for plagiarism will naturally increase. To combat this problem, a professor will check each paper using an "originality analyzer." This system will compare a submitted work with related sources available to the student and will flag passages which appear to be copied or suspiciously unlike that student's previous style. Mencken said that "Conscience is the little voice inside of you that says someone may be watching." Without invoking images of Big Brother, Tablet will be watching.

One educational trend that is bound to continue is the emphasis on simulation. Through simulation, any student can get the feeling of being there. Historical simulations will enable high school students to run for president in 1920 and see why Harding would have beaten them, too. In economics classes, students can erect trade barriers and watch the effect of the ensuing depression. Laboratory science can also be effectively simulated. Ray traced graphics will enable anyone to dissect a frog without the frog minding. Many experiments which could not be performed because of cost or safety considerations can easily be done using the computer.

However, an important aspect of simulations is seldom given enough thought. No simulation is better than its underlying mathematical model of the world. Every model is biased by its designer, by its politics, and by its goals. Some simulations are just plain wrong—their underlying model is fundamentally flawed. Placing trust in the outcomes of simulations is misplacing trust. Students will have to be taught a critical eye for evaluating the results gleaned from simulation. Historical simulations are simply one man's theory, and, despite the need to maintain students' interest, scholarly ideals must be maintained. Further, it is self-defeating to simulate certain aspects of laboratory science. Learning laboratory technique is an important part of experimental science, and it is impossible to realistically model Murphy's Law.

Interactive simulation, treated with the proper reverence, does have its role in education. Exercises will more likely be done when they resemble a video game than a homework assignment. Integrating video, speech and text, these programs will adapt to a student's likes and dislikes. For example, an explanation of harmonic waves would be described to a musician via the analogy of the vibration of a guitar's strings. The same explanation would be made to an avid sailor using the waves of the sea as a metaphor. Ideally, the computer will be able to detect weaknesses in a student's understanding of a particular area and will target problems to attack the weakness. However, it will remain the teacher's job to monitor their student's progress.

THE SOCIAL ASPECTS OF EDUCATION

The biggest flaw in many visions of the future is the failure to account for the fact that people are social creatures. One of the negative aspects of increased use of computers is the corresponding reduction in human interaction. If it is not necessary to spend time in the library for research, one of the traditional gathering sites for students will be empty. The same can be said for open classrooms. The solution is that students will take their work to where other students are, instead of taking themselves to where the classes are. Students will not be limited to working in the library or at home. Why not do your calculus in the park or at a museum or in a cafe?

Electronic mail will be a major communication medium for students in the year 2000. Unlike today's email, it will be possible to incorporate audio and video along with text in the mail message. Electronic mail is a wonderful medium for ideas and does not intrude the way a telephone does upon its recipient. It sits there quietly waiting to be read. The cellular telephone built into Tablet will allow students to converse with other students from any location. Using the infrared interface, a computer will be able to talk to other computers. A student's personal computer will be able to continually broadcast what the owner wishes the world to know about him or her: perhaps a name, a face, interests, and sexual preference for openers. Setting your machine in "get-acquainted mode" will display the location of all machines in the vicinity and who their owners are. While sitting in a museum or restaurant, you can find out about other people nearby, with the possibility of meeting a person with similar interests. Just imagine turning this loose in a singles bar!

Local computer bulletin boards will be constantly monitored by your computer looking for events you would be interested in. For example, a bulletin board listing upcoming concerts would try to find matches with your music collection. If you had a recording by an artist that was appearing locally, the computer would notify you of the event and present you with the opportunity to order tickets.

It is amusing to consider that the next generation of computer geeks is more likely to consist of artists than programmers! Tablet will be a creative medium which will lend itself to the creation of new art forms. Descendents of programs like today's hypertext system will lead to a redefinition of what exactly literature is. Initial efforts to create hypertext novels will no doubt be artistic failures, but with time legitimate hyperliterature will be created. The time will come, perhaps not by 2000, when the Nobel Prize for Literature will be awarded for hyper instead of linear text.

Using CCD cameras and ray traced graphics, home movies take on a new meaning. By digitally splicing home "footage" with simulated scenery, the amateur will be able to produce professional looking movies the way any author can now typeset his own material. As the technical and financial obstacles to entry for such arts fall, more and more people will participate.

From the social perspective, where is the audience who will appreciate all this new art? Some form of shareware video might arise. Other distribution channels will sprout up, but much of this art will be for private consumption only. An analogous situation already exists, as publishers have known for years that more people write poetry than read it. So it might be with shareware video. Just having a studio available doesn't make everyone an artist!

ECONOMIC IMPACTS ON EDUCATION

At no point in American history have sufficient resources been allocated to education. It doesn't take a visionary to know this will still be the case in the year 2000. Putting a price tag on Tablet is pure speculation, but $2,000 could be in the ballpark. We must find a way to get Tablet into the hands of the student. Who is going to pay for these computers and the software to run on them?

Some universities currently require their students to purchase a computer in addition to the costs of books, tuition, and other items. The limited resources of students are strained enough that this additional cost is not often appreciated. Despite assurances that the naive freshman is buying a "productivity tool for life," by senior year it will be obsolete and suitable for use only as a planter. Something, either economic or technological, must happen to get us out of this rut.

What will happen is that in the university of the year 2000, students will be given a computer on their first day. Over the years that they spend at the university, a fixed cost will be assessed each term. This cost will pay for the computer, tuition, access to a myriad of database services, and online textbooks. By the time students leave the university, Tablet will be theirs to keep. The reason this scenario is different from today is that by 2000, the technology will have reached saturation; the way typewriter technology had reached saturation by World War II. Tablet is a complete tool which will integrate into people's lives and maintain its value. Manual typewriters maintained their value after electrical typewriters came around, finally meeting their match with the word processor. It will take another product generation, several years down the road, to do in Tablet. We have difficulty imagining what Tablet's successor will be able to do—but given time we will think of something.

CONCLUSIONS

Tablet will have a tremendous impact on education by the year 2000, but it will require effort in many different directions to make it happen. Technologists will have to build the thing, but that is the easy part. The educational community will have to use its imagination to decide what is desirable and struggle with the technologists to make it work.

THINKING AND RE-READING

1. As you re-read this piece, think about the ways in which the students' story of a day in the life of first-year student Alexis Quesada and Professor Xiao-Lin Zhang agrees or departs from your own experiences. List the similarities and differences.

2. Many of the ideas about education presented here seem quite radical (e.g., accessing a professor's lecture in a park instead of attending class), but others seem quite traditional (e.g., the notion of a lecture as accepted pedagogy). Make two columns either on paper or in a word processing file. In one column, jot down instances in which you think the students' ideas of college classes are innovative; in the other column jot down instances in which they seem conventional. In which instances does the use of computers have the ability to improve the learning experience? Why or why not?

3. In the fourth paragraph, the students write:

> However, there is reason to hope that technical progress by the year 2000 will animate the human side of education. As computers become more powerful, it becomes reasonable to mold them in the image of people. The computer as a tool will fit naturally into the lives of the masses instead of being shoehorned in under the oxymoron of "computer literacy."

List and analyze the various claims in this sentence. Think carefully about what it means to "animate the human side of education." Does this seem to happen in the scenarios presented in the article? What does it mean to mold computers "in the image of people"? Do computers today "fit naturally into the lives of the masses"? What problems still exist that aren't touched upon here? Why is "computer literacy" an oxymoron for these students? How do you understand the term?

WRITING AND LEARNING

1. Prepare a list of questions for a faculty member in the computer science department regarding the kinds of computer technology available in 1987 when the students wrote their future scenario. If possible, interview a faculty member or friend who is in the computer science department. Also talk with a friend or relative who was attending college at this time. Find out which of the innovations seemed particularly spectacular for the times. Are there developments that have occurred in computer technology that the students didn't foresee? Which? Now write a scenario for a day in the life of a student in the year 2015 that would be appropriate for a magazine like *Wired* or another magazine of your choice.

2. In John Murphy's article on distance learning, he describes the Carnegie Unit instructional model. According to Murphy, the model requires a student's occupying a place in a classroom for approximately forty-five hours a semester with the lecture functioning as the primary mode of instruction. He goes on to add that in the Carnegie Unit model students customarily "listen to" a professor rather than interact with her or him. Go back through Murphy's article and jot down other characteristics that mark the Carnegie Unit model. Find out if this is the model employed in your school. Then

formulate an argument in which you argue either that the students' view of education in the year 2000 conforms to the model or that it bears little resemblance to it. As you review the articles, try to come up with a vision of learning that not only makes use of the new technologies but also fits with your ideas of a stimulating and democratic intellectual environment. Present your "philosophy of learning" to your instructor and other classmates in your course.

EXTENDED WRITING ACTIVITIES

BUILDING ON WRITING AND LEARNING

SAC   Writing and learning activities that can be done on a stand-alone computer with access to word processing software

LAN   Writing and learning activities that can be done on local area network with access to synchronous or asynchronous conferencing software

WAN   Writing and learning activities that can be done on a wide-area network, like the Internet, with access to Netscape or Gopher software

ASSIGNMENT 1: RE-IMAGINING COMPUTERS IN SCHOOLS

As you read the selections in this section, you were probably not surprised to read that school days, even in the college students' future scenario, are usually compartmentalized into a series of courses. In high school, you often "took" five classes that met each day; in college, you have a similar schedule although your classes meet less frequently and you are not confined to a single school building for most of the day. In some respects, schools seem to be patterned on the industrial, assembly-line model in which one instructor can "teach" many students by delivering the same lecture repeatedly to a series of classes. Even the class "room" is designed to compartmentalize learning, with students going from room to room, from subject to subject, as the school day progresses. Despite society's moving away from an industrial model toward an information economy, today's schools bear a close resemblance to the schools your great-grandparents attended—except perhaps for the presence of computers.

For this assignment, you are asked to design a school using a drawing program such as SUPER-PAINT or another program that you have handy. You can represent "school" in any way you like, but learning must be one of its essential components. Other requirements are that you incorporate the new technologies into the school day and that you convince your classmates that your school will prepare them adequately for the future. To accompany the graphic representation of your school, you will also write a description of your vision for schooling and tell your classmates about the school's activities. Also describe the students who will attend the school. What will the students learn? How? For this assignment, you're to think about what's good and bad about schools and how technology can in some instances be used to exacerbate the current problems or in others to provide rich opportunities for educational reform.

To begin, think about your school experiences with computers before coming to college and about computers in relation to schooling overall. What educational function did computers serve in your school? How did they do so? The challenge here is to introduce computers into school settings in such a way that the quality of life and learning for all students and teachers improves.

Another challenge is to view schooling as something different from a series of courses that you have to pass through. How might you re-imagine the school day? How might your representation of school change the way society views computers? What steps might communities take to help schools benefit from today's information technologies?

Your task, then, is to design a school that depends on the new technologies but that may depart radically from current conceptions of what a school is. Use any selections in this reader for your assignment and conduct any interviews you think appropriate in order to construct your vision of schooling. When you finish, synthesize your thinking by creating a brochure to advertise your school, and ask your classmates to judge and discuss whether your school is one that they would attend and why. **(SAC)**

ASSIGNMENT 2: USING NETWORKED DISCOURSE

Computers can be networked in such a way as to support real-time written discussion, using programs like ASPECTS or Daedalus's INTERCHANGE. One advantage to these programs is that you can save and print out the transcripts to use as resources for your other writing. If you have a real-time program available, we suggest that you use it for this assignment. If you don't, set up an e-mail discussion group with your class and use the transcripts that the discussion generates to inform the document you will write. Conceivably, you could also carry out this assignment with a single disk with a file for discussion that your classmates contribute to during the week. With whatever discussion method you use, make sure that your classmates know that you will be using their comments for your written assignment.

For this assignment you will construct a set of principles or guidelines that school officials and instructors should read and follow in regard to the instructional use of computers at your school. Certainly these principles should be informed by the reading you've done on computers and education, but they should also grow out of local concerns—of yours and your classmates' experiences at your own college. Some of the questions you might want to consider are the following:

- When does the use of computers feel like busy work?
- In what classes has your work with computers been really worthwhile? Why?
- Are some applications of computers particularly noteworthy for certain classes and not for others?
- Do all students seem to benefit equally when computers are used instructionally? Why or why not?
- In general, what criteria should be applied in adapting the information technologies for instruction?

Certainly, you will think of other questions to add to these, but the online discussion you conduct should serve as a rich resource for compiling and composing the guidelines. Essentially, your classmates will need to decide on the kinds of thinking that must be done if computers are to be used effectively in educational contexts.

At some point you will also want to ask straight out what guidelines your classmates think should be in place at your school. After you've drafted the guidelines, send them out to the online discussion. What suggestions do your classmates offer for adding to or revising them?

Now compose a proposal aimed at the faculty senate, explaining why the guidelines are needed, and attach the guidelines. If you, your instructor, and classmates think it appropriate, also write a letter to the school newspaper and send the editors the guidelines as well. (LAN, WAN)

ASSIGNMENT 3: A GLOBAL PERSPECTIVE ON SCHOOLING

Each fall, visions of the new school year conjure up all sorts of cultural expectations for us as Americans—football games, new fall clothes, book bags, new instructors, even the smell of autumn leaves. In other parts of the world, however, schools are quite different, and sporting events, for example, are not connected in any way to schooling. From a global perspective, you might find it interesting to look at how different colleges and universities not only organize their studies but also at how they represent themselves to the rest of the world on the World Wide Web. For this assignment, you will analyze the web sites of several colleges and universities in this country and around the world. Your final report will be an overview of post-secondary education viewed from a global perspective.

Using a browser such as NETSCAPE, select ten schools and find the URLs (Uniform Resource Locators) that will let you access their web sites. Choose a variety of schools that are different in size, location, specialties, makeup of the student body, and so on. Five of the schools should be in other countries, but the others can be anywhere in the United States.

Here are some suggestions and questions to guide your analysis. If your instructor has set up groups for your class, you should also brainstorm with other members of your writing group to come up with other questions. You may also want to narrow the topic of your report, with different members of the class reporting on various aspects of post-secondary education from a global perspective.

- List the schools and URLs for which you were able to find web sites.
- For which schools or locations couldn't you find URLs?
- What information do the ten schools offer on their home pages?
- What links have they set up to connect to other sites?
- What information at the various sites do you find interesting or valuable? Why?
- What information is less interesting or less valuable? Why?
- What kinds of courses are offered?
- What are the names of some of the academic departments featured?
- What can you glean about the student body from the web site?
- What language(s) are in evidence at the particular sites?
- What visual images do the schools use to represent themselves on the Web?
- What, if anything, can you infer about the use of computers at the various schools you've chosen to analyze?

- What other inferences can you draw about school life at the colleges based on the information at the web site?
- Who constructed the various pages at the web sites? E-mail those persons responsible for the different web sites and ask what purposes they had in mind in creating World Wide Web pages.

Using a word processing package, type up your notes. Incorporate the information you've gathered (attaching any relevant images you've captured and printed) into a three-to-five-page report on what you've learned. Choose an issue that you think will interest the rest of your class and prepare an oral report based on the written document you've composed. Be sure to use the correct form for citing electronic sources (see appendix on the bibliographic citation of electronic materials). **(WAN)**

PART III

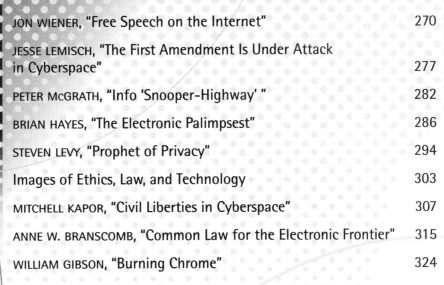

ETHICS, LAW, AND TECHNOLOGY

INTRODUCTION

CYBERSPACE, it has been often claimed during the past decade, is a liberated territory, an unlegislated frontier, a growing and uncharted territory open to millions of individuals, groups, and organizations who want to cruise and use its rapidly expanding resources. Cyberspace is also one of the fastest-growing literacy environments on the planet—the Internet, for example, links approximately 159 countries with electronic mail (Internet Index #5, 31 December 1994), supports more than 3,864 computer hosts as they exchange information (Internet Index #4, 5 November 1994), and registers a new information domain every two minutes (Internet Index #6, 12 February 1995).

A recent publication about the Internet (Abbott, 1994) identifies more than 8,000 different communicating groups that occupy this electronic landscape: groups formed around national allegiances (e.g., Native Americans, Greeks, Algerians, Croatians, Brazilians, Cubans, Russians, Ecuadorians, Estonians, Romanians, and Hungarians), literary works (e.g., Chicano literature, Hebrew literature, Islamic literature, Latin American literature, Greek literature, and German literature), religious topics (e.g., Coptic Orthodoxy, Old Testament, New Testament, Eastern Orthodoxy, Christianity, Buddhism, Bahai, Pagan, and Quaker), political interests (e.g., immigration, human rights, policy making, government information, disabilities, national security, communism, feminism, family studies, gay and lesbian topics, and hazardous waste management), and current events (e.g., the Bosnian conflict, Somalia, Grochz Kapusta, earthquakes, cyberspace, and nuclear war).

Because cyberspace, in its function as an information environment, allows users to broadcast and narrowcast information (to send a message to millions of people or to a single individual), to alter and re-distribute information and images, and to seek and locate information in public and private databases, it has generated a range of legal and ethical concerns. Our country and other nations are now engaged in the project of reconsidering laws and ethical stances on freedom of speech and First Amendment rights, privacy and the public nature of electronic communications, encrypted information and information filtering, civil liberties and cybertheft, accountability and libel, as well as copyright law and digital plasticity (the ability to manipulate digitized images).

This section—Ethics, Law, and Technology—illustrates how many dilemmas are introduced when the basis of communication (written, graphics, audio, or video) becomes digital, and information can be communicated within an environment like the Internet. We begin the section with two essays that discuss freedom of speech in electronic environments. One author, Jon Wiener, maintains that we may need to implement guidelines for censorship, libel, and defamation on the Internet, just as we do in the real world. On the other hand, another author, Jesse Lemisch, claims that free speech should have no limits in cyberspace.

To complement this focus on freedom of speech, we have also included three key pieces on electronic privacy issues. The first of these, by Peter McGrath, compares the privacy concerns connected with computers with those allied with the telephone and other technologies and claims that electronic environments have encouraged us to compromise our individual right to privacy. In the second contribution, "The Electronic Palimpsest," Brian Hayes discusses encryption technologies—technologies that attach a digitized signature to documents thereby helping authors protect the integrity of their messages—and why these technologies are so important to online language users who seek privacy and rely on message integrity. The third contribution, an article by author Steven Levy, focuses on the life and work of Whitfield Diffie, a pioneer of encryption technology. Diffie, according to Levy, has always had a "visceral interest in personal privacy" and is now an outspoken critic of governmental control of encryption technologies.

Also included in this section are two contributions that discuss the ways in which laws relevant to language and information use need to change in electronic environments. Both essays are written by two outspoken technology advocates. Both focus on the complicated cultural intersection formed by electronic language exchanges, our paper-based legal system, and the ethics of computer-based communication. In one selection, Mitchell Kapor, who founded Lotus Development Corporation in 1982 and was the designer of Lotus 1-2-3, writes about the civil liberties (e.g., due process, freedom of the press, and copyright protection) we should accord to individuals in cyberspace. In the other selection, Anne Branscomb, a past chair of the Communication Law Division of the American Bar Association, writes about the need to create new laws to govern information, authorship, and ownership in electronic environments.

Finally, we end this section with a glimpse of the future—"Burning Chrome," a short story by science fiction author William Gibson. In this piece, Gibson extrapolates from current social and technological practices to predict scenes that we'll encounter in the next millennium. He paints a grim picture of the Matrix, supercharged offspring of the Internet, controlled by corporate interests, inhabited by roving console cowboys, and up for sale to the highest bidder. In Gibson's Matrix, laws are made by those who can pay to have them enforced.

As a collection, these pieces are intended to encourage thinking about the law, about ethics, and about language in technological contexts. Indeed, the explosion of popular computer use in the last decade and the rapid expansion of the Internet have created a situation in which humans *must* re-think almost everything that they know about communicating with one another. It is an exciting and terrifying project to undertake. The authors and the works in this section help us begin the task.

Free Speech on the Internet

Jon Wiener

> *Congress shall make no law respecting an establish-*
> *ment of religion, or prohibiting the free exercise thereof: or*
> *abridging the freedom of speech, or of the press; or the*
> *right of the people peaceably to assemble, and to petition*
> *the government for a redress of grievances.*
>
> Bill of Rights, December 15, 1791

IN THIS ARTICLE, ORIGINALLY PRINTED in *The Nation* on June 13, 1994, and aimed at a general audience, Jon Wiener explores the implications of free speech as it exists on the Internet. In a relatively short essay, he expresses concern about the need for electronic gag orders suppressing public discussions of sensitive legal cases, the nature and value of "unmoderated" speech on open discussion lists, and the possibility of needing new libel laws for cyberspace. This article indicates the level of concern that increasing numbers of Americans are feeling as they watch the Internet expand at an exponential rate.

Wiener makes an interesting claim that will be explored from various perspectives in different parts of this reader: that cyberspace is not a new world but a reflection, an artifact really, of our existing world—"VR mirrors RL" (virtual reality mirrors real life). Consequently, much as we would like to think of cyberspace as a new world, the values, problems, practices, and relationships that we see in real life are also apparent on the nets.

At a time when Paramount Communications and Time Warner and Rupert Murdoch's News Corporation have achieved near-total domination over all hitherto existing media, many people have come to view the Internet—the computer network linking millions of users in a hundred countries—as a free space where critical and independent voices can communicate, liberated from the mainstream media's obsession with profits and hostility to the unpopular. It's "the most universal and indispensable network on the planet," *The New York Times Magazine* recently proclaimed, because, at a time when the "giant information empires own everything else," the Internet is "anarchic. But also democratic." *Harper's Magazine* joined the utopian talk: The Internet marks "not the beginning of authority but its end." Computer networks create "a country of decentralized nodes of governance and thought," in which "the non-dogmatic—the experimental idea" and "the global perspective" all work to undermine centralized power and official opinion. *U.S. News & World Report* declared in January that, on the Internet, "everyone has a virtually unlimited right to express and seek information on any subject."

The "Net" is a free space, the argument continues, because no one controls it and no one owns it; it has no center. Instead, it has thousands of nodes, each of which permits those with access to a computer, a modem and a modest budget to send and receive messages and to read, copy and distribute documents, manifestoes, essays and exposés. No one is excluded because of race, ethnicity, creed or gender. And it's growing like kudzu. The Internet Society reported last year that 1.7 million host computers provided gateways for 17 million users to enter the Infobahn. Those who operate computer bulletin board systems ("bbs"), newsgroups and mailing lists are mainly volunteers working for free. According to Harley Hahn and Rick Stout, authors of *The Internet Complete Reference*, the Net provides "living proof that human beings who are able to communicate freely and conveniently will choose to be social and selfless."

It all sounds great. But despite the claims made for the Net, its freedoms are restricted in familiar ways; it reproduces many problems and obstacles found outside cyberspace, in what the hackers disparagingly term "real life."

The largest collection of news and discussion groups on the Net is Usenet, which involves millions of people reading and posting messages on more than 5,000 topics, ranging from "artificial intelligence" (comp.ai) to "Japanese animation" (rec.arts.anime). Usenet bulletin boards recently dramatized the power of the Internet as a weapon to fight government censorship. The Canadian government has been trying to prevent Canadians from learning about the sensational sex-torture-murder trial of Karla Homolka and her husband/accomplice, Paul Bernardo. Homolka pleaded guilty in July 1993 after confessing gruesome details of two murders and naming her husband as the instigator. The Ontario court imposed a gag order on the media, seeking to prevent potential jurors in her husband's separate trial from learning about the case. None of the Canadian media challenged the ban, but industrious computer networkers in Toronto set up a Usenet newsgroup, alt.fan.karla-homolka, on which they posted daily news of the trial. (Putting it in the "alternative-fan" area was a macabre touch.)

Then "the Royal Canadian Mounted Police (R.C.M.P.) showed up in the newsgroup and said we were all going to jail," recalled Joel Furr, a Usenet moderator responsible for editing messages on some bulletin boards. "They said they were recording our names and contacting our site administrators." Most Canadian institutions on the Net, including all universities, shut down local access to the bulletin board. Undeterred, the hackers started a new one, "alt.pub-ban.homolka," on which they continued to post news of the trial. "It took the R.C.M.P. about a month to find that hiding place," Furr said. When that one was shut down, they started posting Karla Homolka information on still other bulletin boards.

Space for all, from neo-Nazis to anti-censorship activists, but how free is the speech?

The gag order remains in effect, since jury selection in Bernardo's trial won't begin until fall. But as a result of the postings on computer bulletin boards, Stephen Kimber wrote in the *Halifax Daily News*, "the ban has become a joke." Global communications systems "are now beyond the short arms of narrow-minded Ontario judicial regulators." Kimber, a journalism professor at the

maze

University of King's College in Halifax, got the banned information "through an electronic labyrinth from a double-blind anonymous posting service based, I believe, in Finland—a service often used by those who discreetly post adult personal classified messages on the Internet." Every effort by court authorities to prevent trial news from reaching the public "has simply led individuals to find more innovative ways to distribute it." (I got the grisly story by e-mail from a gentleman in Texas with the address abdul@io.com. A lot of what was posted included rumors, hearsay and people indulging their taste for bizarre news, which is an inevitable consequence of such an open forum.)

certain to happen

Canadian gov banned issue of wired because of price about trial

When *Wired* magazine did a short piece on the story in its April issue, the Canadian government banned the issue and confiscated copies from distributors. *Wired* fought back in cyberspace, making the text of the banned article available on the Internet through their own "infobot"—a software program that provides information on demand—and on networks accessible to any Canadian with a modem.

Fighting the Mounties presents the Net at its best, and shows how people could obtain other more significant information their governments might want to keep secret. But the same strategy for resisting government authority is available to more malevolent forces. A news item on the "SN GrapeVine" bulletin board, datelined Munich and headlined "Nazis Online," reports that German neo-Nazis have established their own bulletin boards on which users can "exchange ideas on how to rid Germany of foreigners, coordinate illegal rallies and swap bomb-making recipes." The "Thule Network," named after a 1920s proto-Nazi group, consists of a dozen bulletin boards in three states, access to which is protected by passwords. Neo-Nazis are using the network to avoid detection by police who are not yet familiar with the new technology.

For everyone from neo-Nazis to anti-censorship activists, cyberspace does indeed provide a free space. But how free is the speech on the Internet? Most of the Usenet bulletin boards are completely open to anyone with any message—a rich information anarchy, limited only by self-regulation, that can't be found in any other medium. But this utopian ideal is abandoned in bulletin boards that are "moderated" by volunteer system operators who have the power to edit or refuse to post messages they consider irrelevant or objectionable.

To see what an unmoderated bulletin board looks like, I checked the Usenet Bosnia discussion group (soc.culture.bosna-herzgvna). The first posting read, "Serbs in world wars? O yes, I remember. . . . Russians come and liberated Belgrade. Serbs were so grateful that they did not mind, let say, missbehaviour of Russian soldiers towards local women. Or was raping a kind of a sign of frendship." It was signed by Damir Sokcevic, Department for Theoretical Physics, Rudjer Boskovic Institute, Zagreb, Croatia.

The next message read, "Why should we let you 'holy Armenian crooks' get away with the Muslim Holocaust's cover-up? . . . The ex-Soviet Armenian government got away with the genocide of 2.5 million Muslim men, women and children and is enjoying the fruits of that genocide." It had been posted by "Serdar Argic." This is the ugly side of freedom of speech. Garbage postings like these can devastate regions of cyberspace. The Usenet discussion group soc.history "has been absolutely destroyed by Serdar Argic," Usenet moderator Joel Furr wrote in April on an internal news bulletin board. "Upon reading the group today, I found 200+ active articles, of which 175 were from Serdar Argic and 20 were complaining about him." That group has now been replaced by one with a moderator who censors Serdar Argic. (His 175 messages on soc.history were all different, but all had the same nutty theme: Turks didn't kill Armenians in 1915, it was the other way around.)

requiring considerable time & effort

Al's Autoresponder

The Internet's advocates describe it as a new force for democracy because it provides millions of ordinary people with a means of instantaneous communication with our nation's leaders. The Clinton Administration set up an electronic address on the Internet. No more *laborious* addressing of envelopes, licking stamps and hiking to the mailbox to tell the President what's on your mind; no more waiting weeks for a reply. Now you can e-mail him and he will receive the message within minutes.

At least that's the promise. I sent a two-sentence e-mail to vice.president@whitehouse.gov, urging Gore to "keep access to the Internet free and universal." Within five minutes I had a reply! Unfortunately, it didn't come from Gore himself but from "autoresponder@whitehouse.gov." "Thank you for writing to the Vice President via Internet," the autoresponder told me. "This Administration is committed to integrating this new medium into the White House, and we hope to begin responding electronically to your messages in the near future.

"Unfortunately, the very large volume of mail received by the Vice President from citizens around the nation prevents him from sending a more detailed and direct response at this time." After thanking me for my "patience as we fine-tune the response system," the message concluded with the stirring words, "You will only receive one automated response per day."

I e-mailed Joel Furr for more details, and he replied with a startlingly archaic suggestion: I ~ *belonging to former & ancient times* should telephone him, so we could "talk." On the phone, he explained that " 'Serdar Argic' seems to be several people, anti-Armenian Turks, with software that scans bulletin boards for keywords and automatically generates responses out of a database of megabytes of messages. Several universities have kicked him off their networks, but he's currently got access through a firm called UUNet in Virginia. There's nothing we can do about him from a legal standpoint." Other Usenet groups have had problems with freedom of electronic speech: The "guns" discussion group (rec.guns), which is moderated, "flat out prohibits ANY discussion on gun control," reports Usenet moderator Cindy Tittle Moore, "because they know from experience that's just one long flame war." (To *flame* is to hurl abuse on-line.) If you are against guns, you are not allowed to tell it to the Usenet "guns" discussion group. And the gun nuts have virtually taken over the *Mother Jones* Usenet bulletin board (alt.motherjones), swamping it with pro-gun diatribes ~ *a harsh and forceful verbal attack* crosslisted from talk.politics.guns and alt.fan.rush-limbaugh. The energy of these people is astounding: The unmoderated group talk.politics.guns had 2,096 new postings in the week I checked—300 a day. *a quantity representing the power to which that must be raised to produce a given no.*

The underlying problem, Furr says, is that "the Internet is expanding at logarithmic rates. A million new users will bring a few sociopaths. Until recently we had complete anarchy with self-regulation. Now some human will have to look at everything and decide what to post. It's unfortunate."

But it's not necessarily censorship. The moderated bulletin board or newsgroup is edited like a magazine letters-to-the-editor page: Relevant material is posted, objectionable or useless or loony stuff is kept out. In this respect communication in cyberspace is closer to ordinary publishing than to a new realm of freedom. (On the other hand, the extent of communication possible is far richer and freer than in any letters page.)

Commercial advertising presents a different threat to the freedom of the Internet. Attorney Laurence Canter of Phoenix showed how to do it: In April he placed an ad for his services as a "green card" immigration lawyer on Usenet—not just on bulletin boards where it might be relevant, like misc.legal and alt.visa.us, or the "business" area, but on every one of more than 5,000 discussion groups. It appeared on rec.arts.erotica and on the anti-Barney alt.tv-dinosaurs.barney.die.die.die. This ambulance chasing on the information superhighway resulted in "a nuclear level flame," Furr said. The network was bombarded with thousands of protest messages from outraged users. Despite his violation of "netiquette," Canter is unrepentant; he told *The New York Times*, "We will definitely advertise on the Internet again." *showing no regreat for ones wolding*

There's no good way to stop him. "These things that are written into the Internet culture are not written into the law," said James Gleick, who runs a commercial Internet gateway in Manhattan called the Pipeline. Usenet groups could be swamped with advertisements that would drown out noncommercial speech, and the rich discussion of common interests that now takes place would wither away. *some one who studies sociury & cutural olglns of humans* *damage the good repstation of*

In real life, freedom of speech is also limited by libel laws. But is there libel in cyberspace? A federal court ruled in 1991 that CompuServe couldn't be sued for libel for a message it transmitted. That case (*Cubby v. CompuServe*) set a vital precedent for free speech in the electronic age: U.S. District Court Judge Peter Leisure of New York ruled that, since computer networks do not exercise editorial control over the messages they transmit, they are not liable for defamation.

Individuals, however, are still responsible for their own words communicated through cyberspace. The first trial for libel by e-mail—held in Australia—concluded with a substantial fine being imposed on the offending e-mailer. In that case, an anthropologist fired by the University of Western Australia sued another anthropologist, claiming he had been defamed in a computer bulletin board message. The case went to the West Australian Supreme Court, which ruled in April that libel in cyberspace is actionable. David Rindos, who has a doctorate from Cornell University, was dismissed last June because of insufficient productivity. A supporter of Rindos posted news of the firing on the DIALx science anthropology international computer bulletin board; many colleagues e-mailed their support for him, but Gil Hardwick, an anthropologist working in the field in Western Australia, posted a message criticizing Rindos. According to Justice David Ipp, it declared that Rindos's career was based not on academic achievement "but on his ability to berate and bully all and sundry." The message also contained "allegations of pedophilia," in the words of Rindos's lawyer, and falsely implied that sexual misconduct had some bearing on his firing by the university. *a perso who is sexualy attracted to children*

Twenty-three thousand people around the world have access to the bulletin board on which Mr. Hardwick's message appeared, and most of them are professional anthropologists and anthropology students. "The defamation caused serious harm to Dr. Rindos's personal and professional reputation," Justice Ipp declared. "The publication of these remarks will make it more difficult for him to obtain appropriate employment.... The damages award must compensate him for all these matters and vindicate his reputation to the public."

Although it's easier to win a libel case in Australia than in the United States, the same circumstances here would produce the same result, according to Martin Garbus, an attorney and a libel law authority. The Internet is not a free space when it comes to libel; it is subject to the same libel law as any publication.

In the Australian case, the libelous message had been posted on a bulletin board available to thousands; but even individual e-mail messages can cause legal problems. The day is not too

[margin annotations]: Lawgivin Sufficient reason to Illega Action; scoled or criticize angerly; of various kinds; clear of blame or suspicion

[handwritten annotations at top: "N. a writ ordering a person to attend a court" with arrow pointing to "subpoena"; "this is a verb — summon w/ a subpoena"]

distant when an e-mailer will find himself or herself in court, perhaps in an employment discrimination suit, for a statement uttered only in a single e-mail message. E-mail messages, like other written communications, are discoverable in legal proceedings, according to William Parker, director of the office of academic computing at the University of California, Irvine—they can be subpoenaed and presented as evidence in court. And that's only the beginning: It turns out that your old e-mail is not necessarily gone just because you deleted it. At my campus of the University of California, and probably at most universities as well as private corporations, backup copies of most e-mail messages are retained on tape as part of the nightly backup of the main computer. Ollie North was unable to destroy evidence of the Iran/*contra* cover-up because the White House maintained a backup copy of the e-mail system on which he had plotted his crimes. Erasing his hard drive and shredding his paper copies didn't help. Most e-mailers are as vulnerable today as North was. Parker's advice: "You should not say anything via e-mail that you would not say publicly."

[handwritten: "clear & detailed, w/ no room for confusion or doubt" and "a characteristic of / inherent quality of / feature"]

Those who see the Internet as a free space neglect another important limitation to that freedom: Cyberspace is still a male space. Despite the universal access and nondiscrimination on the Internet, despite the fact that physical appearances and attributes are absent, the great majority of users are men, and women's voices tend to get drowned out in cyberspace. Even in feminist discussion groups, says Ellen Broidy, history bibliographer at the U Cal, Irvine, library, "two or three men will get on and dominate the conversation—either by being provocative, or by flooding the system with comments on everything. It's like talk radio, only worse." Cindy Tittle Moore, a moderator on Usenet's soc.feminism, says, "It should be mandatory for every male on the Net to seriously pretend being female for two weeks to see the difference." They will get sexually explicit invitations from other men, she says, "some polite, some gross." And the styles of disagreement are different. When a man disagrees with another man on a bulletin board, "he's likely to go for a point by point argument and pretty much stay on topic," Moore says. "With a female, he's likely to call her a bull-dyke bitch and leave it at that." Cyberspace, concludes Katherine Hayles, who teaches English at U.C.L.A., will not "free us from the straitjacket of physically marked categories such as race, class and gender."

The Internet has demonstrated its effectiveness as a weapon against government censorship and as a means of communication untrammeled by corporate control. It makes available immense information resources on an unprecedented scale. It makes instantaneous communication easy, which could strengthen democracy. It's also fun. But it's not a new world of freedom, significantly different from our own; in terms of free speech and censorship, libel and defamation, gender and social hierarchies, not to mention advertising and commerce, the moral of this story seems to be, in cybertalk, "VR mirrors RL"—virtual reality hasn't escaped the bounds of real life.

THINKING AND RE-READING

1. As you re-read this piece, think about Wiener's words, "despite claims made for the Net, its freedoms are restricted in familiar ways." Think about your own freedom of speech. In what ways is it constrained? By what factors and values? From what sources do these values come?

2. Why do you think that some people spend hours and hours surfing the Internet, corresponding with people on electronic bulletin boards, talking to others via e-mail? What are the differences between this kind of communication and face-to-face exchanges? Telephone conversations? An exchange of letters?

WRITING AND LEARNING

1. Wiener notes that "No one is excluded [from the Internet] because of race, ethnicity, or gender." In a letter to the editor of your school newspaper or your local city newspaper, state whether you agree with this claim. Explain your reasoning to this general audience and explain why this topic is important for citizens in the twenty-first century to think about critically and carefully.

2. Relate a story about someone you know who does not use computers and explain why this is so. Write this response from his or her point of view using the words that he or she might use. Imagine that the person telling this story is talking to someone else who is highly dependent on computers and who loves to use them. Imagine that the storyteller's purpose is to get his or her high-tech listener to consider and appreciate the perspective of a person who has chosen to take a very different approach to life and technology.

3. What do you think about Wiener's claim that "Cyberspace is still a male space"? What experiences have you had that corroborate or disaffirm this claim? Write an argument based on your experiences to a member of the opposite sex. Imagine that your audience has had experiences that have initially convinced him or her of the opposite point of view. Your job is to provide your audience with additional perspectives from your own experiences to broaden his or her outlook on this issue.

4. Write a letter to a member of your family who lived during the early part of this century—describe what the Internet is, what one can do on it, and why one would want to cruise it. Your dual purpose is to describe and inform.

The First Amendment Is Under Attack in Cyberspace

Jesse Lemisch

IN THIS SHORT ESSAY, PUBLISHED in the *Chronicle of Higher Education* on January 20, 1995, Jesse Lemisch tries to persuade readers that their First Amendment rights are "under attack in cyberspace." To accomplish this purpose, he describes the many obstacles to free speech that he has encountered: "censorship, capricious rejection of messages, and a sacrifice of freedom to personal messages."

Lemisch is echoing the concerns of an increasing number of Americans who perceive a widespread erosion of their right to free speech as guaranteed by the Bill of Rights. These individuals want to make sure that the rights afforded to citizens in other public spheres—in politics, in news media, and in public address situations—are mirrored in the public sphere of the Internet. Balancing these views, other Americans, often parents of young children, are becoming increasingly concerned and vocal about what they consider to be dangerous and offensive material on the Internet—material ranging from information on how to build bombs and other destructive devices to examples of child pornography, offensive jokes, or newsletters from religious or racial hate groups. Individuals offended by these materials believe that there should be some controls or constraints available on the Internet. Such measures would aid parents in keeping children from being exposed to objectionable material.

Both groups are concerned with how the Internet will develop within the legal, ethical, and political framework that already exists in our culture and that continues to shape our lives. You might be interested to note that the *Chronicle of Higher Education* is a newspaper widely read by educators in colleges and universities—namely, professors, university presidents, deans, and educational program administrators.

There is no First Amendment in cyberspace. Right now, in the thousands of Internet discussion groups, we find a cyberspace full of gatekeepers and fiefdoms, where those who would disagree must learn the oblique expression of the dissident under autocracy. This marvelous form of electronic communication—whose essence is spontaneous, informal, unconstrained, and speedy interactivity—is being trammeled and tranquilized. If this new medium is to be a place of freedom for ideas, all of the classic First Amendment issues must be revisited: censorship, pornography, hate speech, the costs of freedom versus the costs of suppression.

I have been a dissenter in cyberspace. My adventures are important because dissent defines the system's limits. I have been an active participant in 13 Internet groups, known as bulletin boards or discussion lists, to which subscribers electronically submit queries, notices, and opinions. I frequently receive 75 or more messages a day. I have participated in both academic and non-academic groups covering history, American studies, and issues concerning women, left-wing politics, labor, science, and health. In "unmoderated" groups, everything submitted is distributed electronically to the entire membership; in others, moderators decide what will and will not be distributed or "posted."

For example, a man who directs several networks told me that he had killed a submission from a graduate student who asserted that some noted historians did not know their historiography. The director said that he was saving the student from "real professional trouble." On a network devoted to women's studies, a female folklorist attempted to solicit jokes about Lorena Bobbitt's attack on her husband, for a research project the scholar was conducting. The moderator refused to post such material, fearing that it would just aid the spread of sexist jokes. To me, both these actions prevented critical scrutiny and discussion, one of the Internet's most valuable features.

These problems are not peculiar to a specific field or to academic lists. On a list devoted to discussion of chronic-fatigue syndrome (largely a support group for those who suffer from the illness and those who care for sufferers), I suggested that we prepare and distribute a leaflet summarizing the variety of ways that government agencies obstruct treatment and understanding of the illness. Many participants on the list hit the roof, describing my adversarial approach as "terrorism." One particularly enraged member mounted racist, anti-Semitic, obscene, and threatening attacks on me, both on and off the net (and with impassioned frequency). As a First Amendment absolutist, I locked my door and made it clear to the list's moderator that I had no desire to suppress such heinous expression.

But the hate mail distressed me less than the response of the moderator, who lectured me on provocation and required that both I and my attacker submit any future messages to him ahead of time so that he could decide whether to post them. "Messages that challenge the patient/reader to serious and complex contemplation," he wrote to me, "will be asking them to use talents whose exercise may negatively impact their health." The health concerns of participants in the discussion group, he added, "necessitate a limitation on 'freedom of speech.'"

A list devoted to American studies, in which anything submitted is screened by its moderator, is governed by similar reflexes. In response to a note stating that the National Endowment for the Humanities was soliciting nominees for its prestigious annual Jefferson Lecture, I noted that a couple of recent lecturers were well-known conservative scholars. I voiced no objection to them, but suggested that people debating political correctness should note such possible right-wing P.C. by a leading cultural institution. A good discussion ensued, but it was sidetracked by a sociologist who clearly didn't even recognize the names of the conservative historians I had cited.

I sent a message pointing that out, noting that he had "only the most narrow and idiosyncratic notion of P.C., which makes him incapable of comprehending the simple notion of right-wing political correctness."

That was the extent of my crime. Two hours later I got a private e-mail message from the moderator of the list, saying that he wouldn't post the message unless I changed it. "This kind of 'flaming' is unnecessary and counterproductive," he wrote. "X's responses have been courteous; yours should be likewise."

Privately feeling that I *had*, in fact, been discourteous but surprised to see discourtesy offered as a rationale for rejection, I sent a brief message to the moderator—for posting—which described his refusal and suggested that the list discuss censorship. He refused to post it, suggesting that the discussion would amount to little more than "navel gazing." I later discovered that the moderator first sends some submissions to the people whose views are being criticized so that he can take their feelings into account in deciding whether or not to post the material.

These are just two examples of lists in which the obstacles to free debate are clear: censorship, capricious rejection of messages, and a sacrifice of freedom to personal feelings. Those who moderate and direct discussion groups seem not to understand what more than 200 years of debate about the First Amendment have shown, most recently with hate speech and pornography: There is absolutely no way to ban valueless or offensive speech without banning valuable speech as well.

Moreover, no clear, agreed-upon definition of "flaming" exists. Moderators repeatedly have accused me of flaming, while list members, including those whom I was debating, found nothing objectionable. One person's meat is another person's poison. But the problem is not simply the lack of a consensus on what constitutes appropriate decorum on the Internet. Net moderators and participants who make much of the horrors of flaming always seem to have an approved target against whom flaming is condoned and even encouraged. For example, on lists in which I participate, I've noticed that it is all right to attack "anti-Semitic loonies" or people who erroneously assert that chronic-fatigue syndrome is psychosomatic. Thus flaming is in the eye of the beholder. I would argue that it is the price that we pay for free expression. Attempts to prevent it are analogous to attempts to ban "irresponsible" media.

Legally, it is an open question whether existing laws regulating free speech—including bans on certain types of expression such as slander, libel, and obscenity—apply to the Internet. The system currently operates in a gray area between what is considered public speech and personal correspondence. I'm skeptical about placing limits on speech in general; I listen sympathetically to those who oppose libel laws. But the moderators who are imposing restrictions aren't really concerned with issues of libel or other legal limits on free speech. Many are unilaterally placing repressive limits on communications in the name of decorum and civility.

Too often, guidelines for moderators of discussion groups offer them no positive statement about free expression to aid them in making decisions. My experience on the American-studies list, for example, might have been caused in part by an overzealous moderator; like many others, he is a graduate student, with limited experience in scholarly debate. But the American-studies list is only one of 43 history-oriented discussion groups that make up "H-net." That network is an influential model; with the support of the American Historical Association, H-net recently received a six-figure grant from the humanities endowment.

The only time that the H-net guidelines mention free speech is in a passage that justifies constraint rather than freedom: "It is so easy to set up a (free) printing press that control over messages on H-net lists does not stifle the free flow of information."

The director of the history network, Richard Jensen, professor of American history at the University of Illinois at Chicago, has stated his position unambiguously to me in correspondence: "Internet provides rather too much freedom right now." He also said that "excessive freedom" seriously hinders the ability to improve communications among scholars, and that the net should "emphasize gentility, politeness, and courtesy, and *demand* it of the participants." He wants postings written "in the style of dispassionate nonpartisans" and instructs moderators who are confronted with flaming to use a "quick DELETE finger."

How far we have come since the American Historical Association issued a Statement of Professional Standards in 1974 that endorsed "candor, forcefulness, or persistence" in the "expression of differences of opinion"! It rejected "civility" as a standard, on the grounds that it would interfere with free debate.

Mr. Jensen's position sacrifices freedom to sensitivity. It also seems to me that attempts to enforce civility place many moderators *in loco parentis,* treating scholars and other Internet users as children to be protected from their supposed indiscretions.

I come from a school that believes that ridicule of ridiculous ideas is a legitimate debating strategy. It might be possible to express my ideas less dramatically—maybe even within somebody's prescribed limits of gentility and decorum. But would they then be the same ideas and present the same critique? I don't think so. Ban the medium of flaming, and you ban the message of dissent. It's time to remember our sacred and distinctive traditions of academic freedom and open debate and to ask basic questions about who will control the Internet and how. If the Internet is to be free, the default position must be ON.

THINKING AND RE-READING

1. As you re-read this article, think about Lemisch's words, "If the Internet is to be free, the default position must be on." Think about whether this machine metaphor (i.e., a switch that is either off or on) is appropriate for a complex set of issues, including freedom of speech. How many situations, issues, or circumstances in real life are either off or on? In what ways does this metaphor work well? In what ways does it fail to work?

2. As you read, imagine somebody sending out a public message about you posted somewhere online. This message accuses you of some action that you may or may not have committed or ascribes to you an intellectual position that you may or may not hold. Perhaps it accuses you of a motivation that you may or may not have. Imagine this message going out to thousands of people. Should freedom be balanced with protection at any level? If so, how? If not, why?

WRITING AND LEARNING

1. For your own knowledge, describe at least two key experiences that you have had that taught you important information concerning the use of computers to communicate with other people. To gain insight, write about those conceptions that you like most about communicating via the computer. Also write about those elements you like least. For yourself, try to articulate why these experiences make you feel the way that you do.

2. Pretend that you are asked to write some rules for the language exchanges that occur on the Internet, either on your classroom network or on your campus network. Under the section entitled "Rules of Speech," what rules would you include? State these rules in language that student users, in general, are able to understand.

3. Write about an experience you have had in which someone was hurt because another person exercised his or her right to free speech. As an alternative, write about an experience you have had in which you exercised your right to free speech despite the possibility of unpleasant consequences. Your purpose in telling these stories is to provide an object lesson for someone younger than yourself. Imagine a younger person that you know well—a friend, a sibling, or a cousin—as the audience for your written storytelling.

4. Think about the following claim by Lemisch, "If the Internet is to be free, the default position must be on." For your own insight, brainstorm two lists of arguments, one supporting this statement, one opposing it. You might even identify more than two sides to this issue; complex issues sometimes have three, four, or more different perspectives. Include at least five arguments for each perspective that you identify. Use your own words, but let your thinking be informed by other readings in this text as well. When you're finished, write a paragraph—for yourself as the audience—stating your stance on this matter, choosing one of the positions over the other(s). Articulate why you chose the position that you did.

talk> how freedom of speech
needs to find its self on the net
pretty much every where
first line hert is whole argument

Info "Snooper-Highway"

Peter McGrath

THIS SHORT PIECE, AUTHORED by Peter McGrath, was published in *Newsweek* on February 27, 1995, as a "special report" on the growing dangers associated with surveillance tactics on the Internet. In the article, which was written for a general, non-specialist audience, McGrath attempts to convince readers that our culture's increasing reliance on computers and networks jeopardizes the privacy of individuals in some very dangerous and disturbing ways.

In this article, McGrath employs a common persuasive technique that you may recognize. He supports his primary claims (our increasing reliance on computers and the compromising of individual privacy by computer networks) with a series of hard-hitting examples designed to illustrate their validity. Examples include a hacker who snoops an individual's e-mail, a private investigator who tracks people using only computer records, and a software company that surreptitiously scans its customers' hard drives without their permission. As you read this article, consider how successful McGrath is in establishing his case.

Every keystroke can be monitored. And the computers never forget. Two cautions for the Information Age.

Of all the effects of high-speed global data networks, none seems quite as insidious as the noose they draw around traditional American notions of personal privacy. Just ask the members of the WELL, a small but cutting-edge online service based in Sausalito, Calif. Last week they were alarmed to learn that Kevin Mitnick, a notorious hacker in North Carolina, allegedly had not only broken into the service's computers and begun reading their electronic mail but also used the WELL as a screen behind which he was able to launch anonymous attacks on networks throughout the Internet. Before being arrested, he even taunted WELL administrators by stashing stolen computer files on one of their servers, in a directory entitled "Computers, Freedom and Privacy."

It was a bracing reminder of the fragility of privacy on what is fast becoming known as the "information snooper-highway." "With the new online services, we're all excited that this is going to be our window on the world, to movies, consumer services, for talking with our friends," says Marc Rotenberg, director of the Washington-based Electronic Privacy Information Center. "The reality is that this may be a window looking *in*."

Intimate Details: Concern about computers and privacy dates back to the 1960s, when governments first began to store their files on the room-filling machines then in use. As computerized record-keeping spread to the private sector, the machines became repositories for the most intimate details of people's lives. Anyone who opened a bank account was leaving electronic traces of his or her house payments, buying habits, visits to the doctor. Telephone service created trails leading to families and friends. Even a social-security number was a potential liability: with it, a dedicated sleuth could pry the holder's tax returns loose from government computers.

Since then, invading privacy has become steadily easier, almost as a corollary of Moore's Law, a Silicon Valley maxim that computer power doubles every two years. More and more personal data take digital form. Driver's-license numbers provide electronic links to the licensee's physical characteristics and driving record. Credit cards and automated-teller-machine cards make financial records even more accessible. At the same time, computers themselves operate at speeds that were unthinkable a few years ago: personal computers running Intel's Pentium chip are more than 300 times faster than machines with the same company's first-generation PC chip, the 8086. Today, anyone with $3,000 can buy essentially the same search-and-retrieve facility as in all but the most advanced government and business systems.

As a result, surveillance is now a brokerage business. Where once this was the domain of experts in such arts as wiretapping, the barriers to entry have been lowered. Consider Sandy Martin, a private investigator in Wilmette, Ill., who was asked last year to track down an elderly man based on nothing but his name. The client was the man's daughter, a New Jersey woman anxious to know if the father she had never met was a carrier of a blood disorder. Martin collated nine database searches, all of them legal, to locate a man in Florida with the right name and the right approximate age, 84. A phone call confirmed that he was the woman's father. The entire search took four days from a desktop computer and cost the client $1,500. Martin says the pre-PC way would have consumed two months and more than $10,000.

As computer power increases, so does the information available. Commercial online services routinely ask members to submit personal profiles along with their credit-card numbers. These might include not only names and addresses but hobbies—items that could be used to create mailing lists of great value to advertisers and marketers. The services typically check members' computer hard drives every time they log on; the purpose is to determine any need for software updates, but the scan can also surreptitiously record valuable information about the way members have configured their machines and what software they use. Until customer protests forced it to back down, a Beaverton, Ore.-based company called Central Point Software did just that, as part of registering its PC Tools for Windows.

Every online keystroke leaves its fingerprint on the service's central computers. Over time, system operators could build detailed profiles of members based on their electronic mail, the Internet newsgroups they subscribe to, the kinds of software they download. Such profiles could then be sold to telemarketers or others using online services to send demographically targeted commercial messages. These records are vulnerable to penetration from outside, too. Last month, 28 Harvard students were mortified to learn that the campus newspaper, the Crimson, had identified them as consumers of pornography simply by tracking their Internet activities through the university's network.

Newsweek Poll

85% are concerned about pornography being too available to young people through the Internet

80% are concerned about being harassed by "virtual stalking" through unwanted messages on the Internet

76% are concerned about being harassed by real stalking from someone they first meet on the Internet

The Newsweek Poll, Feb. 16–17, 1995

---

we leave
trails
on comp
& net

In the end, we compromise ourselves. We leave traces of our lives in databases everywhere. Computers are built to recognize patterns, to find coherence in individually insignificant details. If we then lose our privacy, it's because we volunteered.

THINKING AND RE-READING

1. As you re-read this piece, think about the metaphor that McGrath includes as a quote from Marc Rotenberg, the director of the Electronic Privacy Information Center (see Rotenberg's comments on privacy later in this section): "We're all excited that this [the Internet] is going to be our window on the world. . . . The reality is that this may be a window looking *in*." Think about those projects you do online that you would not want others to see, know about, or have access to.

2. There are as many perspectives on technology as there are on personal relationships and sports. Some people believe that technology represents progress—that the more and more sophisticated our society becomes as a result of technology, the more problems we are able to solve, such as overpopulation, exploitation of natural resources, disease, and lack of education. Some people think that technology itself contributes to such situations—encouraging us to pin our hopes on the next fix discovered by scientists and engineers, increasing the pace of natural resource exploitation, as well as exacerbating educational inequalities. As you re-read this piece, start to formulate your own opinion.

WRITING AND LEARNING

1. For your own insight, describe a time when someone invaded your privacy—or you invaded someone else's privacy. What was the motivation? What were the consequences? What do you think of the whole situation now? Consider this a chance to learn more about yourself, your experiences, and your intellectual positions through writing.

2. Generally, when people talk about computers, they present technology as a means of enhancing people's lives, efforts, and environments. But when Peter McGrath writes about technology—specifically about the ways in which computer technology has supported a less secure sense of privacy for individuals—he says, "In the end, we compromise ourselves." What do you think he means? Write a short essay designed to help other students in your class answer this question. In the first paragraph of this essay, re-state McGrath's argument in your own words. Then, in the next few paragraphs, write about whether you agree or disagree with his assessment; give specific examples; tell specific stories from your own experiences that support your position.

3. Visit your central campus computing office and inquire about whether it has specific guidelines/policies/rules for individuals' use of campus computing services, especially any guidelines/policies/ rules that deal with issues of privacy. Read these guidelines carefully concerning what they have to say regarding the protection of the privacy of individuals. For your campus newsletter, write a response to these guidelines, specifying whether you agree or disagree with them and why. In this response, express your opinion on whether you think these guidelines are adequate or inadequate to protect individuals' online privacy—give specific examples and arguments from your own experience. In writing your response, you might want to try paraphrasing, summarizing, as well as quoting from some of the readings in this section. (Be sure to check your grammar handbook to find the correct citation format for paraphrasing, quoting, and summarizing.) If guidelines dealing with the protection of privacy online do not exist on your campus, or if you consider those guidelines that do exist to be inadequate for protecting privacy, write a draft of more adequate guidelines/policies/rules. These guidelines should be written so that student users will find them useful in understanding the issues connected with privacy.

The Electronic Palimpsest

Brian Hayes

> *pal-imp-sest (pal' imp sest'), n: a parchment from which writing has been partially or completely erased to make room for another text*
>
> The Random House Dictionary, *1980, p. 634*

BRIAN HAYES, THE AUTHOR of the following contribution, notes, "As a writing instrument, the computer is not so much a better pencil as a better eraser." In this article, Hayes describes some of the current controversies surrounding encryption devices—such as electronic signature devices designed to protect the authenticity of important messages, or messages that demand extraordinary security measures. He notes that although encryption devices provide some protection from fraudulent communications, they do not address the unauthorized duplication of messages, nor do they indicate when a document was written or received. Hayes also points to the ways in which archival techniques and techniques of document scholarship may be changed by computers.

This article appeared in a magazine called *The Sciences,* in the September/October issue of 1991. This magazine, aimed at a broadly informed audience, covers the advances, issues, and challenges associated with science.

As a writing instrument, the computer is not so much a better pencil as a better eraser. Although it serves well enough to put words on the page, where it really excels is in wiping them out again. Writing with a computer affords you the luxury of changing your mind, again and again, without penalty. The excised word leaves no scar; the page never becomes gray or tattered from rubbing; the margins do not fill up with afterthoughts; there is no tangle of arrows showing how sentences are to be rearranged. When you write on the glass screen, the world need never know how you labored to achieve that easygoing prose style. Indeed, this very paragraph conceals the tortured history of its own composition: you the reader cannot see in the space between the lines how I have revised it, a dozen times or more, until hardly a word of the first draft survives.

When I got my first chance to write with a computer, it was an exhilarating experience. I would insert a word into the middle of a paragraph and marvel as all the following words automatically rearranged themselves to make room, cascading from line to line in a kind of domino effect. Or I would hold down the delete key and suck up whole sentences like spaghetti. Suddenly prose became a kind of clay that never hardens, a medium that one can always reshape yet again.

But if the plasticity of electronic text is a great liberation for the author, it can also license the forger, the plagiarist, the swindler, the impostor; and it is not an unmixed blessing for the scholar, the historian or even the ordinary reader. Words stored in electronic form are in certain ways less secure and less permanent than words on paper. When writing is inscribed in the magnetic domains of a spinning disk, can one trust its integrity? Fifty years from now, will anyone even be able to read it? As more of the world's documents migrate from memo pads and filing cabinets and bookshelves into computer memories, those questions are going to take on considerable importance.

One way of exploring the issues is to imagine a world without paper, in which all documents are electronic. Such a world is not far off. True, the "paperless office" has so far turned out to be a bad joke, as office paper consumption doubles every four years. But all those pages spewing out of all those laser printers are coming from computers. In many cases the computer files are already the primary versions of the documents, and the printouts are just a means of distribution or archival storage. In the long run, paper will surely be supplanted in those roles as well.

The first thing you notice in a paperless world is that certain awkward situations become even more awkward:

You receive a letter (in the form of a computer file) in which your long-lost sister claims she is being held in a Turkish prison for crimes she didn't commit: Please send her $20,000 to bribe the prosecutor. How do you establish that the letter was written by your sister?

A Washington friend asks you to take a discreet look around someone else's office late one night. In case you get into any trouble, he gives you a letter, stored on a computer disk, that explains the importance of your work to the nation's security. When you are charged with burglary, however, the friend disclaims all knowledge of the letter—and of you. How can you prove the letter is not a forgery? Note that this task is harder than the first one. With the letter from your sister, you need only convince *yourself* of its authenticity; to avoid jail—or at least to take your friend with you—you must convince a judge and a jury of the letter's provenance.

You pick up a hitchhiker in the desert, and in gratitude for that small kindness he gives you a floppy disk bearing a promise of millions of dollars upon his death. How do you prove the bequest is from Howard Hughes? Again, you must demonstrate to others that the document is genuine. Furthermore, you may well have to show not only that Hughes wrote the note but also that you have not altered it (changing "two million" to "two hundred million," say).

In the world of paper documents the primary tool for settling such controversies is the examination of handwriting. You know the letter is from your sister because you recognize her hand; experts compare your cover letter from the White House or your note from Howard Hughes with specimens known to be authentic. But the bits and bytes of a computerized document are all alike, with none of the idiosyncrasies that might identify individual authorship. Anyone could have typed those letters, on almost any computer.

The introduction of "pen"-based computers, which substitute a stylus for a keyboard, will not solve the problem. On such a machine one might confect an ornate and quite inimitable *signature, ending with the most swashbuckling paraph, but a document signed in that way offers only a weak warrant of authenticity. The reason is that such a digitized signature—or any other graphic object—can be copied in an instant with the help of a computer. Give me one "signed" electronic document, and I can forge your name to anything I please. As a matter of fact, the widespread availability of high-resolution scanning and printing equipment raises questions about the security of signatures on paper. There is nothing the modern forger might need that can't be found at the local Kinko's.*

Digital documents *can* be signed, however; what is needed is not a digitized signature but a truly digital one. A technique for creating such signatures was proposed in 1976 by Whitfield Diffie and Martin E. Hellman, both then at Stanford University, as part of their ingenious public-key cryptosystem; the idea was refined a few years later by Ronald L. Rivest, Adi Shamir and Leonard Adleman (a triumvirate known as RSA), all then at MIT. In the RSA cryptosystem each user has two keys, one of which is made public and the other is held in secret. A message encrypted with the public key can be decrypted with the private key, and vice versa.

When the system is used for secrecy, a message is encrypted with the recipient's public key (which anyone can look up in a directory); then only the recipient can decrypt the message with the corresponding private key. A simple variation on the protocol yields highly secure digital signatures. To sign a document, you encrypt a copy of it with your private key. Anyone can then verify the signature by decrypting it with your public key. The mechanism works like Cinderella's slipper: whoever owns the key that fits must be the author of the document.

A further refinement has since been added to the digital-signature protocol. If you encrypt an entire document in order to sign it, the signature is as large as the document itself. To reduce the bulk, and at the same time avoid a subtle weakness lurking in the original scheme, the document is collapsed to a "digest" of just 160 bits, and then only the digest is signed. The digesting is done in such a way that even the slightest change to the document is almost certain to yield an entirely different digest. The recipient verifies the signature by applying the digesting algorithm to the document and decrypting the digest with the sender's public key; the result should match the supplied signature.

> The decrypting mechanism works like Cinderella's slipper: whoever owns the key that fits must be the author of the document.

The National Institute of Standards and Technology is at work on a digital-signature standard based on the public-key principle. The standard-setting process has been going on for years, buffeted by much controversy, but it now appears to be nearing a conclusion.

Digital signatures would probably deal quite well with the three situations described above. If signatures accompanying the letter from the Turkish prison and the note from Howard Hughes could be decrypted with the appropriate public keys, that would count as strong evidence for the documents' authenticity. Similarly, your Washington friend would have a hard time disowning a letter that had been signed by means of encryption with his own private key. The signatures also protect against after-the-fact tampering. There is no way you could have exaggerated Hughes's generosity in the signed bequest without knowing his private key.

Although digital signatures are dashed clever, they fall short of solving all the problems of the paperless society.

It might seem at first that digital signatures would provide all the security necessary for a system of electronic checks. To pay your rent, you would merely type a note on the computer, or fill in a template, stating the date, the amount and the payee and identifying your bank and your account number; then you would sign the check with your private key and send it off by electronic mail; the recipient would sign it as an endorsement and mail it on to his own bank. You would be confident that your unscrupulous landlord could not alter the amount, because the bank would detect the change when it verified your signature. Unfortunately, you would remain vulnerable to a cruder kind of fraud. The computer is not only a good eraser but also a flawless copier, and your landlord could simply duplicate your check (along with its signature) and deposit multiple copies, all of which would appear equally authentic. Rivest, Shamir and Adleman suggest including a unique serial number in each signed check and requiring banks to accept only one check with a given serial number. But that puts the onus of vigilance and record keeping on the banks, which may be reluctant to accept it.

Another problem arises when readers must verify not only the authorship and the integrity of a document but also its time of composition. In your computerized laboratory notebook you record the discovery of a new comet or a new virus, and you apply a digital signature to the entry. Later, a rival challenges your claim to priority. Naturally you included the date in your signed notebook entry, but your opponent is not much impressed by that evidence. He points out that the digital signature prevents others from tampering with the document, but since you know your own secret key, you could alter the date—or alter other parts of the document—at any time, then resign it. In other words, the signature proves that you wrote the notebook entry, but it cannot establish when you wrote it.

With paper documents there are at least two ways of dealing with the problem. First, important documents are witnessed as well as signed, and the witnesses can later be called to attest to the dating of the material. That practice can be adopted just as easily with digital signatures. Second, laboratory notes are generally kept in a bound volume with numbered pages, so that sheets cannot be inserted or removed. When disputes arise, the notebook will be credible evidence only if it can be read as a complete, continuous and contemporaneous record of laboratory activity. The pages must be filled up in sequence, without leaving gaps where back-dated entries might be inserted. In the recent controversy over the work of Thereza Imanishi-Kari of Tufts University, the U.S. Secret Service was asked to examine certain notebooks in an attempt to verify the chronology of the entries.

A laboratory record kept on a computer is more like a loose-leaf notebook than like a bound volume. New entries can be inserted anywhere in the sequence, or existing entries can be moved around; dates can be misstated or changed after the fact. But a solution is at hand. Inspired by the Imanishi-Kari case, Stuart A. Haber and W. Scott Stornetta of Bell Communications Research (Bellcore), in Piscataway, New Jersey, have devised a time-stamping service for electronic documents. The scheme is conceptually similar to public-key cryptography. When your notebook needs to be validated, you submit a digest to the time-stamping computer, which returns a "certificate" that encodes the time of receipt and other information.

But what if the time-stamping service itself cannot be trusted? For example, someone might tamper with the time-stamping computer, perhaps resetting the clock for long enough to create a fraudulent certificate, then restoring the clock to the correct current value. As protection against such deceptions, each certificate is combined with others issued at about the same time in a treelike structure; the single certificate at the root of the tree, whose value depends on all the individual certificates, is publicly posted. During preliminary trials of the service, documents are being time-stamped in weekly batches, and the root certificates are being published every Sunday in the Public Notices section of *The New York Times*. A certificate for any document stamped in the past week can be verified by rederiving the published root value. (A question that remains for the future is what will happen when *The New York Times* is published electronically instead of on paper.)

Even documents that no one would dream of having time-stamped or witnessed sometimes come under scrutiny. For example, George Bush has made public some of his private diaries in an attempt to establish what he didn't know (and when he didn't know it) about the sale of arms to Iran during his vice-presidency. Suppose Bush had kept his diary on a computer instead of on paper: he would have had great difficulty convincing his critics that no entries had been altered, deleted or back-dated.

Of course another major cache of documentary evidence in the Iran-Contra affair was in electronic form: the electronic mail messages of Oliver North. Curiously, those messages were accepted as authentic and unaltered precisely because North had deleted them (or rather had tried to delete them) from the disk memory of his computer. They were recovered through a sector-by-sector examination of the contents of the disk. If North had instead copied all the files onto floppy disks and voluntarily handed them over to congressional investigators, the messages would surely have been viewed with greater skepticism. (The hard-core conspiracy theorist knows that the supposed deletion and subsequent recovery of the messages was all a carefully staged means of increasing the credibility of concocted evidence. That some of the recovered messages were incriminating counts for nothing, apart from demonstrating that the real messages must have been much worse.)

The handling of legal documents is certainly not the only domain in which a conversion to electronic storage and transmission will change the nature of writing. Even personal correspondence is affected. For example, consider the art of the deft postscript. At the end of a chatty letter home, below the signature, you add, "P.S. I've just heard from Stockholm. Good news." Now, it may be that word of your Nobel prize reached you in the moments after the letter was finished but before it was sealed, but it's also possible that you turned the announcement into a casual afterthought purely for rhetorical effect. With a letter on paper, the recipient could never be quite sure. But with an electronic letter, "P.S." is almost certainly an artifice. After all, with a word processor it is no more trouble to add a sentence at the beginning than at the end.

Other rhetorical devices also lose a bit of their impact. In a letter on paper you might write, "Say hi to ~~dreary~~ dear old Dad," where the strike-through is very much a part of the joke. With a computer, since any mistake can be silently and invisibly corrected, the same trick seems more contrived, less spontaneous.

When a manuscript is being prepared for publication, the kind of invisible mending made possible by computers is often a handicap. Traditionally an editor would return to the author a marked-up copy of the original manuscript, showing all the proposed changes and corrections. When the editing is done with a computer, that record of alterations generally disappears. In fact, software solutions are available for that problem; they are just not widely used. Many word-processing programs offer a "red-lining" mode, which displays insertions and deletions explicitly (though seldom as clearly as they can be with a red pencil). There are also special-purpose programs for annotating text, and the contributions of multiple editors are identified by color.

Such tools may capture an editor's changes, but what about the author's transformations of the work during its composition? Few writers have the patience to document every stage in the creation of a novel or a poem (much less a love letter or a business memorandum). Indeed, some authors would cite as an advantage of computerized writing the end of old drafts and scribbled notes; all that remains of those scraps is now seamlessly integrated into the final text. From the scholar's point of view, however, a valuable source of information is being lost.

Take William Wordsworth's long autobiographical poem *The Prelude*. Fragments of the poem are known from as early as 1798; several versions were composed between 1799 and 1804; Wordsworth made sporadic revisions until 1839; various further emendations were introduced by others before a new edition was published soon after the poet's death in 1850. Dozens of manuscript sources survive, and they have enabled scholars to reconstruct the poem's compositional history in detail. There is no consensus among modern readers that the final state of the poem is the best; indeed, the 1805 version has many partisans. Yet if Wordsworth had had a PC, the history of the poem would probably be lost.

Lord Byron is another intriguing case. He presented himself to the world as an aristocrat of letters whose verses were casual, offhand productions, which he would not deign to correct or revise. Had he been writing with a computer (I imagine him toting the latest laptop model across the Alps into Italy), he might have gotten away with that fib. But recently published facsimiles of his manuscripts show just how labored his process of composition was. A reviewer describes the manuscripts as "bristling with added stanzas, overwritten crosswise, with false starts, impatient deletions, emendations and adjustments of rhymes." A modern Byron can readily conceal all signs of such unseemly labor, and as a result readers of the next century will likely find that manuscript sources for authors of the 1990s are rather scanty. Information that might well have been preserved on paper is being lost on disk.

The loss is not inevitable, and the cause is not really technological. As a matter of fact, keeping a complete archive of a life's work is surely easier with a computer than it is with a filing cabinet. One approach—one of many—is the WORM drive: a disk memory that can be written on and read from but never erased. (WORM stands for "write once, read many.") WORM drives have ample storage capacity; a single disk would hold all the versions of all the works of a Wordsworth or a Byron, along with all his journals and correspondence. The trouble is, adopting such a device amounts to a declaration that one's every word is worth preserving—which is even more obnoxious than the pose of the poet who claims he never cancels a line.

Still, somewhere in America today there must be a writer of merit who is either meticulously or absentmindedly saving her complete œuvre as a series of computer files. Fifty years from now some lucky scholar will sit down in a library carrel to unseal the treasure. There they'll be, packed in a cardboard carton: 600 eight-inch floppy disks from a Radio Shack TRS-80 Model 1. What is the probability anyone will be able to read them? Even supposing the information encoded on the disks has survived, where would one go in the year 2043 to find a working TRS-80? And a copy of the Electric Pencil, the word-processing program the author used to create her works?

It is curious that archival longevity seems to be the last thing anyone worries about when choosing computer hardware and software. In picking a word processor for my own use, for example, I have focused mainly on ease and speed of editing, and the elegance of the on-screen display; I've thought very little about how I will read my own files a few decades from now, when I will have gone on to another computer, another word processor, another disk format (if indeed the very notion of "word processor" or "disk format" is still meaningful). I should know better. I've changed computers five times in ten years. Every few months I need to resurrect a document from some long-gone system, and I spend an exasperating hour puzzling over cryptic formatting commands that were once intimately familiar. What does "@|" mean again? And "◆HYØ◆"?

I'm not the only one with such a narrowly constrained time horizon. The computer I'm writing on at this moment thinks the world will end in 2040.

Both buyers and sellers of software pay a good deal of attention to the transfer of information between different programs and computer systems, but the emphasis is on synchronic rather than diachronic transfers. We worry about how to move a WordPerfect file on an IBM PC onto an Apple Macintosh equipped with Microsoft Word; we don't pause to ask how our descendants will read any of those files in a century or two, when WordPerfect, IBM, Apple Computer and even Microsoft are only dim memories.

Given all the drawbacks and disadvantages of electronic documents, why not just stick with paper? The best way of answering that question is to look back on the one other occasion in human history when a writing medium was replaced. To societies accustomed to writing on stone or clay, paper must have seemed terribly ephemeral stuff, vulnerable to fire and water, with inscribed marks that all too easily smudged or bleached away. And yet paper prevailed. Moses' tablets were stone, but the story of Moses was told on paper. The economic incentives were just too powerful to be ignored: with paper, information became far cheaper to record, to store and to transport. Exactly the same considerations argue that a transition to paperless, electronic writing is now inevitable.

In any case, eternity is too much to ask of any storage medium. Libraries are full of disintegrating paper books; graveyards are full of stone tablets eroded to illegibility; even languages die. Perhaps the best advice, if you must write for the ages, is this: Write very well. In the centuries to come no one will be reading your verses or your novels because they are stored as WordStar files on 1.2 megabyte floppy disks; but maybe someone will preserve the equipment needed to decipher those files and disks if that's the only way to read your deathless works.

THINKING AND RE-READING

1. As you re-read this piece, think about the ways in which computer technology has influenced the way we think about authorship, authority, ownership, and reproduction. Think about people who lived before computer-based writing was possible—people who wrote by hand on paper and those who wrote on a typewriter. How might their perceptions of language production and reproduction differ from your own?

2. Hayes writes, "The excised word leaves no scar." Consider these words in terms of your own composing habits and processes. Do you agree or disagree? Think about the effort that is attached to words erased, words revised, and even words unexpressed.

WRITING AND LEARNING

1. Hayes makes the following claim in his article, "Both buyers and sellers of software pay a good deal of attention to the transfer of information between different programs and computer systems but the emphasis is on synchronic rather than diachronic transfers.

... we don't pause to ask how our descendants will read any of those files." Write a letter to a descendant of yours, to be opened in the year 2097. In the letter, mention the writing technologies that you have at your disposal currently and speculate about the capabilities that your descendant may have available.

2. Make an appointment to interview someone who works with a computer-intensive business that requires long-term archiving of documents: a librarian, a specialist on your campus computing staff, a clerical worker who deals with computer files, and so on. Ask this person about his or her electronic archiving techniques and about the precautions taken to ensure that important files will be available even after a certain brand/model/type of technology has become obsolete. In this interview, summarize your questions and answers in writing. Your purpose in writing this is to inform your classmates about what you have learned through this interview experience.

3. For insight into your own life and experiences, write an account of how you organize your work on electronic documents to keep from writing over important information, to preserve documents in various drafts, and to keep your computer files accessible and in order. How do you organize these files? Name them? Store them? Back them up?

4. Talk to someone who lived before computers were used for the purpose of writing. Ask this person to tell you about his or her writing processes and habits—frequency of writing, recipient(s) of writing, writing methods, revision processes and changes made, and writing instruments. Record in writing your findings from this conversation. Your purpose in detailing this is to provide people in your generation with a lesson drawn from history.

Prophet of Privacy

Steven Levy

IN THIS CONTRIBUTION, STEVEN LEVY (author of *Hackers* and *Insanely Great* and a Fellow at the Freedom Forum Media Studies Center) writes about the life and the work of Whitfield Diffie, a pioneer of modern encryption technologies and the father of the public key encryption system. Levy describes how Diffie came to crack the problems of public key cryptography, and why he devoted so much time and effort to the project. In a fundamental sense, Levy notes, Diffie believes in a citizen's right to privacy, but he is afraid that communication technologies—including his own public key system—may be used to erode that right. This article appeared in *Wired,* a magazine aimed at an audience that is highly literate in its knowledge of computers and interested in some of the more controversial issues raised by the new age of technology.

Diffie's life, you will note, has been an unusual one—it has not followed the traditional patterns of the "promising youth" or the "successful college scholar" stories with which we are all familiar. Diffie did not learn to read until he was ten years of age, spent much of his younger years drifting from one interest to another, left a good job and a steady salary to travel across the country for two years visiting libraries, and chose to spend some of his most productive years as a researcher serving part time as a house husband. As you read, consider the ways in which these non-traditional life choices contributed to Diffie's unique approach to solving problems in cryptography.

The heat on this steamy June day is oppressive, but Whitfield Diffie doesn't seem to notice. He strides across the street from his hotel to the Washington, DC, Convention Center like a smart bomb homing in on a bunker. He has prepared for the Armed Forces Communications and Electronics Association Expo and Convention with his usual compulsive vigor. Some days before, in his office at Sun Microsystems Computer Corporation in Mountain View, California—where he holds the title of distinguished engineer—Diffie examined the list of exhibitors and methodically charted a course through the convention center that would take him past every vendor or organization that offers something related to the field he has helped revolutionize: cryptography.

Diffie is quite at home in Washington. In the past 15 months he has testified three times before Congress and participated in a blue-ribbon panel on the future of crypto. This swing started two days ago, on his 50th birthday. He celebrated by having a quiet dinner with his wife, Egyptologist Mary Fischer. The following day he denounced the Clipper Chip at a conference organized by the Electronic Privacy Information Center. Now—accompanied by a small entourage of authors, including David Kahn (The Codebreakers), Bruce Schneier (Applied Cryptography), and me—he is ready to hit the convention floor of the Armed Forces show, where the theme of the day is "Digitizing the Battlefield."

Even if he weren't leading a crew of cypherscribes, Diffie would cut an imposing figure. From the neck down, he fits the conservative mode of the bureaucrats, techies, and spooks in attendance: blue suit with a neatly knotted tie over a blue shirt. But hovering over the suit are piercing blue eyes framed by shoulder-length blonde hair and a beard worthy of Buffalo Bill. Then there's his unforgettable voice: Diffie speaks in a cutting tremolo that heightens the effect of his words, which are often already provocative.

Diffie has a chance to exercise these vocal proclivities as he jaunts from booth to booth, happily bantering with the purveyors of surveillance systems, crypto-protected jeep communications, and "situation awareness" helmets with built-in quanta-ray sensors. At one modest display he jokes, "For an outfit of your formidability, you've managed an economical booth." The exhibitors wilt. At another booth he is offered a chance to try out an encryption-equipped walkie-talkie. "Presumably, we'll discover it works just fine," says Diffie, refusing the demo.

Then Diffie reaches Booth 660, let by the National Security Agency. The agency is the world's largest repository of information about cryptography and usually operates under total secrecy. In these après Cold War days, however, the agency has been experimenting with a more public posture, and at the conference it has fronted two booths: this one, with its banner proudly unfurled, and an exhibit room off the show floor.

A helpful NSA employee shows Diffie and company to the latter. It's hardly different from any other vendor's operation at a high-tech convention—except that visitors must provide social security numbers and proof of US citizenship. The room is filled with several elaborate demos of cryptosystems running off PC nets. Diffie examines a system that allows several levels of encryption to coexist on a network. The young agency technician running the demo is obviously bright, perhaps even a bit haughty as he runs the system through its paces. As Diffie turns away, someone asks the technician if he recognized that bearded fellow.

"Who?" the technician asks.

"That's Whitfield Diffie. He invented public key cryptography."

The technician's eyes widen to the size of video monitors. For a second he is paralyzed. Then he bolts forward. "Dr. Dif-fffffie. . . ," he shouts, "Dr. Dif-fffeeeeee. . ." When he catches up, his attempt to describe his awe comes out in a jumble. For a moment it looks like he might outstretch his arms and execute knee-bend bows, à la Wayne and Garth: "I'm not worthy!"

It was in 1976 that Diffie and Stanford University electrical engineering professor Martin Hellman blew open the cryptographic world by announcing a new way to protect secrets: the public key. It was a profound discovery: historian David Kahn (still in tow as Diffie leaves the booth) called it "the most revolutionary new concept in the field since the Renaissance." A

Prophet of Privacy   295

pursuit formerly limited to the domain of spies, diplomats, and the military now had the potential to enhance the privacy of the masses. Public key has the potential to change the way we work, even the way we live.

Compared to ordinary encryption, public key is a type of magic. By splitting the scrambling-and-descrambling "key" into two components, a widely distributed public key and a closely held private key, it enables users to communicate in complete secrecy with people they've never met. And when that person replies, only the user will be able to read that message. Even more remarkable, it makes possible a "digital signature," assuring that an electronic message was generated by the person who claims responsibility for it. Together, these features allow us to create new forms of digital commerce with an unprecedented level of privacy. These possibilities also present a challenge to government, particularly to the NSA, which is accustomed to controlling the nation's cryptosystems. As cryptography slips into the mainstream, the agency is faced with a dramatic reassessment of its mission.

And looking over the agency's shoulder is Whit Diffie, who has emerged as a passionate and public critic of government cryptographic policy. His eloquence alone would make him a formidable figure in the debate over whether the feds should limit the spread of crypto, but his credentials make him a figure truly to be reckoned with. "I would say he is the elder statesman of cryptography," says Jim Bidzos, president of RSA Data Security. "Few people have the kind of insights he does."

Yet at one time, it looked like Diffie might slip into obscurity as an eccentric hacker who never made much of his genius for math and his laser-focus mind. As his wife tells it, on the very eve of the historic discovery of public key crypto, Diffie was virtually despondent. "He was telling me that he should do something else," recalls Mary Fischer, "that he was a broken-down researcher."

This was 1975. Diffie was 31, with only a bachelor's degree, and he had reached a point in life where, he says, "I was worried that I wasn't particularly remarkable as a programmer and that my lot in life would get progressively worse if things continued going as they were." All his life Diffie had jigged in perfect cadence to an internal tune, heeding little of convention. Had the music led him to a dead end?

Whit Diffie, it seems, had always been different. Born in 1944, he was the sole offspring of Bailey Wallace Diffie and Justine Louise Whitfield. They had met as foreign service workers in Madrid in the 1920s and married in Paris in 1928. Diffie senior became a City College of New York history professor specializing in Iberia and its colonies, and Whit grew up in Queens, in perhaps the only atheist Camelite household in a mostly Jewish neighborhood. "One of Whit's oldest friends told me he had an alternative lifestyle at age 5," says Mary Fischer.

Diffie didn't learn to read until he was 10 years old. There was no question of disability; it was obvious he was a bright, curious child. He simply didn't read, and no one considered it a horrible problem. During the fifth grade he spontaneously worked his way through a tome called *The Space Cat* and immediately progressed to one of the *Wizard of Oz* books. Later that year, his teacher at PS 78—"Her name was Mary E. Collins and if she is still alive I would like to find her," says Diffie—spent an afternoon on the subject of ciphers, and Diffie was so taken he had his father check out all the cryptography books in the City College library. But his code mania soon faded, and he pursued other interests—castles, camouflage rockets, and poison gases. (As late as his junior year in high school, he considered a career in the military.) Diffie also became interested in math—"I thought of myself as a mathematician in high school," he says.

At the Massachusetts Institute of Technology, he harbored contempt for computers—he thought himself too pure a mathematician to have much truck with them. This began to change after he earned his degree in 1965. The Vietnam War dampened Diffie's military enthusiasm, and he became a self-described "peacenik," with no desire to deploy the armed rockets and poison gases that had entranced him in his youth. Like many, he found a way to avoid the draft—working for a defense contractor. It was the Mitre Corporation, a Massachusetts systems engineering company that worked for the Defense Department. The job was a plum—while technically a Mitre employee, he would write LISP code at the MIT Artificial Intelligence Lab. There Diffie was exposed to the best computer hackers in the world. By the time he left Mitre in 1969, Diffie was over his contempt for computers.

Ever since his freshman year at MIT, though, when he spent the summer in Berkeley, Diffie had been pining to move west. "I hung out with the red diaper set in New York, the frontier of the sexual revolution. I'd been used to having a full social life—folk singing parties and stuff like that. There were such scenes in Cambridge, but I fell in with what was easy: hanging out with these guys at MIT's East Campus—with 25 women in a class of 950, it was a Boy Scout camp. But when I went back to Berkeley, immediately I was in among what I thought of as the real people. I have always believed the thesis that one's politics and the character of one's intellectual work are inseparable."

Diffie got his chance to go west when he heard that artificial intelligence pioneer John McCarthy was interested in a mathematical problem that fascinated Diffie: proof of correctness of programs. Diffie was hired to work at Stanford's Artificial Intelligence Lab, where McCarthy was a professor. But he now conjectures, "In his view, McCarthy probably hired me as the LISP system programmer." Nonetheless, Diffie's work in proof of correctness (funded, ironically, by the NSA) apparently met with McCarthy's approval. Then McCarthy, in essence, lost Diffie as a worker by urging him to consider crypto once more. Diffie's long-dormant penchant for cryptography was quickly rekindled, and he began working on crypto obsessively.

There are several reasons that cryptography so entranced Diffie. He has always had a visceral interest in personal privacy. Though he prefers not to label them as such—after trying several labels to characterize his views, Diffie finally decided none applied—his politics are strongly libertarian. There was also the challenge of investigating a problem that was, in a sense, forbidden. "It was a whole secret field," he says. "Ostensibly my reason for getting interested in it was that I thought it was important to personal privacy. It seems to me now that I was also fascinated with investigating this business that people wouldn't tell you about. But it was unlike a lot of other secret things where it was very, very hard to get at real evidence because somebody else had control of the information and you had to try to get informants or something like that. With cryptography, there was a certain amount of solid information one could figure out merely by doing mathematics."

Finally, there was Diffie's personal quest—his belief that solving the problems of crypto would provide some meaning to things. "I think somewhere deep in my mind is the notion that if I could just learn the right thing I would be saved," Diffie says, laughing at his own struggles. "So I've been looking all my life for some great mystery. And this is the most successful one I've investigated. I mean, I certainly feel the lure of things that are in some way mysterious. I felt that if I could just get to the bottom of this it would somehow be incredibly satisfying."

Diffie pored over David Kahn's 1,164-page 1967 opus, *The Code-breakers.* "It must have taken me a year to read it," he says. "I read it more carefully probably than anyone had ever read it. It's like the Veda—in India if a man loses his cow, he looks for it in the Veda. In any event, by the spring of 1973, I was doing nothing but cryptography."

Diffie took a leave from the AI lab and embarked on an epic sojourn to discover cryptographic truths. It was a lonely quest. True, NSA headquarters at Fort Meade, Maryland, was teeming with people working on these problems, but all the results were classified. Precious little information about the subject existed in the public domain. If someone did publish something, or try to patent a cryptographic innovation, the agency might attempt to classify that information. "My attitude was to keep my head down at first," says Diffie.

For two years, Diffie crisscrossed the country in a Datsun 510. He hit every library that might have some information and attempted to talk to anyone whose ideas might inform his own. Some people refused to talk to him. But the journey helped in establishing the key problems Diffie needed to tackle in cryptography. (Besides, the trip wasn't all cryptography: he managed to take in several Skylab launches and, most significantly, to hook up with Fischer, who became his traveling companion.)

When Diffie and Fischer finally returned to the West Coast in the fall of 1974, Diffie heard about a Stanford prof named Martin Hellman who was also interested in crypto. Diffie gave him a call; Hellman agreed to a half-hour meeting.

"There was an immediate meeting of the minds," Hellman recalls. "I'd been working in a vacuum and getting disappointed and wondering whether it was really worth it. So meeting Whit was just fantastic. He had some ideas I'd already had and vice versa, and we each had some ideas that were different, and it was just an interplay." The half-hour meeting lasted the rest of the afternoon, moved to Hellman's house, and didn't break up until late at night.

Hellman and Diffie agreed that Hellman would hire Diffie as a research programmer, and Diffie would eventually enroll as a Stanford graduate student—but in truth they were collaborators. (Diffie, who describes himself as incapable of working on anything that doesn't interest him, never took his formal graduate studies seriously and eventually dropped out of the program. It was not until 1992 that he received a doctorate from the Swiss Federal Institute of Technology for his public key work.)

At that point Diffie was thinking mainly about two problems that plagued cryptography. One was encryption, the practice of using codes to protect information over insecure channels. How could one get around the problem of key management, which required passing a secret key from one party to another? The second problem was that of authentication—was it possible to concoct a method whereby a recipient of a message could know without question that it came from a certain person, in the same way a written signature indelibly identifies a document?

Pondering some ideas that came from techniques in military "identification friend or foe" systems, and combining them with an innovative scheme of protecting computer passwords using a mathematical technique called one-way functions, Diffie came up with a method to solve the authentication problem—a true digital signature. Two weeks later, he realized that by cracking that puzzle, he had also uncovered a way to solve the encryption problem—an amazing solution that used not one but two cryptographic keys.

He clearly remembers that day in May 1975. He and Fischer were living in John McCarthy's house, with the understanding that Diffie would act as a househusband, taking care of McCarthy's daughter and watching the house, while McCarthy was on leave. His routine at the time was to fix Mary breakfast before she went to work at her job analyzing geologic findings at British Petroleum. Then he would spend the rest of the day alternating between domestic chores and research. Sometime during that afternoon he altered the course of cryptographic history by "splitting the key."

"The thing I remember distinctly is that I was sitting in the living room when I thought of it the first time and then I went downstairs to get a Coke and I almost lost it," he says. "I mean, there was this moment when—I was thinking about something. What was it? And then I got it back and didn't forget it."

That night, he went over to Hellman's and told his collaborator about the idea. Hellman recalls during the brief conversation that he first thought Diffie's heretical idea "was a little bit crazy." But as he thought about it later that night, he began to get excited. Maybe it could work. "I started to think of some analogies," he says. "It still wasn't like 'This is it,' because it wasn't at all clear that you could do it. We now had to figure out how to do it."

Over the next few months they did just that, working together to mathematically flesh out the conceptual skeleton that Diffie had envisioned. By the time they were ready to publish, both were aware of the significance of what they had. The first line of their paper, which eventually appeared in *IEEE Transactions on Information Theory,* in November 1976, said it all:

"We stand today on the brink of a revolution in cryptography."

Now that the aforementioned revolution is well under way, no prospective cryptographer will ever experience the isolation in which Whit Diffie worked in the early 1970s. The Diffie-Hellman breakthrough was a contributing factor to the establishment of an independent nonmilitary movement in cryptography. At 50, Diffie is an elder figure in this community. His advice and comments are eagerly sought from all quarters. He has been a key participant in the work of the Digital Privacy and Security Working Group, an aggregation of more than 50 computer, communications, and public interest groups looking at the problems of privacy in the computer age. He is held in high esteem at meetings of the crypto-rebel Cypherpunks.

Diffie has managed all this while largely skirting jobs with either of the two most common employers of cryptographers—the government and academia. In 1978 he took a job as manager of secure systems research for Northern Telecom, the Canadian equivalent of Western Electric, working in its laboratory in Mountain View, California. One of the best pieces of work he did there was designing a secure phone system; it never saw commercial use, but part of its design became the heart of an innovative product called PDSO, or packet data security overlay, used to provide end-to-end security between hosts on packet data networks. In 1991, Diffie moved to Sun Microsystems, where he became a sort of internal consultant, a companywide resource on security issues. And, of course, a crypto researcher.

"You know, I never know exactly what I do," Diffie says of the latter work. "I mean, every now and then, of course, I produce something, so I can say, 'I did that,' but most of the time I can't remember anything except sort of looking off into space.

"I've been thinking about the problem of evaluating systems," he says, referring to the challenging problem of probing a cryptosystem to see if it has a "trapdoor" built in by its creators. "Who needs to trust systems? It's customers, and sort of by definition, they don't design the systems. It may be an insoluble problem—how in the hell can you ever trust any system independent of trusting the designers? I'm not convinced you can in principle find the flaws in things that way. Hiding a trapdoor in a cryptosystem is a much more difficult mathematical problem than just designing a cryptosystem, but it's not obvious to me that you can't create a trapdoor that is in principle unfindable."

In the past year, with Sun's blessing, Diffie has focused on the public-policy issues of crypto. "I've been making a living off of politics," he says, half-jokingly. But to those who advocate limiting a strong crypto to preserve the wiretapping capabilities of law enforcement and intelligence agencies, Diffie's new job description isn't very funny. He has emerged as an authoritative opponent of these schemes, particularly the Clipper Chip.

"The key escrow proposal is dreadful," he says, "because the big thing we've gotten away from in contemporary cryptographic technology is the vulnerability that grows out of having to maintain secret keys for longer than you actually need them. Prior to Aldrich Ames, two of the most damaging spy scandals of the last 20 years in the US—Boyce and Lee at TRW and the Walker ring in the Navy—resulted from the fact that keys existed for longer than they needed to exist, and somebody got a chance to siphon some of them off.

If you use public keys correctly, particularly in interactive channels like telephones, you can avoid having this hazard. The keys exist only in the equipment, only for the duration of the call, and after that they go away. And so key escrow is just rescuing a dreadful vulnerability."

The Clipper Chip is even less attractive, says Diffie, when one considers who's pushing it. "We're moving our society into a telecommunications environment. I think security mechanisms are fundamental social mechanisms, and what is needed is widespread trust in them—but there's no trusting secret mechanisms designed by an organization most of whose budget goes to spying."

One would think that this sort of talk would place Diffie's picture at the top of an NSA enemy list. But relations between the agency and its most eloquent opponent are cordial. Clinton Brooks, an important architect of the NSA's key escrow scheme, has worked with Diffie on the Association of Computing Machinery's panel on crypto policy. "We came to this from quite different perspectives," says Brooks, with some understatement. "During this experience, my esteem and regard for Whit considerably increased. I found him open, considerate, and eager to listen to others' points of view."

The respect is mutual. Even Diffie has tempered his opinion of the organization. "I started out being very antagonistic to them, but after a decade of studying their technology and history, I came to like and respect them much more. I believe I recognize and have for a long time been sympathetic to NSA's goals. I think from a purely nationalistic point of view those goals are certainly understandable. That does not mean that there are not other objectives that seem even more important. Personal privacy certainly seems to me as important as ever, maybe more so. I'm firmly convinced that human freedom can't stand in the long run against improving communications technology, that that will utterly destroy the independence of people." As it stands, he says, "right now people lack freedom in a way that they had it a century or two ago."

How is this? Diffie explains that in the days of the Founding Fathers, there was no technological surveillance—when two people had a conversation, they communicated with confidence that no one was secretly recording their words. But with every advance in communications technology—telegraph, telephone, fax machine, computer networking, ATM machine, e-mail—more and more information that was once transmitted securely became drawn into these relatively insecure channels. And future advances will continue this trend. Thus, Diffie argues, even if the government permits us the use of strong crypto, law enforcement and intelligence agencies will thrive on a continual bonanza of new technologies that will expose our secrets. The least we can have is some crypto to protect ourselves.

"Basically," Diffie says, "one of the things that frightens me about this Clipper sort of thing is that if it's accepted, society can have far more influence over people by governing what technology is available to them than it can by making laws about what they do and punishing them if they don't obey the laws."

Earlier this spring, Diffie had the opportunity to explain some of these ideas to the Senate Judiciary Subcommittee on Technology and the Law, chaired by Senator Patrick Leahy, D-Vermont, who shares Diffie's skepticism about the Clipper Chip. It was interesting testimony. People from both sides of the issue had spoken on the matter, but their arguments were rather *pro forma*. This changed when Diffie, dressed in a bespoke blue suit from Sam of Nathan Road in Kowloon, with his hair flowing down his back, leaned into the microphone and began talking about the deeper implications of the government's policy. It was as if a creature from a smarter species had somehow been introduced into the Kabuki of congressional protocol. He walked the committee through the privacy problem from the 1790s to the present day and beyond and laid out the Clipper controversy in dazzling context. Crypto, he argued, will not upset the balance of power by giving the individual a huge edge over the government—instead we should see it as one of the few resources available to the individual who wants some privacy. "It has been thoughtlessly said . . . that cryptography brings the unprecedented promise of absolute privacy," testified Diffie. "In fact, it only goes a short way to make up for the loss of an assurance of privacy that can never be regained."

In the flurry of concepts, however, few appreciated the resonance of Diffie's opening sentences. They summed up Whitfield Diffie's progress since he began his quest more than two decades ago.

"I first began thinking about cryptography in 1972," he testified. "My feeling was that cryptography was vitally important for personal privacy, and my goal was to make it better known. I am pleased to say that if I have succeeded in nothing else, I have achieved that goal."

In spades.

THINKING AND RE-READING

1. As you re-read this article, think about the picture that Levy paints of Diffie. What characteristics of this man does Levy admire? Why does he consider Diffie a "prophet"? What kinds of personality traits and operating methods does Diffie share with hackers? How do Diffie and the hackers position themselves with regard to the establishment? The government? Mainstream society? How do you think Levy positions himself in the act of writing about Diffie?

2. How does Levy portray the United States government? The government's efforts to control encryption? The National Security Agency? The mainstream of computer science? The military? In what ways is this a David and Goliath story? Why might it provide some readers with a sense of comfort?

WRITING AND LEARNING

1. In a review of this reading, discuss whether you agree or disagree with Diffie's claim that "human freedom can't stand in the long run against improving communications technology." Explain why you feel the way that you do and what evidence, drawn from your own life experiences, convinces you. You are writing the review for a student audience that has not yet read this piece. Your purpose is to convince this audience that

Steven Levy's article includes some important insights that should be considered carefully, even if they don't agree with these thoughts.

2. Go to the library and research source material referring to the National Security Agency (NSA) and the work that it does. For your own insight, write a relatively brief summary of your findings—no more than two pages. (Be sure to check your grammar handbook to find out the correct citation format for paraphrasing, quoting, and summarizing.)

3. To increase your own understanding about the life choices that you have made and continue to make, write a short essay that deals with the way in which Diffie went about his work—at times avoiding the traditional routes of higher education and focusing, instead, on the subject that most excited him. Do you have any project or interest that is this important or fascinating to you? Something that you want to or feel that you must excel in? If so, describe this endeavor and your plans for continuing your work on it. If not, explain why you think you might not yet have identified such an area of interest.

4. In an editorial suitable for publication in your college newspaper, explain your impression of hackers. Would you compare them to outlaw heroes or terrorists? Or both? Explain your answer and provide examples from your own experience. Pretend that you are writing this editorial right after an incident in which a student hacker has been caught doing damage to the computerized record-keeping system used by your college.

IMAGES OF ETHICS, LAW, AND TECHNOLOGY

THINKING AND RE-READING

1. In Appendix A of this reader, you will find a list of questions that will help you read and understand this set of images and other images that you see, in new ways. Read the questions in this list carefully and use them to "read" the images in this section, carefully and with an increasing sense of thoughtfulness.

WRITING AND LEARNING

1. Choose at least two of the three images to analyze more carefully. For these images, write down your answers to the questions listed in Appendix A.

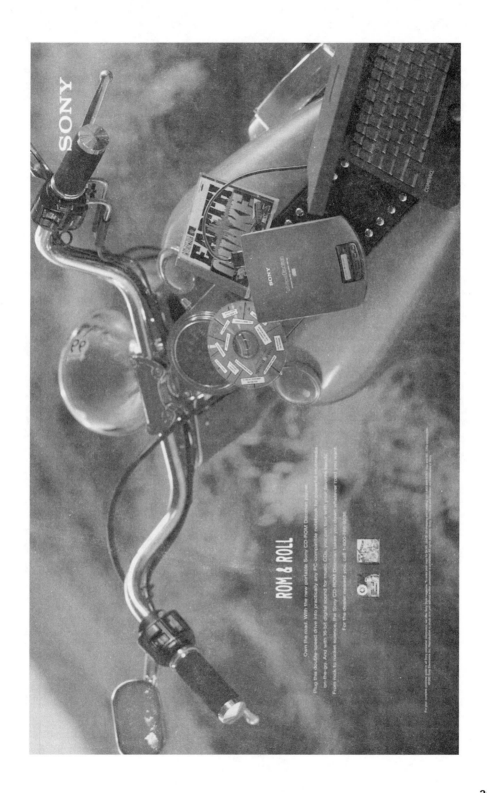

ROM & ROLL

YOU CAN GET

16-BIT HIGH-END SOUND.

YOU CAN GET

16.8 MILLION COLORS.

YOU CAN GET

GOOD MORNING AMERICA.

Some people really know how to wake you up. Namely, the engineers here at NEC. Introducing the new Versa M, a truly spectacular multimedia notebook computer.

Your multimedia applications will come to life with NEC's first-of-a-kind, photo-quality, 24-bit True Color screen which displays some 16.8 million colors. Or select the first-ever high resolution 800 x 600 color display, or one of our enhanced TFT or DSTN screens. With each, you get the Versa's famous reversible 9.5" display screen.

Rest assured, the dockable Versa M comes packed. It's

powered by an Intel 486 DX/4 75 MHz or 100 MHz processor with 8 MB of RAM, up to 810 MB of hard disk drive storage, and 16-bit high-fidelity sound. It features the innovative VersaBay, which is configured with a removable 1.44 MB floppy drive that you can replace with any number of options. Like a PCMCIA Pak, which gives you a total of four PCMCIA slots. Or a Video Pak, which plugs right into your notebook and allows you to watch television.

And thanks to something called VersaConnect, you can add cellular capability to your notebook. This means you can now send faxes and e-mail, hook up to on-line information services, or send out broadcast pages from virtually anywhere.

Plus, as always, you get the reliability of NEC's UltraCare service program and three-year limited warranty. Call 1-800-NEC-VERSA for more details. And see why the new Versa M is receiving attention, compliments, and TV.

SEE, HEAR
AND FEEL THE
DIFFERENCE.

NEC

Civil Liberties in Cyberspace

Mitchell Kapor

MITCHELL KAPOR, IN THIS ARTICLE, tries to sort out some of the complicated issues connected with the exercise of civil liberties in cyberspace, including protection from unreasonable search and seizure, freedom of speech, and protection of individual privacy rights. He reminds readers—taking a page out of *Technologies of Freedom,* Ithiel de Sola Pool's influential book—that communication in digital environments, such as cyberspace, incorporates different and sometimes contradictory features of three systems of control: print, common carrier, and broadcast media.

The fundamental assumptions about control vary broadly in each of these areas, and problems in cyberspace are now springing from the contradictory values associated with each traditional area. As a result, the civil laws of cyberspace are badly in need of attention. Kapor claims that citizens' organizations such as the Electronic Frontier Foundation—a not-for-profit organization founded in 1990 that focuses its efforts on civil liberties in electronic environments—may be able to help in this important cultural project. Kapor published this piece in a special issue of *Scientific American* devoted to an exploration of "Communications, Computers, and Networks." This issue, aimed at an informed but broad readership, appeared in September 1991.

On March 1, 1990, the U.S. Secret Service raided the offices of Steve Jackson, an entrepreneurial publisher in Austin, Tex. Carrying a search warrant, the authorities confiscated computer hardware and software, the drafts of his about-to-be-released book and many business records of his company, Steve Jackson Games. They also seized the electronic bulletin-board system used by the publisher to communicate with customers and writers, thereby seizing all the private electronic mail on the system.

The Secret Service held some of the equipment and material for months, refusing to discuss their reasons for the raid. The publisher was forced to reconstruct his book from old manuscripts, to delay filling orders for it and to lay off half his staff. When the warrant application was finally unsealed months later, it confirmed that the publisher was never suspected of any crime.

Steve Jackson's legal difficulties are symptomatic of a widespread problem. During the past several years, dozens of individuals have been the subject of similar searches and seizures. In any other context, this warrant might never have been issued. By many interpretations, it disregarded the First and Fourth Amendments to the U.S. Constitution, as well as several existing privacy laws. But the government proceeded as if civil liberties did not apply. In this case, the government was investigating a new kind of crime—computer crime.

The circumstances vary, but a disproportionate number of cases share a common thread: the serious misunderstanding of computer-based communication and its implications for civil liberties. We now face the task of adapting our legal institutions and societal expectations to the cultural phenomena that even now are springing up from communications technology.

Our society has made a commitment to openness and to free communication. But if our legal and social institutions fail to adapt to new technology, basic access to the global electronic media could be seen as a privilege, granted to those who play by the strictest rules, rather than as a right held by anyone who needs to communicate. To assure that these freedoms are not compromised, a group of computer experts, including myself, founded the Electronic Frontier Foundation (EFF) in 1990.

In many respects, it was odd that Steve Jackson Games got caught up in a computer crime investigation at all. The company publishes a popular, award-winning series of fantasy role-playing games, produced in the form of elaborate rule books. The raid took place only because law enforcement officials misunderstood the technologies—computer bulletin-board systems (BBSs) and on-line forums—and misread the cultural phenomena that those technologies engender.

Like a growing number of businesses, Steve Jackson Games operated an electronic bulletin board to facilitate contact between players of its games and their authors. Users of this bulletin-board system dialed in via modem from their personal computers to swap strategy tips, learn about game upgrades, exchange electronic mail and discuss games and other topics.

Law enforcement officers apparently became suspicious when a Steve Jackson Games employee—on his own time and on a BBS he ran from his house—made an innocuous comment about a public domain protocol for transferring computer files called Kermit. In addition, officials claimed that at one time the employee had had on an electronic bulletin board a copy of *Phrack*, a widely disseminated electronic publication, that included information they believed to have been stolen from a BellSouth computer.

The law enforcement officials interpreted these facts as unusual enough to justify not only a search and seizure at the employee's residence but also the search of Steve Jackson Games and the seizure of enough equipment to disrupt the business seriously. Among the items confiscated were all the hard copies and electronically stored copies of the manuscript of a rule book for a role-playing game called GURPS Cyberpunk, in which inhabitants of so-called cyberspace invade corporate and government computer systems and steal sensitive data. Law enforcement agents regarded the book, in the words of one, as "a handbook for computer crime."

A basic knowledge of the kinds of computer intrusion that are technically possible would have enabled the agents to see that GURPS Cyberpunk was nothing more than a science fiction creation and that Kermit was simply a legal, frequently used computer program. Unfortunately, the agents assigned to investigate computer crime did not know what—if anything—was evidence of criminal activity. Therefore, they intruded on a small business without a reasonable basis for believing that a crime had been committed and conducted a search and seizure without looking for "particular" evidence, in violation of the Fourth Amendment of the Constitution.

Searches and seizures of such computer systems affect the rights of not only their owners and operators but also the users of those systems. Although most BBS users have never been in the same room with the actual computer that carries their postings, they legitimately expect their electronic mail to be private and their lawful associations to be protected.

The community of bulletin-board users and computer networkers may be small, but precedents must be understood in a greater context. As forums for debate and information exchange, computer-based bulletin boards and conferencing systems support some of the most vigorous exercise of the First Amendment freedoms of expression and association that this country has ever seen. Moreover, they are evolving rapidly into large-scale public information and communications utilities.

These utilities will probably converge into a digital national public network that will connect nearly all homes and businesses in the U.S. This network will serve as a main conduit for commerce, learning, education and entertainment in our society, distributing images and video signals as well as text and voice. Much of the content of this network will be private messages serving as "virtual" town halls, village greens and coffeehouses, where people post their ideas in public or semipublic forums.

Yet there is a common perception that a defense of electronic civil liberties is somehow opposed to legitimate concerns about the prevention of computer crime. The conflict arises, in part, because the popular hysteria about the technically sophisticated youths known as hackers has drowned out reasonable discussion.

Perhaps inspired by the popular movie *WarGames*, the general public began in the 1980s to perceive computer hackers as threats to the safety of this country's vital computer systems. But the image of hackers as malevolent is purchased at the price of ignoring the underlying reality—the typical teenage hacker is simply tempted by the prospect of exploring forbidden territory. Some are among our best and brightest technological talents: hackers of the 1960s and 1970s, for example, were so driven by their desire to master, understand and produce new hardware and software that they went on to start companies called Apple, Microsoft and Lotus.

> **If our legal and social institutions fail to adapt, access to electronic media could be a privilege, rather than a right.**

How do we resolve this conflict? One solution is ensure that our scheme of civil and criminal laws provides sanctions in proportion to the offenses. A system in which an exploratory hacker receives more time in jail than a defendant convicted of assault violates our sense of justice. Our legal tradition historically has shown itself capable of making subtle and not-so-subtle distinctions among criminal offenses.

There are, of course, real threats to network and system security. The qualities that make the ideal network valuable—its popularity, its uniform commands, its ability to handle financial transactions and its international access—also make it vulnerable to a variety of abuses and accidents. It is certainly proper to hold hackers accountable for their offenses, but that accountability should never entail denying defendants the safeguards of the Bill of Rights, including the rights to free expression and association and to freedom from unreasonable searches and seizures.

We need statutory schemes that address the acts of true computer criminals (such as those who have created the growing problem of toll and credit-card fraud) while distinguishing between those criminals and hackers whose acts are most analogous to noncriminal trespass. And we need educated law enforcement officials who will be able to recognize and focus their efforts on the real threats.

The question then arises: How do we help our institutions, and perceptions, adapt? The first step is to articulate the kinds of values we want to see protected in the electronic society we are now shaping and to make an agenda for preserving the civil liberties that are central to that society. Then we can draw on the appropriate legal traditions that guide other media. The late Ithiel de Sola Pool argued in his influential book *Technologies of Freedom* that the medium of digital communications is heir to several traditions of control: the press, the common carrier and the broadcast media.

The freedom of the press to print and distribute is explicitly guaranteed by the First Amendment. This freedom is somewhat limited, particularly by laws governing obscenity and defamation, but the thrust of First Amendment law, especially in this century, prevents the government from imposing "prior restraint" on publications.

Like the railroad networks, the telephone networks follow common-carrier principles—they do not impose content restrictions on the "cargo" they carry. It would be unthinkable for the telephone company to monitor our calls routinely or cut off conversations because the subject matter was deemed offensive.

Meanwhile the highly regulated broadcast media are grounded in the idea, arguably mistaken, that spectrum scarcity and the pervasiveness of the broadcast media warrant government allocation and control of access to broadcast frequencies (and some control of content). Access to this technology is open to any consumer who can purchase a radio or television set, but it is nowhere near as open for information producers.

Networks as they now operate contain elements of publishers, broadcasters, bookstores and telephones, but no one model fits. This hybrid demands new thinking or at least a new application of the old legal principles. As hybrids, computer networks also have some features that are unique among the communications media. For example, most conversations on bulletin boards, chat lines and conferencing systems are both public and private at once. The electronic communicator speaks to a group of individuals, only some of whom are known personally, in a discussion that may last for days or months.

But the dissemination is controlled, because the membership is limited to the handful of people who are in the virtual room, paying attention. Yet the result may also be "published"—an archival textual or voice record can be automatically preserved, and newcomers can read the backlog. Some people tend to equate on-line discussions with party (or party-line) conversations, whereas others compare them to newspapers and still others think of citizens band radio.

In this ambiguous context, free-speech controversies are likely to erupt. Last year an outcry went up against the popular Prodigy computer service, a joint venture of IBM and Sears, Roebuck and Co. The problem arose because Prodigy management regarded their service as essentially a "newspaper" or "magazine," for which a hierarchy of editorial control is appropriate. Some of Prodigy's customers, in contrast, regarded the service as more of a forum or meeting place.

When users of the system tried to protest Prodigy's policy, its editors responded by removing the discussion. When the protestors tried to use electronic mail as a substitute for electronic assembly, communicating through large mailing lists, Prodigy placed a limit on the number of messages each individual could send.

The Prodigy controversy illustrates an important principle that belongs on any civil liberties agenda for the future: freedom-of-speech issues will not disappear simply because a service provider has tried to impose a metaphor on its service. Subscribers sense, I believe, that freedom of speech on the networks is central for individuals to use electronic communications. Science fiction writer William Gibson once remarked that "the street finds its own uses for things." Network service providers will continue to discover that their customers will always find their own best uses for new media.

Freedom of speech on networks will be promoted by limiting content-based regulations and by promoting competition among providers of network services. The first is necessary because governments will be tempted to restrict the content of any information service they subsidize or regulate. The second is necessary because market competition is the most efficient means of ensuring that needs of network users will be met.

The underlying network should essentially be a "carrier"—it should operate under a content-neutral regime in which access is available to any entity that can pay for it. The information and forum services would be "nodes" on this network. (Prodigy, like GEnie and CompuServe, currently maintains its own proprietary infrastructure, but a future version of Prodigy might share the same network with services like CompuServe.)

Each service would have its own unique character and charge its own rates. If a Prodigy-like entity correctly perceives a need for an electronic "newspaper" with strong editorial control, it will draw an audience. Other, less hierarchical services will share the network with that "newspaper" yet find their own market niches, varying by format and content.

The prerequisite for this kind of competition is a carrier capable of high-bandwidth traffic that is accessible to individuals in every community. Like common carriers, these network carriers should be seen as conduits for the distribution of electronic transmissions. They should not be allowed to change the content of a message or to discriminate among messages.

This kind of restriction will require shielding the carriers from legal liabilities for libel, obscenity and plagiarism. Today the ambiguous state of liability law has tempted some computer network carriers to reduce their risk by imposing content restrictions. This could be avoided by appropriate legislation. Our agenda requires both that the law shield carriers from liability based on content and that carriers not be allowed to discriminate.

All electronic "publishers" should be allowed equal access to networks. Ultimately, there could be hundreds of thousands of these information providers, as there are hundreds of thousands of print publishers today. As "nodes," they will be considered the conveners of the environments within which on-line assembly takes place.

None of the old definitions will suffice for this role. For example, to safeguard the potential of free and open inquiry, it is desirable to preserve each electronic publisher's control over the general flow and direction of material under his or her imprimatur—in effect, to give the "sysop," or system operator, the prerogatives and protections of a publisher.

But it is unreasonable to expect the sysop of a node to review every message or to hold the sysop to a publisher's standard of libel. Message traffic on many individually owned services is already too great for the sysop to review. We can only expect the trend to grow. Nor is it appropriate to compare nodes to broadcasters (an analogy likely to lead to licensing and content-based regulation). Unlike the broadcast media, nodes do not dominate the shared resource of a public community, and they are not a pervasive medium. To take part in a controversial discussion, a user must actively seek entry into the appropriate node, usually with a subscription and a password.

Anyone who objects to the content of a node can find hundreds of other systems where they might articulate their ideas more freely. The danger is if choice is somehow restricted: if all computer networks in the country are restrained from allowing discussion on particular subjects or if a publicly sponsored computer network limits discussion.

This is not to say that freedom-of-speech principles ought to protect all electronic communications. Exceptional cases, such as the BBS used primarily to traffic in stolen long-distance access codes or credit-card numbers, will always arise and pose problems of civil and criminal liability. We know that electronic freedom of speech, whether in public or private systems, cannot be absolute. In face-to-face conversation and printed matter today, it is commonly agreed that freedom of speech does not cover the communications inherent in criminal conspiracy, fraud, libel, incitement to lawless action and copyright infringement.

If there are to be limits on electronic freedom of speech, what precisely should those limits be? One answer to this question is the U.S. Supreme Court's 1969 decision in *Brandenburg v. Ohio.* The court ruled that no speech should be subject to prior restraint or criminal prosecution unless it is intended to incite and is likely to cause imminent lawless action.

In general, little speech or publication falls outside of the protections of the Brandenburg case, since most people are able to reflect before acting on a written or spoken suggestion. As in traditional media, any on-line messages should not be the basis of criminal prosecution unless the Brandenburg standard is met.

Other helpful precedents include cases relating to defamation and copyright infringement. Free speech does not mean one can damage a reputation or appropriate a copyrighted work without being called to account for it. And it probably does not mean that one can release a virus across the network in order to "send a message" to network subscribers. Although the distinction is trickier than it may first appear, the release of a destructive program, such as a virus, may be better analyzed as an act rather than as speech.

Following freedom of speech on our action agenda is freedom from unreasonable searches and seizures. The Steve Jackson case was one of many cases in which computer equipment and disks were seized and held—sometimes for months—often without a specific charge being filed. Even when only a few files were relevant to an investigation, entire computer systems, including printers, have been removed with their hundreds of files intact.

Such nonspecific seizures and searches of computer data allow "rummaging," in which officials browse through private files in search of incriminating evidence. In addition to violating the Fourth Amendment requirement that searches and seizures be "particular," these searches often run afoul of the Electronic Communications Privacy Act of 1986. This act prohibits the government from seizing or intercepting electronic communications without proper authorization. They also contravene the Privacy Protection Act of 1980, which prohibits the government from searching the offices of publishers for documents, including materials that are electronically stored.

> **Implementing a civil liberties agenda for computer networks will require participation by technically trained people.**

We can expect that law enforcement agencies and civil libertarians will agree over time about the need to establish procedures for searches and seizures of "particular" computer data and hardware. Law enforcement officials will have to adhere to guidelines in the above statutes to achieve Fourth Amendment "particularity" while maximizing the efficiency of their searches. They also will have to be trained to make use of software tools that allow searches for particular files or particular information within files on even the most capacious hard disk or optical storage device.

Still another part of the solution will be law enforcement's abandonment of the myth of the clever criminal hobbyist. Once law enforcement no longer assumes worst-case behavior but looks instead for real evidence of criminal activity, its agents will learn to search and seize only what they need.

Developing and implementing a civil liberties agenda for computer networks will require increasing participation by technically trained people. Fortunately, there are signs that this is beginning to happen. The Computers, Freedom and Privacy Conference, held last spring in San Francisco, along with electronic conferences on the WELL (Whole Earth 'Lectronic Link) and other computer networks, have brought law enforcement officials, supposed hackers and interested members of the computer community together in a spirit of free and frank discussion. Such gatherings are beginning to work out the civil liberties guidelines for a networked society.

There is general agreement, for example, that a policy on electronic crime should offer protection for security and privacy on both individual and institutional systems. Defining a measure of damages and setting proportional punishment will require further good-faith deliberations by the community involved with electronic freedoms, including the Federal Bureau of Investigation, the Secret Service, the bar associations, technology groups, telephone companies and civil libertarians. It will be especially important to represent the damage caused by electronic crime accurately and to leave room for the valuable side of the hacker spirit: the interest in increasing legitimate understanding through exploration.

We hope to see a similar emerging consensus on security issues. Network systems should be designed not only to provide technical solutions to security problems but also to allow system operators to use them without infringing unduly on the rights of users. A security system that depends on wholesale monitoring of traffic, for example, would create more problems than it would solve.

Those parts of a system where damage would do the greatest harm—financial records, electronic mail, military data—should be protected. This involves installing more effective computer security measures, but it also means redefining the legal interpretations of copyright, intellectual property, computer crime and privacy so that system users are protected against individual criminals and abuses by large institutions. These policies should balance the need for civil liberties against the need for a secure, orderly, protected electronic society.

As we pursue that balance, of course, confrontations will continue to take place. In May of this year, Steve Jackson Games, with the support of the EFF, filed suit against the Secret Service, two individual Secret Service agents, an assistant U.S. attorney and others.

The EFF is not seeking confrontation for its own sake. One of the realities of our legal system is that one often has to fight for a legal or constitutional right in the courts in order to get it recognized outside the courts. One goal of the lawsuit is to establish clear grounds under which search and seizure of electronic media is "unreasonable" and unjust. Another is to establish the clear applicability of First Amendment principles to the new medium.

But the EFF's agenda extends far beyond litigation. Our larger agenda includes sponsoring a range of educational initiatives aimed at the public's general lack of familiarity with the technology and its potential. That is why there is an urgent need for technologically knowledgeable people to take part in the public debate over communications policy and to help spread their understanding of these issues. Fortunately, the very technology at stake—electronic conferencing—makes it easier than ever before to get involved in the debate.

THINKING AND RE-READING

1. As you re-read this article, think about the people in this country who don't have access to computers. Who are they? Where are they? Why might they not have access? What does the split between the technological haves and have-nots mean for our culture? Our society? Our future? Why does such a situation exist? Kapor claims that the creation of a strong civil liberties agenda for cyberspace will require the involvement and input of citizens and specialists in communication, law, and computers. As you read, think about who might be included in these groups and who might be left out.

2. Kapor refers to two different approaches to civil liberties on the Internet: one approach is held by official law enforcement agencies, such as the U.S. Secret Service, and some corporate managers, such as the owners of Prodigy; the other approach is espoused by members of the Electronic Frontier Foundation, many net users, and game players. As you re-read, try to sketch out the positions, key points, and motivations of these two approaches.

WRITING AND LEARNING

1. Kapor claims that the first step in making a reasonable set of laws for cyberspace involves articulating the "kinds of values we want to see protected in the electronic society we are now shaping." Think of your own campus or class computing environment; make a list of the values that you think should influence the environment you choose. In an editorial suitable for publication in your school newspaper, list and describe these principles.

2. Make an appointment to interview a systems administrator (a sysop)—someone who administers a major computer network at the central campus computing office, in an academic department, or in the library. Interview this person regarding the rights and responsibilities that systems administrators have for accessing private files on the computer systems for which they are responsible. Find out about their concerns in connection with security, privacy, and liability. In writing, summarize the questions and answers addressed in this interview. Your purpose in this assignment is to inform your classmates about the insights you have gathered pertaining to privacy issues.

3. Go to the library and look up several references that describe the work of the Electronic Frontier Foundation (EFF) and the work that it does. To inform students who are not familiar with the EFF, write a relatively brief summary of your findings—no more than two pages. (Be sure to check your grammar handbook to find out the correct citation format for paraphrasing, quoting, and summarizing.)

4. It is obvious that though many people do use computers around the world, there are also many who do not. To increase your own understanding regarding this situation, make a list of the characteristics or conditions that keep people from using computers and the Internet.

Common Law for the Electronic Frontier

Anne W. Branscomb

IF YOU HAVE EVER CONSIDERED studying to become an attorney, you might want to think about practicing communications law, especially as it applies to the new electronic environments. According to Anne Branscomb, there should be enough work in this field to keep the legal profession busy for some time to come. Branscomb notes, "As networks become less the toys of the console cowboys and more ubiquitous in the daily lives of ordinary computer users, a new breed of lawyers is trying to adapt existing laws to the electronic frontier." But "lawmaking is a complicated process," especially in the unsettled environment of cyberspace, and anyone thinking of going into this field had better be prepared for a creative set of career challenges.

This contribution touches on many of the same issues that we have covered in other selections; among the topics mentioned are privacy rights, freedom of speech, protection from broad powers of search and seizure, and censorship. Similar to many of the articles in this collection, this particular piece might be described as journalistic in its approach but substantive in its treatment of technology issues for an informed and serious readership. Branscomb published this piece in *Scientific American* in September 1991, for a special issue devoted to an exploration of "Communications, Computers, and Networks."

"Cyberspace," says John P. Barlow, computer activist and co-founder of the Electronic Frontier Foundation, "remains a frontier region, across which roam the few aboriginal technologists and cyberpunks who can tolerate the austerity of its savage computer interfaces, incompatible communications protocols, proprietary barricades, cultural and legal ambiguities, and general lack of useful maps or metaphors."

It looks much the same to the legal profession. As networks become less the toys of the console cowboys and more ubiquitous in the daily lives of ordinary computer users, a new breed of lawyers is trying to adapt existing laws to the electronic frontier.

The behavior of computer users in cyberspace, a term for electronic space coined by science fiction writer William Gibson, confounds the carefully honed skills of lawyers to make sense of the morass of new uses of information technology. The electronic environment of computer networks is marked by versatility, complexity, diversity and extraterritoriality. All these characteristics pose challenges to the laws that govern generating, organizing, transmitting and archiving information.

Today the exchange of information in a network can defy efforts to stop distribution by the very speed with which the deed is accomplished via satellites and optical fibers. In 1988 it took only a matter of hours for the Worm, a rogue computer program, designed by Cornell University graduate student Robert T. Morris, Jr., to circulate through and disable the Internet, the network used by scientists.

The ease with which electronic impulses can be manipulated, modified and erased is hostile to a deliberate legal system that arose in an era of tangible things and relies on documentary evidence to validate transactions, incriminate miscreants and affirm contractual relations. What have been traditionally known as letters, journals, photographs, conversations, videotapes, audiotapes and books merge into a single stream of undifferentiated electronic impulses.

The complex environment and fluid messages make it difficult to determine which version of a document or electronic envelope is the draft or review or "published" copy. The diversity of inputs and outputs also makes it difficult to determine who is author, publisher, republisher, reader or archivist.

Under the 1976 revision of the Copyright Law, one must assume that any original work is protected by an unpublished copyright until published. Consequently, when precisely a work is published and under what proviso it is released are matters of considerable legal interest. Is the electronic record a copyrightable "writing"? If so, by an individual or a group? Suppose some members wish to extract portions of the conversation and transmit them to others. Would that constitute fair use or misuse?

Thus, the information industry, which has thrived on a convenient arrangement between vested interests of authors, publishers and libraries, is now confronting a different economic environment. Computer users have greater freedom to reach out and draw from a digital environment chunks of data in different forms. It is difficult to sort out who is entitled to compensation or royalties from which use of data. Moreover, when a distributed network has multiple participants, it will be more complicated to determine who is entitled to claim recompense for value added.

Lawyers, for whom legal jurisdiction involves the statutory reach of persons residing within certain boundaries, are further confounded by the extraterritoriality (or nonterritoriality) of cyberspace. Electronic communities abound as nodes tied together in a network, be they independent computer bulletin boards or information network providers such as CompuServe, Prodigy Services Company or the Electronic Information Exchange System (EIES).

The earliest global networks, such as the Society for Worldwide Interbank Financial Telecommunication (SWIFT), a system that transfers funds electronically, operate under very stringent rules to which member banks subscribe when entering the system. University network services are scurrying to set up their own codes of conduct in the aftermath of the Internet Worm. How these codes of conduct will mesh with local, state and national laws will prove challenging.

A dialogue held on the Whole Earth 'Lectronic Link (WELL), a computer network operated out of Marin County, Calif., by Stewart Brand of *Whole Earth Catalog* fame, suggests that "computer crackers" will push the outer limits of network security as long as any barrier exists to the free flow of information. A recent revolt of Prodigy subscribers protesting censorship of electronic messages indicates that users want more voice in determining the rules under which they will participate.

Yet what information should be free? Weather forecasts, perhaps news of impending disasters, epidemics, pests, volcanic eruptions? It is inconceivable that we should contemplate a society in which everybody must pay a meter to learn that a hurricane is on the way. But as more and more information is provided by the private rather than the public sector, the line between what is public and what is private blurs.

Moreover, the demarcation between public and private seems to change constantly. What was yesterday freely obtainable (network sporting events) comes today on a pay-as-you-go basis (on cable channels). Indeed, one obstacle to networked videotex services has been a reluctance of consumers to pay for information in electronic form when it is available in printed form at lower cost.

The privatization and commercialization of information do not sit well with computer hackers, who look on computer networks as an open, sharing society in which the skilled contribute to the welfare of the cooperative. Yet, like pioneers on the Western frontier, they are confronted by those who wish to fence in their private domains.

Many computer professionals, for example, have objected to the proprietary control of user interfaces, which programmers need to design compatible and sometimes competitive products. One such group, known as the nuPrometheus League (for the Titan who stole fire from the gods and gave it to humankind), distributed some of the source code of Apple Computer's Macintosh to a variety of computer professionals.

The distribution was apparently a protest against aggressive litigation Apple had instigated against Hewlett-Packard Company and Microsoft Corporation. Apple claimed copyright infringement of its source code on the grounds that software sold by the defending companies appropriated the "look and feel" of its user interface.

The letter accompanying the distribution of the source code was signed "nuPrometheus League (Software Artists for Information Dissemination)" and stated: "Our objective at Apple is to distribute everything that prevents other manufacturers from creating legal copies of Macintosh. As an organization, the nuPrometheus League has no ambition beyond seeing the genius of a few Apple employees benefit the entire world, not just dissipated by Apple through litigation and ill will."

Apple management, which had once encouraged the sharing of software on floppy disks to encourage the use of its computers, promised to prosecute "to the full extent of the law." It declared that those in possession of the code were recipients of stolen property and could be prosecuted under federal laws that prohibit mailing stolen property across state lines.

But U.S. law also has traditionally recognized that much information is freely available for all the world to take and develop as a shared resource. Indeed, the recent Supreme Court decision of *Feist Publications v. Rural Telephone Service Company* confirms that the concept of shared information is alive and well.

In this case, an independent telephone company refused to license the use of its telephone directory to Feist Publications, which packaged wider-area directories. So Feist extracted the numbers, claiming they were facts that were not susceptible to copyright protection.

The Supreme Court agreed, putting to rest the labored efforts of a long line of lower courts that attempted to craft a "sweat of the brow" theory to cover the substantial investment made by data base providers in gathering, processing, packaging and marketing their information products.

The application of intellectual property concepts to data bases may become more complex as a result of the Feist decision. Under the copyright rubric, only original expression may be copyrighted, not facts or ideas. Computers can scan pages of data, and, presumably, as long as they do not copy the exact organization or presentation or the software programs used to sort the information, they may not be infringing the copyright of the "compilation," the legal hook on which data bases now hang their protective hats.

Unless Congress or the states clarify what in a data base can be protected, information providers will have to continue to rely largely on contracts with their users. It is not entirely clear, however, whether a contract that appears momentarily on the screen prior to use is valid if the user has had no opportunity to negotiate the terms. Surely, information will not be shared with competitors unless some quid pro quo is offered or some eleemosynary motive is apparent. Giving away the fruits of intellectual labor without fair and equitable compensation is a policy not destined to survive the rigors of a marketplace economy.

At the other end of the spectrum of the debate over public and private information are the protesters who would like to control the distribution of personal information about themselves. As more computer networks come on line, more users are becoming aware that personal data are being gathered and correlated for someone else's purposes. The regulation of transaction-generated information, such as the records from telephone calls or credit card purchases, is a legal nightmare waiting to happen.

> **The ease with which electronic impulses can be manipulated, modified and erased is hostile to a deliberate legal system.**

This issue caught the public interest through the controversy over caller I.D., or automated number identification, which allows holders of "800" numbers—or anyone subscribing to the service—to read a caller's number from a video terminal. This feature permits marketers to greet callers by their first names but, more important, to correlate their names and addresses with purchasing habits.

In fact, the telephone number is fast becoming at least as important an identifier as the social security card or the driver's license number (which is one and the same in many states). Transaction-generated information can be mixed and matched with census data, postal codes and such other publicly available information as automobile and boat registrations, birth registrations and death certificates.

This information, which has long been available to small marketers at a prohibitive cost from such large corporate information gatherers as Equifax Marketing Decision Systems, can provide precise profiles of potential buyers. But when Equifax joined forces with Lotus Development Corporation to offer an inexpensive product called Lotus Marketplace, a set of optical disks containing data on 80 million households and more than 120 million individuals, 30,000 people wrote in to have their names removed from the data base.

Yet that data base is typical of the type of information that is available when credit cards or any electronically readable media are used to make a purchase. K-Mart Corporation, Sears, Roebuck and Co. and J. L. Hudson Company collect point-of-sale data from credit card customers and either reward frequent buyers or appeal to their tastes and buying habits. One of the most aggressive of the new "relationship marketers" is Quaker Oats, which has a data base of 35 million households to whom it sends discount coupons and tracks their redemption. Citicorp has been experimenting with a data base of two million consenting customers who shop at supermarket chains across the country.

Clearly, the uproar over Lotus Marketplace, which caused it to be canceled, indicates that citizens are becoming apprehensive about the information about them that is being collected and correlated. Yet digital data are almost totally unregulated because they do not neatly fit into any of the legal boxes we have developed over the past 100 years. Traditionally the established laws governing communications apply specifically to mail, newspaper, cable television and radio broadcasting, in their separate legal pigeonholes. Signals in a digital environment do not differentiate among voice, video and data.

Already the lines between cable and broadcasting are becoming indistinct, as are the lines between what constitutes a common carrier (the telephone network) and a content provider (newspapers, journals and books). The common carriers, such as Bell operating companies, are petitioning to become information providers as a quid pro quo for installing optical fiber to the home that will facilitate the fully digital and networked environment of the future.

Ironically, the telephone companies are being besieged by demands to exercise control over the obscenity and pornography offered on the "900" paid-access calls, as anxious parents deplore salacious conversations as well as excessive charges on their telephone bills. But in late 1990, when Prodigy, an on-line service owned by IBM and Sears, admitted to controlling the content of messages posted on electronic bulletin boards, it met with just the opposite reaction from users.

Prodigy was accused of censorship for curtailing an on-line discussion critical of its rates and for discontinuing several controversial computer conferences involving sexual preferences. The public debate blossomed into a full-fledged airing of the nature of open discussion on electronic media.

Prodigy contended that it had the right to screen public messages posted on bulletin boards and conferences, on the basis that it was similar to the Walt Disney Productions cable channel, a family service. Many users disagreed. They likened the electronic forums in which they participated to the coffeehouses of Paris or a street corner or a private gathering in one of their homes.

Indeed, electronic bulletin boards (many operated by individuals who allow access only to their friends) have grown up in an atmosphere of open, uninhibited discussion. The WELL, for example, operates under the assumption that each person owns and is responsible for whatever he or she says.

Whether the law will recognize such individual responsibility and control in electronic media remains to be seen. Nor is it certain that the law will absolve the network provider from liability for messages it allowed to be "published" or distributed. Indeed, there is considerable danger that the law will attempt to cover all electronic media under the same rubric without recognizing the vast diversity of networks—and diverse forms of communication within the same service—that are currently developing, some with unique cultures.

Law enforcement agents are stepping up the efforts to arrest computer hackers, a term that has come to mean unscrupulous youngsters who wreak havoc with computer systems. In February 1990 members of a hacker group called the Legion of Doom were arrested and charged with breaking into the computers of BellSouth. Three of the targets later pleaded guilty to stealing a BellSouth text file for its 911 emergency telephone system.

Then, in May 1990, a two-year Secret Service operation called Sundevil culminated in 27 simultaneous searches in which 40 computer systems were seized. One indictment for publishing the information was dropped because the defendant's lawyer convinced the authorities that the material was already published. Others are still awaiting indictment without the return of equipment that was seized.

Sundevil precipitated an outcry from computer professionals that constitutional rights were being trampled on, and the Electronic Frontier Foundation, devoted to protecting those rights, was established. The incident itself, however, is indicative of the confusion surrounding legal concepts that have survived the test of time in the noncomputer world but may not stand up to scrutiny in the electronic context.

Property has traditionally been something that can be transferred from place to place or person to person. Theft is defined as "depriving the owner of the use thereof." In an electronic environment, although a piece of software or a component of a data base may be valuable, the intruder who accesses it without authorization is not depriving the owners or authorized users of its use, unless the data are maliciously destroyed or distorted.

Some forms of miscreant behavior, such as introducing a message bearing a virus into a network, may not be destructive. Still, they may clog the computer's memory, denying authorized users access to their data. Any unauthorized entry alarms network managers because they fear some undesirable and deleterious consequence.

> Cyberspace is a frontier where territorial rights are being established and electronic environments are being differentiated.

A "hacker" law recently enacted in the U.K. makes unauthorized entry punishable as a misdemeanor and entry with malicious intent a felony. In the U.S., several states have passed special legislation to expand their computer crime laws to cover the insertion of viruses and other rogue programs into software or network systems.

Proposed federal legislation would expand the Computer Fraud and Abuse Act of 1986 to cover "reckless disregard" for the consequences in addition to specific intent to cause damage or harm. There is also a move to enlarge the definition of venue. Such legislation would make it possible to try an alleged perpetrator in any state through which, from which or into which some part of the transmission is found to have occurred.

Another potential legal issue surrounds the ability of computers to alter and distort data and images. With computerized capability to cut and paste images, what you see may not be what actually took place. An incident that occurred in the weeks just before the election of November 6, 1990, in Massachusetts may be a harbinger of more widespread controversies. A popular Boston television journalist, Natalie Jacobson, interviewed the two contenders in the gubernatorial race. Both candidates, John Silber and William Weld, were filmed in their homes to let the viewers see the intimate sides of their characters and family lives.

During the interview, however, Silber berated the audience for denigrating those women who, like one of his daughters (as well as his wife), chose to dedicate their lives to the care of husband, home and children. The implication of his comments was that working mothers who left children in day care were selfish and uncaring.

The outburst so ruffled working women, a large voting bloc, that the Weld campaign incorporated this segment into a political advertisement. The image of Silber, however, was enlarged and slightly distorted, so that he appeared more menacing than in the original shot. In addition, taking the conversation out of context made his words sound more threatening. The ad was widely criticized, and the Silber campaign took immediate action to have it withdrawn.

lies being spread about someone through media "liable"

The incident raises interesting political as well as legal issues about the ease with which voice, data and images can be downloaded and manipulated almost instantaneously for retransmission. Should a temporary restraining order have been available to prevent television stations from broadcasting the spot or would that have constituted prior restraint? Should Silber have a case against Weld for libel or slander? If so, what is the appropriate penalty, recompense or sanction?

On the other hand, should the television station have a right of action against the Weld campaign or other broadcasters for copyright infringement for carrying an excerpt from a copyrighted newsmagazine? Should the television correspondent have a right of action against Weld for distorting the image or changing its context? Was the copying and rebroadcast of the segment a "fair use" of her work product?

Still other relatively unexplored legal territory surrounds the way companies conduct business over networks. A recent California case, *Revlon v. Logisticon, Inc.*, was the computer-age equivalent of shutting off the phones for nonpayment. On October 16, 1990, Logisticon, a software firm, brought the operations of Revlon, the cosmetics firm, to a dead halt by remotely disabling the software that managed the distribution of products from warehouse to retail stores. Logisticon justified the *curtailment* of service because Revlon had refused to make the next scheduled payment under its contract.

Logisticon's action, which was characterized by a Revlon vice president as "commercial terrorism," resulted in a loss of three days of activity at Revlon's main distribution centers. Revlon raced to court, accusing Logisticon of extortion, breach of contract and trespass, among other complaints. Logisticon claimed a right to disable the software because Revlon had refused to honor the next payment.

The legal issues are myriad. Who "owned" the software installed within the Revlon business offices? Was the agreement a "purchase" of software or a "license" to use software? And does it make a difference? Did Logisticon act improperly by disengaging its software so precipitously, or was it acting within its legal rights in disabling the use of its proprietary product? Should it have disclosed to Revlon the existence of the remote capability to disable the software?

Even more important than the substance of the legal issues that will arise from data networks is the question of what group will determine which laws or operating rules shall apply. Nowhere is this more clear than in the emergence of computer bulletin boards such as the WELL.

Without question, computer bulletin boards are an electronic hybrid, parts of which may be looked on either as public or private, depending on the desires of the participants. These are *analogous* to mail, conversations, journals, chitchat or meetings. Under normal circumstances, this electronic environment might be considered more like a street corner where one is entitled to make informal remarks to one's intimate friends.

But many bulletin boards are accessed by users intent on "publication" for the record— scientists pursuing common interests in a research project, for instance. The cooperative writing may therefore have substantial historical, political or scientific value as a publishable research paper or journal article or treatise or textbook.

A community is usually governed by its duly enacted laws, which represent the ethical values of the group. But what if the computer conference or electronic bulletin board crosses the borders of two or more states or nations? In that case, more than one legal system may apply with rules that differ within the separate legal dominions. Should the community's laws be those of the geographic or the electronic *locus*? If the latter, how should the laws be promulgated?

Who should administer them? What sanctions should enforce them? What institutions are responsible for resolving disputes in the global information marketplace?

Cyberspace is a frontier where territorial rights are being established and electronic environments are being differentiated in much the way the Western frontier was pushed back by voyageurs, pioneers, miners and cattlemen. And the entrepreneurs are arriving with their new institutions and information technology, in much the same way as the pony express and railroads pioneered communications networks during the 19th century.

Lawmaking is a complicated process that takes place in a larger universe than the confines of legislatures and courts. Many laws are never written. Many statutory laws are never enforced. Legal systems develop from community standards and consensual observance as well as from litigation and legislative determination. So, too, will the common law of cyberspace evolve as users express their concerns and seek consensual solutions to common problems.

THINKING AND RE-READING

1. In re-reading this article, note the stylistic presentations that Branscomb makes of the legal cases and the positions of the two sides within these cases. How does she portray the positions of each party? How does she discuss motivation and concern? In what way is this manner of presentation tied to Branscomb's career as an attorney? In what way does the law determine the manner in which Branscomb represents issues?

2. A number of authors in this section have pointed out the influences of commercialization in cyberspace. As you re-read this piece, try to identify the relationships between commercial interests and the conflicts that Branscomb describes. Trace the methods in which commercial interests generate and shape the issues that Branscomb mentions. Think also about the ways in which attorneys and the law are affected by commercial interests.

WRITING AND LEARNING

1. Write a response about the case of censorship on the Prodigy network. Do you think Prodigy should be allowed to censor e-mail messages (similar to the manner in which the Disney channel censors television content for its family channel)? Do you believe that freedom of speech is a right that should not be abridged other than under narrowly defined guidelines? Or do you believe in absolute freedom of speech in cyberspace? Explain your stance and your reasoning.

2. What kind of information do you think should be free on the Internet—available to all citizens who have access to technology—and what kind of information do you think needs to have some fee attached to it? Who should establish the free services you name, and who should fund them?

3. Write a response about the Lotus and Equifax case. Do you think that Equifax/Lotus should be allowed to gather and then sell marketing data concerning individual citizens (e.g., names, addresses, purchasing preferences) *without* their knowledge? Only *with* their knowledge? Or not at all? Explain and support your position.

4. Go to the library and look up several sources that describe the Equifax/Lotus case. Write a relatively brief summary of your findings—no more than two pages. (Be sure to check your grammar handbook to find out the correct citation format for paraphrasing, quoting, and summarizing.)

Burning Chrome

William Gibson

WILLIAM GIBSON, THE AUTHOR of *Neuromancer, Count Zero,* and *Mona Lisa Overdrive,* is a winner of both the Hugo and the Nebula awards for science fiction. During the 1980s and 1990s, Gibson has become increasingly respected for his ability to evoke a gritty, realistic vision of the future—one based on the continuing emergence of post-modern human values manifested in the chaos and beauty of the Matrix, the global collection of computer entities and systems that girds the world of the future. Gibson's stories of the future provide a compelling connect-the-dots picture for us—one that gives a dark and visionary glimpse of where our intimate marriage with technology, our faith in the scientific fix, and many of our resultant global challenges (e.g., overpopulation, the destruction of natural resources, and the toleration of poverty and starvation) are leading us. Gibson portrays "Big Science," fellow author Bruce Sterling notes, not as a "source of quaint Mr. Wizard marvels, but an omnipresent, all-permeating, definitive force. It is a sheet of mutating radiation pouring through a crowd, a jam-packed Global Bus roaring wildly up an exponential slope" (Preface, *Burning Chrome,* 1986, p. xi). The short story was first published by Omni publications in 1981 before being anthologized in 1986 in a collection of Gibson's short stories named *Burning Chrome* after the short story.

As you read this story, think about how humans are re-making their world with technology and what kind of world it is that they are shaping. Think about the roles that you play, and want to play, in this strange and fascinating project.

It was hot, the night we burned Chrome. Out in the malls and plazas, moths were batting themselves to death against the neon, but in Bobby's loft the only light came from a monitor screen and the green and red LEDs on the face of the matrix simulator. I knew every chip in Bobby's simulator by heart; it looked like your workaday Ono-Sendai VII, the "Cyberspace Seven," but I'd rebuilt it so many times that you'd have had a hard time finding a square millimeter of factory circuitry in all that silicon.

We waited side by side in front of the simulator console, watching the time display in the screen's lower left corner.

"Go for it," I said, when it was time, but Bobby was already there, leaning forward to drive the Russian program into its slot with the heel of his hand. He did it with the tight grace of a kid slamming change into an arcade game, sure of winning and ready to pull down a string of free games.

A silver tide of phosphenes boiled across my field of vision as the matrix began to unfold in my head, a 3-D chessboard, infinite and perfectly transparent. The Russian program seemed to lurch as we entered the grid. If anyone else had been jacked into that part of the matrix, he might have seen a surf of flickering shadow roll out of the little yellow pyramid that represented our computer. The program was a mimetic weapon, designed to absorb local color and present itself as a crash-priority override in whatever context it encountered.

"Congratulations," I heard Bobby say. "We just became an Eastern Seaboard Fission Authority inspection probe. . . ." That meant we were clearing fiberoptic lines with the cybernetic equivalent of a fire siren, but in the simulation matrix we seemed to rush straight for Chrome's data base. I couldn't see it yet, but I already knew those walls were waiting. Walls of shadow, walls of ice.

Chrome: her pretty childface smooth as steel, with eyes that would have been at home on the bottom of some deep Atlantic trench, cold gray eyes that lived under terrible pressure. They said she cooked her own cancers for people who crossed her, rococo custom variations that took years to kill you. They said a lot of things about Chrome, none of them at all reassuring.

So I blotted her out with a picture of Rikki. Rikki kneeling in a shaft of dusty sunlight that slanted into the loft through a grid of steel and glass: her faded camouflage fatigues, her translucent rose sandals, the good line of her bare back as she rummaged through a nylon gear bag. She looks up, and a half-blond curl falls to tickle her nose. Smiling, buttoning an old shirt of Bobby's, frayed khaki cotton drawn across her breasts.

She smiles.

"Son of a bitch," said Bobby, "we just told Chrome we're an IRS audit and three Supreme Court subpoenas. . . . Hang on to your ass, Jack. . . ."

So long, Rikki. Maybe now I see you never.

And dark, so dark, in the halls of Chrome's ice.

Bobby was a cowboy, and ice was the nature of his game, *ice* from ICE, Intrusion Countermeasures Electronics. The matrix is an abstract representation of the relationships between data systems. Legitimate programmers jack into their employers' sector of the matrix and find themselves surrounded by bright geometries representing the corporate data.

Bobby came in with a girl I hadn't seen before, and usually I feel a little funny if a stranger sees me working that way, with those leads clipped to the hard carbon studs that stick out of my stump. She came right over and looked at the magnified image on the screen, then saw the waldo moving under its vacuum-sealed dust cover. She didn't say anything, just watched. Right away I had a good feeling about her; it's like that sometimes.

"Automatic Jack, Rikki. My associate."

He laughed, put his arm around her waist, something in his tone letting me know that I'd be spending the night in a dingy room in a hotel.

"Hi," she said. Tall, nineteen or maybe twenty, and she definitely had the goods. With just those few freckles across the bridge of her nose, and eyes somewhere between dark amber and French coffee. Tight black jeans rolled to midcalf and a narrow plastic belt that matched the rose-colored sandals.

But now when I see her sometimes when I'm trying to sleep, I see her somewhere out on the edge of all this sprawl of cities and smoke, and it's like she's a hologram stuck behind my eyes, in a bright dress she must've worn once, when I knew her, something that doesn't quite reach her knees. Bare legs long and straight. Brown hair, streaked with blond, hoods her face, blown in a wind from somewhere, and I see her wave goodbye.

Bobby was making a show of rooting through a stack of audio cassettes. "I'm on my way, cowboy," I said, unclipping the waldo. She watched attentively as I put my arm back on.

"Can you fix things?" she asked.

"Anything, anything you want, Automatic Jack'll fix it." I snapped my Duralumin fingers for her.

She took a little simstim deck from her belt and showed me the broken hinge on the cassette cover.

"Tomorrow," I said, "no problem."

And my oh my, I said to myself, sleep pulling me down the six flights to the street, *what'll Bobby's luck be like with a fortune cookie like that? If his system worked, we'd be striking it rich any night now.* In the street I grinned and yawned and waved for a cab.

Chrome's castle is dissolving, sheets of ice shadow flickering and fading, eaten by the glitch systems that spin out from the Russian program, tumbling away from our central logic thrust and infecting the fabric of the ice itself. The glitch systems are cybernetic virus analogs, self-replicating and voracious. They mutate constantly, in unison, subverting and absorbing Chrome's defenses.

Have we already paralyzed her, or is a bell ringing somewhere, a red light blinking? Does she know?

Rikki Wildside, Bobby called her, and for those first few weeks it must have seemed to her that she had it all, the whole teeming show spread out for her, sharp and bright under the neon. She was new to the scene, and she had all the miles of malls and plazas to prowl, all the shops and clubs, and Bobby to explain the wild side, the tricky wiring on the dark underside of things, all the players and their names and their games. He made her feel at home.

"What happened to your arm?" she asked me one night in the Gentleman Loser, the three of us drinking at a small table in a corner.

"Hang-gliding," I said, "accident."

"Hang-gliding over a wheatfield," said Bobby, "place called Kiev. Our Jack's just hanging there in the dark, under a Nightwing parafoil, with fifty kilos of radar jammed between his legs, and some Russian asshole accidentally burns his arm off with a laser."

I don't remember how I changed the subject, but I did.

I was still telling myself that it wasn't Rikki who was getting to me, but what Bobby was doing with her. I'd known him for a long time, since the end of the war, and I knew he used women as counters in a game, Bobby Quine versus fortune, versus time and the night of cities. And Rikki had turned up just when he needed something to get him going, something to aim for. So he'd set her up as a symbol for everything he wanted and couldn't have, everything he'd had and couldn't keep.

I didn't like having to listen to him tell me how much he loved her, and knowing he believed it only made it worse. He was a past master at the hard fall and the rapid recovery, and I'd seen it happen a dozen times before. He might as well have had NEXT printed across his sunglasses in green Day-Glo capitals, ready to flash out at the first interesting face that flowed past the tables in the Gentleman Loser.

I knew what he did to them. He turned them into emblems, sigils on the map of his hustler's life, navigation beacons he could follow through a sea of bars and neon. What else did he have to steer by? He didn't love money, in and of itself, not enough to follow its lights. He wouldn't work for power over other people; he hated the responsibility it brings. He had some basic pride in his skill, but that was never enough to keep him pushing.

So he made do with women.

When Rikki showed up, he needed one in the worst way. He was fading fast, and smart money was already whispering that the edge was off his game. He needed that one big score, and soon, because he didn't know any other kind of life, and all his clocks were set for hustler's time, calibrated in risk and adrenaline and that supernal dawn calm that comes when every move's proved right and a sweet lump of someone else's credit clicks into your own account.

It was time for him to make his bundle and get out; so Rikki got set up higher and farther away than any of the others ever had, even though—and I felt like screaming it at him—she was right there, alive, totally real, human, hungry, resilient, bored, beautiful, excited, all the things she was. . . .

Then he went out one afternoon, about a week before I made the trip to New York to see Finn. Went out and left us there in the loft, waiting for a thunderstorm. Half the skylight was shadowed by a dome they'd never finished, and the other half showed sky, black and blue with clouds. I was standing by the bench, looking up at that sky, stupid with the hot afternoon, the humidity, and she touched me, touched my shoulder, the half-inch border of taut pink scar that the arm doesn't cover. Anybody else ever touched me there, they went on to the shoulder, the neck. . . .

But she didn't do that. Her nails were lacquered black, not pointed, but tapered oblongs, the lacquer only a shade darker than the carbon-fiber laminate that sheathes my arm. And her hand went down the arm, black nails tracing a weld in the laminate, down to the black anodized elbow joint, out to the wrist, her hand soft-knuckled as a child's, fingers spreading to lock over mine, her palm against the perforated Duralumin.

Her other palm came up to brush across the feedback pads, and it rained all afternoon, raindrops drumming on the steel and soot-stained glass above Bobby's bed.

Ice walls flick away like supersonic butterflies made of shade. Beyond them, the matrix's illusion of infinite space. It's like watching a tape of a prefab building going up; only the tape's reversed and run at high speed, and these walls are torn wings.

Trying to remind myself that this place and the gulfs beyond are only representations, that we aren't "in" Chrome's computer, but interfaced with it, while the matrix simulator in Bobby's loft generates this illusion. . . The core data begin to emerge, exposed, vulnerable. . . . This is the far side of ice, the view of the matrix I've never seen before, the view that fifteen million legitimate console operators see daily and take for granted.

The core data tower around us like vertical freight trains, color-coded for access. Bright primaries, impossibly bright in that transparent void, linked by countless horizontals in nursery blues and pinks.

But ice still shadows something at the center of it all: the heart of all Chrome's expensive darkness, the very heart . . .

It was late afternoon when I got back from my shopping expedition to New York. Not much sun through the skylight, but an ice pattern glowed on Bobby's monitor screen, a 2-D graphic representation of someone's computer defenses, lines of neon woven like an Art Deco prayer rug. I turned the console off, and the screen went completely dark.

Rikki's things were spread across my workbench, nylon bags spilling clothes and makeup, a pair of bright red cowboy boots, audio cassettes, glossy Japanese magazines about simstim stars. I stacked it all under the bench and then took my arm off, forgetting that the program I'd brought from the Finn was in the right-hand pocket of my jacket, so that I had to fumble it out left-handed and then get it into the padded jaws of the jeweler's vise.

The waldo looks like an old audio turntable, the kind that played disc records, with the vise set up under a transparent dust cover. The arm itself is just over a centimeter long, swinging out on what would've been the tone arm on one of those turntables. But I don't look at that when I've clipped the leads to my stump; I look at the scope, because that's my arm there in black and white, magnification 40 ×.

I ran a tool check and picked up the laser. It felt a little heavy; so I scaled my weight-sensor input down to a quarter-kilo per gram and got to work. At 40 × the side of the program looked like a trailer truck.

It took eight hours to crack: three hours with the waldo and the laser and four dozen taps, two hours on the phone to a contact in Colorado, and three hours to run down a lexicon disc that could translate eight-year-old technical Russian.

Then Cyrillic alphanumerics started reeling down the monitor, twisting themselves into English halfway down. There were a lot of gaps, where the lexicon ran up against specialized military acronyms in the readout I'd bought from my man in Colorado, but it did give me some idea of what I'd bought from the Finn.

I felt like a punk who'd gone out to buy a switchblade and come home with a small neutron bomb.

Screwed again, I thought. *What good's a neutron bomb in a streetfight?* The thing under the dust cover was right out of my league. I didn't even know where to unload it, where to look for a buyer. Someone had, but he was dead, someone with a Porsche watch and a fake Belgian passport, but I'd never tried to move in those circles. The Finn's muggers from the 'burbs had knocked over someone who had some highly arcane connections.

The program in the jeweler's vise was a Russian military icebreaker, a killer-virus program.

It was dawn when Bobby came in alone. I'd fallen asleep with a bag of takeout sandwiches in my lap.

"You want to eat?" I asked him, not really awake, holding out my sandwiches. I'd been dreaming of the program, of its waves of hungry glitch systems and mimetic subprograms; in the dream it was an animal of some kind, shapeless and flowing.

He brushed the bag aside on his way to the console, punched a function key. The screen lit with the intricate pattern I'd seen there that afternoon. I rubbed sleep from my eyes with my left hand, one thing I can't do with my right. I'd fallen asleep trying to decide whether to tell him about the program. Maybe I should try to sell it alone, keep the money, go somewhere new, ask Rikki to go with me.

"Whose is it?" I asked.

He stood there in a black cotton jump suit, an old leather jacket thrown over his shoulders like a cape. He hadn't shaved for a few days, and his face looked thinner than usual.

"It's Chrome's," he said.

My arm convulsed, started clicking, fear translated to the myoelectrics through the carbon studs. I spilled the sandwiches; limp sprouts, and bright yellow dairy-produce slices on the unswept wooden floor.

"You're stone crazy," I said.

"No," he said, "you think she rumbled it? No way. We'd be dead already. I locked on to her through a triple-blind rental system in Mombasa and an Algerian comsat. She knew somebody was having a look-see, but she couldn't trace it."

If Chrome had traced the pass Bobby had made at her ice, we were good as dead. But he was probably right, or she'd have had me blown away on my way back from New York. "Why her, Bobby? Just give me one reason. . . ."

Chrome: I'd seen her maybe half a dozen times in the Gentleman Loser. Maybe she was slumming, or checking out the human condition, a condition she didn't exactly aspire to. A sweet little heart-shaped face framing the nastiest pair of eyes you ever saw. She'd looked fourteen for as long as anyone could remember, hyped out of anything like a normal metabolism on some massive program of serums and hormones. She was as ugly a customer as the street ever produced, but she didn't belong to the street anymore. She was one of the Boys, Chrome, a member in good standing of the local Mob subsidiary. Word was, she'd gotten started as a dealer, back when synthetic pituitary hormones were still proscribed. But she hadn't had to move hormones for a long time. Now she owned the House of Blue Lights.

"You're flat-out crazy, Quine. You give me one sane reason for having that stuff on your screen. You ought to dump it, and I mean *now*. . . ."

"Talk in the Loser," he said, shrugging out of the leather jacket. "Black Myron and Crow Jane. Jane, she's up on all the sex lines, claims she knows where the money goes. So she's arguing with Myron that Chrome's the controlling interest in the Blue Lights, not just some figurehead for the Boys."

" 'The Boys,' Bobby," I said. "That's the operative word there. You still capable of seeing that? We don't mess with the Boys, remember? That's why we're still walking around."

"That's why we're still poor, partner." He settled back into the swivel chair in front of the console, unzipped his jump suit, and scratched his skinny white chest. "But maybe not for much longer."

"I think maybe this partnership just got itself permanently dissolved."

Then he grinned at me. The grin was truly crazy, feral and focused, and I knew that right then he really didn't give a shit about dying.

"Look," I said, "I've got some money left, you know? Why don't you take it and get the tube to Miami, catch a hopper to Montego Bay. You need a rest, man. You've got to get your act together."

"My act, Jack," he said, punching something on the keyboard, "never has been this together before." The neon prayer rug on the screen shivered and woke as an animation program cut in, ice lines weaving with hypnotic frequency, a living mandala. Bobby kept punching, and the movement slowed; the pattern resolved itself, grew slightly less complex, became an alternation between two distant configurations. A first-class piece of work, and I hadn't thought he was still that good. "Now," he said, "there, see it? Wait. There. There again. And there. Easy to miss. That's it. Cuts in every hour and twenty minutes with a squirt transmission to their comsat. We could live for a year on what she pays them weekly in negative interest."

"Whose comsat?"

"Zürich. Her bankers. That's her bankbook, Jack. That's where the money goes. Crow Jane was right."

I stood there. My arm forgot to click.

"So how'd you do in New York, partner? You get anything that'll help me cut ice? We're going to need whatever we can get."

I kept my eyes on his, forced myself not to look in the direction of the waldo, the jeweler's vise. The Russian program was there, under the dust cover.

Wild cards, luck changers.

"Where's Rikki?" I asked him, crossing to the console, pretending to study the alternating patterns on the screen.

"Friends of hers," he shrugged, "kids, they're all into simstim." He smiled absently. "I'm going to do it for her, man."

"I'm going out to think about this, Bobby. You want me to come back, you keep your hands off the board."

"I'm doing it for her," he said as the door closed behind me. "You know I am."

And down now, down, the program a roller coaster through this fraying maze of shadow walls, gray cathedral spaces between the bright towers. Headlong speed.

Black ice. Don't think about it. Black ice.

Too many stories in the Gentleman Loser; black ice is a part of the mythology. Ice that kills. Illegal, but then aren't we all? Some kind of neural-feedback weapon, and you connect with it only once. Like some hideous Word that eats the mind from the inside out. Like an epileptic spasm that goes on and on until there's nothing left at all. . .

And we're diving for the floor of Chrome's shadow castle.

Trying to brace myself for the sudden stopping of breath, a sickness and final slackening of the nerves. Fear of that cold Word waiting, down there in the dark.

I went out and looked for Rikki, found her in a café with a boy with Sendai eyes, half-healed suture lines radiating from his bruised sockets. She had a glossy brochure spread open on the table, Tally Isham smiling up from a dozen photographs, the Girl with the Zeiss Ikon Eyes.

Her little simstim deck was one of the things I'd stacked under my bench the night before, the one I'd fixed for her the day after I'd first seen her. She spent hours jacked into that unit, the contact band across her forehead like a gray plastic tiara. Tally Isham was her favorite, and with the contact band on, she was gone, off somewhere in the recorded sensorium of simstim's biggest star. Simulated stimuli: the world—all the interesting parts, anyway—as perceived by Tally Isham. Tally raced a black Fokker ground-effect plane across Arizona mesa tops. Tally dived the Truk Island preserves. Tally partied with the superrich on private Greek islands, heartbreaking purity of those tiny white seaports at dawn.

Actually she looked a lot like Tally, same coloring and cheekbones. I thought Rikki's mouth was stronger. More sass. She didn't want to *be* Tally Isham, but she coveted the job. That was her ambition, to be in simstim. Bobby just laughed it off. She talked to me about it, though. "How'd I look with a pair of these?" she'd ask, holding a full-page headshot, Tally Isham's blue Zeiss Ikons lined up with her own amber-brown. She'd had her corneas done twice, but she still wasn't 20-20; so she wanted Ikons. Brand of the stars. Very expensive.

"You still window-shopping for eyes?" I asked as I sat down.

"Tiger just got some," she said. She looked tired, I thought.

Tiger was so pleased with his Sendais that he couldn't help smiling, but I doubted whether he'd have smiled otherwise. He had the kind of uniform good looks you get after your seventh trip to the surgical boutique; he'd probably spend the rest of his life looking vaguely like each new season's media front-runner; not too obvious a copy, but nothing too original, either.

"Sendai, right?" I smiled back.

He nodded. I watched as he tried to take me in with his idea of a professional simstim glance. He was pretending that he was recording. I thought he spent too long on my arm. "They'll be great on peripherals when the muscles heal," he said, and I saw how carefully he reached for his double espresso. Sendai eyes are notorious for depth-perception defects and warranty hassles, among other things.

"Tiger's leaving for Hollywood tomorrow."

"Then maybe Chiba City, right?" I smiled at him. He didn't smile back. "Got an offer, Tiger? Know an agent?"

"Just checking it out," he said quietly. Then he got up and left. He said a quick goodbye to Rikki, but not to me.

"That kid's optic nerves may start to deteriorate inside six months. You know that, Rikki? Those Sendais are illegal in England, Denmark, lots of places. You can't replace nerves."

"Hey, Jack, no lectures." She stole one of my croissants and nibbled at the top of one of its horns.

"I thought I was your adviser, kid."

"Yeah. Well, Tiger's not too swift, but everybody knows about Sendais. They're all he can afford. So he's taking a chance. If he gets work, he can replace them."

"With these?" I tapped the Zeiss Ikon brochure. "Lot of money, Rikki. You know better than to take a gamble like that."

She nodded. "I want Ikons."

"If you're going up to Bobby's, tell him to sit tight until he hears from me."

"Sure. It's business?"

"Business," I said. But it was craziness.

I drank my coffee, and she ate both my croissants. Then I walked her down to Bobby's. I made fifteen calls, each one from a different pay phone.

Business. Bad craziness.

All in all, it took us six weeks to set the burn up, six weeks of Bobby telling me how much he loved her. I worked even harder, trying to get away from that.

Most of it was phone calls. My fifteen initial and very oblique inquiries each seemed to breed fifteen more. I was looking for a certain service Bobby and I both imagined as a requisite part of the world's clandestine economy, but which probably never had more than five customers at a time. It would be one that never advertised.

We were looking for the world's heaviest fence, for a non-aligned money laundry capable of dry-cleaning a megabuck online cash transfer and then forgetting about it.

All those calls were a waste, finally, because it was the Finn who put me on to what we needed. I'd gone up to New York to buy a new blackbox rig, because we were going broke paying for all those calls.

I put the problem to him as hypothetically as possible.

"Macao," he said.

"Macao?"

"The Long Hum family. Stockbrokers."

He even had the number. You want a fence, ask another fence.

The Long Hum people were so oblique that they made my idea of a subtle approach look like a tactical nuke-out. Bobby had to make two shuttle runs to Hong Kong to get the deal straight. We were running out of capital, and fast. I still don't know why I decided to go along with it in the first place; I was scared of Chrome, and I'd never been all that hot to get rich.

I tried telling myself that it was a good idea to burn the House of Blue Lights because the place was a creep joint, but I just couldn't buy it. I didn't like the Blue Lights, because I'd spent a supremely depressing evening there once, but that was no excuse for going after Chrome. Actually I halfway assumed we were going to die in the attempt. Even with that killer program, the odds weren't exactly in our favor.

Bobby was lost in writing the set of commands we were going to plug into the dead center of Chrome's computer. That was going to be my job, because Bobby was going to have his hands full trying to keep the Russian program from going straight for the kill. It was too complex for us to rewrite, and so he was going to try to hold it back for the two seconds I needed.

I made a deal with a streetfighter named Miles. He was going to follow Rikki the night of the burn, keep her in sight, and phone me at a certain time. If I wasn't there, or didn't answer in just a certain way, I'd told him to grab her and put her on the first tube out. I gave him an envelope to give her, money and a note.

Bobby really hadn't thought about that, much, how things would go for her if we blew it. He just kept telling me he loved her, where they were going to go together, how they'd spend the money.

"Buy her a pair of Ikons first, man. That's what she wants. She's serious about that simstim scene."

"Hey," he said, looking up from the keyboard, "she won't need to work. We're going to make it, Jack. She's my luck. She won't ever have to work again."

"Your luck," I said. I wasn't happy. I couldn't remember when I had been happy. "You seen your luck around lately?"

He hadn't, but neither had I. We'd both been too busy.

I missed her. Missing her reminded me of my one night in the House of Blue Lights, because I'd gone there out of missing someone else. I'd gotten drunk to begin with, then I'd started hitting Vasopressin inhalers. If your main squeeze has just decided to walk out on you, booze and Vasopressin are the ultimate in masochistic pharmacology; the juice makes you maudlin and the Vasopressin makes you remember, I mean really remember. Clinically they use the stuff to counter senile amnesia, but the street finds its own uses for things. So I'd bought myself an ultraintense replay of a bad affair; trouble is, you get the bad with the good. Go gunning for transports of animal ecstasy and you get what you said, too, and what she said to that, how she walked away and never looked back.

I don't remember deciding to go to the Blue Lights, or how I got there, hushed corridors and this really tacky decorative waterfall trickling somewhere, or maybe just a hologram of one. I had a lot of money that night; somebody had given Bobby a big roll for opening a three-second window in someone else's ice.

I don't think the crew on the door liked my looks, but I guess my money was okay.

I had more to drink there when I'd done what I went there for. Then I made some crack to the barman about closet necrophiliacs, and that didn't go down too well. Then this very large character insisted on calling me War Hero, which I didn't like. I think I showed him some tricks with the arm, before the lights went out, and I woke up two days later in a basic sleeping module somewhere else. A cheap place, not even room to hang yourself. And I sat there on that narrow foam slab and cried.

Some things are worse than being alone. But the thing they sell in the House of Blue Lights is so popular that it's almost legal.

At the heart of darkness, the still center, the glitch systems shred the dark with whirlwinds of light, translucent razors spinning away from us; we hang in the center of a silent slow-motion explosion, ice fragments falling away forever, and Bobby's voice comes in across light-years of electronic void illusion—

"Burn the bitch down. I can't hold the thing back—"

The Russian program, rising through towers of data, blotting out the playroom colors. And I plug Bobby's homemade command package into the center of Chrome's cold heart. The squirt transmission cuts in, a pulse of condensed information that shoots straight up, past the thickening tower of darkness, the Russian program, while Bobby struggles to control that crucial second. An unformed arm of shadow twitches from the towering dark, too late.

We've done it.

The matrix folds itself around me like an origami trick.

And the loft smells of sweat and burning circuitry.

I thought I heard Chrome scream, a raw metal sound, but I couldn't have.

Bobby was laughing, tears in his eyes. The elapsed-time figure in the corner of the monitor read 07:24:05. The burn had taken a little under eight minutes.

And I saw that the Russian program had melted in its slot.

We'd given the bulk of Chrome's Zürich account to a dozen world charities. There was too much there to move, and we knew we had to break her, burn her straight down, or she might come after us. We took less than ten percent for ourselves and shot it through the Long Hum setup in Macao. They took sixty percent of that for themselves and kicked what was left back to us through the most convoluted sector of the Hong Kong exchange. It took an hour before our money started to reach the two accounts we'd opened in Zürich.

I watched zeros pile up behind a meaningless figure on the monitor. I was rich.

Then the phone rang. It was Miles. I almost blew the code phrase.

"Hey, Jack, man, I dunno—what's it all about, with this girl of yours? Kinda funny thing here . . ."

"What? Tell me."

"I been on her, like you said, tight but out of sight. She goes to the Loser, hangs out, then she gets a tube. Goes to the House of Blue Lights—"

"She what?"

"Side door. *Employees* only. No way I could get past their security."

"Is she there now?"

"No, man, I just lost her. It's insane down here, like the Blue Lights just shut down, looks like for good, seven kinds of alarms going off, everybody running, the heat out in riot gear. . . . Now there's all this stuff going on, insurance guys, real-estate types, vans with municipal plates. . . ."

"Miles, where'd she go?"

"Lost her, Jack."

"Look, Miles, you keep the money in the envelope, right?"

"You serious? Hey, I'm real sorry. I—"

I hung up.

"Wait'll we tell her," Bobby was saying, rubbing a towel across his bare chest.

"You tell her yourself, cowboy. I'm going for a walk."

So I went out into the night and the neon and let the crowd pull me along, walking blind, willing myself to be just a segment of that mass organism, just one more drifting chip of consciousness under the geodesics. I didn't think, just put one foot in front of another, but after a while I did think, and it all made sense. She'd needed the money.

I thought about Chrome, too. That we'd killed her, murdered her, as surely as if we'd slit her throat. The night that carried me along through the malls and plazas would be hunting her now, and she had nowhere to go. How many enemies would she have in this crowd alone? How many would move, now they weren't held back by fear of her money? We'd taken her for everything she had. She was back on the street again. I doubted she'd live till dawn.

Finally I remembered the café, the one where I'd met Tiger.

Her sunglasses told the whole story, huge black shades with a telltale smudge of fleshtone paintstick in the corner of one lens. "Hi, Rikki," I said, and I was ready when she took them off.

Blue, Tally Isham blue. The clear trademark blue they're famous for, ZEISS IKON ringing each iris in tiny capitals, the letters suspended there like flecks of gold.

"They're beautiful," I said. Paintstick covered the bruising. No scars with work that good. "You made some money."

"Yeah, I did." Then she shivered. "But I won't make any more, not that way."

"I think that place is out of business."

"Oh." Nothing moved in her face then. The new blue eyes were still and very deep.

"It doesn't matter. Bobby's waiting for you. We just pulled down a big score."

"No. I've got to go. I guess he won't understand, but I've got to go."

I nodded, watching the arm swing up to take her hand; it didn't seem to be part of me at all, but she held on to it like it was.

"I've got a one-way ticket to Hollywood. Tiger knows some people I can stay with. Maybe I'll even get to Chiba City."

She was right about Bobby. I went back with her. He didn't understand. But she'd already served her purpose, for Bobby, and I wanted to tell her not to hurt for him, because I could see that she did. He wouldn't even come out into the hallway after she had packed her bags. I put the bags down and kissed her and messed up the paintstick, and something came up inside me the way the killer program had risen above Chrome's data. A sudden stopping of the breath, in a place where no word is. But she had a plane to catch.

Bobby was slumped in the swivel chair in front of his monitor, looking at his string of zeros. He had his shades on, and I knew he'd be in the Gentleman Loser by nightfall, checking out the weather, anxious for a sign, someone to tell him what his new life would be like. I couldn't see it being very different. More comfortable, but he'd always be waiting for the next card to fall.

I tried not to imagine her in the House of Blue Lights, working three-hour shifts in an approximation of REM sleep, while her body and a bundle of conditioned reflexes took care of business. The customers never got to complain that she was faking it, because those were real orgasms. But she felt them, if she felt them at all, as faint silver flares somewhere out on the edge of sleep. Yeah, it's so popular, it's almost legal. The customers are torn between needing someone and wanting to be alone at the same time, which has probably always been the name of that particular game, even before we had the neuroelectronics to enable them to have it both ways.

I picked up the phone and punched the number for her airline. I gave them her real name, her flight number. "She's changing that," I said, "to Chiba City. Thatright. Japan." I thumbed my credit card into the slot and punched my ID code. "First class." Distant hum as they scanned my credit records. "Make that a return ticket."

But I guess she cashed the return fare, or else didn't need it, because she hasn't come back. And sometimes late at night I'll pass a window with posters of simstim stars, all those beautiful, identical eyes staring back at me out of faces that are nearly as identical, and sometimes the eyes are hers, but none of the faces are, none of them ever are, and I see her far out on the edge of all this sprawl of night and cities, and then she waves goodbye.

THINKING AND RE-READING

1. Gibson frequently refers to the characters in his stories as "console cowboys." What similarities and differences does this story have with the traditional genre of Hollywood Westerns? Who is the hero and what characteristics does he have? What are the typical gender roles that women play? What is the plot? What is the conflict that this plot revolves around? Who wins the conflict and why? What is the relationship between the protagonist and his buddy?

2. As you re-read this story, consider what characterizes the relationships that human beings have established with technology in Gibson's story. What is Jack's relationship with his console? Rikki's relationship with her simstim deck or the Zeiss Ikons? Bobby's with the Matrix? Tiger's with his Sendais? Also consider the human relationships that Gibson portrays—Bobby's and Jack's partnership, Rikki's relationship with Bobby and Jack, or Tiger's relationship with Rikki. What do you think of these relationships? How do they compare with relationships you observe today?

WRITING AND LEARNING

1. In this story, Gibson predicts a number of events, situations, and occurrences. As a further exercise in prediction, for your own insight, make a list of those situations that you find most interesting or likely to happen. In writing, to clarify your reasoning, explain why you think each one is likely to come about.

2. Gibson uses a number of common and made-up words in this story that are not immediately familiar to readers in the context that he uses them (e.g., the grid, matrix, ice, cowboy, waldo, simstim). Using the context provided by the story, your own understanding of technology, and some informed guessing (based on the current meanings of these words), write a glossary for Gibson's story. Try to define at least twenty words. Write this glossary for other readers who are just becoming acquainted, through this work, with Gibson as an author.

3. Although the setting of "Burning Chrome" is certainly futuristic and jarringly unfamiliar, the success of the story rests on the credible and realistic nature of Gibson's

extrapolations—how he builds the future on the foundations of the present. In other words, many of the values, trends, and activities that Gibson portrays in the future can be observed in the present. Make a list of the trends, values, and activities that you see now—especially those associated with our increasingly technologically dependent society—that might well lead to the world that Gibson envisions. From this list, write a cautionary letter to the younger generation telling them what to watch out for and what courses of productive action you would urge them to take in order to avoid the bleak future that Gibson predicts.

EXTENDED WRITING ACTIVITIES

BUILDING ON WRITING AND LEARNING

SAC   Writing and learning activities that can be done on a stand-alone computer with access to word processing software

LAN   Writing and learning activities that can be done on local area network with access to synchronous or asynchronous conferencing software

WAN   Writing and learning activities that can be done on a wide-area network, like the Internet, with access to Netscape or Gopher software

ASSIGNMENT 1: IDENTIFYING AND ARTICULATING CLAIMS

1. Making a carefully constructed catalog of the claims and controversies that are related to a complex set of issues can sometimes help you see the issues more clearly. This assignment is designed to help you understand those issues associated with technology and the law.

   Re-read the pieces you have been assigned in this section. As you read, using a word-processing package on a stand-alone computer, compile a list of at least twenty *claims* that the authors make about computers, the NREN, or the Internet and their effect on our current laws concerning copyright, privacy, freedom of speech, search and seizure, and so on. By *claims*, we mean statements offered as informed opinions, which may or may not be facts. The following items are examples of claims from other sources:

Quoted Claim

- "Most online denizens consider the Net a social resource" (46).

   Roberts, Steven K. "Technomadness and the Internet." *Internet* 5.1 (1994): 44–51.

Paraphrased Claim

- Lear-Newman claims that many of the online manuals available on the Internet are written for users who have considerable experience with computers (61).

   Lear-Newman, Elizabeth. "How to Be a Supported User," *Internet* 5.1 (1994): 60–67.

Summarized Claim

- Computers—the machines themselves, their linear logic, and the warlike language associated with them—have grown out of a masculine culture that does not encourage the participation of women. Computer scientists interested in ameliorating this situation have encouraged explorations of non-linear models of mental processing in artificial intelligence work, more computer use and access by girls and women, and programming approaches that acknowledge multiple ways of making meaning (46).

Van Bergen, Marilyn. "Electronic Citizenship and Social Responsibility." *EDUCOM Review* 28.3 (1993): 45–47.

2. As you list these claims, make sure that you record the full bibliographical information you need for *each* of the claims you list. If you are unfamiliar with the term "full bibliographic information," consult your handbook. In fact, even if you think you know what this term means, read those pages carefully for review. If you are citing electronic material that is not covered in the regular handbook that your teacher has assigned, turn to the appendix on the bibliographic citation of electronic materials for additional information concerning citation and reference formats.

   Make sure that in your list of claims, you include some claims that you quote (as in the first bullet), some claims that you paraphrase (as in the second bullet), and some claims that you summarize (as in the third bullet). Make your list of claims as comprehensive as possible.

3. Meet with your writing group and exchange your lists of claims. Check for completeness—help each other by pointing out the claims that have been omitted or missed. Check for the correctness of citation forms as well (quoted, summarized, and paraphrased material), and for bibliographic references. Help each other out by making sure that these forms are correct according to your handbook. **(SAC)**

ALTERNATIVE ASSIGNMENT

When your small writing group meets, get on a computer and, using the word-processor's ability to cut and paste information, combine your lists into one large group document, eliminating redundant material or placing similar items under headings showing their relationships. Follow the same procedures as outlined above for critiquing, revising, and correcting this group document. **(SAC or LAN)**

ASSIGNMENT 2: OBSERVING AND WRITING ABOUT AN ONLINE CONVERSATION AND FREE SPEECH

1. In most cases, our freedom of speech is not curtailed by law but rather by factors such as custom, habit, and politeness. In most group conversations, for example, we are free to say almost anything, but we *choose* or *select* what we say according to the topic and the nature of the conversation (e.g., a formal introduction to a friend of your mother, a study session in the dorm on a calculus problem, or a conference with your teacher about a test), according to the individuals with whom we are speaking (e.g., their

gender, age, or background). Also, we choose what we say according to the circumstances in which we are talking (e.g., a cocktail party, a dorm-room chat, a conversation with a member of a church congregation, or a road trip with friends) and many other factors as well (e.g., how we are raised, what mood we are in, or how we perceive others). In this sense, our speech is never really free—it is always socially determined and shaped. Most of the time, we are so used to responding to such factors that we do so unconsciously as a natural response to our social environment.

In this assignment, you will observe an online conversation and identify some of the social factors that serve to limit and shape speech. Some of these factors may operate differently online than they do in face-to-face conversations. For example, gender, age, and race are not necessarily evident online—especially when people use pseudonyms.

On your campus computer network, find a public discussion or bulletin board that interests you. Make sure that this discussion is *absolutely open to the public,* that there are no formal, published constraints on membership, and no rules about who can join or participate or simply read what is going on. Moreover, there should be no rules about the use of the information that is posted in the ensuing discussion.

2. Subscribe to this discussion and monitor its contents for at least one week. Your purpose is to describe this discussion as fully as possible—as both a linguistic and cultural phenomenon—to someone who has never participated in one but who might be interested in learning about what occurs in the discussion. In connection with this section's focus on freedom of speech, you will also be looking for those social factors that serve to place constraints or limits to speech, attempting to move it in certain directions.

3. Acting as an anthropologist, observe the contents of the discussion and take notes relating to the following questions, as well as others that may interest you:

- Who participates in this conversation (e.g., age, gender, interest group, orientation, or knowledge level)?
- Who seems to be left out of this conversation?
- What topics are brought up and why?
- How long are the topics maintained and why?
- What topics are ignored and why?
- Are taboos observed? If so, what are they?
- What are the subjects that people avoid? What kinds of language, topics, or directions do they shun?
- What kinds of messages are sent (e.g., informational, humorous, questions and answers, or diatribes)?
- What kinds of language behaviors (e.g., flaming, lurking, or dominating the conversation) are tolerated? Encouraged? Discouraged? How?
- What characteristics do these messages have (e.g., length, tone, style, conventions, or references)?
- From where or whom do the messages come (e.g., geographical location, interest group, or organization)?
- What relationships do participants have with each other (e.g., do they refer to one another? each other's ideas? Do they seem to know each other in person or only online?)?

- How does the conversation change directions? Who determines this?
- Are there patterns, trends, or conventions that you are able to see in the discussion? Broad movements or group dynamics that seem to order the discussion in some way (e.g., problem-solving efforts, storytelling, displaying knowledge, or reporting on events)?
- Why do people seem to participate in this discussion? What do they seem to get out of it?

4. Using a word-processing package, type up your notes after observation for one week.

5. Next, write a message to members of the online discussion to introduce yourself. Share your observations with participants of the discussion after "listening" in on it for a week. Ask participants to comment on the accuracy of your observations and to add input or suggest revisions to information that you may have missed or misread.

6. Incorporate this information into a more formal description of the discussion, a one-to-four-page report, which describes what you have learned. This description should be informative and suitable for sharing with both the participants of the discussion group that you have studied and the members of your class who are informed concerning the technology issues. Try to give your readers the fullest possible sense of the discussion by including carefully selected details relevant to the discussion, the rich description of the content, and the stories of pertinent events that happened during your observations. Be sure to reflect, as well, on what you have learned regarding how speech is socially constrained and shaped in the online discussion that you observed.

7. Share a draft of this assignment with your writing group or a trusted reader. Ask these readers to write questions in the margins of your description to point out what is unclear, confusing, or incomplete. Use these comments to revise your description again before you hand it in. **(LAN)**

ALTERNATIVE ASSIGNMENT

Complete this assignment collaboratively, from start to finish, with your writing group. Choose an online discussion on which you can all observe and report. **(LAN)**

ASSIGNMENT 3: DESIGNING AND WRITING A MOCK-UP HOME PAGE

1. Increasingly, people are settling in cyberspace by occupying a small piece of this landscape and customizing it to suit their own purposes. On the World Wide Web, individuals mark these virtual locations with their own personal or organizational home pages—locations in cyberspace that provide information relative to individuals for interested readers. These home pages introduce the individual or the organization that designed them. They also include some highlighted links that yield additional information when a user clicks on them.

To personal home pages, people link their résumés, lists of hobbies, pointers to the WWW sites they find most interesting, autobiographies, educational history, stories of their family, pictures, favorite quotes, video clips of their graduation, as well as representations of their family tree—however they choose to represent themselves. Home pages can also be created for businesses (utilizing advertisements, merchandise information, ordering information, hours, services, philosophy, employees' pictures, and expertise); pets (with stories, video clips, veterinary history, show history, and audio sound tracks); schools (with catalogs of courses and curricula, descriptions of departments and courses of study, campus maps, histories, registration information, campus directory); clubs and organizations (with lists of public-service projects, past and present members, ongoing discussions, financial information, contact numbers and addresses, meeting schedules and times); and cities (with town maps, town histories, tour guides, listings of local sights and attractions, famous citizens, and public services).

An important aspect to remember concerning home pages is that they are *very public* documents, potentially open to viewing by millions of people of all types. It is important to think carefully about what sort of information you would actually want to include in these online documents. When you create a home page for a business, for an organization, or for yourself, you must be careful not to include any information that you would worry about becoming general public knowledge. The issues surrounding privacy covered by the authors in this section should provide you with some help in determining a cautious approach in this regard.

For this assignment, use a word-processing package to create a *mock-up* of a home page focusing on one of three topics: (1) a business that you would like to start and run; (2) an organization to which you belong or which you support; or (3) yourself. You might choose to create a mock-up home page for your major academic department, for your writing class, for your smaller writing group, for your sorority or fraternity, for your pet, for a club or organization to which you belong, for your family, for a real or imaginary business, for your home town, for your old high school, or for yourself. This home page will not necessarily be the real thing (a home page that resides and works on the World Wide Web); however, it can be a simulation of such a document. There are four major stages to the assignment.

For the first stage of the assignment, create a word-processing file that contains the text as you want it to appear on the mock-up home page. If you know how, use different type fonts and other graphic design features (e.g., boxes, icons, and subheads) to make the information on your home page visually interesting and clearly organized for readers.

On this home page, be sure to identify at least ten links that will lead to additional information that you want your readers to know. These links can lead to anything—advertisements, pictures, resumes, other web sites, a family tree, a video clip, a letter from a relative, or an audio clip of a speech—but *at least three of these links must lead to short (one to three pages) documents that you will write yourself as a part of this assignment.* For the remaining seven links, you have to be able to produce the items to which the links lead; although you need not author them yourself. On the mock-up home page, type the reference text for each link in capital letters to make it stand out.

2. **For the second stage of the assignment,** draft the three short, original documents that you will link to the home page you create. These documents should provide information useful to individuals who are browsing the home page that you conceived. Be sure the information is suitable and is of a kind that you don't mind sharing with others. Think about how you will represent yourself, your organization, or your business with the input that you choose to link to this home page. Think, as well, about the information you choose not to include.

   Next, gather up and clearly label the other seven documents or items that you have identified as being linked to the home page. These items may be on any subject that you like, as long as they may be scanned into a computer: a picture of the members of an organization, a report card from the first grade, a letter from a friend, a story about the history of a business, a video clip of an arts performance, the score of a favorite piece of music, and so on.

3. **For the third stage of the assignment,** meet with your writing group to provide revision feedback for each other's home pages and linked documents. Have *at least two members of your writing group read and comment on your work*—not only on your home page but also on the three additional short documents that you have authored. In providing feedback on these drafts, focus on the following tasks:

   - Prepare written notes on the tone and impression that the home page and the three documents convey to a reader. What does the information contained in these documents suggest? When you are finished, show these notes to the author. Do these impressions match the intent of the author/designer? If not, where are the mismatches?

   - Consider how the home page is organized, arranged, and presented. As a reader, underline or highlight the three most important sentences on the home page. In addition, have the author perform the same task on a separate copy of the home page. When you are both finished, compare the sentences that each of you has underlined. Are the sentences the same? If not, try to figure out why, and provide the author with some guidance in setting down his or her main ideas.

   - How are each of the original documents by the author organized, arranged, and presented? As a reader, underline or highlight the three most important sentences in each document. Have the author undertake the same task on a separate copy of each document. When you are both done, compare the sentences you have both underlined. Are the sentences the same? If not, try to figure out why and provide the author with some guidance in presenting his or her main ideas.

   - In the margins of the home page and in each of the author's original documents as well, draft questions to the author where the text is unclear, incomplete, or confusing for a reader/browser.

   Your readers can look at the seven additional linked items, but they need not comment on them, unless it is to ask questions to clarify their purpose or to query the references to these items on the home page.

4. **For the fourth stage,** revise your home page and the three originally authored documents. Before you hand in a final copy of your mock-up home page, be sure to highlight the links with a colored marking pen and clearly label the linked items to which each refers.

ALTERNATIVE ASSIGNMENT

If you have access to the World Wide Web (WWW), create an *actual* home page (along with its ten links) and then publish this document. If you aren't already familiar with the procedures for creating and publishing documents on the WWW, you will need to consult with someone who is—a technical consultant, a friend who has experience with the WWW, or a systems manager in your department or on your campus. **(WAN)**

PART IV

GENDER AND TECHNOLOGY

INTRODUCTION

The global Internet ... has suddenly become the most universal and indispensable network on the planet. ... It's a wild frontier, befitting its origins—amorphous, unruly, impolite and anarchic.

James Gleich

IF, as James Gleich notes, the Internet is an "indispensable network" and a "wild frontier," it is a good bet that women should participate online but that they may not always find themselves welcome. As several of the authors in this section note, frontiers have never been especially friendly places for women, and it is probable that cyberspace, similar to the ordinary spaces both genders inhabit daily, will not treat the sexes equally. The gender disparity in computing exists, of course, not only on the Internet—it runs through the whole of the computer culture despite the fact that some of its early programming pioneers were identified with names such as Grace Hopper and Ada Lovelace.

But each new technology, as feminist Dale Spender reminds us, tends to exclude women from positions of influence. When writing became part of Western culture, few women were scribes and fewer yet authors. Moreover, in the ascendancy of print, women were not known to hold positions of power in the major publishing companies. Today, as electronic media move to center stage, women commonly are not in control of broadcasting companies or of the major software companies, nor are they among the policymakers who are setting the agenda for the national information infrastructure, NII, or its educational counterpart, the National Research and Education Network, NREN. How then are women able to make room for themselves in the computer culture? In what ways can they have a beneficial influence on cyberspace and in what ways can cyberspace be made more hospitable toward them? Will they remain every bit as excluded from the production of information in the electronic age as they were in the early years of print? These are some of the issues that the authors present in this section.

To begin, we've included a provocative, academic piece titled "Women and Men on Electronic Networks," by Cheris Kramarae and H. Jeanie Taylor. In this article Kramarae and Taylor provide a critical framework through which to view one particular computer technology: electronic communication on the net. In doing so, they present a list of recommendations for making cyberspace a tamer, more hospitable locale. As you read, we ask that you decide whether their recommendations have the power to change e-spaces for the better—and whether you think the suggestions are workable. In "Sex and the Cybergirl," the short piece from *Mother Jones* that follows, Julie Petersen offers one strong recommendation: get more women online! As you read the other articles, however, you will see that the problem of women's underrepresentation on the net, similar to many other social dilemmas, has no easy solution.

To give you a wider perspective on women and computers, we have also included three pieces that focus on very diverse settings. The first of these, Elisabeth Gerver's "Computers and Gender," depicts computing as a "male preserve" that is not restricted to the United States but is prevalent also in other English-speaking countries—it is a problem of global proportions. She presents several initiatives that women's groups throughout the developed world have taken in order to encourage women to use computers. These include, among others, computer literacy projects in the United States, a women's technology training workshop in the United Kingdom, and a Women and Technology month sponsored by an Israeli organization. The next article, "Becoming a Computer Scientist," authored by a group of computer scientists—all women—tackles the problem of gender disparity within one professional field. It is a carefully researched article that ends with seventeen recommendations for change. Also included here is an article that focuses on the workplace, specifically the employment patterns in the computer industry in Silicon Valley, California. It will not surprise you that the proportion of women in professional positions is considerably smaller than the proportion of those who hold clerical positions or work in unskilled jobs. In describing gender inequities in computing within the different countries for a particular educational field as well as for the workforce in Silicon Valley, all three pieces point to sites where women can begin to act effectively as agents for change.

To complement these articles, we then turn to selections that have appeared in the popular press: specifically, Paula Span's "The On-Line Mystique" and Stephanie Brail's "Take Back the Net!" Both articles present disturbing pictures of the treatment of women in cyberspace while at the same time assuring women that they are capable of negotiating cyberspace and urging them to participate.

The last three contributions in this section are very different from one another. The first, Nancy Kaplan and Eva Farrell's ethnographic study of a small group of adolescent girls, has been published only electronically up until now. The girls observed in this reading seem quite at home with computers and inspire hope for the future of women's involvement in computing. The second is a cartoon, which seems most appropriate in connection with Kaplan and Farrell's research. We hope that you enjoy it. And the third is a disturbing piece of fiction by James Tiptree Jr. who, in reality, is Alice B. Sheldon. Her short story, "The Girl Who Was Plugged In," ostensibly not about computers, reminds us of a combination of the Internet and virtual reality, and we wonder whether Sheldon's piece, originally written in 1969, might qualify as an early example of cyberpunk fiction.

As you read through the contributions in this portion of the book, you will note that all of the authors are women. We wish that we had been as successful in bringing women into the whole of the book as we have been in this section on Gender and Technology. In many respects, our text illustrates the pervasiveness of the problem of the underrepresentation of women in computing. Of the 60 or so authors in the book, 21 are women, surely a number that must increase in future editions. We believe, however, that the overall growth of the number of women in technology will not happen by chance—it will occur only because of the concerted and persistent efforts of women such as those represented in this section, along with the support of farsighted men.

Women and Men on Electronic Networks: A Conversation or a Monologue?

Cheris Kramarae and H. Jeanie Taylor

IN THE OPENING PIECE TO THIS SECTION, Cheris Kramarae and Jeanie Taylor inform us that despite the promise of electronic networking technology, cyberspace itself may not always offer a friendly or safe haven for women. Focusing on the university setting, the authors outline specific problems that women and other underrepresented groups on campuses encounter online and present several recommendations that they would like to see colleges and universities follow. Kramarae and Taylor's article first appeared in a 1993 publication called WITS, named after a group that the authors founded at the University of Illinois, Urbana-Champaign. WITS, which stands for Women, Information Technology and Scholarship, is an organization consisting of academic women who support one another in the learning and using of new information technologies. This selection provides you with an opportunity to think about electronic groups in relation to sexism and to decide what, if any, actions need to be taken on your own campus.

The promises of the new technologies are enticing: Electronic networks provide low-cost communication systems that enable an increasing number of people (in the wealthier countries) who have access to them to cross barriers of space, time, and social categories. These popular networks use computer tools and long-distance telecommunication lines to provide high-speed information exchange, linking individuals and groups. The examples of the benefits to many people using the networks are growing.[1]

For example, women and other marginalized people in many places and occupations are using the electronic networks to maintain easy, quick connections to kindred souls with shared interests, nearby or far away. Rural students and teachers in the U.S. state of Montana are linking their computerized bulletin board and electronic mail system (called Big Sky

[1]A woman from Estonia points out that this discussion presumes that users live in a democracy where people basically consider access to the nets a right or privilege. In some societies network use could become a requirement or duty, and could be used to separate people rather than link them.

Telegraph) with Internet, an international computer networking service, enabling these people, at least theoretically, to communicate and share ideas with thousands of communities all over the world. Judy Smith, project director of the Women's Opportunity and Resource Development (WORD) center in Missoula, Montana, uses Big Sky Telegraph to "message" other women's centers and coordinates efforts to attend key legislative meetings (Evan Brown, 1991). Women participating in the Women's Studies network are exchanging concerns, information, and action suggestions. SeniorNet, a small research project in the U.S., has provided the opportunity for at least a few elders to "talk"[2] across geographical areas about such topics as health and fitness, gardening, and recreation (Richard Adler, 1988). In 1989 students from China studying abroad used computer bulletin boards and electronic mail to share their worries, anger, and information about the revolution and the efforts to suppress it in their homeland.

In general, these networks are available to people who work for organizations with investments in computers and their promises.[3] Lee Sproull and Sara Kiesler report that these new forms of communication are changing the ways that large organizations in the "Western" countries function–increasing, they argue, a democratic free exchange of information (Lee Sproull and Sara Kiesler, 1991, p. 13).

If people's uses of these networks are indeed bringing about major changes in organizations, we are particularly interested that women and other marginalized people are included in the conversations about, and on, the nets. We are already seeing problems, including sexual harassment, that work against that equal exchange for all promised by so many of the experts.

Here, we focus on what is happening in the universities, organizations that have a particular interest in freedom of speech, openness, innovation, and the free exchange of ideas. Universities may have more of a chance to institute change "at home" and thus to influence change in the larger world. Many other large organizations have a greater stake in encouraging a common corporate voice–and thus more interest in silencing dissension in the ranks. We focus on the university because that is where we have experience and because universities could set an example not only for dealing with abusive behavior on the networks but also encouraging inclusive and collaborative communication. The concerns we have about computers and educational settings are many. For example, elsewhere Cheris Kramarae (1989) has documented the mismatch between the types of educational problems that computer software companies propose to correct and the types of problems which are given attention by women and "minorities." Here, we focus on problems women are experiencing on electronic networks, and suggest some guidelines to help minimize the problems for women and "minorities" on the nets.[4]

---

[2]Participants at the Gender, Technology and Ethics conference, held on June 1–3, 1992, in Lulea, Sweden, where a version of this paper was presented, pointed out that using talk terminology may affect the way we conceptualize words on the network. Judy Smith and Ellen Balka (1988) use the term "chatting," and do not reread or rewrite to correct spelling or grammar errors in their messages, to deliberately maintain an informality that invites people of many educational levels and interests to enter into a discussion.

[3]We are focusing on seemingly volunteer uses of networks. Of course, in many organizations electronic networks are used to distribute company messages and employees are required to read them.

[4]A few of the problems are also being addressed by the Ethics Case Studies, sponsored by Educational Uses of Information Technology, a program of EDUCOM, a consortium of more than 600 colleges and universities concerned about ethics in computing. The director of the Ethics study is Sarah P. Webster, assistant professor of computer applications at the State University of New York College of Environmental Science and Forestry. She says that ethical problems reported range from "students using a computer network to threaten or harass someone, to a department chairman's ordering faculty members to participate in software theft, to university officials' breaking into professors' computer files" (David L. Wilson, 1991).

Increasingly, universities will be judged by whether they have state-of-the-art computing equipment to support staff, students, and faculty work. Increasingly, universities will be judged by how they use this equipment. This report suggests some ways to avoid the misuse and abuse of the new electronic technologies that are transforming universities but often forming patterns that replicate or intensify previous problems. While we write here only about the networks that are used daily by millions of faculty, staff, and students on campuses across the nation (and around the world), we, along with the other participants of the Women, Information Technology and Scholarship (WITS) colloquium at the University of Illinois,[5] have related concerns about the uses of computers in classrooms and in libraries.

THE SETTINGS FOR THE NEW TECHNOLOGIES

The resistance of most universities to change what has been characterized as a "chilly climate" for women and minorities is well documented (Roberta Hall and Bernice Sandler, 1982). After several decades of feminist documentation and explanation, even *The New York Times* has recognized, in a front page story, that bias against girls is "rife" in schools, resulting in "lasting damage" (Susan Chira, 1992). (The *Times* report is based on a report commissioned by the American Association of University Women Educational Foundation that in turn is based on work by hundreds of individual women and research groups.) What the report concludes for girls is also accurate for most women at most coeducational universities. Teachers pay less attention to girls than to boys. Boys talk more than girls in classrooms. Reports indicate that sexual harassment by peers is increasing. Textbooks still ignore or stereotype women. Girls learn almost nothing in their formal instruction about many issues critical for their lives, such as sexual harassment, violence against women, discrimination, and depression. At the moment, there is nothing to suggest that the new information technologies on campuses, from which so much is expected, will change this situation.

Lee Sproull and Sara Kiesler (1991) and others suggest that people who are peripheral in large organizations (e.g., because of low rank in the hierarchy) do relatively well on the nets. Indicators of race, age, physical abilities, and physical appearance disappear in "real-time chats" or in messages sent to be stored for later reading. Divisions, Sproull and Kiesler write, disappear. Except one. The signatures on most networks indicate the sex of the writer. As Angela Gunn (1991) argues in her article "Computer Bulletin Boards: Not Just Boy Toy," women are still The Other on most of the computer network systems in the world.

NEW TECHNOLOGY AS OLD SOCIAL PROCESS

We do not question whether computer discussions could have a liberating influence within the university structure. These are frameworks for communicating that could offer new, inviting changes in the presently very gendered structure of academe. Computer conferences "exist on the intellectual margins of most traditional academic discourse communities in a new medium that is as wild and unsettled as any frontier" (Marilyn Cooper and Cynthia L. Selfe, 1990). However, if it is treated as a "frontier," to be conquered, subdued, and brought into line, we can be very sure that what we will soon have is more of the same practices that are repressive for women.

[5]WITS is a faculty and administrator colloquium, meeting two or three times a month, sponsored by the Center for Advanced Study at the University of Illinois at Urbana-Champaign. Cheris Kramarae and Jeanie Taylor are co-organizers of the colloquium. Maureen Ebben is the research assistant for the project.

Despite all the potential the nets have for equalizing the influence of participants, we have evidence that women are experiencing on the nets much of the same kinds of trouble they experience in other conversations (see Barrie Thorne, Cheris Kramarae, and Nancy Henley [1983]; Karen Foss and Sonja Foss [1991]; Casey Miller and Kate Swift [1989]). If university administrators are really interested in providing a welcoming, comfortable climate for women in the office, classroom, and research lab, they can usefully turn attention now to the nets, as these are increasingly the places where education of many kinds happens. In fact, the problems that women experience in other conversations may be intensified on the nets. Beth Kevies, a user-services consultant at the Massachusetts Institute of Technology, says that "[p]eople do things on computers that they wouldn't dream of doing on any other medium." Obscenities, racial slurs, and vicious personal attacks are recorded from people who might not say such things in face-to-face interaction (quoted in David Wilson, 1991).[6]

Of course, not all conversations on electronic networks are the same.[7] Most public conversations take place on network bulletin boards such as Usenet, the Unix-based bulletin board network that can be accessed by any system connected to the Internet with the proper operating system. (In the U.S. there are an estimated 60,000 public access bulletin boards and an estimated 10 million people who are regular callers to these public access bulletin board services.) Less public are the mailing lists, which are postings sent via the network to a specific list of people. The most private electronic conversations take place through private electronic mail (although, as with telephone conversations, electronic conversations can be "listened in on"). We suspect that the kind and extent of problems experienced by women and other "minorities" on these networks will vary depending on how public the forum and how cohesive the community of users. Bulletin boards as open networks have the most potential for abusive behavior. Lists are likely to retain more sense of community and sense of purpose, but exclusion from the conversation is more likely to have career repercussions for marginal groups. Private e-mail is similar to communication by telephone or letter, but the absence of aural cues and the speed of transmission may cause problems for communication.

SOME SPECIFIC PROBLEMS

1. In almost any open network, men monopolize the talk.[8] The reasons are probably several. Young men may have more time to spend in front of their computers. Men, in general, are

---

[6]We have many examples from networks of women's concern with this problem. On a sociology network we found discussion of whether those who use concealing nicknames rather than their real names in making comments about affirmative action should even be replied to, and whether those who "flame" (send hot-tempered messages) should be "flamed back." The members of Systers, a network for women in computer science, are often harassed on other nets, and exchange information on how to deal with it (e.g. sending a copy of the offending message, along with a complaint, to the "postmaster" at the node from which the message originated).

[7]We thank WITS member Jenny Barrett for her contribution to this part of the discussion.

[8]When a draft of this paper was circulated among participants in the Lewis and Clark College Electronic Salon in April 1992, this point elicited numerous comments. Everyone seemed to have a study that verified our observations. For example, Jane Fraser made the following comments: "Here at Ohio State, we recently started osu.women. The consensus is that it is working fine, but only as a place for notices of meetings, etc. It is not a place where women can talk because—you guessed it—the men dominate and tend to pick apart word-by-word any woman's posting. We have recently started a private mailing list for women faculty and grad students in engineering—requests to be added will be verified." "Blade X," a male participant in the Electronic Salon, commented, "Cyberspace is elitist; cyberspace is exclusionary. For all the rhetoric and propaganda of eliminating barriers to participation it still remains the eminent domain of white, middle-class males."

accustomed to talking more than women do in public conversations of various sorts (see annotated bibliography in Barrie Thorne, Cheris Kramarae, and Nancy Henley [1983]). If the topics women raise are seldom taken up by men on the networks, women may become less interested in network talk or feel that their issues are not very important. As Cynthia Selfe (1992) reports, students who are already assertive about their verbal group input, often because they enjoy a confidence born of privilege, feel freer to take more verbal space. WITS participant Ramona Curry notes that network members who want to take more time to think about responses or don't want to take up too much of others' time may find that discussions sweep by them.

Even open networks where the topic is women's issues are, we have found, over-run by men. For example, on this campus, we've checked the network called soc.women and have noticed that on some days only men have posted messages. On a national soc.women board, dominated by comments from men, one woman noted that even the women-only boards are not respected by men who cross-post to the women from other boards.[9]

The moderators of the newsgroup soc.feminism have noted that the men and women posting often have protracted disagreements on gender-neutral language, on the actual statistics on spouse-beating in comparing which sex is "worse off," and in the propriety of "women-only" events. These arguments have led many women to complain that soc.feminism is "too hostile" for them.

Women's topics and concerns are often not considered or taken seriously. Further, the "conversations" that take place may assume a degree of homogeneity that does not reflect the reality of the particular network.[10]

These should be concerns of anyone interested in collaboration and democracy. However, working toward gender equality in conversation, or in any setting, has not yet been made an important goal in most institutions.

2. Sexual harassment on the networks is a problem being reported by many women at many sites. The forms of sexual harassment vary. In some cases, women on the networks experience the types of sexist jokes and limericks that were once a part of many classroom lectures but now are

[9]From a 1988 soc.women network discussion:
Robert N. Lately in my reading of soc.men and soc.women, I've been noticing two phenomena:
—Articles (like this one, in fact:-) [smiley face] are heavily crossposted between soc.men and soc.women. In a recent batch, all but 5 of 40 articles in soc.men were crossposted to soc.women.
—Various soc.women readers complain that men are trying to dominate soc.women, when the group should be a forum for women's perspectives. Other readers think that the group should be a discussion of gender issues from anybody's point of view, and complain that they are being shoved out. (These men's articles are often among the articles crossposted to both groups.)
It might be a good idea, then, to create another . . . newsgroup . . . so that soc.women and soc.men could go more towards being more a forum for the personal perspectives of women or men. . . .
Mary: Go right ahead, Robert. . . . But you know what? I was here, on the net, the last time this was tried. We had a net.women, and a net.women-only. Guess what? Articles were crossposted to net.women-only from net.women by men. Net.women-only was NOT respected by men. . . .
[10]Deborah Heath, organizer of the April 1992 Lewis and Clark College Electronic Salon, remarked, "In the absence of more complete cues about who is in our audience, some of us will assume that all share the same worldview . . . and . . . those who occupy privileged or "unmarked" social positions [male or white or straight or English-speaking, etc.] may be even more inclined to presume that their perspective is natural and universal."

increasingly discouraged by university administrators.[11] In other cases, women's complaints about the harassment they experience lead to hostile comments about the women.[12] Women who want to be respected scholars (which means avoiding being known as a trouble-maker, or as someone who questions the actions of respected men in the field) will be very hesitant about publicly pointing to sexist behavior. This silencing has serious consequences for interaction on individual nets, for disciplines and for the academy in general.

3. The climate of the nets may exclude many women and minorities from participating fully in the conversation. Men tend to use more assertive behavior than women. In addition to sending more messages, and introducing more new topics than do women, men tend to disagree more frequently with others. (See Cynthia L. Selfe and Paul R. Meyer [1990] for one valuable study; more research is needed on this.) "Flaming" (sending hot-tempered messages) is an issue that has received some attention by people on the networks. Yet seldom discussed is sex-related behavior on the networks and the impact of this kind of dominant behavior on women's participation.

4. We can expect an increase in high-tech titillation. *Penthouse*, with a circulation of 1.5 million, is one of the first mass media publications to become available electronically (Deirdre Carmody, 1991). The widespread interest in mass media pornography has always had implications for universities. For example, female students at universities across the country are increasingly daring to complain about *Playboy*-type posters in professors' offices and research labs, concerned about what

---

[11]In 1990 Peg Jennings wrote an open letter on a scientific network " . . . to those of you who assume that men are [scientists] and women are whores" after a series of limericks was posted. The discussion that followed was sometimes acrimonious. Some people sending messages said that the author of a particularly offending limerick was a staunch supporter of women in science and that it was a shame that he was being criticized in this way. Some women sent e-mail messages to individuals in the discussion, relating their own experiences of sexism in academe. After dozens of messages on this topic, the moderator decided that the issue of the limericks did not belong on the bulletin board: "[This] mailing list is a private mailing list for the discussion of 'technical' issues only." He included the following directive: "Persons who continue this limerick thread will be removed from the list."

The woman who first complained about sexist limericks watched her computer screen as many of the network users commented on her action. A few examples: "If we let [her] get away with this raving attack on an innocent bit of humor, the next thing will be women trying to rewrite the English language, and then rewrite history, abolish men's and women's bathrooms. . . ." "Get a grip . . . and stop treating men as all alike (simply because you are too blinded by your anger to think)." "By being a reactionary to limericks, you give a bad message about women. And that is exactly a cause that I fight. Your open letter is a condescending knee-jerk reaction." "[You contributed] to the stereotype of advocates of nonsexist writing as being brainless flakes."

[12]After women students and faculty brought complaints, a notice was finally posted in the computer laboratory of the Computer and Information Science Department at the University of Oregon that states, in part, as follows: "The CIS Department has received reports of incidents of offensive and unprofessional behavior [in the lab]. Much of this behavior can be described as sexual harassment. At the very least, a small group of students has made it a very uncomfortable working environment and effectively driven away a large number of other students from the only place they can work on their class projects. Not surprisingly, this behavior also violates the University's Student Conduct Code. . . . The department views these reports very seriously, and is in the process of investigating them, as well as preparing an explicit statement of department policy regarding behavior in the workplace. In the meanwhile, reports of offensive behavior should be directed to [several names] or to any CIS faculty member. Please remember that the appearance and atmosphere of the University facilities (that includes computing labs) should be conducive to their educational goals. Professional courtesy and respect are not only the norm but the rule to be enforced." (We thank Sarah Douglas, CIS Department, University of Oregon, for this material, and for her comments on an earlier version of this paper.)

the posters convey about the professors' attitudes toward women. Only recently have university administrators at many universities shown concern about these practices (and then usually only after women complain, often after they have changed courses or majors). Female scholars on campuses are also concerned about related electronic practices. University nets have been used to transmit pornography. At times this has been blatant, as when Usenet at the University of Washington carried electronically transferred digitized pornographic pictures (Elaine Richardson, 1991). In this case, the "sexually explicit drawings and photographs" were distributed to selected faculty members and students by the director of the university's Microcomputer Evaluation Center (*Chronicle of Higher Education*, Nov. 13, 1991, p. A22). At the University of Oregon the photographs were available on high-resolution display machines in the student computer labs. Women at many other universities are reporting similar situations. Many of us have received unrequested body-parts "visuals" (e.g., "breasts" composed of computer keyboard letters and punctuation marks).

IMPLICATIONS FOR UNIVERSITY POLICY

Universities have the unique opportunity at this moment to change the structure of interaction on campuses. Without new policies guiding the use of these public nets, we will be losing a chance to plan new structures to benefit everyone in the university. Policies will need to deal not only with freedom of speech but also the protection of women and "minorities" on campus. (At times in the U.S. the First Amendment is discussed as if it is the Only Law of the Land. The laws provide for a variety of protections.) Computer networks provide a forum for many kinds of debates. University policy could encourage open debate for everyone, including women, but this would entail revisions in policies and behavior. A few suggestions to begin discussions:

1. Women-only forums for speech. The literature is clear: men are more interested in having mixed-sex conversations than women are. Women are more likely to give men plenty of time, space, and consideration than vice versa. Separatism is not necessarily what women want for their discussions, but until gender equality becomes a reality in a wide variety of settings, women need both access to the public nets and some safe forums for their conversations. (In case some readers believe that only "those radical feminists" want women-only forums, they should know that there are all kinds of women-only nets, including a fundamentalist-Christian board [Angela Gunn, 1991].) On women-only nets, the talk is more candid and the topics, unlike those on "regular" boards, are controlled by women.[13] Because impostors are present, perhaps prevalent, on the nets, university policies should deal with those who gain trust and confidences by presenting themselves as other than they are, sometimes with devastating results to those who trusted (Lindsy Van Gelder, 1985).

2. Training, including instruction in the issues above, for the moderators, who decide what is allowed on the nets and who have the right to censor material they do not think belongs there. The moderators would learn about the issues introduced above and about ways of dealing with people who express disrespect for others on the nets.

---

[13]One man who spends a great deal of time on the nets said, in response to discussions of women-only nets, something like this: "I spend about four hours a day on the net, talking to my girlfriend, and on the scuba diving bulletin board, etc. It's all there for me. Then I hear you talking about these other nets that I can't access—your Handsnet, and dog and cat net or whatever. And I find it really *frightening* that you are out there communicating with each other, and I can't get to it."

For many women, of course, access to nets—and time to use them—is very limited.

3. Warnings for new participants and reminders for long-time participants. We could make a part of the responsibilities of organizers and "owners" of networks the warning to users that the networks are not totally private or safe. Deborah Heath, in the Electronic Salon, pointed out that "[t]he informal mode of most communiqués, the rapidity of response, and the fact that many of us can send and receive messages within the familiar surroundings of home all work to create, it seems to me, a sense of intimacy or connectedness with others in a discussion group. But ... this 'safe' intimacy is partial and to some extent illusory." Unknown others, with more interest in playing games with the systems than in ensuring confidentiality of discussions can, for example, "listen in" and send "fake messages" with false names and addresses.

4. A grievance procedure for complaints of sexual harassment on the nets. This should be part of the sexual harassment policy of any institution that sponsors (or allows) electronic network communication. Users should be told that sexual harassment will not be tolerated, the prohibited behaviors should be defined, and punishments should be spelled out. Users should be given details on how, when, and where they can complain about harassment. The policy should also take a strong, explicitly detailed stand against retaliation; otherwise many people experiencing harassment will fear reporting it. (See William Petrocelli and Barbara Kate Repa [1992] for excellent information on how effective policies can be written and enforced.)

5. Periodic reports, to a central body, on the number and types of complaints and action taken. These reports could also include assessment of the conversations on the nets—number and length of postings and control of topics by women and men. They could also include a yearly profile of the subscribers and the participants, so network users could find out who was participating and who was silently listening in. The reports and assessments would differ depending upon the makeup and issues of the network. Some models are available. For example, one national network community (discussing aspects of the research field of computers and writing) decided to try a period of 20 days during which participants used real names and 20 days during which participants could use their real name or a pseudonym. The researchers (Cynthia L. Selfe and Paul R. Meyer, 1991) who decided to analyze the interaction during those days found that messages were sent by 18 men and 15 women from 16 states. Men contributed twice as many messages and 40% more words; high-profile (determined in part by publications) members contributed more than twice the number of messages and words than did low-profile members. Participation by both women and men increased during the pseudonym-optional period. While the option of using pseudonyms seemed to have a particular appeal for women, it did not result in any restructuring of conference power relationships. Perhaps of most importance, the experiment prompted more explicit attention and discussion of power issues.

6. Clarification of what will be considered offensive messages. (Who will decide whether something is repugnant and objectionable?) Universities concerned about the prevailing chilly climates for women on campus could organize guidelines for behavior that show particular concern with the problems which women and "minorities" often experience in conversations with others. The guidelines offered by Howard Rosenbaum and Gregory Newby (1990) might be used as an aid in establishing the agreed-upon etiquette of network communications. Other useful examples are available from some of the nets, such as DOROTHYL, a network discussion group, organized by a group of women librarians, for lovers of the mystery genre. (They considered limiting DOROTHYL [named after Dorothy L. Sayers, the writer of mysteries] to women participants, but realized that it was likely that "men would sneak on with anonymous [identifications] to join in DOROTHYL's energizing discussions.") Among the directions they include is "Be tolerant of newcomers. Do not abuse new users of computer networks for their ignorance—be patient. . . . "

7. Explicit explanations about determining who can create a network bulletin board on what topics.[14] The person in charge of approving and setting up new bulletin boards and newsgroups generally uses his [sic] own judgment. One such person on a university campus states: "I have to make continuing choices based on what provides the best value to the University community. . . . My general theory is that if a group has some value to myself or [the computer center], I'll create it soon after the newsgroup is posted once it shows signs of life."

8. Explicit discussion of the differing access to networks, both inside and outside academe. Men are overwhelmingly the primary users of the nets. Many male students expect to use them in jobs outside the academy, and ask about access in job interviews. What are the implications of this differential use for women's jobs of the future? We know that women, in very low-paying and physically debilitating jobs, are making the computer chips that middle-class men are using for recreation, communication, and job fulfillment. What is happening with the sex hierarchies in academe is not divorced from the sex hierarchies worldwide. The increasing number of city Freenets (free to users, supported by community individuals, groups, or businesses) does not solve all access problems. Some people can afford modems for home use; others can't afford the bus fare to get to the modems in the libraries or other public places. Also, women, especially older women, often trained to think that they will break machinery if they try to use it, may not feel as comfortable using the networks unless special efforts are made to involve them in the Freenet programs.

Getting even these initial relatively minor responses from the academy would not be a simple matter. As women's studies research has made very clear, universities (and most other institutions) have taught sex discrimination, if not explicitly at least very well. The rhetoric about the importance of diversity and equality in universities has been in place for some time, but equity in practice has been very slow in following. Now, with the so-called electronic-information revolution in the "West," we have a wonderful opportunity for some administrators, staff, faculty, and students to take specific actions that could have an edifying influence on every member of academia—and many others.

ACKNOWLEDGMENTS

We worked with Maureen Ebben during the first year of the WITS colloquium. We appreciate the discussions with her that contributed to this paper. We also appreciate the comments of WITS member Jenny Barrett, Sarah Douglas at the University of Oregon, and of the participants in the Electronic Salon of the Gender Symposium at Lewis and Clark College, April 1992.

REFERENCES

Adler, Richard (1988). *Seniornet: Toward a National Community of Computer-Using Seniors. Forum Report #5, Aspen Institute Project on Enhancing the Social Benefits of New Electronic Technologies.* New York, N.Y., Aspen Institute.

Brown, Evan (1991). "On Line in the Big Sky." *Missoula Independent*, November 14, 10.

Carmody, Deirdre (1990). "New President at *Penthouse* Looks Beyond Printed Page." *The New York Times*, December 1, C1, C8.

[14]During the Electronic Salon, "Blade X" (a man) commented, "I have yet to see a post by a migrant farm worker or a homeless person. Both groups who are fairly immune to the viruses of feminism and/or communication technology. When dealing with technology, always ask who is invited? and who is excluded?"

Chira, Susan (1992). "Bias Against Girls Is Found Rife in Schools, With Lasting Damage." *The New York Times,* February 12, A1, A10.

Cooper, Marilyn M. and Cynthia L. Selfe (1990). "Computer Conferences and Learning: Authority, Resistance, and Internally Persuasive Discourse." *College English,* 52:8, 847–869.

Foss, Karen and Sonja Foss (1991). *Women Speak: The Eloquence of Women's Lives.* Prospect Heights, Ill.: Waveland Press.

Gunn, Angela (1991). "Computer Bulletin Boards Not Just Boy Toy." *New Directions for Women,* November–December, 7.

Hall, Roberta M. and Bernice Sandler (1982). "The Classroom Climate: A Chilly One for Women." *Project on the Status and Education of Women.* Washington, D.C.: Association of American Colleges.

Kramarae, Cheris (1989). "Computers, Communication and Education: Science Fiction and Fantasies." Conference on Rhetoric and Technology, Houghton, Mich., Michigan Technological University, October.

Miller, Casey and Kate Swift (1989). *Words and Women: New Language in New Times,* 2nd ed. Garden City, N.Y.: Doubleday.

Petrocelli, William and Barbara Kate Repa (1992). *Sexual Harassment on the Job.* Berkeley: Nolo Press.

Richardson, Elaine (1991). "U. Washington deletes erotica from computer network." *The Daily Illini,* October 31, 4.

Rosenbaum, Howard and Gregory B. Newby (1990). "An Emerging Form of Human Communication: Computer Networking." *ASIS '90: Proceedings of the 53rd ASIS Annual Meeting,* v. 27. November 4–8, Toronto, Ontario.

Selfe, Cynthia L. (1992). "Computer-based Conversations and the Changing Nature of Collaboration." In Janis Forman (Ed.), *New Visions of Collaborative Writing.* Portsmouth, N.H.: Boynton/Cook, 147–169.

Selfe, Cynthia and Paul R. Meyer (1991). "Testing Claims for On-line Conferences." *Written Communication,* 8:2, 162–192.

Smith, Judy and Ellen Balka (1988). "Chatting on a Feminist Computer Network." In Cheris Kramarae (Ed.), *Technology and Women's Voices.* New York: Routledge & Kegan Paul/Methuen, 82–97.

Sproull, Lee and Sara Kiesler (1991). *Connections: New Ways of Working in the Networked Organization.* Cambridge, Mass.: Massachusetts Institute of Technology Press.

Thorne, Barrie, Cheris Kramarae, and Nancy Henley (Eds.) (1983). *Language, Gender and Society.* Rowley, Mass.: Newbury House.

Van Gelder, Lindsy (1985). "The Strange Case of the Electronic Lover." *Ms.* October, 94–104, 117, 123, 124.

Wilson, David L. (1991). "Computer-related Ethical Problems Are Focus of Conference on Values." *The Chronicle of Higher Education,* September 4, A31.

THINKING AND RE-READING

1. As you re-read this piece, list the discriminatory practices against women that the authors encountered in various settings. How do these experiences correspond with online behavior you've observed on the nets at your own campus?

2. Review the authors' eight recommendations. Which do you think are especially promising for your own campus? Which seem less promising?

WRITING AND LEARNING

1. On your campus, contact a member of a student or faculty committee that is devoted to women's issues. Set up a meeting with the representative to find out what steps your campus is taking to address some of the problems Kramarae and Taylor consider. Also include other issues that you think are important and are not mentioned in the article. Prepare a written report for your classmates in which you discuss the types of resources that are available on your campus for those individuals who encounter hostile online environments in classes or in other online settings. If your instructor thinks it appropriate, write a letter from your class to the appropriate school officials apprising them of your findings and recommending measures to be taken to ensure gender equality online.

2. Make a list of ways in which you think online environments may discriminate against men. Write a report to your class whereby you argue against sexism of any kind. What, in your mind, constitutes sexism? As you prepare your statement, be sure to include examples of the varieties of online behavior in classes that you believe detract from learning or that make the net an unfriendly place for all students regardless of gender.

3. As you review Kramarae and Taylor's eight recommendations, decide which ones are likely to be effective on your campus. Why? Which ones are less likely to be effective? Why? Choose one that you think needs to be enacted on your campus and develop it into a workable plan. Send the plan, along with a letter, to the director of computing on your campus or to another college representative whom you deem appropriate, arguing for the need for such action on your campus. Your letter and plan might also be appropriate to send to your school newspaper.

Sex and the Cybergirl

Julie Petersen

THIS SELECTION FIRST APPEARED in 1994 in *Mother Jones*, a magazine known for its liberal views. In the article, Julie Petersen provides illustrations to demonstrate the kinds of sexual harassment and other rude behaviors that are found in public discussions on the Internet. As you read the article, you will see that some people believe that this type of behavior will subside over time; however, others see the necessity of taking action of some sort. Re-read the short selection a second time and decide where you stand on this issue.

Using the handle MaryHJones, MoJo recently logged on to a "live chat" session to check out the on-line action. She told her newfound friends that she did union work and was fairly new on the "net." "Are you married?" asked Jim. "How tall are you and what color hair do you have?" And later, "When was the last time you really enjoyed sex? Was it *gooooooooddd?*"

Though the "information superhighway" has been heralded as a great equalizer, where race, class, gender, sexual preference, and physical appearance make no difference, many women are finding otherwise. Females who surf the Internet's vast, male-dominated network of computer databases or join in public discussions are often subjected to sexism and harassment—occurring most frequently in live chat and via "talk" requests where people can send private messages to anyone on-line at the same time.

Things can turn ugly. After apparently offending someone in an Internet newsgroup discussion, Stephanie Brail received an untraceable e-mail "bomb" containing hundreds of sexual and violent messages—the mildest of which was "Shut up, bitch." Brail is calling for action. "It's against the law to harass people on the phone, in person, or in the mail," she says. "Personally threatening e-mail messages should be against the law."

Other women have reported similar incidents; some refused to identify themselves for fear of on-line retaliation. Though laws pertaining to phone threats likely extend to e-mail, they remain untested. But Howard Rheingold, author of "The Virtual Community," believes the problem will diminish with time. "It will be regarded as uncool. There are people who do uncool things, [but] that's not the medium, that's a larger social issue."

Meanwhile, several on-line groups have taken matters into their own hands. Women's Wire penalizes repeat offenders by suspending their accounts. MIT-based Cyberion City (a "bar" of sorts in cyberspace) warns customers that

> When Mother Jones stepped out onto the electronic superhighway, so did a few cyberpigs.

"unwanted advances of a hostile or forward nature are unacceptable. If you think someone [wants] a closer personal relationship, make absolutely sure before saying or doing anything that would be considered inappropriate in real life."

Will the promise of cyberspace fall to a few sexist cyberpigs? The only way to change the present course, as nearly everyone in cyberspace agrees, is to get more women on-line. In the meantime, it's a sty out there.

THINKING AND RE-READING

1. As you review "Sex and the Cybergirl," think about times when you received unwanted messages on the Internet or when friends felt that they had been threatened in some way in real life (IRL) or online. How did you or your friends respond? Petersen's article was written in 1994. Have the spaces you participate in online changed much since then? Why or why not?

WRITING AND LEARNING

1. In her piece on "Sex and the Cybergirl," Julie Petersen comes to the conclusion that the one surefire way to combat online sexism is to get more women to participate online. Decide whether you agree or disagree with this assessment. Why? If you agree, what sorts of measures need to be taken on your campus to encourage women to participate? How is it possible for women to be made to feel more comfortable with the new technologies? Construct a written plan for action that you present to an undergraduate or graduate student group, accompanied by a letter in which you request their help to implement your plan.

Computers and Gender

Elisabeth Gerver

IN THIS SELECTION, ELISABETH GERVER gives us an international look at gender equity and computers during the 1980s. She maintains that gender bias exists in students' access to computers in schools, in the kinds of work each sex performs with computers in jobs, and, overall, in almost every venue throughout the industrial world's computer culture. After she discusses several instances demonstrating various gender inequities regarding computers, she discusses organized efforts to encourage women to engage more in the use of computers. Gerver's article provides an excellent introduction to wider, global perspectives on the use of computer technology insofar as women are concerned. As you read, keep in mind the countries about which she is writing and those that she might be neglecting. This selection is taken from Gerver's 1985 book titled *Humanizing Technology.*

> *Why does computing appear to be a male preserve? The author provides an impressive survey of the evidence on gender imbalance in computing and looks at the reasons behind it—in particular, the ways in which girls are "turned off" computer studies at school. Gerver then describes some projects created for women to learn about computing in New Zealand, Britain and the United States.*
> *Taken from chapter 2 of Elisabeth Gerver's book* Humanizing Technology *(Plenum Press, London and New York, 1985).*
>
> *Microcomputers offer a golden, and perhaps unprecedented, opportunity to women.*
> *Rose Deakin*, Women and Computing

In the initial enthusiastic introduction of computers into various forms of community education in many parts of the developed world, grandiose claims were sometimes made for the beneficial effects that computerization could have on entire communities. It was against such a background of enthusiasm that I started to work in 1981 in the Scottish Community Education Microelectronics

Project (SCEMP). Two impressions of that time are particularly vivid. The first is that there was already an extraordinarily high level of interest in using computers for individualized learning and for community information. The second is that, among the large number of people who expressed interest in the project, there were very few women. As a collaborative venture, the project drew heavily on the help of volunteers to create computer programs to demonstrate some of the possibilities of using individualized learning in community education. Nearly all of the volunteer programmers were men and boys. The project also required the help of voluntary organizations to coordinate and manage computer exhibitions which would give ordinary people a chance to experience the machines for themselves. Nearly all of the individuals who offered to help with these exhibitions were men. At that time, there were no women among the senior staff and computer programmers employed by the government-funded project to introduce computers into schools in Scotland, a project with which SCEMP was closely associated, and most of the visitors to both projects appeared to be men.

When the public exhibitions of computer programs began, their most notable feature at first was the large number of young people who wanted to use the equipment, and who often had to be tactfully or even bluntly steered away so that the adults, for whom the exhibitions were primarily intended, could also sample the programs. Almost all the young people were young and adolescent boys, and most of the adults for whom they made way were young men. Yet, the exhibitions were intended as an educational experience for adults, and in Britain, as in most of the developed world, most of the students in adult education are women.

At first glance, then, the phenomenon was puzzling. The programs used in the exhibitions were intended to have a reasonably wide appeal; they included programs on managing personal finance, assessing one's current state of health, choosing well-balanced meals, answering quiz questions about road safety, and a number of programs illustrating the kinds of educational games which children often played at school. Several exhibitions even included a program designed to help women make well-informed decisions about whether to breast or to bottle feed their babies! On the face of it, then, there was no explicit appeal primarily to male users.

Yet the users were predominantly male. At about the same time, I attended a conference for providers of computer literacy courses in support of the BBC Computer Literacy Project, which was expected to, and did, rouse a great deal of public interest in computers. Again, despite the fact that there are many female tutors in adult education, nearly all of those present were men.

The next evidence of the strangely single-gendered world of computers was visual. The overwhelming impression created by all the computer magazines and advertisements for microcomputers in Britain in the early 1980s was that this was a world only for men and their sons. "Son, where's my Epson?" demanded a happy father in an advertisement, as his schoolage child sheepishly hid the computer behind his back. Early figures for sales of the extraordinarily popular BBC Computer indicated that over 90 percent of the purchasers were male (BBC, 1983).

Printed material for the computer hobbyist or for the serious computer educationalist seemed to assume that its reader would be a man. In magazines in 1983, there were about ten males to every one female, and she was usually there in a decorative capacity (Gerver, 1984). Even in the Open University, which usually avoids explicitly sexist material, the original leaflet for a course for teachers to learn about computers depicted far more men than women (Gerver, 1984). These visual impressions are confirmed by Bernstein (1984), who has found that there are three types of advertisements for computers: "men as decision-makers; women as attention-getters; and family-oriented ads which do not include the whole family." Those women who are included in advertisements portraying family life are shown only as being in charge of young children. Where the children are older, women tend to disappear, and girls, where they are depicted at all, are merely shown as watching the boys admiringly.

Advertisers are now beginning—more so in the United States than in Britain—to include women more often as users of computers. Deakin (1984) cites one advertisement on television in the UK in which a mother and father were shown as creeping down to use the home computer when they thought the children were not around. The commercial need for new markets for computers means that the representation of women in advertisements for computers is likely to increase, as women form 50 percent of the potential market. But until the mid-1980s, the message of most computer advertising was that computers were for men and boys.

The phenomenon seemed to me not merely striking, because unexpected, but also very dangerous, because it appeared to be so little noticed in the world of community education. Attention had already been drawn to the under-representation of women in the field of computing as a whole (Simons, 1981), but the largely male tutors of computer courses and the male observers at computer exhibitions seemed not even to notice that the great majority of the participants were men. Since then, increasing attention has been paid to the single gender of computers in publications (Deakin, 1984; Gerver and Lewis, 1984; among many others), at international conferences on the new information technologies, in action groups, and in many projects which have been started to try to redress the sexual balance in this field. Before considering the various ways in which adult educators and feminist groups have been trying to address the problem, however, I should like first to sketch the dimensions of the situation which has caused so much concern.

GENDER BIAS IN LEARNING ABOUT COMPUTERS

The land of computing is a frontier country, and, as in the development of most frontier territories, there are many more men than women. Indeed, it appears that at all levels of learning about computers—in school, in higher education, in further education, in training, in adult education classes, and in independent learning—women tend to be strikingly underrepresented. The extent of their under-representation varies from sector to sector and to some extent from country to country, but the fact of it is so ubiquitous that the evidence tends to become monotonous. The statistical evidence that follows gives an indication of the scope of the problem, but it does not attempt to cover the phenomenon at all comprehensively.

Anyone observing the use of computers in schools in the UK and the United States will find many male teachers and students—and few females—among the enthusiasts. Even in the recently developing use of computers in primary school, there is already evidence in the UK that "girls are failing to seize the opportunity. There seems to be a preponderance of boys even in the more imaginative and exciting courses ... designed for primary schools and intended to stimulate children before there is any firmly recognizable division of activities according to gender" (Deakin, 1984). In the United States, the pattern appears to be that seen in California, where at elementary school both sexes participate nearly equally in using computers, but by the time of junior high school, girls form only 37 percent of the users (Beyers, 1983).

In courses in computing in American secondary schools, males outnumber females by nearly 2:1 in a pattern that remains remarkably similar over a number of states (PEER, 1983). In the UK, the sexual bias in computing in schools may be seen in the finding that computer studies are assumed by many schools to be boys' subjects, along with nearly all the other sciences (Rogers, 1983). At the most senior level of work in computer studies in schools in England and Wales—that of A level examinations in computer science—the ratio of boys to girls is 4:1 (EOC, 1984).

In the more informal uses of computers in schools, the same pattern is evident. In the UK, "there are a few schools where an imaginative teacher has managed to stimulate girls into using computers, but in general there is a distressingly low take-up" (Deakin, 1984). The situation described by Deakin in one school is emblematic:

> At one north London comprehensive school, the current fifth-year computer studies group has no girls at all. The current fourth year shows an improvement with six girls, but alongside them are seventeen boys. . . . A computer was available in the library, and here again boys tended to dominate. In the opinion of the deputy head, this was because "girls were not assertive or confident enough to resist the boys' 'helpful' suggestions about programming and gradually the girls would be eased out. . . ." Girls would not join the lunchtime computer club.

At the university level of study, in 1970–80 in the United States, only 30.3 percent of all first degrees in computer and information sciences were earned by women (National Science Foundation, undated). In the same year, only 20.9 percent of all masters degrees in the same subject were awarded to women, while at the doctoral level, the figure falls to 11.2 percent. In the UK in 1979, women formed only 27 percent of all the applicants for computer science undergraduate courses at the university level (Simons, 1981).

The pattern is not restricted to the level of undergraduate work. In the UK where the shortage in computing skills led the government to fund a 500 percent increase in places for postgraduate studies in information technology in 1983–4, only 10 percent of those qualifying in 1984 were women (Women's National Commission, 1984). The low percentage is unexpected and striking, especially as some of the new courses are "conversion" courses for graduates with degrees in the arts or social sciences and, therefore, could have offered women an opportunity to change direction and to enhance their chances of employment.

In computer courses within adult education, the pattern at first seems encouragingly less sexist: in the UK in 1982–3 the proportion of males to females in enrollment in adult education classes in computing appeared to be about only 2:1 (Banks, 1983; Gerver, 1984). In 1983–4, there was an encouraging increase in the number of women in computer classes in at least one local authority area, where the proportion of women rose to 43 percent (Banks, 1984). These figures, however, need to be treated with some caution. They should be seen in the light of the fact that, whereas there are roughly equal numbers of boys and girls in the school population, far more women than men traditionally take part in adult education classes, so that the population, from which such an apparently encouraging proportion of women is drawn, does not consist equally of men and women.

Among the providers of education in computers, there appears to be an even more pronounced male bias. Within schools in the UK, most work with computers is carried out by teachers of mathematics and physics, by far the great majority of whom are male. In 1983–4 in the UK, no woman was among the "new blood" university appointments in information technology.

Within the field of training unemployed people for new careers, the same pattern seems to persist. In Scotland in 1983, for instance, there was a striking difference in the numbers of unemployed men and women who completed training in higher level computer skills: 83 percent of those completing courses in computing at higher levels were male (Gerver, 1984). At the new Information Technology Centers, which have been established in the UK to provide skills in computing for school-leavers, there are far more young men than young women: in 1984, less than one-third of the trainees at these centers were women (Women's National Commission, 1984). The manager of one such center reported that he "is rather concerned about the lack of female applicants. . . . Girl[s] . . . are just not interested enough to apply" (Deakin, 1984).

Among those who are addicted to working with computers—the "compulsive programmers" or "computer junkies"—there appear to be no women. Research being currently conducted into the social pathology of computer addiction, has so far failed to uncover any examples of women who fall into this category (Shotton, 1984). In the United States, the compulsive programmers described by Weizenbaum (1976) are all "bright young *men* of disheveled appearance."

At the level of leisure pursuits, there is ample evidence that fascination with computers is largely a male phenomenon. Almost all the users of computer-based games are boys and young men, and the games appeal primarily to traditionally male preferences. In a review of computer games on the market for sale at Christmas in the UK, Hetherington (1984) noted that "all of the games have heroes, not heroines, and are in other ways oriented toward boys. This unfortunately reflects the current market, which apart from a few patronizing 'games for girls' is almost entirely aimed at boys." The predominantly male appeal of most leisure computer magazines is overwhelmingly evident. The articles, written mainly by men, assume that the reader is male; the advertisements sometimes verge on being offensive to women; the illustrations are primarily of men using computers, with women occupying a lesser, mainly picturesque, role.

Studies on the use of computers at home also show a pronounced sexual imbalance. Beyers (1983) reports that interviews with typical computer-owning families in the United States "indicated that sons used the machine most. They spent an average of two to three hours a day playing and programming games. The father used the computer regularly for business, while the mother did not use it at all."

In the informal learning that takes place in computer camps, where learning about computers is chosen purely as a form of pleasure, there are fewer girls than boys in the UK (Deakin, 1984) and in the United States (Beyers, 1983). In American computer camps, in 1983, "boys outnumbered girls by three to one. The proportion of girls in beginning and intermediate classes was 27 percent. This dropped to 14 percent in advanced programming classes and to 5 percent in higher level courses teaching assembly language" (Beyers, 1983).

In the setting of the public library, whose users tend to be female, it has been shown by Yeates (1982) that far more men than women will use computer-based systems to provide information. At central lending libraries in the UK, the ratio of users of Prestel (a computer-based information system) was seven men to every three women, while at reference libraries the gender imbalance was even more pronounced, with nearly four men to every one woman.

Such an apparently ubiquitous gender imbalance in the use of computers cries out for systematic research which would allow informed speculation about the reasons as a firm basis for trying to redress the imbalance. The field of computing is relatively new, and the studies which directly address the very complex problem of the reasons for the imbalance are scattered. Nevertheless, sufficient evidence has already been accumulated to provide indicators of some of the major factors at work.

FACTORS IN THE GENDER IMBALANCE OF COMPUTER USE

In trying to assess the major sources of the difficulties here, one might be tempted to look at the world of employment as the overriding factor, and at the ability of girls and women to use computers effectively as a second major factor. As I shall suggest, however, both of these approaches lead to blind alleys, and one has to seek elsewhere for possible explanations.

At first sight it appears as if the situation in employment is one of the chief factors: women are significantly underrepresented in employment at most levels of working with computers. At the lowest levels—that of merely entering data into computers—there are far more women than men. In 1980 in the United States, women formed 78 percent of those employed as keypunchers or computer operators (Wider Opportunities for Women, 1983), while, in the UK of the same year, a survey showed that between 75 and 100 percent of all workers at the lowest level of computing were women (Simons, 1981).

At the more advanced levels of working with computers, in the United States in 1980, only 29 percent of computer programmers and 22 percent of systems analysts were women (Wider Opportunities for Women, 1983). In the UK, the gender imbalance was even more dramatic: females comprised only between 5 and 15 percent of all computer programmers, and less than 5 percent of systems analysts (Simons, 1981). In Germany in 1979, female systems analysts, programmers, and sales staff comprised only 18 percent of the total employed in these areas of computing (Simons, 1981).

But there is evidence that companies involved in the computer industry, far from discriminating against women, are trying actively to encourage their participation. Moreover, there are certain characteristics of working with computers which make such work particularly attractive to women who place a high value on their domestic roles. In the UK, the Women's National Commission (1984) has found that:

> The new technology industries are the least resistant to the employment of women at all levels, provided qualified women come forward. Some companies have made special efforts to make their recruitment literature attractive to women. Companies like "F International" which employ women computing experts as "home workers," together with women managers of this now large-scale operation, show that skills in computing can offer women a special kind of compatibility between home and work responsibilities; isolation is also alleviated by the high-powered nature of much of the work and the need for periods of working contact with the client firm. Many women working for such companies have been able to make geographical moves following their husband's career without jeopardising their own; levels of work commitment can be varied over time, and there are opportunities to take wider responsibilities for managing others.

In the United States, evidence adduced in the mid-1970s suggested that the computer industry represented a relatively favorable employment environment for women (Simons, 1981), and the position appears, if anything, to have improved since that time. In varying degrees, throughout the developed world, women still suffer from multifarious patterns of stereotyping and of direct and indirect discrimination, and their progress up the hierarchy of the world of computing is often as tenuous as it is in many other fields. But, as Simons (1981) suggests, "compared with other, older industries, it is arguable that women have done well in data processing"; indeed, as Chivers (1984) reports, "some of the large high technology companies in computing and electronics ... have actively supported the very able women technologists entering their ranks."

It appears, then, as if the reasons for the under-representation of women at all levels of computing do not stem primarily from discriminatory practices within the computer industry itself. Perhaps, then, women simply have less ability to use computers? There often appear to be connections between using computers and using mathematical ideas, and women and girls seem to perform less well at mathematics than men and boys. Perhaps, then, the problem lies in the lesser mathematical ability of females?

So far, nearly all the evidence available seems to suggest that women have abilities to work with computers which are at least equal to those of men. As Deakin (1984) points out, "computing is a discipline that requires some (but not necessarily great) mathematical ability, logic, ... and a grasp of the principles of language systems and communication methods."

But even the assumption that girls and women are "bad" at mathematics needs further investigation. More females than males do say that they are afraid of mathematics and of technology, but there is evidence to suggest that such anxiety is a learned rather than an innate response. At primary school level, it appears that girls and boys perform almost equally in mathematics. It is only after elementary school that there appears to be a decline in the aptitude and achievement of girls. Thus, girls' attitudes toward mathematics tend to take a turn for the worse during the years of their early adolescence, at a time when they tend not to want to compete with boys. It has been shown that, in the United States, where mathematically gifted boys often take advanced courses, mathematically gifted girls are reluctant to do so because of their fear of social rejection (Stanley, 1973).

From the UK, there is a growing body of evidence to suggest that, when girls are taught mathematics in single-sex settings, their academic results are at least equal to those of boys taught in mixed-sex groupings, where boys have consistently been shown to be superior to girls in their results in mathematics. In a cautious review of the evidence in the UK so far, Smith (1984) concluded that "secondary school girls are likely to do better at maths when segregated from boys." This finding was confirmed in an experiment in England at Stamford High School, where a single-sex setting for the teaching of mathematics appeared to have a pronounced beneficial effect on the final marks of the girls during the two years in which it operated. It appears then, that, at least in mathematics, the performance of girls is at least as good as that of boys. The factors affecting the apparent decline in secondary school appear to be social rather than innate.

But the significant dropout of girls from computer courses discussed above seems to imply that they may have less ability at working with computers than boys. In the United States, as Rossen (1982) shows, girls have been doing slightly less well than boys on computer programming tests. However, when they have good exposure to computers, the girls perform as well as, or better than, boys (Rossen, 1982). Here again as in the question of mathematical performance, social factors rather than innate abilities appear to be the main cause of the apparent lesser performance by girls. There is now a mass of anecdotal evidence to suggest that girls will be discouraged from computing by the attitudes of their male peers. In one US high school, for instance, adolescent boys harassed the girls in order to discourage them from registering for the after-school computer courses. The boys admitted that they were doing this deliberately to limit enrollment, so that they could have more computer time for themselves (Rossen, 1982). In the UK, the Equal Opportunities

Commission has graphically depicted one example of a ubiquitous problem with mixed-sex teaching of computer courses in secondary school:

> Because the number of boys in the course far outweighed the number of girls, the girls felt as though they were interlopers, and that they had fewer rights than the boys when the computers were being used.
> There was not enough time in class for adequate programming on the computers. The boys compensated for this by using the computer room at other times, but they did this in a way that forced the girls out or discouraged them from entering at all. This caused many girls to drop out of the course as they felt they had little or no chance of completing their project work. The sheer size and power of the average boy, determined to take more than his fair share of computer time, gradually forced the more timid girls to give up altogether. (EOC, 1983)

It appears, then, that the factors involved in the under-representation of women in computing can be traced neither to the beginning of their formal learning at school nor to their employment at the end of their formal education. Instead, the first of our clues may lie in the interaction that takes place between girls and computers at school.

GIRLS AND COMPUTERS

Even where girls do choose to take part in computer studies and in other ways of using computers at school, they have a particularly pronounced dropout rate. In one local education authority in England, for instance, twice as many girls as boys failed to take the final, qualifying examination in Computer Studies (EOC, 1983). As we have already seen, the ways in which boys effectively exclude girls from using the few machines available in many schools clearly contribute to such a wastage rate; competition between boys and girls for what is still a relatively scarce resource is likely to benefit those who are more aggressive and competitive. But other factors seem to interact with such sexist exclusion to create a situation in which girls choose to exclude themselves from the specific opportunities that are available to them.

A number of features about the way in which computer studies are presented in school seem to alienate girls. Indeed, it appears that some of the same characteristics are at least partially responsible for the extent to which many women also feel alienated from the new information technologies, including computers.

In the first place, work with computers in schools often focuses primarily on the machine itself, the theories behind its functioning and the electronics that implement those theories. The Deputy Director of the Microelectronics Education Programme in England and Wales, for instance, believes that Computer Studies should emphasize "the concepts which underlie electronic systems, electronics, and the binary logic of a system" (EOC, 1983). Since many local authorities in those two countries depend on MEP for in-service training and advice in using computers in schools, such an emphasis will presumably be reflected in practice at the grass-roots level in the schools themselves.

The fact that computing studies tend to be taught, at least in the UK, by teachers of physics and mathematics reinforces the tendency to emphasize the theory and the electronics of the technology itself, and may contribute to the speed at which girls, who tend to have much less affinity with machines as a whole, often opt out of such courses. Moreover, the problems set for pupils to solve by using computer programs tend to be mathematically based, and may thus create gratuitous difficulties for girls who are insecure about their mathematical abilities in the first place.

Other possible reasons for girls' withdrawal from computers emerge from the responses given by girls in England who had chosen Computer Studies at the end of their third year in secondary school. EOC (1983) cited some typical answers to questions which the girls were asked:

Q: Has the course been of use to you? Why?

A: Yes, it helps me practice my typing.

Q: Do you think the course was aimed mainly at boys, girls, or both equally? Explain why.

A: Boys - all the teachers are men.

Q: Has the course turned out as you expected? (Explain fully.)

A: No. I expected to be taught more practical use of the computers; more lessons on actual programming.

Q: Can you suggest any changes in the course which could have helped out?

A: 1: More practical programming. 2: The present course is very dull. A more active lesson would create greater interest on the pupil's part.

Q: Has the course been of use to you? Why?

A: No, I have found the majority of the work uninteresting and the concepts difficult to understand and grasp.

Q: Can you suggest any changes in the course which would help you?

A: More explanation and practice of computer language and terms.

This sample of pupil responses draws unflattering attention to the effect of the quality of teaching in work on computer studies. Because computer studies form a new area of academic study—an area where in many cases teachers are not even a single step ahead of their more able pupils—it is perhaps inevitable that standards of presentation may not be as high as in more traditional subjects. There is now evidence to suggest, however, that this apparent lack of high quality does discourage more girls than boys.

Why? Here again there seems to be a variety of interlocking factors. In the first place, boys seem to have a much stronger motivation to engage with computers for their own sake and will, therefore, probably be more tolerant of difficulties placed in their path, such as poor quality teaching. Girls, with their stronger practical bent, will often wonder what the point of it all is, when, in many cases, the power of the computer is used to perform trivial tasks which could be carried out more efficiently by hand or by using a calculator. Indeed, as McClain (1983) has shown, while men are more interested in computer games and graphics, females tend to see the computer as a tool—a means to an end. Where they fail to find sufficient evidence of the efficacy of the computer as a tool, girls are likely to lose interest quickly.

Secondly, much of the material actually available to children in connection with computers is oriented primarily toward boys. Textbooks for Computer Studies in the UK tend to present a world in which computers are mainly for men and boys. The graphics in one textbook, for example, contained ten men to every woman, while those in another contained 11 men to the one woman, a barely clothed girl on a screen (EOC, 1983).

But children both at home and at school tend to use computer games far more than computer textbooks. And, as we have seen, those games tend to be for boys only. The noneducational games have titles like "Armageddon," "Dracula," "Space Invaders," or "War Games" (after the film of the same name in which an adolescent boy nearly destroys the world as a result of breaking into a computer defense system). Nearly all girls are repelled by the violence in both the concept and the actuality of these games. Descriptions of two recent games from a review of them illustrate their typical characteristics:

> *Along with a nimble fire-button, you also need a keen sense of strategy, if you're to survive in its alien universe. You are a trader who will deal in anything in order to buy weapons and defenses to defend you from anything from galactic pirates to the police.*
>
> *The atmosphere is created by the spoken start of the game when an evil voice welcomes you with the chilling words, "Another visitor, stay awhile, stay forever!" This voice belongs to [a man] . . . who will destroy the world unless you crack his security code, but to do that you will have to outwit the most fiendish robots." (Hetherington, 1984)*

But much of the imagery used in educational programs is also either boring or unattractive to girls. Zimmerman (1983) reports on a game used to teach fractions to young children, which showed an arrow piercing a floating balloon when the pupil made a correct answer. "The girls, unlike the boys, did not care much about popping the balloons. When the reward image changed to a little puppy, girls' scores rose significantly."

A further difficulty often arises because most computer games foster a spirit of intense, often speed-ridden competitiveness either between the individual and the machine or between two individuals. There is a considerable body of evidence to suggest that females tend to view competitive success as dangerous (Whiting and Pope, 1973; Maccoby and Jacklin, 1974; Pollak and Gilligan, 1982; Gilligan, 1983; among many others). Games that appeal primarily to competitiveness rather than to the pleasures of interpersonal relationships may, therefore, tend to alienate girls and women.

Other social factors in girls' experience are also likely to alienate them from engaging with computers at school, as at home. It appears that many teachers and careers advisors still perceive science and technology, including computing, as subjects predominantly for boys. In the United States, for instance, women have consistently reported that the careers counseling which they received at school not only failed to encourage their participation in nontraditional fields but, in many cases, actually attempted to discourage them from study that would lead to mathematical and scientific careers (Luchins and Luchins, 1980). In the UK, concern about an analogous problem about careers counseling of girls led in 1984 to the establishment of the WISE (Women into Science and Engineering) campaign, designed to increase awareness of opportunities for girls in science and engineering, including the new information technologies.

All of these factors which contribute toward the alienation of girls from computers at school may also be found in the experiences of many women, with an even more pronounced adverse effect. Women have less money and less time to spend on themselves than men; many social factors conspire to make it more difficult for women to advance upwards in careers; the computer world itself tends to be composed primarily of young men rather than of middle-aged women. All of these factors make it unlikely that women will, of their own accord, contribute fully to the world of computing.

Does this relative exclusion matter? Well, there are compelling arguments that can be made about the need for our economies to use to the fullest the talents of both men and women. The moral arguments in favor of gender equality are becoming more generally accepted. But there are also specific reasons why the participation of women in the world of computing is necessary both for that world and for the economic position of women themselves. It is to these that I shall now turn, before considering some of the ways that have already been found to enable women to interact more fully with computers.

REDRESSING THE GENDER IMBALANCE

It is essential to encourage more women to engage in computers, both for their economic survival and for the ways in which their greater participation may help to make computers more responsive to human needs. Throughout most of the developed world, computerization seems to be having an apparently contradictory effect on employment: many new jobs are created in the new information technologies, at the same time as the demand for many older skills appears to be decreasing. To an even greater extent than men, women are trapped by this contradictory effect. The situation in Canada, as described by Menzies (1981), seems to be replicated in most other developed countries: "Informatics is creating new work and employment, but largely in the professional and technical ranks where men predominate and women are still in a minority." In particular, Menzies argues, there is likely to be an "alarmingly high rate of structural unemployment among female clerical workers ... unless appropriate measures are taken by governments, employers, and women."

The same conclusion appears elsewhere in the growing literature of this field. Thus, Feldberg and Glenn (1982) find that "the expansion of computer-related occupations has increased the total number of jobs and created some new higher paid occupations. However, the workers displaced by automation do not appear to benefit: the new jobs are technical level and largely held by males." The finding is substantiated by Menzies, who cites the fact that, in the Canadian corporation which she examined, only two out of the 130 workers displaced from clerical work moved upwards to professional or managerial levels.

The extent of the potential wastage of female staff may be seen in the fact that "in most industrialized countries ... the reduction of staff predicted in offices and banks is in the region of 30 to 50 percent" (Trudel and Belanger, 1982). By far the vast majority of these workers are women, and, as Menzies bleakly notes, "the supply of clerical labour is projected to outstrip demand."

But it is not only the quantity of female jobs which are affected adversely by computerization. There is also evidence that the quality, particularly of the kinds of clerical work traditionally undertaken by women, may be suffering in the process. Examining four representative fields in which computerization has affected work—a large, broadly diversified corporation, an insurance company, banking, and supermarkets—Menzies concludes that:

> *The continuing standardization, streamlining, and fragmentation of work functions,*
> *which was observed in all of the case studies, suggests that clerical work is becoming*

more like an assembly line. . . . Monitoring tends to place quantity of output over sophistication of input, and thereby subtly degrades the scope of the work involved. . . . The operation of a word processor terminal does not require a great deal of skill on the part of the operator.

As a homely illustration, my word processor makes it possible for me no longer to need traditional typing skills: I can readily correct the many errors that arise from inaccurate typing before I print out a final version; I can, if I wish, use a spelling program to indicate to me words that I have unwittingly misspelled; indeed, the only loss may be stylistic, in that my computer cannot tactfully suggest where I have communicated unclearly in the way that a sympathetic typist might have done! The final result is to upgrade my incompetent typing skills and thereby to devalue the skills of a conventional typist, whose speed, accuracy, and neatness are largely redundant. Thus, Feldberg and Glenn (1982) conclude that "women have been differentially and more negatively affected than men by changes accompanying office automation." The clerical skills by which many women have earned their living, then, are no longer likely to ensure their economic survival.

But there are other reasons why women need to engage more readily with computers. The fact that some computing firms are actively recruiting and supporting their female staff is not altruistic. In certain respects, women tend to make better computer programmers than men. Women's traditional ability to master languages with apparent ease extends also to the mastery of computer languages, and women's tendency toward linear logic also stands them in good stead in this field. McClain (1983) has found that women are more likely to write good computer programs with the user in mind. Women's tendency to ignore extraneous factors and to concentrate on the task at hand also leads to good programming technique. Indeed, there is a considerable amount of evidence that, while males tend to be more curious and more likely to take risks, females are better able to screen out irrelevancies, carry out tasks, and be better problem-solvers under stress (Weizman, 1975; Safran, 1983; among others). All of these qualities again are conducive to good computer techniques.

The advantages that women bring to computing have also been spelled out by the course tutor in a computing school (Women's National Commission, 1984). She noted first that women provided a disproportionate share of the really able and most tenacious students and that they demonstrated an ability to serve industry well. In particular, she reported that women "frequently showed a clear advantage over men as project managers/systems analysts, as they communicated better with non-computing staff, an absolute requirement of the future."

Deakin (1984) notes that women are often as good as, or better than, men at selling computers. She analyzes her own experience as a sales consultant:

> *Now that I work as a sales consultant, I still feel that there are some ways in which I have something special to offer by being female. I think that I have been able to advise and assist the male customers particularly well because they do not feel threatened by me, because I have learned to communicate and because I am concerned with the practicalities of their needs rather than the beauty of any particular machine. As one person said, I am "into customer solutions." This may not be the preserve of women, but it is their very special contribution and one which the whole industry needs. This is one reason why it is as important for men as it is for women that women become more involved in computers and computing.*

Although such comparisons are probably invidious, there are also snippets of evidence that women may be perceived as better than men in teaching computing to adults. Banks (1984) found that nearly half of the students whom he interviewed about their experiences of computing courses for adults did not consider their tutor to be a good teacher but that "generally students were less critical of female tutors than male." Salkeld (1983) has also suggested that the few female tutors on introductory computer courses for adults seemed to be particularly popular as teachers. Any rash hypothesis that most of the students were male and, therefore, preferred to have women tutors is nullified by the fact that nearly half of the students interviewed by Banks were female.

Finally, simply because of their traditional proficiency in clerical skills—especially in typing—women have a distinct advantage in using computer keyboards. Familiarity with the QWERTY keyboard and accuracy in pressing keys are practical skills, the lack of which are often disadvantageous to male users, particularly male users who wish to use computers for practical applications rather than to write programs or design computer architectures. It is largely for such male users that various devices such as the "mouse" have been designed, but, for sheer practical ease, using the keyboard remains the most efficient way to harness the power of a computer. And more women are better placed than most men to do so.

For their own economic good and for the economic good of the computer industry, then, there are clear advantages in a closer interaction between women and computers. Beyond these economic considerations, however, a more far-reaching case also exists for the need for more women to become involved in computing.

At least part of the world dominated by computers is pathological—obsessed by power and ruled by instrumental reason. There are many reasons why such characteristics have emerged. The relative scarcity of women in computing is probably only a minor factor in creating a situation where computers are used primarily for military purposes and commercial profit rather than to help to meet the real needs that people have to find out more about their local communities, to keep in touch with each other and their compassionate desires to help one another, and to nurture the young, the handicapped, and the frail. As later chapters will suggest, computer applications can provide valuable help in all of these traditionally "female" areas of concern. It may be, then, that when women play a substantially increased part in computing, greater attention will be given to ways in which computers can actively help people.

Many of the characteristics that women currently find so alienating about computers are not inevitable in the technology itself. There is no absolute reason why using computers has to be accompanied by smokescreens of jargon or delight in the machines themselves: women have used automatic washing machines for decades without feeling any need to worship the object which replaces unpleasant physical labor. Most women, too, bring to computers a hard core of common sense, based on a lack of time to waste. They tend to recognize that, just as there are many tasks which can be performed more efficiently and effectively on a computer, so there are many more which can be performed, but which are not worth performing. If women were to play an increased role in using computers, then, it is possible that a more humanly balanced view of the uses and nonuses of computers might result.

Despite these arguments for redressing the gender imbalance in using computers, however, strong counter-arguments have been advanced against any greater involvement by women. Some radical feminists in particular believe that technology is not simply a neutral means whereby individuals, groups, and societies can achieve their goals.

In the first place, the argument runs, women throughout the world are often exploited by computer technology, particularly in Third World countries where they tend to be employed in the production and assemblage of computer and microprocessor equipment. And there appear to be certain dangers to women's health when they are required to use computer terminals for long periods of time. In these ways, women are seriously disadvantaged by computer technology.

More broadly, radical feminists argue that:

> Women must not forget that the range and nature of a society's technology is a reflection of the dominant socio-economic system. And in the Western culture that means that it is a process guided by the values of the various patriarchies and one which owes its very existence to the requirements of the military–industrial complex. At its furthest development their argument challenges the whole nature of technology and the societies that spawned it, asking the . . . question: can feminists use technology as it stands at all, or does using it involve fatal compromise and collusion with the forces of patriarchy? (Women and Computing, 1981)

Such a stance, however, involves the acceptance of premises that are not shared by all feminists. I should like to argue, more pragmatically, that women who exclude themselves from learning about and using computers risk experiencing even greater vulnerability in a world that is increasingly dependent on the power of computers and telecommunications. In a similar belief that education and training, rather than withdrawal from the world of technology, are more likely to empower women, many individuals and organizations are now responding to what they see as the need to help women to use computer technology for their own ends. During the 1980s, there has thus been a dramatic growth in the number of opportunities which have been created for women to learn about computers.

WOMEN LEARNING ABOUT COMPUTERS

We have already seen that girls' mathematical and computer performance tends to increase when they are taught in single-sex settings. And women tend to use computers in greater numbers in women-only groups. Most of the opportunities currently being created for women to come to terms with computers, therefore, tend to be for women only and, more frequently than not, taught by women only. The one major exception to the general pattern—that of the BBC's Computer Literacy Project—appealed more or less equally to men and women, partly because it was careful to show that all ages and both sexes could use computers with equal facility and efficacy (Radcliffe and Salkeld, 1983), but also possibly because the television programs could be watched at home rather than in adult education classes composed predominantly of men.

The range of courses to enable women to learn about computers is wide, encompassing formal training courses, as well as formal courses in educational institutions and nonformal adult education classes. They seem clearly to be meeting a felt need: the demand for them almost invariably exceeds provision. Three case studies of courses in the UK, the United States, and New Zealand may illustrate the range and suggest some of the essential characteristics of successful courses of this type.

"Computers for Women" in New Zealand

In 1984 in Wellington, New Zealand, a course called "Computers for Women" was organized, according to one of the women course leaders,

> *To provide a "safe" environment where women can happily expose their ignorance and try things out and ask elementary questions without being or feeling put down. There has certainly been a lot of interest and a good response from a wide variety of women. We have pointed out to all enrolling that this is indeed a course for absolute beginners, and if they know anything about computers they are too advanced for the course. The usual response is "Oh good, that's just what I want—I've never even seen a computer" ... We hope women who become interested through our courses will go on to take others in special fields of their own choosing.... Once they know a little, they can cope better with the "male expert" syndrome and feel less inadequate faced with all that jargon. (Else, 1984a)*

The attractively elementary nature of the course would be very likely to appeal to women who feel uneasy about coming to terms with computers. Following the completion of the course, an analysis of completed questionnaires showed that participants

> *Appreciated the friendly supportive atmosphere and the availability of an all-women class. They liked feeling able to ask any questions at all without feeling threatened or put down. They liked the variety of speakers arranged and the exchange of ideas between course members and lecturers; also the chance to hear about others' problems with computers. They enjoyed the hands-on experience.... Three stated their approval/enjoyment of the way political issues to do with women, computers, and society were raised, as well as the technical points.... On the whole, the response was one of positive enjoyment and enhanced confidence. (Else, 1984b)*

The difficulties experienced were largely those created by this being the first course of its kind in the country:

> *It was clear that we had not really broken down the initial instruction sessions into small or simple enough chunks for some people. We were still using too much jargon in places or moving too quickly over basic points, e.g., use of keyboard. We needed one more person to help the participants when all were present and using the computers, and should also have provided more written material as simple manuals and hand-outs. There were also some problems with the [computer equipment] breaking down. Not everyone liked politics being included—they would have preferred a straight technical approach. Time was a constant problem. (Else, 1984b)*

The crucial element in this course was clearly the provision of an all-female environment in which women felt free to start from the very beginning. The second characteristic is that of utility, with an emphasis on what the computer can be used for rather than on the details of what exactly it is in itself. For many women, however, such a course may have created practical problems, both because it was relatively expensive, and because it made no provisions for the care of their children. Both of these issues have been directly addressed in Sheffield, UK, in a new scheme designed to introduce women to computing.

A WOMEN'S TECHNOLOGY TRAINING WORKSHOP IN THE UK

The purpose of this workshop, which is funded jointly by Sheffield City Council and the European Social Fund, is:

> *To provide basic and more advanced training in microelectronics and computing fields, where women are under-represented. The training . . . is intended for women over 25 who are unemployed, threatened with unemployment, or wishing to return to work after a period of child-rearing. The courses are specifically tailored to suit unskilled women who have been unable to take advantage of existing training facilities in the field. To this end . . . there are no formal entry requirements; the courses are part-time; child-care allowances are available; the courses are administered by, and taught by, women. (Sheffield City Council, 1984)*

As soon as the course was advertised, despite the fact that its initial intake consisted only of 28 places, there were thousands of telephone enquiries which provided evidence of an unsuspected scale of demand for such training (Miller, 1984a). Over 500 women completed application forms, and trainees were selected primarily on a quota system of age, status, ethnic origin, and "social need." Over two-thirds of the women had no qualifications at all (Miller, 1984b).

The course which the women are following has four main components. The Return to Work component aims "to develop confidence and to provide support for the new training environment" and "to provide a critical appreciation of the social impact of New Technology." The Computing component aims to enable trainees "to gain familiarity and confidence in using both mini- and microcomputers, to gain an understanding of programming in a high-level language (BASIC), to gain skills in using software packages . . . , to become computer literate." The Microelectronics part of the course develops a range of technical knowledge and skills. Mathematics, ranging from basic numeracy to certificate standard, is also taught to enable the students to understand fully the technical course components (Miller, 1984b).

By late autumn of 1984, the response of the trainees, who began in March, was seen as "extremely encouraging. All the trainees, including those with small children, have not only shown considerable enthusiasm and dedication while attending the Workshop, but have also specifically requested that homework be set and assessed on a regular basis, despite the fact that this was not intended to be a requirement of the course" (Miller, 1984b).

However, an analysis of the course has indicated that, while lack of formal qualifications has been no bar to satisfactory performance, some women who lacked numeracy and literacy skills have been unable to grasp essential background concepts. The course organizer has accepted that "these basic skills cannot be taught concurrently with main courses. Moreover teaching of these skills is both a specialized and lengthy process and cannot always be done on an intensive basis. Accordingly, literacy and numeracy must figure in the criteria for admission to the course" (Miller, 1984b).

This problem is not dissimilar to that which emerged from the course in New Zealand, where the initial concepts were not simple enough for some people. Indeed, the Sheffield findings reflect elements in the experience of some girls in computer studies in schools, where they reported that "the concepts [were] difficult to understand and grasp" and that the course was "much more complicated, detailed and theoretical than I imagined" (EOC, 1983).

This issue of the interrelationships between computer literacy and more traditional forms of literacy and numeracy also arises in the use of computers in nonformal adult basic education, and is obviously a matter to which much more thought and research needs to be addressed. It is already clear, however, that women, disadvantaged as they often seem to be in numeracy, may also be disadvantaged in coming to terms with computers unless ways can be found of tackling the combined problem of computer illiteracy and general lack of numeracy.

Meanwhile, it appears as if the prospect of enhanced employment and training opportunities at the end of the course, together with the provision of child-care arrangements and the payment of training expenses to the trainees, have been significant factors in the overwhelming demand for the course. The Women's Technology Training Workshop appears to have demonstrated that, once socioeconomic factors are taken realistically and sensitively into account, women are very willing indeed to come to terms with computers.

The Women's Computer Literacy Project in the United States

This project to enable women to acquire computer literacy was set up as "an alternative to the computer classes many women found alienating" (Marohn, undated). As one of the organizers of the courses saw the situation, "many women have an approach-avoidance attitude toward computers, . . . and most men are not very good at teaching women. We've heard all kinds of horror stories about classes at city colleges and computer stores where smart women have been made to feel stupid and have been given the sense that they can't do it" (Marohn, undated).

The Project offers two-day, full-time, and four-week part-time courses in San Francisco and two-day courses in New York "for those who know nothing about computers and prefer to learn in a woman-centered environment." As is the course in New Zealand and that in Sheffield, it is highly practically oriented, as the leaflet proclaims:

> At the end of the course you will know what microcomputers can and cannot do; you will be able to operate a microcomputer with confidence; and you will be able to read and understand most operations manuals for computer hardware and software systems. You will also understand the differences between various microcomputer systems so that you can shop for the correct system to meet your personal, business, or organizational needs.

Unlike the course in Sheffield, however, the American course, like most others in the United States, has to be self-financing; it is expensive, at least for women who do not have much money at their disposal. Clearly, however, it meets considerably more needs than the courses in programming in BASIC which formed the staple diet of computing courses for adults in the UK and other countries in the first years of using microcomputers (Gerver, 1984).

Other Ways of Encouraging Women to Use Computers

Even where no computer is actually provided as part of an introduction to the new technologies, there is now substantial international evidence that women will respond in large numbers to events and material which are prepared specifically for them about computers. In Israel, NA'AMAT, the largest women's organization in the country, chose "Women and Technology" as the theme for its annual Status of Women Month in 1983. The movement designed a portfolio designed to give women a feeling of familiarity with computers, selected films showing high technology at work in various fields, and used both print and television media to reinforce its message about ways in which women could link up to the new technology. The result was that, even though they themselves were not providing computer experiences or training opportunities, they received more enquiries than they could handle (NA'AMAT, undated). The same experience of demand exceeding supply has been almost invariably repeated in other countries.

As well as burgeoning opportunities in education and training, there has also been a number of important developments in other ways for women to use computers. The WISE Campaign in the UK exemplifies campaigns designed to encourage girls to choose computing as a career;

groups to support women in computing have mushroomed in the past few years throughout the developed world; and books and conferences are increasingly addressing the question of the under-representation of women in computing.

The WISE Campaign promoted by the Equal Opportunities Commission in the UK in 1984 aimed to encourage girls themselves to consider positively the opportunities for careers in science and technology, including particularly information technology. The EOC's (1984) booklet "Working with Computers" exemplifies the approach, in its careful selection of biographies of women who have achieved significant success in the world of the new technologies. Throughout, its approach is one of demystifying. It points out, for example, that for one girl, "the key to coping with computers for her was much more to do with being able to use the English language than to do with maths"; it draws attention to various cooperative ways of using computers and it highlights women who have come into the field from apparently unrelated disciplines and interests.

Such an approach to girls and women to help themselves in coming to terms with computers is likely, of course, to lead to only very limited change. WISE has placed great stress on what can be achieved "simply by a change to more positive attitudes by all concerned.... Girls leaving school simply need the interest and energy to find out and fully appreciate the many incentives and opportunities available in engineering and science" (WISE, 1984). As this present discussion has suggested, however, the matter cannot be resolved merely by altering the attitudes of girls, who, in many cases, are merely responding adversely to characteristics of the world of technology which are genuinely alienating.

Other organizations in Britain and the United States are trying to use the technology itself to offer more concrete help to those women and girls who feel they would like to use computers but are not sure how to go about it. One of the best examples of such supportive use of computers for women who feel that they may want to use computers may be seen in Microsyster, a London-based organization which was set up in 1982.

Microsyster "aims to encourage women to think about positive ways of making computers work for women. We are aware that many women feel alienated and excluded by new technology and are worried by the threat they do pose to our jobs and privacy. We not only want to provide a service for women, but also to open up these debates in the Women's Liberation Movement" (Microsyster, 1984). Microsyster, therefore, aims to "provide computing services to women and women's groups; make contact with and support other feminists working in computing; provide a feminist perspective on new technology; to introduce the skills and knowledge necessary for women to benefit from and critically assess new technology" (Microsyster, 1984).

As with the computer courses offered by women for women, so also the computer services offered by Microsyster are highly practical. They offer advice about whether a computer would really help an individual or a group; they help determine the system that would be most suitable and they even help with the writing out of the applications for grants to buy it. They also offer to help to set up systems and to teach women how to use the software packages which they have bought or acquired; the presentation of information in most computer manuals makes such informed help mandatory!

Support for women who want to use computers and for women who might want to use them if they were presented in a nonthreatening way has also come from an increasing number of books and conferences which, in the mid-1980s, have addressed the problem directly. In the UK in 1981, Simons' account of *Women in Computing* aimed "to encourage a search for constructive policies on the part of managers, employers, politicians, and others." Deakin's *Women and Computing: The Golden Opportunity* (1984) looks "first at the special benefits that exist for women in computing and then . . . at the ways in which the arrival of microcomputers can be a heaven-sent opportunity for them." Both books rely heavily on illuminating case studies of women who have successfully made careers for themselves in the world of computing.

Academic investigations of the problem of the under-representation of women in the new technologies generally and in computing in particular have multiplied during the 1980s. Work has been particularly concentrated on the adverse effects of computerization on the employment of women (Menzies, 1981; Rothschild, 1982; Werneke, 1983; among many others). The educational implications of the under-representation of women in computing are attracting European concern. In 1984, at least two European conferences devoted a substantial amount of time to the question of women and new technology, and there are plans to consider the subject in at least four conferences to be held in the UK in 1985. The awareness of the subject in the United States is also indicated by the growing numbers of academic publications on the topic (Gerver and Lewis, 1984). The International Council for Adult Education, which is based in Canada, also has plans to investigate the topic.

Those adult educators who feel that there is an overwhelming case for making it possible for more women to engage with computers are thus, at least in the mid-1980s, well supported. But much much more remains to be done, as the enormous over-subscription to the Women's Technology Training Workshops in Sheffield suggests.

One potentially worrying development is that the current pressures on higher and further education throughout most of the developed world are likely to exclude more and more women from formal study. One indicator of the full extent of the emerging problem may be seen in a report from the UK from the Computing School of Thames Polytechnic in London. In 1980–1, women formed 25 percent of the intake to courses in computing. In 1983–4, women formed only 16.9 percent of those admitted, and applications from women were down to 18 percent. The course tutor speculated that "the main reason was the increasingly competitive entry to courses . . . which activated women's diffidence, dislike of competition, and belief that a high-powered prestigious profession was 'for men only' " (Women's National Commission, 1984).

As places in higher education continue to be cut back in many developed countries, so one can safely predict that this pattern in London will be replicated many times. The onus will, therefore, lie even more heavily on those who provide informal education in the community. Adult educators need to become more aware of the extent of the problem, its main causes, and their possible solutions, so that they can offer greater gender equality than that which presently exists in most educational experiences involving computers.

REFERENCES

Banks, David (1983), "Adult classes in computing: a survey," *Adult Education*, vol. 56, p. 1.

Banks, David (1984), "The effectiveness of introductory computing evening classes," *Adult Education*, vol. 57(3), pp. 255–61.

BBC (1983), "BBC's computer literacy project: an evaluation," unpublished BBC Broadcasting Research Special Report, London: British Broadcasting Corporation.

Bernstein, Danielle (1984), "The invisible woman," *Practical Computing*, January, p. 189.

Beyers, Charlotte (1983), "Growing sex gap shows up in computer tastes," *The Times Educational Supplement*, November 18, p. 15.

Chivers, G. E. (1984), "A comparative international study of intervention studies to reduce girls' disadvantages in science and technology education and vocational training," paper presented to Conference on Interests in Science and Technology Education, 12th IPN Symposium in cooperation with UNESCO, Kiel, West Germany, April 2–6.

Deakin, Rose (1984), *Women and Computing: the Golden Opportunity*, London: Macmillan.

Else, Anne (1984a), Written communication to the author from Wellington, New Zealand, August 31.

Else, Anne (1984b), Written communication to the author from Wellington, New Zealand, November 29.

EOC (1983) *Information Technology in Schools: Guidelines of Good Practice for Teachers of IT*, produced by the London Borough of Croydon for the Equal Opportunities Commission, Manchester, UK.

EOC (1984), "Attract more girls to information technology," news release, Manchester, UK, January 19.

Feldberg, Roslyn and Glenn, Evelyn (1982), "Technology and work degradation: effects of office automation on women clerical workers," in Joan Rothschild (ed.), *Machina ex Dea: Feminist Perspectives on Technology*, New York: Pergamon Press.

Gerver, Elisabeth (1984), *Computers and Adult Learning*, Milton Keynes, UK: Open University Press.

Gerver, Elisabeth and Lewis, Linda (1984), "Women, computers, and adult education: liberation or oppression?" *Convergence*, vol. 17, p. 4.

Gilligan, C. (1983), *In a Different Voice*, Cambridge, MA: Harvard University Press.

Hetherington, Tony (1984), "Guy's games," *The Times Educational Supplement*, December 12, p. 40.

Luchins, E. H. and Luchins, A. S. (1980), "Female mathematicians: a contemporary appraisal," in L. H. Fox, L. Brody, and D. Tobin (eds), *Women and the Mathematical Mystique*, Baltimore, MD: Johns Hopkins University Press.

Maccoby, E. and Jacklin, C. (1974), *The Psychology of Sex Differences*, Stanford, CA: Stanford University Press.

Marohn, Stephanie (undated), "Computer age feminists," *Woman News*, San Francisco, CA.

McClain, E. (1983), "Do women resist computers?" *Popular Computing*, January.

Menzies, Heather (1981), *Women and the Chip: Case Studies of the Effects of Information on Employment in Canada*, Montreal: Institute for Research on Public Policy.

Microsyster (1984), Written communication to the author from London, November 13.

Miller, Wendy (1984a), Personal communication to the author at Women's Technology Training Workshop, Sheffield, May 8.

Miller, Wendy (1984b), "Women's Technology Training Workshop—Progress Report," report to Board of Directors, City Center Training Limited, October 24.

NA'AMAT (undated), "Working women and technology," leaflet produced by the Status of Women Division, Movement of Working Women and Volunteers, Tel Aviv.

National Science Foundation (undated), "Science and engineering education: data and information," prepared for the National Science Board Commission on Pre-college Education in Mathematics, Science and Technology by the Office of Scientific and Engineering Personnel and Education, Washington, DC.

PEER (1983), "Microcomputers in the classroom: are girls getting an even break?" Washington, DC: Project on Equal Education Rights for the NOW Legal Defense and Education Fund.

Pollak, S. and Gilligan, C. (1982), "Images of violence in thematic apperception test stories," *Journal of Personality and Social Psychology*, vol. 42, p. 1.

Radcliffe, John and Salkeld, Roberts (1983), *Towards Computer Literacy: The BBC Computer Literacy Project 1979–1983*, London: British Broadcasting Corporation.

Rogers, Rick (1983), "Pick a winning combination," *The Guardian*, August 16.

Rossen, P. (1982), "Do schools teach computer anxiety?" *Ms. Magazine,* December.

Rothschild, Joan (1982), (ed.), *Women, Technology, and Innovation,* Oxford: Pergamon Press.

Safran, C. (1983), "Hidden lessons," *New York Daily News,* October 9.

Salkeld, Roberts (1983), Personal communication at the British Broadcasting Corporation, London, on June 7.

Sheffield City Council (1984), "Report of the employment coordinator, Women's Technology Training Workshop," unpublished report for the Employment Program Committee, March 26.

Shotton, Margaret (1984), Personal communication at the University of Loughborough, June 15.

Simons, G. L. (1981), *Women in Computing,* Manchester, UK: National Computing Centre Limited, 1981.

Smith, Stuart (1984), "Single-sex setting," in Rosemary Deem (ed.), *Co-education Reconsidered,* Milton Keynes, UK: Open University Press.

Stanley, J. C. (1973), "Comparison of men's and women's behaviors in high school math classes," California: SRI International.

Trudel, Lina and Belanger, Paul (1982), "Computerization: for better and for worse," paper prepared for International Council of Adult Education Conference, Paris, October.

Weizenbaum, Joseph (1976), *Computer Power and Human Reason,* San Francisco: Freeman.

Weizman, Lenore (1975), "Sex-role socialization," in Jo Freedman (ed.), *Women: A Feminist Perspective,* Palo Alto, CA: Mayfield Publishing.

Werneke, Diane (1983), *Microelectronics and Office Jobs: The Impact of the Chip on Women's Employment,* Geneva: International Labour Office.

Whiting, B. and Pope, C. (1973), "A cross cultural analysis of sex differences in the behavior of children age three to eleven," *Journal of Social Psychology,* vol. 91.

Wider Opportunities for Women (1983), "Bridging the skills gap: women and jobs in a high tech world," Washington, DC: Wider Opportunities for Women, April.

WISE (Women into Science and Engineering) (1984), "When I chose engineering, my friends thought it was a joke . . ." Equal Opportunities Commission leaflet, Manchester, UK.

Women and Computing (1981), "Are computers feminist?" London.

Women's National Commission (1984), "The other half of our future," report of the WNC's Ad-Hoc Working Group on training opportunities for women, London: Cabinet Office.

Yeates, Robin (1982), *Prestel in the Public Library: Reaction of the General Public to Prestel and Its Potential for Conveying Local Information,* Library and Information Research Report 2, London: British Library.

Zimmerman, Jan (1983), cited in Charlotte Beyers, "Growing sex gap shows up in computer tastes," *The Times Educational Supplement,* November 18, 1983.

THINKING AND RE-READING

1. As you re-read this selection, make a list of the areas in which girls or women do not seem to fare as well as boys or men in their usage of computers. Think about whether your own experiences coincide with or contradict the claims you extract from the article.

2. Jot down some of the recommendations Gerver makes for dealing with the issues she raises. How do these suggestions compare with those advanced by Kramarae and Taylor? Are there any claims that Gerver makes with which you disagree? Which? Why? What suggestions would you add to the list?

3. Which countries does Gerver include in her article? What does her choice of countries suggest? How do you think women are faring with computers in countries that she fails to mention?

4. Gerver writes, "It is essential to encourage more women to engage in computers, both for their economic survival and for the ways in which their greater participation may help to make computers more responsive to human needs." What examples can you give from your own experiences on campus or at work of computers used or presented in such a way that they're not responsive to human needs? What changes might you suggest in order to make them more responsive?

WRITING AND LEARNING

The overwhelming impression created by all the computer magazines and advertisements for microcomputers in Britain in the early 1980s was that this was a world only for men and their sons. "Son, where's my Epson?" demanded a happy father in an advertisement, as his school-age child sheepishly hid the computer behind his back. Early figures for sales of the extraordinarily popular BBC Computer indicated that over 90 percent of the purchasers were male.

1. In this statement, Gerver depicts a very male world as far as computers are concerned. Two paragraphs later, however, Gerver makes the interesting point that "the representation of women in advertisements for computers is likely to increase." What is her reasoning here? Is the inclusion of other underrepresented groups likely to increase as well? Why? Go through the advertisements in one of the popular computer magazines in either this country or elsewhere, looking at one magazine from the early 1980s and another from today. What differences, if any, do you see in who gets represented in the advertisements and how? Write a report of your findings to a women's group on campus, giving your assessment as to whether women and other groups are represented more equally and more fairly today in the computer culture than they were when Gerver wrote her article.

2. Like Kramarae and Taylor, Gerver argues that the very language that is used in depicting cyberspace attracts men and tends to exclude women. When the "land of computing" is referred to as a "frontier," more men than women are likely to stake out a claim. Go through several articles on computing in this collection or in a popular computer magazine like *Wired* or a trade magazine. List the metaphors you come across that are used to represent cyberspace. Write a memo to share with your class and send it to us or to the editors of a magazine stating your findings and making suggestions for language that you would like to see used in connection with computers.

3. When you finish re-reading Gerver, go back through Bush's article that we've included at the Web site. Make two columns on paper or in a word processing file. What similar points do the two authors make? Where does their thinking diverge? (Consider two

claims that they both make and think about their relevance for your own community. For example, has the introduction of computers shifted the kinds of jobs available in your community? Has the use of computers changed the kinds of "techniques" or skills required for the job? Are there instances in which jobs are "deskilled," as Michael Apple suggests in his article in the Education and Technology section? Write an account of your observations to the local school board in your community, reporting on your findings and explaining why they have relevance to local school curricula. If your community has an electronic bulletin board, such as FreeNet or another public access network, make sure that those who work with the network also receive a copy of your report.

Becoming a Computer Scientist

Amy Pearl, Martha E. Pollack, Eve Riskin,
Becky Thomas, Elizabeth Wolf, and Alice Wu

HOW DOES ONE CHOOSE an academic career in computer science, especially if one is a woman? With great difficulty, the authors of this selection tell us. As professional women with advanced degrees, the authors present convincing evidence that roadblocks appear on every corner for women aspiring to academic positions in computing. Not only are young girls brought up in a culture in which computers hold little allure for their sex, but, as women, they are also discriminated against in visible and not so visible ways at every level of their education. Although the authors concede that many of the sciences pose similar problems for women, this fact holds little consolation for women seeking careers in computer science. Originally published in the Communications of the Association for Computing Machinery (ACM), this article challenges both men and women to take steps to remedy—or at least improve—conditions that existed for women when the article first appeared in 1990 and which, unfortunately, are likely to exist in many schools today.

It is well known that women are significantly underrepresented in scientific fields in the United States, and computer science is no exception. As of 1987–1988, women constituted slightly more than half of the U.S. population and 45% of employed workers in the U.S., but they made up only 30% of employed computer scientists. Moreover, they constituted only 10% of employed doctoral-level computer scientists. During the same time period, women made up 20% of physicians and, at the doctoral level, 35% of psychologists, 22% of life scientists, and 10% of mathematicians employed in the U.S. On the other hand, there are some disciplines in which women represent an even smaller proportion at the doctoral level: in 1987–88, 8% of physical scientists, and only 2.5% of engineers were women [21].[1] The underrepresentation of women in computer science is alarming for at least

[1]Statistics were also acquired from the U.S. Bureau of Labor Statistics in a telephone conversation.

two reasons. First, it raises the disturbing possibility that the field of computer science functions in ways that prevent or hinder women from becoming part of it. If this is so, those in the discipline need to evaluate their practices to ensure that fair and equal treatment is being provided to all potential and current computer scientists. Practices that exclude women are not only unethical, but they are likely to thwart the discipline's progress, as potential contributors to the field are discouraged from participation.

The second reason for concern about the underrepresentation of women in computer science relates to demographic trends in the U.S., which suggest a significant decrease in the number of white males entering college during the next decade. At the same time, the number of jobs requiring scientific or engineering training will continue to increase. Because white males have traditionally constituted the vast majority of trained scientists and engineers in this country, experts have predicted that a critical labor shortage is likely early in the next century [4, 25]. To confront this possibility, the federal government has begun to expend resources to study the problem further. A notable example is the establishment of a National Task Force on Women, Minorities, and the Handicapped in Science and Technology. Their final report, issued in December of 1989, lists a number of government and industrial programs aimed at preventing a labor shortage by increasing the number of women and minorities trained as scientists and engineers [5].

In light of these facts, the Committee on the Status of Women in Computer Science, a subcommittee of the ACM's Committee on Scientific Freedom and Human Rights, was established with the goal of studying the causes of women's continued underrepresentation in the field, and developing proposed solutions to problems found. It is the committee's belief that the low number of women working as computer scientists is inextricably tied up with the particular difficulties that women face in *becoming* computer scientists.

Studies show that women in computer science programs in U.S. universities terminate their training earlier than men do. Between 1983 and 1986 (the latest year for which we have such figures) the percentage of bachelor's degrees in computer science awarded to women was in the range of 36–37%, while the percentage of master's degrees was in the range of 28–30%. During the same time span, the percentage of doctoral degrees awarded to women has only been in the range of 10–12%, and it has remained at that level, with the exception of a slight increase in 1989 [16, 21]. Moreover, the discrepancy between the numbers of men and women continues to increase when we look at the people who are training the future computer scientists: women currently hold only 6.5% of the faculty positions in the computer science and computer engineering departments in the 158 Ph.D.-granting institutions included in the 1988–1989 Taulbee Survey (see *Communications* September 1990). In fact, a third of these departments have no female faculty members at all [16]. This pattern of decreasing representation is generally consistent with that of other scientific and engineering fields [4, 25]. It is often described as "pipeline shrinkage": as women move along the academic pipeline, their percentages continue to shrink.

The focus of this report is pipeline shrinkage for women in computer science. We describe the situation for women at all stages of training in computer science, from the precollege level through graduate school. Because many of the problems discussed are related to the lack of role models for women who are in the process of becoming computer scientists, we also concern ourselves with the status of women faculty members. We not only describe the problems, but also make specific recommendations for change and encourage further study of those problems whose solutions are not yet well understood.

Of course, our focus on computer science in the university by no means exhausts the set of issues that are relevant to an investigation of women in computer science. Most notably, we do not directly address issues that are of concern exclusively or primarily to women in industry. Although some of the problems we discuss are common to all women computer scientists, there are, without doubt, other problems that are unique to one group or the other. Nonetheless, the committee felt that an examination of the process of becoming a computer scientist provided a good starting point for a wider investigation of women in the field. Clearly, to increase the number of women in industrial computer science, one must first increase the number of women trained in the discipline. Thus, we need to consider why women stop their training earlier than men: too few women with bachelor's degrees in computer science translates into too few women in both industry and academia. Moreover, because of the documented positive effects of same-sex role models [12], it is also important to consider why women drop out in higher numbers than do men even later in their academic training: too few women with doctorate degrees results in too few women faculty members. This in turn means inadequate numbers of role models for younger women in the process of becoming computer scientists.

WHAT IS SPECIAL ABOUT COMPUTER SCIENCE?

There are many professions in which women are underrepresented. Indeed, as we noted earlier, underrepresentation of women is a fact in most scientific disciplines, and the pipeline shrinkage pattern seen in computer science is common to most sciences. Thus, one of the first questions we need to ask is: what, if anything, is different about computer science? Are there any special characteristics of the discipline that lead to unusual problems for women? Studies addressing these questions have been undertaken by both computer scientists and social scientists, and have identified cultural factors that are significant contributors to women's special experience in computing. These factors range from influences present in elementary-school educational software through the experiences of computer science graduate students.

Computers are encountered today by most children in this country more so than the artifacts of other science and engineering fields, even if they never study computer science in a formal educational setting. The earliest computer artifacts that children encounter are not gender neutral. Recreational and educational software programs reflect the gender biases and stereotypes of their designers, and studies reveal that educational software is generally designed to appeal to boys. For a host of reasons that are beyond the scope of this report, girls and boys have been shown to prefer different kinds of software programs. It is thus disturbing that, in an experimental setting, teachers instructed to design software for students tended to build programs that have the characteristics that boys prefer, and few characteristics that girls prefer—even when they are aware of these differences [13].

In addition to abstract characteristics of software use, the cultural values embedded in educational software and computer games that target adolescents almost exclusively reflect what is commonly identified as adolescent male culture. The predominant themes of recreational computer games are war, battles, crimes, destruction, and traditionally male-oriented sports and hobbies [14]. Thus, it is not surprising that boys use computers in courses and summer camps both earlier and more often than do girls.

Experience in computer use, and a resulting comfort with and affinity for computing, have a strong effect on the study of computer science in the university. When college students encounter computer science, they already perceive its strong cultural component. Those who are knowledgeable about computers are differentiated by special names (wizards, hackers, wheels), and are expected to have distinguishing characteristics, language, and behaviors. This "hacker elite" system, along with the relatively new academic structure of computer science which may seem chaotic and confusing to students, results in many "computing dropouts" who are alienated by the foreign culture [23]. Of course, these problems may affect male as well as female students, but the situation is likely to be more pronounced for females who, because of the differences in early experiences with computers, are less likely to be a part of the elite.

The cultural factors we have described thus far appear to have an effect even on women who are making their way successfully through the computer science pipeline. A study of doctoral students in a world-class computer science department found that while male and female students exhibited comparable performance quality in their studies, the women students felt much less comfortable, confident, and successful than did the men [3].

[margin annotation: women less confident than men w/comp]

It is important to acknowledge the significance of cultural influences in the acceptance and success of women in computer science. The studies we referred to show that there are a number of aspects of the computer science culture that may act against women. Unfortunately, there are no easy solutions to this problem. There are a few specific and obvious recommendations that can be made; for instance, more educational software appealing to girls should be developed. Similarly, educators and educational institutions must make a concerted effort to ensure equal access to computers for boys and girls. However, more far-reaching solutions are less tangible. What appears to be needed is increased sensitivity on the part of male computer scientists to their female students and colleagues, an increased awareness by women so that they will not be easily discouraged, and quite simply, an increased number of women in the field.

[margin annotation: male CSci need to be more sensitive to female students & colleagues so they don't get turned away from comp]

In addition to the cultural barriers women face, they also encounter issues of physical safety. This is because, as is also the case for those in the laboratory sciences, computer scientists must often be at their workplace after dark. This is particularly true of students who often do not have computers or terminals at home. The inability to use public terminal areas after hours not only makes it difficult to complete one's assignments, but also precludes informal interactions with other students, an integral part of one's education. For more senior computer scientists after hours access to sophisticated computing systems that cannot be duplicated at home may be necessary.

All computer scientists, male and female, require safe access to the workplace, particularly at night. Yet, for obvious reasons, such access is even more essential for women. Availability of a well-lit, short route to the office from well-lit, safe parking and a sense of safety in the department at night are crucial. It is accepted academic and professional practice to work at night, and women should be able to do so safely. As noted previously, working at home is not always possible. If working at night in the department or on public terminals is not feasible, a woman's working hours are restricted to a subset of those available to her male colleagues. As one woman professor put it, "in many places it is a real problem to do work at night for security reasons, but it is a necessity for professional reasons" [16, p. 32].

One partial solution to this problem is to make campus administrators aware of the issue, so that they will address it when planning new buildings and parking areas. Also useful are services that provide escorts for those walking around campus after dark. In addition, because the issue of safety inside the office at night is equally important, it is crucial that safety procedures such as keeping the building locked at night always be followed. Consciousness-raising within computer science departments may help guarantee that safety procedures are developed and consistently followed. Finally, we should find ways to take advantage of the fact that much computer science research can be done remotely. One recommendation is that funding agencies, such as the National Science Foundation (NSF), provide small grants to female professors to purchase terminals or workstations, printers, and modems for home use, to redress partially the problem of unequal access to resources [16, p. 32]. Male and female faculty advising female graduate students might also find ways to loan such equipment to them. Access to computing equipment at home can also help women who are attempting to balance their careers with family responsibilities that require them to be home in the evenings. As we will describe, the conflict between these two sets of responsibilities is another source of difficulty for many women.

OTHER OBSTACLES FOR WOMEN

Previously we described special characteristics of our discipline that present challenges to women who are attempting to become computer scientists or who are training future computer scientists. The majority of obstacles for women in the discipline are also shared by other women scientists and engineers, and to a lesser degree, by all other women employed outside the home. In our view, there are four primary and interrelated challenges facing women:

- Difficulties with self-esteem,
- Lack of mentoring and role models,
- Gender discrimination, and
- Difficulties balancing career and family responsibilities.

We discuss each of these problems in turn, attempting again to suggest ways to combat them. Of course, since these problems are not unique to women becoming computer scientists, the solutions we propose may also have wider applicability.

Diminished Self-Esteem

Several studies of college students have shown that women experience a much greater lack of self-esteem during their college years than do men. In the 1988 American Association for the Advancement of Science Presidential Lecture [25], Sheila Widnall noted that a recent survey of graduate students in medicine, science, and engineering at Stanford University [26] found that

> "the women were indistinguishable from the men in objective measures of preparation, career aspirations, and performance in graduate school. They differed significantly in their perceptions of their preparation for graduate study, in the pressures and roadblocks that they experienced, and in the strategies that they developed for coping with these pressures. ... 30% of the women versus 15% of the men questioned their ability to handle the work; 27% versus 12% found criticism difficult to accept; only 30% of the women versus 57% of the men felt confident speaking up in class; and 33 versus 9% feared that speaking up would reveal their inadequacies [25, pp. 1741, 1744]."

Widnall also reports on the Illinois Valedictorian Project, which followed 80 high school valedictorians (46 women, 34 men) through their college years [1]. At the end of their college careers, the women had a slightly higher final grade point average than the men (3.6 vs. 3.5). But the women had experienced a significantly higher loss of self-esteem. As high school seniors, about 20% of both men and women ranked themselves as "far above average," and about 45% as "above average." As college sophomores, about 20% of the men thought they were "far above average," as opposed to about 3% of the women; about 50% of the men and a little more than 40% of the women ranked themselves "above average." By their senior year, 25% of the men and *none* of the women thought they were "far above average," with about 55% of the men and 70% of the women considering themselves "above average." Overall, the self-confidence of the men increased slightly during college, while that of the women decreased significantly.

It seems clear that the diminished self-esteem of female college students contributes to the pipeline shrinkage problem. Indeed, while the studies that Widnall reports on refer to self-esteem problems of undergraduates, similar problems may be even more significant at the graduate level, where students receive primarily subjective feedback from their advisors and peers, as opposed to the more objective feedback of test scores and course grades available to undergraduates. An additional complicating factor is the differing communication styles of men and women. Studies have shown that in group settings, women are interrupted more frequently than men, and their contributions are often either attributed to men or ignored altogether [10, 11, 25]. Such experiences are likely to exacerbate an existing lack of self-confidence.

Diminished self-esteem may well cause a woman to not consider valid career options, because she believes that she is not sufficiently well qualified. Even women who consider themselves to be as well qualified as most of their male peers may lower their career goals when they recognize the additional problems that women may face. As Widnall points out:

> "A second trend noted in [the Illinois Valedictorian Project] was the lowering of career ambitions by the women students. The researchers linked lowered career ambitions in part to the unresolved dual-career problem. . . . One of the most effective antidotes for these uncertainties about career goals was the opportunity for successful professional experiences: independent research, professional employment, opportunity for interaction with graduate students, and the support and encouragement of a faculty mentor [25, p. 1743]."

Those who train women to become computer scientists need to become aware of the problem of diminished self-esteem, and work to combat it. Toward this end, it is important to give students unambiguous feedback concerning the quality of their work, to provide equal attention to and have equal expectations of female and male students, and to increase awareness of different, especially less aggressive, communication styles. In addition, it is essential to provide women with the opportunity for successful professional experiences. Computer science faculty need to make an effort to draw women into their research projects. While this is of course true of faculty members training graduate students, efforts to include females in research projects should ideally begin at the undergraduate level. Support must therefore be given to funding that will facilitate this, both at the national and institutional levels. An example of a model program is the National Science Foundation's Research in Undergraduate Institutions (RUI) program [19], the goal of which is to provide research opportunities for undergraduates in the sciences. RUI awards are limited to projects that include significant undergraduate participation. By using programs such as the RUI to bring women to research early in their careers, faculty members may help combat diminished self-esteem in women and its impact on attrition.

Mentoring and Role Models

Another major problem facing women in the process of becoming computer scientists is a shortage of mentors. Mentors play a crucial, though usually informal, role in the training of young computer scientists. In general, a mentor shares with a less experienced colleague information about how to get research funding, avenues for publication, the informal power structure within a department and within the discipline as a whole, and so on. Mentors may invest a good deal of time in their junior colleagues and may offer them important opportunities for research collaboration.

Currently, women are much more likely than men to be mentored by female faculty members [1, 19]. However, there is no reason that men cannot serve as mentors for women, given an appropriate sensitivity to the problems that women in computer science may face. Indeed, because the number of women computer scientists shrinks as one progresses through the pipeline, it is unreasonable to expect senior women to mentor all of the junior women. Men in computer science must also support younger women.

Related to mentoring is the issue of role models. While young computer scientists can benefit from mentors of either gender, it is desirable for women to be exposed to female role models. A role model can serve as evidence that a successful career in computer science is not only a possibility, but a normal and unremarkable option for women. The existence of role models *does* matter, and it matters to women at all stages of their careers. For students, female faculty members prove, by their very existence, that Ph.D. degrees and faculty slots can be attained by women [11, 12]. A similar phenomenon is true of female faculty members who serve as role models for their more junior colleagues. Junior women who have access to senior female faculty members adjust to their positions and establish research programs more quickly than those who do not [7].

Of course, the only real solution to the lack of role models is to increase the number of women in computer science: recall that only 6.5% of computer science and computer engineering faculty at the Taulbee institutions are female. However, until this situation improves, programs that make successful women more visible can help. Examples are programs that bring women scientists to campuses for a short period of time to give a talk, or for a longer period of time in a visiting faculty position. Activities of the former sort can be encouraged by anyone who is involved in a departmental colloquium or seminar series. Invitation for a longer period requires additional funding; one source of support is the NSF's Visiting Professorships for Women program [22].

At the undergraduate level, it is useful to design programs in which undergraduates are paired with female graduate students and/or faculty. Examples of successful programs of this kind include one run by the Women's Science and Engineering Network at Stanford University [24] and the Women in Science Program at the University of Michigan [25]. Such programs can have the additional benefit of providing graduate women with the experience of being viewed as capable and successful scientists.

Finally, we should point out that role models are important even to precollege women. Without sufficient role models, high school girls may end their mathematics and science training prematurely, thus precluding a major in science or engineering before they even begin college. High school guidance counselors and math and science teachers can play a role here by encouraging capable young women to consider science and engineering as valid career options. Several programs have been developed to encourage high school girls to acquire sufficient training to keep their options open. Perhaps the most extensive program of this kind is administered by the Math/Science Network, a non-profit organization that organizes conferences under the title of "Expanding Your Horizons in Science and Mathematics" [7]. These conferences bring high school girls together with local female scientists. Other more local programs include science fairs, sponsored by schools, scouting troops, or similar organizations, in which women are included among the judges. To increase the influence of science fairs, they may be augmented with career awareness workshops in which participating students can meet with local scientists and engineers to learn about career paths and the educational prerequisites for technical careers.

Discrimination

The issue of gender discrimination is of course a large one, which cannot be discussed in great depth here. By gender discrimination, we mean patronizing behavior and assumptions that women are less qualified and/or committed than men, regardless of whether the assumptions are conscious or unconscious. A detailed discussion of the problem of gender discrimination as it relates to women in computer science departments can be found in the 1983 report "Barriers to Equality in Academia," which was written by a group of female graduate students and research staff in the computer science department at MIT [2]. This influential report notes that the cumulative effects of subtle discrimination may be even more harmful than relatively infrequent incidents of overt discrimination:

> "Often, subtle behavior is not recognized as discriminatory, for two reasons. First, the actions often are not intended to be discriminatory; the people who convey biased attitudes toward women may be well-intentioned. Nevertheless, the effect of their behavior is to undermine the professional image of women held by their colleagues and the women themselves. Second, any particular incident might appear trivial when viewed by itself. However, when women experience such incidents daily, the overall effect of the environment is much greater than the sum of the individual incidents. Because subtle discrimination is harder to recognize than overt discrimination, it sometimes does more damage. Constant exposure to negative comments diminishes a woman's self-esteem and may lead her to believe that she cannot succeed [2, p. 3]."

Several reports issued by the Project on the Status and Education of Women (PSEW) of the Association of American Colleges address the subject of gender discrimination as it relates to women undergraduates, graduate students, and faculty [10, 11]. These reports concur with the MIT report's observations on the chilling effect of cumulative incidents of discrimination:

> "Overtly disparaging remarks about women, as well as more subtle differential behaviors, can have a critical and lasting effect. When they occur frequently—especially when they involve "gatekeepers" who teach required courses, act as advisors, or serve as chairs of departments—such behaviors can have a profound negative impact on women's academic and career development by: . . . causing students to switch majors or subspecialties within majors . . . ; minimizing the development of the individual collegial relationships with faculty which are crucial for future professional development; dampening career aspirations; and undermining confidence [10, p. 3]."

The PSEW reports, by documenting manifestations of both overt and subtle gender discrimination throughout academia, provide evidence that the problems described in the MIT report are not unique to computer science.

A recent study of several science and engineering departments also draws the connection between gender discrimination and the effective exclusion of women from first-class citizenship in their departments. The study states that "differential attention to women students was felt to promote performance stress while exclusion from informal relations was . . . a career handicap" [6].

A particular manifestation of the differential attention paid to females in the field is what has been called the "invisibility syndrome." Not only is the percentage of women in computer science smaller than the percentage of women in the general population, but also, even within the field, women are underrepresented in many important professional activities. Ideally, the representation of women in the perceived power structure of a community should reflect their numbers in that community. One would expect reasonable, nontoken representation of women on the editorial boards of technical journals; as guest editors of special issues of journals; on program committees of technical conferences; as invited speakers both at conferences and at departmental colloquia; on executive boards of professional organizations such as ACM and IEEE; and on policy boards such as the Computing Research Association (formerly the Computer Research Board) and the Computer Science and Technology Board.

Unfortunately, even those women who have been successful often appear to be invisible, and are not invited to participate in activities of this type to the same degree as their male counterparts. One way to address this problem is to make people aware of it, so that those whose job it is to nominate or appoint people to boards, program committees, etc., can make a conscious effort to include qualified women. Another solution, towards which some women in the field have begun to work, is to compile lists of qualified women in various areas of computer science who can be suggested to those who are responsible for issuing invitations and nominations.

Not only do women often find themselves subject to the type of unintentional discrimination described so far, but they may also be confronted with instances of more overt discrimination or even sexual harassment. It is therefore necessary that departments and universities develop and institute grievance procedures that guarantee confidentiality and freedom from retaliation. We recommend further study of already implemented grievance procedures to determine policies necessary to ensure their effectiveness.

The authors of the MIT study, like those of the PSEW reports, state that "responsibility for change rests with the entire community, not just with the women," and that "many problems would be alleviated by increasing the number of women" [2, p. 1]. We agree completely, and recommend that the kinds of actions we have proposed elsewhere in the report be adopted to help increase women's representation in the field.

Balancing Responsibilities

A final issue that is of central concern involves the difficulties in balancing the responsibilities of a career in computer science with the responsibilities of raising a family. Concern with this problem may lead young women to abandon the possibility of a career in computer science (or any other science) at a very early stage in their training, as indicated in the quotation from the Widnall report noted earlier ("researchers linked lowered career ambitions in part to the unresolved dual-career problem"). Actual difficulties encountered in achieving this balance may result in women leaving computer science later in their careers. Of course, in their concern with this problem, women considering or pursuing careers in computer science are not very different from women in a wide range of other careers—or, for that matter from many men in those careers. Last April, a *New York Times* article noted, "fathers, too, are seeking a balance between their families and careers." However, while achieving such a balance may be difficult for people pursuing many different careers, there are certain aspects of a tenure-track position in a scientific field that render the balancing act particularly difficult [18].

The typical "tenure-track" career path appears to be generally incompatible with outside interests and responsibilities including, but not limited to, childbearing and rearing. Junior faculty in tenure-track positions (like junior lawyers working towards partnerships, junior investment bankers trying to become vice presidents, etc.) are expected to devote enormous amounts of time and energy to their careers: so much time and energy that serious outside interests are precluded or at least greatly constrained. The model for an academic career was developed during a time in which faculty positions were primarily occupied by men who had wives to tend to their home responsibilities. We call this the *helpmate-in-the-background* model. It is one that is still present today: an illustration can be found in the acknowledgments statement of many academic books. An example, from a recent book authored by a male computer scientist, includes a statement of gratitude to his wife "for sheltering [him] from the travails of the real world."

The problem is that the helpmate-in-the-background model is inappropriate for today's society, in which both men and women should have the right, and often have the obligation, to have careers. The model is most obviously inappropriate for women. Women *were* the helpmates-in-the-background: they do not typically have helpmates of their own.

Further complicating the situation is the fact of women's "biological clocks." Most students do not complete the Ph.D. until the middle or late 20s and tenure is typically not granted until the middle 30s. Hence, the childbearing years directly coincide with the period of time during which a woman is completing her Ph.D. and working towards tenure. Both rearing small children and achieving tenure are tremendously time-consuming efforts; doing both at the same time seems to many women to be exceptionally difficult, if not impossible [6].

There are a number of things that can be done to help women achieve a balance between family responsibilities and career demands. For example, universities can and should provide affordable, quality childcare. Sufficient maternity leave policies are also necessary. Many universities have no formal leave policy at all, while others grant only minimal leaves (e.g., one month or less). A few will allow women a semester off from teaching responsibilities, at reduced pay. At those universities that do not offer this option, female faculty are often put in the position of having to try to "time" their babies for semesters that they had planned to take off anyway, such as summer semesters, sabbatical periods, or semesters during which they used grant money to "buy out" of teaching. However, the first of these options is often not viable, since most computer science faculty do not have the summer off; instead, they use this period to work on research grants, generally a requirement for tenure. The latter two options generally require that the woman already have tenure or at least be fairly close to it. Moreover, attempts to schedule a baby's arrival are far from reliable, and often fail. Thus, better maternity leave policies are obviously needed.

But solutions like these do not go far enough. Fundamental changes in the patterns of academic careers are required. These changes must rest on a realization that it is the responsibilities of *parenting* a small child, and not the responsibilities of *mothering* a small child, that are incompatible with current work requirements. The model of a helpmate-in-the-background should be as untenable for men in today's society as it is for women.

It is true that there are issues that will always be specific to women—pregnancy, childbirth, and lactation—and career paths must be designed with these in mind. But there are other realities of women's lives that should be seen merely as traditionally women's. Many of these can and should be shared by men. For example, universities must develop not just maternal policies, but parental policies that will allow male as well as female faculty members to be involved in the rearing of small children. Many universities today provide no parental leave at all. Yet, fathers not only need time off immediately after the birth of a child, but also, like mothers, need reduced workloads for an extended period of time, to enable them to participate in the rearing of their small children. Thus, another important policy that must be developed, for both men and women, involves changing the way in which the tenure clock operates.

As with maternity leaves, different universities have different policies regarding slowing the tenure clock to allow a faculty member to care for a small child. Differences involve: (1) whether any slowing of the tenure clock is allowed at all; (2) whether it is permitted only for the "primary caretaker" or whether it is permitted for both parents; (3) whether it is permitted for adoptions; (4) the period of time for which the clock is stopped (typically, one semester); (5) the number of children for which this is allowed (typically one, sometimes two). In our view, some kind of reduced work load is essential to permit faculty members who wish to do so to better balance their family responsibilities with their careers. Moreover, this option should be available to fathers as well as mothers. There have been some doubts expressed about this solution: the claim is that fathers will "take advantage" of the situation by stopping the tenure clock even though they are not participating heavily in the rearing of their child. The worry is that if this happens, the default tenure period will simply become seven years instead of six, and women who do take primary responsibility for the rearing of their children will once again be at a disadvantage.

In our view, this possibility must be faced, but it appears that one solution is to make a strong effort not to change the standards for tenure. That is, departments must continue to impose the same tenure requirements as they do now, but must assume that some faculty members will take seven or eight years to meet those requirements rather than six. We need to expect that, at least in the beginning, some faculty members may take the extra year or two even if they do not have additional child-rearing demands. As long as the standards are not raised, which would penalize those with additional responsibilities, this is not a dire consequence.

Because the issues surrounding leave policies, deferred tenure, and related issues are so complex, we recommend a systematic study of policies in academic departments, to better evaluate the options. It is even possible that the conclusion of such a study will be that the entire tenure process is incompatible with the demands of a dual-career society. After all, the demands of rearing a small child do not stop after six weeks or one semester or even one year of a leave. When the helpmate-in-the-background model is thrown out, it needs to be replaced with a much more flexible one in which people are free to move on and off of a "fast track" at different stages in their career, without those moves permanently jeopardizing that career. This is exactly what tenure precludes: if a faculty member is not fully committed to his or her academic career during the very same period of time in which he or she is most likely to face the demands of raising small children, tenure is unlikely to be granted and the academic career will be permanently stalled.

Although we have emphasized that the traditional helpmate-in-the-background model works against women with children, we believe it also works against women without children and men with employed wives. Few of these people have such helpmates.

In our view, it is important to work to change the helpmate-in-the-background model. It must be possible for both women and men to work hard and well at a career, without neglecting their personal lives. We believe this will eventually be advantageous for both men and women. There is great satisfaction to be found in one's work, but there is also great satisfaction to be found in one's personal life. No one should have to choose one at the expense of the other.

REOPENING THE PIPELINE

As a result of the kinds of problems we have discussed, many women have dropped out of the computer science pipeline prematurely. Although we have been focusing on ways to reverse this trend, an additional approach to correcting the problem of underrepresentation is to help women reenter the pipeline after dropping out of it early. One example of a particularly successful reentry program is the University of California at Berkeley program, which has been in existence since 1983. It is aimed at making graduate study in computer science possible for women and minority students who have received a bachelor's degree in another field. Students in the Berkeley reentry program take regular computer science courses along with undergraduates, and in addition receive a host of support services. The program has been producing graduates for seven years now, and students who have completed the program have been quite successful in gaining admission to competitive graduate programs in computer science [9].

A second set of women for whom reopening the pipeline may be useful are those with science degrees who are not employed in science. A 1976 NSF program, called the Science Career Facilitation (SCF) Projects, was aimed at such women. This extensive program, which was later discontinued, funded 21 projects in fields where women were poorly represented even though jobs were readily available. Three of these 21 projects dealt with women reentering computer science.

An evaluation of the SCF projects led to several important findings. The primary reasons most women cited for having dropped out of science involved family responsibilities. Research supported by the SCF projects surveyed more than 2000 organizations providing potential employment to scientists, and revealed that none of them attended to the needs of reentering women. Yet programs that do address this would appear to be very useful: after all, more than 585,000 women scientists expressed an interest in retraining and reentry. Finally, the SCF projects that provided this retraining were quite successful: in total, 65% of the participants were reemployed in science while another 10% became full-time graduate students [15].

CONCLUSIONS

We have presented some of the problems facing women who are in the process of becoming computer scientists, as well as the women who are training them, and we have made recommendations for change. There appear to be clear and relatively easily implemented solutions for some problems, while for others, such as the apparent conflict between child-rearing and gaining tenure, the issues are more complex and further study is required to develop effective solutions. Indeed, complete resolution of some of these problems will depend upon significant societal changes. Ultimately, everything hinges on increasing the number of women in the field. We must make sure that increased representation of women is not stalled because of policies or practices of computer science educators or employers.

Obviously, this article is not comprehensive. We have not, for example, addressed problems unique to women in industrial computer science, nor have we considered how the problems we have described are exacerbated for women of color or disabled women. We believe it is important that these issues be examined, but we leave them for other articles.

ACKNOWLEDGMENTS

The authors wish to thank Barbara Simons for suggesting and initiating this work and Sheila Humphreys for her support and input. In addition, we would like to thank Nita Goyal, Paula Hawthorn, Kathy McCoy, Shari Pfleeger, Anthony Ralston, Eric Roberts, Candy Sidner, the Systers list for helpful comments and discussions, and the Committee on Scientific Freedom and Human Rights for its support. We also thank those who participated in a pilot survey that we conducted to try to elicit additional information about women in the process of becoming computer scientists.

REFERENCES

1. Arnold, K. Retaining high-achieving women in science and engineering. In AAAS *Symposium on Women and Girls in Science and Technology,* (July 1987). Univ. of Michigan, Ann Arbor, Michigan.
2. Barriers to equality in academia: Women in computer science at M.I.T. Laboratory for Computer Science and the Artificial Intelligence Laboratory at M.I.T., 1983.
3. Burton, M. D. Gender differences in professional socialization: A study of women and men becoming computer scientists. Tech. Rep., Carnegie-Mellon University, Pittsburgh, PA, June 1987. Committee on Social Science Research in Computing, Social and Decision Sciences Department.
4. Changing America: The new face of science and engineering–Interim Rep. The Task Force on Women, Minorities, and the Handicapped in Science and Technology, Washington, D.C., 1988.
5. Changing America: The new face of science and engineering–Final Rep. The Task Force on Women, Minorities, and the Handicapped in Science and Technology, Washington, D.C., 1989.
6. Etzkowitz, H., Kemelgor, C., and Neuschatz, M. The final disadvantage: Barriers to women in academic science and engineering. Tech. Rep., Rensselaer Polytechnic Inst. Center for Science and Technology.
7. Failor, B. The History of EYH. *Math/Science Network Broadcast,* (Winter 1990), 5.
8. Gilbert, L., Gallesich, J. M., and Evans, S. L. Sex of faculty role model and students' self-perceptions of competency. *Sex Roles* 9, 5 (597–607), 1983.
9. Grigolia, M. Computer Science Reentry Program. *Comp. Res. News,* 2, 2 (April 19, 1990).
10. Hall, R. M. and Sandler, B. R. The classroom climate: A chilly one for women? Project on the Status and Education of Women, Association of American Colleges, Washington, D.C., 1982.
11. Hall, R. M. and Sandler B. R. The classroom climate revisited: Chilly for women faculty, administrators, and graduate students. Project on the Status and Education of Women, Association of American Colleges, Washington, D.C., 1986.
12. Hornig, L. S. Women in science and engineering: Why so few? *Tech. Rev.,* 87, 8 (31–41), 1984.
13. Huff, C. and Cooper, J. Sex bias in educational software: The effect of designers' stereotypes on the software they design. *J. Applied Soc. Psych.,* 17, 6 (1987), 519–532.
14. Kiesler, S., Sproull, L., and Eccles, J. S. Pool halls, chips, and war games: Women in the culture of computing. *Psych. of Women Q.,* 9 (1985), 451–462.
15. Lantz, A. An Evaluation of Programs for Reentry of Women Scientists. In S. Humphreys, Ed., *Women and Minorities in Science: Strategies for Increasing Participation.* Westview Press, 1982.
16. Leveson, N. Women in computer science: A Report for the NSF CISE Cross Directorate Activities Advisory Committee, 1989.
17. Long, J. S. The origins of sex differences in science. *Social Forces.* To be published.
18. Marriage, family, and scientific careers: Institutional policy versus research findings. American Association for the Advancement of Science. In *Proceedings of a Symposium at the Annual Meeting of the AAAS* (1989).
19. NSF. Research in undergraduate institutions (RUI). Program Announcement, Directorate for Scientific, Technological, and International Affairs, 1989.
20. NSF. Visiting professorships for women. Grants for Research and Education in Science and Engineering Program Announcement, October 1989.
21. Report on women and minorities in science and engineering. National Science Foundation, Washington, D.C., 1988.

22. Sloat, B. Women in science: A university program of intervention, out-reach, and research. In *Second International Interdisciplinary Congress on Women* (April 1984. Gorningen, the Netherlands).

23. Sproull, L. S., Kiesler, S., and Zubrow, D. Encountering an Alien Culture. *J. of Soc. Issues* 40, 3 (1984), 31–48.

24. Sursock, A. The women's science and engineering network. *European Journal of Physics*, 8, 2 (1987), 151–152.

25. Widnall, S. E. AAAS Presidential Lecture: Voices from the pipeline. *Science*, 241 (1988), 1740–1745.

26. Zappert, L. T., and Stanbury, K. In the pipeline: A comparative analysis of men and women in graduate programs in science, engineering, and medicine at Stanford University. Tech. Rep. Working Paper 20, Institute for Research on Women and Gender, Stanford University, Stanford, CA, 1984.

CR Categories and Subject Descriptors: K.3.2 **[Computers and Education]**: Computer and Information Science Education—*computer science education;* K.4.2 **[Computers and Society]**: Social Issues—Employment; K.7.1 **[The Computing Profession]**: Occupations

Additional Key Words and Phrases: Academic occupations, educational pipeline, equality of opportunity, recommendations for change, women in computer science

THINKING AND RE-READING

1. As you re-read the article, list the reasons the authors give as to why society should take heed of women's underrepresentation in computer science. Does one have to major in computer science to be a significant player in the computer world today? Then why is it important to have women in the field? List the problems that the authors give regarding difficulties women will face in entering—and remaining in—a field largely dominated by men.

2. The authors write that "the earliest computer artifacts that children encounter are not gender neutral." Why do they say this? Try to remember your first experience with a computer. For what purposes were you using the computer? After your first experience, did you want to experiment with a computer again? Why or why not?

3. Safety issues are not, of course, restricted to those women who major in computer science. Think about your requirements for access to computer labs on campus. Do you need to go to the labs or are you able to access computer services from your dormitory or apartment? What steps does your college need to take, if any, in order to ensure safe routes and spaces for those needing to work in campus facilities? What has it done so far to make it less hazardous to find adequate computer services?

WRITING AND LEARNING

1. Why do the authors say that there are no easy solutions to the problem of gender equity in computer science? What are the "obvious" recommendations that they give? Like the other professionals in this section, these authors argue that a prime solution would be simply to increase the number of women in the field. How would you go about recruiting

women to computer science programs? What would make you interested in computer science as a profession? How can the field be made more attractive to women and other underrepresented groups in general? As you're thinking about these questions, contemplate developing an "ad campaign" to recruit women into the computing field. Go through several magazines aimed at women and look over those advertisements for positions considered appropriate or even glamorous for women. Now design a poster, preferably with a software program, aimed at attracting women into the field of computer science. Make an appointment with a faculty member in the computer science department or in the women's studies program to determine their responses to your poster. Revise your poster, if necessary, and decide with the rest of your class whether it would be appropriate to place any of the advertisements your class has constructed in the school newspaper, on the World Wide Web, or on the walls of your student union.

2. As the authors note, women often drop out of computer science programs, contributing to an effect they've called "pipeline shrinkage." In other words, there are fewer women in the pipeline to receive degrees in computer science at the end of a course of study than there were at the start. Another phrase, "the glass ceiling," is also used to describe a similar problem in business settings. The glass ceiling usually denotes an invisible barrier that prevents women and other underrepresented groups from rising as high in the corporate hierarchy as their white male counterparts. It would be interesting to find out how widespread these two phenomena are and whether they mark a field that you are interested in entering. Make an appointment with a person working in a potential career field and find out whether the professional climate is conducive to the success of either women or men. Go to the library and find articles that discuss gender issues in the field; look for those readings that give statistics on the number of men and women working in this area as well. If there are no articles on the subject, what might you infer? Write a report for your class in which you stipulate the advantages and disadvantages for men and women in the field that you've chosen. Check again with the person to whom you spoke earlier and see whether he or she agrees with your report. Also be sure to list a series of recommendations that have the potential to improve the climate of the field for both sexes.

3. Collect words and phrases that are used a great deal in the computer world. For example, in this article you encounter such terms as "wizards," "hackers," and "wheels," but there are many others you can add to the list. You should be able to come up with a minimum of twenty-five or fifty. Trade magazines, such as *Wired*, and popular press pieces are excellent resources for finding different uses of language, along with books on computing in your library. First note the meaning of the words and then decide how the terminology might favor one sex over the other. (Even the computer science organizational title of the Association for Computing Machinery may be offputting to some.) Then share your written response with other members of your class or writing group. Are there terms you and your classmates might substitute for those currently in use? With your classmates, write a letter to *Wired*'s reader feedback section, "Rants and Raves," in which you apprise the editors of your findings and make possible recommendations for change.

High-Tech Employment Patterns in Silicon Valley, 1990

Pacific Studies Center

IN OCTOBER 1992, THE PACIFIC STUDIES CENTER published a short report and set of statistics in an effort to represent employment patterns in the high-tech workforce of Silicon Valley, California. The report and statistics give a statistical overview of the work for one area of the country in 1990 based on gender, ethnic group, education, and race.

Employment in electronics manufacturing in Silicon Valley (Santa Clara County, California) follows the same general patterns found in other high-tech centers. **The workforce is sharply stratified**, with white men in positions of power and high income, and women and nonwhites holding down the low-level positions, such as operatives—that is, semi-skilled production workers.

White men make up 62.8% of the officials and managers and 50.9% of the professionals, but they only account for 9.7% of the operatives. Women of all races make up 79.1% of the clerical workers and 60.7% of the operatives, yet they comprise only 38.1% of the high-tech manufacturing workforce. Nonwhite women account for 45.0% of the operatives, although they only represent 16.3% of the workforce at the same companies. Nonwhites (men and women) account for 74.6% of the operatives.

Asians (including immigrants and Asian Americans) are overrepresented in most Silicon Valley job categories. Though they make up 16.8% of the area's population, they comprise 23.6% of the high-tech manufacturing workforce. Their share of technicians (30.8%), craft workers (30.3%), semi-skilled operatives (47.0%), and unskilled laborers (41.2%) is even greater than their rate of participation in the high-tech workforce, and they also make up a substantial fraction of the professional workforce (21.5%). EEOC data does not break down the different Asian/Pacific national origins, but the higher level Asians appear to be preponderantly of Japanese, Chinese, and South Asian descent, while the lower level Asians tend to be Filipino, Indochinese, and Korean.

Many factors contribute to the segregation of the high-tech workforce by race and gender. Education plays an important role, since most of the high-level employees have one or more college degrees. However, even among wage workers companies often practice race and gender discrimination. While

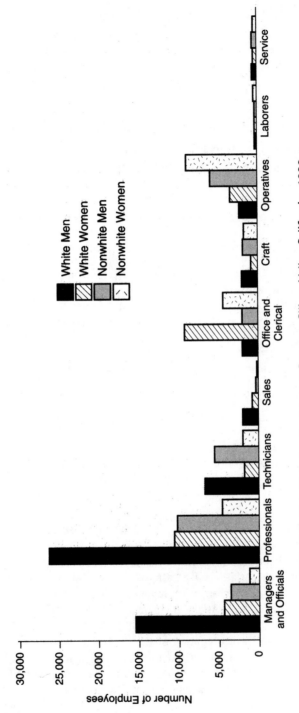

High–Tech Manufacturing Employment Patterns: Silicon Valley, California—1990

Legend:
- White Men
- White Women
- Nonwhite Men
- Nonwhite Women

Number of Employees (y-axis): 0, 5,000, 10,000, 15,000, 20,000, 25,000, 30,000

Categories (x-axis): Managers and Officials, Professionals, Technicians, Sales, Office and Clerical, Craft, Operatives, Laborers, Service

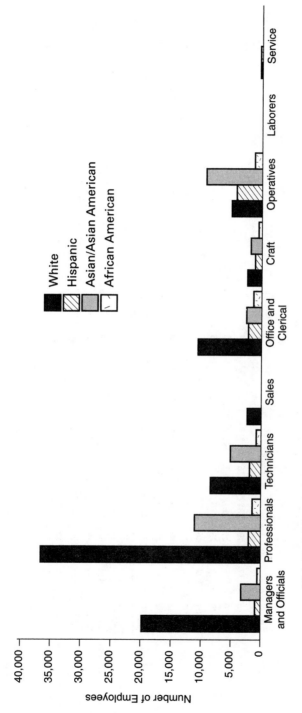

High-Tech Manufacturing Racial Employment Patterns: Silicon Valley, California—1990

High-Tech Manufacturing Employment in Silicon Valley, California—1990

	Population	Number of Employees										% Pop.	Percentage of Job Category									
		Total	Mgrs	Profs	Techs	Sales	Clerks	Craft	Oper	Lab	Serv		Total	Mgrs	Profs	Techs	Sales	Clerks	Craft	Oper	Lab	Serv
ALL	1,497,577	136,909	24,737	51,468	16,078	2,580	16,598	5,278	18,951	374	845	100.0	100.0	100.0	100.0	100.0	100.0	100.0	100.0	100.0	100.0	100.0
Men	759,503	84,699	19,158	36,373	12,191	1,911	3,474	3,264	7,452	188	688	50.7	61.9	77.4	70.7	75.8	74.1	20.9	61.8	39.3	50.3	81.4
Women	738,074	52,210	5,579	15,095	3,887	669	13,124	2,014	11,499	186	157	49.3	38.1	22.6	29.3	24.2	25.9	79.1	38.2	60.7	49.7	18.6
Whites	869,874	85,739	19,902	36,747	8,460	2,297	10,688	2,377	4,817	69	382	58.1	62.6	80.5	71.4	52.6	89.0	64.4	45.0	25.4	18.4	45.2
Men		55,820	15,525	26,198	6,638	1,722	1,773	1,754	1,841	50	319		40.8	62.8	50.9	41.3	66.7	10.7	33.2	9.7	13.4	37.8
Women		29,919	4,377	10,549	1,822	575	8,915	623	2,976	19	63		21.9	17.7	20.5	11.3	22.3	53.7	11.8	15.7	5.1	7.5
Nonwhites		51,170	4,835	14,721	7,618	283	5,910	2,901	14,134	305	463		37.4	19.5	28.6	47.4	11.0	35.6	55.0	74.6	81.6	54.8
Men		28,879	3,633	10,175	5,553	189	1,701	1,510	5,611	138	369		21.1	14.7	19.8	34.5	7.3	10.2	28.6	29.6	36.9	43.7
Women		22,291	1,202	4,546	2,065	94	4,209	1,391	8,523	167	94		16.3	4.9	8.8	12.8	3.6	25.4	26.4	45.0	44.7	11.1
African American	52,583	5,495	600	1,429	767	49	1,221	296	1,051	16	66	3.5	4.0	2.4	2.8	4.8	1.9	7.4	5.6	5.5	4.3	7.8
Men		2,938	407	910	583	35	360	179	404	9	51		2.1	1.6	1.8	3.6	1.4	2.2	3.4	2.1	2.4	6.0
Women		2,557	193	519	184	14	861	117	647	7	15		1.9	0.8	1.0	1.1	0.5	5.2	2.2	3.4	1.9	1.8
Hispanic	314,564	12,753	1,062	2,071	1,811	77	2,254	973	4,096	134	275	21.0	9.3	4.3	4.0	11.3	3.0	13.6	18.4	21.6	35.8	32.5
Men		6,201	710	1,306	1,266	51	581	584	1,422	61	220		4.5	2.9	2.5	7.9	2.0	3.5	11.1	7.5	16.3	26.0
Women		6,552	352	765	545	26	1,673	389	2,674	73	55		4.8	1.4	1.5	3.4	1.0	10.1	7.4	14.1	19.5	6.5
Asian	251,496	32,349	3,084	11,066	4,947	149	2,329	1,599	8,901	154	120	16.8	23.6	12.5	21.5	30.8	5.8	14.0	30.3	47.0	41.2	14.2
Men		19,425	2,458	7,848	3,638	98	740	731	3,749	67	96		14.2	9.9	15.2	22.6	3.8	4.5	13.8	19.8	17.9	11.4
Women		12,924	626	3,218	1,309	51	1,589	868	5,152	87	24		9.4	2.5	6.3	8.1	2.0	9.6	16.4	27.2	23.3	2.8
Native American	6,694	573	89	155	93	8	106	33	86	1	2	0.4	0.4	0.4	0.3	0.6	0.3	0.6	0.6	0.5	0.3	0.2
Men		315	58	111	66	5	20	16	36	1	2		0.2	0.2	0.2	0.4	0.2	0.1	0.3	0.2	0.3	0.2
Women		258	31	44	27	3	86	17	50	0	0		0.2	0.1	0.1	0.2	0.1	0.5	0.3	0.3	0.0	0.0
	2,366											0.2										

This table was prepared by Lenny Siegel of the Pacific Studies Center from data provided by the U.S. Equal Employment Opportunity Commission. Population figures are from the 1990 U.S. Census. The figures include high-tech manufacturing, but not services.

Terms: Silicon Valley = Santa Clara County; Mgr.= Officials & Managers; Prof.= Professionals; Techs = Technicians; Sales = Sales Workers; Clerks = Office & Clerical Workers; Craft = Blue-Collar Skilled Production; Operatives= Semi-Skilled Blue-Collar; Labor = Laborers/Unskilled Blue-Collar; Service = Service Workers

employers do not openly admit such discrimination in the U.S., where it is illegal, they overtly discriminate when hiring at their overseas plants. Furthermore, discrimination and other cultural factors appear to reduce the management opportunities for qualified Asian professionals.

The above analysis is based upon data provided by the U.S. Equal Employment Opportunity Commission. Major employers are required to submit data each year, but the EEOC does not generally verify the accuracy of the data. Thus, the information gives a good general picture of the industries covered, but the precision is limited.

PSC has prepared this information, as well as similar reports on the high-tech workforce in Albuquerque, Austin, Boston, Colorado Springs, Dallas, Phoenix, and Portland metropolitan areas, for the Electronics Industry Good Neighbor Campaign, a collaboration of the Southwest Network for Environmental and Economic Justice and the Campaign for Responsible Technology. The industrial sectors covered in this report are listed [in the table]. For Silicon Valley, PSC also has analyzed data for the entire high-tech workforce, including services as well as manufacturing.

THINKING AND RE-READING

1. As you re-read the report and study the statistics, list some of the claims you can make that grow out of the data. Try to envision the various kinds of jobs that the statistics represent.

2. Locate Silicon Valley (Santa Clara, California) on a map. According to the statistics, how many people live in the area and how many work in a computer-related industry? How does this compare with your own community?

WRITING AND LEARNING

1. The report and statistics indicate that many more men than women are employed as "officials" and "managers," whereas more women than men work as "clericals" and "operatives"; however, there's no description of what the actual jobs entail. Other terms used in representing the data in the graphs include "technicians," "sales," "craft," and "laborers," but again they are not defined. Go to your library or even to your local computer store and find out what sorts of work people perform in the computer industry. What does it mean to be an "operative"? Why is it that the largest segment of "operatives" are nonwhite women? What does a "laborer" do in the computer industry? What's the difference between an "official" and a "professional"? From your written notes, prepare an oral presentation for your writing group or the entire class in which you explore these issues.

2. Edward Tufte, author of *The Visual Display of Quantitative Information,* gives us some guidelines for displaying statistical graphics. Among his suggestions, he states that graphical displays should

- show the data
- induce the viewer to think about the substance rather than about methodology, graphic design, the technology of graphic production, or something else
- present many numbers in a small space
- avoid distorting what the data have to say
- make large data sets coherent
- encourage the eye to compare different pieces of data
- reveal the data at several levels of detail, from a broad overview to the fine structure
- serve a reasonably clear purpose: description, exploration, tabulation, or decoration
- be closely integrated with the statistical and verbal descriptions of the data set

Consider the Pacific Studies Center's report in relation to Tufte's criteria. Can you think of ways in which you might want to re-organize the data? Using a graphics software program, re-represent the data in the report so that they are more in line with Tufte's recommendations.

3. Alternately, collect statistics on your campus as to the numerical breakdown of students and employees studying in computer science or working in the computing services offices and labs. Construct a short report along with a graphical representation of the statistics to present to the rest of the class. If your instructor agrees, after revising your report, send it to the school newspaper to illustrate the employment patterns in computer-related work at your college.

Works Cited

Tufte, Edward R. *The Visual Display of Quantitative Information.* Cheshire, CT: Graphics Press, 1983.

IMAGES OF GENDER AND TECHNOLOGY

THINKING AND RE-READING

1. In Appendix A of this reader, you will find a list of questions that will help you read and understand this set of images and other images that you see in new ways. Read the questions in this list carefully and use them to "read" the images in this section—carefully and with an increasing sense of thoughtfulness.

WRITING AND LEARNING

1. Choose at least two or three images to analyze more carefully. For these images, write down your answers to the questions listed in Appendix A.

I'm rebuilding City Hall using the tools in my kitchen.

Rome wasn't built in a day. But my clients think a
building can be. Luckily, my new Acer® Aspire™

helps me do the impossible. If I need to be across

town at a planning meeting, Aspire's

integrated speakerphone puts me

right in the boardroom. But, I

can still be at my desk at home,

working on a materials budget at the same time.

In fact, Aspire is loaded with features that help

me get things done. Like the full color, CD-ROM

multimedia presentation that wowed the City

Council, and got me into this mess in the first

place. Acer must understand I'm busy, because

they simplified setup and preloaded all the soft-

ware. I didn't have much more than the five

minutes it took to get Aspire up and running.

But now I've got all the time in the world to

build my career from the ground up.

Aspire. To Do More.

*A few more things
I can do with my Aspire:
Do environmental studies.
Negotiate the best prices.
Keep up with architectural news.
Search for interior designers.
And cruise around the Internet.*

ACER ◆ *Everything You Aspire To.*

*For the location of the Acer Aspire dealer nearest you,
call 1-800-529-ACER. Or visit us on the World Wide Web
at http://www.acer.com/aac/*

I wanted to work here.

In the spare room.

At first my work said no way.

The equipment I'd need would be
too expensive.

So I bought it all myself.

A modem, speakerphone, fax machine,
the works. Even a voicemail system
with more mailboxes than the local
Post Office.

They think I spent a small fortune.

Truth is, I got all that by plugging a
single, affordable device inside my PC.

My small fortune is still
in a college fund.

What kind of people design this stuff?

REVEAL
THE POWER OF COMPUTER UPGRADING™

The On-Line Mystique

Paula Span

IN THIS SELECTION, PAULA SPAN, a journalist writing for the *Washington Post Magazine,* offers readers a view of her experiences in cyberspace while, at the same time, pointing to the inequities that exist between the sexes in the computer culture. As you read this piece, intended for a general audience, think of your own experiences with computers and of how they compare with those described by the author in 1994.

The love affair between men and computers was something I knew about but didn't really get, until that morning at the local coffee shop. My pal Pam and I were gabbing in the front booth when in walked Michael, a friend and journalist about to take a leave from his newspaper to write a book. His first step, naturally, was to sink a significant chunk of his book advance into a shiny new computer. It was a beauty: worked faster than a speeding locomotive, boasted many megabytes of RAM, brewed cappuccino, etc.

Pam and I exchanged glances. This sounded familiar. She had written several books on an Apple so antediluvian that the company no longer manufactures it, and abandoned it only when it got damaged by clumsy movers. Yet her husband was about to invest in a pricey new CD-ROM rig, making unconvincing noises about how useful their daughter would find it for schoolwork. My own husband, as it happened, was also taking advantage of a new work assignment and plunging computer prices to replace the system he'd purchased just two years before, though his new machine wasn't as powerful as Michael's. ("Mike could fly to Chicago with that thing," he would later remark, wistfully.)

More speed. Better performance. With names like Quadra and Performa, computers even *sound* like cars these days. (Quick, is it a fastback or a sedan?) The women I know, who all primarily use these things for work, don't give them two seconds' thought unless they encounter some problem. On the other hand, a lot of the men I know ogle weird software in the MacWarehouse catalogue and always seem to require some new $200 gizmo that quacks.

"It's a guy thing," Pam and I decided, virtually in unison. Women treat computers like reliable station wagons: Learn how to make them take you where you want to go, and as long as they're functioning properly, who cares about pistons and horsepower? Computers are useful but unexciting. When something goes wrong, you call a mechanic.

> **Right now, the culture of computing is over-whelmingly male. What will it take for women to succeed in cyberspace?**

Whereas guys, even those who never learned how to change an oil filter, are enamored of computers, want to play with them, upgrade them, fix them when they falter, compare theirs with the other guys'.

As an admitted technoklutz, I initially figured this observation might simply reflect my own prejudice, not to mention a small sample size. Computers, after all, were initially thought to be a field in which women would triumph. Computers had no history of discrimination. They had no history at all. They did not require biceps. They wouldn't be, to adopt the social science term, *gendered.*

Well. It turned out—as I started looking into the whole evolving subject of women, computers, on-line communications and other matters I had previously been unconcerned about—that computing is even more of a guy thing than I knew. That's worth paying attention to, not only for women but for our daughters (mine's 12). Yet I would also learn, as I ventured hesitantly into the computer communications realm dubbed cyberspace, that things don't have to stay this way.

Warning: The following article contains assorted generalizations and risks gender stereotyping.

For there are, no question, numerous males who are phobic about or merely uninterested in computing. And there are plenty of techie females, women who know their algorithms, who run major software companies, and who can clean the cat hair out of a trackball in 30 seconds or less.

But it's hard to overlook the stats. Who studies computer science? The Chronicle of Higher Education's latest numbers show that fewer than 30 percent of the people getting bachelor's and master's degrees are women and that fewer than one in seven doctorates is earned by a woman.

Who works in the industry? The Bureau of Labor Statistics reports that the percentage of women who are computer systems analysts and scientists has barely budged in a decade: It's still under 30 percent, even though nearly half a million more people have entered the field. Fewer than a third of computer programmers are women, as well, another statistic little changed since 1983.

Who pants over those fat, glossy computer magazines (PC World, Byte, MacUser) whose lust-inspiring displays of software and laptops have been dubbed, by writer James Fallows, compu-porn? Eighty percent of their readers are male, says the research firm Simmons MRI. (So are 85 percent of those who buy the newer and hipper Wired.)

Millions of women use computers at their jobs, of course, though often in routinized ways that leave the machines' more intriguing possibilities unexplored. But home computers, which after several years of significant growth still are found in only 31 percent of American homes, remain largely a male preserve. (And a middle-class preserve, but that's another story.) LINK Resources, a New York consulting firm, has found that in only a quarter of those homes is the primary user a woman.

As for cyberspace, about which more later, no one's hung a "No Girls Allowed" sign on the door. It's often a male clubhouse nonetheless, one girls can enter provided they are willing and able to scramble through the briers, shinny up the tree, ignore the skinned knees and announce that they can spit a watermelon seed just as far as the guys inside can. Figuratively speaking.

All of this reflects attitudes toward computers that form at unnervingly young ages. Ten years ago, not long after Time magazine had declared the computer its Person of the Year, education journals started to fill with reports about the way schoolaged boys embraced computers while girls avoided them. Boys were more likely to have home computers and use them, to enroll in computer camps and summer programs, to take advantage of school computer labs, to elect high school computer courses. Academics who pay attention to these things say they haven't seen much dramatic change since.

So much for parents' assuring themselves that kids who've grown up in the Super Mario Era won't inherit their elders' anxieties and biases. The old patterns show considerable staying power. As early as first grade, according to a 1990 study in the Journal of Research and Development in Education, computer use is seen, by both boys and girls, as masculine. Reading and writing, on the other hand, have no perceived gender associations.

Researchers offer various explanations, including the well-documented aversion that many girls develop to math and science, the ever-popular lack-of-role-models theory, and the fact that many boys are introduced to computers through those kill-and-maim computer and video games that girls very sensibly disdain. (Who dubbed the control a joystick, anyway?) The disparity, however triggered, intensifies with age; by high school, girls may use computers to write their term papers (tests show that they're as competent at it as the guys), but deeper interest is suspect.

Computing's male aura may be one of the enduring legacies of the mythic hackers and nerds who patched together the early personal computers, hammered out breakthrough programs and invented computer bulletin boards. (A notorious few also dabbled in phone and credit-card fraud.) They were true trailblazers. In addition, they and their descendants are, as a subculture, so unappetizing—pale geeks without social skills who lose themselves in binary code, sci-fi sagas and chess gambits—that women develop "computational reticence" in response.

This, at least, is the theme developed by well-known MIT sociologist Sherry Turkle in an essay that's part of a 1988 collection called *Technology and Women's Voices.* Basing her analysis on interviews with college women who were doing well in computer courses but resisted identifying themselves as "computer science types," Turkle says that women "observe [the hackers'] obsessions, observe their antisensuality, observe the ways in which they have put things rather than people at the center of their lives and count themselves out."

It's not hard to understand why an adolescent boy might find computing seductive. At a time when sexual pressures and social demands loom threateningly large, the hacker culture offers autonomy, mastery, safety. "The hook is the feeling of power that it gives you: You control a world of your own making," says my friend Steve Adamczyk, an MIT grad who owns a software company called the Edison Design Group. (I'd call Steve a former nerd except that, he explains, "it's like being an alcoholic: You're always a nerd but you're a *recovering* nerd.") Staying up all night coding software in FORTRAN, as Steve did in high school, was "terrifically appealing to people who don't do so well at controlling the real world, maintaining relationships and all that."

Girls, though of course also buffeted by adolescence, have by that point been culturally programmed to maintain relationships. And those who withdraw generally seem to find safe havens other than computer labs.

As a small but influential cadre, hackers are also something of an alien species to non-nerd men. But men, Turkle writes, are apt to view hackers' achievements with admiration. Women, however many magazine stories they read about Bill Gates's net worth, are more likely to bolt.

The good news is that unlike some stubborn power imbalances requiring generations to redress (the composition of the U.S. Congress comes to mind), computer attitudes appear to be rather dramatically revisable. And such attempts are underway: This year, the National Science Foundation has more than tripled its funding for programs aimed at pulling girls and women into science, math and engineering. The boys-will-be-nerds paradigm "is just a throwback to separate spheres, simply a vestigial anachronism," announces Jo Sanders, of the Center for Advanced Study, City University of New York.

Sanders ran the NSF-funded Computer Equity Expert Project, a 30-month-long guerrilla campaign to increase girls' participation in math, science and technology by, well, gently but firmly smashing sexism. Sanders convened 200 teachers and administrators, representing every state, for week-long seminars on the causes and consequences of the gender gap and strategies for closing it. Back in their middle and high schools, these people taught computer equity workshops to their own faculties and recruited girls with everything from guest speakers to pizza parties.

The project, which ended last year, got results with startling speed. Reports flooded in: Within a year, an all-male advanced PASCAL class in Virginia turned 50 percent female and an all-male elective computer course in Oklahoma was nearly a third female, while a West Virginia computer club increased its female membership tenfold. "When you change attitudes," Sanders concludes, "the resistance just evaporates."

As for us grown-up women no longer facing math and science requirements, our resistance is also susceptible to change. What has been missing until recently, however, isn't just spine-stiffening; it's a motivation, some *reason* to acquire or cozy up to a computer, an incentive to struggle past the inevitable glitches.

For years, if you didn't need a computer for work, it has been hard to see what it would do for you. No one really needs to make that sort of investment in time and money to balance her checkbook, file her recipes (to cite one early personal-computer application that was supposed to turn us on) or handle ordinary correspondence. The love of gadgetry and tinkering that draws some men to computers as a hobby hasn't had much measurable impact on women.

What's been missing is the Killer App.

That's the term Silicon Valley types use for the breakthrough use, the irresistible application that finally makes a technological advance not just a toy but a useful tool, so that ordinary people look at it and say, "We need one of those." The Killer App for the desktop computer itself was the Lotus 1-2-3 spreadsheet. The Killer App for microwave ovens, now in 80 percent of homes, was probably reheating leftovers, or maybe popping corn.

The Killer App that draws women into computer use in significant numbers, researchers tell me, will be communication. With a cheap modem and a few commands that connect you to a network, you can reach out and touch people you know and hundreds of thousands of people you don't and discuss everything from breastfeeding to foreign policy. This isn't technology, this is expression, relationships, community, all the things women are taught to be skilled at.

Cyberspace isn't as brave-new-world as the name makes it sound. Reva Basch, whom I've recently met-by-modem on a computer conferencing system called the WELL, told me this story: "My mother-in-law, who's 80, was visiting and expressed curiosity about the WELL. I showed it to her, showed her some of the conferences. She said, 'Why, honey, it's just *talking*, isn't it?' She got it."

My daughter, Emma, was my guide at first. Growing up with parents who use computers (however rudimentarily) and encourage her to do likewise, plus hours of playing Nintendo and computer games with friends who are boys, seems to have immunized her against computer-aversion. She's not fascinated by the things, exactly, but she's entirely unthreatened by them. So, six weeks before I began writing this essay, I nervously sat down at the Macintosh bequeathed to her when my husband, partly for that very reason, bought his latest. She patiently showed me how to log on to America Online, the country's third largest computer communications system.

America Online is easy to use, even for a neophyte. It has a welcoming "interface," a display of onscreen symbols to point to and click at, so that you can read highlights from USA Today and the Atlantic, send electronic mail ("E-mail") to friends and strangers, scroll through 406 messages from fans of Smashing Pumpkins and add your own in the RockLink Forum, or join as many as 22 other users all typing away at each other in "real time" in each of dozens of "lobbies" and "chat areas." It's gotten so popular and grown so fast that the system grew temporarily choked and sluggish this winter from overuse by its 600,000 subscribers.

I found AOL reassuringly simple but not particularly simpatico and so, two weeks later, I logged onto the WELL, a Sausalito-based network founded in 1985 by the folks who published the Whole Earth Catalogue. This was *not* simple, and resulted in the humiliation of repeatedly having to dash down two flights of stairs to ask my husband (already a WELLbeing), "How do you get to an OK prompt?," then dash back up. But I've figured out enough to be able to send and receive E-mail and join in the conversation. I've entered cyberspace.

It's become part of the daily routine: I brush my teeth; I go to my aerobics class; I dial the WELL. Once there, I check my E-mail box (an on-line friend from Massachusetts says revisions on her novel are going well; an on-line friend and new dad in California says the baby slept five hours last night). I usually visit Women on the WELL first (no guys allowed) to learn the latest depressing or exhilarating details of the lives of women I've never met but am coming to know anyway, to commiserate or cheer them on, to complain that I've gained three pounds.

Then I venture out to see who's arguing about what topic in the media conference and who's soliciting advice in the parenting conference. If I care to, I add my own comments, stories, jokes, requests for information and general two cents' worth. If I had hours to spend at this, as some folks seem to, I could join conferences where people are yakking about politics, bicycling, sex, Judaism, AIDS, the Grateful Dead and a zillion other passions and problems.

I haven't yet dared the next step, which is using the WELL to access the Internet, the vast global aggregation of computer networks that would allow me to use countless libraries and databases, join hundreds more conferences, and tell *millions* of people that I've gained three pounds. But I could. And someday, depending on how much of the prattling about the "information superhighway" and its services one chooses to believe, I'll use a computer (attached discreetly to my television) to make rental movies pop up on my TV screen, buy everything from groceries to mutual funds, take the courses I need to finish my master's degree. It all looks quite prosaic at this point—just lines of text appearing on my screen—but it feels very exciting.

At the moment, cyberspace is populated primarily by—did you guess this?—men. The WELL has only about 15 to 18 percent women among its 8,000 subscribers, its managers believe, a proportion considered representative of most conferencing or "bulletin board" systems (BBSs). Even the big on-line services that spend bundles on advertising and direct mail have drawn few female subscribers (though they believe that many women and children log on using men's accounts). Most of CompuServe's 1.5 million subscribers are guys (90 percent) and so are most of America Online's (85 percent); Prodigy claims to be the most egalitarian of the big on-line services with a 30 percent female membership.

Yet these are numbers that could change quickly and dramatically, as women learn that even those who don't know bauds from broads can use a BBS (believe me when I tell you) and—more significantly—learn that there are reasons to.

I give you Sarah Randolph, the poet who co-hosts the WELL's writers conference, who lives in a small seaside town and was "just really hungry for conversation and life" when she bought a modem and joined this odd little community. Through it she's made friends, picked up writing jobs, and learned how to increase her garden's broccoli yield. It isn't a substitute for having real people around, yet it has its own rewards. "In the real world, there's your body. Your body is shy and needs something to hold on to at a party," she muses. On-line, "I feel fairly transparent . . . I feel like I can go anywhere in that world."

I give you Patrizia DiLucchio, who read about the WELL a few years ago while writing her dissertation "on an extremely dry topic" and thought "it sounded like having pen pals . . . like putting messages in bottles and sending them out to alien shores." Now, because she lives in the San Francisco area, the WELL's home port, "half the people I hang out with in real life I met on the WELL." She also had a heavy-duty romance of several years' duration with a fellow WELLperson, and she's hardly the only one: "To some extent, all bulletin boards are interactive personals ads."

I give you Ellen Pack, president of a new on-line service that reverses the usual stats (10 percent of its members are male) called Women's Wire. Along with the databases on women's health, the updates on legislation and such, Women's Wire lets Pack, a San Franciscan, stay in touch with her parents and sisters in New York via E-mail. "My mom is 65 and not particularly computer-literate, but I got her a Mac and now she logs on," Pack reports. "It doesn't replace face-to-face or the occasional phone call, but I communicate with them so much more now because it's sooo easy." E-mail is cheaper and more convenient than long distance telephoning, and, Pack points out, "it lets you have all the incremental communications, things you wouldn't pick up the phone for."

I give you, moreover, my friend Pam, who sallied into cyberspace about the same time I did and is busily researching her new book via America Online. We agree that our most serious current problem with computer networks is that work and family obligations can really cut into the time we spend on-line.

And yet. The thing about cyberspace is that although sometimes it feels like a sophisticated graduate seminar or a good-natured pub, it can also, for women, feel like a walk past a construction site or a wrong turn down a dark street. Like life itself, it requires tactical decisions about how to proceed in a not-always-welcoming sphere: Do you opt for a strategic retreat into protected bunkers? Lobby for reform? Take a deep breath and wade in swinging?

For cyberspace is not an alternate, genderless universe. College women report dopey sexist limericks and images of breasts sent via computer nets. Women can be publicly propositioned or stalked by E-mail suitors who hurl abuse when they get rejected. My daughter, visiting an America Online gathering called Teen Chat, is regularly invited by the teenaged boys who predominate therein to enter a private "room." Sometimes she sees whether they have anything interesting to say. Sometimes she Just Types No.

I have watched as someone named Stacey logged onto an AOL book discussion group, introduced herself as a newcomer, then disappeared from the screen for a while. She came back long enough to type out, "What are all these messages?" She'd been flooded with IMs—instant messages directed only to her. The other women in the group pointed out that her female ID had made her a target for attention. It was at this point that, although I had not encountered such treatment, I changed my own ID to something offering no gender clues. The problem, hardly limited to America Online, is widely reported. "You seek out your friends and places you know are safe and harassment-free," an AOL subscriber named Citywoman tells me via E-mail.

You don't have to sit still for such annoyances, of course. Many on-line systems have some sort of recourse, hosts or monitors who chastise offenders, or policies that can toss a persistent harasser off the net. On the WELL, a "bozofilter" command allows you to simply never hear from a given user again, an option I'd find useful in everyday existence. You can change an ID like Citywoman to a string of numbers or to JackSpratt. You can confront jerks.

Still, if cyberspace were a workplace, this stuff would qualify as creating a hostile environment. "Hearing that incidents happen probably discourages some women who haven't even tried going on-line," worries Reva Basch, who co-hosts the cozy Women on the WELL conference. "They'll say, 'Oooh, you'll get cruised and hit on. Who needs it? I get enough of that on my job.' "

It was Basch who alerted the WELL at large to another way in which cyberspace can mirror life: the discovery last summer that a "cybercad" had been romancing several WELLwomen simultaneously, exchanging erotic E-mail with each of them without the others' knowledge, going so far as to visit one woman using a plane ticket she helped pay for. The incident, first reported in this newspaper, sparked weeks of heated discussion about whether and how this sort-of community should respond. The cad eventually resigned his account voluntarily, but left behind a lot of unanswered questions about what the differences between behavior on-line and behavior IRL (in real life) are and ought to be.

And if it's tough to figure out what to do about virtual knavery, what to do about a virtual rape? It happened in a computer-generated environment developed by Xerox researchers in Palo Alto, Calif., reachable through the Internet and called LambdaMOO. In this fantasy domain, a kind of multi-authored fictional work-in-progress known to its denizens as "the MOO," a motley array of characters glide through many rooms, doing and saying what users sitting at their terminals (mostly college and graduate students in their late teens and early twenties, three-fourths of them male) tell them to do and say. Last year, in an incident vividly reported in the Village Voice, a crude jester named Mr. Bungle sexually assaulted several other LambdaMOO characters in a rampage of intensifying verbal violence. The ensuing sociopolitical debate was fierce and prolonged.

Civilization—as designed by Pavel Curtis, who heads the Xerox Social Virtual Reality Project— has now come to the MOO. An arrangement of petitions and ballots allows users to modify the system, request arbitration, seek justice. In the on-line world, Curtis concludes, "the medium is different, but the people are the same."

Less dramatic than rape or harassment, but a deterrent nevertheless to bringing women into cyberspace, is the matter of style. Here again, the hackers of yore have left their fingerprints all over the world they helped create. Hackers were known for a strong anti-authoritarian streak, a libertarian philosophy that resisted rules, controls, the restrictive codes of real life. They also adopted on-line a style of expression that reflected all the maturity, nuance and nurturing qualities of 17-year-old boys. (A recent press release about a book on women and information technology, for example, posted on a University of Illinois network, brought immediate and snarky attacks on the woman who'd written the release. "Who is she, a cow who belongs to NOW?" "A member of Dykes on Bikes?")

This is the clubhouse atmosphere that greets the tentative newcomer of either gender. Nets and conferences have their own varying personalities, but many of them offer no-holds-barred arguments and aggressive put-downs, a rambunctious interplay (known as "flaming") in which women, vastly outnumbered, find their contributions derided or simply ignored. Academics analyzing "netiquette" have pointed out that both men and women respond more to men's messages. Some women charge in and give as good as they get; others retreat.

The WELL, for instance, seems a reasonably civil place with an egalitarian tradition, where conflict-avoidance abbreviations like "imho" (in my humble opinion) and "YMMV" (your mileage may vary) abound. Yet even here, there are women who feel more comfortable in the supportive confines of the women's conference and rarely leave it (though others find it earnest and too polite and rarely enter). During an on-line flap about "male discourse," a woman named Tigereye kept the history conference at a boil for weeks with remarks about the "traditional male style of communication involving gratuitous one-upmanship, insult and posturing we can readily observe on the WELL."

What if women dominated the net and set the tone? To find out, Nancy Baym, a University of Illinois doctoral candidate, has immersed herself in a Usenet group called rec.arts.tv.soaps, devoted to discussion of soap operas. (And referred to as RATS, which is why Baym hopes to title her dissertation "Of RATS and Women.") Its participants are largely female engineers, techies and academics who like to break up their workdays with discussions on such topics as, "Is Dixie a Ho'?"

Wading through 7,000 posted messages on the subject of "All My Children," Baym found a language of elaborate courtesy. "They use a lot of politeness strategies to make disagreement nonthreatening," she reports. "They'll try to build the esteem of the person they're disagreeing with: 'Jane, I see your point of view, but I must say ...' Alternately, they'll diminish the force of their disagreement, qualify things: 'I could be wrong but ...' In the soap group, the netiquette is, don't insult people. If you look at groups discussing 'Star Trek,' they'll say, 'Stay off the 'Net, you Nazi!' "

Groans all around. Somewhere between enforcing Nice Networks for women, and having women set upon by wolf packs roaming the Internet, there must be a workable middle ground. I count myself among the optimists, partly because there are systems that demonstrate the possibility of egalitarianism. It doesn't happen by accident, but it does happen.

ECHO, a New York-based bulletin board, is more than 50 percent female, an achievement attributed to its founder's determination to lure women in by means of tutorials, a mentoring program and reduced rates. Arlington's Metasystems Design Group operates the Meta Network, a conferencing system that is also more than half female—and aspires to be a no-flame zone.

"We do all the things good moderators do in person," says Metasystems partner Lisa Kimball. On the Meta Net, new members get buddies, flamers get a private talking-to, welcomes are issued the first time someone speaks up on-line, yet the opinions fly. "It's like arriving at a big party with lots of people," Kimball says. "One issue is finding out where the bar is, but it's even better when the hostess says, 'I'm so glad you're here. There's someone over on the other side of the room I think you'd like to meet.' "

One of the elders of cyberspace, who has founded bulletin boards in many places, is Dave Hughes, a k a the Cursor Cowboy. He now runs the Old Colorado City Electronic Cottage, based in Colorado Springs, from which perspective he can see the analogy between that onetime frontier and this one. "It's the same as going into the gold rush towns," the Cowboy observes. "Males jump onto their horses, set up these roistering places, saloons and all. As soon as you begin to approach one-third to one-half of the population being women ... you still have the saloons and the hoop-de-doo, but you also have the schools.

"It's the same in the on-line world, dominated by men, their language, their interests ... The moment a woman goes on-line, she's a target for all sorts of things, like the gal that came into town on the stage ... [On-line women] have to be like frontier women, a little tougher-skinned ... They have to master all kinds of skills they didn't know before. But as the numbers increase, the language changes, the subjects begin to reflect a more balanced society."

Does it matter? I vote yes.

True, people of either gender can still live meaningful lives without computers. If I never progressed beyond the half-dozen commands necessary to send my stories to The Washington Post, I might suffer little handicap. I don't think that will be true for my daughter, though, or any of our daughters. They're entering a world in which card catalogue drawers have already vanished from the public library, replaced by terminals and keyboards.

Perhaps they won't need to be whiz-bang programmers (though it wouldn't hurt). But they can't afford to see computers as toys for boys, to see ignorance as feminine, to wring their hands over the keyboard and worry that they'll break something.

"A sense of yourself as a technologically competent person is no small shakes in this world," Jo Sanders of City University says. "It builds confidence in yourself as a problem-solver. It's important on a résumé whether or not the job you're interested in uses computers . . . It's proof that you are able to learn things, a certificate of capability."

I recall, 20 years ago—as women were trying to free themselves from a set of social expectations that has already changed startlingly—a brief vogue for feminist courses in auto repair. Whether or not you could afford to have someone change your oil or your tire, a sense of independence and mastery of the world demanded that you take on the guy things. You wanted to demonstrate to yourself and others that you could change spark plugs even if, once having proven it, you went back to dropping your VW Bug off at the local garage.

More and more, the computer world feels like that. Women have to be in it because incompetence is an unattractive trait. Women have to be in it because decisions about language and culture and access are being made and we should be involved in making them. Women have to be in it because, although nobody really knows what form all this technology will take, there shouldn't be any clubhouse we're afraid to climb into.

I think that because of timely early intervention, Emma will handle the clubhouse just fine.

As for myself, I'm not afraid of the guys inside, but I dread the technical challenge of climbing the tree. Still, a couple of weeks ago, I logged on and typed in "support" and ordered the WELL User's Manual, Version 5.1a. It arrived recently, a fat and daunting volume that tells you when to use "!sz -a *" as opposed to "!xm stky my*." I'm sure there are dozens of elegant functions in it that I don't need and may never master, just as I doubt that I'll ever drool over the compu-porn in Byte or order RAM-doublers by mail.

But I need to know how to download. I've got to learn how to move files around. So I'm going to wade in. It was sort of a kick, late the other night, when Tigereye taught me, via E-mail, how to extract. It wasn't so difficult; I just typed "!extract -u tigereye history" and the stuff poured forth in waves.

THINKING AND RE-READING

1. As you re-read the selection, jot down the verbs, adjectives, and other language Span uses to evoke images suggesting that "computers are more of a guy thing." Span also labels displays of software and laptops in computer magazines as "lust-inspiring." Why does she say this?

2. Similar claims and statistics have been presented in other articles in this section. We read, for example, that fewer women than men earn degrees in computer science; fewer women are systems analysts and programmers; and that mostly men read the computer magazines. Go back through either the Gerver or Pearl and her colleagues' articles on women in computer science and write down the sentences that make the same claims. Whose arguments do you find more convincing? Why? Who are the audiences for each of the articles?

3. Jot down some of the measures Span says are being taken for changing attitudes about computers and for "smashing sexism." Do you agree that computer-mediated communication is the "Killer App" whereby women will be drawn into the computer culture? Why or why not? What advantages does the WELL offer the author? Do you think that there "ought to be" differences in behavior online and IRL? Why can't women afford to see computers "as toys for boys"?

WRITING AND LEARNING

1. The selection by Paula Span is part narrative or story in which the author describes how she came to access cyberspace and what she found there. As she relates her experiences, she notes that although computers are somewhat intimidating for her, her twelve-year-old daughter, who sometimes serves as her guide, feels no such trepidation. Write a letter to a younger sister or female friend in which you describe your first online experiences. In the letter, you should also tell her why you think it important that she become a part of the computer culture. If you prefer, you might, instead, write to a younger brother, again relating your online experiences but this time suggesting how you would expect him to behave toward women in cyberspace.

2. Shortly into the selection, Span alerts readers with "Warning: The following article contains assorted generalizations and risks gender stereotyping." Make two columns on paper or in a word processing file. Now re-read the article and list the generalizations and stereotypes that Span makes concerning the two sexes. Think of examples that confirm or refute her images of men and women. Compose an e-mail message to your classmates or writing group in which you discuss the dangers or advantages in the use of such stereotypes. Convey your message as a prompt to lead an extended discussion on the topic.

Take Back the Net!

Stephanie Brail

IN THIS 1994 *ON THE ISSUES* SELECTION aimed primarily at women, the author draws a grim picture of online sexual harassment at the same time that she describes the different kinds of online services available commercially and through the Internet. In the end, she urges women to join the net, suggesting that online life is not very different from ordinary everyday living—fraught with dangers, perhaps, but well worth any risk it may entail.

You are at home, sitting at your computer, reading the latest messages, via electronic- or e-mail, from friends and family around the country. You're tired and have been scanning the screen quickly—when suddenly one message leaps out at you: "Why don't you get a life you on-the-rag, stuck up cunt? Geez, you really need to get fucked in the ass."

That's what happened to me a few months ago. I was shaken and scared. The message was signed "Hemroid," and it was the first of many such communications to scroll across my screen, telling me what an "evil cunt" I was and how my opinions were worthless. The man, who also called himself "Mike," sent me reams of pornographic text. And I couldn't do a thing about it. Mike's fake e-mail addresses protected him from even my nasty rejoinder, let alone punitive actions by computer authorities.

My life in cyberspace, as the electronic world is sometimes known, hasn't always been this eventful. I began going "on-line" when my dad insisted I get a computer account at college so he could send e-mail messages to me and save on long distance phone charges. When messages are sent using a computer modem, each party only has to connect to a local network phone number.

NO MORE SNAIL MAIL

I joined the university network and my dad belonged to CompuServe; the two are connected through the Internet, a vast publicly supported supernetwork—part of that information superhighway Al Gore always talks about. Once I learned how to get mail from my father ("Hi, Stephanie, I hope you are doing well in English") and send messages to him ("I'm getting all A's. Please send money."), I was hooked.

After college I found a commercial Internet provider in my area. With that I could send and receive e-mail, "telnet" to other computer networks and join newsgroups. I also got my own CompuServe account, which gave me news, special interest forums and access to databases.

WE ARE TALKING WORLD-WIDE

If commercial networks are like bookstores, the Internet (known as "the net") is like a vast well-funded public library, with access to the best and biggest libraries everywhere. It connects thousands of computer systems—from businesses and universities to the Library of Congress. There are 15 million users worldwide—some say it's expanding by a million new members a month—and so far women comprise only an estimated 10 to 15 percent of users. Millions of members access the Internet every day for research, e-mail and, perhaps . . . sexual harassment.

Being a personal victim of electronic harassment made me wonder if other women have the same experiences. Was high-tech harassment such as this the reason why so few women connect to the Internet?

In a survey taken by Dr. Anita Borg, founder and administrator of the Systers mailing list, a group of 1,500 women computer system operators, one in five of the 500 respondents said they had been sexually harassed on-line. Half of the women surveyed felt that changes in the systems were needed "to make them more conducive to the participation of women and girls."

REAL-LIFE ANARCHY

There's no central authority on the net, which is an anarchic conglomerate of thousands of smaller networks. As a small but visible minority, the problems women run into there are not surprising, but simply a reflection of Real Life. We get to experience the common problem of having our ideas ignored, for example, while a man gets lauded for saying the same thing. We can also be the object of unwanted requests for dates or sex, known on the net as "wanna fucks."

Some women have even had men look up their on-line names in phone books and call them on the telephone. In order to escape such attention, some have adopted gender-neutral or male on-line pseudonyms. When Patricia Currier, a 19-year-old computer science major at Worcester Polytechnic Institute, changed her moniker to Terrylee, sexual harassment stopped.

E-mail is not the only site of on-line harassment. Chats, talk requests and other real-time communications in which participants type in whatever they want to say and it is read by others simultaneously, are often used as virtual pick-up joints. Internet Relay Chat (IRC) is one such place.

Melinda Shore, a 37-year-old software engineer at the Cornell Theory Center, has used the net for decades. She finds it an invaluable resource for maintaining friendships with people all over the world. But as a member of soc.motss, the gay and lesbian newsgroup, she's received some "truly nasty" e-mail. Finally she stopped responding to talk requests from strangers. "It's not uncommon for undergraduate men to cruise the network late at night, looking for women and trying to talk to them," she says. "I know it's loneliness but it's annoying, too."

The Denver Free-Net is one of a growing number of free public access-to-Internet sites across the country. Open only since January 1993, Free-Net already has 6,000 users. After just three months of operation, it began receiving complaints about sexually suggestive conversations. Male staff entered the system under assumed female names, to see if the complaints had merit. They found plenty of evidence, and solved the problem by closing down IRC completely in July.

SOMEONE IS WATCHING OVER YOU

Women who want to test the waters might want to begin in a closed commercial system like CompuServe or Prodigy. Given the rich resources available there, they might never need to venture into Internet's newsgroups. They are certainly less likely to receive obscene messages.

Prodigy, a large commercial service with the highest complement of female users—40 percent—has a strict policy regarding obscenity and harassment, according to Debra Borchert, manager of communications. Obscene messages posted to bulletin boards are sent back to the poster for rewriting. If a member receives an obscene message in e-mail, Prodigy managers will contact the offender and ask that the messages stop. One more instance results in a terminated account.

ECHO (East Coast Hang Out), founded by Stacy Horn in 1990, is well-known for its woman-friendly atmosphere and has attracted 40 percent female participation. Fifty percent of ECHO's conferences are moderated by women, and that includes not only traditional women's forums but also conferences of a technical nature. Horn also gave free one-year accounts to female charter members.

That alone was enough to cause resentment among some male cyberspace users. After a favorable article about ECHO appeared in the hip computer magazine *Wired,* male readers passed around a parody entitled "The Evil Cunts Hang Out." Horn was not surprised, but finds that most men members like ECHO.

The men on ECHO are actually "terribly civilized," Horn explains. "Men have found it valuable that women feel comfortable here. These women stick around and get to know them and it's like a real community. So they have a vested interest in keeping it this way."

SAY NO TO YO?

ECHO has its occasional problems, especially with a real-time talk feature called "yo" which Horn says is not very popular. "One thing we've noticed is that men 'yo' more than women, and when a new woman comes on-line, they'll, like, 'yo her up,' " Horn explains. "It can be annoying, so we'll say 'Look, chill out.' "

ECHO also has a special place for women to report harassment and hassles. If a member has a complaint about another member, Horn's system operators often will talk to the person who sent the offending message. Most cases are resolved easily. "Usually they're very embarrassed," Horn says. They had no idea that some women resented their flirting.

Horn doesn't consider this censorship; she says most users can be trusted to abide by the tone of individual conferences. In ECHO's three years of existence she has only had to force two people out. Both were men who were offending and harassing the rest of ECHO's members.

Following Horn's lead, Ellen Pack and Nancy Rhine founded WIRE (Women's Information Resource and Exchange), a new commercial on-line service based in San Francisco, created to fill the void of women's information on on-line services. Rhine describes the service as a practical place where women can find all the information they need in one stop. She considers this particularly helpful for women with work and family responsibilities who often don't have as much time as men do to play on different services.

The service, which opened in October, offers an easy-to-use Windows interface. Databases such as "Herstory," a news feed which brings in articles about women's issues, women's health topics, and networking for women business owners, activists, and others, are services decidedly different from the usual on-line fare.

If such women-owned and women-designed services become the norm, perhaps more on-line communications will become like Horn's ideal of ECHO. "It's not like just the one or two strong voices ... women who would be heard no matter what ... but here women are generally heard in pretty much every topic and every conference," Horn explains. "There is a different tone and atmosphere to the place because of the presence of women."

Sexual harassment instances should not obscure the fact that there are a lot of satisfied women network users. "It bothers me that women aren't taking more advantage of these services," says Judith Broadhurst, a freelance writer who specializes in psychology and is heavily involved in on-line communications. "It's the new good ole boys network. And women are depriving themselves of it. A lot of wheeling and dealing is now going on in cyberspace ... the whole nature of work and communication has changed forever." If women don't learn to navigate in cyberspace, Broadhurst predicts, "we're going to end up back in the typing pool."

Perhaps the best advice about dealing with the male-dominated net comes from Desiree McCrorey, a 38-year-old computer-user interface designer: "I wouldn't give any serious consideration to not using the net based on any disturbing events. If I did, I wouldn't use a phone or go into public. In fact, I've been telling all my friends about the Internet.... They find it fascinating and full of potential."

THINKING AND RE-READING

1. As you re-read this piece, jot down examples that Brail includes that make the net an attractive space for you, and then note those factors that make it unpleasant and sometimes downright hostile. After reading over your notes, decide the sorts of online services you would be interested in. Why? Why does Brail think that women should be connected online? Why does she title her piece, "Take Back the Net!"? Is it an appropriate title?

WRITING AND LEARNING

1. To increase your own skill in journalistic writing, compose a piece that relates your first experiences on the World Wide Web. As you write, try to imagine that you are corresponding with a group of on-campus friends or acquaintances who have little knowledge of the Web. (When Brail wrote her article in 1994, the Web was still not easily accessible; moreover, it was not the huge commercial enterprise that it is fast becoming.) In your essay, relate what you found exciting regarding your experiences on the Web but also include your thoughts concerning somewhat intimidating or offputting encounters. What is easy and difficult for you on the Web? How does the Web differ from the sites Brail describes? Aim your essay at a particular group on campus to which

you belong and share your perceptions with members of the group. In your essay, set forth a plan in which you offer to help other women and men—older or younger— become savvy net surfers.

2. At the end of the article, Brail quotes a free-lance writer and psychologist who offers the following opinion: " 'It bothers me,' Judith Broadhurst asserts, 'that women aren't taking more advantage of [online] services. . . . It's the new good ole boys network. And women are depriving themselves of it. A lot of wheeling and dealing is now going on in cyberspace,' " and if women don't get involved, she argues, they're "going to end up back in the typing pool." Write an editorial piece for your school newspaper in which you argue for women's online participation. Go back through the articles in this section and choose the evidence that you think the student body—both men and women— will find convincing and use it to strengthen your arguments. Look over other editorials in both the school newspaper and other newspapers that you read so that you will be able to determine the ways in which an editorial, for instance, differs from a representative "letter to the editor."

Weavers of Webs: A Portrait of Young Women on the Net

Nancy Kaplan and Eva Farrell

THIS SELECTION, ORIGINALLY PUBLISHED on the World Wide Web in *The Electronic Journal of Virtual Culture,* is a 1994 study that looks at the online activities of a small group of adolescent girls in upstate New York. The two authors, Nancy Kaplan and Eva Farrell, are mother and daughter: Kaplan, a scholar of rhetoric at the University of Baltimore, and Farrell about to enter her first year at the University of Texas, Austin, when the article was written. The study differs from the other articles in this section in that it focuses on how young women see themselves in relation to the computer culture in which they participate.

ABSTRACT

Gender imbalances within networking culture have prompted an array of interesting research questions about communication practices—who speaks and to whom, who sets conversational agendas, who "dominates" a discourse. Such studies have generally confirmed the negative experiences of professional women who participate actively in network culture, but what they have not yet examined is the persistence of women in this apparently hostile culture, nor have they generally asked how those women who participate despite male dominance understand their own activities. This study begins to address those questions—why women seek electronic spaces, what they articulate as their aims, expectations, and desires, how women make their electronic communication practices meaningful to themselves—by investigating a small community of adolescent women.

The study's population has as yet no professional stake in the activity. Instead the subjects "discovered" electronic communications in relation to leisure time. Their desires, rather than specific institutional pressures, have brought them into networking culture. By examining the subjects' narratives about their activities, we construct a picture of the group's understanding of electronic discourse. What meaning does the electronic discussion have in the lives of the young women who have taken up this activity and how do they understand their participation? What brought them to this activity and what sustains them in it? How do they see themselves and each other in relation to other participants?

This study helps us understand women's stake in electronic networks. It also illuminates some generational issues by exploring how a cohort acquainted with electronic technologies from a relatively early age conceptualizes computing tools and their relations to these instruments.

INTRODUCTION

In some fields, notably rhetoric and composition, women have been early and persistent participants in the professional electronic culture that began emerging in the mid-1980s. Many of the early software developers for writing instruction—Helen Schwartz, Christine Neuwirth, Nancy Kaplan, and Susan Kirschner—as well as the founders of the central professional journal on the subject of computers and composition—Kate Kiefer, Dawn Rodrigues, Cindy Selfe, and Gail Hawisher—have been women. Still, there is little doubt that women are "underrepresented" in many areas of social and economic life, especially those related to electronic technologies.

The figures circulating on various electronic discussion lists show that women are largely absent from computer-related activities: women make up only 20% of the readership of popular computing magazines like *PC World*, 15% of subscribers to *Wired*, 15–18% of subscribers to the WELL (a surprisingly low figure since many of us *believe* women are more likely to be engaged in computing when the technology engages the arts in some way), 10% of CompuServe subscribers, 15% of AOL subscribers, 30% of Prodigy subscribers.[1]

The paucity of women is noticeable not only in arenas of cultural consumption but also in arenas of knowledge production. In the social studies of technology, gender barely figures in important accounts of technologies and social practices. In the earliest and still one of the most important works on electronic networks (Hiltz & Turoff, 1978; revised 1993), the implications of electronic technologies for women occupies only a single, three-paragraph segment. It concludes:

> Our own hope is that the potential of this medium for work at home and for making the sex of participants totally inconsequential will mean that it will lead to a reorganization of occupational and household sex roles. However, it may also reinforce current distinctions. (1993 edition, pp. 438–439)

In *The Social Construction of Technological Systems* (Bijker, Hughes, & Pinch, 1987), gender figures in only two articles: a brief mention in an account of the development of the bicycle (Pinch & Bijker, 1987) and an almost inadvertent focus in an article on the diffusion of home heating and cooking technologies in the United States (Cowan, 1987). This second article, the only one in the collection authored by a woman, proposes to focus on what Cowan calls "the consumption junction" as an important research site in the social studies of technology: it just so happens that the technologies she studies—devices for heating homes and cooking—are consumed in domestic settings and are therefore primarily in the domain of women. It is probably no accident that, both in the work of Hiltz and Turoff and in Cowan's study, the accounts of technological change bring women into focus largely in the context of their traditional domestic sphere.

Women and gender issues loom somewhat larger when researchers stop constructing an epic tale about sweeping technological impacts on the whole culture and begin to tell a narrower story about specific practices and the groups who engage in them. The gender imbalance so obvious to students of networking culture has prompted an array of interesting research investigating many dimensions of gender's intersection with networking practices, primarily asking questions such as who speaks and to whom, who sets conversational agendas, who "dominates" a discourse. Studies of sociolinguistic behaviors in electronic conversations—both those carried on through listserv lists and those occurring in "realtime spaces," such as synchronous conferencing software and MUDs/MOOs—have begun to show that despite the early explorations and sometimes ground-breaking work women have done in computing, women in many rapidly technologizing fields have felt increasingly discouraged by the discursive practices they encounter on the "nets." As many studies have shown, male participants outnumber female, and male participation dominates female in most electronic environments, even on such lists as MBU^2 where the participation of women is remarkable for its vigor (Selfe & Meyer, 1991; Herring, Johnson, & DiBenedetto, 1992). These studies serve to confirm anecdotal evidence from professional women who have participated actively in network culture: women frequently feel ignored, silenced, even abused in electronic conversations.

Most of the published work on issues surrounding gender and networks emphasizes areas of tension or exclusion (see Turkle & Papert, 1990; Taylor, Kramarae, & Ebben, 1993). Typically, studies of discourse on electronic discussion lists examine numbers of messages, turn-taking, topic-setting, and other markers of status and power to show that women do not necessarily encounter the democratizing space so many pioneers of electronic discourse prophesied. Turkle (1988) speculates that women fall prey not to computer phobia but to what she calls "computer reticence," a fear of the intimate machine. The research agenda these studies outline stresses the obstacles women may face in their electronic communications practices. The studies tell us a great deal about what keeps women out of electronic discourse and what discourages their full and fulfilling participation.

What these studies generally overlook (or fail to take into account), however, is that some women persist despite the barriers to entry and the problems they find. They also generally overlook generational issues that may become increasingly important as a cohort of young women for whom computers have been everyday objects since childhood begins to reach maturity. Focusing predominantly on communications practices in two sites—among professional women or in school settings, both elementary and secondary—most studies have yet to take into account the entrance of young women into electronic discourse especially when their participation occurs outside of formal educational settings. In other words, we have been so busy noticing what hinders and repels us that we have failed to ask what draws some of us (but not others). We need to know more about what attracts women to electronic environments and what features of the activities we engage in sustain us in these new spaces. And we need to find out what might account for the presence of some adolescent women, a "next generation" of electronic communicators: how do those adolescents who gravitate to electronic spaces and seem to thrive there come into the subculture and find pleasure, amusement, and interest there?

The gender patterns present in subscriber lists and in electronic behaviors may have roots in the gendered divisions of work and play evident (and reinforced?) in the activities of young children. Girls seek cooperative play, while boys prefer competitive play; girls choose dolls, boys weapons and machinery; girls prefer literature, boys math (Gilligan, 1982; see also Turkle & Papert, 1990; Tannen, 1990). As Turkle (1988) astutely notes, "The computer has no inherent gender bias. But the computer culture is not equally neutral" (p. 41). However these "preferences" and associations arise (and there are a number of competing theories), the effects of gendering various arenas are evident by the time children are in the early years of education and are settled habits by the time children reach their teens. Still, there are always some young women willing to test the construction of gendered spaces. It seems fruitful, then, to begin to look at how some young women, especially those who find the "intimate machine" (Turkle, 1982) congenial and useful for their purposes, understand and make sense of their own behaviors as denizens of electronic spaces.

PURPOSE OF THE STUDY

To begin to address these gaps in our understanding, the authors have undertaken a study of a small community of young women who choose to spend some part of their leisure time participating in the local electronic culture in their town. The study sketches some facets of how these young women use computing, and especially electronic messaging, in their worlds of work (school) and play (home and other venues of social life). As all ethnographic work seeks to do, this study tries to tease out the meanings its subjects construct, to situate their participation in electronic communications within the framework of their lives, to tell the story of how electronic mail and electronic bulletin boards function and fit within the totality of their daily activities and especially within the choices they make about how to spend their leisure time (Van Maanen, 1988). Another goal is to understand how these women see themselves in relation to others, both those using the same or similar b-boards and those who do not engage in this activity. The observations we have been able to make preclude answering many of the global questions we might ask: the number of subjects in the study and their atypicality make it impossible to generalize from this ethnography to other settings or groups of adolescents. Nevertheless, this description can provide a glimpse of some useful research questions the scholarly community could begin to address.

DESCRIPTION OF THE STUDY'S METHODS

Conducted by a scholar of rhetoric (Kaplan) and a participant-observer who is also one of the study's chief informants (Farrell), this study examines some of the electronic communications practices of five young women. The information sources consist of questionnaires, interviews, journal entries, and our observations of messaging behaviors on the electronic bulletin boards the subjects use. Because electronic behaviors depend quite directly on the varieties of technology available to users, we describe the environment of the bboards fairly completely. Yet our main focus remains the activities and choices of the study's subjects.

Rather than examining the messages these women send and receive or the distribution of gender in the totality of messages on any one of the bulletin boards these women use, we decided to focus on the ways the young women see themselves in relation to the technologies and activities they choose. Taking a cue from Cowan (1987), we elicited the information for the study from a "consumption junction" represented by the words and perceptions of those who have chosen this activity among the others competing for their time and attention.

The study began with the questionnaire, asking for some demographic information as well as some self-descriptions of preferred activities and interests. Those who did not write out their answers were interviewed by Farrell. We also asked the participants to keep a log or journal of their electronic lives for a few weeks, but only one participant managed to do so consistently. Over the course of five months, one other participant—Farrell herself—wrote three extensive meditations describing herself and her use of electronic discourse. This study, then, focuses primarily on the two young women who wrote at length, using the other three as a kind of backdrop.

WOMEN WHO WEAVE THE WEB: AN ANALYSIS

1. *Who "we" are.* The subjects of this study are a fairly homogenous set: all are white and middle class, ranging in age from 15 to 18; they live in a small town in upstate New York. Their town is dominated economically and culturally by a major university. Four subjects have one or more parent connected in some way to the university. All live at home with some family (although three are children of divorced and/or reconstituted nuclear families). All but one have a computer and modem at home.

All of the subjects have above average scores on the SATs. All of them will go to college. All of the women in this study attend an alternative school, that is, one where students have considerable say about governance and curriculum and where the educational agenda includes fostering independent thinking and creativity as well as students' sense of responsibility for their own learning. Nevertheless, as a public school this one must meet the general requirements of the state and the local school board, including math and science requirements as well as computer literacy goals. All took a computer literacy course either in high school or in middle school.

Although we suspected that many young women who use computers extensively might also have less math and science aversion than other girls their age, this hypothesis was not in fact supported by the subjects' self-assessments. Some have enjoyed math and science in high school and intend to study these subjects in college while others lean toward the humanities and social sciences. Our two focal cases divide along these disciplinary leanings: "Fish" (a nickname for one of the young women) intends to study science; Farrell prefers literature or perhaps psychology. Fish takes computer classes and writes computer code; Farrell does not and has shown no interest in programming. In fact, she describes herself as math-averse and yet shows an intense interest in computers as communication tools.

All of the young women in the study identify some shared interests with each other and with those they "meet" on the bboards. These interests center on leisure activities, including a canon of science fiction and fantasy texts (*Hitchhiker's Guide to the Galaxy* and *Star Trek* were mentioned most frequently) and similar tastes in music (what these young women generally characterized as "alternative" music). Four of the five mentioned that the people they meet on the bboards tend to be politically liberal, but since their town is also generally more liberal than the surrounding towns, this perception is hardly surprising and quite likely to be accurate for the local electronic community.

The questionnaire/interview asked the subjects to describe some of their preferred activities and to characterize these preferences in gender terms where appropriate. Not surprisingly, most of these young women characterized some of the activities they enjoy, including b-boarding, as male-identified. For example, all said they enjoy some role-playing games—three of them actively and the other two only occasionally—though none engage in the most violent type, which Farrell terms "wargaming"; three of the five admit to greater or lesser degrees of interest in math and/or science and characterize these interests as more typical of males they know than of females. Only one, Fish, describes herself as a programmer, though. One of these young women claims to hate math (except for the conceptual parts) but confesses to a fondness for fixing things, like cars. Although the survey did not elicit a great deal of information and we did no comparisons with other young women who are not engaged in electronic communications nor with any young men whether or not they participate in computer culture, these brief descriptions suggest a cohort of young women who are aware of the gendering of typical adolescent activities but who feel comfortable identifying themselves with some activities and preferences they associate with maleness.

Although we will treat this feature of the subjects' use of electronic messaging more fully in section 4 below, one other common point of connection among these women deserves mention here: all of these young women were introduced to electronic conversations by one or more friends. Several mentioned the same friend, a young woman whom we will call Jane for the purposes of this study. Jane had also attended the alternative high school but is now in college in California. It is unclear how Jane became involved in b-boarding or what her role in spreading this activity among women was, but the personal connection to people (especially other young women no more than a few years older than they) who are already engaged in the local b-board scene seems vital to the story of our subjects' use of the medium. In most cases, members of the subjects' families (fathers, mothers, older siblings) use computers in their work or leisure activities. For example, Farrell's mother has been using computers professionally and at home since Farrell was seven years old. But Farrell began using them in earnest, for herself and her own purposes, only when she was 14 or 15 years old. Even those who mention a family member's computer use connect their own introduction to the bulletin board scene with a specific friend or two. The role modelling a mother might play, then, seems much less potent than the engagement of those within the cohort.

In her first musings about this project and the kinds of questions she would like it to explore, Farrell speculated that girls join the subcultures of role-playing games and electronic communications through different avenues and at a different developmental stage than boys do. She believes that boys begin role-playing when they are quite young (six and seven years old, she guesses). One of her good buddies, Neville, had tried to get her involved in role playing when she was about 10 years old, but she was not interested because the pictures on the role playing materials struck her as sexist. Girls, Farrell observes, join this activity (if they ever do) when they are mid-adolescent, fourteen or fifteen, with active social lives including male friends or even boyfriends, who, as Farrell puts it, "induct them." Similarly, she feels that young men who participate in the b-board subculture engage in it in ways she does not, for purposes she does not share:

> I have noticed that girls tend to be less hard-core [users of computer technologies], usually not being programmers and the like, and not dedicating all their time to the 'boards like some guys do. For most females, it's a hobby, not a lifestyle. I don't know why it is for other people, but for me it's because I have other interests.

Farrell's reflections suggest that young women may enter the related subcultures of role-playing games and electronic b-boarding because of and by means of their immediate social worlds: chiefly their daily companions at school. Young women, Farrell believes, may join these activities precisely because they see them as an extension of, rather than escape from, those immediate social worlds. Clearly, the presence and strength of this connection needs further exploration.

2. *Where we meet electronically.* These young women are participants in a number of local bulletin boards: Memory Alpha, The Color Connection, Total Perspective Vortex, and The Magic Shop are some favorites. These electronic spaces are local in the sense that they do not fully connect to the entire range of utilities and services of the Internet. All of these bboards require users to obtain special permission from the bboard's owner/operator to use an Internet connection. Most with any sort of connection limit users to an electronic mail gateway so that local users can send email to people who are not based in their town or who for various reasons tend to log in to a different bboard. The Internet connection serves as access to local newsgroups, but not to the national and international smorgasbord of newsgroups for which the Internet is so renowned.

Typically, these electronic facilities offer participants a number of different spaces or options for use. The one Farrell uses most often, for example, offers participants a range of discussion topics as well as games and other files users can download. In addition to offering information about the technological underpinnings and a brief history of this bboard, the "sysop" (system operator) invites new users into the activity with this logon message:

> [O]ver the years and through various incarnations of bulletin board software, [this BBS] has evolved into (more-or-less) a general-interest communications system. Here, one often finds references to things such as Star Trek and the Hitchhiker's Guide to the Galaxy trilogy (of four books) by Douglas Adams, as well as debates and arguments on all topics. There are also online games (Tradewars) and files available, but the heart of this board is the message base.
>
> Almost everything is permitted here, unless, of course, it is too weird.
>
> Why it's here:
>
> It's here for you to express your feelings, insights, comments, remarks, annoyances, high-tech computer information and what ever else may crop up in your life, on a public medium, as well as to read the above as related by others. In short, the Total Perspective.
>
> What is expected of you:
>
> Nothing too extensive. A couple of messages here and there, a file or two for every five or ten files downloaded, etc. Let people know you're here, and not simply as one of the "Top Ten Downloaders!"

The end of this introduction suggests the owner's desire that users of his system "message" more and download less, a preference that no doubt speaks about the most common uses of electronic spaces like this one.

All the electronic b-boards, including the one detailed above, are owned and operated by men, often by young men in their teens, who have set up computers, modems, and phone lines in their homes. Most of these b-boards can support only one user at a time (or at most one user and the sysop). These limits on access constrain users' behaviors while they are connected as well as their choices about when and how often to log on. Most of the b-boards our subjects use limit access time for any one user to an hour a day. The competition for access can be stiff at preferred times of the day, too, so at least two of our subjects (Farrell and Fish) often log on at 5:30 or 6:00 in the morning. To do this, of course, they must get up even earlier than the start of the school day would dictate.

The mailing facilities provide for both public and private postings so that users can reply to a message on the General Subboard, the name of the most commonly used discussion space on Vortex, either by posting to that list or by sending the mail directly to the author of the original message. Thus, users choose whether to talk publicly or privately each time they write a message. Since all participants use "handles" or pseudonyms for the purposes of sending messages, a certain measure of privacy (or anonymity) *could* be maintained if users wished, but in fact (as we will discuss later) users of these BBS come to know each other in contexts beyond the virtual spaces of the b-boards. Moreover, at least among the subjects of this study, it is the common practice to use the same pseudonym on all the b-boards to which one belongs, suggesting that these self-selected names have little to do with participants' desires to conceal identity or to construct multiple electronic roles for themselves. In fact, the handle Fish uses on the b-boards—"Madame Poisson"—is the origin of the nickname her "face-to-face" friends often use for her. Farrell's standard handle is "Lady Enigma" or "Lady E."

3. *What we do and why we do it.* To capture some sense of life in this small electronic world, Kaplan informally sampled the message traffic of Vortex on three occasions and Fish supplied a representative sample of her messages (both ones received and ones written) on Color Connection. These glimpses suggest that the most common conversational dynamic consists of a series of interlocking or intertwined dyadic conversations. Farrell explains that typically she carries on several extended, publicly posted, simultaneous conversations, each with one main interlocutor. Thus, she will be "talking with" one other person on topic A and with a different person on topic B and so on. As strings extend through time, they either peter out or are joined by another person who may take over the role of chief conversational partner.

This sort of pairing seems quite different in character than the more general conversational pattern Kaplan has witnessed on email lists serving professional communities, where many participants engage one or two topics of general interest at a time. On MBU, for example, it seems that as topics engaging six or seven participants "run their course," the whole community shifts to new subjects. As the topics shift, some conversants fall silent while new conversants take their place. But only rarely does the forum consist chiefly of two voices trading commentary while countless others read along in silence. The pattern on Vortex and Color Connection, however, might well resemble common patterns on some wider bboards and newsgroups. This structure should be investigated further.

The conversations among these young women and their contacts on the b-boards often seem, at least to an outsider, driven more by the desire of the participants to keep the conversation going than by their desire to achieve understanding of or consensus about some topic or issue. Often the messages are quite short—almost like conversational rejoinders. The participants routinely include the message to which they are responding so that if an outsider drops into one of these dyadic threads for a time, the sequence of messages reads rather like a script from a dramatic scene: several conversational "turns" appear in each posting. (It takes a little while, moreover, to become acclimated to the conventions for cueing different speakers in the conversation.) Here, for example, is a short exchange between Fish and one of her partners that occurred in the "public" area of the bboard Fish favors:

```
Message #14387 - Nothing In Particular (Received)
Date: 03-22-94 18:15
From: Gangrene
To: Madame Poisson
Subject: A Sad Day
Replies: #14090 <- -> #14592
>>> That'll be an awful long time, my friend!
TTThat's ok, I have an awfully big nose. Bah-dum dum.
((unenthused clapping, and the hurling of various objects from the peanut
gallery)
```

I wrote a really long and witty reply to this, but my modem farted out before I saved it. So use your imagination.

Message #14898 - Nothing In Particular
Date: 03-26-94 15:18
From: Madame Poisson
To: Gangrene
Subject: A Sad Day
Replies: #14592 <-

>>> That'll be an awful long time, my friend!
TTTThat's ok, I have an awfully big nose. Bah-dum dum.
((((unenthused clapping, and the hurling of various objects from the peanut gallery)
> I wrote a really long and witty reply to this, but my modem farted out before I saved it. So use your imagination.

Okay.

Wow, that was impressively witty. I am, therefore, impressed.

The sociability of this exchange seems its sole reason for being. Even though the conversational partners seem to be engaged in a dialog carried on over several days, or even weeks, the exchange itself has some of the qualities and functions of rapid repartee. A more extensive examination might in fact show that these conversants are engaged in what Tannen (1990) calls "rapport" talk, a style of conversation more common among women than men, rather than "report" talk, a style men tend to favor.

Although we cannot judge "Gangrene's" stake in this form of exchange, Fish's journal sheds a little light on her use of this conversational form. Describing herself as a shy person "in real life," she writes that she "feels more comfortable typing out my feelings. My mind doesn't work quite fast enough that I feel comfortable in a normal conversation, but typing messages, I can express myself very well." Fish's account of her behavior and the conversational style she and others employ may well yield additional insights into why some young women like electronic environments: the absence of social cues (appearance, for example) and of immediately perceptible power differentials (gender, age, and so on) create a more comfortable social space, Fish believes, for many people like her.

> I must say that since I'm shy and perhaps a little 'nerdy,' I feel a kind of kinship with other people who seem like they might be shy and nerdy [a description of at least some of the people Fish encounters on the nets]. . . . So meeting these people often made me feel strangely comfortable, even though I rarely spoke much to them in person.

> On the bulletin boards, people who are considered misfits can sort of let go [because] on the bulletin boards . . . there are no preconceived ideas about who you are. That was the original attraction of the bulletin boards for me, and I think for many others. . . . It's hard to feel like a 'dork,' or misfit there, somehow. The BBS users of [my town] have even taken back the word 'geek,' the way some women try to take back words like 'babe.' For example, there are now monthly 'GeekFests,' which is often the first place that 'geeks' meet other 'geeks' with whom the only previous contact . . . has been in cyberspace.

Farrell's reflections echo key elements: "I am odd. The people I meet through the medium of the Net are odd." But Farrell characterizes her netcompanions not as social misfits, but as social, or at least verbal, adepts. Farrell's journals and descriptions of herself and her interactions with others on the network show that she loves the net primarily because she loves the word—spoken and written. For her, "Net people are people in love with knowledge. In love with information and words. Debaters, jokers, storytellers, discussers, users of the paths insomnia carves, along with solitude, in the wee hours." The sense of the human connection and its value to them emerges strongly from the words of both these young women. The net seems to extend their connectedness to others, to work for them precisely because it connects them to others.

In addition to facilitating phatic conversations—those dialogs intended to maintain connection rather than to convey information—the b-boards serve a range of traditional communicative functions. In her journal, Fish describes seeking help with a programming problem from Color Connection's Sysop, a young man about her age whom she describes as "a good friend of mine and a very experienced programmer." In her picture of the interaction, he wasn't around when she first logged on. She writes,

> so I hung around waiting for him. I also posted messages addressed to 'All' about that stack overflow error." When the Sysop makes his appearance, Fish says, "We chatted for several hours. We talked for a long time about my computer problems . . . it was funny: when I asked him what a stack overflow error might come from, he said 'Bad programming, mostly,' adding a smilie to let me know he was just kidding.

The help is important to her, of course, but the human connection seems just as valued: "as it got late, we started talking about making eight-key or even two-key keyboards. We also discussed my personal life. . . . Anyway, it was nice to have a person to consult. . . . "

The b-boards constitute an important social space and an information resource for Fish, but they also facilitate other social arrangements. On one occasion, Farrell wrote to Fish to try to arrange an after-school get-together of a group of friends to form a role-playing game (RPG). Farrell writes (rather than just calling her friend Fish on the telephone) because Fish is in school while Farrell is home sick. (For reasons best known to the participants, this conversation took place in the private format of direct electronic mail. Possibly, the technological arrangement has determined this feature. Fish writes on Color Connection—a b-board with two nodes so that it can support "chat" or synchronous messaging between two simultaneous users as well as asynchronous mail messages. Farrell writes on Vortex because she can connect to it via a local telephone call while Color Connection is for her a long distance call.)

As the exchange between Farrell and Fish makes clear, the communication failed in its purposes because Fish didn't receive the message in a timely fashion:

```
Message #15162 - Internet Mail (Private)
(Received)
Date: 03-28-94 13:34
From: ladye@xxxx.yyyy.us
To: FISH
Subject: RPG friday?
Replies: -> #15992
```

Hi, Fishi! It's Afid. I'm just writing in case Wolf doesn't run into you today and for some odd reason you decide to log on before I see you in school tomorrow. Hazel is desperate for a game that she does not GM, so it looks like Wolf may be GMing a present/near future-type campaign on Friday afternoon, before the Illuminati fest at Julius's house. We wanna know if you can and want to play. You could talk to me and/or Wolf to confirm or apologize or whatever, and if you feel like calling Haze, that would be cool. I wish I remembered her number, I realize that I am in a perfect position to call her at the moment, me being home sick and all with very little to do. Maybe I'll try her after I log off, I will try the number that seems to be floating about in my head loosely in connection with her name. . . . But I babble severely. Okay, bye-bye, and I'm sorry I couldn't show up at Drama today, I tried but it didn't work.
Blessed be,
Aiofe.

Eva (Aiofe) Elizabeth - ladye@xxxx.yyyy.us

Message #15992 - Internet Mail (Private)
Date: 04-04-94 18:54
From: FISH
To: ladye@xxxx.yyyy.us
Subject: RPG friday?
Replies: #15162 <-

Aiofe,

Well, I got your message a bit late for the purposes intended, but that's okay. I was looking forward to playing, but it was nice enough to be able to lounge around instead of worrying about plans and such. So whenever it happens, it happens, as they say. Should be nice.

Anyhow, well, thanks for arranging and all.

FISHIE THE WONDERFUL!!

—

*Origin: The Color Connection, Ithaca, New York (0:0/0)

It seems that the arrangement for the RPG on April 1st did not work out, but in the interim between Farrell's March 28th invitation and Fish's April 4th response, these two women had seen each other several times in school and perhaps in the context of other activities, like the drama group to which they both belong. Moreover, at any point, they could have used more direct communications by telephone in the evening. The other plan, to meet at Julius's house for "an Illuminati fest," did bear fruit, however; the nature and role of this event forms the subject of section 4.

4. *Living our lives.* Clearly, electronic mail connections serve a number of functions for these participants, among which is its supplementation of their almost daily contact with each other

at school and in other venues. In fact, the degree to which electronic life permeates the daily habits and activities of these women is perhaps the most fascinating, and the most distinguishing, characteristic of the electronic community they have joined. For them, material ("real") life is entirely continuous with virtual life. Nowhere is this continuity more evident than in the monthly gatherings their electronically extended community calls "GeekFests" and in the "Illuminati fest" Farrell arranged in the exchange with Fish quoted above.

GeekFests or parties are organized by the Sysop of Color Connection but they include denizens of Vortex, Memory Alpha, and the Magic Shop as well. Such gatherings are possible, of course, only because this cluster of electronic communities occupies a geographic site as well as serving as a nexus of shared interests. Fish describes receiving mail from all over the country—from friends away at college and her brother in New Jersey—and Farrell corresponds electronically with her mother in Texas from time to time, but most of their electronic communications circulate locally. The bboards enable these young women to meet new people virtually, but the electronic meeting is usually only a prelude to some face-to-face encounter at one of the monthly fests. Or vice versa: they sometimes meet people who interest them at a GeekFest and then continue the relationship electronically.

Many of the people these young women encounter on the local nets are not high school students: they work in local companies (as Gangrene does) or pursue advanced degrees at the university (Armpit studies electrical engineering). In other words, these are people the subjects of our study would be unlikely to meet in any other way. The net allows these young women to cross social boundaries, an adventure they appear both to enjoy immensely and, curiously, to take for granted. But the crossing seems to have to occur both virtually and materially for it to meet the needs of these young women.

Throughout her journal, Fish describes GeekFests as a central element of her b-boarding. In an early entry (January 22, 1994), she first mentions these regular gatherings as part of her explanation of why she likes bboarding. Two days later, she reports attending one, describing the general scene:

> There was a GeekFest the other night, which was actually a lot of fun.
> There were a lot of geekier looking geeks there, which pleased me to no
> end. One of my friends brought a Newton. . . . That amused several of us
> for quite a while, seeing how it interpreted things we wrote. Other big
> activities were ping-pong, pool, and playing a game called 'Doom.' (Good
> Lord, but programmers are sick little puppies! This is one of those super-
> violent games; you go around killing things quite graphically with any of
> a bunch of weapons; the weapon of choice last night was the chainsaw.
> There's something called 'God Mode,' in which you can walk through walls
> and you can't be hurt by anything, so they were playing the adventure
> 'Knee-Deep in the Gore' (though I can't imagine there's too much
> difference between the adventures, or at least none of the users of the
> game would really care) at the 'Ultra-Violent' level in 'God Mode'. . . . This
> is what geeks do for fun!:-))

Describing another such gathering, Fish mentions that she was one of only two women who regularly join the "cluster of geeks surrounding the computer. . . . I may be the only female BBSer in the local cyber-community ... who programs." Fish's awareness of social differences—gender differences, in particular—seems to operate in tension with a more compelling sense of social solidarity, a sense of "kinship with other people who seem like they might be shy and nerdy."

The safety of the social space partially insulates Fish from a gendered social awkwardness. On one occasion, when she meets Armpit for the first time, she is aware of the kind of gender sensitivity and anxiety familiar to those who cruise MUDs and MOOs.

> The person I met the other day chatting has the alias 'Armpit.' I realize
> that as we were chatting, I had the idea he was male before I had any
> real reason to do so. I suppose part of it was the alias: very few females
> would pick the alias 'Armpit.' Also, he had some ways of being that
> seemed more male; for example, he responded to my 'Hello!' message with
> something like 'Yes, Madame?' Yes, that is part of my alias, but females
> don't generally respond that way.

The conversation seems to turn on a *double entendre* associating "madame" with "madam," a word Fish takes to mean "a woman who runs a brothel." As she chats with Armpit, Fish talks about the GeekFests, urging Armpit to attend one. The face-to-face meetings these parties afford are, after all, a central feature of the activity for Fish and Farrell and the other subjects of this study. Armpit seems reluctant to show interest in meeting Madame Poisson, though. Finally, he writes Fish that he has to go make dinner for his wife and himself. Fish records this episode in her journal as an instance of confusion: "Of course, he probably did [have to go make dinner], but the inclusion of 'my wife' makes me wonder whether he was worrying about my intentions." In this little drama, the "safe" electronic space can be violated, from Armpit's perspective, by the threatened collapse of the distinction between electronic and material worlds. But for Fish, that collapse seems really to be the point, as a subsequent discussion of "virtual romances" reveals.

About two weeks after she records her first meeting with Armpit, Fish writes that she has had some

> virtual romances of a sort. I was 'asked out' in chat mode at around two
> thirty 'in the ayem' once, which I found to be quite a silly situation. . . . I
> don't suppose it was a proper virtual romance because I did have
> relatively significant interaction with him in the 'real world,' but I think it
> counts anyway. I'm also developing a relationship with someone who I
> met via the BBS, but I think that, at least in the last year or so, I haven't
> messaged with him so much and have actually hung out with him in the
> real world a fair amount, so again, not quite a perfect example.

While working out these various distinctions and her own gendered behaviors, Fish ends the entry by noting that she does know some people who have connected romantically through bulletin boards, but that because b-boarding in her town organizes itself around two locations—cyberspace and GeekFests, "there's a healthy dose of reality thrown in by GeekFests, allowing people to meet face-to-face instead of losing themselves in their computer screens."

A locus of social exploration extending through both virtual and material experiences, the electronic bulletin board scene in this town can seem like an organizing principle for a host of otherwise disparate leisure activities, including literacy practices apparently quite divorced from the reading and writing these women pursue on the nets. At one all-night party, not technically a GeekFest but populated, as Farrell puts it, by "electronically minded people," Farrell and Fish began reading *The Illuminatus Trilogy* aloud to each other. Because the two of them "are morning people to a truly disgusting degree, we were sitting on the hostess's couch at seven in the morning, each of us running on about 2 hours of sleep." Farrell casually picked up a copy of the book that had been lying on the floor, read the first page aloud to Fish, and then handed her the book. Fish read the next page aloud to Farrell. And so they continued until others began to awake and decided to watch a movie.

The activity resumed at another party some weeks later, this one a birthday party for Fish and for Steve, another friend who is also deeply engaged in local b-boarding. Farrell found a copy of the book in Steve's room and she and Fish disappeared into a back room to read. Soon they were joined by another. In this way, they managed to read 130 pages or so, Farrell estimates. Fish's account of this event also links the reading to the culture of geeks with which she identifies: "There were a lot of geeky sorts at that birthday party, which was rather comforting. I ended up reading aloud with a few other people for the entire time, but then, that's the sort of thing I would do." Farrell and Fish have actively created opportunities to continue the reading inadvertently begun at these two other social events. Some of their negotiations about meetings, as we have seen, take place through the bboard system.

Farrell typically associates electronic activities with literacy and literary practices.

> *The Web is a reality of constantly shifting virtual truths: Identity, language, talk, programs, even a deadly virus or two, circling through these invisible pathways of the information jungle out there. It is a book forever being written, rewritten, revised and erased; a world that is inside one dimension of text on a screen, and yet does not exist in physical space. Is it any wonder I feel a surge of power through me when I exercise even my pitiful skill?*

This strange literacy practice—a throwback to a reading practice not common since the early twentieth century—connects Farrell, Fish, and Steve to the electronic community because the novel they read belongs to the community's self-selected cultural literacy texts. That is, *The Illuminatus Trilogy* and *Hitchhiker's Guide* and *Star Trek* form a set of common texts and experiences which, though unlikely to show up on Hirsch's list of what every citizen needs to know (see Hirsch, 1987), makes up a portion of the shared interests and values underwriting the connections among these people in the first place. While linking Fish, Steve, and Farrell to the electronic world they frequent, the oral reading takes place in the ordinary material and social world quite typical of adolescents in small towns everywhere.

DIRECTIONS FOR RESEARCH

In a recent posting on the Systers electronic list (a list for women computer scientists, systems analysts, and the like), Carolyn Seaman brought an article from the February 27, 1994 edition of the Washington *Post* to the attention of the list's denizens because the article discussed the question whether it matters that women be well represented in cyberspace. In the bit of the article Seaman quotes, it becomes clear that Paula Span, the author of the *Post* article, saw a generational issue within the gendered one:

> *True, people of either gender can still live meaningful lives without computers. . . . I don't think that will be true for my daughter, though, or any of our daughters. They're entering a world in which card catalogue drawers have already vanished from the public*

library, replaced by terminals and keyboards. . . . [T]hey can't afford to see computers as toys for boys, to see ignorance as feminine, to wring their hands over the keyboard and worry that they will break something. . . .

The daughters who have let us study their habits are joining the world Span sketches. They seem to be successfully overcoming at least some of the reticence toward the intimate machine that Turkle describes in her research on women learning to program (1988). As this preliminary description of a small community makes clear, however, there is much to study in their practices and much to learn about the attractions of electronic communications for the young women who will be the professional women of the next generation.

The young women who participated in this study, sharing bits of their adolescent world with us, are aware that the communication practices described in this article set them apart from other young women their age, girls who do not use electronic communications in their leisure time. But our subjects do not see themselves as especially male-identified, either. Instead, they have rearticulated their relations to the technologies, transforming what the wider culture codes as male into a tool they themselves identify with characteristically female traits and capacities. We found no trace, then, of Turkle's "computational reticence," except insofar as these young women do not feel compelled to learn programming or other aspects of computing they may see as irrelevant to their own interests in using the technology.

What needs further investigation, then, is what differentiates these girls from others in their cohort, both from other girls who show no interest in using computers and from the young men who tend to dominate computer use in schools and in the leisure spaces we have studied. How have the subjects in this study succeeded in redefining the machine where others have, apparently, failed? To understand this, we would need to explore in fuller detail when young women who take to the networks first begin to do so, and how they become acquainted with networking culture. In particular, it would be valuable to know what role other adolescent girls play in inducting new members. By the same token, it is clear that we need to know more fully what roles family members and schools play. Computing in educational settings is most often affiliated with the math and science curriculum, but the young women we have studied suggest that defining computers as tools of communication and connection would draw more girls to them. Further study might reveal that in settings where computers are used as fully in the language arts curriculum as they tend to be in the math and science areas, young women feel more interested in and positive about using computers.

Ethnographies focus on the meanings its subjects articulate, and it is important that those meanings arise from the young women and the young men who should become the subjects of future studies. Although such work will always be methodologically challenging, this study shows the importance of situating research on communication practices at the points where those practices arise: in the context and texture of women's lives. The Webs they weave, after all, consist not just of the warp and woof of their electronic messages but of the totality of their lived experiences, combining virtual and material worlds.

What is especially suggestive in the words and thoughts of our subjects is the connection between electronic culture and other gendered behaviors, like role-playing games, and the routes young children and then older adolescents find into a whole, linked set of activities. It seems likely, from Farrell's and Fish's thoughts, that neither role-playing games nor electronic practices necessarily serve the same functions for girls as they do for boys. But those differences do not necessarily exclude girls from these activities: as Farrell says about her participation in the net, "I noticed that even as I was inducted into this world, I invoked changes in it. . . . You create the net in the act of accessing it." Do young men think about, reflect on their net experiences in the same ways? And what do those young women who never make it into cyberspace choose instead? What communications practices serve as their looms for the Webs of their lives?

These are the sorts of questions further and more extensive ethnographic work, situated in the convergence of adolescents' worlds of work and play, can help us answer. That it is vital to understand both what keeps women out and what invites them in hardly needs arguing: as Paula Span observed, "Women have to be in [the computer world] because decisions about language and culture and access are being made and we should be involved in making them. Women have to be in it because, although nobody really knows what form all this technology will take, there shouldn't be any clubhouse we're afraid to climb into."

WORKS CITED

Bijker, W., Hughes, T., & Pinch, T. (1989). *The social construction of technological systems: New directions in the sociology and history of technology.* Cambridge, MA: MIT.

Cowan, R. (1987). The consumption junction: A proposal for research strategies in the sociology of technology. In Wiebe Bijker, Thomas Hughes, and Trevor Pinch (Eds.), *The social construction of technological systems: New directions in the sociology and history of technology.* Cambridge, MA: MIT, 261–280.

Gilligan, C. (1982). *In a different voice: Psychological theory and women's development.* Cambridge, MA: Harvard University Press.

Herring, S., Johnson, D., & DiBenedetto, T. (1992). Participation in electronic discourse in a "feminist" field. Paper presented at the Berkeley Women and Language Conference, April 1992, University of California at Berkeley.

Hiltz, R., & Turoff, M. (1993). *The network nation: Human communication via computer.* Cambridge, MA: MIT.

Hirsch, E. D. Jr. (1987). *Cultural literacy: What every American needs to know.* Boston: Houghton Mifflin.

Pinch, T., & Bijker, W. (1987). The social construction of facts and artifacts: Or how the sociology of science and the sociology of technology might benefit each other. In Wiebe Bijker, Thomas Hughes, and Trevor Pinch (Eds.), *The social construction of technological systems: New directions in the sociology and history of technology.* Cambridge, MA: MIT, 17–50.

Selfe, C., & Meyer, P. (1991). Testing claims for online conferences. *Written Communication,* 8(2), 162–192.

Tannen, D. (1990). *You just don't understand: Women and men in conversation.* New York: Ballantine.

Taylor, H. J., Kramarae, C., & Ebben, M. (1993). *Women, information technology, and scholarship.* Urbana: Center for Advanced Study, University of Illinois.

Turkle, S. (1984). *The second self: Computers and the human spirit.* New York: Simon & Schuster.

Turkle, S. (1988). Computational reticence: Why women fear the intimate machine. In Cheris Kramerae (Ed.), *Technology and women's voices: Keeping in touch.* New York: Routledge & Kegan Paul, 41–61.

Turkle, S., & Papert, S. (1990). Epistemological pluralism: Styles and voices within the computer culture. *Signs: Journal of Women in Culture and Society,* 16(1), 128–157.

Van Maanen, J. (1988). *Tales of the field: On writing ethnography.* Chicago: University of Chicago Press.

NOTES

Nancy Kaplan, Associate Professor in the School of Communication at the University of Baltimore, teaches rhetoric and technology. Eva Farrell, a high school senior at the Alternative Community School and principal investigator on this project, will be a first year student at the University of Texas at Austin in September, 1994. She is also Kaplan's daughter.

1. These figures come via a long chain of postings on various email lists: the original posting came from "Bruce Siceloff <bsicelof@nando.net>," a virtual person whose information came to us through a friend who subscribes to the MIT Media Lab's electronic list. Siceloff's message was reposted there, perhaps from online-news@marketplace.com, one of several virtual locations to which Siceloff originally sent his message on March 10, 1994.

2. MBU or Megabyte University is an unmoderated list for rhetoric and composition specialists interested in electronic technologies for writing and teaching.

THINKING AND RE-READING

1. As you re-read the article, compare your own experiences in high school on computer networks with those of the teenagers in the study. How were you "inducted" into the world of computers? How are the experiences of these young women similar and dissimilar from yours?

2. Find the place in the text where the authors write of Fish's and Armpit's experiences with the collapse of "the distinction between electronic and material worlds." What exactly do they mean by this? Has this ever happened to you? How? Do you know of others to whom it's happened? Is it a common occurrence on campus? Why do you think this is or is not the case?

WRITING AND LEARNING

1. Collect, through e-mail, stories of your classmates' adolescent or early experiences on the Internet. Compare their experiences with the young women in Kaplan and Farrell's study. Are your classmates' experiences different from the adolescent women's? What did you find that was similar concerning the early online activities of the men and women in your class? Dissimilar? Write a report of your informal survey that you will share with your classmates or members of your writing group.

2. Join a listserv or Internet discussion group that your instructor or classmates recommend. Keep a record of the participation of men and women in the discussion over the course of one week. Collect data on the topics that are discussed, the number of messages all told, the number from men and women, the names of the people who are referenced in the messages, the length of the messages, and anything else you think noteworthy relating to the conversations. Also do a "review" command of the listserv participants to find out how many people belong to the list

and who they are (e.g., percentage of men, women, academics, and organization or company people and geographical distribution). You should be able to tell a great deal from the participants' e-mail addresses, with .edu denoting an educational affiliation, .org an organization, and so forth. Draw conclusions from the data to generate your claims and put together a research report that uses either Kaplan and Farrell's study as a guide or is based on another piece of research with which you're familiar. The audience for your study should be a broad-based group of writing instructors who use the Internet for their own work and pleasure. Part of your task will be to let them know how friendly the list is for their own needs as well as for their students'.

New Yorker **Cartoon**

"Darling, trust me. Santa isn't going to give you a network."

The Girl Who Was Plugged In

James Tiptree Jr. (Alice B. Sheldon)

AS MENTIONED IN THE INTRODUCTION to this section, James Tiptree Jr. is really Alice B. Sheldon, a science fiction writer who was born in 1915 and died in 1987. During the years 1968–1977, before she revealed her true identity, she is said to have written some of her finest and most energetic prose. "The Girl Who Was Plugged In" is a short story that originally appeared in 1973 in *New Dimensions 3*, edited by Robert Silverberg. The story tells us of a time in the future when advertising is outlawed, and common people emulate the "stars" by acquiring the same material goods or accoutrements that these stars or "godlings," as the narrator in the story calls them, find alluring. As you read the story, think of how the times depicted may compare to our own contemporary networked lives, and of why Sheldon thought it necessary even in the seventies to assume a pseudonym.

L isten, zombie. Believe me. What I could tell you—you with your silly hands leaking sweat on your growth-stocks portfolio. One-ten lousy hacks of AT&T on twenty-point margin and you think you're Evel Knievel. AT&T? You doubleknit dummy, how I'd love to show you something.

Look, dead daddy, I'd say. See for instance that rotten girl?

In the crowd over there, that one gaping at her gods. One rotten girl in the city of the future (That's what I said.) Watch.

She's jammed among bodies, craning and peering with her soul yearning out of her eyeballs. Love! Oo-ooh, love them! Her gods are coming out of a store called Body East. Three youngbloods, larking along loverly. Dressed like simple street-people but . . . smashing. See their great eyes swivel above their nose-filters, their hands lift shyly, their inhumanly tender lips melt? The crowd moans. Love! This whole boiling megacity, this whole fun future world loves its gods.

You don't believe gods, dad? Wait. Whatever turns you on, there's a god in the future for you, custom-made. Listen to this mob. "I touched his foot! Ow-oow, I TOUCHED Him!"

Even the people in the GTX tower up there love the gods—in their own way and for their own reasons.

The funky girl on the street, she just loves. Grooving on their beautiful lives, their mysterioso problems. No one ever told her about mortals who love a god and end up as a tree or a sighing sound. In a million years it'd never occur to her that her gods might love her back.

She's squashed against the wall now as the godlings come by. They move in a clear space. A holocam bobs above, but its shadow never falls on them. The store display-screens are magically clear of bodies as the gods glance in and a beggar underfoot is suddenly alone. They give him a token. "Aaaaah!" goes the crowd.

Now one of them flashes some wild new kind of timer and they all trot to catch a shuttle, just like people. The shuttle stops for them—more magic. The crowd sighs, closing back. The gods are gone.

(In a room far from—but not unconnected to—the GTX tower a molecular flipflop closes too, and three account tapes spin.)

Our girl is still stuck by the wall while guards and holocam equipment pull away. The adoration's fading from her face. That's good, because now you can see she's the ugly of the world. A tall monument to pituitary dystrophy. No surgeon would touch her. When she smiles, her jaw—it's half purple—almost bites her left eye out. She's also quite young, but who could care?

The crowd is pushing her along now, treating you to glimpses of her jumbled torso, her mismatched legs. At the corner she strains to send one last fond spasm after the godlings' shuttle. Then her face reverts to its usual expression of dim pain and she lurches onto the moving walkway, stumbling into people. The walkway junctions with another. She crosses, trips and collides with the casualty rail. Finally she comes out into a little bare place called a park. The sportshow is working, a basketball game in three-di is going on right overhead. But all she does is squeeze onto a bench and huddle there while a ghostly free-throw goes by her ear.

After that nothing at all happens except a few furtive hand-mouth gestures which don't even interest her bench mates.

But you're curious about the city? So ordinary after all, in the FUTURE?

Ah, there's plenty to swing with here—and it's not all that *far* in the future, dad. But pass up the sci-fi stuff for now, like for instance the holovision technology that's put TV and radio in museums. Or the worldwide carrier field bouncing down from satellites, controlling communication and transport systems all over the globe. That was a spin-off from asteroid mining, pass it by. We're watching that girl.

I'll give you just one goodie. Maybe you noticed on the sportshow or the streets? No commercials. No ads.

That's right. NO ADS. An eyeballer for you.

Look around. Not a billboard, sign, slogan, jingle, sky-write, blurb, sublimflash, in this whole fun world. Brand names? Only in those ticky little peep-screens on the stores, and you could hardly call that advertising. How does that finger you?

Think about it. That girl is still sitting there.

She's parked right under the base of the GTX tower, as a matter of fact. Look way up and you can see the sparkles from the bubble on top, up there among the domes of godland. Inside that bubble is a boardroom. Neat bronze shield on the door: Global Transmissions Corporation—not that that means anything.

I happen to know there are six people in that room. Five of them technically male, and the sixth isn't easily thought of as a mother. They are absolutely unremarkable. Those faces were seen once at their nuptials and will show again in their obituaries and impress nobody either time. If you're looking for the secret Big Blue Meanies of the world, forget it. I know. Zen, do I know! Flesh? Power? Glory? You'd horrify them.

What they do like up there is to have things orderly, especially their communications. You could say they've dedicated their lives to that, to freeing the world from garble. Their nightmares are about hemorrhages of information; channels screwed up, plans misimplemented, garble creeping in. Their gigantic wealth only worries them, it keeps opening new vistas of disorder. Luxury? They wear what their tailors put on them, eat what their cooks serve them. See that old boy there—his name is Isham—he's sipping water and frowning as he listens to a databall. The water was prescribed by his medistaff. It tastes awful. The databall also contains a disquieting message about his son, Paul.

But it's time to go back down, far below to our girl. Look!

She's toppled over sprawling on the ground.

A tepid commotion ensues among the bystanders. The consensus is she's dead, which she disproves by bubbling a little. And presently she's taken away by one of the superb ambulances of the future, which are a real improvement over ours when one happens to be around.

At the local bellevue the usual things are done by the usual team of clowns aided by a saintly mop-pusher. Our girl revives enough to answer the questionnaire without which you can't die, even in the future. Finally she's cast up, a pumped-out hulk on a cot in the long, dim ward.

Again nothing happens for a while except that her eyes leak a little from the understandable disappointment of finding herself still alive.

But somewhere one GTX computer has been tickling another, and toward midnight something does happen. First comes an attendant who pulls screens around her. Then a man in a business doublet comes daintily down the ward. He motions the attendant to strip off the sheet and go.

The groggy girl-brute heaves up, big hands clutching at body-parts you'd pay not to see.

"Burke? P. Burke, is that your name?"

"Y-yes." Croak. "Are you . . . policeman?"

"No. They'll be along shortly, I expect. Public suicide's a felony."

" . . . I'm sorry."

He has a 'corder in his hand. "No family, right?"

"No."

"You're seventeen. One year city college. What did you study?"

"La—languages."

"H'mm. Say something."

Unintelligible rasp.

He studies her. Seen close, he's not so elegant. Errand-boy type.

"Why did you try to kill yourself?"

She stares at him with dead-rat dignity, hauling up the gray sheet. Give him a point, he doesn't ask twice.

"Tell me, did you see Breath this afternoon?"

Dead as she nearly is, that ghastly love-look wells up. Breath is the three young gods, a loser's cult. Give the man another point, he interprets her expression.

"How would you like to meet them?"

The girl's eyes bug out grotesquely.

"I have a job for someone like you. It's hard work. If you did well you'd be meeting Breath and stars like that all the time."

Is he insane? She's deciding she really did die.

"But it means you never see anybody you know again. Never, *ever*. You will be legally dead. Even the police won't know. Do you want to try?"

It all has to be repeated while her great jaw slowly sets. *Show me the fire I walk through.* Finally P. Burke's prints are in his 'corder, the man holding up the big rancid girl-body without a sign of distaste. It makes you wonder what else he does.

And then—THE MAGIC. Sudden silent trot of litterbearers tucking P. Burke into something quite different from a bellevue stretcher, the oiled slide into the daddy of all luxury ambulances—real flowers in that holder!—and the long jarless rush to nowhere. Nowhere is warm and gleaming and kind with nurses. (Where did you hear that money can't buy genuine kindness?) And clean clouds folding P. Burke into bewildered sleep.

. . . Sleep which merges into feedings and washings and more sleeps, into drowsy moments of afternoon where midnight should be, and gentle businesslike voices and friendly (but very few) faces, and endless painless hyposprays and peculiar numbnesses. And later comes the steadying rhythm of days and nights, and a quickening which P. Burke doesn't identify as health, but only knows that the fungus place in her armpit is gone. And then she's up and following those few new faces with growing trust, first tottering, then walking strongly, all better now, clumping down the short hall to the tests, tests, tests, and the other things.

And here is our girl, looking—

If possible, worse than before. (You thought this was Cinderella transistorized?)

The disimprovement in her looks comes from the electrode jacks peeping out of her sparse hair, and there are other meldings of flesh and metal. On the other hand, that collar and spinal plate are really an asset; you won't miss seeing that neck.

P. Burke is ready for training in her new job.

The training takes place in her suite and is exactly what you'd call a charm course. How to walk, sit, eat, speak, blow her nose, how to stumble, to urinate, to hiccup—DELICIOUSLY. How to make each nose-blow or shrug delightfully, subtly, different from any ever spooled before. As the man said, it's hard work.

But P. Burke proves apt. Somewhere in that horrible body is a gazelle, a houri, who would have been buried forever without this crazy chance. See the ugly duckling go!

Only it isn't precisely P. Burke who's stepping, laughing, shaking out her shining hair. How could it be? P. Burke is doing it all right, but she's doing it through something. The something is to all appearances a live girl. (You were warned, this is the FUTURE.)

When they first open the big cryocase and show her her new body, she says just one word. Staring, gulping, "How?"

Simple, really. Watch P. Burke in her sack and scuffs stump down the hall beside Joe, the man who supervises the technical part of her training. Joe doesn't mind P. Burke's looks, he hasn't noticed them. To Joe, system matrices are beautiful.

They go into a dim room containing a huge cabinet like a one-man sauna and a console for Joe. The room has a glass wall that's all dark now. And just for your information, the whole shebang is five hundred feet underground near what used to be Carbondale, Pa.

Joe opens the sauna cabinet like a big clamshell standing on end with a lot of funny business inside. Our girl shucks her shift and walks into it bare, totally unembarrassed. *Eager.* She settles in face-forward, butting jacks into sockets. Joe closes it carefully onto her humpback. Clunk. She can't see in there or hear or move. She hates this minute. But how she loves what comes next!

Joe's at his console, and the lights on the other side of the glass wall come up. A room is on the other side, all fluff and kicky bits, a girly bedroom. In the bed is a small mound of silk with a rope of yellow hair hanging out.

The sheet stirs and gets whammed back flat.

Sitting up in the bed is the darlingest girl child you've EVER seen. She quivers—porno for angels. She sticks both her little arms straight up, flips her hair, looks around full of sleepy pazazz. Then she can't resist rubbing her hands down over her minibreasts and belly. Because, you see, it's the god-awful P. Burke who is sitting there hugging her perfect girl-body, looking at you out of delighted eyes.

Then the kitten hops out of bed and crashes flat on the floor.

From the sauna in the dim room comes a strangled noise. P. Burke, trying to rub her wired-up elbow, is suddenly smothered in *two* bodies, electrodes jerking in her flesh. Joe juggles inputs, crooning into his mike. The flurry passes; it's all right.

In the lighted room the elf gets up, casts a cute glare at the glass wall, and goes into a transparent cubicle. A bathroom, what else? She's a live girl, and live girls have to go to the bathroom after a night's sleep even if their brains are in a sauna cabinet in the next room. And P. Burke isn't in that cabinet, she's in the bathroom. Perfectly simple, if you have the glue for that closed training circuit that's letting her run her neural system by remote control.

Now let's get one thing clear. P. Burke does not *feel* her brain is in the sauna room, she feels she's in that sweet little body. When you wash your hands, do you feel the water is running on your brain? Of course not. You feel the water on your hand, although the "feeling" is actually a potential-pattern flickering over the electrochemical jelly between your ears. And it's delivered there via the long circuits from your hands. Just so, P. Burke's brain in the cabinet feels the water on her hands in the bathroom. The fact that the signals have jumped across space on the way in makes no difference at all. If you want the jargon, it's known as eccentric projection or sensory reference and you've done it all your life. Clear?

Time to leave the honeypot to her toilet training—she's made a booboo with the toothbrush, because P. Burke can't get used to what she sees in the mirror—

But wait, you say. Where did that girl-body come from?

P. Burke asks that too, dragging out the words.

"They grow 'em," Joe tells her. He couldn't care less about the flesh department. "PDs. Placental decanters. Modified embryos, see? Fit the control implants in later. Without a Remote Operator it's just a vegetable. Look at the feet—no callus at all." (He knows because they told him.)

"Oh . . . oh, she's incredible. . . . "

"Yeah, a neat job. Want to try walking-talking mode today? You're coming on fast."

And she is. Joe's reports and the reports from the nurse and the doctor and style man go to a bushy man upstairs who is some kind of medical cybertech but mostly a project administrator. His reports in turn go—to the GTX boardroom? Certainly not, did you think this is a *big* thing? His reports just go up. The point is, they're green, very green. P. Burke promises well.

So the bushy man—Dr. Tesla—has procedures to initiate. The little kitten's dossier in the Central Data Bank, for instance. Purely routine. And the phase-in schedule which will put her on the scene. This is simple: a small exposure in an off-network holo-show.

Next he has to line out the event which will fund and target her. That takes budget meetings, clearances, coordinations. The Burke project begins to recruit and grow. And there's the messy business of the name, which always gives Dr. Tesla an acute pain in the bush.

The name comes out weird, when it's suddenly discovered that Burke's "P." stands for "Philadelphia." Philadelphia? The astrologer grooves on it. Joe thinks it would help identification. The semantics girl references *brotherly love, Liberty Bell, main line, low teratogenesis,* blah-blah. Nicknames Philly? Pala? Pooty? Delphi? Is it good, bad? Finally, "Delphi" is gingerly declared goodo. ("Burke" is replaced by something nobody remembers.)

Coming along now. We're at the official checkout down in the underground suite, which is as far as the training circuits reach. The bushy Dr. Tesla is there, braced by two budgetary types and a quiet fatherly man whom he handles like hot plasma.

Joe swings the door wide and she steps shyly in.

Their little Delphi, fifteen and flawless.

Tesla introduces her around. She's child-solemn, a beautiful baby to whom something so wonderful has happened you can feel the tingles. She doesn't smile, she . . . brims. That brimming joy is all that shows of P. Burke, the forgotten hulk in the sauna next door. But P. Burke doesn't know she's alive—it's Delphi who lives, every warm inch of her.

One of the budget types lets go a libidinous snuffle and freezes. The fatherly man, whose name is Mr. Cantle, clears his throat.

"Well, young lady, are you ready to go to work?"

"Yes, sir," gravely from the elf.

"We'll see. Has anybody told you what you're going to do for us?"

"No, sir." Joe and Tesla exhale quietly.

"Good." He eyes her, probing for the blind brain in the room next door.

"Do you know what *advertising* is?"

He's talking dirty, hitting to shock. Delphi's eyes widen and her little chin goes up. Joe is in ecstasy at the complex expressions P. Burke is getting through. Mr. Cantle waits.

"It's, well, it's when they used to tell people to buy things." She swallows. "It's not allowed."

"That's right." Mr. Cantle leans back, grave. "Advertising as it used to be is against the law. *A display other than the legitimate use of the product, intended to promote its sale.* In former times every manufacturer was free to tout his wares any way, place, or time he could afford. All the media and most of the landscape was taken up with extravagant competing displays. The thing became uneconomic. The public rebelled. Since the so-called Huckster Act sellers have been restrained to, I quote, displays in or on the product itself, visible during its legitimate use or in on-premise sales." Mr. Cantle leans forward. "Now tell me, Delphi, why do people buy one product rather than another?"

"Well . . . " Enchanting puzzlement from Delphi. "They, um, they see them and like them, or they hear about them from somebody?" (Touch of P. Burke there; she didn't say, from a friend.)

"Partly. Why did *you* buy your particular body-lift?"

"I never had a body-lift, sir."

Mr. Cantle frowns; what gutters do they drag for these Remotes?

"Well, what brand of water do you drink?"

"Just what was in the faucet, sir," says Delphi humbly. "I—I did try to boil it—"

"Good god." He scowls; Tesla stiffens. "Well, what did you boil it in? A cooker?"

The shining yellow head nods.

"What *brand* of cooker did you buy?"

"I didn't buy it, sir," says frightened P. Burke through Delphi's lips. "But—I know the best kind! Ananga has a Burnbabi. I saw the name when she—"

"Exactly!" Cantle's fatherly beam comes back strong; the Burnbabi account is a strong one, too. "You saw Ananga using one so you thought it must be good, eh? And it is good, or a great human being like Ananga wouldn't be using it. Absolutely right. And now, Delphi, you know what you're going to be doing for us. You're going to show some products. Doesn't sound very hard, does it?"

"Oh, no, sir . . . " Baffled child's stare; Joe gloats.

"And you must never, *never* tell anyone what you're doing." Cantle's eyes bore for the brain behind this seductive child.

"You're wondering why we ask you to do this, naturally. There's a very serious reason. All those products people use, foods and healthaids and cookers and cleaners and clothes and cars—they're all made by *people*. Somebody put in years of hard work designing and making them. A man comes up with a fine new idea for a better product. He has to get a factory and machinery, and hire workmen. Now. What happens if people have no way of hearing about his product? Word of mouth is far too slow and unreliable. Nobody might ever stumble onto his new product or find out how good it was, right? And then he and all the people who worked for him—they'd go bankrupt, right? So, Delphi, there has to be *some way* that large numbers of people can get a look at a good new product, right? How? By letting people see you using it. You're giving that man a chance."

Delphi's little head is nodding in happy relief.

"Yes, sir, I do see now—but sir, it seems so sensible, why don't they let you—"

Cantle smiles sadly.

"It's an overreaction, my dear. History goes by swings. People overreact and pass harsh unrealistic laws which attempt to stamp out an essential social process. When this happens, the people who understand have to carry on as best they can until the pendulum swings back." He sighs. "The Huckster Laws are bad, inhuman laws, Delphi, despite their good intent. If they were strictly observed they would wreak havoc. Our economy, our society, would be cruelly destroyed. We'd be back in caves!" His inner fire is showing; if the Huckster Laws were strictly enforced he'd be back punching a databank.

"It's our duty, Delphi. Our solemn social duty. We are not breaking the law. You will be using the product. But people wouldn't understand, if they knew. They would become upset just as you did. So you must be very, very careful not to mention any of this to anybody."

(And somebody will be very, very carefully monitoring Delphi's speech circuits.)

"Now we're all straight, aren't we? Little Delphi here"—he is speaking to the invisible creature next door—"little Delphi is going to live a wonderful, exciting life. She's going to be a girl people watch. And she's going to be using fine products people will be glad to know about and helping the good people who make them. Yours will be a genuine social contribution." He keys up his pitch; the creature in there must be older.

Delphi digests this with ravishing gravity.

"But sir, how do I—?"

"Don't worry about a thing. You'll have people behind you whose job it is to select the most worthy products for you to use. Your job is just to do as they say. They'll show you what outfits to wear to parties, what suncars and viewers to buy, and so on. That's all you have to do."

Parties—clothes—suncars! Delphi's pink mouth opens. In P. Burke's starved seventeen-year-old head the ethics of product sponsorship float far away.

"Now tell me in your own words what your job is, Delphi."

"Yes, sir. I—I'm to go to parties and buy things and use them as they tell me, to help the people who work in factories."

"And what did I say was so important?"

"Oh—I shouldn't let anybody know, about the things."

"Right." Mr. Cantle has another paragraph he uses when the subject shows, well, immaturity. But he can sense only eagerness here. Good. He doesn't really enjoy the other speech.

"It's a lucky girl who can have all the fun she wants while doing good for others, isn't it?" He beams around. There's a prompt shuffling of chairs. Clearly this one is go.

Joe leads her out, grinning. The poor fool thinks they're admiring her coordination.

It's out into the world for Delphi now, and at this point the up-channels get used. On the administrative side account schedules are opened, subprojects activated. On the technical side the reserved bandwidth is cleared. (That carrier field, remember?) A new name is waiting for Delphi, a name she'll never hear. It's a long string of binaries which have been quietly cycling in a GTX tank ever since a certain Beautiful Person didn't wake up.

The name winks out of cycle, dances from pulses into modulations of modulations, whizzes through phasing, and shoots into a giga-band beam racing up to a synchronous satellite poised over Guatemala. From there the beam pours twenty thousand miles back to Earth again, forming an all-pervasive field of structured energics supplying tuned demand-points all over the CanAm quadrant.

With that field, if you have the right credit rating, you can sit at a GTX console and operate an ore-extractor in Brazil. Or—if you have some simple credentials like being able to walk on water— you could shoot a spool into the network holocam shows running day and night in every home and dorm and rec site. *Or* you could create a continentwide traffic jam. Is it any wonder GTX guards those inputs like a sacred trust?

Delphi's "name" appears as a tiny analyzable nonredundancy in the flux, and she'd be very proud if she knew about it. It would strike P. Burke as magic; P. Burke never even understood robot-cars. But Delphi is in no sense a robot. Call her a waldo if you must. The fact is she's just a girl, a real-live girl with her brain in an unusual place. A simple real-time on-line system with plenty of bit-rate—even as you and you.

The point of all this hardware, which isn't very much hardware in this society, is so Delphi can walk out of that underground suite, a mobile demand-point draining on omnipresent fieldform. And she does—eighty-nine pounds of tender girl flesh and blood with a few metallic components, stepping out into the sunlight to be taken to her new life. A girl with everything going for her including a meditech escort. Walking lovely, stopping to widen her eyes at the big antennae system overhead.

The mere fact that something called P. Burke is left behind down underground has no bearing at all. P. Burke is totally unselfaware and happy as a clam in its shell. (Her bed has been moved into the waldo cabinet room now.) And P. Burke isn't in the cabinet; P. Burke is climbing out of an airvan in a fabulous Colorado beef preserve, and her name is Delphi. Delphi is looking at live Charolais steers and live cottonwoods and aspens gold against the blue smog and stepping over live grass to be welcomed by the reserve super's wife.

The super's wife is looking forward to a visit from Delphi and her friends, and by a happy coincidence there's a holocam outfit here doing a piece for the nature nuts.

You could write the script yourself now, while Delphi learns a few rules about structural interferences and how to handle the tiny time lag which results from the new forty-thousand-mile parenthesis in her nervous system. That's right—the people with the leased holocam rig naturally find the gold aspen shadows look a lot better on Delphi's flank than they do on a steer. And Delphi's face improves the mountains too, when you can see them. But the nature freaks aren't quite as joyful as you'd expect.

"See you in Barcelona, kitten," the headman says sourly as they pack up.

"Barcelona?" echoes Delphi with that charming little subliminal lag. She sees where his hand is and steps back.

"Cool, it's not her fault," another man says wearily. He knocks back his grizzled hair. "Maybe they'll leave in some of the gut."

Delphi watches them go off to load the spools on the GTX transport for processing. Her hand roves over the breast the man had touched. Back under Carbondale, P. Burke has discovered something new about her Delphi-body.

About the difference between Delphi and her own grim carcass.

She's always known Delphi has almost no sense of taste or smell. They explained about that: only so much bandwidth. You don't have to taste a suncar, do you? And the slight overall dimness of Delphi's sense of touch—she's familiar with that, too. Fabrics that would prickle P. Burke's own hide feel like a cool plastic film to Delphi.

But the blank spots. It took her a while to notice them. Delphi doesn't have much privacy; investments of her size don't. So she's slow about discovering there's certain definite places where her beastly P. Burke body *feels* things that Delphi's dainty flesh does not. H'mm! Channel space again, she thinks—and forgets it in the pure bliss of being Delphi.

You ask how a girl could forget a thing like that? Look. P. Burke is about as far as you can get from the concept *girl*. She's a female, yes—but for her, sex is a four-letter word spelled P-A-I-N. She isn't quite a virgin. You don't want the details; she'd been about twelve and the freak lovers were bombed blind. When they came down, they threw her out with a small hole in her anatomy and a mortal one elsewhere. She dragged off to buy her first and last shot, and she can still hear the clerk's incredulous guffaws.

Do you see why Delphi grins, stretching her delicious little numb body in the sun she faintly feels? Beams, saying, "Please, I'm ready now."

Ready for what? For Barcelona like the sour man said, where his nature-thing is now making it strong in the amateur section of the Festival. A winner! Like he also said, a lot of strip mines and dead fish have been scrubbed, but who cares with Delphi's darling face so visible?

So it's time for Delphi's face and her other delectabilities to show on Barcelona's Playa Nueva. Which means switching her channel to the EurAf synchsat.

They ship her at night so the nanosecond transfer isn't even noticed by that insignificant part of Delphi that lives five hundred feet under Carbondale, so excited the nurse has to make sure she eats. The circuit switches while Delphi "sleeps," that is, while P. Burke is out of the waldo cabinet. The next time she plugs in to open Delphi's eyes it's no different—do you notice which relay boards your phone calls go through?

And now for the event that turns the sugarcube from Colorado into the PRINCESS.

Literally true, he's a prince, or rather an Infante of an old Spanish line that got shined up in the Neomonarchy. He's also eighty-one, with a passion for birds—the kind you see in zoos. Now it suddenly turns out that he isn't poor at all. Quite the reverse; his old sister laughs in their tax lawyer's face and starts restoring the family hacienda while the Infante totters out to court Delphi. And little Delphi begins to live the life of the gods.

What do gods do? Well, everything beautiful. But (remember Mr. Cantle?) the main point is Things. Ever see a god empty-handed? You can't be a god without at least a magic girdle or an eight-legged horse. But in the old days some stone tablets or winged sandals or a chariot drawn by virgins would do a god for life. No more! Gods make it on novelty now. By Delphi's time the hunt for new god-gear is turning the earth and seas inside-out and sending frantic fingers to the stars. And what gods have, mortals desire.

So Delphi starts on a Euromarket shopping spree squired by her old Infante, thereby doing her bit to stave off social collapse.

Social what? Didn't you get it, when Mr. Cantle talked about a world where advertising is banned and fifteen billion consumers are glued to their holocam shows? One capricious self-powered god can wreck you.

Take the nose-filter massacre. Years, the industry sweated years to achieve an almost invisible enzymatic filter. So one day a couple of pop-gods show up wearing nose-filters like *big purple bats.* By the end of the week the world market is screaming for purple bats. Then it switched to bird-heads and skulls, but by the time the industry retooled the crazies had dropped bird-heads and gone to injection globes. Blood!

Multiply that by a million consumer industries, and you can see why it's economic to have a few controllable gods. Especially with the beautiful hunk of space R & D the Peace Department laid out for and which the taxpayers are only too glad to have taken off their hands by an outfit like GTX, which everybody knows is almost a public trust.

And so you—or rather, GTX—find a creature like P. Burke and give her Delphi. And Delphi helps keep things *orderly,* she does what you tell her to. Why? That's right, Mr. Cantle never finished his speech.

But here come the tests of Delphi's button-nose twinkling in the torrent of news and entertainment. And she's noticed. The feedback shows a flock of viewers turning up the amps when this country baby gets tangled in her new colloidal body-jewels. She registers at a couple of major scenes, too, and when the Infante gives her a suncar, little Delphi trying out suncars is a tiger. There's a solid response in high-credit country. Mr. Cantle is humming his happy tune as he cancels a Benelux subnet option to guest her on a nude cook-show called Wok Venus.

And now for the superposh old-world wedding! The hacienda has Moorish baths and six-foot silver candelabra and real black horses, and the Spanish Vatican blesses them. The final event is a grand gaucho ball with the old prince and his little Infanta on a bowered balcony. She's a spectacular doll of silver lace, wildly launching toy doves at her new friends whirling by below.

The Infante beams, twitches his old nose to the scent of her sweet excitement. His doctor has been very helpful. Surely now, after he has been so patient with the suncars and all the nonsense—

The child looks up at him, saying something incomprehensible about "breath." He makes out that she's complaining about the three singers she had begged for.

"They've changed!" she marvels. "Haven't they changed? They're so dreary. I'm so happy now!"

And Delphi falls fainting against a gothic vargueno.

Her American duenna rushes up, calls help. Delphi's eyes are open, but Delphi isn't there. The duenna pokes among Delphi's hair, slaps her. The old prince grimaces. He has no idea what she is beyond an excellent solution to his tax problems, but he had been a falconer in his youth. There comes to his mind the small pinioned birds which were flung up to stimulate the hawks. He pockets the veined claw to which he had promised certain indulgences and departs to design his new aviary.

And Delphi also departs with her retinue to the Infante's newly discovered yacht. The trouble isn't serious. It's only that five thousand miles away and five hundred feet down P. Burke has been doing it too well.

They've always known she has terrific aptitude. Joe says he never saw a Remote take over so fast. No disorientations, no rejections. The psychomed talks about self-alienation. She's going into Delphi like a salmon to the sea.

She isn't eating or sleeping, they can't keep her out of the body-cabinet to get her blood moving, there are necroses under her grisly sit-down. Crisis!

So Delphi gets a long "sleep" on the yacht and P. Burke gets it pounded through her perforated head that she's endangering Delphi. (Nurse Fleming thinks of that, thus alienating the psychomed.)

They rig a pool down there (Nurse Fleming again) and chase P. Burke back and forth. And she loves it. So naturally when they let her plug in again Delphi loves it too. Every noon beside the yacht's hydrofoils darling Delphi clips along in the blue sea they've warned her not to drink. And every night around the shoulder of the world an ill-shaped thing in a dark burrow beats its way across a sterile pool.

So presently the yacht stands up on its foils and carries Delphi to the program Mr. Cantle has waiting. It's long-range; she's scheduled for at least two decades' product life. Phase One calls for her to connect with a flock of young ultrariches who are romping loose between Brioni and Djakarta where a competitor named PEV could pick them off.

A routine luxgear op, see; no politics, no policy angles, and the main budget items are the title and the yacht, which was idle anyway. The storyline is that Delphi goes to accept some rare birds for her prince—who cares? The *point* is that the Haiti area is no longer radioactive and look!—the gods are there. And so are several new Carib West Happy Isles which can afford GTX rates, in fact two of them are GTX subsids.

But you don't want to get the idea that all these newsworthy people are wired-up robbies, for pity's sake. You don't need many if they're placed right. Delphi asks Joe about that when he comes down to Barranquilla to check her over. (P. Burke's own mouth hasn't said much for a while.)

"Are there many like me?"

"Nobody's like you, buttons. Look, are you still getting Van Allen warble?"

"I mean, like Davy. Is he a Remote?"

(Davy is the lad who is helping her collect the birds. A sincere redhead who needs a little more exposure.)

"Davy? He's one of Matt's boys, some psychojob. They haven't any channel."

"What about the real ones? Djuma van O, or Ali, or Jim Ten?"

"Djuma was born with a pile of GTX basic where her brain should be, she's nothing but a pain. Jimsy does what his astrologer tells him. Look, peanut, where do you get the idea you aren't real? You're the realest. Aren't you having joy?"

"Oh, Joe!" Flinging her little arms around him and his analyzer grids. "Oh, *me gusto mucho, muchísimo!*"

"Hey, hey." He pets her yellow head, folding the analyzer.

Three thousand miles north and five hundred feet down a forgotten hulk in a body-waldo glows.

And is she having joy. To waken out of the nightmare of being P. Burke and find herself a peri, a star-girl? On a yacht in paradise with no more to do than adorn herself and play with toys and attend revels and greet her friends—her, P. Burke, having friends!—and turn the right way for the holocams? Joy!

And it shows. One look at Delphi and the viewers know: DREAMS CAN COME TRUE.

Look at her riding pillion on Davy's sea-bike, carrying an apoplectic macaw in a silver hoop. Oh, *Morton, let's go there this winter!* Or learning the Japanese chinchona from that Kobe group, in a dress that looks like a blowtorch rising from one knee, and which should sell big in Texas. *Morton, is that real fire?* Happy, happy little girl!

And Davy. He's her pet and her baby, and she loves to help him fix his red-gold hair. (P. Burke marveling, running Delphi's fingers through the curls.) Of course Davy is one of Matt's boys—not impotent exactly, but very *very* low drive. (Nobody knows exactly what Matt does with his bitty budget, but the boys are useful and one or two have made names.) He's perfect for Delphi; in fact the psychomed lets her take him to bed, two kittens in a basket. Davy doesn't mind the fact that Delphi "sleeps" like the dead. That's when P. Burke is out of the body-waldo up at Carbondale, attending to her own depressing needs.

A funny thing about that. Most of her sleepy-time Delphi's just a gently ticking lush little vegetable waiting for P. Burke to get back on the controls. But now and again Delphi all by herself smiles a bit or stirs in her "sleep." Once she breathed a sound: "Yes."

Under Carbondale P. Burke knows nothing. She's asleep too, dreaming of Delphi, what else? But if the bushy Dr. Tesla had heard that single syllable, his bush would have turned snow-white. Because Delphi is TURNED OFF.

He doesn't. Davy is too dim to notice, and Delphi's staff boss, Hopkins, wasn't monitoring.

And they've all got something else to think about now, because the cold-fire dress sells half a million copies, and not only in Texas. The GTX computers already know it. When they correlate a minor demand for macaws in Alaska the problem comes to human attention: Delphi is something special.

It's a problem, see, because Delphi is targeted on a limited consumer bracket. Now it turns out she has mass-pop potential—those macaws in *Fairbanks*, man!—it's like trying to shoot mice with an ABM. A whole new ball game. Dr. Tesla and the fatherly Mr. Cantle start going around in headquarters circles and buddy-lunching together when they can get away from a seventh-level weasel boy who scares them both.

In the end it's decided to ship Delphi down to the GTX holocam enclave in Chile to try a spot on one of the mainstream shows. (Never mind why an Infanta takes up acting.) The holocam complex occupies a couple of mountains where an observatory once used the clean air. Holocam total-environment shells are very expensive and electronically superstable. Inside them actors can move freely without going off-register, and the whole scene or any selected part will show up in the viewer's home in complete three-di, so real you can look up their noses and much denser than you get from mobile rigs. You can blow a tit ten feet tall when there's no molecular skiffle around.

The enclave looks—well, take everything you know about Hollywood-Burbank and throw it away. What Delphi sees coming down is a neat giant mushroom-farm, domes of all sizes up to monsters for the big games and stuff. It's orderly. The idea that art thrives on creative flamboyance has long been torpedoed by proof that what art needs is computers. Because this showbiz has something TV and Hollywood never had—*automated inbuilt viewer feedback.* Samples, ratings, critics, polls? Forget it. With that carrier field you can get real-time response-sensor readouts from every receiver in the world, served up at your console. That started as a thingie to give the public more influence on content.

Yes.

Try it, man. You're at the console. Slice to the sex-age-educ-econ-ethno-cetera audience of your choice and start. You can't miss. Where the feedback warms up, give 'em more of that. Warm—warmer—*hot!* You've hit it—the secret itch under those hides, the dream in those hearts. You don't need to know its name. With your hand controlling all the input and your eye reading all the response, you can make them a god ... and somebody'll do the same for you.

But Delphi just sees rainbows, when she gets through the degaussing ports and the field relay and takes her first look at the insides of those shells. The next thing she sees is a team of shapers and technicians descending on her, and millisecond timers everywhere. The tropical leisure is finished. She's in gigabuck mainstream now, at the funnel maw of the unceasing hose that's pumping the sight and sound and flesh and blood and sobs and laughs and dreams of *reality* into the world's happy head. Little Delphi is going plonk into a zillion homes in prime time and nothing is left to chance. Work!

And again Delphi proves apt. Of course it's really P. Burke down under Carbondale who's doing it, but who remembers that carcass? Certainly not P. Burke, she hasn't spoken through her own mouth for months. Delphi doesn't even recall dreaming of her when she wakes up.

As for the show itself, don't bother. It's gone on so long no living soul could unscramble the plotline. Delphi's trial spot has something to do with a widow and her dead husband's brother's amnesia.

The flap comes after Delphi's spots begin to flash out along the world-hose and the feedback appears. You've guessed it, of course. Sensational! As you'd say, they IDENTIFY.

The report actually says something like InskinEmp with a string of percentages, meaning that Delphi not only has it for anybody with a Y chromosome, but also for women and everything in between. It's the sweet supernatural jackpot, the million-to-one.

Remember your Harlow? A sexpot, sure. But why did bitter hausfraus in Gary and Memphis know that the vanilla-ice-cream goddess with the white hair and crazy eyebrows was *their baby girl?* And write loving letters to Jean warning her that their husbands weren't good enough for her? Why? The GTX analysts don't know either, but they know what to do with it when it happens.

(Back in his bird sanctuary the old Infante spots it without benefit of computers and gazes thoughtfully at his bride in widow's weeds. It might, he feels, be well to accelerate the completion of his studies.)

The excitement reaches down to the burrow under Carbondale where P. Burke gets two medical exams in a week and a chronically inflamed electrode is replaced. Nurse Fleming also gets an assistant who doesn't do much nursing but is very interested in access doors and identity tabs.

And in Chile, little Delphi is promoted to a new home up among the stars' residential spreads and a private jitney to carry her to work. For Hopkins there's a new computer terminal and a full-time schedule man. What is the schedule crowded with?

Things.

And here begins the trouble. You probably saw that coming too.

"What does she think she is, a goddamn *consumer rep?*" Mr. Cantle's fatherly face in Carbondale contorts.

"The girl's upset," Miss Fleming says stubbornly. "She *believes* that, what you told her about helping people and good new products."

"They are good products," Mr. Cantle snaps automatically, but his anger is under control. He hasn't got where he is by irrelevant reactions.

"She says the plastic gave her a rash and the glo-pills made her dizzy."

"Good god, she shouldn't swallow them," Dr. Tesla puts in agitatedly.

"You told her she'd use them," persists Miss Fleming.

Mr. Cantle is busy figuring how to ease this problem to the feral-faced young man. What, was it a goose that lays golden eggs?

Whatever he says to Level Seven, down in Chile the offending products vanish. And a symbol goes into Delphi's tank matrix, one that means roughly *Balance unit resistance against PR index.* This means that Delphi's complaints will be endured as long as her Pop Response stays above a certain level. (What happens when it sinks need not concern us.) And to compensate, the price of her exposure-time rises again. She's a regular on the show now and response is still climbing.

See her under the sizzling lasers, in a holocam shell set up as a walkway accident. (The show is guesting an acupuncture school shill.)

"I don't think this new body-lift is safe," Delphi's saying. "It's made a funny blue spot on me—look, Mr. Vere."

She wiggles to show where the mini-grav pak that imparts a delicious sense of weightlessness is attached.

"So don't leave it *on,* Dee. With your meat—watch that deck-spot, it's starting to synch."

"But if I don't wear it it isn't honest. They should insulate it more or something, don't you see?"

The show's beloved old father, who is the casualty, gives a senile snigger.

"I'll tell them," Mr. Vere mutters. "Look now, as you step back bend like this so it just shows, see? And hold two beats."

Obediently Delphi turns, and through the dazzle her eyes connect with a pair of strange dark ones. She squints. A quite young man is lounging alone by the port, apparently waiting to use the chamber.

Delphi's used by now to young men looking at her with many peculiar expressions, but she isn't used to what she gets here. A jolt of something somber and knowing. *Secrets.*

"Eyes! Eyes, Dee!"

She moves through the routine, stealing peeks at the stranger. He stares back. He knows something.

When they let her go she comes shyly to him.

"Living wild, kitten." Cool voice, hot underneath.

"What do you mean?"

"Dumping on the product. You trying to get dead?"

"But it isn't right," she tells him. "They don't know, but I do, I've been wearing it."

His cool is jolted.

"You're out of your head."

"Oh, they'll see I'm right when they check it," she explains. "They're just so busy. When I tell them—"

He is staring down at little flower-face. His mouth opens, closes. "What are you doing in this sewer anyway? Who are you?"

Bewilderedly she says, "I'm Delphi."

"Holy Zen."

"What's wrong? Who are you, please?"

Her people are moving her out now, nodding at him.

"Sorry we ran over, Mr. Uhunh," the script girl says.

He mutters something, but it's lost as her convoy bustles her toward the flower-decked jitney.

(Hear the click of an invisible ignition-train being armed?)

"Who was he?" Delphi asks her hairman.

The hairman is bending up and down from his knees as he works.

"Paul. Isham. Three," he says and puts a comb in his mouth.

"Who's that? I can't see."

He mumbles around the comb, meaning, "Are you jiving?" Because she has to be, in the middle of the GTX enclave.

Next day there's a darkly smoldering face under a turban-towel when Delphi and the show's paraplegic go to use the carbonated pool.

She looks.

He looks.

And the next day, too.

(Hear the automatic sequencer cutting in? The system couples, the fuels begin to travel.)

Poor old Isham senior. You have to feel sorry for a man who values order: when he begets young, genetic information is still transmitted in the old ape way. One minute it's a happy midget with a rubber duck—look around and here's this huge healthy stranger, opaquely emotional, running with god knows who. Questions are heard where there's nothing to question, and eruptions claiming to be moral outrage. When this is called to Papa's attention—it may take time, in that boardroom—Papa does what he can, but without immortality-juice the problem is worrisome.

And young Paul Isham is a bear. He's bright and articulate and tender-souled and incessantly active, and he and his friends are choking with appallment at the world their fathers made. And it hasn't taken Paul long to discover that *his* father's house has many mansions and even the GTX computers can't relate everything to everything else. He noses out a decaying project which adds up to something like, Sponsoring Marginal Creativity (the free-lance team that "discovered" Delphi was one such grantee). And from there it turns out that an agile lad named Isham can get his hands on a viable packet of GTX holocam facilities.

So here he is with his little band, way down the mushroom-farm mountain, busily spooling a show which has no relation to Delphi's. It's built on bizarre techniques and unsettling distortions pregnant with social protest. An *underground* expression to you.

All this isn't unknown to his father, of course, but so far it has done nothing more than deepen Isham senior's apprehensive frown.

Until Paul connects with Delphi.

And by the time Papa learns this, those invisible hypergolics have exploded, the energy-shells are rushing out. For Paul, you see, is the genuine article. He's serious. He dreams. He even reads—for example, *Green Mansions*—and he wept fiercely when those fiends burned Rima alive.

When he hears that some new GTX pussy is making it big, he sneers and forgets it. He's busy. He never connects the name with this little girl making her idiotic, doomed protest in the holocam chamber. This strangely simple little girl.

And she comes and looks up at him and he sees Rima, lost Rima the enchanted bird girl, and his unwired human heart goes twang.

And Rima turns out to be Delphi.

Do you need a map? The angry puzzlement. The rejection of the dissonance Rima-hustling-for-GTX-My-Father. Garbage, cannot be. The loitering around the pool to confirm the swindle . . . dark eyes hitting on blue wonder, jerky words exchanged in a peculiar stillness . . . the dreadful reorganization of the image into Rima-Delphi *in my Father's tentacles*—

You don't need a map.

Nor for Delphi either, the girl who loved her gods. She's seen their divine flesh close now, heard their unamplified voices call her name. She's played their god-games, worn their garlands. She's even become a goddess herself, though she doesn't believe it. She's not disenchanted, don't think that. She's still full of love. It's just that some crazy kind of *hope* hasn't—

Really you can skip all this, when the loving little girl on the yellow-brick road meets a Man. A real human male burning with angry compassion and grandly concerned with human justice, who reaches for her with real male arms and—boom! She loves him back with all her heart.

A happy trip, see?

Except.

Except that it's really P. Burke five thousand miles away who loves Paul. P. Burke the monster down in a dungeon smelling of electrode paste. A caricature of a woman burning, melting, obsessed with true love. Trying over twenty-double-thousand miles of hard vacuum to reach her beloved through girl-flesh numbed by an invisible film. Feeling his arms around the body he thinks is hers, fighting through shadows to give herself to him. Trying to taste and smell him through beautiful dead nostrils, to love him back with a body that goes dead in the heart of the fire.

Perhaps you get P. Burke's state of mind?

She has phases. The trying, first. And the shame. The SHAME. *I am not what thou lovest.* And the fiercer trying. And the realization that there is no, no way, none. Never. *Never* . . . A bit delayed, isn't it, her understanding that the bargain she made was forever? P. Burke should have noticed those stories about mortals who end up as grasshoppers.

You see the outcome—the funneling of all this agony into one dumb protoplasmic drive to fuse with Delphi. To leave, to close out the beast she is chained to. *To become Delphi.*

Of course it's impossible.

However, her torments have an effect on Paul. Delphi-as-Rima is a potent enough love object, and liberating Delphi's mind requires hours of deeply satisfying instruction in the rottenness of it all. Add in Delphi's body worshiping his flesh, burning in the fire of P. Burke's savage heart—do you wonder Paul is involved?

That's not all.

By now they're spending every spare moment together and some that aren't so spare.

"Mr. Isham, would you mind staying out of this sports sequence? The script calls for Davy here."

(Davy's still around, the exposure did him good.)

"What's the difference?" Paul yawns. "It's just an ad. I'm not blocking that thing."

Shocked silence at his two-letter word. The script girl swallows bravely.

"I'm sorry, sir, our directive is to do the *social sequence* exactly as scripted. We're having to respool the segments we did last week, Mr. Hopkins is very angry with me."

"Who the hell is Hopkins? Where is he?"

"Oh, please, Paul. *Please.*"

Paul unwraps himself, saunters back. The holocam crew nervously check their angles. The GTX boardroom has a foible about having things *pointed* at them and theirs. Cold shivers, when the image of an Isham nearly went onto the world beam beside that Dialadinner.

Worse yet, Paul has no respect for the sacred schedules which are now a full-time job for ferret boy up at headquarters. Paul keeps forgetting to bring her back on time, and poor Hopkins can't cope.

So pretty soon the boardroom data-ball has an urgent personal action-tab for Mr. Isham senior. They do it the gentle way, at first.

"I can't today, Paul."

"Why not?"

"They say I have to, it's *very* important."

He strokes the faint gold down on her narrow back. Under Carbondale, Pa., a blind mole-woman shivers.

"Important. Their importance. Making more gold. Can't you see? To them you're just a thing to get scratch with. A *huckster*. Are you going to let them screw you, Dee? Are you?"

"Oh, Paul—"

He doesn't know it, but he's seeing a weirdie; Remotes aren't hooked up to flow tears.

"Just say no, Dee. No. Integrity. You have to."

"But they say, it's my job—"

"Will you believe I can take care of you, Dee? Baby, baby, you're letting them rip us. You have to choose. Tell them, no."

"Paul . . . I w-will. . . . "

And she does. Brave little Delphi (insane P. Burke). Saying, "No, please, I promised, Paul."

They try some more, still gently.

"Paul, Mr. Hopkins told me the reason they don't want us to be together so much. It's because of who you are, your father."

She thinks his father is like Mr. Cantle, maybe.

"Oh, great. Hopkins. I'll fix him. Listen, I can't think about Hopkins now. Ken came back today, he found out something."

They are lying on the high Andes meadow watching his friends dive their singing kites.

"Would you believe, on the coast the police have *electrodes in their heads?*"

She stiffens in his arms.

"Yeah, weird. I thought they only used PP on criminals and the army. Don't you see, Dee— something has to be going on. Some movement. Maybe somebody's organizing. How can we find out?" He pounds the ground behind her: "We should make *contact!* If we could only find out."

"The, the news?" she asks distractedly.

"The news." He laughs. "There's nothing in the news except what they want people to know. Half the country could burn up, and nobody would know it if they didn't want. Dee, can't you take what I'm explaining to you? They've got the whole world programmed! Total control of communication. They've got everybody's minds wired in to think what they show them and want what they give them and they give them what they're programmed to want—you can't break in or out of it, you can't get *hold* of it anywhere. I don't think they even have a plan except to keep things going round and round—and god knows what's happening to the people or the Earth or the other planets, maybe. One great big vortex of lies and garbage pouring round and round, getting bigger and bigger, and nothing can ever change. If people don't wake up soon we're through!"

He pounds her stomach softly.

"You have to break out, Dee."

"I'll try, Paul, I will—"

"You're mine. They can't have you."

And he goes to see Hopkins, who is indeed cowed.

But that night up under Carbondale the fatherly Mr. Cantle goes to see P. Burke.

P. Burke? On a cot in a utility robe like a dead camel in a tent, she cannot at first comprehend that he is telling *her* to break it off with Paul. P. Burke has never seen Paul. *Delphi* sees Paul. The fact is, P. Burke can no longer clearly recall that she exists apart from Delphi.

Mr. Cantle can scarcely believe it either, but he tries.

He points out the futility, the potential embarrassment, for Paul. That gets a dim stare from the bulk on the bed. Then he goes into her duty to GTX, her job, isn't she grateful for the opportunity, etcetera. He's very persuasive.

The cobwebby mouth of P. Burke opens and croaks.

"No."

Nothing more seems to be forthcoming.

Mr. Cantle isn't dense, he knows an immovable obstacle when he bumps one. He also knows an irresistible force: GTX. The simple solution is to lock the waldo-cabinet until Paul gets tired of waiting for Delphi to wake up. But the cost, the schedules! And there's something odd here . . . he eyes the corporate asset hulking on the bed and his hunch-sense prickles.

You see, Remotes don't love. They don't have real sex, the circuits designed that out from the start. So it's been assumed that it's *Paul* who is diverting himself or something with the pretty little body in Chile. P. Burke can only be doing what comes natural to any ambitious gutter-meat. It hasn't occurred to anyone that they're dealing with the real hairy thing whose shadow is blasting out of every holoshow on Earth.

Love?

Mr. Cantle frowns. The idea is grotesque. But his instinct for the fuzzy line is strong; he will recommend flexibility.

And so, in Chile:

"Darling, I don't have to work tonight! And Friday too—isn't that right, Mr. Hopkins?"

"Oh, great. When does she come up for parole?"

"Mr. Isham, please be reasonable. Our schedule—surely your own production people must be needing you?"

This happens to be true. Paul goes away. Hopkins stares after him, wondering distastefully why an Isham wants to ball a waldo. How sound are those boardroom belly-fears—garble creeps, creeps in! It never occurs to Hopkins that an Isham might not know what Delphi is.

Especially with Davy crying because Paul has kicked him out of Delphi's bed.

Delphi's bed is under a real window.

"Stars," Paul says sleepily. He rolls over, pulling Delphi on top. "Are you aware that this is one of the last places on Earth where people can see the stars? Tibet, too, maybe."

"Paul . . . "

"Go to sleep. I want to see you sleep."

"Paul, I . . . I sleep so *hard,* I mean, it's a joke how hard I am to wake up. Do you mind?"

"Yes."

But finally, fearfully, she must let go. So that five thousand miles north a crazy spent creature can crawl out to gulp concentrates and fall on her cot. But not for long. It's pink dawn when Delphi's eyes open to find Paul's arms around her, his voice saying rude, tender things. He's been kept awake. The nerveless little statue that was her Delphi-body nuzzled him in the night.

Insane hope rises, is fed a couple of nights later when he tells her she called his name in her sleep.

And that day Paul's arms keep her from work and Hopkins's wails go up to headquarters where the weasel-faced lad is working his sharp tailbone off packing Delphi's program. Mr. Cantle defuses that one. But next week it happens again, to a major client. And ferret-face has connections on the technical side.

Now you can see that when you have a field of complexly heterodyned energy modulations tuned to a demand-point like Delphi, there are many problems of standwaves and lashback and skiffle of all sorts which are normally balanced out with ease by the technology of the future. By the same token they can be delicately unbalanced too, in ways that feed back into the waldo operator with striking results.

"Darling—what the hell! What's wrong? DELPHI!"

Helpless shrieks, writhings. Then the Rima-bird is lying wet and limp in his arms, her eyes enormous.

"I . . . I wasn't supposed to . . . " she gasps faintly. "They told me not to. . . ."

"Oh, my god—*Delphi.*"

And his hard fingers are digging in her thick yellow hair. Electronically knowledgeable fingers. They freeze.

"You're a *doll!* You're one of those PP implants. They control you. I should have known. Oh, god, I should have known."

"No, Paul," she's sobbing. "No, no, no—"

"Damn them. Damn them, what they've done—you're not *you*—"

He's shaking her, crouching over her in the bed and jerking her back and forth, glaring at the pitiful beauty.

"No!" she pleads (it's not true, that dark bad dream back there). "I'm Delphi!"

"My father. Filth, pigs—damn them, damn them, damn them."

"No, no," she babbles. "They were good to me—" P. Burke underground mouthing, "They were good to me—AAH—AAAAH!"

Another agony skewers her. Up north the sharp young man wants to make sure this so-tiny interference works. Paul can scarcely hang on to her, he's crying too. "I'll kill them."

His Delphi, a wired-up slave! Spikes in her brain, electronic shackles in his bird's heart. Remember when those savages burned Rima alive?

"I'll *kill* the man that's doing this to you."

He's still saying it afterward, but she doesn't hear. She's sure he hates her now, all she wants is to die. When she finally understands that the fierceness is tenderness, she thinks it's a miracle. *He knows—and he still loves!*

How can she guess that he's got it a little bit wrong?

You can't blame Paul. Give him credit that he's even heard about pleasure-pain implants and snoops, which by their nature aren't mentioned much by those who know them most intimately. That's what he thinks is being used on Delphi, something to *control* her. And to listen—he burns at the unknown ears in their bed.

Of waldo-bodies and objects like P. Burke he has heard nothing.

So it never crosses his mind as he looks down at his violated bird, sick with fury and love, that he isn't holding *all* of her. Do you need to be told the mad resolve jelling in him now?

To free Delphi.

How? Well, he is, after all, Paul Isham III. And he even has an idea where the GTX neurolab is. In Carbondale.

But first things have to be done for Delphi, and for his own stomach. So he gives her back to Hopkins and departs in a restrained and discreet way. And the Chile staff is grateful and do not understand that his teeth don't normally show so much.

And a week passes in which Delphi is a very good, docile little ghost. They let her have the load of wildflowers Paul sends and the bland loving notes. (He's playing it coony.) And up in headquarters weasel boy feels that *his* destiny has clicked a notch onward and floats the word up that he's handy with little problems.

And no one knows what P. Burke thinks in any way whatever, except that Miss Fleming catches her flushing her food down the can and next night she faints in the pool. They haul her out and stick her with IVs. Miss Fleming frets, she's seen expressions like that before. But she wasn't around when crazies who called themselves Followers of the Fish looked through flames to life everlasting. P. Burke is seeing Heaven on the far side of death, too. Heaven is spelled P-a-u-l, but the idea's the same. *I will die and be born again in Delphi.*

Garbage, electronically speaking. No way.

Another week and Paul's madness has become a plan. (Remember, he does have friends.) He smolders, watching his love paraded by her masters. He turns out a scorching sequence for his own show. And finally, politely, he requests from Hopkins a morsel of his bird's free time, which duly arrives.

"I thought you didn't *want* me anymore," she's repeating as they wing over mountain flanks in Paul's suncar. "Now you *know*—"

"Look at me!"

His hand covers her mouth, and he's showing her a lettered card.

> DON'T TALK THEY CAN HEAR EVERYTHING WE SAY. I'M TAKING YOU AWAY NOW.

She kisses his hand. He nods urgently, flipping the card.

> DON'T BE AFRAID. I CAN STOP THE PAIN IF THEY TRY TO HURT YOU.

With his free hand he shakes out a silvery scrambler-mesh on a power pack. She is dumbfounded.

> THIS WILL CUT THE SIGNALS AND PROTECT YOU DARLING.

She's staring at him, her head going vaguely from side to side, No.

"Yes!" He grins triumphantly. "Yes!"

For a moment she wonders. That powered mesh will cut off the field, all right. It will also cut off Delphi. But he is *Paul*. Paul is kissing her, she can only seek him hungrily as he sweeps the suncar through a pass.

Ahead is an old jet ramp with a shiny bullet waiting to go. (Paul also has credits and a Name.) The little GTX patrol courier is built for nothing but speed. Paul and Delphi wedge in behind the pilot's extra fuel tank, and there's no more talking when the torches start to scream.

They're screaming high over Quito before Hopkins starts to worry. He wastes another hour tracking the beeper on Paul's suncar. The suncar is sailing a pattern out to sea. By the time they're sure it's empty and Hopkins gets on the hot flue to headquarters, the fugitives are a sourceless howl above Carib West.

Up at headquarters weasel boy gets the squeal. His first impulse is to repeat his previous play, but then his brain snaps to. This one is too hot. Because, see, although in the long run they can make P. Burke do anything at all except maybe *live*, instant emergencies can be tricky. And—Paul Isham III.

"Can't you order her back?"

They're all in the GTX tower monitor station, Mr. Cantle and ferret-face and Joe and a very neat man who is Mr. Isham senior's personal eyes and ears.

"No, sir," Joe says doggedly. "We can read channels, particularly speech, but we can't interpolate organized pattern. It takes the waldo op to send one-to-one—"

"What are they saying?"

"Nothing at the moment, sir." The console jockey's eyes are closed. "I believe they are, ah, embracing."

"They're not answering," a traffic monitor says. "Still heading zero zero three zero—due north, sir."

"You're certain Kennedy is alerted not to fire on them?" the neat man asks anxiously.

"Yes, sir."

"Can't you just turn her off?" The sharp-faced lad is angry. "Pull that pig out of the controls!"

"If you cut the transmission cold you'll kill the Remote," Joe explains for the third time. "Withdrawal has to be phased right, you have to fade over to the Remote's own autonomics. Heart, breathing, cerebellum, would go blooey. If you pull Burke out you'll probably finish her too. It's a fantastic cybersystem, you don't want to do that."

"The investment." Mr. Cantle shudders.

Weasel boy puts his hand on the console jock's shoulder, it's the contact who arranged the no-no effect for him.

"We can at least give them a warning signal, sir." He licks his lips, gives the neat man his sweet ferret smile. "We know that does no damage."

Joe frowns, Mr. Cantle sighs. The neat man is murmuring into his wrist. He looks up. "I am authorized," he says reverently, "I am authorized to, ah, direct a signal. If this is the only course. But minimal, minimal."

Sharp-face squeezes his man's shoulder.

In the silver bullet shrieking over Charleston Paul feels Delphi arch in his arms. He reaches for the mesh, hot for action. She thrashes, pushing at his hands, her eyes roll. She's afraid of that mesh despite the agony. (And she's right.) Frantically Paul fights her in the cramped space, gets it over her head. As he turns the power up she burrows free under his arm and the spasm fades.

"They're calling you again, Mr. Isham!" the pilot yells.

"Don't answer. Darling, keep this over your head damn it how can I—"

An AX90 barrels over their nose, there's a flash.

"Mr. Isham! Those are Air Force jets!"

"Forget it," Paul shouts back. "They won't fire. Darling, don't be afraid."

Another AX90 rocks them.

"Would you mind pointing your pistol at my head where they can see it, sir?" the pilot howls.

Paul does so. The AX90s take up escort formation around them. The pilot goes back to figuring how he can collect from GTX too, and after Goldsboro AB the escort peels away.

"Holding the same course." Traffic is reporting to the group around the monitor. "Apparently they've taken on enough fuel to bring them to towerport here."

"In that case it's just a question of waiting for them to dock." Mr. Cantle's fatherly manner revives a bit.

"Why can't they cut off that damn freak's life-support," the sharp young man fumes. "It's ridiculous."

"They're working on it," Cantle assures him.

What they're doing, down under Carbondale, is arguing.

Miss Fleming's watchdog has summoned the bushy man to the waldo room.

"Miss Fleming, you will obey orders."

"You'll kill her if you try that, sir. I can't believe you meant it, that's why I didn't. We've already fed her enough sedative to affect heart action; if you cut any more oxygen she'll die in there."

The bushy man grimaces. "Get Dr. Quine here fast."

They wait, staring at the cabinet in which a drugged, ugly madwoman fights for consciousness, fights to hold Delphi's eyes open.

High over Richmond the silver pod starts a turn. Delphi is sagged into Paul's arm, her eyes swim up to him.

"Starting down now, baby. It'll be over soon, all you have to do is stay alive, Dee."

" . . . stay alive . . . "

The traffic monitor has caught them. "Sir! They've turned off for Carbondale—Control has contact—"

"Let's go."

But the headquarters posse is too late to intercept the courier wailing into Carbondale. And Paul's friends have come through again. The fugitives are out through the freight dock and into the neurolab admin port before the guard gets organized. At the elevator Paul's face plus his handgun get them in.

"I want Doctor—what's his name, Dee? Dee!"

" . . . Tesla . . . " She's reeling on her feet.

"Dr. Tesla. Take me down to Tesla, fast."

Intercoms are squalling around them as they whoosh down, Paul's pistol in the guard's back. When the door slides open the bushy man is there.

"I'm Tesla."

"I'm Paul Isham. *Isham.* You're going to take your flaming implants out of this girl—now. Move!"

"What?"

"You heard me. Where's your operating room? Go!"

"But—"

"Move! Do I have to burn somebody?"

Paul waves the weapon at Dr. Quine, who has just appeared.

"No, no," says Tesla hurriedly. "But I can't, you know. It's impossible, there'll be nothing left."

"You screaming well can, right now. You mess up and I'll kill you," says Paul murderously. "Where is it, there? And wipe the feke that's on her circuits now."

He's backing them down the hall, Delphi heavy on his arm.

"Is this the place, baby? Where they did it to you?"

"Yes," she whispers, blinking at a door. "Yes . . . "

Because it is, see. Behind that door is the very suite where she was born.

Paul herds them through it into a gleaming hall. An inner door opens, and a nurse and a gray man rush out. And freeze.

Paul sees there's something special about that inner door. He crowds them past it and pushes it open and looks in.

Inside is a big mean-looking cabinet with its front door panels ajar.

And inside that cabinet is a poisoned carcass to whom something wonderful, unspeakable, is happening. Inside is P. Burke, the real living woman who knows that HE is there, coming closer—Paul whom she had fought to reach through forty thousand miles of ice—PAUL is here!—is yanking at the waldo doors—

The doors tear open and a monster rises up.

"Paul darling!" croaks the voice of love, and the arms of love reach for him.

And he responds.

Wouldn't you, if a gaunt she-golem flab-naked and spouting wires and blood came at you clawing with metal-studded paws—

"Get away!" He knocks wires.

It doesn't much matter which wires. P. Burke has, so to speak, her nervous system hanging out. Imagine somebody jerking a handful of your medulla—

She crashes onto the floor at his feet, flopping and roaring *PAUL-PAUL-PAUL* in rictus.

It's doubtful he recognizes his name or sees her life coming out of her eyes at him. And at the last it doesn't go to him. The eyes find Delphi, fainting by the doorway, and die.

Now of course Delphi is dead, too.

There's a total silence as Paul steps away from the thing by his foot.

"You killed her," Tesla says. "That was her."

"Your control." Paul is furious, the thought of that monster fastened into little Delphi's brain nauseates him. He sees her crumpling and holds out his arms. Not knowing she is dead.

And Delphi comes to him.

One foot before the other, not moving very well—but moving. Her darling face turns up. Paul is distracted by the terrible quiet, and when he looks down he sees only her tender little neck.

"Now you get the implants out," he warns them. Nobody moves.

"But, but she's dead," Miss Fleming whispers wildly.

Paul feels Delphi's life under his hand, they're talking about their monster. He aims his pistol at the gray man.

"You. If we aren't in your surgery when I count three, I'm burning off this man's leg."

"Mr. Isham," Tesla says desperately, "you have just killed the person who animated the body you call Delphi. Delphi herself is dead. If you release your arm you'll see what I say is true."

The tone gets through. Slowly Paul opens his arm, looks down.

"Delphi?"

She totters, sways, stays upright. Her face comes slowly up.

"Paul . . . " Tiny voice.

"Your crotty tricks," Paul snarls at them. "Move!"

"Look at her eyes," Dr. Quine croaks.

They look. One of Delphi's pupils fills the iris, her lips writhe weirdly.

"Shock." Paul grabs her to him. "*Fix* her!" He yells at them, aiming at Tesla.

"For god's sake . . . bring it in the lab." Tesla quavers.

"Good-bye-bye," says Delphi clearly. They lurch down the hall, Paul carrying her, and meet a wave of people.

Headquarters has arrived.

Joe takes one look and dives for the waldo room, running into Paul's gun.

"Oh, no, you don't."

Everybody is yelling. The little thing in his arm stirs, says plaintively, "I'm Delphi."

And all through the ensuing jabber and ranting she hangs on, keeping it up, the ghost of P. Burke or whatever whispering crazily, "Paul . . . Paul . . . Please, I'm Delphi . . . Paul?"

"I'm here, darling, I'm here." He's holding her in the nursing bed. Tesla talks, talks, talks unheard.

"Paul . . . don't sleep. . . ." The ghost-voice whispers. Paul is in agony, he will not accept, WILL NOT believe.

Tesla runs down.

And then near midnight Delphi says roughly, "Ag-ag-ag—" and slips onto the floor, making a rough noise like a seal.

Paul screams. There's more of the *ag-ag* business and more gruesome convulsive disintegrations, until by two in the morning Delphi is nothing but a warm little bundle of vegetative functions hitched to some expensive hardware—the same that sustained her before her life began. Joe has finally persuaded Paul to let him at the waldo-cabinet. Paul stays by her long enough to see her face change in a dreadfully alien and coldly convincing way, and then he stumbles out bleakly through the group in Tesla's office.

Behind him Joe is working wet-faced, sweating to reintegrate the fantastic complex of circulation, respiration, endocrines, mid-brain homeostases, the patterned flux that was a human being—it's like saving an orchestra abandoned in midair. Joe is also crying a little; he alone had truly loved P. Burke. P. Burke, now a dead pile on a table, was the greatest cybersystem he has ever known, and he never forgets her.

The end, really.

You're curious?

Sure, Delphi lives again. Next year she's back on the yacht getting sympathy for her tragic breakdown. But there's a different chick in Chile, because while Delphi's new operator is competent, you don't get two P. Burkes in a row—for which GTX is duly grateful.

The real belly-bomb of course is Paul. He was *young,* see. Fighting abstract wrong. Now life has clawed into him and he goes through gut rage and grief and grows in human wisdom and resolve. So much so that you won't be surprised, sometime later, to find him—where?

In the GTX boardroom, dummy. Using the advantage of his birth to radicalize the system. You'd call it "boring from within."

That's how he put it, and his friends couldn't agree more. It gives them a warm, confident feeling to know that Paul is up there. Sometimes one of them who's still around runs into him and gets a big hello.

And the sharp-faced lad?

Oh, he matures too. He learns fast, believe it. For instance, he's the first to learn that an obscure GTX research unit is actually getting something with their loopy temporal anomalizer project. True, he doesn't have a physics background, and he's bugged quite a few people. But he doesn't really learn about that until the day he stands where somebody points him during a test run—

—and wakes up lying on a newspaper headlined NIXON UNVEILS PHASE TWO.

Lucky he's a fast learner.

Believe it, zombie. When I say growth, I mean *growth.* Capital appreciation. You can stop sweating. There's a great future there.

THINKING AND RE-READING

1. For your own practice, summarize the story as you re-read. Who is Isham? What happens to P. Burke? Who is Delphi? Who is Paul? What does the following passage—presented early on in the story—have to do with anything?

> What they do like up there is to have things orderly, especially their communications. You could say they've dedicated their lives to that, to freeing the world from garble. Their nightmares are about hemorrhages of information; channels screwed up, plans misimplemented, garble creeping in. Their gigantic wealth only worries them, it keeps opening new vistas of disorder. Luxury? They wear what their tailors put on them, eat what their cooks serve them. See that old boy there—his name is Isham—he's sipping water and frowning as he listens to a databall. The water was prescribed by his medistaff. It tastes awful. The databall also contains a disquieting message about his son, Paul.

   At one point, the narrator says, "P. Burke does not *feel* her brain is in the sauna room, she feels she's in that sweet little body. When you wash your hands, do you feel the water is running on your brain? Of course not." What meaning does this quotation have for the rest of the story? Are P. Burke and Delphi the same entity? What's the relationship between them?

2. Readers also learn shortly thereafter that "[a]dvertising as it used to be is against the law. *A display other than the legitimate use of the product, intended to promote its sale.*" What implication does this policy have for the action that takes place in the story? How does corporate America hawk its wares in this brave new world of Alice Sheldon's?

WRITING AND LEARNING

1. Unlike Gibson's *Neuromancer,* there is no mention of the "console cowboy" in this short fiction, but readers do encounter the term "system matrices," not unlike *matrix,* which Gibson uses to refer to the net or what we might also call cyberspace. Only in this case, P. Burke is the system matrix. Another way to think of "The Girl Who Was Plugged In" is to imagine P. Burke as a woman sitting at her computer on the Internet while Delphi is the persona she sends out to the MOO or other online contexts in which she participates. For your own practice, describe the person that you become when you participate online with different people on different lists or on IRC (Internet Relay Chat). Is this the same person you are offline with your friends? With your family? If you have more than one persona online, describe those as well. Where does the analogy with P. Burke break down?

2. Re-read the last page or so of the short story and decide what you think about the ending. Can you think of another that might be more appropriate and more to your liking? Using a style much like Sheldon's, rewrite the ending convincingly so that other readers are unable to detect that Sheldon didn't write it. Read the ending aloud to your classmates or writing group.

EXTENDED WRITING ACTIVITIES

BUILDING ON WRITING AND LEARNING

SAC   Writing and learning activities that can be done on a stand-alone computer with access to word processing software

LAN   Writing and learning activities that can be done on local area network with access to synchronous or asynchronous conferencing software

WAN   Writing and learning activities that can be done on a wide-area network such as the Internet, with access to Netscape or Gopher software

ASSIGNMENT 1: A WOMAN'S GUIDE TO CYBERSPACE

1. Several authors in this section suggest that cyberspace is often an unfriendly environment for women. Yet women and girls continue to persist in their use of networks regardless of the barriers they face. Eventually, many of them find that the nets are neither egalitarian utopias nor sites devoid of influence for their sex, but they might have found it helpful to have some guidance early on. For this assignment, you are asked to design along with your classmates or writing group a handbook to guide women in their use of the networks. You should assign specific tasks to different classmates so that all of you contribute to writing and compiling various documents for your guide. Be sure, also, to use some of the ideas from the readings that you think appropriate.

   In your guide, you will want to let women know what they can expect from various electronic discussion groups, and you will want to include cautionary as well as uplifting stories of women on the nets. The style that your guide develops is completely up to you, but you may want your handbook to contain a section on advice: a list of resources women would find helpful; listservs and news groups exclusively for women and those notoriously unfriendly toward women; MOOs and the customary conventions participants follow; and other sections that you and your group think important.

2. When you finish writing and collecting documents to include in your guide, design a format for it using a powerful word processing program or desktop publishing software. Then contact your college's publications office or another campus group that is concerned with student affairs to see about publishing it. Try, also, to meet with those people who might be interested in making the guide a part of an orientation packet that new students would be given as they begin their first year of college. Your dorm leaders might also consider it an appropriate publication that they would like to hand out to new students. (SAC)

ASSIGNMENT 2: DISCUSSING OUR DIFFERENCES

1. As a class or group project, run a series of real-time discussions with your class or with several classes at your college. (Conceivably, you could also do this through an e-mail discussion group if you'd prefer.) Your goal is to find out what kind of e-space both women and men might find to their liking and what kind of behavior or "netiquette" most of your classmates find desirable. Prepare five to ten questions to lead the discussion over a course of a week or two. At the end of a prescribed period of time (previously stipulated to the participants), print out the transcripts and do an analysis of the material that the students have contributed. In other words, are there any particular themes that seem to run through the transcripts? Can you set up categories and tally the number of times a particular recommendation was made during the discussion? What conclusions can you and your classmates draw from the transcripts? If your instructor thinks it appropriate, write a group report based on the series of discussions and present it to your college's network committee or publish it through the web site of your class or school. The report should be aimed at other college students who have an interest in the kinds of e-spaces that society ultimately creates on the Internet.

ASSIGNMENT 3: CONSTRUCTING A WOMAN'S WEB SITE

1. For this assignment, you and members of your class or writing group will create a World Wide Web site that is devoted entirely to women's issues. First create in a word processing file the text that you want to appear on your mock-up home page. Use different types of fonts and other graphic design features (e.g., boxes, icons, and subheads) to make the information on your home page visually interesting and clearly organized for readers.

2. On this home page, be sure to identify at least ten links that will lead to additional information that you want women to be able to access. These links can lead to any resources you think appropriate: online journals, particular articles, or resources designed especially for women—but at least four of these links must lead to short (one to three page) documents that each member of your group will write for the women. For the remaining links, you must be able to produce the items to which the links lead, but you need not author them yourself. On the mock-up home page, type the reference text for each link in capital letters to make it stand out.

3. Next, each of you needs to draft one of the four short, original documents that you will link to your home page. These documents should apprise women of something you have learned in your experiences on the net that you think will be especially interesting for them. You and your group members will need to decide together what these documents should be and who should write each piece. When you have finished, you and your

group should meet (or exchange drafts electronically) so that you are able to help one another with revisions.

4. Finally, gather up and clearly label the other documents or items to be linked to the home page—these items can be anything you like as long as they can be scanned into a computer or accessed on the World Wide Web. Now construct your group's home page and web site online, publishing it for the rest of your class to read and enjoy. If you desire and your instructor thinks it appropriate, you may also advertise your web site to various Internet discussion groups. (WAN)

PART V

GOVERNMENT AND TECHNOLOGY

INTRODUCTION

WHAT role should a government assume in the development, distribution, and use of technology? Or should these efforts be left entirely up to corporate and commercial entities in our culture? In the United States, the government has chosen to assume a leading role in fashioning a national information infrastructure (NII), a system of linked computers and networks that supports the computing needs of university researchers and corporations working on government contracts, government agencies and organizations that want to exchange information, colleges and schools that want to share resources, and private citizens who seek information. Not only is the government leading the effort to establish the public policy and standards that will form the basis of this infrastructure, but it is also serving as a role model for employing the technology. In 1993, the White House announced that citizens would have direct access to the president and the vice president through e-mail, and in 1994 the vice president conversed directly with citizens in a real-time electronic town meeting. The current administration believes that the government must take an active role in shaping the NII to ensure a fair, equitable, and flexible computer system that will help support the economic growth of the country and the democratic involvement of a wide range of citizens.

In the end, what attracts governments to computer technology is power—the same force that attracts individuals to computers. In this section, we examine the relationship between government and technology by presenting thirteen different perspectives on this topic, from artifacts to analyses.

Four of the pieces in this section are artifactual documents. We have included, for example, a now famous letter from the White House announcing the advent of the White House e-mail system that allows citizens direct access to the offices of the vice president and president. The questions following this piece ask readers to consider what message this move conveys to citizens regarding the administration's interest and involvement in technology. Also included is a transcript of the first electronic town meeting involving the vice president of the United States and a group of citizens. Additional artifacts include a speech on the Global Information Infrastructure (GII) delivered by the vice president to the International Telecommunications Union in Buenos Aires in 1994; a statement that science fiction author Bruce Sterling made to the House of Representatives Subcommittee on Telecommunications and Finance in 1993; and a Bill of Rights and Responsibilities for Electronic Learners created by members of EDUCOM, a not-for-profit consortium of six hundred colleges, universities, and corporate partners interested in technology for use in institutions of higher education.

Two of the pieces in this section can be characterized as analyses of the larger social issues raised by the relationship between government and technology. Roger Karraker, for example, in "Highways of the Mind or Toll Roads Between Information Castles," discusses whether the NII should be designed based on the privatized model of the railroad system or the public utility model of the interstate highway system, and in "Direct Democracy," Evan I. Schwartz explores the benefits and drawbacks of electronic town meetings.

Other analytical pieces in this section look into the relationship between government and technology from a slightly different perspective, focusing on the perspective of community and citizen involvement. Doug Schuler, for example, in "Community Networks: Building a New Participatory Medium" debates the concept of community or free nets that support the democratic involvement of citizens; and Rob Glaser and Peter Huber discuss the concept of universal access to the computer resources.

Two additional pieces focus on the relationship between government and technology as it is played out in countries other than our own. "When Words Are the Best Weapon," by Russell Watson and colleagues, discusses how information technologies change the relationships between governments and citizens. "Making Every Vote Count," by Erik Nilsson, tells the story of the first nationwide election in postapartheid South Africa and the role that technology played in this endeavor.

Finally, we have included a historical and fictional perspective on the relationship between government and technology—Franz Kafka's "In the Penal Colony," the metaphorical story of how governments use technology to enforce the law, and how citizens come to believe so willingly in the soundness of such a system.

Letter from the President and Vice President in Announcement of White House Electronic Mail Access

William Clinton and Albert Gore Jr.

ON JUNE 1, 1993, THE WHITE HOUSE issued a public announcement that many citizens considered remarkable—individuals now had direct access to the president and vice president via e-mail. To many computer users in this country, this announcement was the first acknowledgment by an American head of state that communications in this country were changing in dramatic ways, and that citizens in the twenty-first century should be able to take advantage of computers to establish direct contact with elected officials.

In the minds of many Americans, this historic announcement and other initiatives to which the Clinton-Gore administration committed itself heralded a new era focusing directly on electronic communications. Vice President Albert Gore, for example, had already announced a major initiative to involve the nation in thinking about—and building—a national information infrastructure (NII) that would support computing at the end of the twentieth century, along with a global information infrastructure (GII) that would support global electronic communications. With these initiatives, America went electronic in a new way.

Dear Friends:

Part of our commitment to change is to keep the White House in step with today's changing technology. As we move ahead into the twenty-first century, we must have a government that can show the way and lead by example. Today, we are pleased to announce that for the first time in history, the White House will be connected to you via electronic mail. Electronic mail will bring the Presidency and this Administration closer and make it more accessible to the people.

The White House will be connected to the Internet as well as several on-line commercial vendors, thus making us more accessible and more in touch with people across this country. We will not be alone in this venture. Congress is also getting involved, and an exciting announcement regarding electronic mail is expected to come from the House of Representatives tomorrow.

Various government agencies also will be taking part in the near future. Americans Communicating Electronically is a project developed by several government agencies to coordinate and improve access to the nation's educational and information assets and resources. This will be done through interactive communications such as electronic mail, and brought to people who do not have ready access to a computer.

However, we must be realistic about the limitations and expectations of the White House electronic mail system. This experiment is the first-ever e-mail project done on such a large scale. As we work to reinvent government and streamline our processes, the e-mail project can help to put us on the leading edge of progress.

Initially, your e-mail message will be read and receipt immediately acknowledged. A careful count will be taken on the number received as well as the subject of each message. However, the White House is not yet capable of sending back a tailored response via electronic mail. We are hoping this will happen by the end of the year.

A number of response-based programs which allow technology to help us read your message more effectively, and, eventually respond to you electronically in a timely fashion will be tried out as well. These programs will change periodically as we experiment with the best way to handle electronic mail from the public. Since this has never been tried before, it is important to allow for some flexibility in the system in these first stages. We welcome your suggestions.

This is an historic moment in the White House and we look forward to your participation and enthusiasm for this milestone event. We eagerly anticipate the day when electronic mail from the public is an integral and normal part of the White House communications system.

President Clinton   Vice President Gore

THINKING AND RE-READING

1. As you re-read this letter, think about the implications of the fifth paragraph, in particular the sentence "However, the White House is not yet capable of sending back a tailored response via electronic mail." What are the expectations that people have when they write a traditional letter? What social actions does the exchange of letters traditionally involve? What changes in this social compact does this paragraph project? What are the implications of these changes?

2. What does it mean to the United States to "keep the White House in step with today's changing technology"? What are the costs—fiscal, intellectual, political, and social—of such a policy? What are the implications—both positive and negative?

WRITING AND LEARNING

1. Write an e-mail message to the president or the vice president with regard to the technology issues that concern you as a student and taxpayer. Focus on the most important political issues that touch your life—limit your comments to one, two, or three such issues. Make sure to provide not only your analysis of these issues but cite examples of how these technological issues have touched your life or the lives of those close to you.

2. Not everybody in this country can afford a computer. Moreover, not everyone can afford the cost of hooking a computer up to the Internet. In addition, not everyone in this country wants to communicate via computer or has access to the training that would allow him or her to communicate via technology. Go to the library and, with the help of a reference librarian, look up several kinds of statistics pertaining to computer use: How many Americans now own computers? Use them? How many do not own or use them? How many schools now have access to computers? How many do not? How many Americans have access to the Internet? How many do not? How much time do Americans spend on computers? On subscribing to online services such as America Online, Prodigy, or CompuServe? Write a summary of what you have found—no more than one or two pages. Be sure to check your handbook for correct citations and bibliographical form. Your purpose for this summary is to increase your own understanding of this issue through research and then to inform classmates regarding your findings. Be sure that the statistics you use are as up-to-date as possible—the computer scene changes rapidly. Finally, for your own insight and that of your classmates, include a discussion of the implications that you are able to draw from your examination of the statistics.

3. Evan I. Schwartz, a journalist for *Wired,* noted in December 1994:

   > The Net is not just a mechanism for conducting the country's political affairs. While the vast majority of the public gets its dose of political information from television and newspapers, the citizens of the Net are plugged directly into their government. On a daily basis, subscribers to America Online, CompuServe, and Prodigy, as well as other denizens of the Internet, can download and read a stack of new policy papers, speeches, and transcripts of conversations put out by dozens of departments within the Clinton administration. In the past, only reporters and lobbyists saw these documents.
   >
   > All this surfs the line between information and propaganda. And it could be viewed as either, depending on your political persuasion. White House staffers tend to view the Net as ballast against the out-of-control mass media and Washington press corps. And they believe the public is sympathetic—that there is as much anger against the media as there is against government. These days, it is easy to argue that the prevailing tone of the political press—one of detached skepticism—has not only outlived its usefulness, but has grown into an infectious brand of cynicism that permeates society.

   Write a brief response to Schwartz's claim that e-mail changes the dynamics of government for citizens—compose this in the form of a letter written directly to Schwartz. Focus this response not on the functioning of government at the national level but rather the functioning of government in the lives of individual citizens. Has e-mail changed any of the political dynamics for your family? For any individuals that you know? For any other families you know? If so, how and why? If not, why not?

Highways of the Mind or Toll Roads Between Information Castles?

Roger Karraker

AT TIMES, IT HELPS TO TAKE a historical look at how technology develops and how technological structures come into being—how such projects are shaped by (and, in turn, help shape) various forces in our culture: governmental policy, business and manufacturing trends, military goals, public opinion, historical experiences, and so on.

In this article for *Whole Earth Review*, written in the spring of 1991, Roger Karraker describes the debate surrounding the development of a new high-performance computer network (the National Research and Education Network, or NREN) that would replace the BITNET/Internet computer network created by the Defense Department's Advanced Research Projects Agency (DARPA) in the 1960s. As Karraker describes the debate over the NREN, "The battle is about who will build, own, use and pay for the high-speed data highways of the future and whether their contact will be censored." The *Whole Earth Review*, as you may know, is a magazine read primarily by a liberal, educated audience of baby boomers, especially those who had formative experiences during the 1960s.

Interestingly, the debate about the NREN was begun by Albert Gore who, as a democratic Senator from Tennessee, introduced a national networking bill into Congress for the first time in 1990. Both the bill and the debate led to related discussions about a new National Information Infrastructure (NII) after the Clinton administration was elected. The NII, in turn, was a project that led to the Clinton administration's discussion of and implementation of the Global Information Infrastructure (GII).

T his is not an article about technology. It's an article about human needs. For example:

A doctor telecommunicates a CAT scan from her small hospital to the nearest major medical center.

An MIT professor uses his desktop computer in Cambridge to tutor a talented young physicist on a reservation in rural Montana.

Biologists scattered around the world exchange data on an hourly basis, coordinating their effort to map the human genetic code.

A grassroots political organization gets the word out about a meeting, just in time to mobilize for a municipal legislative session.

Each of these activities, science-fiction as they might sound, actually are happening today, courtesy of computer-mediated telecommunication networks. The future of this technology is a matter of much behind-the-scenes maneuvering. Roger Karraker, instructor in journalism and Macintosh at Santa Rosa Junior College, has teased out the key issues from a politically and technically complex debate.

—Howard Rheingold

A quiet but crucial debate now under way in Congress, in major corporate boardrooms, and in universities, has the potential to shape America in the 21st century and beyond. The outcome may determine where you live, how well your children are educated, who will blossom and who will wither in a society where national competitiveness and personal prosperity will likely depend on access to information.

The battle is about who will build, own, use and pay for the high-speed data highways of the future and whether their content will be censored. These vast data highways, capable of sending entire libraries coast-to-coast in a few seconds or sending crucial CAT scans from a remote village to urban specialists, could be linked in a vast network of "highways of the mind."

The backbone of these communications networks will be built of fiber optics, hair-thick strands of glass, transmitting digital pulses thousands of times faster than ever before. In addition to their speed, fiber optics bring with them an environmental bonus: fiber optics are made of silicon, the earth's most common element, and the growing use of optical fibers will mean much less demand for traditional cables composed of copper, an element whose fabrication causes much environmental damage.

Futurist Alvin Toffler says the future of the United States depends upon the creation of these networks. "Because so much of business now depends on getting and sending information, companies around the world have been rushing to link their employees through electronic networks. These networks form the key infrastructure of the 21st century, as critical to business success and national economic development as the railroads were in [Samuel] Morse's era."

These data highways connecting schools, colleges, universities, researchers and industry could help create high-quality education in the smallest schools, or start a society-wide revolution as important as the invention of printing.

Conversely, if access to such data networks is restricted to only those who already have money, power and information, then the highways of the mind might become nothing more than a classic case of economic imperialism, taxation without communication, that one critic has dubbed "toll roads between information castles."

Virtually all sides to the controversy agree that such networks are essential. The future belongs to those who have ready access to huge amounts of accurate information. The Japanese government and industry are actively building such a network. The Japanese government estimates that in 20 years 35 percent of Japan's gross national product will be dependent on information that flows across this web.

In the United States there is only a vague consensus that this high-bandwidth network is vital. In place of the unity of purpose evident in Japan, there is internecine squabbling over who has the right to do what/to where/to whom.

FOUR QUESTIONS

At issue are vastly different visions of the roles of government, education and corporations. Four key questions dominate the debate:

1. Who will build the network? (Will the federal government create the infrastructure or will it be left to private enterprise?)

2. Who will have access to network services? The debate here is between those who would restrict the network's services to the nation's research leaders and those who believe in access to anyone with a modem.

3. Who will pay for all this? Everyone concedes that the federal government will pay the lion's share of getting the network underway. But should it do so by directly funding the infrastructure or by paying the user fees of just the big research organizations working on federal projects?

4. What kind of information will be allowed on the network? If the federal government owns the network, the First Amendment is in place and unpopular speech and art will be protected. If private enterprise owns and runs the network, freedom of electronic speech is less clear. Conceivably, a corporation owning the network could refuse to allow discussion of controversial topics.

So far, two models or metaphors—"highways" and "railroads"—have been proposed to frame the debate. Both borrow from transportation examples in U.S. history. Both, I believe, fall short of the mark. And we suggest that a little tweaking of the two, the best solution for the U.S., might be found in a kind of synthesis of these different visions.

THE INTERSTATE HIGHWAY MODEL

One vision, championed most visibly by U.S. Sen. Albert Gore (D-Tenn.), is to create a National Research and Education Network (NREN) that will link the nation's top research, education, corporate and governmental researchers. Gore's bill to create NREN died in the last Congress but was re-introduced in January, 1991, with more coordinated support among governmental agencies. The NREN proposal is just one part of the government's five-year, $2 billion High Performance Computing Program, which includes supercomputers, software, networking and education.

Gore speaks of a "catalyst" role for the Federal Government akin to the creation of the interstate highway system in the 1950s. The interstate transportation system was seen as a national resource and national tax monies were used to finance the infrastructure, which benefited all Americans through more far-flung, decentralized distribution of goods and services.

The highway model—that government recognizes the communications infrastructure as a vital national resource—is the norm throughout Japan, Europe and most of the world.

THE RAILROAD MODEL

IBM, MCI and other private firms prefer a different model: private enterprise and quasi-monopolies such as America's railroads of the 19th century.

The decision in the 19th century to give private transportation monopolies to the railroads and let them determine the nation's destiny created the 20th century landscape of America. Not surprisingly towns and farms accessible to the railroads prospered and grew. Areas ignored by the railroads withered and died.

Under the railroad model, the public and the government weren't consulted; private interest, not national interest, determined who got what. It was pure free market capitalism with no government regulation, no direct governmental investment and led to some ugly excesses. Yet at a time when federal budget deficits approach $300 billion per year the idea of letting private enterprise foot the whole bill is powerfully attractive.

And that is essentially what IBM, MCI and Merit, an agency of the state of Michigan have proposed. Last September they formed ANS (Advanced Network Services), a not-for-profit joint venture that proposes to build and maintain a private network. But the federal government would need to guarantee that the research institutions would have annual budgets sufficient to pay their ANS bills.

WHY DECIDE NOW?

The existing national research communication system is woefully inadequate to today's needs and must be updated soon; this technical obsolescence lends urgency to the need for finding answers to these policy questions.

The question is how best to modernize and expand the DARPA/Internet network. In the late 1960s, the Defense Department's Advanced Research Projects Agency (ARPA) created a network of telephone lines connected to large research institutions in government, education, private enterprise and the military to allow researchers to exchange computerized information.

Over the next decade and a half the number of researchers grew significantly. As computers grew more powerful and easier to use, researchers outside the computer sciences began to use remote terminals and telecommunication networks to exchange messages and share computing resources from their homes, offices, and laboratories. Each research center supported dozens or hundreds of users, and each local center was plugged into the overall network; thus, both the number of nodes in the network and the number of users at each node proliferated. The number of regional networks in government, business and education skyrocketed, as did connections to ARPANet's main lines, or "backbone." Most importantly, the type of data exchanged by researchers changed dramatically. Where once simple electronic mail messages were sufficient, collaborators across the nation now needed to exchange high-density data like sounds, CAT scans, other graphic images, even video images.

By 1987 the ARPANet suffered data gridlock and the last of its 1970s state-of-the-art lines (56,000 digital "bits" per second—about 50,000 words per minute) were laid to rest. ARPANet's successor is NSFNET, funded until 1993 by the National Science Foundation, another government agency. NSFNET's original lines were so-called T-1 or 1.544 million bits per second—28 times the capacity of ARPANet. These lines lasted just three years, and are now being replaced by a newer T-3 (45 million bits per second) backbone—another 28-fold increase. No one expects it to last for long.

The growth of the so-called Internet—those machines connected to the NSFNET backbone—has been phenomenal. In 1989, the number of networks attached to the NSFNET/Internet increased from 346 to 997; data traffic increased five-fold. The latest estimate, itself probably wildly out-of-date, is that 100,000 to 200,000 main computers are directly connected to NSFNET, with perhaps a total of two million individuals able to exchange information.

For example, the WELL, Whole Earth's computer conferencing system, is not connected directly to either the NSFNET backbone or the so-called Internet of sites on the backbone. But the WELL's computer is linked to Apple Computer's mainframes, and to Pacific Bell's computers and to the University of California at Berkeley—all of them on the Internet. So the WELL's 3,500 customers can send electronic mail to millions of other computer users around the country and, via connections between the Internet and other countries, all around the world.

NSFNET's phenomenal growth in 1989 was, evidently, just a prelude for the data deluge that is now in full flood. Traffic more than doubled between September 1989 and September 1990. It is projected to double again this year. It won't take too long to exhaust even those T-3 lines that carry 800+ times the data of the pre-1987 lines.

That's where the NREN proposal comes in. As proposed by the Coalition for the National Research and Education Network and championed by Senator Gore, Congress would authorize the network and provide $400 million over five years to put it in place. The universities and research centers would pay the additional costs for the local area networks that would connect their scholars to the network.

When completed in 1995 the network would have a 3-gigabit backbone—3 billion bits per second, a 66-fold increase over the current T-3 capacity, a 50,000-fold increase over the old ARPA lines. That's about 300 million times faster than the clattering state-of-the-art teletypes I used at the Associated Press a quarter-century ago.

FROM CAT SCANS TO INSTANT ENCYCLOPEDIAS

What can you do with 3 billion bits per second? The NREN Coalition likens it to sending 100 three-dimensional x-rays and CAT scans every second for 100 cancer patients, or sending 1,000 satellite photographs to researchers investigating agricultural productivity, environmental pollution or weather prediction. Reduced to just words, it would be 100,000 typed pages per second, or as the Coalition dangles tantalizingly before us, "making it possible to transmit the entire Encyclopedia Brittanica in a second. . . ."

Now before you begin salivating at the thought of every book, every magazine article available instantaneously at your slightest whim, here's the rub: as currently designed, NREN's 3-gigabit data lines aren't coming to your house, or your kids' school, or even your local library. NREN will connect only the largest research universities and consortia, at least one in every state. From there, lower-speed regional networks would connect nearby institutions. At the bottom of NREN's proposed three-tier system would be local campus networks. There's no plan or provision for K-12 schools or local libraries in the NREN proposal.

One doesn't need the vast capacity of NREN to exchange simple electronic mail. There are many alternative, if slower, networks available. Using super-sophisticated NREN for such mundane tasks might be like trying to get a drink out of a fire hose. And it's problematic whether local schools and libraries would be able to pay for the equipment needed to exchange items much more complex than simple electronic mail. There's the potential here for the creation of information haves and information have-nots. As Apple Computer librarian Steve Cisler puts it, "If this is going to be a data superhighway, how would you like to have to go to a computer company, military base, or university to find an onramp?"

Dave Hughes, a Colorado telecommunications pioneer, takes a more cautious view of the slimmed-down NREN that Gore and others are trying to push through Congress. An ex-Army colonel and former aide to Defense Secretary Robert McNamara, Hughes believes that NREN's plan, with local schools not even mentioned, could perpetuate educational elitism, where the already-prosperous research universities get additional taxpayer-paid subsidized service and the already-poor local schools get short shrift.

Which doesn't mean that Dave Hughes doesn't want to see a high-speed data network. To the contrary, he wants it to reach every corner of America, terminating in at least each of the 16,000 local school districts. Such as the 114 one-room school houses in Montana which he and Frank Odasz of Western Montana College have managed to connect up, after a fashion, through their Big Sky Telegraph system, and from there out to the rest of the world. And over which a theoretical physicist from MIT has been able to teach a course in chaos theory mathematics to students in these schools—which the physicist cannot do through the Internet workstation on his MIT desk, Hughes says. Hughes and Odasz already have created a grassroots online culture in the wide-open spaces where physical isolation reinforces the lack of ready access to national sources of information.

Hughes wants either to flatten NREN's three tiers of service into a single tier, or have guarantees of affordable access and compatible protocols between the three tiers to and from every educational/political subdivision in America. From observing online behavior nationally for the past 11 years, he thinks talent will find its own level on the network, and that those with neither the talent nor motivation will be satisfied with local bulletin-boards and video games. He believes all schools in the country should have the right of access under the law, including either affordable rates, or appropriate subsidies down to the local level.

"The implicit assumptions behind the NREN proposal," Hughes says, "are that it will only link large research (which also may be 'educational' in the sense of higher education) institutions. As currently conceived NREN will NOT extend to the 16,000 K–12 school districts in America, much less foster the vision of a nation of people learning all their lives by mixing institutional (edifice-centered) education and training, and learning, formally and informally, from home, library, place of business or study.

"So the metaphor of the need for 'Highways of the Mind' across this land is very deceptive. It really could turn out to mean 'Super Toll Roads Between Castles.' That is not my vision of a Network Nation."

THE NETWORK NATION

What would a real Network Nation be like? Conservative theorist/author George Gilder, like Hughes, foresees a renaissance in education caused by the "telecomputer": the merger of fiber optic telephone service to the home and new ultra-powerful multimedia computers.

"The telecomputer could revitalize public education by bringing the best teachers in the country to classrooms everywhere," Gilder says. "More important, the telecomputer could encourage competition because it could make home schooling both feasible and attractive. To learn social skills, neighborhood children could gather in micro-schools run by parents, churches or other local institutions. The competition of home schooling would either destroy the public school system or force it to become competitive with rival systems . . . "

High-speed data communications to the home might also revolutionize where and how we live. Data communications could allow rural tele-commuting, ending two centuries of "brain drain" from the countryside to the cities.

Gilder says, "Every morning millions of commuters across America sit in cars inching their way toward cluttered, polluted and crime-ridden cities," he says.

"Or they sit in dilapidated trains rattling toward office towers that survive as business centers chiefly because of their superior access to the global network of computers and telecommunications. With telecomputers in every home attached to global fiber network, why would anyone commute? People would be able to see the boss life-size in high-definition video and meet with him as easily at home as at the office. They would be able to reach with equal immediacy the head of the foreign subsidiary or the marketing chief across the country. They would be able to send and receive documents almost instantly from anywhere."

WHO PAYS THE BILL?

Whether it's the $400 million Gore's NREN bill calls for or the untold billions required for fiber optics to the home, high-speed data communications will cost a bundle and the major political battle is over who will pay.

For Gilder and for many of us who hope to benefit from fiber-to-the-home, the answer is clear: let the local telephone companies install fiber to every home, amortize the cost and add it to our monthly telephone bills.

To consumer groups and many state public utilities commissions that reeks of reverse Robin Hood-ism: stealing from the poor, retired and elderly who may never be able to utilize the capabilities of the new system in order to subsidize the corporations, universities and a well-educated few. Indeed, that's already underway. Much of the U.S. telephone system, especially in the central cities and along corporate "data corridors" has already been converted to fiber optic service and the costs rolled into the local telephone rate.

Another option: last September IBM and MCI, who already operate NSFNET under contract, proposed to build a "private Internet" backbone that would require less governmental funding, but would involve user fees. Advanced Network Services, the IBM/MCI non-profit joint venture, would build and operate the network.

The benefit, as IBM exec Allan H. Weis, president/chief executive officer of ANS puts it, is "Because we are broadening the community of those using the network, the fixed costs of national networking will be more widely distributed. This will free up funds which could then be allocated to assist the neediest organizations to connect to the national network, as well as to continue to support and enable the national network to remain in the vanguard of new technology."

That doesn't sit well with Dave Hughes. "With this Administration, the budget crunch, and general ignorance of the implications, I'm afraid that the decision makers—including Congress—will welcome 'private enterprise' with open arms. And overlook such minor details as 'equal access.' No, it will be 'if you got the bucks you can buy it.' Kiss off the idea that all K–12 schools will have 'educational' access."

Mitch Kapor, the co-founder of Lotus Computing and the president of the Electronic Frontier Foundation, also believes that universal access should be a central tenet of any national network policy.

"Whatever infrastructure we create," Kapor says, "should incorporate a notion of 'universal digital service,' much as AT&T pioneered, and which later became national policy, with respect to voice telephony in the early 20th century. Everyone should be able to connect to the net."

Hughes and Kapor approach the NREN controversy from substantially different perspectives. Hughes is suspicious of turning the nation's infrastructure over to the agendas of private enterprise.

As Hughes terms it, "I am concerned about the U.S. mind-set which, without thinking, says that the 'private sector' should provide telecommunications in the U.S. simply because that is the way it always has been, while in a couple other key areas—sewage, highways, and education—that is not the case.

"If we believe so mightily that our national future is very much wrapped up in computing and telecommunications—and that especially 'research and education' are going to have to be improved mightily for us to compete—then we ought to be thinking a lot more carefully than we are now about which portion of telecommunications should be government provided/subsidized/regulated and which portion pure profit-and-loss commercial."

Kapor, one of the country's most respected entrepreneurs, suggests that one way to satisfy both Big Scientists and Universalists is to have, in effect, two networks, achieved by "overlaying" lower-bandwidth networks onto an NREN-like backbone.

"These high-end and low-end visions of the NREN are strikingly different. There is no assurance that one size network fits all. Some important public policy choices will therefore be made, one way or the other," he says.

While he lauds the IBM/MCI/ANS group for its donations of millions of dollars to NSFNET computing, Kapor is concerned that ANS policies may become, by default, national polices concerning telecommunications without the benefit of public debate. ANS, he says, is already establishing policies for measuring network traffic, billing and accounting, and setting access charges for new information entrepreneurs, all without the normal hearing and rule-setting process required of public utilities.

"What ANS does in the way of setting up commercial access to the national information infrastructure may well become, in effect, national policy," Kapor says. "But there is no guarantee of public accountability.

"We are dependent on the continued good will of ANS in setting its policies. We don't know, for instance, whether the technology for counting traffic on the net that ANS develops will be as enabling for would-be information entrepreneurs as it will for big corporate information providers. Without an open public process for getting input in the development of the net, the resulting choices are less likely to be in the public interest."

Kapor also sees that a purely private enterprise such as ANS may not be fully in consonance with the goals of the Electronic Frontier Foundation's goals, including First Amendment guarantees for electronic speech and guaranteed access to communications services at fair prices.

EFF's recent newsletter noted that Prodigy, a national computer communications system half owned by IBM, has been embroiled in disputes because of its policy of reading and censoring postings made to Prodigy's public forums.

"I believe it's important to establish the legal principle that businesses which offer a network service which is principally that of a conduit—moving bits from here to there—may not restrict the content of the information they carry. The ability to restrict content, whether conducted by the government in the form of censorship, or by a private carrier for whatever reason, is not conducive to the free and open flow of information," he says.

SO WHAT'S THE ANSWER?

Now let's play Chinese menu, taking a few items from column A (Gore's NREN/Big Scientists bill) and column B (the Universalists approach).

A workable national network might include the following features:

Built and managed by private enterprise

Federal start-up subsidies for colleges, universities, libraries and schools

First Amendment free speech guarantees

Guaranteed interconnection to other data services offered by telephone companies and other locally regulated businesses

Guaranteed universal digital access for everyone who wants to connect

Fair rates and policies subject to regulatory review

In short, we'd have a regulated public utility: precisely the system that the U.S. used over the past century to develop the best—and cheapest—public telephone system in the world.

The problem, as usual, is in how one defines the purpose of the national network. Laura Breeden, a network group manager at Bolt Beranek and Newman (a private research and development company that was one of the original ARPANet contractors), frames the issues this way:

"If you think of data networking as a public utility, then it seems important to regulate it in some of the same ways that other utilities are regulated, i.e. to make sure that basic services are provided to everyone and not withdrawn unreasonably.

"If you think of it as a strategic resource, important for insuring U.S. competitiveness and technological progress, then you put it where it can do the most good strategically.

"If you believe that it is important to education generally, then you put it at as many schools as possible.

"If you think data networking is some of all of these, you have to balance the trade-offs among them."

The National Network is a complex issue. It's safe to say only a handful of representatives understand the issue in depth. A letter from you to your elected representatives asking for reasonable rates, guaranteed free speech rights and access for local schools, libraries and homes might make a lot of difference.

For more information concerning NREN, consult the following sources:

The WELL, Whole Earth's computer conferencing system, has extensive coverage of NREN/Internet issues and the Info, Telecommunications and Electronic Frontier Foundation conferences. Call 415/332-4335 (voice) or 415/332-6106 (modem) for more information on how to join the WELL. On the WELL you will find: Dave Hughes (dave@well.sf.ca.us), Steve Cisler (sac@well.sf.ca.us), Tom Valovic (tvacorn@well.sf.ca.us), Mitch Kapor (mkapor@well.sf.ca.us), and Roger Karraker (roger@well.sf.ca.us).

Mike Nelson, Senate Commerce Committee, U.S. Capitol, Washington, DC 20510; 202/224-9360.

Sen. Albert Gore, U.S. Senate, Washington, DC 20510 (Gore's office, or the Senate Commerce Committee, can send you a copy of Gore's article, "Networking the Future," published in the July 15, 1990 Outlook section of the Washington Post.

Coalition for the National Research and Education Network: Mike Roberts, Vice President/Networking, EDUCOM, 1112 16th Street NW, #600, Washington, DC 20036; roberts@educom.edu

Research & Education Networking, a commercial publication devoted to developments related to NREN, is published nine times a year. Volume I, Number 1 is eight pages long. Institutional rate is $59 annually; personal rate is $39. Available from Meckler, 11 Ferry Lane West, Westport, CT 06880; 203/226-6967; Fax 203/454-5840.

THINKING AND RE-READING

1. Karraker notes, "The question is how best to modernize and expand the DARPA/Internet network." It is interesting that he does not say, "whether or not to expand." There is an underlying assumption in Karraker's article about the need to keep up the pace of technological improvements. As you re-read this article, try to question this assumption—are there reasons not to invest in this system? Or to modify our investment as a culture? Try to articulate, for yourself, a few of these reasons.

2. In this article, Karraker notes that, "it's problematic whether local schools and libraries would be able to pay for the equipment needed to exchange items much more complex than simple electronic mail." As you re-read this article, think back to your own high school and junior high school—and those of people you know. Describe the kinds of computer equipment available in your schooling experience. In what courses did you use this equipment? Why? What courses were not computer-intensive? Why? Did you have computers in every classroom? A computer laboratory? Did all students use these computers? Why or why not?

WRITING AND LEARNING

1. In one part of this article, Karraker discusses some of the implications of creating a society in which some citizens have access to technology and are trained to use it, whereas others do not. Imagine that the city council in your town has just proposed a city sales tax that would generate revenues to pay for public-access computers in public libraries around the city. Write an editorial to the local paper that is either supportive or non-supportive of this tax proposal. Provide reasons why it should or should not be passed; use your own experiences with technology to provide support as well. Think about whether such a project would eliminate the gap between the technological haves and

have-nots in your local community. If you are unfamiliar with the genre of editorials (how long they are, what tone they take, and what counts as evidence in arguments), be sure to study a few editorials in your local paper to get ideas.

2. Respond to the controversy sketched out in this article regarding whether universal access to the NREN/NII should be paid for by government (with the help of taxpayers) or should be provided by the private sector and charged to the citizens. Write an editorial for your local paper on this topic. If you are unfamiliar with the genre of editorials (how long they are, what tone they take, and what counts as evidence in arguments), be sure to study a few editorials in your local paper to get ideas.

3. Take a careful look at the examples of computer technology that are presented at the beginning of this article as indications of social and technological progress. To develop your own critical insight on this matter and to sharpen your persuasive skills, brainstorm the downside of some of these achievements and write a note that argues against the funding of such projects. Convey this informative report to the members of the district's school board. If you need to do some research in order to get alternative perspectives on these debates, go to the library and do some reading on the rising costs of high-tech medical care or on high-tech education. Be sure to check your handbook for the proper format for summarizing, paraphrasing, and quoting from these articles and for providing the bibliographic citations for them.

Remarks Prepared for Delivery by Vice President Al Gore Jr.

International Telecommunications Union

IN MARCH 1994, VICE PRESIDENT ALBERT GORE traveled to Buenos Aires to give a speech before a gathering of the International Telecommunications Union, a group of representatives from a consortium of countries that cooperate on the exchange of telecommunications and the establishment of telecommunications infrastructures on a global scale. Soon after his presentation, the following remarks were posted on the Internet by the White House.

As you read the remarks prepared for Gore, identify and think about the arguments that Gore makes for the GII. Which do you find compelling? Why? Which do you consider less strong? Why?

I have come here, 8,000 kilometers from my home, to ask you to help create a Global Information Infrastructure. To explain why, I want to begin by reading you something that I first read in high school, 30 years ago.

"By means of electricity, the world of matter has become a great nerve, vibrating thousands of miles in a breathless point of time . . . The round globe is a vast . . . brain, instinct with intelligence!"

This was not the observation of a physicist—or a neurologist. Instead, these visionary words were written in 1851 by Nathaniel Hawthorne, one of my country's greatest writers, who was inspired by the development of the telegraph. Much as Jules Verne foresaw submarines and moon landings, Hawthorne foresaw what we are now poised to bring into being.

The ITU was created only 14 years later, in major part for the purpose of fostering an internationally comparable system of telegraphy.

For almost 150 years, people have aspired to fulfill Hawthorne's vision—to wrap nerves of communications around the globe, linking all human knowledge.

In this decade, at this conference, we now have at hand the technological breakthroughs and economic means to bring all the communities of the world together. We now can at last create a planetary information network that transmits messages and images with the speed of light from the largest city to the smallest village on every continent.

I am very proud to have the opportunity to address the first development conference of the ITU because the President of the United States and I believe that an essential prerequisite to sustainable development, for all members of the human family, is the creation of this network of networks. To accomplish this purpose, legislators, regulators, and business people must do this: build and operate a Global Information Infrastructure. This GII will circle the globe with information superhighways on which all people can travel.

These highways or, more accurately, networks of distributed intelligence—will allow us to share information, to connect, and to communicate as a global community. From these connections we will derive robust and sustainable economic progress, strong democracies, better solutions to global and local environmental challenges, improved health care, and—ultimately—a greater sense of shared stewardship of our small planet.

The Global Information Infrastructure will help educate our children and allow us to exchange ideas within a community and among nations. It will be a means by which families and friends will transcend the barriers of time and distance. It will make possible a global information marketplace, where consumers can buy or sell products. I ask you, the delegates to this conference, to set an ambitious agenda that will help all governments, in their own sovereign nations and in international cooperation, to build this Global Information Infrastructure. For my country's part, I pledge our vigorous, continued participation in achieving this goal—in the development sector of the ITU, in other sectors and in plenipotentiary gatherings of the ITU, and in bilateral discussions held by our Departments of State and Commerce and our Federal Communications Commission.

The development of the GII must be a cooperative effort among governments and peoples. It cannot be dictated or built by a single country. It must be a democratic effort.

And the distributed intelligence of the GII will spread participatory democracy.

To illustrate why, I'd like to use an example from computer science. In the past, all computers were huge mainframes with a single processing unit, solving problems in sequence, one by one, each bit of information sent back and forth between the CPU and the vast field of memory surrounding it. Now, we have massively parallel computers with hundreds—or thousands—of tiny self-contained processors distributed throughout the memory field, all interconnected, and together far more powerful and more versatile than even the most sophisticated single processor, because they each solve a tiny piece of the problem simultaneously and when all the pieces are assembled, the problem is solved.

Similarly, the GII will be an assemblage of local, national, and regional networks, that are not only like parallel computers but in their most advanced state will in fact be a distributed, parallel computer.

In a sense, the GII will be a metaphor for democracy itself. Representative democracy does not work with an all-powerful central government, arrogating all decisions to itself. That is why communism collapsed.

Instead, representative democracy relies on the assumption that the best way for a nation to make its political decisions is for each citizen—the human equivalent of the self-contained processor—to have the power to control his or her own life.

To do that, people must have available the information they need. And be allowed to express their conclusions in free speech and in votes that are combined with those of millions of others. That's what guides the system as a whole.

The GII will not only be a metaphor for a functioning democracy, it will in fact promote the functioning of democracy by greatly enhancing the participation of citizens in decision-making.

And it will greatly promote the ability of nations to cooperate with each other. I see a new Athenian Age of democracy forged in the fora the GII will create.

The GII will be the key to economic growth for national and international economies. For us in the United States, the information infrastructure already is to the U.S. economy of the 1990s what transport infrastructure was to the economy of the mid-20th century. The integration of computing and information networks into the economy makes U.S. manufacturing companies more productive, more competitive, and more adaptive to changing conditions and it will do the same for the economies of other nations.

These same technologies are also enabling the service sectors of the U.S. economy to grow, to increase their scale and productivity and expand their range of product offerings and ability to respond to customer demands.

Approximately 60% of all U.S. workers are "knowledge workers"—people whose jobs depend on the information they generate and receive over our information infrastructure. As we create new jobs, 8 out of 10 are in information-intensive sectors of our economy. And these new jobs are well-paying jobs for financial analysts, computer programmers, and other educated workers.

The global economy also will be driven by the growth of the Information Age. Hundreds of billions of dollars can be added to world growth if we commit to the GII. I fervently hope this conference will take full advantage of this potential for economic growth, and not deny any country or community its right to participate in this growth.

As the GII spreads, more and more people realize that information is a treasure that must be shared to be valuable. When two people communicate, they each can be enriched—and unlike traditional resources, the more you share, the more you have. As Thomas Jefferson said, "He who receives an idea from me, receives instruction himself without lessening mine; as he who lights his taper at mine, receives light without darkening me."

Now we all realize that, even as we meet here, the Global Information Infrastructure is being built, although many countries have yet to see any benefits.

Digital telecommunications technology, fiber optics, and new high-capacity satellite systems are transforming telecommunication. And all over the world, under the seas and along the roads, pipelines, and railroads, companies are laying fiber optic cable that carries thousands of telephone calls per second over a single strand of glass.

These developments are greatly reducing the cost of building the GII. In the past, it could take years to build a network. Linking a single country's major cities might require laying thousands of kilometers of expensive wires. Today, a single satellite and a few dozen ground stations can be installed in a few months—at a much lower cost.

The economics of networks have changed so radically that the operation of a competitive, private market can build much of the GII. This is dependent, however, upon sensible regulation.

Within the national boundaries of the U.S. we aspire to build our information highways according to a set of principles that I outlined in January in California. The National Information Infrastructure, as we call it, will be built and maintained by the private sector. It will consist of hundreds of different networks, run by different companies and using different technologies, all connected together in a giant "network of networks," providing telephone and interactive digital video to almost every American.

Our plan is based on five principles: First, encourage private investment; Second, promote competition; Third, create a flexible regulatory framework that can keep pace with rapid technological and market changes; Fourth, provide open access to the network for all information providers; and Fifth, ensure universal service.

Are these principles unique to the United States? Hardly. Many are accepted international principles endorsed by many of you. I believe these principles can inform and aid the development of the Global Information Infrastructure and urge this Conference to incorporate them, as appropriate, into the Buenos Aires Declaration, which will be drafted this week.

Let me elaborate briefly on these principles.

First, we propose that private investment and competition be the foundation for development of the GII. In the U.S., we are in the process of opening our communications markets to all domestic private participants.

In recent years, many countries, particularly here in Latin America, have opted to privatize their state-owned telephone companies in order to obtain the benefits and incentives that drive competitive private enterprises, including innovation, increased investment, efficiency and responsiveness to market needs.

Adopting policies that allow increased private sector participation in the telecommunications sector has provided an enormous spur to telecommunications development in dozens of countries, including Argentina, Venezuela, Chile, and Mexico. I urge you to follow their lead.

But privatization is not enough. Competition is needed as well. In the past, it did make sense to have telecommunications monopolies.

In many cases, the technology and the economies of scale meant it was inefficient to build more than one network. In other cases—Finland, Canada, and the U.S., for example—national networks were built in the early part of this century by hundreds of small, independent phone companies and cooperatives.

Today, there are many more technology options than in the past and it is not only possible, but desirable, to have different companies running competing—but interconnected—networks, because competition is the best way to make the telecommunications sector more efficient, more innovative—and more profitable as consumers make more calls and prices decline.

That is why allowing other companies to compete with AT&T, once the world's largest telephone monopoly, was so useful for the United States. Over the last ten years, it has cut the cost of a long-distance telephone call in the U.S. more than 50%.

To promote competition and investment in global telecommunications, we need to adopt cost-based collection and accounting rates. Doing so will accelerate development of the GII.

International standards to ensure interconnection and interoperability are needed as well. National networks must connect effectively with each other to make real the simple vision of linking schools, hospitals, businesses, and homes to a Global Information Infrastructure.

Hand in hand with the need for private investment and competition is the necessity of appropriate and flexible regulations developed by an authoritative regulatory body.

In order for the private sector to invest and for initiatives opening a market to competition to be successful, it is necessary to create a regulatory environment that fosters and protects competition and private sector investments, while at the same time protecting consumers' interests.

Without the protection of an independent regulator, a potential private investor would be hesitant to provide service in competition with the incumbent provider for fear that the incumbent's market power would not be adequately controlled.

Decisions and the basis for making them must also be made public so that consumers and potential competitors are assured that their interests are being protected.

This is why in the U.S., we have delegated significant regulatory powers to an independent agency, the Federal Communications Commission. This expert body is well-equipped to make difficult technical decisions and to monitor, in conjunction with the National Telecommunications and Information Administration and the Department of Justice, changing market conditions. We commend this approach to you.

We need a flexible, effective system for resolution of international issues, too—one that can keep up with the ever-accelerating pace of technological change.

I understand that the ITU has just gone through a major reorganization designed to increase its effectiveness. This will enable the ITU, under the able leadership of Mr. Tarjanne, to streamline its operations and redirect resources to where they are needed most. This will ensure that the ITU can adapt to future and unimaginable technologies.

Our fourth principle is open access. By this I mean that telephone and video network owners should charge non-discriminatory prices for access to their networks. This principle will guarantee every user of the GII can use thousands of different sources of information—video programming, electronic newspapers, computer bulletin boards—from every country, in every language.

With new technologies like direct broadcast satellites, a few networks will no longer be able to control your access to information—as long as government policies permit new entrants into the information marketplace.

Countries and companies will not be able to compete in the global economy if they cannot communicate instantly with customers around the globe. Ready access to information is also essential for training the skilled workforce needed for high-tech industries.

The countries that flourish in the twenty-first century will be those that have telecommunications policies and copyright laws that provide their citizens access to a wide choice of information services. Protecting intellectual property is absolutely essential.

The final and most important principle is to ensure universal service so that the Global Information Infrastructure is available to all members of our societies. Our goal is a kind of global conversation, in which everyone who wants can have his or her say.

We must ensure that whatever steps we take to expand our worldwide telecommunications infrastructure, we keep that goal in mind.

Although the details of universal service will vary from country to country and from service to service, several aspects of universal service apply everywhere. Access clearly includes making service available at affordable prices to persons at all income levels. It also includes making high quality service available regardless of geographic location or other restrictions such as disability.

Constellations of hundreds of satellites in low earth orbit may soon provide telephone or data services to any point on the globe. Such systems could make universal service both practical and affordable.

An equally important part of universal access is teaching consumers how to use communications effectively. That means developing easy-to-use applications for a variety of contexts, and teaching people how to use them. The most sophisticated and cost-efficient networks will be completely useless if users are unable to understand how to access and take full advantage of their offerings.

Another dimension of universal service is the recognition that marketplace economics should not be the sole determinant of the reach of the information infrastructure.

The President and I have called for positive government action in the United States to extend the NII to every classroom, library, hospital, and clinic in the U.S. by the end of the century.

I want to urge that this conference include in its agenda for action the commitment to determine how every school and library in every country can be connected to the Internet, the world's largest computer network, in order to create a Global Digital Library. Each library could maintain a server containing books and journals in electronic form, along with indexes to help users find other materials. As more and more and more information is stored electronically, this global library would become more and more useful.

It would allow millions of students, scholars and business people to find the information they need whether it be in Albania or Ecuador.

Private investment . . . competition . . . flexibility . . . open access . . . universal service.

In addition to urging the delegates of this conference to adopt these principles as part of the Buenos Aires Declaration, guiding the next four years of telecommunications development. I assure you that the U.S. will be discussing in many fora, inside and outside the ITU, whether these principles might be usefully adopted by all countries.

The commitment of all nations to enforcing regulatory regimes to build the GII is vital to world development and many global social goals.

But the power of the Global Information Infrastructure will be diminished if it cannot reach large segments of the world population.

We have heard together Dr. Tarjanne's eloquent speech setting forth the challenges we face. As he points out: the 24 countries of the OECD have only 16 percent of the world's population. But they account for 70 percent of global telephone mainlines and 90 percent of mobile phone subscribers.

There are those who say the lack of economic development causes poor telecommunications. I believe they have it exactly backwards. A primitive telecommunication system causes poor economic development.

So we cannot be complacent about the disparity between the high and low income nations, whether in how many phones are available to people or in whether they have such new technologies as high speed computer networks or videoconferencing.

The United States delegation is devoted to working with each of you at this Conference to address the many problems that hinder development.

And there are many. Financing is a problem in almost every country, even though telecommunications has proven itself to be an excellent investment.

Even where telecommunications has been identified as a top development priority, countries lack trained personnel and up-to-date information.

And in too many parts of the world, political unrest makes it difficult or impossible to maintain existing infrastructure, let alone lay new wire or deploy new capacity.

How can we work together to overcome these hurdles? Let me mention a few things industrialized countries can do to help.

First, we can use the Global Information Infrastructure for technical collaboration between industrialized nations and developing countries. All agencies of the U.S. government are potential sources of information and knowledge that can be shared with partners across the globe.

The Global Information Infrastructure can help development agencies link experts from every nation and enable them to solve common problems. For instance, the Pan American Health Organization has conducted hemisphere-wide teleconferences to present new methods to diagnose and prevent the spread of AIDS.

Second, multilateral institutions like the World Bank, can help nations finance the building of telecommunications infrastructure.

Third, the U.S. can help provide the technical know-how needed to deploy and use these new technologies. USAID and U.S. businesses have helped the U.S. Telecommunications Training Institute train more than 3500 telecommunications professionals from the developing world, including many in this room.

In the future, USTTI plans also to help business people, bankers, farmers, and others from the developing world find ways that computer networking, wireless technology, satellites, video links, and other telecommunications technology could improve their effectiveness and efficiency.

I challenge other nations, the development banks, and the UN system to create similar training opportunities.

The head of our Peace Corps, Carol Bellamy, intends to use Peace Corps volunteers both to help deploy telecommunications and computer systems and to find innovative uses for them. Here in Argentina, a Peace Corps volunteer is doing just that.

To join the GII in the effort to protect and preserve the global environment, our Administration will soon propose using satellite and personal communication technology to create a global network of environmental information. We will propose using the schools and students of the world to gather and study environmental information on a daily basis and communicate that data to the world through television.

But regulatory reform must accompany this technical assistance and financial aid for it to work. This requires top-level leadership and commitment—commitment to foster investment in telecommunications and commitment to adopt policies that ensure the rapid deployment and widespread use of the information infrastructure.

I opened by quoting Nathaniel Hawthorne, inspired by Samuel Morse's invention of the telegraph.

Morse was also a famous portrait artist in the U.S.—his portrait of President James Monroe hangs today in the White House. While Morse was working on a portrait of General Lafayette in Washington, his wife, who lived about 500 kilometers away, grew ill and died. But it took seven days for the news to reach him.

In his grief and remorse, he began to wonder if it were possible to erase barriers of time and space, so that no one would be unable to reach a loved one in time of need. Pursuing this thought, he came to discover how to use electricity to convey messages, and so he invented the telegraph and, indirectly, the ITU.

The Global Information Infrastructure offers instant communication to the great human family.

It can provide us the information we need to dramatically improve the quality of our lives. By linking clinics and hospitals together, it will ensure that doctors treating patients have access to the best possible information on diseases and treatments. By providing early warning on natural disasters like volcanic eruptions, tsunamis, or typhoons, it can save the lives of thousands of people.

By linking villages and towns, it can help people organize and work together to solve local and regional problems ranging from improving water supplies to preventing deforestation.

To promote ... to protect ... to preserve freedom and democracy, we must make telecommunications development an integral part of every nation's development. Each link we create strengthens the bonds of liberty and democracy around the world. By opening markets to stimulate the development of the global information infrastructure, we open lines of communication.

By opening lines of communication, we open minds. This summer, from my country cameras will bring the World Cup Championship to well over one billion people.

To those of you from the 23 visiting countries whose teams are in the Finals, I wish you luck—although I'll be rooting for the home team.

The Global Information Infrastructure carries implications even more important than soccer.

It has brought us images of earthquakes in California, of Boris Yeltsin on a tank in Red Square, of the effects of mortar shells in Sarajevo and Somalia, of the fall of the Berlin Wall. It has brought us images of war and peace, and tragedy and joy, in which we all can share.

There's a Dutch relief worker, Wam Kat, who has been broadcasting an electronic diary from Zagreb for more than a year and a half on the Internet, sharing his observations of life in Croatia.

After reading Kat's Croatian diary, people around the world began to send money for relief efforts. The result: 25 houses have been rebuilt in a town destroyed by war.

Governments didn't do this. People did. But such events are the hope of the future.

When I began proposing the NII in the U.S., I said that my hope is that the United States, born in revolution, can lead the way to this new, peaceful revolution. However, I believe we will reach our goal faster and with greater certainty if we walk down that path together. As Antonio Machado, Spanish poet, once said, "Pathwalker, there is no path, we create the path as we walk."

Let us build a global community in which the people of neighboring countries view each other not as potential enemies, but as potential partners, as members of the same family in the vast, increasingly interconnected human family.

Let us seize this moment. Let us work to link the people of the world. Let us create this new path as we walk it together.

THINKING AND RE-READING

1. As you re-read, think about the aptness of Gore's claim that "the GII will be a metaphor for democracy itself." Gore bases his claim on this reasoning: "Representative democracy relies on the assumption that the best way for a nation to make its political decisions is for each citizen—the human equivalent of the self contained processor—to have the power to control his or her own life." Do you think the GII, as Gore explains it here, provides such decentralized power to individuals? What role does Gore sketch out for governments in this project? How does this role reconcile with his metaphor?

2. Gore proposes that "private investment and competition" and governmental "regulation" should provide the tripartite foundation for the GII. As you read, think about those countries that might be unable or unwilling to take these steps and the reasons that this might be so. What alternative socioeconomic methods can you think of for building the GII?

WRITING AND LEARNING

1. What are the implications of Gore's comment, "As the GII spreads, more and more people realize that information is a treasure that must be shared to be valuable"? How is this notion related to the claim that we now live in an age of information rather than in an age of manufacturing? What do we mean when we say that information has

become a commodity? Who sells information? Who is buying it? Who is involved in making, transferring, and interpreting information? For the answers to these questions, go to the library and do a periodical search on the "information age." Choose two or three key articles to read from this search—make sure that these pieces are informative and that they provide you with a general introduction to the concept of the *information age*. With the insights that you derive from this search, write a letter to someone (e.g., a relative or an imaginary citizen) who lived between 1850 to 1950 during the manufacturing age in American history. Explain to this person in your own words and through experiences drawn from your own life and from those around you what the information age is and how it has affected people in the future.

2. Interview a person from another country—if possible, someone from a non-European or non–North American country. Describe Gore's vision of the GII and the tenets that should inform its structure (e.g., private investment, competition, and governmental regulation). Ask your interviewer what people in his or her country would think of this proposal, this vision, or these beliefs. Ask about whether such a proposal is feasible or not and why. Try to get a sense of how this person's culturally informed vision of technology might differ from your own. In a letter to the vice president, summarize your questions and the answers in writing, giving as full an interpretation of the person's responses as possible.

3. The use of metaphors is always a tricky business. In some ways, good metaphors illuminate unfamiliar subjects—showing how something that is unknown is similar to something that is quite well known. In other ways, however, metaphors can blind us to dissimilarities between things—glossing over important ways in which they differ. In a written response that sharpens your own critical insights regarding technology, explore Gore's metaphor of "the great human family." Is the metaphor apt? Why or why not? In what ways? Also write about those matters or aspects that the metaphor may conceal. Who might benefit from the use of such a metaphor? Who might not? Why?

Opening Statement to the House Subcommittee on Telecommunications and Finance

Bruce Sterling

IN THIS SECTION, YOU HAVE READ a number of pieces that place the current efforts to build the NREN or the NII in historical and social contexts. The piece that follows—the remarks that author Bruce Sterling gave before the House Subcommittee on Telecommunications and Finance—provides a context set in the future. The remarks are meant to be a persuasive wake-up call to the members of this important subcommittee, which is responsible for making recommendations about communication technologies that will eventually form part of our national policy concerning such matters.

These remarks extrapolate from current conditions the challenges that citizens of the future will face in connection with computer networks. This is not surprising if you know that Bruce Sterling is a science fiction and nonfiction author. You might be familiar with his *Hacker Crackdown: Law and Disorder on the Electronic Frontier, Mirrorshades*, and *The Artificial Kid.* Sterling's remarks might surprise you, and similar to most good science fiction, they may make you think more clearly about the technology challenges facing our culture right now.

Hello everyone and thanks for inviting me here. My name is Bruce Sterling and I'm a science fiction writer and sometime science journalist. Since writing my nonfiction book *Hacker Crackdown: Law and Disorder on the Electronic Frontier,* I have returned to writing science fiction. And I've returned to that with some relief, frankly, since the world of science fiction is in most ways rather less strange and less bizarre than the contemporary world of telecommunications policy.

I hope therefore that you will forgive me if I testify today as a science fiction writer. It's one of the perks of my profession to write about the future, or attempt to, and I thought you might like to meet someone from the telecommunications future that you are so busy creating.

With your kind indulgence for my novelist's whimsy then, the rest of my brief presentation today will be given by a Mr. Bob Smith, who is an NREN network administrator from the year 2015. I present Mr. Smith.

"Thank you, Mr. Sterling. It's a remarkable privilege to talk to the legislators who historically created my working environment. As a laborer in the fields of 21st Century cyberspace I of course would have no job without NREN, and my wife and small son and I are all properly grateful for your foresight in establishing the Information Superhighway.

"Your actions in this regard have affected American society every bit as strongly as did the telegraph, the railroads, the telephone, the highway system, and television. In fact, it's impossible for me to imagine contemporary life in 2015 without the Global Net; living without the Net would be like trying to live without electricity.

"However, it's a truism in technological development that no silver lining comes without its cloud. Today I'd like to mention two or three trifling problems that have come up that were not entirely obvious from the perspective of the early 1990s.

"First of all, this 'Research and Education' aspect. Since communications *is* power in an Information Society, giving fantastically advanced communications to the Research and Education communities did in fact empower those communities quite drastically by comparison with interest-groups lacking that advantage. Today, one of the most feared political organizations in the world is the multi-national anarchist libertarian group called the Students for an Utterly Free Society.

"Of course, there have always been campus radicals, but thanks to their relative lack of financial clout, and lack of even a steady home address, these young fanatics once found it very difficult to organize politically. Therefore, they were easy for the powers-that-be to ignore, except during occasional spasms of violent campus unrest.

"Thanks to NREN, however, spasms of student unrest can now spread like lightning across entire continents. Advanced AI translation programs installed on the Net only made matters worse, since in 2015 the global leaders of the student movements are not only extremely radical, but French.

"Attempts by campus authorities to control this unrest have failed miserably. In 2015, NREN sites are always the first buildings occupied during a campus strike. Campus chancellors and faculty are themselves so utterly dependent on NREN that they become quite helpless off-line.

"A second major problem has been the growth of unlicensed encryption, which has proved quite unstoppable. Today some seventy-five percent of NREN archives are material that no one in authority can read. Countries that attempted to control and monitor network traffic have lost market share and service revenue as data processing simply moves offshore.

"The United States has profited by this phenomenon to a great extent as people worldwide have flocked to the relative liberty of our networks. Unfortunately many of these electronic virtual immigrants are not simply dissidents looking for free expression but in fact are organized criminals.

"Take for instance a recent FBI raid on an enormous archive of encrypted Iranian files, illicitly stored in an obscure NREN node in North Dakota. Luckily the FBI was able to decrypt these files thanks to an inside informant. Deciphering these archives revealed the following contraband:

"Eighty percent graphic image files of attractive young women without veils on, or, in fact, much clothing of any kind.

"Fifteen percent digitally stored pirated copies of Western pop music and Western videos, still illegal to possess in Teheran.

"And, five percent text files in the Farsi language describing how to build, deliver and park truck-bombs in major urban areas.

"I can't conclude my brief remarks today without a mention of a particularly odd development having to do with *wireless* computer telecommunications. Since it is now possible to transact business entirely in cyberspace, including financial transactions, many information entrepreneurs in 2015 have simply given up any physical home. Basically, they have become stateless people, 21st Century gypsies.

"A recent tragic example of this occurred in the small town of North Zulch, Texas. There some rural law enforcement officers apprehended a scruffy vagabond on a motorcycle in a high-speed chase. Unfortunately he was killed. A search of his backpack revealed a device the size of a cigarette pack. In searching the dead man's effects, the police officers, who were not computer literate, accidentally broke the device. This tiny device was actually a privately owned computer bulletin board system with some 15,000 registered users.

"Many of the users were wealthy celebrities, and the apparent outlaw biker was actually an extremely popular and nationally known system operator. These 15,000 users were enraged by what they considered the wanton destruction of their electronic community. They pooled their resources and took a terrible vengeance on the small town of North Zulch, which, by contrast, had only 2,000 residents, none of them wealthy or technologically sophisticated. Through a combination of harassing lawsuits and sharp real-estate deals, the vengeful board users bankrupted the town. Eventually the entire township was bulldozed flat and purchased for parkland by the Nature Conservancy.

"Thanks in part to the advances that you yourselves set in motion, violent conflicts between virtual and actual communities have become a permanent feature of the cultural landscape in 2015."

Thank you for your patience in entertaining my speculations. I'll be happy to take any questions—though only in my real-life persona. Thank you very much.

THINKING AND RE-READING

1. As you re-read, think about how likely you consider the scenario that Sterling paints. What elements from your own experience and those of other people whom you know convince you that his predictions are likely or less likely?

2. Consider the purpose of science fiction as a literary genre. Some people think that science fiction is so appealing because it serves as a cultural looking glass, showing us—if only dimly and with distortion—where our current social trajectories might take us. Some people say that science fiction fascinates us because it provides a setting for social criticism, but at a temporal distance, thus making the exercise of criticism more palatable. Some people think that science fiction is simply entertaining. As you read, consider the purpose and value of this particular piece of writing—why might it be useful to a legislative body?

WRITING AND LEARNING

1. In a written response, test your own predictive powers. Imagine that you are a student on your college or university campus in the year 2015. Much as Bruce Sterling did, extrapolate from your experiences and those of others whom you know to predict what kinds of technological environment and challenges students will face in the future. Write your remarks as if you were a student from the future addressing your campus computer coordinating committee or university president.

2. Consider the story that Sterling tells of the violence against North Zulch, Texas. To sharpen your own powers of critical observation, identify the current technology-related trends and patterns you are able to observe in our culture that could eventually result in such a situation happening. If necessary, go to the library and read a few recent copies of *Wired* or *Mondo 2000* to inspire your thinking. In this assignment, you are writing for yourself and speculating on what the future might bring. When you are finished with this assignment, put this piece of writing away in a scrapbook or album so that you are able to re-read it and test its validity in twenty years.

3. Make an appointment to interview someone at your central campus computing network or sit down to read your school's written technology policy. Focus on the policy that your campus has formulated regarding online pornography. Interview three or four of your friends (equal numbers of men and women) concerning this policy and elicit their comments on whether they agree with it and how they might like to see it improved. Finally, write a letter to the committee or the individual administrator who devises the campus computer policy regarding pornography. Discuss whether this policy addresses the issue of pornography on the nets in a way that seems responsible and fair to you and to your friends. Using the comments of your friends (appropriately cited), your understanding of technology, and your own understanding of free speech and pornography issues (as informed by various articles in the Law and Technology section of this book), suggest improvements to this policy.

Direct Democracy: Are You Ready for the Democracy Channel?

Evan I. Schwartz

IN THE 1992 PRESIDENTIAL ELECTION, Ross Perot, running as a third-party candidate, made the Electronic Town Hall—nationwide town meetings supported by computer technology—an important and high-profile issue in his campaign. Although Perot did not win the election, many voters—especially those who felt removed from national policy discussions and decision-making processes and frustrated with the country's government—considered the concept of the Electronic Town Hall a promising and innovative use of technology.

In this piece, Evan Schwartz discusses some of the benefits and drawbacks of such electronic democracy projects. In reading this piece, try to imagine what it would mean to be connected electronically to local, state, and national governments—and to have them connected directly to you!

This piece was originally published in *Wired* in 1993. This popular magazine is aimed at the educated and professional generation of baby boomers who have grown up and become comfortable in an increasingly technological world.

Good evening, citizens. The electronic town meeting is about to begin. Everyone take your seats and make sure your voter ID number is handy and your touch-tone phone or remote control device is by your side. Those of you tuning in via computer please click on the "start" icon on the top of your screen.

Today's topic is gun control. We assume everyone has read the issue brochure sent to all of your electronic mailboxes one month ago. Our first speaker will be Robert Corbin, executive director of the National Rifle Association, followed by Sarah Brady, president of Handgun Control Incorporated. We will follow that up with a discussion among a panel of twelve randomly selected citizens and an impartial moderator. At the end of the meeting, we will ask you to vote on the proposed legislation.

Ever since Ross Perot made the concept of an Electronic Town Hall a central part of his stop-and-go bid for the presidency, the idea has been catching on. The Texas tycoon is still talking up electronic democracy as something that would not only restore the American Dream but also give us something useful to do after work. "If we ever put the people back in charge of this country and make sure they understand the issues," Perot has said, "you'll see the White House and Congress, like a ballet, pirouetting around the stage and getting things done in unison."

The idea of holding these events regularly is now being carried into the future by people not associated with Perot. In September, the Public Agenda Foundation, a nonprofit group, hosted a two-hour electronic town meeting (ETM) in San Antonio, Texas over that city's new interactive cable system (special software and set-top boxes allow the user to send signals upstream—"I'd like to order this," or "I disagree with that.") That forum allowed the locals to deliberate the health care crisis and use their remote controls to vote on solutions. Future forums all over the country could attack everything from the federal budget deficit to abortion to foreign policy.

And Public Agenda is hardly alone in its quest to popularize such events. There are now dozens of foundations and entrepreneurs forging an entire ETM industry. There's even a cable executive at John Malone's Denver headquarters who is quietly planning to launch the Democracy Channel as a sort of 24-hour branch of government.

Mixing television, politics, and interactive electronics could be a formula for either new public enlightenment or a country run by push-button impulse. It all depends on how the concept is executed.

No doubt, it will run into some opposition. Big Media hates the idea of giving the public too much of a voice because that would diminish its own role as arbiter of opinion. Fully half of registered voters don't even bother to show up to pick their president, press veterans argue. Why would anyone think the public would be interested in, not to mention capable of, wading through complex issues? When the idea was broached on his Sunday morning talk show a while back, David Brinkley's lips crinkled. "What do we do with all the senators and congressmen?" he asked. "Send them home?"

But ask the average person on the street whether he or she can do a better job than the average politician, and the answer will usually be: Hell yes! In fact, Eon Corporation of Reston, Virginia did something of that sort. One of several companies planning a 1994 rollout of interactive TV in major media markets, Eon commissioned a survey of 1,465 random television viewers and found that people are substantially more interested in using two-way TV for political opinion purposes (85 percent) than they are interested in using it for electronic shopping (70 percent) or playing along with game shows (64 percent) or sporting events (42 percent). The public seems to be saying this: We are already deluged with results from opinion polls in which uninformed people are abruptly telephoned and questioned. Why not give us a chance to take part in voting on topics we have taken the time to understand?

Madison and Hamilton might retch at the vision of sofa spuds choosing to ratify or eradicate NAFTA with a click-click of their remote controls or a beep-beep of their touch-tone phones. Our Founding Fathers, in their white wigs, feared that the lower classes would vote to seize their property. So they intentionally created a representative republic, not a full-fledged democracy, to keep power out of the hands of the masses. But others at the Constitutional Convention were notably less paranoid. Thomas Jefferson might find electronic town meetings an absolute scream.

Since those heady days in Philadelphia, the trend has been to expand the power of the people, not limit it. First, non-property holders were given the right to vote, then African Americans, then women, then those between ages 18 and 21. Twenty-three states have amended their constitutions to allow referenda on election ballots. With California leading the pack, citizens now commonly vote directly on a few issues per year. Sometimes, they vote in favor of what may well be harebrained ideas, such as Colorado's 1992 choice to turn back the clock on homosexual rights. But Congress has also passed some clunkers in its day. It's all part of the inherent messiness of democracy.

The notion of a nationwide network for participatory politics goes back to the 1940s, when scientist Buckminster Fuller first proposed voting on the issues of the day via telephone. Psychologist Erich Fromm, in his 1955 book *The Sane Society*, wrote of "a true House of Commons," where citizens would vote on the issues "with the help of the technical devices we have today." In 1982, futurist Alvin Toffler wrote that such a system "would strike a devastating blow at the special interest groups and lobbies who infest most parliaments." Perot, in fact, has been advocating the electronic town hall for twenty years. It's just that no one took him seriously—that is, until public frustration with ineffective government reached a crescendo in 1992.

The main worry among the ETM crowd is that Perot, in popularizing the idea, has also co-opted the concept. When he bought a half-hour of time on ABC last March and asked millions of people to fill out ballots in TV Guide, the information he presented and the way he worded his questions amounted to a form of teletyranny. A typical ballot question was: "Do you feel trade agreements have cost this country jobs?" Ted Becker, an Auburn University political science professor who has been running experiments on ETMs for fifteen years, calls what Perot does "electronic town manipulation." Becker also notes that what President Clinton has been calling ETMs are simply glorified versions of Donahue, as there is no real interaction with viewers. Any legitimate ETM, he believes, must be based on the New England town meetings of yore, when ordinary citizens debated the issues of the day and then voted yea or nay.

What distinguished the San Antonio forum on health care was its form of interactive deliberation. Eight ordinary citizens were selected to appear on a panel, which was moderated by two people from Public Agenda. The panel, and the wider TV audience, reviewed seven options for cutting health care costs, from regulating drug prices to rationing expensive procedures to eliminating fraud and waste. Viewers watched mini-documentaries on each option and then saw the panel debating them.

Of course, this form of ETM has its drawbacks. First, the typical channel-surfer would not find these panelists the most telegenic or articulate folks on the dial. Second, of the 18,000 San Antonio households watching, only 200 were selected to be part of the cross-sectional sample whose votes were tabulated by computers and quickly flashed on the TV screen. All the others could have voted with remote control—or a mail-in newspaper ballot if they didn't have the latest cable gear. But they weren't part of the immediate action.

Still, the experiment yielded some interesting results. As the panel discussion raged on, the group at least seemed to appreciate what a bitch the health care issue is. And many among the voting sample—during the course of the event itself—actually changed their minds on certain options as they learned more about the issues. The first time they were asked, only 27 percent said that hospitals should ration expensive procedures like organ transplants. But by the time all the information was presented, when the same question was asked again, that number had jumped to

43 percent. This suggests that many people are willing to accept limits when they understand the reasons for them. Says Public Agenda's Jean Johnson: "Some of the worst problems in public policy arise when people think there is a cost-free solution."

The ETM in San Antonio represents only one of many models for interactive politics. Electronic bulletin boards on the Internet and other computer networks already allow people to voice political views, take part in electronic polls, even send e-mail to the White House. The Community Service Foundation, a non-profit group in Pipersville, Pennsylvania, has formed the Electronic Congress. Citizens call an 800 number, punch in their ID codes, and register their opinions on national issues. In the city of Reading, Pennsylvania, the locals use video-conferencing and cable call-in shows to debate city, state, and national issues. And under an agreement with Eon, ABC's World News Tonight and Nightline programs have plans to pose instant opinion questions on the day's events to the viewing audience.

Then there's Jeffrey Reiss, the man working with Malone. A former Viacom executive, and co-founder of the Showtime and Lifetime cable networks, Reiss has already drawn up plans for the Democracy Channel. He is now in the process of tapping Malone's Tele-Communications Inc., the world's biggest cable company, for the tens of millions of dollars it will take to get the venture off the ground. The venture will also be partly funded by advertising and membership fees from a new organization in charge of lobbying Congress with poll results from the channel's ETMs.

The very thought of living in an electronic democracy raises fundamental issues. While Reiss and other proponents see it as a way to create consensus, democratize debate, and energize the electorate, the sticky questions remain: Won't it be harder than ever for Congress and the President to stand up for what's right, rather than what's popular? Can voter privacy be maintained, or will marketers get hold of everyone's voting records? Will everyone have access to the latest technology? Will the people really be getting their say, or will the whole process be controlled by moguls like Malone? And perhaps most important, what would happen if votes somehow became binding, rather than just advisory?

Most advocates of ETMs, including Reiss, see the technology as a way to supplement, not supplant, the existing system. Yet, could it be possible that we've simply outgrown our current model of government? In the early days of the republic, each House member represented about 30,000 people. Today, each member represents an unwieldy 575,000 constituents. To better represent the views of all those people, the US Constitution could be amended to place national issues such as gun control on federal election ballots—to be voted on either electronically or in the conventional way. In fact, there was an ill-fated bill to do just that in the late 1970s. The bill, which never made it to a floor vote, specified that an issue could appear on the ballot if 3 percent of the public signed a petition to place it there. It was co-sponsored by 55 members of Congress, including Jack Kemp, who wrote in a 1981 book: "I feel strongly about this reform because I believe it goes to the heart of our national malaise."

One thing most everyone agrees on is this: Democracy in America has always been a living, breathing experiment. And no one knows just where the experiment will lead. Reiss, for one, says, "I would not rule out transforming our government into a direct democracy. Maybe that's where government evolves, when we truly have an enlightened public." How will we know when the public is at last enlightened? That's hard to say. But if the electronic town meetings of the future start pulling better ratings than Roseanne, Seinfeld, or Beavis and Butt-head, watch out!

THINKING AND RE-READING

1. As you re-read this article, consider what Schwartz means by the "inherent messiness of democracy." Think about both the benefits and drawbacks of electronic democracy and try to form your own opinion on the feasibility and the desirability of such an approach. Think also of the effects that an electronic town meeting might have on the people you know, the people in your family, the people in your neighborhood, or your friends.

2. Many individuals who once considered e-mail fun and novel are now being inundated with so many messages that they limit their exposure to online communications. As you read this piece, consider whether this same phenomenon might happen with electronic democracy. If so, what might the results be? How might such effects be ameliorated?

WRITING AND LEARNING

1. Electronic town meetings are not without drawbacks. Choose an issue of local importance to your campus or community. Choose an issue that you are familiar with and that you know quite a bit about. Then imagine an electronic town meeting with individuals representing many of the perspectives on the issue you have chosen. Write a script for a portion of a short presentation at that electronic town meeting. In your script, be sure to represent the perspectives of at least three or four individuals in a substantive way.

2. Write a letter to one of your congressional representatives and let him or her know about your stance on electronic town meetings. Tell your representative the reasons that you have taken this position and present the evidence that has informed your reasoning. If appropriate, urge your representative to take specific action.

3. Write a letter to your central campus computing policy committee (or to another organization on your campus—for example, the student government, the dorm council, the inter-fraternity/sorority council) urging it to consider setting up an electronic campus meeting forum for students. Give reasons why such a forum would be both desirable and useful. Also deal with the issues that would have to be addressed before such a meeting could function effectively to provide students with a useful place to meet, learn, and talk.

Transcript of Vice President Al Gore Jr. in Convention Center, January 13, 1994

ON JANUARY 13, 1994, A HISTORIC MEETING took place: the first electronic town hall in which the vice president of the United States, then Albert Gore Jr., appeared in a real-time, online conference with American citizens.

As we noted, the concept of an "electronic town meeting" had been popularized by Ross Perot during the 1992 presidential election (see "Direct Democracy," by E. Schwartz, in this section). This idea caught the imagination of an American public disenchanted with public policy-makers and politics inside the Washington beltway. Initially, the electronic town hall was perceived as a corrective to political infighting, the influence of lobbyists, governmental gridlock, and a government grown too big to be answerable to its citizens. The electronic town hall offered democratic involvement, a direct line to policy-makers, and a means for demanding accountability among elected officials.

Although the promise was great, in reality, the first electronic town hall was an experiment marred by a lack of experience on the part of its participants, technological glitches, and the limitations of computers. Great ideas often have rocky beginnings, though, and promise is often proven only by time. What are your thoughts regarding the first electronic meeting with the vice president?

Welcome to the live "electronic town meeting" with Vice President Al Gore, hosted by U.S. News Online and CompuServe. I am William F. Allman, a Senior Writer at U.S. News & World Report, and I will be the moderator this afternoon.

Vice President Gore will join us online from his office in the West Wing of the White House in a few minutes; in the meantime, I'd like to make some suggestions as to how to make this historic first appearance of a Vice President in a live, online conference go smoothly. If you would like to ask a question once the conference is underway, please type a slash followed by the word "question" [/question], which will put you in the question queue. When you get the message that it is your turn to ask a question, please begin by telling us where you are from. It is not necessary to state your name, as this appears automatically. You should keep your question as short as possible—only a sentence or so. It also helps to type your question as a series of very short lines—about 65 characters long—followed by carriage returns. This helps others follow along as you type, as well as presenting a readable text. If your question goes on too long, I may have to move on to the next question. For technical reasons, those of you who have entered into GORE2 or GORE3 will not be able to ask questions.

Vice President Gore will be typing his own responses from his office in the White House, and should be online shortly. This conference is also being broadcast live on C-SPAN cable television. Greetings from the West Wing of the White House in Washington, DC, for a live, electronic town meeting with Vice President Al Gore, hosted by U.S. News & World Report and CompuServe. Just as President Franklin D. Roosevelt appeared in one of the world's first television broadcasts at the 1939 World's Fair in New York, it is only fitting that Mr. Gore, one of the key proponents of the coming information superhighway, should be making history by being the first U.S. Vice President to participate in a live, interactive conference on a prototype of that information revolution. I am William F. Allman, a Senior Writer at U.S. News & World Report, a sysop for U.S. News Online, and the moderator this afternoon. I'd like to remind everyone to keep their questions to only a sentence or so, type in short lines (less than 65 characters wide), and to please start your question by telling us where you are from. Vice President Gore will be typing his responses on his computer from his office in the White House. Welcome, Mr. Vice President.

> **#11, Vice President Gore:** Welcome to the White House. Let's get started.

> **#10, Bill Allman/US NEWS:** I'd like to start things off with a question that was submitted in advance to the U.S. News Online Forum.

Moderator recognizes question #1, Dion Douglas (46).

> **#46, Dion Douglas:** Mr VP . . . I am from Hammond IN. What are your views on these "Virtual Communities. . . . and are you currently involved in any networks?

> **#11, Vice President Gore:** I think they are terrific. I do a lot of my work in a virtual community.

> **#46, Dion Douglas:** Thank you. . . . and I am currently watching you on C-span.

> **#140, Vice President Gore:** I'm back. Sorry. Anyway, we have a kind of "virtual community" here in the White House that gets a lot of work done but we have not yet established the myriad links outside that we hope to soon.

Moderator recognizes question #2, Aaron Dickey [HelpF (60).

> **#60, Aaron Dickey [HelpF]:** Mr. Vice-President . . . Huntington, WV here I'm a 23-year-old student. . . . Myself, and most of my friends, are finding ourselves spending more and more time . . . in front our computers than in the "real world". Are you at all worried that eventually we ALL may end up spending too much time iba*iuXE>ytoo (line snoise sorry) on the Net, and not enough time in face-to-face conversations/socialization?

> **#140, Vice President Gore:** Yes. But it's better than the same amount of time . . .

#60, Aaron Dickey [HelpF: (line noise was my father picking up an extension, Mr. VP, sorry <grin>)

#196, Vice President Gore: Sorry. . . . in front of a non-interactive

#60, Aaron Dickey [HelpF: No sir, it was my father, not your fault.

#196, Vice President Gore: Plus . . . soon, the nature of the . . . be enriched with full-motion video and much faster links . . . which I predict will lead to a renewed appetite for REAL communities.

#60, Aaron Dickey [HelpF: (Member? I'm a sysop, Bill. <grin>.) Those are . . . very good points, Mr. Vice-President . . . thanks.

Moderator recognizes question #3, Jacquelyn Close (29).

#29, Jacquelyn Close: Hello from Jackson. Would you establish a single-source repository for all environmental data and lab analyses and make that information accessible through the envisioned information super highway?

#196, Vice President Gore: Great idea. A great deal of that information is already accessible but a single-source is worth exploring. I will raise the idea in our weekly environment idea group here in the White House.

Moderator recognizes question #4, Ricardo Bunge (34).

#34 Ricardo Bunge: Ricardo Bunge from Mobile, AL. Good afternoon, Mr. Vice President, and thank you for this historic opportunity. Where (in society) do you see the Information Super Highway having the greatest impact? Business, science, etc?

#196, Vice President Gore: Schools. Classrooms. At-home learning.

Moderator recognizes question #5, Larry H. Lewis (65).

#65, Larry H. Lewis: Mr. Vice-President. . . . . : -) Alta Loma, Ca. I'm handicapped & spend a lot of time on the net. Do you envision home computer jobs & how will that affect the economy?

#196, Vice President Gore: Yes. In fact you may be interested in knowing that the sysop of the White House Forum, Georgia Griffith, is deaf and blind. There will be MANY opportunities.

#65, Larry H. Lewis: Thank you.

#196, Vice President Gore: for the disabled to use their minds productively on networks. In my home state of Tennessee, in Jackson, there is a wonderful place called the Star Center—and there are others elsewhere—that finds ways to link a person's mind to new ways of communicating, no matter what their disability. In fact, they don't even ask what the disability is. They only ask, "What works?"

#65, Larry H. Lewis: I'm looking forward to that Mr. VP.

Moderator recognizes question #6, Glen Falkenstein (102).

#102, Glen Falkenstein: What do you think is going to end the problem in Bosnia?

#196, Vice President Gore: We (the US) have believed for some time that the Bosnian government forces should not be subject to the international embargo on the arms they need to even the odds. And we have proposed airstrikes to prevent the aggressors from taking advantage of the situation while the arms are delivered. But our allies, whose votes we need in the Security Council, don't agree. We will continue to work for peace, though, in other ways—including maintenance of the toughest sanctions against Serbia in history. And the biggest airlift of humanitarian supplies since the Berlin airlift. And if a real agreement can be reached, we will help enforce it.

Moderator recognizes question #7, Sara Arnold (79).

#79, Sara Arnold: I'm from Burlington, MA. I'm a special needs teenager. . . . My town gives my parents . . . a hard time . . . for funding at a . . . theraputic school. . . . Can the government help kids like me?

#196, Vice President Gore: Yes. By enforcing laws against discrimination. And we will do that. Let us know if we can get involved.

#10, Bill Allman/US NEWS: This question was submitted to the U.S. News Online Forum: "Mr. Vice President: Do you see the NII evolving toward a global II so that Europe could be also hooked to the superhighway? My name is George Nahon and I live in Paris.

#79, Sara Arnold: Thank you, sir.

#10, Bill Allman/US NEWS: France. Merci. Bonne chance!"

#196, Vice President Gore: Yes, at least to an extent. In fact, many nations are already hooked up to the internet. And the demand for higher capacity links on an international basis is of course growing very rapidly.

Moderator recognizes question #8, David Rogers (26).

#26, David Rogers: Mr. Vice President . . . Hello from a Houston, Texas, student. . . What effect will the information highway . . . have on our health care system . . . in our future?

#196, Vice President Gore: It will make it possible to conduct remote and to link patients to the right specialist regardless of geographic location . . . And by making the transfer of large volumes of financial information much cheaper, it will save money. In addition it will make possible a MUCH larger role for patients in diagnosing their own problems and finding the help they need much more easily . . . Of course, we have to add a little for extra eyestrain treatments in a few cases.

Moderator recognizes question #9, Scott Dart (30).

#30, Scott Dart: Hello from Valley Forge, PA. For those of us on the "sidelines" watching the emergence of the "information highway", can you tell us what we can do to participate in the construction? Specifically, and tangibly?

#196, Vice President Gore: If you patronize the excellent services now beginning to be available, you will add your demand to the growing national demand that is inexorably pulling the NII toward early completion. Also, contact your member of Congress and your Senators and urge them to support the administration's bill that I unveiled in L.A.

Moderator recognizes question #10, Ben Huntoon (37).

#37, Ben Huntoon: Hello from Reynoldsburg, Home of the tomato! How will the Federal Government see to the fair and equal implementation of Internet technology among wealthy and poor school districts?

#196, Vice President Gore: Two days ago. President Clinton and I began challenging all of the companies that do business in these industries to make a commitment to link up and provide free access to every classroom in their service areas. And some of them are now pledging to do just that. I think we will have every classroom in the country—and every library—on line in the NII by the start of the year 2000.

#37, Ben Huntoon: Thank you.

#10, Bill Allman/US NEWS): We're about out of time, Mr. Vice President. Would you like to make a closing statement?

#196, Vice President Gore: Thanks. I loved it. I'm just sorry that it is impossible to answer everyone. Let's do it again sometime soon.

#10, Bill Allman/US NEWS: Thank you everyone. Our time is up. Thank you, Mr. Vice President, for participating in this historic event, and thank all of you in our virtual electronic community. A transcript of this conference will be available tomorrow in the ON THE RECORD library section of the U.S. News Online Forum. I invite all of you to join in a post-conference discussion which will begin immediately in the U.S. News Online Forum conference room (GO USNFORUM).

#37, Ben Huntoon: exit.

The conference has ended. Thank you for attending.

THINKING AND RE-READING

1. As you re-read this transcript, catalog the difficulties that participants had with technology. Also note, however, what you believe was productive regarding the conversation between Gore and the other participants.

2. As you re-read this transcript, also consider what information the vice president was able and unable to glean about the participants. In comparing these two kinds of information, what conclusions can you arrive at with regard to the effectiveness of such online conversations?

WRITING AND LEARNING

1. Consider the choice of both the sponsor of this conversation (CompuServe and *U.S. News* Online) and the moderator (William Allman, a senior writer for the *U.S. News & World Report*). In the form of a newspaper review of this historic event, write a short piece

that considers both the possible reasons for and the implications of these choices. Why choose a print journalist to moderate the conversation? Why this particular print journalist? (Hint: to answer this last question, you might have to go to the library and read some of Allman's writing in a few back issues of *U.S. News & World Report*.) Why choose a writer from this particular news magazine? Why would CompuServe host such an event? Why the partnership between CompuServe and *U.S. News* Online? Your purpose in writing this newspaper review is to inform citizens regarding the decisions that influenced the final shape of the electronic town hall meeting.

2. Go to the library and locate two or three sources that explain what a traditional town meeting is (try "New England town meeting" as a search term). Find out the purpose of such meetings, the kinds of participants, the nature of issues that were discussed, the kinds of exchanges that were typical at such meetings, the rules that characterized town meetings, as well as their frequency and the duration. In an informational piece of writing aimed at tenth-grade students who are studying this present-day town meeting, analyze the nature of the online exchanges between the vice president and individual participants. Building on your research, discuss how the online town meeting compares with the conventional town meeting. Compare the participants, issues, rules of conduct, and purpose of the two types of meetings. In each instance, discuss why the similarity or the difference might be due to other influences (e.g., historical context, social factors, available technology, local geographical constraints). Be sure to check your class handbook for the proper format for citing the reference materials that you use and for summarizing, paraphrasing, and quoting.

3. Imagine that leaders in your local community are proposing a ballot referendum in the next election regarding the usage of electronic town meetings: "Should *your city's name* hold regularly scheduled electronic town meetings in which city business is conducted?"

4. Write a statement to deliver in front of the next town council meeting regarding your position on this matter. Present your views on whether you believe electronic town meetings would be a productive idea for your city—try to discuss both the benefits and drawbacks to such meetings. Use your knowledge of the local community as much as possible in writing this statement. Provide reasons and evidence to support your final stance on the referendum issue. If you support having electronic town meetings, discuss what specific format they should take. Also discuss whether electronic town meetings should be a complement to a parallel series of face-to-face meetings or a substitute for them.

IMAGES OF GOVERNMENT AND TECHNOLOGY

THINKING AND RE-READING

1. In Appendix A of this reader, you will find a list of questions that will help you read and understand this set of images and other images that you see in new ways. Read the questions on this list carefully and use them to "read" the images in this section—carefully and with an increasing sense of thoughtfulness.

WRITING AND THINKING

1. Choose at least two of the images to analyze more critically. For these images, write down your answers to the questions listed in Appendix A.

With every reincarnation, we hope to draw closer to Nirvana.

But as each generation grows obsolete and dies, Sikander gets madder:

"How come I keep trashing my hardware every 9 months?"

Don't worry about obsolete technology. Worry about obsolete thinking.

Thinking that designs systems that can't expand, can't be networked to emerging technologies.

Thinking you won't find at IBM.

Instead you'll find interchangeable hard drives in our ThinkPads.® You'll find IBM consultants who consider where you are as well as where you're headed.

You'll find long term, big picture thinking.

And soon you'll find that you're hauling in business, instead of tossing out equipment.

Solutions for a small planet®

513

Frauenkirche
Dresden, Germany

IN DRESDEN, FREEDOM RISES FROM THE RUBBLE. Germany's greatest church, the Frauenkirche, was destroyed during Allied bombing in 1945. Where Bach and Wagner once performed, there now lies only broken rock. But recently, stonemason Franz Huber and a team of other artisans and architects began to painstakingly resurrect the city's symbol of harmony. Once IBM reconstructed the Baroque landmark in 3-D cyberspace, the team could begin to rebuild the ruins. Guiding them is an IBM RS/6000™ running CATIA,™ a computer-aided design tool. By 2006, the church will reach to the heavens once more, thanks to 18th-century craftsmanship and a powerful 21st-century tool. What can IBM help you build? Call 1 800 IBM-3333, ext. G102, or visit us on the World Wide Web at http://www.ibm.com

Solutions for a small planet™

515

Community Networks: Building a New Participatory Medium

Doug Schuler

AS YOU HAVE READ IN OTHER contributions in this collection, a central concern of people who are thinking about the design and implementation of the National Information Infrastructure (NII) and the Global Information Infrastructure (GII) is access: Who will have access to the information superhighway? How much will access cost? Will access be affordable to low-income families? Where will access points for citizens be provided? What services should universal access include?

One answer to these concerns is the concept of community-based free nets: computer-based networks maintained by communities that provide citizens with public access to community services and information at little or no cost. In the following article, Doug Schuler describes the concept of these community networks and explores their potential for increasing civic participation at a number of levels.

This article was published in January 1994 in the *Communications of the ACM*, a journal for the computer specialists who are members of the Association for Computing Machinery (ACM). This particular issue of *Communications of the ACM* focused on some of the social implications of technological issues.

> *I know of no safe depository of the ultimate power of the society but the people themselves, and if we think them not enlightened enough to exercise their control with a wholesome discretion, the remedy is not to take it from them, but to inform their discretion.*
>
> —*Thomas Jefferson*

Communities are distinguished by lively interaction and engagement on issues of mutual concern and the well-being of communities contributes to the well-being of the commonweal. There is a growing view, however, that the strands of community life are unraveling—violence, alcohol and drug use, crime, alienation, degradation of the political process, and ineffectual social institutions are increasingly accepted as inevitable. Computers and communication technology are often touted as saviors of the modern age, but the benefits of the "computer revolution" are unevenly distributed and the lack of access to communication technology contributes to the widening gulf between socioeconomic classes [9].

Some advocates believe that computer technology in concert with other efforts could play a role in rebuilding community life by improving communication, economic opportunity, civic participation, and education. Whether these aims are realized will depend to a large degree on computer professionals, whose experience and expertise make them vital participants in the development of future systems.

Community members and activists all over the world have developed and are developing community-oriented electronic bulletin boards of community networks with a local focus. These community networks, some with user populations in the tens of thousands, are intended to advance social goals such as building community awareness, encouraging involvement in local decision making, or developing economic opportunities in disadvantaged communities. They are intended to provide "one-stop shopping" using community-oriented discussions, question-and-answer forums, electronic access to government employees and information, access to social services, email, and in many cases, Internet access. These networks are also beginning to integrate services and information found on existing electronic bulletin board systems and on other remote systems. The most important aspect of their community networks, however, is their immense potential for participation.

An *ad hoc* alliance of librarians, educators, network and bulletin board systems users, community activists, social service providers, government agencies, and concerned computer professionals is developing around the community network issue. Several distribution lists now exist on the Internet providing active forums on these issues. There are an increasing number of conferences and workshops on these topics, including two influential round tables organized by Richard Civille for Computer Professionals for Social Responsibility and for the Center for Civic Networking. Organizations increasingly are rallying around this issue.

In the "Apple Library of Tomorrow for 1993" call for proposals, Steve Cisler noted, "In 1992 it can honestly be called a movement. In many people's minds the model of a citizens-based, geographically delimited community information system has taken hold"[6]. As of this writing, community networks are planned or are in operation in over 100 locations in the U.S.

A SAMPLING OF COMMUNITY NETWORKS

Several existing systems are briefly presented to illustrate the wide range of motivations, services, and approaches to community networking.

Community Memory—A Virtual People's Park. Community Memory of Berkeley, California (see [14]), was the first community network. Initially started in the mid-1970s as a followup to experiments conducted in 1972 and 1973 on unmediated two-way access to a message database through public computer terminals, Community Memory was conceived as a tool to help strengthen the Berkeley community. Their brochure states that "strong, free, nonhierarchical channels of communication—whether by computer and modem, pen and ink, telephone, or face-to-face—are the front line of reclaiming and revitalizing our communities." Their commitment to serving those without ready access to information technology is demonstrated by numerous training programs and their insistence that all Community Memory terminals be in public places: terminals can be found in libraries and in laundromats but cannot be reached via modem or from the Internet. Community Memory has adopted a creative approach to funding. They offer coin-operated terminals which can be read without charge, but require 25 cents to post an opinion and a dollar to start a new forum.

Community Memory has pushed its principles to their logical limits. Anonymity, for example, is possible because users are not required to use their own names or register to use the system. Perhaps the most noteworthy of their convictions is that all of the information on the system is community generated. This has two important implications. The first is that no central authority of any kind establishes what information is available. The other is that information (such as Internet newsgroups) is not imported from other sites. One of their most noteworthy projects is the "Alameda County War Memorial Project" in which information on every deceased veteran in Alameda County is stored on the system. According to their newsletter, "Friends and family can share their thoughts and reminiscences at the memorial screen of their friend or relative. This unique capability enables the Alameda County Veteran's Memorial to become a growing piece of community history."

Cleveland (and other) Free-Nets—Electronic Infrastructure for the 21st Century City. The Cleveland Free-Net, operating out of Case-Western University, has over 35,000 registered users and over 10,000 logins per day and is probably the largest community network in the world. It originated as "St. Silicon's Hospital and Dispensary" in 1986, in an electronic question-and-answer forum devoted to medical topics. This format still persists and is a major part of the system. Doctors, lawyers, automotive mechanics, and others answer questions on-line. The Free-Nets all use a city metaphor to orient users (Figure 1). One has to go to the appropriate "building" to find the desired information or services. Supreme Court decisions, for example, will be found in the Courthouse building. Free-Nets now exist in Peoria, Illinois; Denver, Colorado; Ottawa, Ontario, Canada; Youngstown, Ohio, and many other locations and are linked into a National Public Telecomputing Network (NPTN) (see "National Public Telecomputing Network" sidebar) which includes national as well as international sites.

Big Sky Telegraph—Western Ingenuity Overcoming Rural Long Distances. Frank Odasz of Western Montana University in Dillon started the Big Sky Telegraph [17] in 1988 by electronically linking one- and two-room school houses across Montana. Now a fully distributed system consisting of "Big Skies" and "Little Skies," Big Sky Telegraph is an "action-oriented rural telecomputing testbed" designed to overcome some of the problems of the rural American western states related to sparse population and long distances between communities. Big Sky Telegraph's approach is to use appropriate technology to demonstrate "low-cost, low-tech, high-imagination, scalable networking models." Education is the key and economic opportunity and self-sufficiency are the goals. Big Sky Telegraph offers 600 K–12 lesson plans and serves as a "telecurricular clearinghouse" for K–12 projects running on networks all over the world. It uses the telegraph metaphor, an approach reflecting the influential communication technology of the last century. As their brochure on "Homesteading the Educational Frontier" states, "Teachers in rural Montana serving as circuit riders, community telegraphers, and teletutors have used modems to overcome time, distance, and economic limitations to empower rural education and community survival through the Big Sky Telegraph network."

WELCOME TO THE...

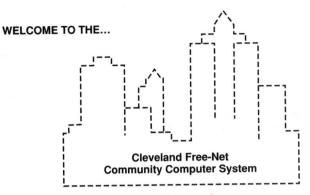

**Cleveland Free-Net
Community Computer System**

brought to you by

Case Western Reserve University
Community Telecomputing Laboratory

<<< CLEVELAND FREE-NET DIRECTORY >>>

1. The Administration Building
2. The Post Office
3. Public Square
4. The Courthouse and Government Center
5. The Arts Building
6. Science and Technology Center
7. The Medical Arts Building
8. The Schoolhouse (Academy One)
9. The Community Center and Recreation Area
10. The Business and Industrial Park
11. The Library
12. University Circle
13. The Teleport
14. The Communications Center
15. NPTN/USA TODAY HEADLINE NEWS

FIGURE 1

Example screen from Cleveland Free-Net utilizing city metaphor
of contents organization

Public Electronic Network (PEN)—A New Urban Polis. The Public Electronic Network (PEN) in Santa Monica, California is a computer system designed to promote community-oriented participatory democracy. Citizens can converse with public officials and civil servants as well as with one another. It was established in 1989 and has over 3,000 registered users and over 500 user logons per month. PEN provides access to local government information, such as city council agendas, reports, public safety tips and the library's on-line catalog, and to local government services, such as obtaining permits. PEN also provides email and conferences on a wide variety of local civic issues. PEN has served as an early test bed for many ideas related to "electronic democracy"and Verley [24] has documented some of the problems that have surfaced using this medium.

Electronic Cafe International—Cultural Explorations with Video Technology. The Electronic Cafe in Santa Monica, California, serves not only food but also live multimedia cultural events with participants at remote sites. Using affordable technology such as slow-scan television over voice-grade telephone lines, Kit Galloway and Sherry Rabinowitz have hosted a multitude of real-time encounters. Most notable perhaps was their 1984 linking of eight family-owned restaurants in the Los Angeles area into a shared video, audio, text, and "sketch" space. This cultural exploration was widely enjoyed by community residents and was a pioneer "groupware" application. Other cafes have been set up at the Telluride IDEAS festival (July 1993) and at CPSR's annual meeting in Seattle (Oct. 1993). The Electronic Cafe's explorations into multimedia, cultural diversity, international communications, and aesthetics serve as excellent reminders of creative opportunities that transcend conventional text and discussion-based approaches.

A Clearinghouse of Information

Assessing the size and scope of the community networking movement is difficult due to the scarcity of data and the rapidly changing situation. This lack of data prevents researchers from adequately investigating the movement and inhibits communication among community network developers. To begin to address these needs I developed a survey and sent it to system administrators and electronic distribution lists (see "Community Network Survey Information" sidebar). Of the over 100 systems that are either operational or planned, completed surveys on over 30 systems (in addition to the survey form and instructions) are available electronically. Each completed survey is dated and developers are encouraged to submit updated surveys when the system changes, so an informal record of system evolution will be available.

From the limited data, some observations can be made. Approximately 63% of the systems are operational with the remainder in the planning or prototype stage. With the exception of the Big Sky Telegraph the systems serve urban or suburban populations and are distributed all over the U.S. and Canada. In the majority of cases (51%) a university is associated with the community network. Libraries have some sort of association with many of the systems (45%). Of the operational community networks the access methods vary: 1 (5%) relies on list servers in which email is sent to the server and is distributed electronically to the list subscribers; 16 (76%) have Internet connections of some kind; 19 (90%) have dial-up connections and two of these, the Boston Peace and Justice Hotline and RTK Net, contain audio information only and a touchtone telephone is the user terminal; finally, Community Memory in Berkeley has public access, dedicated terminals only.

ADDRESSING COMMUNITY NEEDS

Artifacts, being the result of human conscious and subconscious design, necessarily have "politics" that encourage certain attitudes and values and discourage others (see [25]). As with other designed artifacts, input at early stages has stronger and more long-lasting influence on the system than input at later stages. As Winner explains, "Because choices tend to become strongly fixed in material equipment, economic investment, and social habit, the original flexibility vanishes for all practical purposes once the initial commitments are made." He goes on to say that "the same careful attention one would give the rules, roles, and relationships of politics must also be given to such things as the building of highways, the creation of television networks, and the tailoring of seemingly insignificant features on new machines." Community networks are no exception. In fact, the issue of attitudes and values—the politics of community networks—makes participation in community network development important.

The "politics" that are "designed into" community networks must address community needs. In accordance with that philosophy, the Seattle Community Network, "Principles of the Seattle

Community," developed five interrelated needs and summary statements that apply to the community at large as well as smaller communities.

- *Community cohesion.* Communities need to be more cohesive, safer, healthier, and more caring. Opportunities for participation must be developed for all people, and disadvantaged neighborhoods need improved economic opportunity.
- *The informed citizen.* People need and want to be well informed. They need high-quality, timely, and reliable information. They are interested in a wide range of opinions from a wide variety of sources.
- *Access to education and training.* People need training to use technology effectively. They need to be able to learn independently over the course of their lifetimes.
- *Strong democracy.* People need an inclusive, effective, ethical, and enlightened democracy.
- *An effective process.* People need a process by which the preceding needs can be met.

For each need, the Seattle Community Network group generated specific measurable objectives, a procedure for attaining each objective, an evaluation procedure, and a budget. This needs analysis can be used in this way as the basis of specific proposals.

Community Cohesion

Developers must work with community activists and community development organizations to design new services and to support and extend existing services electronically. In Seattle, for example, an "electronic pen-pals" project to promote communication among school children in diverse neighborhoods has been proposed. Participatory Design principles and techniques of strong user participation in design are applicable [23] whether the service is new or an extension.

To truly support community cohesion, access must be universal. The barriers of cost, availability, literacy, and physical disabilities must be bridged. Connecting to community network services must be inexpensive and easy, and use open standards. No-cost or minimal-cost use from the home as well as publicly accessible terminals are required. Potential locations include existing community locations such as libraries, schools, community and senior centers, and parks. Places where people traditionally congregate such as bars, coffeehouses, laundromats, bus stations, and shopping malls are also good candidates. Community network terminals must become as ubiquitous as telephones for use to become a natural, every-day occurrence.

Ray Oldenberg argues in "The Great Good Place" [18] that people need a "third place" away from their home—the "first place"—and away from their place of work—the "second place." Third places are characterized by their location on "neutral ground," a "leveling" tendency where social and economic standings (as well as physical characteristics) of the participants are greatly diminished, and as a place where "conversation is the main activity." Although Oldenberg's "third place" is a physical location such as a coffeehouse or a tavern, many attributes of third places can be applied to community networks [21].

The Informed Citizen

As Paul Resnick and Mel King explain [20], "There is no such thing as a poor community. Even neighborhoods without much money have substantial human resources. Often, however, the human resources are not appreciated or utilized, partly because people do not have information about one another and about what their neighborhood has to offer. For example, a family whose oil heater is broken may go cold for lack of knowledge that someone just down the block knows how to fix it."

Community-oriented "want-ads" could address this need. Other useful information includes calendars of events that are searchable by topic and date; bus schedules and routes; disaster preparation; carpool information; question-and-answer forums conducted by doctors, nurses, lawyers, recycling experts, and automotive mechanics; community maps; and community resources including social services, job banks, and afterschool activities for kids.

Access to Education and Training

Community networks can promote education in structured and unstructured ways. Providing access to community information and network resources helps people pursue their own education. More structured approaches coordinated by professional educators are also possible. Curriculums and network projects can be shared and both students and teachers can participate in forums. Big Sky Telegraph and NPTN's Academy One are involved in many innovative projects. Community networks can also provide a convenient initial access point for training the computer-naive as well as the computer-phobic.

Community networks provide important areas of research but research need not be confined to universities. Community members themselves can propose and conduct meaningful research using Participatory Action Research (PAR) techniques. PAR [11] is an approach to scientific inquiry in which the scientific method is employed to conduct research while simultaneously bringing about desired change, such as improving the quality of political dialogue in a forum. PAR explicitly acknowledges that the dictates of "traditional science" such as repeatability, control variables, and closed-world assumptions are irrelevant in real-world situations involving people [3]. Findings, for example, which are related to current community networks may not be applicable to future systems. Users are full partners in PAR, making it particularly appropriate in the community network context.

Strong Democracy

Signs that the public is interested in pursuing "electronic democracy" include calls for "Electronic Town Meetings," email to President Clinton, and the popularity of radio and television call-in shows. Community networks can increase public participation by improving access to elected officials and agency employees through email and electronic forms [10]. They can also improve access to government information and services and be the home of dozens of community-created forums on local issues. The technology by itself, however, cannot ensure a more strongly democratic culture—thus the policies and processes that we create deserve critical attention.

Voting [13] and other types of democratic participation are practiced infrequently in the U.S. [19]. More disturbing is the common attitude that politics is inherently vile and all politicians are corrupt [19]. This polarization into "us" and "them" undermines democratic potential by discouraging participation. Sad, too, is the evidence that the media that is supposed to help citizens make informed decisions may actually be contributing to degradation of the political process. For example, network television's reliance on "sound bites" (averaging 8.5 seconds in 1992 according to the *New York Times* [Oct. 31, 1992]) trivializes the process. A more serious charge is that of systematic bias. Some critics charge that the media is so structurally biased that democratic "consent" is actually "manufactured" [12]. To counter these discouraging trends, increasing media diversity, citizen participation, and access to communication channels is necessary. It is only then, that the dream of a "strong democracy" [2] marked by the "pleasure of participation" and the "fellowship of civil association" can become realizable.

An Effective Process

As community networks are intended to be developed and maintained by citizens, we must pay special attention to the process that institutionalizes them. The process must guide participation in three major ways: (1) network design and development; (2) the on-line community; and (3) governance.

Networks Design and Development.   The community network organization must develop a shared vision, a shared plan, and a shared voice. It must also establish how work will be organized, assigned, evaluated, and sanctioned. To this end, the SCN Project established five committees—hardware/software, policy, outreach, services, staff and facilities—and a steering committee. Communication approaches that are informative and inclusive are needed to support both internal development and community outreach.

Developing basic documents is another important responsibility. Documents include FAQs (frequently asked questions), statement of purpose, principles, business plan and budget (some examples are available electronically). Other important documents include the policy statement, which addresses a wide range of complex issues including censorship, privacy, dealing with grievances, establishing groups, and other areas and the organization's bylaws, which are legally required and form the basis for system governance over time.

The On-line Community.   Participation in the on-line community can take two forms. Basic participation means participating in forums, including those specifically devoted to discussing the system and how well it meets community needs. Extended use means modifying services, developing new services, or hosting forums.

Network Governance.   Opportunities for participation extend to roles and responsibilities that transcend using the system. These will include (paid) staff roles, board members, advisory board members, and volunteers. Areas of responsibilities include user services such as training and documentation development; system administration, including user accounts and software installation; outreach including publicity, fund-raising, and communication; and executive, including strategic planning, evaluating, and codesigning.

A MODEL FOR COMMUNITY NETWORKS

Community networks that address the preceding needs must be developed within existing social and technological contexts. Pertinent aspects of the contexts of community networks are reflected in a model consisting of two superimposed architectures. The first architecture (Figure 2a) depicts the human context of community networks: how people interact and how social systems (including legal, political, and economic) influence them. The second (Figure 2b) depicts the system's technological infrastructure.

There are five components of the social and political architecture: the on-line community; individual and organizational participants; influencing organizations; the community network organization; and infrastructure providers.

On-line Community.   The group of people who use the community network constitutes the "on-line community." The on-line community is at the center of the social and political architecture—if this element is deficient, the system is deficient. There are three main influences on the on-line

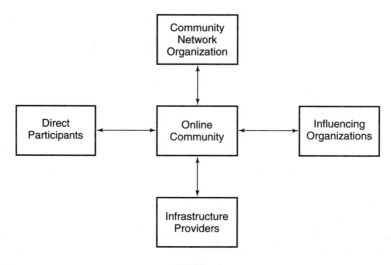

FIGURE 2a

Social and political architecture

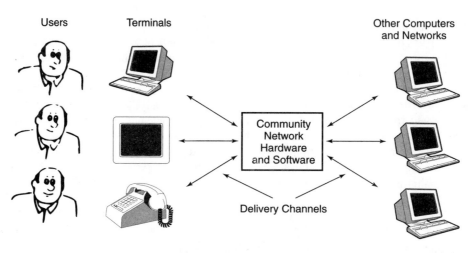

FIGURE 2b

Technological architecture

community: the medium itself—essentially the technical specifications of the system including what information and services are available and the nature of the interaction approach (forums, "chat," or email, for example); the user population or demographics including the number and characteristics of users as well as formal and informal roles assumed by users; and the resulting on-line community or society with its conventions, folkways, interaction patterns, and cast of characters.

John Coate, who worked for the WELL ("Whole Earth 'Lectronic Link") for many years, compares a community network to an inn [7]. While visiting an inn people may talk with people they know or with people they encounter. To Coate, facilitating an on-line community is like "innkeeping"—the innkeeper encourages interchange among patrons but sometimes problems arise and order has to be restored. Much has been written about proper on-line interactions or "netiquette" but Sedgewick's seven rules on the art of conversation may be the most useful.

Participants.   Organizations, such as community associations, or individuals, can provide information or services. Lack of resources or technical expertise may inhibit participation although the promise of increased penetration, reduced communication costs, and the desire to "computerize" their operations may promote participation. Furthermore, organizations that are considering making their information or services available electronically may reduce their costs considerably by not developing an independent system. An existing community network also makes it easier for potential clients by providing a common access point to many services.

Influencing Organizations.   A wide range of organizations influence community network development and coordination. The government's potential for involvement is strongest—it can act as both regulator and supporter. Advocacy groups may include library or educational groups as well as other groups such as NPTN, CPSR, or the Center for Civic Networking. Recently the Corporation for Public Broadcasting has launched an initiative to help develop community networks. Other organizations may offer a competitive influence, including the telephone companies, cable television companies, and various other media and communication companies. These companies are well positioned to address community needs but have not prioritized it.

The Community Network Organization.   The network organization is the primary mechanism ensuring that the community network is functioning well from technical and social points of view. It must see that the five needs previously discussed are being adequately addressed. It must be involved with day-to-day operations, including system maintenance and administration, as well as community outreach, fundraising, and participation in the political process. The organization itself may be a nonprofit organization, a nonprofit/government cooperative venture, a governmental organization, or (if certain guidelines are met) a for-profit organization. The network could also be allied in coalitions, cooperatives, or associations with other organizations. Each of these approaches carries with it a set of values, prerogatives, and methods and with those a set of advantages and disadvantages for participatory community networking.

Infrastructure Providers.   Infrastructure providers including Internet providers, telephone companies, and cable television companies influence individual community networks directly through their rates and policies. Their influence is more global, however, largely due to their strong role in public policy through lobbying and public relations work. The relations between companies of this magnitude have the potential to swamp issues of access and participation on the local level.

Technological Architecture

The technological architecture roughly parallels the social and political architecture. The computer system (including software, CPUs, memory, and interface devices) is at the core of the system, surrounded by different types of users—developers, participants, administrators, information providers, and other on-line information and services—connected through delivery channels and interfaces. The following are among the most relevant aspects:

Hardware.   This may be the least complicated component in the model. The community network computer needs to be an extremely reliable, multiprocessing machine or group of machines whose main role will be gathering input from users, accessing data from disk, and presenting output back to users. The community network computer must also be configured to communicate with a potentially large number of devices. If email and additional storage are offered to participants, disk drives with gigabytes of storage will be required.

Community Network Survey Information

The community network survey contains information on

- Status
- Accessing the system
- Purposes
- Services
- User fees
- Information policy
- System affiliations
- Contacting system developers

Software. A community network at its current state of evolution is essentially a very large electronic bulletin board that ideally can accommodate hundreds of simultaneous users and a user base of tens of thousands. The software services that community networks often provide are forums (moderated and unmoderated); access to static information contained in files; email; download-upload capabilities; chat; remote login; search capabilities; and database facilities. Additionally, a simple menu structure with which to navigate information and services is often used. Furthermore, the systems must easily incorporate new capabilities, such as search engines, multimedia applications, or wide-area information servers, as they become available.

The user interface should be easy to use, consistent, and resistant to user input errors. The requirement that the system be accessible from a wide variety of terminals argues for a simple, text-based interface. The Cleveland Free-Net and other Free-Nets use a city metaphor to organize the contents (Figure 1). Placing the information into "buildings" is straightforward and users generally know where to look to find what they want. One question is how far can or should the metaphor be taken. As the amount of information grows larger, say in the case of legal decisions in the "Legal Center," one might want to divide the buildings into "floors" and the floors into "rooms." As the system grows larger the metaphor *by itself* (i.e., without additional "directories") will fail. Interestingly, the city metaphor offers a degree of user portability: users who are familiar with the city metaphor in their own community network will be comfortable with it in another.

Delivery Channels. The term "delivery channel" is applied loosely to the physical medium plus the protocol plus the interfaces that allow information to pass back and forth between the community network computer and users and other machines. It is important to think of delivery channels in a general sense because the physical substrate, protocols, and policies are currently in a state of flux. For this reason, community network proponents must be active participants in all decisions concerning public uses of delivery channels including voice-grade telephone, fiber optics, ISDN, cable television, or radio transmissions.

National Public Telecomputing Network

Networking the Networks

Following the success of the Free-Net model in Cleveland, Ohio, people from all over the world began to make inquiries about establishing Free-Nets in their cities. Soon there were other Free-Net sites in the Midwestern U.S. The idea that Free-Nets could be established in a number of cities linked into a broader network became institutionalized into NPTN—the National Public Telecomputing Network—under the guidance of Tom Grundner, the originator of the Cleveland Free-Net. NPTN is a nonprofit organization that helps develop free, public-access community systems and helps to integrate them into a common network. NPTN also helps to develop and make available "network-quality" information and services via "cybercasting" to all NPTN affiliates. Currently there are over 20 NPTN affiliates who coordinate operational Free-Nets and over 80 organizing committees that intend to establish Free-Nets in their cities. The NPTN "Blue Book" (16) is an excellent introduction to Free-Nets and describes the vision, the motivation, and the actual tasks involved in building a Free-Net.

The "Academy One" program designed to promote K-12 education using networking technology is an important example of an NPTN service. Academy One events have included "Kid Trek," for young science fiction writers, "Teleolympics" where scores of local athletes are compared with those from other locations using the network, and "Project Common Ground," the purpose of which is "to improve the environment and to foster a student voice in the affairs of their communities."

NEAR-TERM ISSUES AND DECISIONS

The community network movement is currently marked by strong interest and activity. Several issues, however, must be addressed in the short term if community networks will have an effective and long-lived influence. Identifying and addressing these issues are essential to determining what steps—including political action—must be taken to ensure the long-term health and survival of community networks. The following paragraphs offer glimpses of some of these issues.

Funding. Funding is needed for computer and communication equipment as well as office space and office expenses. Funding is also needed for administration, outreach, software development, and maintenance. Volunteers and donated space and equipment cannot meet the need for professional service over the long run. On the other hand, funding for community networks so far has been sporadic and unreliable. Equitable, reliable, and replicable funding approaches from indirect and/or direct participants (Figure 3) must be developed.

Access and Use. Community network developers speculate that community networks in the twenty-first century will become as common as public libraries are now. Currently they are available only in a few locations and accessible to relatively few users. To promote universal use, community networks must be easy to use, easy to access, and free of structural barriers to their use. In addition, the systems must be reliable and responsive, the user interface intuitive and nonintimidating, and special-purpose interfaces must be developed for those with special needs.

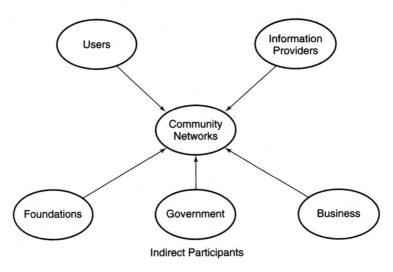

FIGURE 3

Possible funding sources for community networks

While public terminals are critical, penetration into the home is also important. People must be able to easily and inexpensively participate using one or more delivery channels. Telephone, cable television, and radio as well as other approaches are all possible delivery channels and a certain percentage of any spectrum should be reserved for public use. Community networks must also be able to communicate with one another and with other electronic services using high-quality, low-cost technology.

Policy. An information policy must anticipate and address questions and issues such as the following:

- How private is my email?
- Can you ever deny me access to the community network?
- Can I post "adult" material?
- Do I have to use my real name?
- How can I register a complaint against a moderator?
- I'm receiving abusive email. Can you put an end to it?
- I'd like to use the network to advertise my product. Is that OK?
- I have a commercial database service. Can you let people login to it?
- The doctor in your question-and-answer forum gave bad advice. I'm suing you!
- Someone reprinted my posting in a magazine without my permission!
- Somebody on your network posted stolen credit card numbers. We're confiscating your equipment.

These issues and others like them reflect in large part the tension that exists between individual and community rights. They are not unique to community networks whose newness as a medium implies a variety of unresolved issues.

We can begin to devise policies based on other media, but the analogy is often strained. Community networks such as libraries must be champions of free speech. But disagreements in libraries are between library users and contents of books—not between two (or more) library users. Furthermore, libraries do not officially disallow material, but the space limitations on their shelves provide implicit constraints unlike those of cyberspace. Community networks, such as telephones, provide a medium for discourse—discourse that is sometimes acrimonious. Phone calls, however, are fleeting, private, and have few participants. Some "discussions" in public electronic forums are more like fistfights involving potentially large numbers of participants and spectators—and every spectator optionally can record the session which can be disseminated still further.

National Information Infrastructure (NII) and Political Action. The commercial sector is proposing a plethora of innovative programs which, along with their mergers and alliances, have become prominent in national media (see, for example, *Time* magazine cover story on the "Information Superhighway," April 12, 1993). Nearly absent from this coverage is any mention of public-interest, truly interactive, participatory, civic, or community-owned and operated networks. Large computer, telecommunications, and media companies are involved in formal and informal discussions on the future of the NII (in the Commerce Department's Information Infrastructure Task Force, for example), but there is little effort to involve citizens in either education or consultation. Citizens are largely unfamiliar with the issues their tax dollars helped engender and critical decisions may be framed, debated, and resolved without their participation. To redress this oversight the government should convene a series of local and regional meetings *before* critical and potentially irreversible actions are taken.

Encouraging public education and debate at all levels is paramount. This is probably addressed most easily by working with local or national groups and by making your concerns known via individual correspondence and testimony. These groups and others are currently developing vision statements as well as policy recommendations on these issues. The development of free on-line services and information should accompany these efforts. Developing such services benefits community network participants directly while generally strengthening the community network movement. By providing high-quality, free services, commercial information and service providers must increase product value.

DIRECTIONS AND IMPLICATIONS

The world is emerging from a long Cold War that has profoundly influenced the thinking and behavior of its leaders and citizens. To some degree the ending of the Cold War has brought with it an uncertainty of thought and of motivation [5], which prevents us from tackling national and international problems. Addressing current and future needs will require compassion, confidence, and creativity. Here we can only offer glimpses of the issues facing us in the long term.

Universal access and equitable participation must not erode over time. We cannot rely on commercial interests to make the necessary guarantees. The overriding concern of profitability, responsibility to shareholders—not citizens—and a closed decision-making process argue strenuously against it. Furthermore, as Sandra Schickele has demonstrated [22], the requirements of the free-market mechanism are not met in the case of the Internet. She concludes that public subsidy is essential if network resources are to be made widely available. The need for accountability, public participation, and visibility clearly point to some type of public ownership. Increasing the role of government, however, is viewed skeptically by many. Government can be corrupt, beholden to special interests, inefficient, unresponsive, or antagonists to citizen participation and oversight. Lack of funds, technological expertise, and experience further limit government's effectiveness. Nevertheless, community networks in democratic societies must ultimately have a relatively close relationship to government, which *in turn is controlled by citizens. Prescriptions for "reinventing government,"* [19] particularly those involving "community-owned government," "mission-driven government," and "decentralized government," are particularly relevant in considering the role of government.

Consequences for Democracy.   "Electronic democracy" can open new doors for participation, but it is no panacea—and it is not impervious to abuse. Democracy is vulnerable to many threats and "electronic democracy" may be even more vulnerable. Democracy without democratic processes is just a word. New processes will need to be developed (*"Roberts Rules of Order—Revised for Electronic Participation"*) to promote equitable decision making. With many systems, for example, a single individual or group can monopolize a discussion. A powerful group could possibly bombard the community network in a sustained and orchestrated manner designed to overwhelm any opposition. In an even more paranoid scenario, powerful interests could attempt to shut down the entire community network if they objected to certain postings, or moderators.

A Global Community.   A global network is quickly becoming a reality. The Institute for Global Communications, awarded the Norbert Wiener Award by CPSR for its work in developing network technology to empower previously disenfranchised individuals and groups working for progressive change, offers PeaceNet, EcoNet, ConflictNet, LaborNet, and access to several international partner organizations to subscribers in over 70 countries. With truly global networks impending, it is not too early to begin considering the prospects of a global community of communities. NPTN affiliates, for example, already are active in Canada, Mexico, Finland, and Germany. The Community Network Movement should welcome international partners. We should establish "sister networks," hold joint congresses, codevelop electronic services, and generously share information. Reports of the birth of a golden age based on global networking are exaggerated, but any relief from humankind's long history of suffering, death, environmental degradation, and waste that can be promoted through global networking should be welcome.

New technologies including display devices, wireless, multimedia, and the like, coupled with new applications and modes of interacting such as MUDs [8] and conversational email [4], have strong implications for usability, service providing, and participatory democracy. Technical innovations should be introduced into community networks when they will increase the ability to meet user needs. Adopting new technology, however, will necessarily introduce some unfamiliarity or resistance. This translates into disruptions in the user community as prior conventions and patterns of interactions will require modification. Being cognizant of these implications will help alert network developers to the need for training, user preparation, usability testing, and participatory design.

The incorporation of new technology should not dilute universal access. Low-cost text-based terminals must not, for example, be made obsolete with the introduction of new graphics technology. The solution probably will require multiple user interfaces, resulting in an "interface gap" but not sacrificing the basic level of universal access.

Principles of the Seattle Community Network

The Seattle Community Network (SCN) is a free public-access computer network for exchanging and accessing information. Beyond that, however, it is a service conceived for community empowerment. Our principles are a series of commitments to help guide the ongoing development and management of the system for both the organizers and participating individuals and organizations.

Commitment to Access

- Access to the SCN will be free.
- We will provide access to all groups of people, particularly those without ready access to information technology.
- We will provide access to people with diverse needs. This may include special-purpose interfaces.
- We will make the SCN accessible from public places.

Commitment to Service

- The SCN will offer reliable and responsive service.
- We will provide information that is timely and useful to the community.
- We will provide access to databases and other services.

Commitment to Democracy

- The SCN will promote participation in government and public dialogue.
- The community will be actively involved in the ongoing development of the SCN.
- We will place high value on freedom of speech and expression and on the free exchange of ideas.
- We will make every effort to ensure privacy of the system users.
- We will support democratic use of electronic technology.

Commitment to the World Community

- In addition to serving the local community, we will become part of the regional, national, and international community.
- We will build a system that can serve as a model for other communities.

Commitment to the Future

- We will continue to evolve and improve the SCN.
- We will explore the use of innovative applications such as electronic town halls for community governance, or electronic encyclopedias for enhanced access to information.
- We will work with information providers and with groups involved in similar projects using other media.
- We will solicit feedback on the technology as it is used, and make it as accessible and humane as possible.

Control of Technology. We—in a collective sense—do have some control over technology and its effects on us. We attempt to affect the influence and direction of technology through its physical design and through policies surrounding its use. The idea of "controlling" community networks, however, makes little sense. An iterative process of imagining, discussing, prescribing, monitoring, and evaluating is more in line with our aspirations, our limitations, and our habits.

CONCLUSION

The community network movement with its great potential for renewed participation in community life is rapidly gaining momentum. While the potential is significant, the realization of this potential will depend on active, compassionate, creative, and persistent participation of computer professionals and others in technical, social, and political roles. With your help community networks will play a part in a revitalized, richer, and more inclusive future.

ACKNOWLEDGMENTS

I would like to thank Ray Allis, Alan Borning, Steve Cisler, Richard Civille, Andrew Clement, Carl Farrington, Miles Fidelman, Stephanie Fowler, Dave Levinger, Doug McLaren, Todd Newman, Helen Nissenbaum, Andy Oram, Evelyn Pine, David Tallan, and Terry Winograd for their helpful suggestions. I also want to thank the volunteers of the Seattle Community Network.

The articles in this special section were inspired by CPSR's Directions and Implications of Advanced Computing (DIAC) symposia. Also thanks to CPSR for pushing the discussion of computing implications into the public sphere and to Rachelle Hollander in the Ethics and Values Studies office at the NSF for support of previous DIAC symposiums. I also would like to thank all the authors and reviewers of these articles.

REFERENCES

1. Bagdikian, B. *The Media Monopoly.* Beacon Press, Boston, Mass., 1992.
2. Barber, B. *Strong Democracy.* University of California Press, Berkeley, Calif., 1984.
3. Baskerville, R., and Wood-Harper, T. A critical perspective on action research as a method for information systems research. Tech. Rep., State University of New York, Binghamton, N.Y.
4. Borenstein, N. Computational mail as network infrastructure for computer-supported cooperative work. In *Proceedings of 1992 ACM Conference on Computer-Supported Cooperative Work* (Toronto, Canada).
5. Chapman, G. The National Forum on Science and Technology goals: Building a democratic post-Cold War science and technology policy. *Commun. ACM 37,* 1 (Jan. 1994).
6. Cisler, S. Apple Library of Tomorrow Proposal, Apple Computer Corporation, Cupertino, Calif., 1992.
7. Coate, J. Innkeeping in Cyberspace. In *Proceedings of Directions and Implications of Advanced Computing (DIAC-92) Symposium* (Berkeley, Calif., May 2–3, 1992).
8. Curtis, P. MUDDING: Social phenomena in text-based virtual reality. In *Proceedings of Directions and Implications of Advanced Computing (DIAC-92) Symposium* (Berkeley, Calif., May 2–3, 1992).
9. Doctor, R. The National Information Infrastructure—Social Equity Considerations. To be published.
10. Elgin, D. Conscious democracy through electronic town meetings. *Whole Earth Review* (Summer 1991).
11. Foote, W. *Participatory Action Research.* Sage Publications, Beverly Hills, Calif., 1991.
12. Herman, E., and Chomsky, N. *Manufacturing Consent—The Political Economy of the Mass Media.* Pantheon, New York, N.Y., 1988.
13. Levine, M., et al. *The State and Democracy: Revitalizing America's Government.* Routledge, New York, 1988.

14. Levy, S. *Hackers: Heroes of the Computer Revolution.* Dell, New York, 1984.
15. National Public Telecomputing Network, videotape. If it plays in Peoria ... National Public Telecomputing Network, Moreland Hills, Ohio, 1991.
16. National Public Telecomputing Network. A Guide to the Development of Free-Net Community Computer Systems. National Public Telecomputing Network, Moreland Hills, Ohio, 1993.
17. Odanz, F. Big Sky Telegraph. *Whole Earth Review* (Summer 1991).
18. Oldenberg, R. *The Great Good Place.* Paragon House, New York, 1989.
19. Osborne, D., and Gaebler, T. *Reinventing Government.* Plume, New York, 1993.
20. Resnick, P., and King, M. The rainbow pages—Building community with voice technology. In *Proceedings of Directions and Implications of Advanced Computing (DIAC-90) Symposium* (Boston, Mass., July 28, 1990).
21. Rheingold, H. The great equalizer. *Whole Earth Review* (Summer 1991).
22. Schickele, S. The economic case for public subsidy of the Internet. Distributed at the *Public Access to the Internet Conference.*
23. Schuler, D., and Namioka, A., Eds. *Participatory Design: Principles and Practice.* Erlbaum, Hillsdale, N.J., 1993.
24. Verley, P. What's really happening in Santa Monica? *BCS Impact!* (Dec. 1992).
25. Winner, I., *The Whale and the Reactor—A Search for Limits in an Age of High Technology.* University of Chicago Press, Chicago, Ill., 1986.

CR Categories and Subject Descriptors: H.3.4. [Information Storage and Retrieval]: Systems and Software—*Information networks;* H.4.3 [Information Systems Applications]: Communications Applications—*Bulletin boards;* K.8.1 [Personal Computing]: Application Packages—*data communications*

General Terms: Human Factors

Additional Key Words and Phrases: Bulletin board services, community networks

THINKING AND RE-READING

1. As you re-read this piece, think about the access you currently have to the various functions of your local city or county government (e.g., city council meetings, social services, public libraries, public transportation, fire protection, garbage collection, as well as water and sewer services) and how these interactions might change should a community network be set up in your area.

2. The networks described in this article are relatively low cost, but they are not free. As you re-read this piece, think about who should bear the cost of community networks. Should they be funded through increased taxes? If so, what kinds of taxes should be used (e.g., sales taxes, real estate taxes, school taxes)? Should the networks be funded entirely by those who choose to use them? By school systems? By businesses and local services?

WRITING AND LEARNING

1. Write a brief two or three page proposal for a community network in your local area aimed at an audience of city council members. Provide a brief rationale for the network. Describe the organization of such a network, what exactly it would include, how

citizens would have access to it, and how it should be funded. Include, as well, cautions for this network—concerns about access, maintenance, cost, technical assistance, and so on. If you have access to the Internet, you may want to do a bit of research by studying some of the community networks listed in this article before you begin this response.

2. As Schuler points out, "While the potential is significant, the realization of this potential will depend on active, compassionate, creative, and persistent participation of computer professionals and others in technical, social, and political roles." To sharpen your own critical analysis skills, write a response that identifies the difficulties that a community network would face in your city. Make your list as complete as possible and explain why each difficulty might arise.

3. Read the principles of the Seattle Community Network. Draft a revised statement of principles for your own community that might provide vision for a community network. Aim this document at a general audience of users that would possibly benefit from such a service—you might imagine it as part of a brochure on a community network that you have been hired to design and publicize. In this response, also identify the bases on which your principles are founded. As part of the information in this document, describe how the principles in establishing this network differ from or are similar to those informing other community networks that you have read about.

Talk Is Cheap

Peter Huber

Universal Service *Does* Matter

Rob Glaser

THE GOVERNMENT REPRESENTATIVES, the technology critics, and the citizen groups involved in the design of the NII agree on at least one key tenet: universal access to the net. But what, exactly, does *universal access* mean? The two short pieces that follow explore this concept—discussing what universal access and service mean, what technologies are required to ensure such access and services, what barriers currently exist to universal access, and what specific services should be included in basic-access packages.

Both of these pieces are examples of popular journalism on the subject of technology, but they are aimed at very different audiences. Peter Huber's article, "Talk Is Cheap," was published in *Forbes*—a magazine for professionals in the financial and the business community. Technology, for many of these readers, can be perceived as a challenge, both fiscal and social. Rob Glaser's article, "Universal Service *Does* Matter," was published in *Wired* magazine in January 1995. *Wired* is aimed at an informed generation of readers (generally, from the baby boomers forward) who are committed to and comfortable with technology. To many of these readers, technology is a desirable and necessary part of life.

In the endless debate about the information highway, one issue dominates all others: universal service. No politician can talk about telecom policy without first endorsing "equal access." What does that mean? Probably that cable and phone companies deploying upgraded networks will be required to serve some consumers at prices below cost, and to extend wires to

places where other technologies (like satellite, perhaps) would make more sense. It hardly seems to matter that the little red hen has only just begun growing the wheat; politicians seem determined to slice up the loaf now.

The inclusionary emphasis isn't all bad. Networks are inherently collectivist: A broader reach benefits everyone. With that said, policymakers should face some hard facts about poverty and communication in America today. A recent, pathbreaking study of telephone service conducted by San Francisco-based Field Research Corp. is a good place to start.

Already today, with no superhighway in sight, a telephone line is more than some poor households can manage. The reason is simple: A dial tone is an open line of credit. Grandma may be prudent, but her grandchildren barge in and run up long distance bills, so she has to cancel her service. The best thing society can give in such circumstances is not subsidy but help with self-discipline—maybe a service that just doesn't allow more than a dollar a day in outgoing calls.

Second, understand that most poor people are already buying more than basic, "lifeline" local service. The Bell breakup triggered a $10 billion reallocation of charges from long distance toll to local subscription rates. Yet the percentage of households with telephones grew from 91.4% in 1983 to 94.2% in 1991. For the poorest fifth of the population, penetration increased from 80.1% to 83.7%. How come? The poor make long distance phone calls, too. Local rates rose a bit, but long distance rates fell even more. It doesn't help the poor to subsidize the hamburger a nickel by way of a six-cent tax on the sesame-seed bun.

Third, study markets, not metaphors. A highway has as many lanes coming as going, so by analogy every living room, rich and poor, needs 50 megabits per second (or whatever figure we latch onto) outbound as well as inbound. That vision sharply skews the choice of technology. The favored medium for providing symmetric, two-way broadband is glass. And glassing all of America immediately would be very expensive, for the poor and the middle class, too.

But the highway analogy is all wrong, for reasons rooted in basic economics. Solid things obey immutable laws of conservation—what goes south on the highway must go back north, or you end up with a mountain of cars in Miami. By the same token, production and consumption must balance. The average Joe can consume only as much wheat as the average Jane can grow.

Information is completely different. It can be replicated at almost no cost—so every individual can (in theory) consume society's entire output. Rich and poor alike, we all run information deficits. We all take in more than we put out. Networks have to be built accordingly.

The markets have already grasped this, even if the metaphor makers haven't. Smart people are putting their money in asymmetric technologies, with far more bandwidth coming than going. Use direct broadcast satellite, say, to provide tons of capacity down, and then close the loop by telephone or something else narrow going back. Put glass in the backbone, then bundle some coaxial cable and copper side-by-side at the end. Graft asymmetric broadband onto the telephone network itself. Segment the market. A bank and an insurance company don't need the same lines as a library or a home; a hospital needs something different again. Workplaces obviously need capacious outbound channels, just as factories need loading docks. Schools need far more bandwidth in than out.

This sets the stage for the last and most fundamental problem—the paradox of haves and have-nots.

A single mom parked in front of a cabled television swallows a Niagara of bits with every episode of *Beavis and Butt-head*. She is the poorer for it. A cyber-nerd on Internet uses tiny amounts of bandwidth by comparison, for such things as sending E-mail or transferring a file to the office.

Telecommuters manage today with channels a thousand times less capacious than the ones used for television. They need less because they are producing new bits, not just consuming old ones.

The poor, then, are already consuming more bandwidth than the rich. The have-nots inhale low-grade information like greasy hamburgers. The haves thrive on smarter salad. TV-induced stupefaction, like obesity, is a disease of poverty, not wealth. It's unclear how any government policy in a free society can do very much about that.

This much, however, should be clear. With information, one size doesn't fit all. If promoting universal service means pretending that it does, we are going to waste a ton of money, and probably do more harm than good. Politically crazy though the thought may be, the poor would probably be better off if someone shut down all those dozens of inbound, broadband channels from Hollywood. If we're going to subsidize anything at all, it should probably be just a few more plain, narrow-band links to workplaces and schools. The last thing most poor homes need right now is another hundred lanes of television.

> "When I gave food to the poor, they called me a saint. When I asked why the poor were hungry, they called me a Communist."
> —Dom Helder Camara, Brazilian Roman Catholic archbishop, author, and Nobel Peace Prize nominee

Not because you're a bleeding heart, but because you're selfish.

One of the surest ways to get labeled a communist in cyberspace is to merely raise the question of universal service. To many, the idea of universal service—that ubiquitous access in and of itself is a worthy public policy goal—is inextricably linked to an archaic, centralized, paternalistic, and discredited approach to government. Some, such as John Browning—who championed his ideas in *Wired* 2.09—would like to proclaim the concept dead, and be done with it.

But, like apple pie, baseball, and bombast in Oliver Stone movies, universal service is a fundamental part of America, and is not going to go away any time soon. Moreover, it shouldn't. There are good reasons—both selfish and high-minded—why we should try to achieve an effective form of universal service for the infobahn.

The monopoly on local telephone service is being broken up, haltingly but inevitably, and this in turn will break the method by which *nearly* universal phone service has been financed. Rigid, centralized attempts to achieve universal service for *any* future communications infrastructure just won't work in the brave new world of competitive, decentralized broadband networks.

So, fine—let's not be centralized. But let's not throw out the baby with the bath water. The basic reason that universal service has been an important goal of telecom policy since the 1930s is that Americans want the American experience to be inclusive and broadly participatory. Inclusiveness is important for both personal and community reasons, for the same reasons we have public schools and a federally funded interstate highway system.

We all benefit from the legacy of our interstate highway system, which provided money to pave roads in New York and North Dakota alike. Consider what would have happened if we had not established a national highway policy after World War II. Instead, let's say we just licensed right of ways to entrepreneurs, as was done in the 1980s with cellular telephony. We would have gotten some kind of interstate highway system, built by entrepreneurs. Granted, maybe it would have been built for less money. But the pricing and national coverage of this highway system would have resembled today's cellular telephone network. Certain parts of the country, such as the northeast megalopolis, would have developed four-lane roads fairly quickly. Other regional roadways, such as the I-5 corridor linking Seattle to Los Angeles, would have developed organically as well. But less well-trafficked areas would probably have been served by gravel roads for many years.

The biggest problem with locking in on a universal-access plan is that nobody knows what the essence of the infobahn will be. Fiber-optic cable to everyone's home? Specific applications such as video-on-demand or interactive home shopping? Even if we did know, which infobahn services would we consider truly essential? Basic e-mail? The multimedia successor to plain old telephone service? Anyone, including government officials, who deigned to "know" the answer today to any of these questions would be exhibiting only arrogance.

The best practical step we can take now is to broaden the range of trials being undertaken. For instance, why not persuade US West and Time Warner that, in exchange for receiving regulatory approval for video-on-demand trials in places like Omaha, Nebraska, and the wealthy suburbs of Orlando, Florida, they should help subsidize nonprofit efforts to run trials in rural Nebraska and in Harlem. I'd bet that some foundations would kick in a few bucks, too. Such trials—combined with the continued organic growth of freenets, library-access programs, and other community-based projects—would generate meaningful information on which infobahn applications are essential to all Americans, and hence ought to eventually become the focus of universal-service programs.

While none of us knows exactly what services will develop over the nascent broadband network, I'd bet that nearly all *Wired* readers will agree that the infobahn will not be an ancillary service, but will be central to how Americans work, learn, and communicate. It is precisely because of this centrality that we need to talk about universal service—what it should be, what it should not be, and how we can achieve it. For without a thoughtful universal-service policy, cyberspace could well end up as alien and cost-prohibitive to the general public as venturing out of town was during the reign of medieval highway robbers.

THINKING AND RE-READING

1. As you re-read these pieces, think about what the terms "universal access" and "universal service" mean to you. What do the terms mean to Huber and Glaser?

2. While re-reading, think about why "universal access" is such a prime focus in current discussions concerning the design of the NII and the GII. Why are we so worried about this concept? Is our concern justified? Why or why not?

WRITING AND LEARNING

1. What is your definition of "universal access" or "universal service"? What is Glaser's definition? Huber's definition? In a two-page handout, summarize these definitions and explain them to a class of gifted twelfth-grade students taking a summer class on technology and social issues. In your written document, point out both the similarities and the differences between these definitions. Be sure to study your handbook for the correct format for quoting, paraphrasing, and summarizing for this work.

2. In a written letter of response to the editors of *Forbes*—using quotes, paraphrases, and summarized material—consider the picture that Peter Huber paints of "poor people." What characteristics does he attribute to these families? What characteristics does he assume they do not have? How does he portray them? Why? How does this portrait compare with your own personal knowledge of people in such circumstances? Is this portrait accurate or inaccurate? Useful or not useful?

3. To sharpen your own skills in historical scholarship, social research, and journalism, go to the library and look up two or three historical references that cover the early days of public telephone service in this country. In reading this material, focus on those social issues associated with the development of our country's public telephone system—especially those issues now being discussed in connection with the NII (e.g., access, service, cost, technology, government regulation and involvement). Choose two or three of these issues to focus on and state how the public discussion of these matters over the years has remained the same and, conversely, how it has changed. Describe these issues and the findings from your research in an informative feature article for your local newspaper. To get a sense of the feature article as a genre (as opposed, for instance, to news articles or editorials), you should read several examples of feature articles in the newspaper or consult a journalism textbook.

The Bill of Rights
and Responsibilities
for Electronic Learners

AS WE HAVE POINTED OUT in a number of other articles in this collection, citizen groups are becoming increasingly involved in formulating scientific and technology policies, contributing their thinking to the design and implementation of the NII, and voicing their opinions on the needs of citizens in an increasingly electronic age.

EDUCOM, one such organization, is a nonprofit consortium of representatives from institutions of higher education who have invested in the use of technology. One EDUCOM committee took on the task of developing a Bill of Rights and Responsibilities for Electronic Learners. This contribution represents their work; it was published in the *Educom Review* in the summer of 1993.

Before you read this piece, re-read the original Bill of Rights for the American Constitution in Appendix D. As you read the "Bill of Rights and Responsibilities for Electronic Learners," think about the similarities and the differences between the two documents and the reasons that these might exist. Think in terms of historical context, purpose, audience, information, and so on.

The seeds for a Bill of Rights and Responsibilities for Electronic Learners were sown in 1989, in a project to analyze the impact of the National Research and Educational Network (NREN) on our society. The project team labored for some time trying to meld concepts of intellectual property with those of education, the idea of free society with that of controlling knowledge. Although no one on the project was a lawyer, discussion was consistently framed in legal jargon, describing the problem as one of legal rights under intellectual property law. A breakthrough came when the team realized it was going about the analysis backward. Instead of grappling with the question of what was possible and valuable, we were posing the issues in terms of what should be protected and how.

The fruits of these early efforts were presented in a report to the U.S. Congress Office of Technology Assessment titled "A Bill of Rights for Electronic

Citizens." Its main focus was that initial concerns ought to be on values as related to technology (i.e., which of the things society values can be facilitated through technology), and only later should we consider how to use controls (e.g., laws) to help us achieve the things we valued. From these insights the present project springs forth. The goal of this project is to articulate the values and the fundamental rights that accompany them.

Although individual privacy rights receive the most attention in the media, many other issues related to digitized information directly affect the quality of life in electronic communities. The Bill of Rights, which amends the U.S. Constitution, addressed the tension between the rights of individual citizens and the powers of a strong, central government. The challenge in our interconnected and digitized educational community is to find the right balance between protecting individual rights and fostering the creation and sharing of ideas and knowledge in a market-oriented, free society. Just as the original Bill of Rights recognized the existence of individual rights, it also recognized their limits and the responsibilities that came with them—so, too, in our educational communities, electronic or otherwise. This document (and the work that produced it) is an attempt to change the culture of our educational community by extending its traditional values into the new circumstances and relationships that result from information technology.

This bill is presented as a work in progress. It has been drafted by members of the higher education community and proposes to represent the perspective of educators at all levels (K–life). Assuming that such a narrowly drawn group could accurately represent the views, ideas, and intents of the broader population of educators is, indeed, presumptuous. This stance was taken not to exclude those involved in other aspects of education, but rather to complete a draft statement in a timely manner, recognizing that others would be sought out to critique our efforts and would help hammer out and write the next version.

We intend the Bill of Rights and Responsibilities for Electronic Learners to be used as a model that other electronic communities can use to draft similar statements. Even as we develop our model, we are establishing a national board to oversee the development of similar statements for other communities. We intend to urge that the collected statements be the basis for a broad national effort to develop a comprehensive Bill of Rights for Electronic Citizens. As is true with the EDUCOM Code, we expect the end product to be widely distributed, referred to, and used as a guide by organizations and individuals as they develop policy and personnel statements.

PREAMBLE

In order to protect the rights and recognize the responsibilities of individuals and institutions, we the members of the educational community propose this Bill of Rights and Responsibilities for Electronic Learners. These principles are based on a recognition that the electronic community is a complex subsystem founded on the values espoused by the educational community. As new technology modifies the system and further empowers individuals, new values and responsibilities will change this culture. As technology assumes an integral role in education and lifelong learning, technological empowerment of individuals and organizations becomes a requirement and right for students, faculty, staff, and institutions, bringing with it new levels of responsibility that individuals and institutions have to themselves and to other members of the educational community.

ARTICLES

Article I: Individual Rights

The original Bill of Rights explicitly recognized that all individuals have certain fundamental rights as members of the national community. In the same way, the citizens of the electronic community of learners have fundamental rights that empower them.

Section 1. A citizen's access to computing and information resources is a right. Access to computing or information resources shall not be denied or removed without just cause.

Section 2. The right to access includes the right to appropriate training and the tools required to effect access.

Section 3. All citizens shall have the right to be informed about personal information that is being and has been collected about them, the right to review and correct that information, and the right to control the distribution of that information beyond the expressed purpose of its collection.

Section 4. The constitutional right to freedom of speech applies to citizens of electronic communities just as it does to citizens of other communities.

Section 5. All citizens of the electronic community of learners have ownership rights over their own intellectual works.

Article II: Individual Responsibilities

Just as certain rights are given to each citizen of the electronic community of learners, each citizen is held accountable for his or her actions. The interplay of rights and responsibilities within each individual and within the community engenders the trust and intellectual freedom that form the heart of our society. This trust and freedom are grounded on each person's developing the skills necessary to be an active and contributing citizen of the electronic community. These skills include an awareness and knowledge about information technology and the uses of information and an understanding of the roles in the electronic community of learners.

Section 1. It shall be each citizen's personal responsibility to actively pursue needed resources: to recognize when information is needed, and to be able to find, evaluate, and effectively use information.

Section 2. It shall be each citizen's personal responsibility to recognize (attribute) and honor the intellectual property of others.

Section 3. Since the electronic community of learners is based upon the integrity of all information, it shall be each citizen's personal responsibility to be aware of the potential for and possible effects of manipulating electronic information: to understand the fungible nature of electronic information; and to verify the integrity and completeness of information that he or she compiles or uses.

Section 4. Each citizen, as a member of the electronic community of learners, is responsible to all other citizens in that community: to respect and value the rights of privacy for all; to recognize and respect the diversity of the population and opinion in the community; to behave ethically; and to comply with legal restrictions regarding the use of information resources.

Section 5. Each citizen, as a member of the electronic community of learners, is responsible to the community as a whole to understand what information technology resources are available, to remember that the members of the community share them, and to refrain from all acts that waste or prevent others from using these resources.

Article III: Rights of Educational Institutions

Educational institutions have legal standing similar to that of individuals. Our society depends upon educational institutions to educate our citizens and advance the development of knowledge. However, in order to survive, educational institutions must attract financial and human resources. Therefore, society must grant these institutions the rights to the electronic resources and information necessary to accomplish their goals.

Section 1. Educational institutions' access to computing resources and information is a right rather than a privilege. Access to computing resources and information shall not be denied or removed without just cause.

Section 2. Educational institutions in the electronic community of learners have ownership rights over the intellectual works they create.

Section 3. Educational institutions have the right to allocate resources in line with their unique institutional missions.

Article IV: Institutional Responsibilities

Just as certain rights are ensured to educational institutions in the electronic community of learners, so too each is held accountable for the appropriate exercise of those rights to foster the values of society and to carry out each institution's mission. This interplay of rights and responsibilities within the community fosters the creation and maintenance of an environment wherein trust and intellectual freedom are the foundation for individual and institutional growth and success.

Section 1. The institutional members of the electronic community of learners have a responsibility to provide all members of their community with legally acquired computer resources (hardware, software, networks, databases, etc.) in all instances when access to or use of the resources is an integral part of active participation in the electronic community of learners.

Section 2. Institutions have a responsibility to develop, implement, and maintain security procedures sufficient to ensure the integrity of individual and institutional files.

Section 3. The institution shall treat electronically stored information as confidential. The institution shall treat all personal files as confidential, examining or disclosing the contents only when authorized by the owner of the information, approved by the appropriate institutional official, or required by local, state, or federal law.

Section 4. Institutions in the electronic community of learners shall train and support faculty, staff, and students to use information technology effectively. Training includes skills necessary to use the resources, knowledge of the existence of data repositories and techniques for using them, and an understanding of the ethical and legal uses of and responsibility for the resources.

THINKING AND RE-READING

1. As you re-read this piece, think about what the authors mean by the word "learner." How do you define the term? How would your family define it?

2. Upon re-reading, think about what the committee means by a "right." A "responsibility." To whom are these terms meant to apply? Whom do they leave out? Why?

3. This document talks about the rights and responsibilities of both individuals and institutions. As you re-read this piece, think of how these rights and responsibilities will be assured, paid for, and protected. What kinds of infrastructures are needed for these tasks?

WRITING AND LEARNING

1. To sharpen your powers of critical reading and presentation, sketch out the important similarities and differences that you perceive between the original Bill of Rights attached to the United States Constitution (Appendix D) and the Bill of Rights and Responsibilities for Electronic Learners. In a written handout of no more than three pages, identify these key similarities and differences and state why you think they are important. Your audience for this assignment is a group of eleventh-grade students who have recently read both documents. Your essay should help them focus on the relationship between the two.

2. In the introduction to the article, the co-chairs of the EDUCOM committee, Frank Connolly and Sally Webster, note that the main focus of the bill ought to be on those beliefs that our society values that can be facilitated through technology. Write a letter to the U.S. Congress, Office of Technology Assessment (the government office to which this bill was presented) stating why you believe this bill should be adopted as is or revised. In your letter, identify the societal values that the bill expresses—are they your values? The values of your friends? Of students you know? Of your family? Of American citizens in general? Why or why not?

3. Choose your three favorite sections in the Bill of Rights and Responsibilities for Electronic Learners—those sections you consider most important to your life and to your relationship with technology. In a written response, relate why these three sections are so important to you. Your audience for this assignment is yourself; your purpose is to connect this reading to your own life.

When Words Are the Best Weapon

Russell Watson

"WHAT GOVERNMENTS SHOULD REALLY FEAR is a communications expert," Subcomandante Marcos, chief spokesperson for the Zapatista rebels in the Mexican state of Chiapas, notes in this next article. And what might be most dangerous of all is a writer who has the support of technology that can speed up communication and distribute information on a worldwide basis.

The following article describes how communications technologies are being used by minority political groups, dissidents, and repressed populations—as well as by authoritarian regimes, government agencies, and military groups—to accomplish their ends. As Watson points out, communication technologies that are not centrally controlled by a government are now "almost impossible to police or control" and have, as a result, been used to great effect by political groups seeking a broader audience.

This article, written by Russell Watson, was published in *Newsweek* on February 27, 1995 in a special issue on technology. As you are able to tell from the level of specificity and detail, the lack of technical terminology, and the article's tone, *Newsweek* is written for a general audience.

Here's how to wage a revolution in the Information Age: two weeks ago Mexican government troops lunged into the rain forests of Chiapas state in renewed pursuit of the Zapatista rebels. When the federal soldiers reached an insurgent stronghold at Guadalupe Tepeyac, the guerrillas melted into the jungle, leaving behind a few trucks but taking with them their most valuable equipment—fax machines and laptop computers. In retreat, the Zapatistas faxed out a communiqué claiming that the army was "killing children, beating and raping women . . . and bombing us." Soon the government was taking another public-relations beating. It stopped the offensive and allowed reporters into the area. They found no signs of atrocities or bombing. But the government attack had been thwarted, and the rebels were free to fight on, with words as their best weapons.

The Zapatistas' chief spokesman, Subcomandante Marcos (the government says his name is Rafael Guillén), knows that he will never obtain political power from the barrel of a gun. "What governments should really fear," he told a NEWSWEEK reporter last summer, "is a communications expert." Information technology has always been seen as a potentially revolutionary weapon. Almost as soon as the printing press was invented, governments and churches tried to control it, and the Ottoman Empire shunned the technology for almost 300 years. The American Revolution was spurred on by Benjamin Franklin, a printer; Thomas Paine, a pamphleteer; and Samuel Adams, a propagandist. In the modern era, vulnerable governments have been challenged by proliferating means of communication. Long-distance telephone service, for example, helped to undermine the Soviet Union, connecting dissidents to each other and to supporters outside the country. Other Communist regimes have been weakened by radio and television signals: West German programs beamed into East Germany, and broadcasts from Hong Kong feeding the appetite for reform in mainland China.

Violent revolutions, especially those that resort to terrorism, often have the most success with relatively low-tech weapons. But like the Zapatistas, many of today's revolutionaries are better talkers than fighters, accomplishing little or nothing on the battlefield. "These new insurgencies, in the end, are aimed more at high-intensity lobbying and low-intensity fighting," says William LeoGrande of the American University in Washington, an expert on leftist movements. Now they have the tools they need. Older communications technology, such as radio and television, is centralized and subject to government control, if only through the assignment of frequencies and the jamming of unauthorized signals. The latest gear, such as satellite television receivers or computers linked to the Internet, is decentralized, diffused and—so far—almost impossible to police or control.

The Internet is the fastest-growing communication tool, with as many as 30 million subscribers in 92 countries. Even Chinese dissidents are beginning to use e-mail. News about the fight against Chinese repression in Tibet is regularly gathered and circulated by the London-based Tibet Information Network, one of dozens of human-rights organizations using the Information Superhighway. In the Soviet Union, the Internet played a small but vital role in defeating the attempted coup by Communist hard-liners in 1991. Soviet computer scientists had hooked up to the Internet only a few months before. When Boris Yeltsin and his reformists holed up in the White House, the Russian republic's Parliament, someone inside the building started sending bulletins, including Yeltsin's edicts, on the Internet. They were picked up by the Voice of America (VOA), which broadcast them back to the Soviet Union by radio, helping to rally public support for Yeltsin.

Since then, the VOA has made a big investment in the Internet. It now offers computer users written news reports in 47 languages and audio bulletins in 16. Access is obtained through two of the Internet's standard communications protocols: Internet Gopher and FTP (File Transfer Protocol). Those aren't the most advanced access gates, but that's precisely why the VOA chose them; more users overseas are likely to have them. The VOA currently logs about 100,000 uses of its Internet service each week. That's minuscule compared with the 92 million weekly VOA radio listeners. But Christopher Kern, the VOA's director of computer services, says the Internet has "wonderful demographics"; users are educated and influential. They also seem to have sensitive political antennae. Recently, when Washington and Beijing got into a nasty dispute over trade, no one in China logged on to the VOA Internet for an entire week. The next week, with the trade issue under negotiation, they came back online.

On a much more modest scale, the Internet also has become a platform for the Zapatistas. One of the services offering information about the movement is run from Mexico City by Barbara Pillsbury, a 24-year-old American who works for a development organization. She transmits bulletins about the Zapatistas and communiqués from Subcomandante Marcos to subscribers around the world. (Her Internet address: pueblo@laneta.apc.org.) She says interest in the Zapatistas helped introduce many Mexicans to cyberspace. "Beyond their concerns about Chiapas," says Pillsbury, "Mexicans have realized that they need to be part of this technology."

Satellite TV is much easier to use, given the proper dish-shaped antenna and decoding equipment. The technology has become popular in many countries where the native TV menu is limited. There are thought to be more than 150,000 dishes in Saudi Arabia, pulling in programming as varied as CNN, Italian game shows, soft pornography from Turkey, sitcoms from Israel and religious fulminations from Iran, the kingdom's archenemy. China, where dishes are institutionally owned, would seem to be at the opposite end of the scale as a market for satellite TV. But four months ago the VOA began beaming a weekly hour of TV news in Mandarin Chinese from the AsiaSat, which has a good broadcast "footprint" over the mainland. Is anyone watching? The VOA doesn't know yet. "We shot an arrow in the air," says Kern.

Authoritarian governments of all political persuasions would like to shoot down satellite TV. Jamming is much more difficult than with radio, which uses a narrower and more vulnerable bandwidth. A more productive approach is to outlaw the dish antennas. The conservative Saudi government banned them last year, threatening a fine of $130,000 on anyone who continues to use them. Fundamentalist Iran outlawed the dishes last month. The mullahs who rule Iran have been fighting a rear-guard action against communications technology ever since they took power in 1979. Previously they tried—and failed—to suppress videocassettes and camcorders.

The irony is that Ayatollah Ruhollah Khomeini and his followers overthrew the Shah of Iran by using even more primitive communications technology. While Khomeini was still exiled in Paris, his calls to rebel against the shah were disseminated throughout Iran on tape cassettes. Any means of communication can be an instrument of revolution, as long as it's in fairly widespread use. For years, Iraqi dictator Saddam Hussein banned private ownership of typewriters. He remembered the subversive power of the mimeograph machine when he was an ambitious young rebel plotting his own takeover.

The most tightly closed societies, such as North Korea, and the most violently repressive ones, such as Iraq or Libya, may not be susceptible to an Information Age revolution. In North Korea, shortwave radios are unavailable, even to the few who could afford them. Fax machines, privately owned computers and satellite TV are unheard-of. Partly to constrict the flow of information, travel is severely limited, within the country as well as outside it; even bicycles were banned until about three years ago. Iraq and Libya have considerably more open societies, but their regimes remain in power through the most ruthless terror tactics, killing off opponents, real or imagined, and utterly intimidating the rest of the population, which in any case has little access to outside information.

Even in less rigid dictatorships, communications technology cannot make a revolution by itself. The Soviet Union was done in by its own economic failures and a ruinous arms race, not by long-distance phone calls or foreign radio broadcasts. In Iran, the conditions for revolution were created by the shah's brutal repression and his breakneck modernization program, which outraged Muslim tradition. But the flow of information helps to undermine such regimes, and the faster it flows, the more trouble they're in. Few states can afford to opt out of the Information Age; they have to keep up with at least some of the latest scientific, technical and commercial developments. "We have a kind of knowledge market going on which is, in a way, impervious to the efforts of states to control it," says Paul Wilkinson, professor of international relations at the University of St. Andrews in Britain. If dictatorships want to play any part in the modern world, they have to risk exposing themselves to ideas and information that could inspire reform or spark a revolution.

THINKING AND RE-READING

1. As you re-read this piece, consider the role that the circulation of information plays in establishing, maintaining, and changing political relationships within and among countries. Who controls information within a country? How is information controlled? At what sources? At what levels? In what ways? How do individuals subvert a government's control of information?

2. Generally, we think of our country as a place where information is freely exchanged, where censorship does not flourish, and where the government does not exert strict control over the exchange and production of information. As you re-read, test these areas of common sense against your understanding of how our own government works—do they hold true or can you think of ways in which information is controlled and limited by our national government? By the military? By the major media? By educational systems? By libraries?

WRITING AND LEARNING

1. In a letter to the editors of *Newsweek,* convey your thoughts, generally, with respect to this article and, more specifically, regarding the comment made by Subcomandante Marcos, chief spokesperson for the Zapatista rebels in the Mexican state of Chiapas—

"What governments should really fear is a communications expert." Do you agree or disagree? Why? What experiences have you (or those you know) had that have helped you formulate your position on this issue? What have you learned from studying history or reading about current events that convinces you?

2. Go to the campus library and ask the librarian for help in finding a list of works that have been banned by the U.S. government during the last decade. Also locate two or three articles that focus on the government's banning of literary works. If you have access to the Internet and are a member of several worldwide discussion lists, write an electronic post that asks people for examples of works that have been banned over the last decade in their country. Using the information that you receive, write a summary handout (no more than three pages) about this form of government control over information for tenth-grade students who are studying censorship. Among the questions to answer are the following: Why do governments ban books? How long do such bans typically last? What is the real effect of government bans on books? What stance do you think the government should take in connection with banning? Why? Be sure to check your handbook for the correct format for citations, quotes, paraphrases, and summaries.

3. To sharpen your own powers of critical observation and thinking, go to the library and get a copy of your local newspaper (or a copy of a major daily newspaper from a large city in your home state). Also, get a copy of a major daily newspaper from a large city in an English-speaking country outside the United States. In a written response, compare the news stories (ignore the features, editorials, and ads for this assignment) in the two papers. Among the questions you might answer are the following: What kinds of news stories are covered? What types of stories are not covered? Why? What are the datelines for the stories (in the city and country in which they were written)? What kinds of stories never make it into your local paper or the large-city paper in your home state? Why? Your purpose in this assignment is to think systematically and critically about the news coverage that you have access to on a daily basis. Your audience is yourself.

4. Choose an organization to which you belong or with which you are familiar. For this organization, write a brief guide concerning how to use communication technologies for low-cost publicity projects—both publicity projects that go to the organization's members and those that go to the broader public. In this guide, list the various communication technologies available to the organization, and identify the benefits and drawbacks of each in terms of publicity efforts (e.g., cost, distribution, access, audience). List as many kinds of communication technologies as you can. For this document your audience is the members of the organization who will be directly involved in publicity efforts in the future.

Making Every Vote Count

Erik Nilsson

ONE OF THE BENEFITS OF TRAVELING and making friends with people from other countries is the perspective you gain on your own life, on the customs of your own culture, as well as on the situation in your own nation. The article that follows may also help in this regard, because the author—Erik Nilsson—offers a fascinating glimpse of life in South Africa, a country with a rich history, courageous people, active political struggles, and changing social structures. This article helps to illuminate the complex relationship that computer technology has with social situations, political movements, the lives of individuals, and the nature of social interaction. As you read this contribution, think of how your life (and the lives of your friends and family) are both similar and dissimilar to the lives of the people about whom you read.

This article was published in December 1994 in *Wired*. This magazine, aimed at an informed readership of computer enthusiasts, frequently focuses on the global issues associated with technology use.

There wasn't enough time. Not just for building the computer systems, but for everything. The schedule was insane. It was as if we were trying to build a nationwide banking system in six weeks, in a huge, politically unstable country where terrorist bombings are routine. Open 9,000 branch offices all on the same day, run for four days, and then shut down—without losing anybody's money.

Our task, in April 1994, was to help South Africa prepare for its first multiracial elections. The enormous responsibility of these elections would rest with the Independent Electoral Commission, where I would work on computer systems. As a software jockey from the US, and a member of Computer Professionals for Social Responsibility (CPSR), I would be loaned to the South African Commission from the CPSR Computers and Elections project, which assists the US Federal Election commission with voting equipment standards, analyzes elections, and gives advice on election security. Fellow CPSR member Bob Wilcox and I have been running the project for seven years.

In March, I got a phone call from the International Foundation for Electoral Systems, which sends technical and other experts to "difficult" elections, often in the Third World. Were we interested in helping with software for the South African elections? Of course we were—how could we turn down the opportunity to work on the election of the century?

The challenge would be daunting. The South African electorate, newly swelled with the enfranchisement of the huge black majority, was estimated at 25 million, but there was no census to show where they lived. How would we tell people where to vote if we didn't even know where they were? How would we make sure we sent out enough ballots and election workers if we could only guess how many people would show up at the polls? Just directing voters and workers to polling places was difficult with addresses as makeshift as the facilities themselves. (One polling site was officially called "the tent behind Bob's house.") Ballot boxes, polling equipment, entire counting stations, and millions of ballots had to be deployed in a country that encompassed sprawling urban leviathans as well as outposts a day's drive from a telephone. Worse, the elections had only been announced five months earlier. What would normally take a year to complete had to be done in 20 days.

To keep track of these mammoth, frenzied, and changing circumstances, South Africa would need massive databases to follow people, places, and equipment. And massive databases to record protests, incidents of violence, and the election results themselves. Software was needed to manage these databases, enter new information, and produce reports. The task would have been impossible without computers, but even with the technology we could still only hope we'd bought enough time. A common South African expression—"The wheels come off it," meaning something has become a fiasco—seemed to preface far too many conversations around the commission.

I arrived at Jan Smuts airport 20 days before counting started and drove to Johannesburg. April is autumn in South Africa—the rainy season is over, and the weather is pleasant. Like a street hustler, Jo'berg is friendly, threadbare, and menacing. The center of South Africa's mining region, Jo'berg is called the "City of Gold" because its modern, graceful towers were bought with precious ores from beneath the surrounding plateau. But depressed gold prices, a drought, and sanctions have taken their toll. The wealthy white suburbs are tidy and peaceful, but the city itself is run-down and dangerous. The streets reek of garbage and urine. Muggings are common after dark.

I didn't have much time to worry about Jo'berg's decline, however. After I checked into the hotel, I went over to the Independent Electoral Commission headquarters to get started. That's where I would work every day for the next 25 days, an average of 16 hours each, scattered around the clock in an irregular blur. I didn't go through jet lag, I just went to work.

The commission, headquartered in a 10-story building five blocks from our hotel, was a caricature of a busy office building. People were charging around and shouting at each other 24 hours a day. A constant stream of new faces and equipment poured into every office. People shared desks. People shared chairs. The phones were always ringing, the faxes faxing, the elevators jammed, and the air heavy with air-conditioned sweat. The commission didn't hum, it roared—sometimes painfully loud.

Applications were being written and deployed daily, if not hourly, including systems to track 200,000 elections employees, 9,000 polling locations, warehouses full of equipment, and the voting results themselves. Because I was one of the few software people with elections experience, I was quickly assigned to design the vote tabulation system.

This was no small task. In recent white-only elections, the results from the entire country had been produced on a Lotus spreadsheet. But with the black majority swelling the number of voters from about 2 million to 25 million people, this election wasn't a spreadsheet problem. Voting was to take place over three days, from April 26 through 28 and was later extended a day. On the evening of the last day, the polls would close, and all the ballot boxes would be trucked to counting centers to be tallied.

There were roughly 1,000 counting centers. As each batch of ballots was counted, a tally sheet would be filled out, showing the votes for each party. This sheet would then be faxed to the commission. We expected an average of 25 batches from each center, which meant 25,000 tally sheets. It would have taken a month and a half, day and night, to fax these tally sheets on one fax machine. Fortunately, we had dozens at the commission dedicated to receiving the forms.

The tabulation system processed these faxes and entered them into the database. Another program then totaled the results per party and passed these results to a transmission program that sent them to the world's news media. As the count progressed hour by hour, new election results would appear on millions of TV screens minutes after we had received them.

All of these programs for tabulation were written by a small software group inside the Election Administration Directorate. It was the dawn patrol of software. Beside me, there were two other Americans: forms whiz Mario Tejada and Michael Yard: ex-minister, ex-flower child, expert in databases. The South Africans included Etienne Posthumus, a 22-year-old software wonder boy. We worked elbow-to-elbow on laptops set up on rickety, folding metal tables. Power failures sometimes left us working by the light of our screens. A foxhole wouldn't have been a bit more intimate.

We dressed as we pleased, worked the weirdest hours in the building, and survived on Brazilian coffee, Coke, and strange candy bars. I'm not sure how much confidence a bunch of caffeine- and sugar-hyped hackers in dirty jeans inspired, but nobody gave us trouble. Maybe they were afraid to ask.

With 13 days until the count, we of the dawn patrol had designed a software architecture and a paper flow for tabulation. We built databases tracking parties and results. The databases for voting and counting centers should have been complete, but new centers had to be added as huge new chunks of population were uncovered and as prospective centers were bombed or burned down.

"It's a quiet day," a commissioner told me, his dry Scandinavian humor belying the grave situation. "Only one [commission] office was bombed today."

Eleven days before the count, and only a week before voting started, the commission was awash in rumors that the Inkatha Freedom Party, the Zulu political party of some two million voters, would now be participating in the elections. Around 10 A.M. on April 19, I was told to be ready for an unspecified "additional party." By 1 P.M., I got the official word: Inkatha *was* in. Now there were 19 parties in the national election. The problem was, however, that the ballots had 18 parties printed on them; tally forms for counting all the ballots had 18 boxes; computer input screens for these forms had 18 fields; and—you guessed it—electronic records for transmitting results to the news media were built for 18 parties.

The ballots—larger than this magazine page with full four-color pictures of each party's flag and leader beside its box—had been printed weeks earlier in England. It was too late to reprint these elaborate sheets, so a sticker with the Inkatha flag and a picture of the Zulu party leader, Chief Mangosuthu Gatsha Buthelezi, would be affixed. It was also too late to reprint all the thousands of tally forms, so Inkatha's name would be added by hand. The computer screens and the electronic transmission form could be fixed, but it took time, and the software had to have the parties in the same order as the paper forms. Except now we didn't know what those tally sheets would look like. I talked to Lisa Thornton, who was coordinating work on Inkatha. She was meeting with the commission at 5 P.M. to figure out how to get tens of millions of stickers printed and distributed in a matter of days. She'd try to get me answers after the meeting, but she couldn't promise anything. There was so much to do.

"Less than the amount of work emergency-room doctors and nurses and undertakers would have to do otherwise," I said.

"Yes, of course," she said. "This is good news, but—"

"How much more good news can we stand?"

Now, almost the entire political spectrum was participating in the elections; it was all the more important that the elections be credible. It was like living on camera. Billions of people would watch every gesture, every line of code. The whole election funneled through our work. It was as if I were working in a sandwich shop, and God walked in and said, "The fate of 40 million people depends on the salami submarine I'm ordering, and hold the onions." Everything was doable, but the stakes were high enough to be unreal.

Late that night, there was a thunderstorm. I got to the hotel just ahead of the rain, and wrote input routines on my laptop in the dark, watching the lightning. The rain washed away much of Jo'berg's grime and reek. By now I was pacing myself, working only 14-hour days. I would need my strength when counting started.

The next day we completed the data structures, and I got an input system running that expected 19 parties.

With a week left, Bob and I took a rare evening off (which is to say we quit at about 9 P.M.) and went to a party. We returned very late, and I stayed up to do a little work. Consequently, I was sleeping in the hotel the next morning when a white man reportedly left a car containing about 200 pounds of plastic explosives on Bree Street, a block away. The explosion rocked the hotel and wounded 100, killing nine. It was the largest car bomb in South African history.

I immediately thought the bomb might have been targeting the commission—sabotaging it would have delayed the elections and probably started a civil war—but when I called the offices there, Mario answered the phone. I went to a window and looked down on the destruction. A cloud of smoke rose languidly from the bomb site. A water main was broken, carrying the red soil away, resembling a river of blood. There were shattered windows on all sides, and the storefronts were destroyed. The roof on one building had collapsed. Bob and I went out to investigate. It was at once calm and threatening, like being inside the barrel of a gun. Twisted cars were strewn about like neglected toys. Nothing remained of the bomb car.

> I'm not sure how much confidence a bunch of caffeine- and sugar-hyped hackers in dirty jeans inspired, but nobody gave us trouble.

That night, I was wakened by another bomb directly outside the hotel. The hotel was full of foreigners, mostly election observers, and someone was trying to scare us off. I felt like a sleeping target.

Four days before the count, the old South Africa vanished when, at midnight, officials lowered its flag at the Parliament building in Pretoria and hoisted a colorful new one: black, green, gold, blue, red, and white, incorporating the colors from every South African political party.

Voting started the next day. Counting wouldn't start until all voting was finished, in four days, but, feeling this was the last opportunity for violence to derail the elections, everyone was edgy. The authorities ran extra patrols of bomb-sniffing dogs through the commission, and most of us went home early, although I didn't feel much safer in the hotel.

By counting day, everything was ready to go, despite some last minute database changes demanded by our supervisor. About 11 P.M., the first results trickled in.

By 1 A.M., we were reporting a million votes cast. But that struck me as too few—the results weren't being reported fast enough, so I was called upstairs to report on progress. Because of the database changes, we were reporting only half our results to the South African press. The other half couldn't be reported until a tricky program called the Summarizer, which totaled the votes for each party and cross-checked the totals, was fixed to account for the database changes. We were sitting on close to a million votes that weren't being reported to the world. I agreed to have this fixed by 2:30 A.M.

I went back downstairs to a scene of total chaos. Not only did we have a nasty software fix ahead of us, but now the server was refusing connections, so only about a dozen of the 24 data entry stations were working. Faxed tally sheets from the counting centers—hundreds of thousands of votes—were piling up, and the world was waiting. The whole election was inside that server, and if it was sick we could lose everything if we touched it. It was a pretty scary situation, but I decided we'd have to reboot it anyway. We got it down at about 2 A.M.

> It was as if God had walked into a restaurant saying, "The fate of 40 million people depends on this salami submarine. Hold the onions."

Geva Patz was working on the server. He found a hardware fault, pulled the offending unit, and managed to get the server back up in 15 minutes. All the data entry stations worked flawlessly. Neil Cawse fixed the Summarizer in a shade over 15 minutes. There had been no data feed to the media for half an hour, and they would start to scream any minute. We turned the live data feed to the world back on. If any of the sleep-deprived programmers working on the Summarizer had made a mistake, it would show up on millions of TV screens in a few minutes, probably as drastically wrong results. We went over to the transmitting computer and held our breath as we watched the vote totals. Through bleary eyes, we saw reasonable numbers of votes scrolling across the screen. I stayed until Mario and Etienne showed up mid-morning.

Two days later, with results from all over the country showing them getting close to two-thirds of the vote, the African National Congress declared victory. Several of us from the commission crashed the victory party, which was across the street at the Carlton Hotel. Only a month earlier, people had been hacked to death here by machete-wielding rioters. That night, Jo'berg had emptied its population onto the streets, and both the commission and the Carlton were surrounded by a sea of exuberant black faces. I waded in, carrying four paper South African flags—of black, green, gold, blue, red, and white.

As I rounded the corner of the hotel, a middle-aged woman wearing a scarf was thrown against me by the crowd. She saw my flags, looked at me excitedly, and asked, "May I have one?"

I obliged without hesitation, aware of the irony: it was her country, but I was handing out the flags.

THINKING AND RE-READING

1. As you re-read this piece, think about what you know of the continuing political situation in South Africa. Take some time to go to your library and read related newspaper stories from the past five years on this subject. What is the political situation in this country? How is this situation being addressed at this particular time? What are the political issues involved? How are these issues related to economic issues? Issues of race? Issues of political freedom? Issues of foreign affairs?

2. This piece illustrates the folly of thinking that technology manufactured and designed in or for one culture can simply be imported into another culture—without changes, without complications, and without considering the cultural context. As you re-read this piece, think of reasons why this might be true. How are cultural values designed into computers? Why? What specific cultural values are designed into computers manufactured in the United States? Why?

3. As you re-read the narrative of "Making Every Vote Count," trace the plot line in terms of well-known stories that you are familiar with—the cowboy western, the super-hero adventure, and the high-tech science fiction thriller. Who are the heroes in this story? Who are the villains? How does the hero save the day? Who is the trusty sidekick? Who is in trouble? Who is generous? Who is needy? What are the weapons of choice? It may help you to know that Erik Nilsson coordinates the Computers and Elections project for the Computer Professionals for Social Responsibility (CPSR).

WRITING AND LEARNING

1. Some people think of computer technology as an artifact of a culture, an artifact that has designed into it all the values of the particular culture in which it is developed and utilized. For example, because American manufacturers had such an early and continuing influence on the design and manufacture of personal computers during the 1980s and 1990s, these machines are characterized by the many features determined and valued by our culture. Among these features are a default primary interface that relies on English; an exchange standard called the American Standard Code for Information Interchange (ASCII), which does not adequately represent a number of global languages; and a physical makeup and appearance that use materials, colors, and design features determined by American consumer preferences (e.g., plastics readily available in this country, keyboards designed for

twenty-six letters; neutral colors; icons familiar to American users; and power sources designed for Western electric current). In a written response, consider the implications of this concept within the context of the Nilsson article. Pretend that you are a member of a technology team sent to South Africa to prepare the technical infrastructure for the upcoming election. Write a letter home to the chair of the Computer Science Department in your college or university. Describe some of the social and cultural effects that you have observed technology having within the South African culture. In what sense are these effects positive? In what sense are they problematic? Why? What sorts of adjustments and changes do the people in South Africa have to make in order to use imported technology? Why? What necessary changes are warranted by the American technology specialists to work effectively in South Africa? In light of your answers to these questions, discuss what subjects computer scientists should study in the course of their university education.

2. The story that Erik Nilsson recounts in "Making Every Vote Count" has mythical proportions and storylike qualities. It has the same plot features, for example, of a traditional western cowboy movie—although not the same setting, characters, or action. In fact, this might be why American readers find this piece so appealing. Write a letter of response to Erik Nilsson with the purpose of pointing out this fact and its implications to him. In the letter, discuss the similarities that you see between Nilsson's narrative and the narrative plot of a traditional western. In your letter, state how this plot and narrative might be read or interpreted by a black person from South Africa.

3. Go to the library and do a bit of research on the everyday lives of blacks and "Coloreds" when apartheid prevailed in South Africa. Find at least two or three substantive articles that explain the restrictions that such people lived under, the extent to which their lives were controlled by government regulations, as well as the nature of the violence and poverty that characterized black homelands.

4. Write a two or three page summary handout of your findings for twelfth-grade students studying the system of apartheid in a world history class. Imagine that these students have also read this piece by Erik Nilsson. Use the first one or two pages of this handout to describe the system of apartheid. For the remaining pages, speculate on how a black South African might view computer technology, his or her relation to computer technology, and the relative importance of this technology in re-building an open South Africa. Be sure to check your handbook for the correct format for citing these articles and for paraphrasing, quoting, and summarizing material contained in them.

In the Penal Colony

Franz Kafka

IN FICTION, WE SOMETIMES FIND a metaphorical representation of reality that forces us to pay attention to what is going on around us. In "In the Penal Colony," you'll learn about a mechanism, an "apparatus" of torture that inscribes a motto relative to crime onto the body of criminals. You'll also learn about the officers and the administrators who permit this torture to happen, the government that relies on this technology, and the reasoning of citizens who allow such torture to go on.

Kafka meant his writing to be metaphorical in a larger social sense. When you read this story, think about the computer as another form of "apparatus." What messages might this apparatus of the computer be writing on the body of our culture? What is the relationship between the apparatus of the computer and the government of our country? Are we aware of the changes that computers are writing into our society?

Kafka, born on July 3, 1883 of German parents working in Prague, is famous for both his short stories and novels. His work deals with human beings' responses to the challenges posed by the modern industrial world, focusing on themes of alienation, religious judgment, guilt, the influence of governmental authority on individual lives, and technologies of control invented by humans to control other humans. Kafka, a Jew, lived through the First World War and died in 1924. His sister was later to die in 1942 at the concentration camp referred to as Auschwitz.

"It's a remarkable piece of apparatus," said the officer to the explorer and surveyed with a certain air of admiration the apparatus which was after all quite familiar to him. The explorer seemed to have accepted merely out of politeness the Commandant's invitation to witness the execution of a soldier condemned to death for disobedience and insulting behavior to a superior. Nor did the colony itself betray much interest in this execution. At least, in the small sandy valley, a deep hollow surrounded on all sides by naked crags, there was no one present save the officer, the explorer, the condemned man, who was a stupid-looking wide-mouthed creature with bewildered hair and face, and the soldier who held the heavy chain controlling the small chains locked on the prisoner's ankles, wrists and neck chains which were themselves attached to each other by communicating links. In any case, the condemned man looked so like a submissive dog that one might have thought he could be left to run free on the surrounding hills and would only need to be whistled for when the execution was due to begin.

The explorer did not much care about the apparatus and walked up and down behind the prisoner with almost visible indifference while the officer made the last adjustments, now creeping beneath the structure, which was bedded deep in the earth, now climbing a ladder to inspect its upper parts. These were tasks that might well have been left to a mechanic, but the officer performed them with great zeal, whether because he was a devoted admirer of the apparatus or because of other reasons the work could be entrusted to no one else. "Ready now!" he called at last and climbed down from the ladder. He looked uncommonly limp, breathed with his mouth wide open and had tucked two fine ladies' handkerchiefs under the collar of his uniform. "These uniforms are too heavy for the tropics, surely," said the explorer, instead of making some inquiry about the apparatus, as the officer had expected. "Of course," said the officer, washing his oily and greasy hands in a bucket of water that stood ready, "but they mean home to us; we don't want to forget about home. Now just have a look at this machine," he added at once, simultaneously drying his hands on a towel and indicating the apparatus. "Up till now a few things still had to be set by hand, but from this moment it works all by itself." The explorer nodded and followed him. The officer, anxious to secure himself against all contingencies, said: "Things sometimes go wrong, of course; I hope that nothing goes wrong today, but we have to allow for the possibility. The machinery should go on working continuously for twelve hours. But if anything does go wrong it will only be some small matter that can be set right at once."

"Won't you take a seat?" he asked finally, drawing a cane chair out from among a heap of them and offering it to the explorer, who could not refuse it. He was now sitting at the edge of a pit, into which he glanced for a fleeting moment. It was not very deep. On one side of the pit the excavated soil had been piled up in a rampart, on the other side of it stood the apparatus. "I don't know," said the officer, "if the Commandant has already explained this apparatus to you." The explorer waved one hand vaguely; the officer asked for nothing better, since now he could explain the apparatus himself. "This apparatus," he said, taking hold of a crank handle and leaning against it, "was invented by our former Commandant. I assisted at the very earliest experiments and had a share in all the work until its completion. But the credit of inventing it belongs to him alone. Have you ever heard of our former Commandant? No? Well, it isn't saying too much if I tell you that the organization of the whole penal colony is his work. We who were his friends knew even before he died that the organization of the colony was so perfect that his successor, even with a thousand new schemes in his head, would find it impossible to alter anything, at least for many years to come. And our prophecy has come true; the new Commandant has had to acknowledge its truth. A pity you never met the old Commandant!—But," the officer interrupted himself, "I am rambling on, and here stands his apparatus before us. It consists, as you see, of three parts. In the course of time each of these parts has acquired a kind of popular nickname. The lower one is called the 'Bed,' the upper one the 'Designer,' and this one here in the middle that moves up and down is called the 'Harrow.'" "The Harrow?" asked the explorer. He had not been listening very attentively, the glare of the sun in the shadeless valley was altogether too strong, it was difficult to collect one's thoughts. All the more did he admire the officer, who in spite of his tight-fitting full-dress uniform coat, amply befrogged and weighed down by epaulettes, was pursuing his subject with such enthusiasm and, besides talking, was still tightening a screw here and there with a spanner. As for the soldier, he seemed to be in much the same condition as the explorer. He had wound the prisoner's chain round both his wrists, propped himself on his rifle, let his head hang and was paying no attention to anything. That did not surprise the explorer, for the officer was speaking French, and certainly neither the soldier nor the prisoner understood a word of French. It was all the more remarkable, therefore, that the prisoner was none the less making an effort to follow the officer's explanations. With a kind of drowsy persistence he directed his gaze wherever the officer pointed a finger, and at the interruption of the explorer's question he, too, as well as the officer, looked round.

"Yes, the Harrow," said the officer, "a good name for it. The needles are set in like the teeth of a harrow and the whole thing works something like a harrow, although its action is limited to one place and contrived with much more artistic skill. Anyhow, you'll soon understand it. On the Bed here the condemned man is laid—I'm going to describe the apparatus first before I set it in motion. Then you'll be able to follow the proceedings better. Besides, one of the cog wheels in the Designer is badly worn; it creaks a lot when it's working; you can hardly hear yourself speak; spare parts, unfortunately, are difficult to get here.—Well, here is the Bed, as I told you. It is completely covered with a layer of cotton wool; you'll find out why later. On this cotton wool the condemned man is laid, face down, quite naked, of course; here are straps for the hands, here for the feet, and here for the neck, to bind him fast. Here at the head of the bed, where the man, as I said, first lays down his face, is this little gag of felt, which can be easily regulated to go straight into his mouth. It is meant to keep him from screaming and biting his tongue. Of course the man is forced to take the felt into his mouth, for otherwise his neck would be broken by the strap." "Is that cotton wool?" asked the explorer, bending forward. "Yes, certainly," said the officer, with a smile, "feel it for yourself." He took the explorer's hand and guided it over the bed. "It's specially prepared cotton wool, that's why it looks so different; I'll tell you presently what it's for." The explorer already felt a dawning interest in the apparatus; he sheltered his eyes from the sun with one hand and gazed up at the structure. It was a huge affair. The Bed and the Designer were of the same size and looked like two dark wooden chests. The Designer hung about two meters above the Bed; each of them was bound at the corners with four rods of brass that almost flashed out rays in the sunlight. Between the chests shuttled the Harrow on a ribbon of steel.

The officer had scarcely noticed the explorer's previous indifference, but he was now well aware of his dawning interest; so he stopped explaining in order to leave a space of time for quiet observation. The condemned man imitated the explorer; since he could not use a hand to shelter his eyes he gazed upwards without shade.

"Well, the man lies down," said the explorer, leaning back in his chair and crossing his legs.

"Yes," said the officer, pushing his cap back a little and passing one hand over his heated face, "now listen! Both the Bed and the Designer have an electric battery each; the Bed needs one for itself, the Designer for the Harrow. As soon as the man is strapped down, the Bed is set in motion. It quivers in minute, very rapid vibrations, both from side to side and up and down. You will have seen similar apparatus in hospitals; but in our Bed the movements are all precisely calculated; you see, they have to correspond very exactly to the movements of the Harrow. And the Harrow is the instrument for the actual execution of the sentence."

"And how does the sentence run?" asked the explorer.

"You don't know that either?" said the officer in amazement, and bit his lips. "Forgive me if my explanations seem rather incoherent. I do beg your pardon. You see, the Commandant always used to do the explaining; but the new Commandant shirks this duty; yet that such an important visitor"—the explorer tried to deprecate the honor with both hands, the officer, however, insisted—"that such an important visitor should not even be told about the kind of sentence we pass is a new development, which—" He was just on the point of using strong language but checked himself and said only: "I was not informed, it is not my fault. In any case, I am certainly the best person to explain our procedure, since I have here"—he patted his breast pocket—"the relevant drawings made by our former Commandant."

"The Commandant's own drawings?" asked the explorer. "Did he combine everything in himself, then? Was he soldier, judge, mechanic, chemist and draughtsman?"

"Indeed he was," said the officer, nodding assent, with a remote, glassy look. Then he inspected his hands critically; they did not seem clean enough to him for touching the drawings; so he went over to the bucket and washed them again. Then he drew out a small leather wallet and said: "Our sentence does not sound severe. Whatever commandment the prisoner has disobeyed is written upon his body by the Harrow. This prisoner, for instance"—the officer indicated the man—"will have written on his body: HONOR THY SUPERIORS!"

The explorer glanced at the man; he stood, as the officer pointed him out, with bent head, apparently listening with all his ears in an effort to catch what was being said. Yet the movement of his blubber lips, closely pressed together, showed clearly that he could not understand a word. Many questions were troubling the explorer, but at the sight of the prisoner he asked only: "Does he know his sentence?" "No," said the officer, eager to go on with his exposition, but the explorer interrupted him: "He doesn't know the sentence that has been passed on him?" "No," said the officer again, pausing a moment as if to let the explorer elaborate his question, and then said: "There would be no point in telling him. He'll learn it on his body." The explorer intended to make no answer, but he felt the prisoner's gaze turned on him; it seemed to ask if he approved such ongoings. So he bent forward again, having already leaned back in his chair, and put another question: "But surely he knows that he has been sentenced?" "Nor that either," said the officer, smiling at the explorer as if expecting him to make further surprising remarks. "No," said the explorer, wiping his forehead, "then he can't know either whether his defense was effective?" "He has had no chance of putting up a defense," said the officer, turning his eyes away as if speaking to himself and so sparing the explorer the shame of hearing self-evident matters explained. "But he must have had some chance of defending himself," said the explorer, and rose from his seat.

The officer realized that he was in danger of having his exposition of the apparatus held up for a long time; so he went up to the explorer, took him by the arm, waved a hand towards the condemned man, who was standing very straight now that he had so obviously become the center of attention—the soldier had also given the chain a jerk—and said: "This is how the matter stands. I have been appointed judge in this penal colony. Despite my youth. For I was the former Commandant's assistant in all penal matters and know more about the apparatus than anyone. My guiding principle is this: Guilt is never to be doubted. Other courts cannot follow that principle, for they consist of several opinions and have higher courts to scrutinize them. That is not the case here, or at least, it was not the case in the former Commandant's time. The new man has certainly shown some inclination to interfere with my judgments, but so far I have succeeded in fending him off and will go on succeeding. You wanted to have the case explained; it is quite simple, like all of them. A captain reported to me this morning that this man, who had been assigned to him as a servant and sleeps before his door, had been asleep on duty. It is his duty, you see, to get up every time the hour strikes and salute the captain's door. Not an exacting duty, and very necessary, since he has to be a sentry as well as a servant, and must be alert in both functions. Last night the captain wanted to see if the man was doing his duty. He opened the door as the clock struck two and there was his man curled up asleep. He took his riding whip and lashed him across the face. Instead of getting up and begging pardon, the man caught hold of his master's legs, shook him and cried: 'Throw that whip away or I'll eat you alive.'—That's the evidence. The captain came to me an hour ago, I wrote down his statement and appended the sentence to it. Then I had the man put in chains. That was all quite simple. If I had first called the man before me and interrogated him, things would have got into a confused tangle. He would have told lies, and had I exposed these lies he would have backed them up with more lies, and so on and so forth. As it is, I've got him and I won't let him go.—Is that quite clear now? But we're wasting time, the execution should be beginning and I haven't finished explaining the apparatus yet." He pressed the explorer back into his chair, went up again to the apparatus and began: "As you see, the shape of the Harrow corresponds to the human form; here is the harrow for the torso, here are the harrows for the legs. For the head there is only this one small spike. Is that quite clear?" He bent amiably forward towards the explorer, eager to provide the most comprehensive explanations.

The explorer considered the Harrow with a frown. The explanation of the judicial procedure had not satisfied him. He had to remind himself that this was in any case a penal colony where extraordinary measures were needed and that military discipline must be enforced to the last. He also felt that some hope might be set on the new Commandant, who was apparently of a mind to bring in, although gradually, a new kind of procedure which the officer's narrow mind was incapable of understanding. This train of thought prompted his next question: "Will the Commandant attend the execution?" "It is not certain," said the officer, wincing at the direct question, and his friendly expression darkened. "That is just why we have to lose no time. Much as I dislike it, I shall have to cut my explanations short. But of course tomorrow, when the apparatus has been cleaned—its one drawback is that it gets so messy—I can recapitulate all the details. For the present, then, only the essentials.—When the man lies down on the Bed and it begins to vibrate, the Harrow is lowered onto his body. It regulates itself automatically so that the needles barely touch his skin; once contact is made the steel ribbon stiffens immediately into a rigid band. And then the performance begins. An ignorant onlooker would see no difference between one punishment and another. The Harrow appears to do its work with uniform regularity. As it quivers, its points pierce the skin of the body which is itself quivering from the vibration of the Bed. So that the actual progress of the sentence can be watched, the Harrow is made of glass. Getting the needles fixed in the glass was a technical problem, but after many experiments we overcame the difficulty. No trouble was too great for us to take, you see. And now anyone can look through the glass and watch the inscription taking form on the body. Wouldn't you care to come a little nearer and have a look at the needles?"

The explorer got up slowly, walked across and bent over the Harrow. "You see," said the officer, "there are two kinds of needles arranged in multiple patterns. Each long needle has a short one beside it. The long needle does the writing, and the short needle sprays a jet of water to wash away the blood and keep the inscription clear. Blood and water together are then conducted here through small runnels into this main runnel and down a waste pipe into the pit." With his finger the officer traced the exact course taken by the blood and water. To make the picture as vivid as possible he held both hands below the outlet of the waste pipe as if to catch the outflow, and when he did this the explorer drew back his head and feeling behind him with one hand sought to return to his chair. To his horror he found that the condemned man too had obeyed the officer's invitation to examine the Harrow at close quarters and had followed him. He had pulled forward the sleepy soldier with the chain and was bending over the glass. One could see that his uncertain eyes were trying to perceive what the two gentlemen had been looking at, but since he had not understood the explanation he could not make head or tail of it. He was peering this way and that way. He kept running his eyes along the glass. The explorer wanted to drive him away, since what he was doing was probably culpable. But the officer firmly restrained the explorer with one hand and with the other took a clod of earth from the rampart and threw it at the soldier. He opened his eyes with a jerk, saw what the condemned man had dared to do, let his rifle fall, dug his heels into the ground, dragged his prisoner back so that he stumbled and fell immediately, and then stood looking down at him, watching him struggling and rattling in his chains. "Set him on his feet!" yelled the officer, for he noticed that the explorer's attention was being too much distracted by the prisoner. In fact he was even leaning right across the Harrow, without taking any notice of it, intent only on finding out what was happening to the prisoner. "Be careful with him!" cried the officer again. He ran round the apparatus, himself caught the condemned man under the shoulders and with the soldier's help got him up on his feet, which kept slithering from under him.

"Now I know all about it," said the explorer as the officer came back to him. "All except the most important thing," he answered, seizing the explorer's arm and pointing upwards: "In the Designer are all the cogwheels that control the movements of the Harrow, and this machinery is regulated according to the inscription demanded by the sentence. I am still using the guiding plans drawn by the former Commandant. Here they are"—he extracted some sheets from the leather wallet—"but I'm sorry I can't let you handle them, they are my most precious possessions. Just take a seat and I'll hold them in front of you like this, then you'll be able to see everything quite well." He spread out the first sheet of paper. The explorer would have liked to say something appreciative, but all he could see was a labyrinth of lines crossing and re-crossing each other, which covered the paper so thickly that it was difficult to discern the blank spaces between them. "Read it," said the officer. "I can't," said the explorer. "Yet it's clear enough," said the officer. "It's very ingenious," said the explorer evasively, "but I can't make it out." "Yes," said the officer with a laugh, putting the paper away again, "it's no calligraphy for school children. It needs to be studied closely. I'm quite sure that in the end you would understand it too. Of course the script can't be a simple one; it's not supposed to kill a man straight off, but only after an interval of, on an average, twelve hours; the turning point is reckoned to come at the sixth hour. So there have to be lots and lots of flourishes around the actual script; the script itself runs round the body only in a narrow girdle; the rest of the body is reserved for the embellishments. Can you appreciate now the work accomplished by the Harrow and the whole apparatus?—Just watch it!" He ran up the ladder, turned a wheel, called down: "Look out, keep to one side!" and everything started working. If the wheel had not creaked, it would have been marvelous. The officer, as if surprised by the noise of the wheel, shook his fist at it, then spread out his arms in excuse to the explorer and climbed down rapidly to peer at the working of the machine from below. Something perceptible to no one save himself was still not in order; he clambered up again, did something with both hands in the interior of the Designer, then slid down one of the rods, instead of using the ladder, so as to get down quicker, and with the full force of his lungs, to make himself heard at all in the noise, yelled in the explorer's ear: "Can you follow it? The

Harrow is beginning to write; when it finishes the first draft of the inscription on the man's back, the layer of cotton wool begins to roll and slowly turns the body over, to give the Harrow fresh space for writing. Meanwhile the raw part that has been written on lies on the cotton wool, which is specially prepared to staunch the bleeding and so makes all ready for a new deepening of the script. Then these teeth at the edge of the Harrow, as the body turns further round, tear the cotton wool away from the wounds, throw it into the pit, and there is more work for the Harrow. So it keeps on writing deeper and deeper for the whole twelve hours. The first six hours the condemned man stays alive almost as before, he suffers only pain. After two hours the felt gag is taken away, for he has no longer strength to scream. Here, into this electrically heated basin at the head of the bed, some warm rice pap is poured, from which the man, if he feels like it, can take as much as his tongue can lap. Not one of them ever misses the chance. I can remember none, and my experience is extensive. Only about the sixth hour does the man lose all desire to eat. I usually kneel down here at that moment and observe what happens. The man rarely swallows his last mouthful, he only rolls it round his mouth and spits it out into the pit. I have to duck just then or he would spit it in my face. But how quiet he grows at just about the sixth hour! Enlightenment comes to the most dull-witted. It begins around the eyes. From there it radiates. A moment that might tempt one to get under the Harrow oneself. Nothing more happens than that the man begins to understand the inscription, he purses his mouth as if he were listening. You have seen how difficult it is to decipher the script with one's eyes; but our man deciphers it with his wounds. To be sure, that is a hard task; he needs six hours to accomplish it. By that time the Harrow has pierced him quite through and casts him into the pit, where he pitches down upon the blood and water and the cotton wool. Then the judgment has been fulfilled, and we, the soldier and I, bury him."

The explorer had inclined his ear to the officer and with his hands in his jacket pockets watched the machine at work. The condemned man watched it too, but uncomprehendingly. He bent forward a little and was intent on the moving needles when the soldier, at a sign from the officer, slashed through his shirt and trousers from behind with a knife, so that they fell off; he tried to catch at his falling clothes to cover his nakedness, but the soldier lifted him into the air and shook the last remnants from him. The officer stopped the machine, and in the sudden silence the condemned man was laid under the Harrow. The chains were loosened and the straps fastened on instead; in the first moment that seemed almost a relief to the prisoner. And now the Harrow was adjusted a little lower, since he was a thin man. When the needle points touched him a shudder ran over his skin; while the soldier was busy strapping his right hand, he flung out his left hand blindly; but it happened to be in the direction towards where the explorer was standing. The officer kept watching the explorer sideways, as if seeking to read from his face the impression made on him by the execution, which had been at least cursorily explained to him.

The wrist strap broke; probably the soldier had drawn it too tight. The officer had to intervene, the soldier held up the broken piece of strap to show him. So the officer went over to him and said, his face still turned towards the explorer: "This is a very complex machine, it can't be helped that things are breaking or giving way here and there; but one must not thereby allow oneself to be diverted in one's general judgment. In any case, this strap is easily made good; I shall simply use a chain; the delicacy of the vibrations for the right arm will of course be a little impaired." And while he fastened the chains, he added: "The resources for maintaining the machine are now very much reduced. Under the former Commandant I had free access to a sum of money set aside entirely for this purpose. There was a store, too, in which spare parts were kept for repairs of all kinds. I confess I have been almost prodigal with them, I mean in the past, not now as the new Commandant pretends, always looking for an excuse to attack our old way of doing things. Now he has taken charge of the machine money himself, and if I send for a new strap they ask for the broken old strap as evidence, and the new strap takes ten days to appear and then is of shoddy material and not much good. But how I am supposed to work the machine without a strap, that's something nobody bothers about."

The explorer thought to himself: It's always a ticklish matter to intervene decisively in other people's affairs. He was neither a member of the penal colony nor a citizen of the state to which it belonged. Were he to denounce this execution or actually try to stop it, they could say to him: You are a foreigner, mind your own business. He could make no answer to that, unless he were to add that he was amazed at himself in this connection, for he traveled only as an observer, with no intention at all of altering other people's methods of administering justice. Yet here he found himself strongly tempted. The injustice of the procedure and the inhumanity of the execution were undeniable. No one could suppose that he had any selfish interest in the matter, for the condemned man was a complete stranger, not a fellow countryman or even at all sympathetic to him. The explorer himself had recommendations from high quarters, had been received here with great courtesy, and the very fact that he had been invited to attend the execution seemed to suggest that his views would be welcome. And this was all the more likely since the Commandant, as he had heard only too plainly, was no upholder of the procedure and maintained an attitude almost of hostility to the officer.

At that moment the explorer heard the officer cry out in rage. He had just, with considerable difficulty, forced the felt gag into the condemned man's mouth when the man in an irresistible access of nausea shut his eyes and vomited. Hastily the officer snatched him away from the gag and tried to hold his head over the pit; but it was too late, the vomit was running all over the machine. "It's all the fault of that Commandant!" cried the officer, senselessly shaking the brass rods in front, "the machine is befouled like a pigsty." With trembling hands he indicated to the explorer what had happened. "Have I not tried for hours at a time to get the Commandant to understand that the prisoner must fast for a whole day before the execution. But our new, mild doctrine thinks otherwise. The Commandant's ladies stuff the man with sugar candy before he's led off. He has lived on stinking fish his whole life long and now he has to eat sugar candy! But it could still be possible, I should have nothing to say against it, but why won't they get me a new felt gag, which I have been begging for the last three months. How should a man not feel sick when he takes a felt gag into his mouth which more than a hundred men have already slobbered and gnawed in their dying moments?"

The condemned man had laid his head down and looked peaceful, the soldier was busy trying to clean the machine with the prisoner's shirt. The officer advanced towards the explorer, who in some vague presentiment fell back a pace, but the officer seized him by the hand, and drew him to one side. "I should like to exchange a few words with you in confidence," he said, "may I?" "Of course," said the explorer, and listened with downcast eyes.

"This procedure and method of execution, which you are now having the opportunity to admire, has at the moment no longer any open adherents in our colony. I am its sole advocate, and at the same time the sole advocate of the old Commandant's tradition. I can no longer reckon on any further extension of the method, it takes all my energy to maintain it as it is. During the old Commandant's lifetime the colony was full of his adherents; his strength of conviction I still have in some measure, but not an atom of his power; consequently the adherents have skulked out of sight, there are still many of them but none of them will admit it. If you were to go into the teahouse today, on execution day, and listen to what is being said, you would perhaps hear only ambiguous remarks. These would all be made by adherents, but under the present Commandant and his present doctrines they are of no use to me. And now I ask you: because of this Commandant and the women who influence him, is such a piece of work, the work of a lifetime"—he pointed to the machine—"to perish? Ought one to let that happen? Even if one has only come as a stranger to our island for a few days? But there's no time to lose, an attack of some kind is impending on my function as judge; conferences are already being held in the Commandant's office from which I am excluded; even your coming here today seems to me a significant move; they are cowards and use you as a screen, you, a stranger.—How different an execution was in the old days! A whole day before the ceremony the valley was packed with people; they all came only to look on; early in the morning the Commandant appeared with his ladies; fanfares roused the whole camp; I reported that everything was in readiness; the assembled company—no high official dared to absent himself—arranged itself round the machine; this pile of cane chairs is a miserable survival from that epoch. The machine was freshly cleaned and glittering, I got new spare parts for almost every execution. Before hundreds of spectators—all of them standing on tiptoe as far as the heights there—the condemned man was laid under the Harrow by the Commandant himself. What is left today for a common soldier to do was then my task, the task of the presiding judge, and was an honor for me. And then the execution began! No discordant noise spoilt the working of the machine. Many did not care to watch it but lay with closed eyes in the sand; they all knew: Now Justice is being done. In the silence one heard nothing but the condemned man's sighs, half muffled by the felt gag. Nowadays the machine can no longer wring from anyone a sigh louder than the felt gag can stifle; but in those days the writing needles let drop an acid fluid, which we're no longer permitted to use. Well, and then came the sixth hour! It was impossible to grant all the requests to be allowed to watch it from near by. The Commandant in his wisdom ordained that the children should have the preference; I, of course, because of my office had the privilege of always being at hand; often enough I would be squatting there with a small child in either arm. How we all absorbed the look of transfiguration on the face of the sufferer, how we bathed our cheeks in the radiance of that justice, achieved at last and fading so quickly! What times these were, my comrade!" The officer had obviously forgotten whom he was addressing; he had embraced the explorer and laid his head on his shoulder. The explorer was deeply embarrassed, impatiently he stared over the officer's head. The soldier had finished his cleaning job and was now pouring rice pap from a pot into the basin. As soon as the condemned man, who seemed to have recovered entirely, noticed this action he began to reach for the rice with his tongue. The soldier kept pushing him away, since the rice pap was certainly meant for a later hour, yet it was just as unfitting that the soldier himself should thrust his dirty hands into the basin and eat out of it before the other's avid face.

The officer quickly pulled himself together. "I didn't want to upset you," he said, "I know it is impossible to make those days credible now. Anyhow, the machine is still working and it is still effective in itself. It is effective in itself even though it stands alone in this valley. And the corpse still falls at the last into the pit with an incomprehensibly gentle wafting motion, even although there are no hundreds of people swarming round like flies as formerly. In those days we had to put a strong fence round the pit, it has long since been torn down."

The explorer wanted to withdraw his face from the officer and looked round him at random. The officer thought he was surveying the valley's desolation; so he seized him by the hands, turned him round to meet his eyes, and asked: "Do you realize the shame of it?"

But the explorer said nothing. The officer left him alone for a little; with legs apart, hands on hips, he stood very still, gazing at the ground. Then he smiled encouragingly at the explorer and said: "I was quite near you yesterday when the Commandant gave you the invitation. I heard him giving it. I know the Commandant. I divined at once what he was after. Although he is powerful enough to take measures against me, he doesn't dare to do it yet, but he certainly means to use your verdict against me, the verdict of an illustrious foreigner. He has calculated it carefully: this is your second day on the island, you did not know the old Commandant and his ways, you are conditioned by European ways of thought, perhaps you object on principle to capital punishment in general and to such mechanical instruments of death in particular, besides you will see that the execution has no support from the public, a shabby ceremony—carried out with a machine already somewhat old and worn—now, taking all that into consideration, would it not be likely (so thinks the Commandant) that you might disapprove of my methods? And if you disapprove, you wouldn't conceal the fact (I'm still speaking from the Commandant's point of view), for you are a man to feel confidence in your own well-tried conclusions. True, you have seen and learned to appreciate the peculiarities of many peoples, and so you would not be likely to take a strong line against our proceedings, as you might do in your own country. But the Commandant has no need of that. A casual, even an unguarded remark will be enough. It doesn't even need to represent what you really think, so long as it can be used speciously to serve his purpose. He will try to prompt you with sly questions, of that I am certain. And his ladies will sit around you and prick up their ears; you might be saying something like this: 'In our country we have a different criminal procedure,' or 'In our country the prisoner is interrogated before he is sentenced,' or 'We haven't used torture since the Middle Ages.' All these statements are as true as they seem natural to you, harmless remarks that pass no judgment on my methods. But how would the Commandant react to them? I can see him, our good Commandant, pushing his chair away immediately and rushing on to the balcony, I can see his ladies streaming out after him, I can hear his voice—the ladies call it a voice of thunder—well, and this is what he says: 'A famous Western investigator, sent out to study criminal procedure in all the countries of the world, has just said that our old tradition of administering justice is inhumane. Such a verdict from such a personality makes it impossible for me to countenance these methods any longer. Therefore from this very day I ordain . . .' and so on. You may want to interpose that you never said any such thing, that you never called my methods inhumane, on the contrary your profound experience leads you to believe they are most humane and most in consonance with human dignity, and you admire the machine greatly—but it will be too late; you won't even get onto the balcony, crowded as it will be with ladies; you may try to draw attention to yourself; you may want to scream out; but a lady's hand will close your lips—and I and the work of the old Commandant will be done for."

The explorer had to suppress a smile; so easy, then, was the task he had felt to be so difficult. He said evasively: "You overestimate my influence; the Commandant has read my letters of recommendation, he knows that I am no expert in criminal procedure. If I were to give an opinion, it would be as a private individual, an opinion no more influential than that of any ordinary person, and in any case much less influential than that of the Commandant, who, I am given to understand, has very extensive powers in this penal colony. If his attitude to your procedure is as definitely hostile as you believe, then I fear the end of your tradition is at hand, even without any humble assistance from me."

Had it dawned on the officer at last? No, he still did not understand. He shook his head emphatically, glanced briefly round at the condemned man and the soldier, who both flinched away from the rice, came close up to the explorer and without looking at his face but fixing his eye on some spot on his coat said in a lower voice than before: "You don't know the Commandant; you feel yourself—forgive the expression—a kind of outsider so far as all of us are concerned; yet, believe me, your influence cannot be rated too highly. I was simply delighted when I heard that you were to attend the execution all by yourself. The Commandant arranged it to aim a blow at me, but I shall turn it to my advantage. Without being distracted by lying whispers and contemptuous glances—which could not have been avoided had a crowd of people attended the execution—you have heard my explanations, seen the machine and are now in course of watching the execution. You have doubtless already formed your own judgment; if you still have some small uncertainties the sight of the execution will resolve them. And now I make this request to you: help me against the Commandant!"

The explorer would not let him go on. "How could I do that," he cried, "it's quite impossible. I can neither help nor hinder you."

"Yes, you can," the officer said. The explorer saw with a certain apprehension that the officer had clenched his fists. "Yes, you can," repeated the officer, still more insistently. "I have a plan that is bound to succeed. You believe your influence is insufficient. I know that it is sufficient. But even granted that you are right, is it not necessary, for the sake of preserving this tradition, to try even what might prove insufficient? Listen to my plan, then. The first thing necessary for you to carry it out is to be as reticent as possible today regarding your verdict on these proceedings. Unless you are asked a direct question you must say nothing at all; but what you do say must be brief and general; let it be remarked that you would prefer not to discuss the matter, that you are out of patience with it, that if you are to let yourself go you would use strong language. I don't ask you to tell any lies; by no means; you should only give curt answers, such as: 'Yes, I saw the execution,' or 'Yes, I had it explained to me.' Just that, nothing more. There are grounds enough for any impatience you betray, although not such as will occur to the Commandant. Of course, he will mistake your meaning and interpret it to please himself. That's what my plan depends on. Tomorrow in the Commandant's office there is to be a large conference of all the high administrative officials, the Commandant presiding. Of course the Commandant is the kind of man to have turned these conferences into public spectacles. He has had a gallery built that is always packed with spectators. I am compelled to take part in the conferences, but they make me sick with disgust. Now, whatever happens, you will certainly be invited to this conference; if you behave today as I suggest the invitation will become an urgent request. But if for some mysterious reason you're not invited, you'll have to ask for an invitation; there's no doubt of your getting it then. So tomorrow you're sitting in the Commandant's box with the ladies. He keeps looking up to make sure you're there. After various trivial and ridiculous matters, brought in merely to impress the audience—mostly harbor works, nothing but harbor works!—our judicial procedure comes up for discussion too. If the Commandant doesn't introduce it, or not soon enough, I'll see that it's mentioned. I'll stand up and report that today's execution has taken place. Quite briefly, only a statement. Such a statement is not usual, but I shall make it. The Commandant thanks me, as always, with an amiable smile, and then he can't restrain himself, he seizes the excellent opportunity. 'It has just been reported,' he will say, or words to that effect, 'that an execution has taken place. I should like merely to add that this execution was witnessed by the famous explorer who has, as you all know, honored our colony so greatly by his visit to us. His presence at today's session of our conference also contributes to the importance of this occasion. Should we not now ask the famous explorer to give us his verdict on our traditional mode of execution and the procedure that leads up to it?' Of course there is loud applause, general agreement, I am more insistent than anyone. The Commandant bows to you and says: 'Then in the name of the assembled company, I put the question to you.' And now you advance to the front of the box. Lay your hands where everyone can see them, or the ladies will catch them and press your fingers.—And then at last you can speak out. I don't know how I'm going to endure the tension of waiting for that moment. Don't put any restraint on yourself when you make your speech, publish the truth aloud, lean over the front of the box, shout, yes indeed, shout your verdict, your unshakable conviction, at the Commandant. Yet perhaps you wouldn't care to do that, it's not in keeping with your character, in your country perhaps people do these things differently, well, that's all right too, that will be quite as effective, don't even stand up, just say a few words, even in a whisper, so that only the officials beneath you will hear them, that will be quite enough, you don't even need to mention the lack of public support for the execution, the creaking wheel, the broken strap, the filthy gag of felt, no, I'll take all that upon me, and, believe me, if my indictment doesn't drive him out of the conference hall, it will force him to his knees to make the acknowledgment: Old Commandant, I humble myself before you.— That is my plan; will you help me to carry it out? But of course you are willing, what is more, you must." And the officer seized the explorer by both arms and gazed, breathing heavily, into his face. He had shouted the last sentence so loudly that even the soldier and the condemned man were startled into attending; they had not understood a word but they stopped eating and looked over at the explorer, chewing their previous mouthfuls.

From the very beginning the explorer had no doubt about what answer he must give; in his lifetime he had experienced too much to have any uncertainty here; he was fundamentally honorable and unafraid. And yet now, facing the soldier and the condemned man, he did hesitate, for as long as it took to draw one breath. At last, however, he said, as he had to: "No." The officer blinked several times but did not turn his eyes away. "Would you like me to explain?" asked the explorer. The officer nodded wordlessly. "I do not approve of your procedure," said the explorer then, "even before you took me into your confidence—of course I shall never in any circumstances betray your confidence—I was already wondering whether it would be my duty to intervene and whether my intervention would have the slightest chance of success. I realized to whom I ought to turn: to the Commandant, of course. You have made that fact even clearer, but without having strengthened my resolution, on the contrary, your sincere conviction has touched me, even though it cannot influence my judgment."

The officer remained mute, turned to the machine, caught hold of a brass rod, and then, leaning back a little, gazed at the Designer as if to assure himself that all was in order. The soldier and the condemned man seemed to have come to some understanding; the condemned man was making signs to the soldier, difficult though his movements were because of the tight straps; the soldier was bending down to him; the condemned man whispered something and the soldier nodded.

The explorer followed the officer and said: "You don't know yet what I mean to do. I shall tell the Commandant what I think of the procedure, certainly, but not at a public conference, only in private; nor shall I stay here long enough to attend any conference; I am going away early tomorrow morning, or at least embarking on my ship."

It did not look as if the officer had been listening. "So you did not find the procedure convincing," he said to himself and smiled, as an old man smiles at childish nonsense and yet pursues his own meditations behind the smile.

"Then the time has come," he said at last, and suddenly looked at the explorer with bright eyes that held some challenge, some appeal for co-operation. "The time for what?" asked the explorer uneasily, but got no answer.

"You are free," said the officer to the condemned man in the native tongue. The man did not believe it at first. "Yes, you are set free," said the officer. For the first time the condemned man's face woke to real animation. Was it true? Was it only a caprice of the officer's, that might change again? Had the foreign explorer begged him off? What was it? One could read these questions on his face. But not for long. Whatever it might be, he wanted to be really free if he might, and he began to struggle so far as the Harrow permitted him.

"You'll burst my straps," cried the officer, "lie still! We'll soon loosen them." And signing the soldier to help him, he set about doing so. The condemned man laughed wordlessly to himself, now he turned his face left towards the officer, now right towards the soldier, nor did he forget the explorer.

"Draw him out," ordered the officer. Because of the Harrow this had to be done with some care. The condemned man had already torn himself a little in the back through his impatience.

From now on, however, the officer paid hardly any attention to him. He went up to the explorer, pulled out the small leather wallet again, turned over the papers in it, found the one he wanted and showed it to the explorer. "Read it," he said. "I can't," said the explorer, "I told you before that I can't make out these scripts." "Try taking a close look at it," said the officer and came quite near to the explorer so that they might read it together. But when even that proved useless, he outlined the script with his little finger, holding it high above the paper as if the surface dared not be sullied by touch, in order to help the explorer to follow the script in that way. The explorer did make an effort, meaning to please the officer in this respect at least, but he was quite unable to follow. Now the officer began to spell it, letter by letter, and then read out the words. " 'BE JUST!' is what is written there," he said, "surely you can read it now." The explorer bent so close to the paper that the officer feared he might touch it and drew it farther away; the explorer made no remark, yet it was clear that he still could not decipher it. " 'BE JUST!' is what is written there," said the officer once more. "Maybe," said the explorer, "I am prepared to believe you." "Well, then," said the officer, at least partly satisfied, and climbed up the ladder with the paper; very carefully he laid it inside the Designer and seemed to be changing the disposition of all the cogwheels; it was a troublesome piece of work and must have involved wheels that were extremely small, for sometimes the officer's head vanished altogether from sight inside the Designer, so precisely did he have to regulate the machinery.

The explorer, down below, watched the labor uninterruptedly, his neck grew stiff and his eyes smarted from the glare of sunshine over the sky. The soldier and the condemned man were now busy together. The man's shirt and trousers, which were already lying in the pit, were fished out by the point of the soldier's bayonet. The shirt was abominably dirty and its owner washed it in the bucket of water. When he put on the shirt and trousers both he and the soldier could not help guffawing, for the garments were of course slit up behind. Perhaps the condemned man felt it incumbent on him to amuse the soldier, he turned round and round in his slashed garments before the soldier, who squatted on the ground beating his knees with mirth. All the same, they presently controlled their mirth out of respect for the gentlemen.

When the officer had at length finished his task aloft, he surveyed the machinery in all its details once more, with a smile, but this time shut the lid of the Designer, which had stayed open till now, climbed down, looked into the pit and then at the condemned man, noting with satisfaction that the clothing had been taken out, then went over to wash his hands in the water bucket, perceived too late that it was disgustingly dirty, was unhappy because he could not wash his hands, in the end thrust them into the sand—this alternative did not please him, but he had to put up with it—then stood upright and began to unbutton his uniform jacket. As he did this, the two ladies' handkerchiefs he had tucked under his collar fell into his hands. "Here are your handkerchiefs," he said, and threw them to the condemned man. And to the explorer he said in explanation: "A gift from the ladies."

In spite of the obvious haste with which he was discarding first his uniform jacket and then all his clothing, he handled each garment with loving care, he even ran his fingers caressingly over the silver lace on the jacket and shook a tassel into place. This loving care was certainly out of keeping with the fact that as soon as he had a garment off he flung it at once with a kind of unwilling jerk into the pit. The last thing left to him was his short sword with the sword belt. He drew it out of the scabbard, broke it, then gathered all together, the bits of the sword, the scabbard and the belt, and flung them so violently down that they clattered into the pit.

Now he stood naked there. The explorer bit his lips and said nothing. He knew very well what was going to happen, but he had no right to obstruct the officer in anything. If the judicial procedure which the officer cherished were really so near its end—possibly as a result of his own intervention, as to which he felt himself pledged—then the officer was doing the right thing; in his place the explorer would not have acted otherwise.

The soldier and the condemned man did not understand at first what was happening, at first they were not even looking on. The condemned man was gleeful at having got the handkerchiefs back, but he was not allowed to enjoy them for long, since the soldier snatched them with a sudden, unexpected grab. Now the condemned man in turn was trying to twitch them from under the belt where the soldier had tucked them, but the soldier was on his guard. So they were wrestling, half in jest. Only when the officer stood quite naked was their attention caught. The condemned man especially seemed struck with the notion that some great change was impending. What had happened to him was now going to happen to the officer. Perhaps even to the very end. Apparently the foreign explorer had given the order for it. So this was revenge. Although he himself had not suffered to the end, he was to be revenged to the end. A broad, silent grin now appeared on his face and stayed there all the rest of the time.

The officer, however, had turned to the machine. It had been clear enough previously that he understood the machine well, but now it was almost staggering to see how he managed it and how it obeyed him. His hand had only to approach the Harrow for it to rise and sink several times till it was adjusted to the right position for receiving him; he touched only the edge of the Bed and already it was vibrating; the felt gag came to meet his mouth, one could see that the officer was really reluctant to take it but he shrank from it only a moment, soon he submitted and received it. Everything was ready, only the straps hung down at the sides, yet they were obviously unnecessary, the officer did not need to be fastened down. Then the condemned man noticed the loose straps, in his opinion the execution was incomplete unless the straps were buckled, he gestured eagerly to the soldier and they ran together to strap the officer down. The latter had already stretched out one foot to push the lever that started the Designer; he saw the two men coming up; so he drew his foot back and let himself be buckled in. But now he could not reach the lever; neither the soldier nor the condemned man would be able to find it, and the explorer was determined not to lift a finger. It was not necessary; as soon as the straps were fastened the machine began to work; the Bed vibrated, the needles flickered above the skin, the Harrow rose and fell. The explorer had been staring at it quite a while before he remembered that a wheel in the Designer should have been creaking; but everything was quiet, not even the slightest hum could be heard.

Because it was working so silently the machine simply escaped one's attention. The explorer observed the soldier and the condemned man. The latter was the more animated of the two, everything in the machine interested him, now he was bending down and now stretching up on tiptoe, his forefinger was extended all the time pointing out details to the soldier. This annoyed the explorer. He was resolved to stay till the end, but he could not bear the sight of these two. "Go back home," he said. The soldier would have been willing enough, but the condemned man took the order as a punishment. With clasped hands he implored to be allowed to stay, and when the explorer shook his head and would not relent, he even went down on his knees. The explorer saw that it was no use merely giving orders, he was on the point of going over and driving them away. At that moment he heard a noise above him in the Designer. He looked up. Was that cogwheel going to make trouble after all? But it was something quite different. Slowly the lid of the Designer rose up and then clicked wide open. The teeth of a cogwheel showed themselves and rose higher, soon the whole wheel was visible, it was as if some enormous force were squeezing the Designer so that there was no longer room for the wheel, the wheel moved up till it came to the very edge of the Designer, fell down, rolled along the sand a little on its rim and then lay flat. But a second wheel was already rising after it, followed by many others, large and small and indistinguishably minute, the same thing happened to all of them, at every moment one imagined the Designer must now really be empty, but another complex of numerous wheels was already rising into sight, falling down, trundling along the sand and lying flat. This phenomenon made the condemned man completely forget the explorer's command, the cogwheels fascinated him, he was always trying to catch one and at the same time urging the soldier to help, but always drew back his hand in alarm, for another wheel always came hopping along which, at least on its first advance, scared him off.

The explorer, on the other hand, felt greatly troubled; the machine was obviously going to pieces; its silent working was a delusion; he had a feeling that he must now stand by the officer, since the officer was no longer able to look after himself. But while the tumbling cogwheels absorbed his whole attention he had forgotten to keep an eye on the rest of the machine; now that the last cogwheel had left the Designer, however, he bent over the Harrow and had a new and still more unpleasant surprise. The Harrow was not writing, it was only jabbing, and the Bed was not turning the body over but only bringing it up quivering against the needles. The explorer wanted to do something, if possible, to bring the whole machine to a standstill, for this was no exquisite torture such as the officer desired, this was plain murder. He stretched out his hands. But at that moment the Harrow rose with the body spitted on it and moved to the side, as it usually did only when the twelfth hour had come. Blood was flowing in a hundred streams, not mingled with water, the water jets too had failed to function. And now the last action failed to fulfil itself, the body did not drop off the long needles, streaming with blood it went on hanging over the pit without falling into it. The Harrow tried to move back to its old position, but as if it had itself noticed that it had not yet got rid of its burden it stuck after all where it was, over the pit. "Come and help!" cried the explorer to the other two, and himself seized the officer's feet. He wanted to push against the feet while the others seized the head from the opposite side and so the officer might be slowly eased off the needles. But the other two could not make up their minds to come; the condemned man actually turned away; the explorer had to go over to them and force them into position at the officer's head. And here, almost against his will, he had to look at the face of the corpse. It was as it had been in life; no sign was visible of the promised redemption; what the others had found in the machine the officer had not found; the lips were firmly pressed together, the eyes were open, with the same expression as in life, the look was calm and convinced, through the forehead went the point of the great iron spike.

As the explorer, with the soldier and the condemned man behind him, reached the first houses of the colony, the soldier pointed to one of them and said: "There is the teahouse."

In the ground floor of the house was a deep, low, cavernous space, its walls and ceiling blackened with smoke. It was open to the road all along its length. Although this teahouse was very little different from the other houses of the colony, which were all very dilapidated, even up to the Commandant's palatial headquarters, it made on the explorer the impression of a historic tradition of some kind, and he felt the power of past days. He went near to it, followed by his companions, right up between the empty tables which stood in the street before it, and breathed the cool, heavy air that came from the interior. "The old man's buried here," said the soldier, "the priest wouldn't let him lie in the churchyard. Nobody knew where to bury him for a while, but in the end they buried him here. The officer never told you about that, for sure, because of course that's what he was most ashamed of. He even tried several times to dig the old man up by night, but he was always chased away." "Where is the grave?" asked the explorer, who found it impossible to believe the soldier. At once both of them, the soldier and the condemned man, ran before him pointing with outstretched hands in the direction where the grave should be. They led the explorer right up to the back wall, where guests were sitting at a few tables. They were apparently dock laborers, strong men with short, glistening, full black beards. None had a jacket, their shirts were torn, they were poor, humble creatures. As the explorer drew near, some of them got up, pressed close to the wall, and stared at him. "It's a foreigner," ran the whisper around him, "he wants to see the grave." They pushed one of the tables aside, and under it there was really a gravestone. It was a simple stone, low enough to be covered by a table. There was an inscription on it in very small letters, the explorer had to kneel down to read it. This was what it said: "Here rests the old Commandant. His adherents, who now must be nameless, have dug this grave and set up this stone. There is a prophecy that after a certain number of years the Commandant will rise again and lead his adherents from this house to recover the colony. Have faith and wait!" When the explorer had read this and risen to his feet he saw all the bystanders around him smiling, as if they too had read the inscription, had found it ridiculous and were expecting him to agree with them. The explorer ignored this, distributed a few coins among them, waiting till the table was pushed over the grave again, quitted the teahouse and made for the harbor.

The soldier and the condemned man had found some acquaintances in the teahouse, who detained them. But they must have soon shaken them off, for the explorer was only halfway down the long flight of steps leading to the boats when they came rushing after him. Probably they wanted to force him at the last minute to take them with him. While he was bargaining below with a ferryman to row him to the steamer, the two of them came headlong down the steps, in silence, for they did not dare to shout. But by the time they reached the foot of the steps the explorer was already in the boat, and the ferryman was just casting off from the shore. They could have jumped into the boat, but the explorer lifted a heavy knotted rope from the floor boards, threatened them with it and so kept them from attempting the leap.

THINKING AND RE-READING

1. As you re-read this piece of fiction, think about why, in Kafka's words, the officer was such a "devoted admirer of the apparatus," why he had such a commitment to the ways of the "former Commandant," and why, finally, he submitted his own body to the discipline of the apparatus. Think about the ways in which we effectively discipline ourselves through social habits, conventions, accepted ways of thinking, and adherence to government programs. Think about how difficult it is to understand your own culture's familiar habits from the perspective of an outsider, an Explorer.

2. Think about the actions of the prisoner, the condemned man, the soldier, as well as the government of the penal colony—how does each act as a part of the system of punishment surrounding the apparatus? How are their behaviors similar? How do they differ? What, ultimately, keeps this system of punishment going? How is it maintained? Why? How is it ultimately stopped? Why?

WRITING AND LEARNING

1. What messages, what crimes, have been written on the body of society by the invention and use of computers? For your own insight, make a list of them. If you have trouble thinking of the crimes or the ill effects that computers have had on our culture, look back at some of the contributions in this section and in this book. Then compose a message that refers to the correction of the crime—just as Kafka suggested the Commandant had done. Your purpose for this assignment is to increase your critical understanding of the technological culture in which you live and work.

2. Sometimes we learn more about computers when we look at the impact that other technologies have had on our culture, such as telephones, washing machines, automobiles, and a machine called the "apparatus." Make a list of the impact that computers have had on our daily lives. Try to think about some of the social effects that our reliance on computers has generated—the ways in which computers have changed our sense of time, changed our educational systems, or changed the ways in which we communicate with people. Try to list some effects that you believe are positive and some that you believe are negative. Your purpose for this assignment is to increase your critical understanding of the technological culture in which you live and work.

3. Imagine that you are an explorer from another culture—a noncomputer, low-tech culture—who is visiting the campus to observe the workings of the apparatus called "computers." You are intelligent, well educated in your cultural context, and highly civilized and humane in your values. However, your culture does not have access to computers; indeed, many people in your culture consider computers to be harmful influences. Write a letter to your friends at home about what you see happening. How do computers seem to be affecting people? Their tasks? Their time? The places in which they work? The kinds of work they do? The ways in which they interact? Their values? As an alternative assignment, write a speech suitable for presentation at the local Rotary or Kiwanis chapter meeting. These groups have asked you to provide your perspective on the American culture and its technological values.

EXTENDED WRITING ACTIVITIES

BUILDING ON WRITING AND LEARNING

SAC   Writing and learning activities that can be done on a stand-alone computer with access to word processing software

LAN   Writing and learning activities that can be done on local area network with access to synchronous or asynchronous conferencing software

WAN   Writing and learning activities that can be done on a wide-area network such as the Internet, with access to Netscape or Gopher software

ASSIGNMENT 1: DESIGNING A COMMUNITY FREENET

1. In this assignment, you will design the structure for a freenet in your local community and author ten to fifteen screens for this freenet. Using your own knowledge of the concerns that citizens have about local government and community involvement, design the organizational structure for a community freenet that you think could be useful to and popular with citizens in your area. Be certain that they have ready access to networked technology in places such as public libraries, supermarkets, public parks, schools, and laundromats. You'll want to re-read Doug Schuler's article on community networks to familiarize yourself with some of the services that it might be useful to include.

2. In connection with your design of this freenet, complete the following writing assignments:

- Use the outlining function of your word-processing package to create an organizational structure for the freenet you design. At the first level of specificity, identify the major departments or areas of interest that users will have available to choose from when they log onto the freenet and see the main-menu screen. Also include at least two more levels of specificity within each of these major areas—at the most specific level, identify the various services, resources, or discussions that will be offered citizens on your freenet.

- If you have access to a computer-supported drawing package, create an organizational chart for your freenet, showing in chart form how the various parts of the freenet would be related to one another, and how users would get from one area of the net to another.

- Design at least ten menu or explanation screens for the freenet that you have created. You can use any medium—or combination of media—to design and produce these screens: colored pencils, word processing packages, graphics software, crayons, colored paper and paste, and so on. If you have access to the Internet, you may want to do a bit of research by looking at some of the community networks listed in this article before you begin this response. Make sure that at least one of the screens you design provides users with the central rationale for the freenet that you are creating. You should draft this statement several times, because it is very important to the undertaking. **(SAC)**

ALTERNATIVE ASSIGNMENT

1. Complete this project with your writing group. Design a common network; pool the number of screens you produce (at least ten per person). (SAC)

ASSIGNMENT 2: DESIGNING A PAMPHLET

1. In this assignment, you will write and design an introductory pamphlet (maximum six to eight pages) for first-year students on your campus titled, "Computing at _____: An Introduction to Your Electronic Citizenship." The purpose of the pamphlet is to provide useful information on computing for incoming first-year students or for high school students considering your college or university as an educational choice. The assignment consists of the following tasks:

- **Conducting research:** You will need to visit your central campus computing office to obtain copies of any public documents that have already been written for students. You can also obtain information on the campus computing facilities available to students, the campus computing philosophy and long-term plans, rules and regulations that students must follow, computing fee information, and other relevant materials that will help you explain the campus computing environment to incoming first-year students.

- **Writing the pamphlet:** Using the word-processing package on your computer, write the basic text for the pamphlet. The text should introduce students to the computing environment on your campus—describing it generally (e.g., machines, networks, and facilities), talking about how it is funded and from what sources (e.g., lab fees, technology fees, or tuition), and identifying the capabilities it provides the students (e.g., computer labs, Internet access, available software, and applications). You will also want to explain the overall purpose of computing on your campus, the access to technology that students have available to them, and the responsibilities of the students as citizens within the campus computing environment. Be sure to consult existing documents already published by your central campus computing office. If you quote from these documents, be sure to do so correctly, referring to your handbook for the appropriate format.

- **User-testing and revising:** Ask two or three first-year students or local high school seniors to read and critique a draft of your pamphlet. Have them write their questions and comments in the margins of the pamphlet draft and hand these in with your final project. Use these comments to revise your copy. Remember that the purpose of the document is to provide useful information on campus computing that will help orient these students to the electronic community that they will be joining.

- **Designing the pamphlet:** If you have a page-layout program available to you, use it to design your pamphlet, adding graphics and other layout features (e.g., different fonts, borders, illustrations, and icons) if needed. If you don't have access to a page-layout program, design your pamphlet by cutting, pasting, and photocopying a final copy. (SAC)

OPTIONAL ASSIGNMENT

1. Provide the central campus computing office with a copy of your pamphlet and offer to revise it for them if they agree to publish it for the incoming students. (SAC)

ASSIGNMENT 3: INTRODUCING YOUNGSTERS TO THEIR GOVERNMENT ONLINE

1. In this assignment, you will write a booklet for eleventh-grade students enrolled in an American government class to introduce them to various online government resources at the national level. Your purpose in this assignment is to encourage students to become active citizens who know how to access online information concerning the American government and how it operates. The booklet can be no more than eight pages, and it should convince students of its importance to an active and informed citizen online. The assignment consists of the following tasks:

- **Conducting research:** You will need to spend some time online yourself exploring the various governmental resources available to citizens—use either Gopher or Mosaic to navigate the Internet. The first place to go online is Washington, D.C.—after you locate Washington, you'll find numerous listings of government resources. As you explore these resources, think about which ones would be most inviting and interesting to high school students. Take notes on the Universal Resource Locator (URL) addresses for each resource that you select. You will also need to take notes concerning the contents of the various resource locations— what types of subjects are located there, what is the purpose of the resource, and what other resource does it lead to. Try to find resources that you would find interesting yourself as an eleventh grader—this will take some digging. You might also be able to find listings for some government resources in many of the recent books or commercial magazines on cruising the Internet. Try your school library, the magazine rack of a local grocery store, or a local bookstore for this material. Your grade on this pamphlet will depend, in part, on how interesting the resources are that you find—don't be content with the obvious ones; dig hard to find those that might really intrigue and engage the students.

- **Writing the pamphlet:** Using the word processing package on your computer, write the basic text for the pamphlet. The text should start by introducing students to the concept of electronic citizenship—your task here is to explain why citizens should be able to locate and use government resources online. The pamphlet should also introduce the high school students to some of the specific governmental material to explore that you think they will find interesting. You'll want to make a list of these resources, relate something relevant concerning each one, and provide a URL so that students are able to find and explore them on their own. You may want to make the entire project more fun by posing a scavenger hunt for online resources or by identifying some assignments and questions that the students are able to answer, as they access the various resources.

- **User-testing and revising:** Ask two or three eleventh-grade students to read and critique a draft of your pamphlet. Have them write their questions and comments in the margins of the pamphlet draft and hand these in with your final project. Use the comments on this draft to revise your copy. Remember that the purpose of the document is to encourage these students to use the Internet to become more active online citizens.

- **Designing the pamphlet:** If you have a page-layout program, use it to design your pamphlet, adding graphics and other layout features (e.g., different fonts, borders, illustrations, and icons) if needed. If you don't have access to a page-layout program, design your pamphlet by cutting, pasting, and photocopying a final copy. **(WAN)**

ALTERNATIVE ASSIGNMENT

1. Work collaboratively on this assignment in your writing group—multiply the page length of the booklet by the number of people in your group.

OPTIONAL ASSIGNMENT

1. Show your pamphlet to a teacher of American government at a local high school or at the high school you attended. Offer to revise the pamphlet to meet the needs of that teacher's students.

Appendix A
How to Look at an Image

The following questions have been adapted from a list of similar queries at the end of Arthur Asa Berger's "Sex as Symbol in Fashion Advertising and Analyzing Signs and Sign Systems." In *Reading Culture: Contexts for Critical Reading and Writing* (2d edition), Diana George and John Trimbur (eds.), pp. 156–164, HarperCollins, 1992. The questions have been modified, added to, and extended by Cynthia L. Selfe and Diana George, 1995.

Please note that you may not be able to apply all of the questions that follow to every image that you choose for analysis. Some questions will prove more applicable, interesting, or informative than will others for any given image. Select those questions that yield the richest and most textured responses.

> *Every concept in our conscious mind, in short, has its own psychic associations. While such associations may vary in intensity . . . they are capable of changing the "normal" charac-ter of that concept. It may even become something quite different as it drifts below the level of consciousness. (C. Jung,* Man and His Symbols, *1968, p. 29)*

1. What is the general ambiance of the image? What mood does it create? How does it do this? What specific details in the image—or details about the way in which the image is structured—help you come to this conclusion?

2. What is the design of the image? Does it use axial balance or some other form? How are the basic components or elements of the image arranged? Why?

3. What is the relationship that exists among the various pictorial elements and between the pictorial elements and the written material? What is the reason for juxtaposing various elements in the image? What does this representation of elements indicate to a reader? What specific details in the image—or details about the way in which the image is struc-tured—help you come to this conclusion?

4. What is the spatial arrangement of the image? Is there a lot of "white space" or is the image full of graphic and written elements?

5. What signs and symbols are present in the image? What role(s) do the various signs and symbols play individually and together? What specific details in the image—or details about the way in which the image is structured—help you to come to this conclusion?

6. If there are human figures present in the image, what are they like? What can be said about their facial expressions, poses, hairstyles, age, gender, hair color, ethnicity, education, occu-pation, relationships, and so on? What kinds of human figures are not present?

7. What is in the background of the image, and what does the background convey to a reader? Where is the action in the image, and what significance does this action have? (This might be described as the plot of the image.)

8. What theme(s) are present in the image? What is the image about? (The plot of an image may involve a man and a woman drinking, but the theme might be jealousy, faithlessness, ambition, passion, etc.). What specific details in the image—or details about the way in which the image is structured—help you come to this conclusion?

9. What language is used in the image? Does it provide essential information, generate some kind of emotional response, or raise some questions about the image? Or all three? What

specific details in the image—or details about the way in which the image is structured—help you come to this conclusion? What techniques are used by the copywriter: humor, alliteration, "definitions" of life, comparisons, sexual innuendo, and so on?

10. What typefaces are used and what impressions do these convey?

11. Does the image tell a story? If so, what is the plot or text of the story? Is this story a familiar one to you—have you heard other stories that remind you of it? How does the story told by the image connect to other stories that you know or that you have been told? What elements of this story are told, and what is the significance of these elements? What elements of this story are not told and what is the significance of the elements that are not told?

12. What item or human figure is the main focus of the image? What item or human figure seems most important? What specific details in the image—or details about the way in which the image is structured—make you come to this conclusion? What role does this item or human figure regularly play in American culture and society?

13. Is this image historic, contemporary, or futuristic? What specific details in the image—or details about the way in which the image is structured—help you come to this conclusion? What does this information tell you about the image? How does this information help you read the image?

14. What aesthetic decisions are evident in the image? If the image is a photograph, what kind of a shot is it? How does the range of the shot (e.g., long shot, medium shot, or close-up) affect the image? What about the lighting, use of color, or angle of the shot? How would the image change if another shot (or another approach to lighting, color, or angle) were used?

15. What sociological, political, economic, or cultural attitudes are directly or indirectly reflected in the image? What specific details in the image—or details about the way in which the image is structured—help you come to this conclusion?

16. At whom is the image aimed? For whom is it designed? What individuals? Cultures? Races? Ages? Economic status? What specific details in the image—or details about the way in which the image is structured—help you come to this conclusion?

17. What kinds of objects or human figures are left out of the image?

A FINAL RESPONSE

After you used as many of these questions as possible to analyze the image you are studying, write a response to the following final question:

Who benefits from the attitudes, portrayals, representations, or system of signs contained in this image? Who doesn't? What specific details in the image—or details about the way in which the image is structured—make you come to this conclusion?

Appendix B
Bibliographic Citation of Electronic Materials: APA Style

Source: *Computers and Composition: An International Journal for Teachers of Writing*, Gail E. Hawisher and Cynthia L. Selfe, Eds., Ablex Publishing Corporation, 355 Chestnut St., Norwood, New Jersey 07648.

The basic style for this citation handout is that of the *Publication Manual of the American Psychological Association (APA Style Manual*, 4th ed.). As the APA notes, "the goals of an electronic reference are to credit the author and to enable the reader to find the material" (the *Publication Manual of the American Psychological Association [APA Style Manual]*, p. 218). They continue that when the print form and the electronic form are identical, the author should prefer the print citation. However, if the author has used the electronic form, that form should be cited with the intention of assisting the reader in accessing the material.

In some instances, to accommodate specific features of our discipline or where the APA does not provide a style guide, Computers and Composition has modified the APA style.

Basic elements of bibliographic reference for retrievable electronic materials

Author's Last Name, First Name & Middle Name/Initial. (Date). Subject/title line of message. *Name of periodical/source* [Online], *vol.* (if available). Available (method used to find material): Specify path [Note do not end cite with a period; such stray punctuation may hinder retrieval. Last Accessed (provided when a "publication" date cannot be determined): (Date)

Abstract on CD-ROM

Jones, Anne S., & Anderson, Michael K. (1992, March). What should be taught in computer-intensive classrooms? [CD-ROM]. *Computer Applications* [Online serial], *13*(3) 232–242. Abstract from: Wilson Index File: Computer Science Index Item: 8-139232

Brown, James Louis. (1995). *Computer-intensive classroom pedagogy and the rhetoric of argumentation: A comparative study* [CD-ROM]. Abstract from: ProQuest File: Dissertation Abstracts Item 3293293

Abstract, Online

Jones, Anne S., & Anderson, Michael K. (1992). What should be taught in computer-intensive classrooms? [Online]. *Computer Applications, 13,* 231–242. Abstract from: DIALOG File: CompApp Item 32-4234

Computer program, software, or programming language

Viking Island [Computer program]. (1989). Gravesend, Kent, England: Fernleaf Educational Software.

FrameMaker 4 [Computer software]. (1993). San Jose, CA: Frame Technology.

Listserv Message-Archived

Seabrook, Richard H. C. (1994, Dec. 20). Community and progress. In CYBERMIND-L [Online]. Available E-mail: cybermind@jefferson.village.virginia.edu

Listserv Message-Unarchived

Seabrook, Richard H. C. (1994, Dec. 20). Community and progress. [Online]. cybermind@jefferson.village.virginia.edu [Accessed December 25, 1994].

MOOs, MUDs, and OWLs

Teach_Chat. (1995, March 23). Personal Interview. Telnet world.computertalk.edu 3292

Synchronous Communications (MOOs, MUDs, OWLs, IRC, etc.)

Teach_Chat. (1995, March 23). Personal Interview. Telnet world.computertalk.edu 3292

Telnet Sites (Available via telnet protocols)

Jones, Anne S., & Anderson, Michael K. (1992). What should be taught in computer-intensive classrooms? *Computer Chronicle.* telnet angel.compapp.illinois.edu@go#30923, press 12 [Accessed 1995, March 25].

Usenet posting

Jones, Anne S., & Anderson, Michael K. (1992, March 23). What should be taught in computer-intensive classrooms? comp.infosystems.www.users [Usenet newsgroup] No archive known. [Accessed 1995, March 25].

WWW Sites (World Wide Web) (Available via Lynx, Netscape, Mosaic, and other web browsers)

Jones, Anne S., & Anderson, Michael K. (1992, March). What should be taught in computer-intensive classrooms? http://angel.compapp.illinois.edu/comphome.html [Accessed 1995, March 25].

Data file or database, Electronic

National Health Interview Survey-Current health topics: 1991—Longitudinal study of aging (Version 4). [Electronic data tape]. (1992). Hyattsville, MD: National Center for Health Statistics [Producer and Distributor].

E-mail, Archived

Jones, Anne S., & Anderson, Michael K. (1992, March). What should be taught in computer-intensive classrooms? [23 paragraphs]. *Computer Applications* [Online serial], *13*(3). Available E-mail: compapp@uiuc.uc.edu Message: Get compapp 93-xxxxxx.

E-mail (Private) Correspondence, Unarchived

Smith, Karen J. [kjsmith@mtu.edu] (1995, March 23). Use of Multimedia in Editing. [Private e-mail].

FTP

Jones, Anne S., & Anderson, Michael K. (1992, March). What should be taught in computer-intensive classrooms? [23 paragraphs]. *Computer Applications* [Online serial], *13*(3). Available ftp://hostname. Illinois.edu Directory: pub/illcomp/compapp/1992.volume.13 File: compapp.94.13.3.teachquest.33.team

Gopher

Jones, Anne S., & Anderson, Michael K. (1994). What should be taught in computer intensive classrooms? [Online]. Available: gopher://angel.compapp.illinois.edu/comphome [Accessed March 25, 1995].

Quittner, Joshua. (1994, December 5). Far out: Welcome to their world built of MUD. Published in *Newsday*, November 7, 1993. Gopher://university of Koeln/About MUDs, MOOs and MUSEs in Education/Selected Papers/newsday

Journal article, Online and Subscriber Based

Jones, Anne S., & Anderson, Michael K. (1992). What should be taught in computer-intensive classrooms? [93 paragraphs]. *Computer Applications* [Online serial]. Available: Doc. No. 42.

Journal article, Online and Open Access

Jones, Anne S., & Anderson, Michael K. (March 1992). What should be taught in computer-intensive classrooms? [23 paragraphs]. *Computer Applications* [Online serial], *13*(3). Available E-mail: compapp@uiuc.uc.edu Message: Get compapp 93-xxxxxx.

Appendix C
Bibliographic Citation of Electronic Materials: MLA Style

Source: Janice R. Walker (jwalker@chuma.cas.usf.edu), Department of English, University of South Florida, 4202 East Fowler Avenue, CPR 107, Tampa, FL 33620-5550 (Endorsed by the Alliance for Computers & Writing). Modified by Cynthia L. Selfe and Gail Hawisher for this volume.

The *MLA Handbook for Writers of Research Papers,* while giving citation references for Computer Software (135) and information retrieved from computer and information services (136–8), does not address the wealth of information now being made available to teachers (and to students) via the Internet.

This listing includes reference formats for electronically-available information sites that have not been addressed by MLA attempting where possible to adhere to formats already delineated by MLA. Please note, however, that since punctuation is an important part of many Internet addresses, certain conventions of citation punctuation have necessarily been changed and/or adapted (for instance, placing the date in parentheses and omitting trailing periods for Internet addresses).

The basic component of the reference citation offered here is as follows:

> *Author's Last Name, First Name. "Title of Work." Title of Complete Work. [protocol and address] [path] (date of message or visit).*

The pages that follow give more specific examples for following and modifying this format. Please bear in mind, however, that, like the Internet itself, the information sources are in a constant state of flux and, therefore, this work will also need to change as the sites, themselves, proliferate and adapt to the new era of electronic print.

FTP (File Transfer Protocol) Sites

Bruckman, Amy. "Approaches to Managing Deviant Behavior in Virtual Communities." ftp.media.mit.edu pub/asb/papers/deviance-chi94 (4 Dec. 1994).

WWW Sites (World Wide Web) (Available via Lynx, Netscape, Other Web Browsers)

Burka, Lauren P. "A Hypertext History of Multi-User Dimensions." MUD History. http://www.ccs.neu.edu/home/lpb/mud-history.html (5 Dec. 1994).

Telnet Sites (Sites and Files available via the telnet protocol)

Gomes, Lee. "Xerox's On-Line Neighborhood: A Great Place to Visit." Mercury News 3 May 1992. telnet lambda.parc.xerox.com 8888,@go #50827, press 13 (5 Dec. 1994).

Synchronous Communications (MOOs, MUDs, IRC, etc.)

Pine_Guest. Personal Interview. telnet world.sensemedia.net 1234 (12 Dec. 1994).
WorldMOO Christmas Party. telnet world.sensemedia.net 1234 (24 Dec. 1994).

GOPHER Sites (Information available via gopher search protocols)

Quittner, Joshua. "Far Out: Welcome to Their World Built of MUD." Published in *Newsday,* 7 Nov. 1993. gopher/University of Koeln/About MUDs, MOOs and MUSEs in Education/Selected Papers/newsday (5 Dec. 1994).

E-mail, Listserv, and Newslist Citations

Bruckman, Amy S. "MOOSE Crossing Proposal." mediamoo@media.mit.edu (20 Dec. 1994).

Seabrook, Richard H. C. "Community and Progress." cybermind@jefferson.village.virginia.edu (22 Jan. 1994).

Thomson, Barry. "Virtual Reality." Personal e-mail (25 Jan. 1995).

Appendix D
Bill of Rights

Amendment I [First ten amendments ratified December 15, 1791]

Congress shall make no law respecting an establishment of religion, or prohibiting the free exercise thereof; or abridging the freedom of speech, or of the press; or the right of the people peaceably to assemble, and to petition the government for a redress of grievances.

Amendment II

A well regulated militia, being necessary to the security of a free State, the right of the people to keep and bear arms, shall not be infringed.

Amendment III

No soldier shall, in time of peace be quartered in any house, without the consent of the owner, nor in time of war, but in a manner to be prescribed by law.

Amendment IV

The right of the people to be secure in their persons, houses, papers, and effects, against unreasonable searches and seizures, shall not be violated, and no warrants shall issue, but upon probable cause, supported by oath or affirmation, and particularly describing the place to be searched, and the persons or things to be seized.

Amendment V

No person shall be held to answer for a capital or otherwise infamous crime, unless on a presentment or indictment of a grand jury, except in cases arising in the land or naval forces, or in the militia, when in actual service in time of war or public danger; nor shall any person be subject for the same offense to be twice put in jeopardy of life or limb; nor shall be compelled in any criminal case to be a witness against himself, nor be deprived of life, liberty, or property, without due process of law; nor shall private property be taken for public use, without just compensation.

Amendment VI

In all criminal prosecutions, the accused shall enjoy the right to a speedy and public trial, by an impartial jury of the State and district wherein the crime shall have been committed, which district shall have been previously ascertained by law, and to be informed of the nature and cause of the accusation; to be confronted with the witnesses against him; to have compulsory process for obtaining witnesses in his favor, and to have the assistance of counsel for his defense.

Amendment VII

In suits at common law, where the value in controversy shall exceed twenty dollars, the right of a trial by jury shall be preserved, and no fact tried by a jury shall be otherwise reexamined in any court of the United States, than according to the rules of the common law.

Amendment VIII

Excessive bail shall not be required, nor excessive fines imposed, nor cruel and unusual punishments inflicted.

Amendment IX

The enumeration in the Constitution of certain rights shall not be construed to deny or disparage others retained by the people.

Amendment X

The powers not delegated to the United States by the Constitution, nor prohibited by it to the States, are reserved to the States respectively, or to the people.

ALTERNATIVE TABLES OF CONTENTS

Focus on Expression and Form (Prose/Poetry/Short Story)

BY RHETORICAL MODE

Focus on Description

Focus on Narration

Focus on Classification

Focus on Evaluation

BY ISSUE

Access/Universal Service

Workplace Issues

ACKNOWLEDGMENTS

"The New Technology: Is It Part of the Solution or Part of the Problem in Education?" by Michael W. Apple. *Computers in the Schools* 8(1/2/3), 1991:59–77. Haworth Press, Inc., Binghamton, NY. By permission of author and publisher.

"Fly Me to the MOO," by David Bennahum. Reprinted by permission from *Lingua Franca, The Review of Academic Life*, published in New York. Email:76200.414@compuserve.com.

"Take Back the Net," by Stephanie Brail. Originally appeared in *On the Issues: The Progressive Woman's Quarterly*, Winter 1994, 39–42. Reprinted by permission.

"Common Law for the Electronic Frontier," by Anne W. Branscomb. *Scientific American*, 1991. Reprinted with permission. Copyright © 1991 by Scientific American, Inc. All rights reserved.

"A Note from the Future," passed on to us by Cathy Camper. *Wired*, January 1995. By permission of the author.

"The Bill of Rights and Responsibilities for Electronic Learners." *EDUCOM Review*, May/June 1993, 24–27.

"Welcome to Cyberspace," by Philip Elmer-DeWitt. *Time*, Spring 1995, 4–11. © 1995 Time Inc. Reprinted by permission.

"Unplugged," by David Gelernter. *The New Republic*, September 19 and 26, 1994, 14–15. Reprinted by permission of *The New Republic*. © 1994 The New Republic, Inc.

"Social Saturation and the Populated Self," by Kenneth J. Gergen. *The Saturated Self: Dilemmas of Identity in Contemporary Life*. New York: Basic Books, 1991, 48–80. Reprinted by permission.

"Computers and Gender," by Elizabeth Gerver in *Humanizing Technology*. London and New York: Plenum Press, 1985, 481–501. Reprinted by permission.

"Johnny Mnemonic" and "Burning Chrome," by William Gibson. New York: Arbor House Publishing Company, 1986, 1–22, 168–191. © 1986 by William Gibson. By permission of William Morrow & Company, Inc.

"Terror On-Line," by Mark Stuart Gill. *Vogue*, January 1995, 163–167, 195. Mark Stuart Gill is a journalist based in Los Angeles. His work has appeared in *Esquire, The New York Times Magazine, Rolling Stone*, and many others. By permission of the author.

"Universal Service Does Matter," by Rob Glaser. *Wired*, January 1995, 96–98. By permission of the author.

"High-Tech Employment Patterns in Silicon Valley," 1990. *Global Electronics*, Issue 116 (October 1992). (Published by the Pacific Studies Center, 222 B View St., Mountain View, CA 94041.) By permission of the publisher.

"The Electronic Palimpsest," by Brian Hayes. This article is reprinted by permission of *The Sciences* and is from the September/October 1993 issue. Individual subscriptions are $21.00 per year. Write to: The Sciences, 2 East 63rd Street, New York, NY 10021 or call 1-800-THE-NYAS.

"Talk Is Cheap," by Peter Huber. *Forbes*, April 11, 1994, 131. Reprinted by permission of *Forbes* Magazine © Forbes Inc., 1994.

"Feminism and Computers in Composition Instruction," by Emily Jessup, in *Evolving Perspectives on Computers and Composition Studies*, Gail E. Hawisher and Cynthia L. Selfe, Eds. Urbana: NCTE, 1991, 336–355. Copyright 1991 by the National Council of Teachers of English. Reprinted with permission.

"Welcome to Cyberbia," M. Kadi, excerpted from "The Internet Is Four Inches Tall," in *UTNE Reader*, March–April 1995, 57–59. By permission of the author.

From *The Penal Colony* by Franz Kafka, trans. by Willa and Edwin Muir. Copyright © 1948, renewed 1975 by Schocken Books, Inc. Reprinted by permission of Schocken Books, published by Pantheon Books, a division of Random House, Inc.

"The Information Gap," by Barbara Kantrowitz. From *Newsweek*, March 21, 1994, 78. Newsweek, Inc. All rights reserved. Reprinted by permission.

"Weavers of Webs: A Portrait of Young Women on the Net," by Nancy Kaplan and Eva Farrell. First published in *Electronic Journal of VirtualCulture* 2(3), July 1994. http://rdz..stjohns.edu/ejvc/ejvc.html. Reprinted by permission of Nancy Kaplan.

"Civil Liberties in Cyberspace," by Mitchell Kapor. *Scientific American*, September 1991, 158–164. Reprinted with permission. Copyright © 1991 by Scientific American, Inc. All rights reserved.

"Highways of the Mind or Toll Roads Between Information Castles?," by Roger Karraker. *Whole Earth Review*, Issue 70, Spring, 1991. Roger Karraker writes for *MicroTimes, MacWeek, Whole Earth Review*, and others about telecommunications and public policy. He is co-author of *Digital Revolution in the USA* (Tokyo: Yoyansha Publ., 1994). He can be reached at roger@river.org. By permission of the author.

"Computers, Networks and Education," by Alan C. Kay. *Scientific American* (Special Issue: The Computer in the 21st Century), 1995, 148–155. (Reprinted from 1991.) By permission of author.

"Women and Men on Electronic Networks: A Conversation or a Monologue?," by Cheris Kramarae and H. Jeanie Taylor. In H. J. Taylor, C. Kramarae, and M. Ebben, *Women, Information, Technology, and Scholarship*. Center for Advanced Study, University of Illinois at Urbana-Champaign, 1993, 52–61. By permission of authors.

"The First Amendment Is Under Attack in Cyberspace," by Jesse Lemisch. *Chronicle of Higher Education*, January 20, 1995. Copyright © Jesse Lemisch, 1995. By permission of author.

"Prophet of Privacy," by Steven Levy. *Wired*, December 1994, 126–132. Reprinted by permission of Sterling Lord Literistic, Inc. Copyright © 1994 by Steven Levy.

"Info 'Snooper Highway,' " by Peter McGrath. *Newsweek*, February 27, 1995. Copyright © Newsweek, Inc. All rights reserved. Reprinted by permission.

"Virtual Time Computer-Mediated Distance Learning Versus the Carnegie Model," by John D. Murphy. *Journal of Quality Management in Adult-Centered Education*, Summer 1995, 6–11. Reprinted by permission of the author.

"Making Every Vote Count" by Erik Nilsson. *Wired*, December 1994, 68–73. Reprinted with permission of the author.

"From Captain America to Wolverine," by Mark Oehlert. Reprinted from *The Cyborg Handbook*, 219–232, by Chris Hables Gray (1995), by permission of the publisher, Routledge: New York and London.

"Becoming a Computer Scientist," by Amy Pearl, Martha E. Pollack, Eve Riskin, Becky Thomas, Elizabeth Wolf, and Alice Wu. *Communications of the ACM*, 30 (November 1990), 48–57. Copyright © 1990, Association for Computing Machinery. Reprinted by permission.

"Sex and the Cybergirl," by Julie Petersen. Reprinted with permission from *Mother Jones* Magazine, © 1994, Foundation for National Progress.

"Community Networks: Building a New Participatory Medium," by Doug Schuler, 37:1 (January 1994), 39–51. Copyright © 1994, Association for Computing Machinery. Reprinted by permission.

"Are You Ready for the Democracy Channel?," by Evan I. Schwartz. *Wired*, 2.01 (1993). Reprinted by permission of author, a Boston-based science and technology writer.

"The Relationship Between Business and Higher Education: A Perspective on the 21st Century" by John Sculley from *Communications of the ACM*, 32(9), September 1989, 1056–1061.

"We're Teen, We're Queer and We've Got E-Mail," by Steve Silberman. *Wired*, *2.11*, November 1994, 76–80 © 1994 Wired Ventures Ltd. All rights reserved. Reprinted by permission.

"The On-Line Mystique," by Paula Span. *Women and Computers: Is There Equity in Cyberspace. The Washington Post Magazine*, February 27, 1994. © 1994 The Washington Post. Reprinted with permission.

"Computers, Networks and Work," by Lee Sproull and Sara Kiesler. *Scientific American*, September 1991, 116–123. Reprinted with permission. Copyright © 1991 by Scientific American, Inc. All rights reserved.

"Information Systems and Literacy," by Paul A. Strassman. *Literacy for Life*, R. W. Bailey and R. M. Fosheim, eds. New York: MLA, 1983, 115–121. Reprinted by permission of the Modern Language Association of America, © 1983.

"The Girl Who Was Plugged In," by James Tiptree Jr., in *Her Smoke Rose Up Forever*. Sauk City: Arkham House Publishers, Inc., 1990. Reprinted by permission of Arkham House Publishers Inc. © 1973 by James Tiptree Jr. © 1990 *Her Smoke Rose Up Forever*. Est. Alice B. Sheldon

"When Words Are the Best Weapon," by Russell Watson. *Newsweek*, February 27, 1995, 36–40 © 1995, Newsweek, Inc. All rights reserved. Reprinted by permission.

"Can Technology Replace Social Engineering?" by Alvin M. Weinberg. *University of Chicago Magazine*, 59 (October 1966):6–10. © 1966 *University of Chicago Magazine*. Reprinted with permission.

"Free Speech on the Internet," by Jon Wiener. *The Nation*, June 13, 1994. Reprinted with permission from *The Nation* magazine. © The Nation Company, L.P.

"Mythinformation," by Langdon Winner from *The Whale and the Reactor*. University of Chicago Press, 1986, 98–117. By permission of the author and the publisher.

"Surreal Science: Virtual Reality Finds a Place in the Classroom," by Philip Yam. *Scientific American*, February 1993. Reprinted with permission. Copyright © 1993 by Scientific American, Inc. All rights reserved.

"In the Year 2000," by Luke Young et al. *Academic Computing*, May/June 1988:7–12, 62–65. Reprinted by permission of Stephen Wolfram of Wolfram Research.

Cartoon from *The New Yorker*. Drawing by Bruce Eric Kaplan. © 1994 The New Yorker Magazine, Inc.

IMAGES

Part I

Portable Computers, Peripherals and More/Charles Webley Edwards

Net Books-We're Mapping A Whole New World/© Wolff New Media. Creators of the NetBooks and Your Personal Net (www.ypn.com).

Escape the Office Without Leaving It/Fujitsu Microelectronics/Carl Yarborough Photography

Part II

On September 15 in Pontiac, Illinois/Watusi, Inc.

Electronic Learning/©Comstock, Inc.

Have You Ever Studied . . . Classmate/Hunter Freeman Studios

Part III

Xband Is Like Computer Dating . . ./Photograph courtesy of Catapult Entertainment, Inc.

SONY Rom and Roll/©1995 Sony Electronics Inc. All rights reserved.

Grand Canyon/NEC

Part IV

Irma Speaks Fluent Internet/Reprinted with permission of Attachmate Corporation.

European Art Comes to the Screen/Nokia Display Products

I Had to Move On/Created by Buck Labadie and Chris Lombardo for Reveal Computer Products

Part V

Solutions for a Small Planet/IBM, Ogilvy & Mather

Because the World . . . Software/Polyglot International

In Dresden, Freedom Rises . . . Ruble/IBM, Ogilvy & Mather

INDEX